Colloids In Biology And Medicine

AUTHOR'S PREFACE.

THIS book is an attempt to apply the results of colloid research to biology. The reader may find the undertaking somewhat bold, since the number of facts are so few, and the gaps so numerous that a complete picture is impossible I find myself somewhat in the position of a palæontologist who wishes to reconstruct the ancestry of the entire organized world from some chance fragments Each day brings new finds which must be fitted into his plan and which confirm his views or show that he has been on a false trail. From the nature of things, it happens that I must more often indicate problems than report experimental results. This probably will prove a stimulus to those who wish to take active part in the development of our young science.

I wish to state one additional fact. it was not my purpose to make this book exhaustive. I have endeavored to give a general view, and since the work is addressed to *biologists* and *physicians* as well as colloid investigators, I have striven to give a clear picture of the subject, disregarding moot questions — On this account the "Introduction to The Study of Colloids" was abbreviated as much as possible without danger of obscuring the subsequent parts — Those who wish to study more thoroughly pure colloid chemistry, I refer to the excellent books of Herbert Freundlich "Kapillarchemie" Leipzig, 1909, and Wolfgang Oswald "Grundris der Kolloidchemie," Dresden.

Accordingly, in the arrangement of the first part, I have not followed the usual system, but have been guided by a desire to make easy of comprehension the matters most important to biologists and physicians. On this account I have considered it advisable to devote considerable space to the "Methods of Colloid Research "

Some new unpublished experimental data of my own and some placed at my disposal by others have been included

It is finally my privilege to thank all those who have helped me in the preparation of this book, particularly Professors H. Apolant, R. Hober, H. Sachs, and Dr H Siedentopf. I am especially indebted to my dear friend, Professor Richard Lorenz, with whom I have discussed some of the chapters, and to Dr. and Mrs Ziegler, who undertook not only the laborious task of reading the proofs but also checked back the index, page for page. I am also grateful to my publisher, Mr Theodor Steinkopff who, by intelligent cooperation was of great assistance to me.

H BECHHOLD.

FRANKFORT ON THE MAIN

DEDICATED
TO HIS EXCELLENCY
PRIVY MEDICAL COUNCILLOR

PROF DR PAUL EHRLICH

AND

PRIVY SANITARY COUNCILLOR

DR THEODORE NEUBURGER

WITH THE GRATITUDE OF THE AUTHOR

TRANSLATOR'S PREFACE

The translation of the first edition of this book was in hand when Professor Bechhold announced the preparation of a second edition. The translation was therefore delayed awaiting that issue in order to bring the volume up to date, and embody data obtainable from recent literature

The proof sheets were received in 1915 and 1916, but the translation and revision were again delayed by occupation connected with the prosecution of the War. (Local Board Membership)

The translator hopes that Professor Bechhold's presentation of the colloid chemical problems of biology and medicine will serve to stimulate greater interest in colloid chemistry among physicians, biologists, and bio-chemists His own reward, he has already found in the interest attached to interpreting the every-day problems of practice from this angle.

It is to be expected that the application of colloid principles to the phenomena of life will lead to new and more rational theories of their disturbances, and it is hoped that an improved practice of medicine will eventually result The pages of this book indicate the beginnings already made and suggest future studies

The translator acknowledges his debt to Dr. B Michaelovsky for assistance with the translation; to Mrs. D. D. Pool for the author index, and to his publishers, Messrs. D. Van Nostrand Company, for their friendly co-operation

His debts to his friend, Jerome Alexander, he is unable to enumerate. He owes to him, not only his introduction to colloid chemistry, but never failing stimulation, encouragement and assistance with the translations and the proof-reading: Any merit the work possesses is due to his collaboration.

J G M B

February 15, 1919
62 WEST EIGHTY-SEVENTH STREET,
NEW YORK CITY.

TABLE OF CONTENTS

PART I

INTRODUCTION TO THE STUDY OF COLLOIDS

xi

CHAPTER XXIII

PART I.

INTRODUCTION TO THE STUDY OF COLLOIDS.

COLLOIDS IN BIOLOGY AND MEDICINE

CHAPTER I

WHAT ARE COLLOIDS?

In spite of the fact that they have a much wider distribution than crystalloids, it is only a little over fifty years that colloids have been scientifically studied. Plants and animals and all the things we manufacture from them, such as our clothing and the greater part of our household goods, are colloids. In the year 1861, THOMAS GRAHAM,*[1] an Englishman, called attention to the fact that there were substances which, when in solution, diffused through parchment membranes (dialysed). These he called crystalloids because the soluble crystallizable substances (e. g., sugar and salt) possess this property to a marked degree. Substances which were held back by parchment membranes he called colloids, "glue-like," because glue was the most characteristic of this group. Every discoverer of a new fundamental principle is easily led into exaggerations; it so happened with GRAHAM who opposed crystalloids to colloids as "two distinct worlds of matter," though we know now that all sorts of transition stages exist.

In succeeding years very few investigators concerned themselves with colloids. The very fruitful development of organic chemistry occupied the attention of investigators, who neglected, as less important, a field which promised fewer immediate results. Only in the beginning of the new century was there a revival of interest in colloid chemistry.

We shall not follow the historic development further, but shall give a description of colloids in accordance with the present state of the science. It must be noted at the outset that, even to-day, the behavior of a dissolved substance towards a partitioning membrane, that is, inability to diffuse through it, is the chief characteristic of a dissolved colloid.

Many colloids form with liquids, especially with water, a more or less fluid solution. [The term *dispersion* is preferred by ARTHUR W. THOMAS in a recent discussion on Nomenclature. Science, N. S., Vol XLVII, No 1201, p. 10. Tr.] This solution is called a *sol* (from

[1] An * after an author's name refers to the reference in the index of authors.

3

solutio   solution. We speak of silver sols, albumin sols, etc. The dissolved substance in a sol may by various means be separated in an amorphous form that retains more or less water. This form is called a *gel*[1] from similarity to gelatin. If we add salt to a solution of colloidal silver, we obtain a black sediment containing very little water, the silver gel. If we boil a serum solution, the entire mass solidifies to a jelly that does not allow a separation of water and albumin, the albumin gel.

Sols.

As the researches of GRAHAM have already shown, sols in general are substances which subdivide in their solvents into relatively large particles, or which possess very large molecules, so large that, in contrast with the molecules of water or crystalloids, they are unable to pass through the pores of an animal skin or a parchment membrane. Chemical grounds indicate that albumin possesses a very large molecule. Even though we were to assume that it split into single molecules in aqueous solution, these are so large that they are unable to pass through an animal or vegetable membrane. Accordingly, the intact membranes of the organism protect it from loss of albumin, only in pathological conditions as in diseases of the kidneys does albumin pass through.

Substances like albumin,[2] soluble starches, etc., are to a certain extent inherently colloids. Every further subdivision of the colloidally dissolved particles would have to be associated with a splitting of the molecule, and the fragments are certainly no longer albumin, but albumoses, polypeptids, aminoacids, etc.

It is otherwise in the case of certain artificial colloids. According to G. BREDIG and TH. SVEDBERG, gold, silver, platinum and other metals may be electrically pulverized under water or in organic fluids, e.g., absolute alcohol. According to G. WEGELIN, silica, vanadic acid, and other substances may by mere trituration be reduced to suspensions whose particles are so small that they cannot be recognized microscopically. If the electrical pulverization is accomplished in water which is practically free from electrolytes, we obtain a solution which is red in the case of gold, brown in the case of silver, and greenish black with platinum. These solutions remain

[1] Many recent authors make "gel" and "jelly" synonymous. It seems preferable to go to use the expression "gel" for the general comprehensive phenomenon and to reserve the word "jelly" for the gelatinization of a hydrophile colloid.

[2] When I refer to albumin, I mean albumin absolutely unsplit, whether it be egg albumin or globulin, etc., as opposed to albumoses which are classified as albumin in some textbooks.

unchanged for months provided they are preserved in Jena glass, which yields no electrolytes to water. These colloidal gold, silver or platinum solutions consist of more or less fine metal particles, each of which often comprises thousands of metal molecules. By varying the strength and tension of the current, finer or coarser particles may be obtained.

Gold, silver and other sols have been prepared from gold, silver and other salts by chemically liberating the metal. According to the method of preparation, the metal is obtained in a more or less fine state of subdivision. If the metal sol is once produced it is impossible by the solvent alone to make the particles still smaller (without using chemical means). Unlike albumin they do not have the tendency to disintegrate of themselves in the solvent. We can accordingly call them *artificial colloids*, because they can be brought into such fine subdivision only by artificial means. If one were to further subdivide the molecules of such artificial colloids, the molecule would remain intact, gold would remain gold, and silver, silver. R. Zsigmondy * has prepared gold solutions so finely subdivided that they approach molecular dimensions, and Th. Svedberg has shown that, with these gold sols, and also with selenium sols, the finer the subdivision, the nearer these substances approach in color and light absorption their respective molecular solutions. In general, however, the artificial sols which can be seen in the ultramicroscope consist of much coarser particles than the natural sols.

While the chemical constitution of inorganic colloids is revealed by their method of preparation, nothing was known concerning the constitution of natural organic colloids until 1913, when Emil Fischer succeeded in synthetically preparing organic colloids resembling tannin and having molecular weights above 1000. Exact knowledge of the chemical constitution of these substances will reveal much to colloid research.

Suspension, Emulsion, Solution.

By *suspension* we mean the floating of a powder in a fluid, *e. g.*, clay in water. An *emulsion* is the minute division of one fluid in another with which it does not mix, *e.g.*, oil in milk or water. The smaller the particles of the "dispersed phase" [1] (cf. p. 11) of the clay or the fat, the longer it takes for them to separate. Such a suspension or emulsion, in which the dispersed phase is easily distinguished

---

[1] Portions of a structure separated from each other by physical surfaces are called *phases* (What Ostwald). A mixture of oil and water contains two phases. Oil is one phase and water the other. Dispersed means scattered, distributed. In the above examples oil or clay is the "dispersed phase."

microscopically, may last months and even years. Only about a decade ago there was an animated discussion as to whether the known inorganic colloids such as colloidal silver, gold, arsenic sulphid, Prussian blue, etc., were suspensions or true homogeneous solutions. Some evidence was against their being considered homogeneous solutions, other evidence, however, favored this view. Microscopically, they seemed entirely homogeneous, and they could not be separated from their solvents by mechanical means (filtration or centrifugation).

It was only by means of the *ultramicroscope*, invented by H. SIEDENTOPF and R. ZSIGMONDY (1903), that it was convincingly shown that they were suspensions and not homogeneous solutions.

After this point was settled, the further question arose as to whether gelatin, albumin sol and like substances were to be considered true solutions. Under the ultramicroscope, they also showed tiny particles, which, however, were by no means as numerous as might have been expected. Evidently most of them were invisible, and it was uncertain whether this was due to conditions of refraction, or whether the larger part of these substances was in true solution. This question was settled by the method of *ultrafiltration* invented by H. BECHHOLD in 1906. By a sufficiently impermeable jelly filter *ultra filters*, that is, by a purely mechanical process, he was able to separate solutions of albumin, gelatin, enzymes, toxins, etc., from their aqueous solvent. Not only did albumin, gelatin, etc., prove to be suspensions or emulsions, but in addition, substances whose true solubility had hardly been questioned, e.g., most of the albumoses and even dextrin whose molecular weight had been placed at about 1000, and which had practically been classified as a crystalloid.

It is also possible to accomplish such a separation by means of *centrifugation*. By centrifugation at 6,000 revolutions per minute, H. BECHHOLD separated colloidal silver sols (collargol) into coarser and finer particles. H. FREUNDENTHAL has recently constructed centrifuges turning from 10,000 to 30,000 revolutions per minute, by means of which he can separate the casein from cows' milk.

We must here refer to the definition for "homogeneous" and "homogeneous solution" given by H. W. BAKHUIS ROOZEBOOM whose premature death we lament. "We call a system homogeneous, if all its mechanically separable particles possess *the same* composition and the same physical properties. Therefore, this homogeneity of constitution exists in a well-mixed liquid only because of the smallness of molecules and the coarseness of our means of observation."

We cannot speak of a definite *solubility* in respect to suspensions and emulsions, for within certain limits, we are able to suspend as much clay or emulsify as much fat as we wish; the "finer" the clay or the fat is subdivided, the more "dissolves" The same thing holds for colloids, which are characteristically different in this respect from crystalloids, the latter having a sharply defined solubility

As a matter of fact we can get "supersaturated solutions" of crystalloids, and certain small additions increase the solubility disproportionately. Such additions (e g, albumin, albumoses, gelatose, dextrin) when employed in the case of suspensions and colloids, are called *protective colloids* (schutz-kolloide) because they protect the lixiviated clay or finely dispersed silver from separating out

As indicated, many of the pure, inorganic sols, especially the metal sols obtained by electric pulverization, are very sensitive to electrolytes by which they are easily precipitated, whereas on the contrary natural colloids are relatively insensitive It has been shown that the addition of certain natural sols acting as protective colloids gives metal sols etc., properties which cause them to approach the natural sols in stability The inorganic colloids employed in medicine, such as colloidal silver (collargol, lysargin), colloidal calomel (kalomelol), colloidal bismuth, etc., are all *stabilized* by protective colloids.

Thus we see a complete transition from the suspension and emulsion of insoluble substances, to the true solution of crystalloids, where there occurs a disintegration by the solvent, which is so profound in the case of electrolytes, that they separate into their electrically charged atoms (ions) As everywhere in nature, here too there are no sharp lines of demarcation We cannot deny that at a certain size the particles possess the *maximum* colloidal properties, especially those conditioned by surface phenomena. These properties decrease when the particles are larger, i e, if they approach those of true suspensions or emulsions; or when they become smaller, i.e, if they approach the molecular condition.

Th. Svedberg * has shown that the light absorption of colloidal gold and selenium increases as the particles become smaller, reaches a maximum in the amicroscopic field, and again decreases as the particles approach molecular dimensions. It is noteworthy also that at a certain degree of dispersion the tinctorial power reaches a maximum which in the case of gold is forty times stronger than the powerful color fuchsin. The color of colloidal gold having a particle size of 10 to 20 $\mu\mu$ is ruby red, when the particles are smaller it is fuchsin red; but when the particles are still smaller the color becomes yellowish red In other words it approaches the color of gold salts (auric chlorid) in which the gold is molecularly dispersed.

To recapitulate: The chief characteristic of sols is the large size of their particles,[1] which are unable to pass through vegetable or animal membranes. The natural size of the particles accounts for this in the case of *natural sols*, while in *artificial sols* it is due to the defects of our technic, which hitherto has not permitted our preparation of such substances in molecular, or even approximately molecular subdivision.

This criterion is only valid for extreme cases. Between the undoubted colloids, *e.g.*, albumin, and the undoubted crystalloids, *e.g.*, amino acids, there are all kinds of transition forms, which pass through the same membranes more or less rapidly, *e.g.*, albumoses and peptones. There is, indeed, *no sharp line of demarcation* between colloid and crystalloids.

Gels.

It might be inferred from the nomenclature (colloids and crystalloids) that the main distinguishing feature was the ability or inability to crystallize. It is a fact that most crystalloids, *i.e.*, substances which pass through membranes, are crystallizable, whereas most colloids are not able to form crystals when they separate from solution. However, this is not a radical difference, since egg albumin and hemoglobin which are undoubted colloids may be obtained in beautiful crystals, and I have further established by ultrafiltration, the colloidal nature of the solutions of the alkaline salts of the fatty acids, *e.g.*, oleic acid, which also form good crystals. Colloids usually separate from their solution in unformed masses called *gels*.

If the solid phase be separated from crystalloid solutions, it may form either crystals or a slightly or even an entirely amorphous precipitate. Colloidal crystals separate from a solution of common salt on evaporation or addition of alcohol, and crystals of $Na_2SO_4 + 10 H_2O$ separate from solutions of Glauber's salt (sodium sulphate). A white precipitate of barium sulphate, which has hardly any definite form, separates from a sodium sulphate solution upon adding barium chlorid. A substance of constant chemical composition especially as regards water content is obtained if the impurities, especially the extraneous water, are removed by filtration from the crystals or precipitate. To return to our example: the sodium chlorid crystals and the barium sulphate are water-free, whereas the sodium sulphate contains 10 molecules of water to one molecule of Na_2SO_4, but it is water-free above 33° C.

[1] By the passage through a membrane, I mean especially passage *by means of dialysis*. In many cases we may substitute *ultrafiltration*, provided ultrafilters of sufficient tightness are employed (see p. 102).

Gels behave differently; in fact there are a number of colloids which separate from their solution almost water-free. If sols of gold, silver, platinum, arsenious sulphid or antimony sulphid hydrosol, prepared according to the method of BREDIG or the method of SVEDBERG, precipitate, that is, separate from their solutions in the form of flocks, they are almost free from water. Many inorganic sols (i.e., the artificial ones), and according to my knowledge nearly all *natural organic sols*, retain a large quantity of water upon separation.

Gelatin is the most characteristic gel, its aqueous solutions (containing only 1 per cent of water-free gelatin) gelatinize at ice-box temperature. Furthermore, other sols, such as egg albumin, starches, silicic acid, iron oxid, etc., on separation in gel form retain many times their own weight of water, and form jelly-like masses in which the proportion between the solid substance and *the retained solvent is by no means constant*. According to the circumstances attending the separation, the amount of water held fast in the gel has wide limits of variation. This is a cardinal distinction. In accord with it, I have adopted the happily chosen nomenclature of J. PERRIN and call such colloids as throw down a practically water-free hydrogel, *hydrophobe* and those which produce a hydrogel swollen and rich in water, *hydrophile colloids* [1]

The *gels* of hydrosols (cf. p. 11) stabilized by protective colloids are somewhat hydrophile, because very minute quantities of protective colloid are sufficient to give the inorganic sol the properties of the protective colloid.

The Structure of Jellies.

Jellies are formed from their respective solutions by such physical and chemical changes as would cause the separation of crystals in the solution of a crystalloid, e.g., by cooling, by removal of water either by a chemical change or by forming an insoluble substance (e.g., by boiling or by acidifying an albumin sol). It is thus apparent that jellies are to be considered two-phased structures.

Two phases are much more obvious in coagulated egg albumen whose opacity and white color suggest a non-homogeneity of structure. Recently BACHMANN* has demonstrated ultramicroscopically the two-phased structure of transparent jellies such as gelatin and silicic acid. In gelatinizing, it is evident that granular flocculent

[1] I mentioned above that, as far as I knew all natural organic sols are hydrophile. It might be objected that epidermis, hair, feathers, bark and numerous other vegetable structures are deposited from natural sols and become very poor in water. This is met by the assertion that when they are deposited they contain much water and that the loss of water or drying out occurs subsequently.

and even crystalline particles, e.g., in soap jellies, unite to form spongelike structures.

J. M. VAN BEMMELEN compares the process of separation of colloids with the condition deduced from the phase rule governing the separation of two fluids not miscible in all proportions, e.g., water and phenol. In jellies also, we have a phase containing much colloid and little water, and another phase containing little colloid and much water. This conception of the structures of jellies and the process of separation is due to J. M. VAN BEMMELEN, O. BÜTSCHLI, W. B. HARDY, G. QUINCKE, R. ZSIGMONDY and W. BACHMANN. The views of O. BÜTSCHLI are not accepted nowadays. He maintained that jellies are, broadly speaking, foamy structures having microscopic cavities with firm net-like walls filled with fluid. Such a structure can occur only exceptionally.

The conception of jellies as spongy structures gives us a satisfactory explanation of their properties. It explains their solidity and their plasticity, their elasticity, and in short their various physical properties.

The above assumption finds corroboration in another observation, through the fact that jellies also act as ultrafilters and consequently must be penetrated by fine capillaries whose diameter has been determined by BECHHOLD (see p. 99). The penetration of jellies by fine capillaries filled with fluid was demonstrated by another observation. H. BECHHOLD and J. ZIEGLER* allowed salts which would form precipitates with various properties to diffuse towards each other in gelatin, e.g., potassium ferrocyanid and copper sulphate which form a copper ferrocyanid membrane entirely impervious to electrolytes, silver nitrate and sodium chlorid which form a silver chlorid membrane which is permeable for electrolytes if the osmotic pressure is higher on one side than on the other. Microscopic sections through the membranes formed by the precipitates prove that the gelatin is not deformed. Accordingly, when diffusion ceases, it is because the diffusion paths have been obstructed, i.e., a precipitate has been formed in the fluid phase so that the paths are closed and of course the gelatin walls which contain little water are impassable for electrolytes. Remelting is sufficient to reopen the diffusion paths. ANDERSON determined a diameter of $5.2\ \mu\mu$ for the largest pores of silicic acid jelly from the vapor pressure reduction which a fluid undergoes in cylindrical capillaries.

Until now we have assumed that sols exist only as aqueous solutions and that there are only aqueous gels. This is by no means true. Even THOMAS GRAHAM* showed that water could be replaced by alcohol and glycerin. TH. SVEDBERG pulverized numerous metals in organic fluids especially in isobutyl alcohol. R. LORENZ has even made metal sols in red hot solution (pyrosols) by electrolysis of molten lead and cadmium salts, etc To distinguish them from the water soluble *hydrosols* and from the *hydrogels* we call them *organosols* or *organogels* and according to the solvent as alcosols, etc. These do not occur in nature and are therefore of no importance to us

An investigation of such colloids as have *fats*, *lecithin* and *cholesterin* either as a dispersing medium or as a "dispersed phase" (cf. p 12) would certainly be of great importance to biology and medicine The fact that fats and oils, especially mineral oils, may serve as a dispersing medium for colloids has been mentioned by D. HOLDE * in his work on the "physical condition of solid fats" and this was confirmed by investigations of H BECHHOLD,[1] who was able upon ultrafiltration (through a toluol-glacial acetic acid collodion filter) to hold back from a crude oil a part of the asphalt colloidally dissolved in it. Recently C. AMBERGER dissolved a series of metals (gold, silver, platinum, arsenic, etc.) in lanolin. Some of these solutions have therapeutic application

By ultrafiltration H BECHHOLD separated from commercial *chlorophyl* the coloring matter and the wax-like products which were evidently held in colloidal solution.

Protective colloids also exist for organic fluids. Iron oxid gel and iron oxid hydrosol, rennin and trypsin, as well as albumoses which are completely insoluble in chloroform, become soluble in it with the aid of lecithin acting as a protective colloid.

Thus far we have sought to obtain a picture of what we term "colloids" and now we shall strive to elucidate upon what their properties depend In solutions of colloids and in gels, we have mixtures of solids or of fluids with fluids. It has for a long time been known, that at the interface between two substances which do not mix (air and water, oil and water, glass and water) there occur phenomena, called *surface phenomena* For instance, the surface of water in contact with air acts as a pellicle, if we allow water to drip, each drop reaches a considerable size before its weight breaks through the surface skin or pellicle and the drop falls This surface skin is much weaker in the case of alcohol, so that drops of alcohol falling from the same tube are much smaller than those of water The following is another example of a surface phenomenon· oil forms a sphere in a suitable mixture of water and alcohol, if we raise the specific gravity of the water by removing some of the alcohol, the oil rises and spreads out over the surface of the water.

Such surface phenomena are very numerous; they are brought

about by the fact that different conditions exist in the interior than exist on the surface of the fluid or solid body. In two-phase systems, such as colloids, in which the interfaces reach enormous dimensions, surface and capillary phenomena become most prominent; in fact, they are in many ways the most characteristic phenomena of colloids. Two fluids which do not mix are described as two fluid "phases"; it is possible also to speak of a fluid, of a solid and of a gaseous phase. In order to give expression to the great surface development in a *sol* or *gel*, WOLFGANG OSTWALD introduced the very happy expression *dispersed phase*. In a silver sol, silver is the solid dispersed phase, in an oil emulsion, oil is the fluid dispersed phase; in both, water is the *dispersing medium*. Colloidal solutions and gels are all *dispersed systems*.

[Of interest in this connection is the work of G. H. A. Clowes and Martin H. Fischer. Tr.]

CHAPTER II.

SURFACES.

WE have seen in the preceding chapter that both colloidal solutions and jellies are to be regarded as two-phase systems. In dispersed systems, the surfaces of contact acquire an overpowering importance by reason of their enormous development

In order to get an idea of the increased development of surface attending progressive subdivision, I give below a table taken from WOLFGANG OSTWALD:

Edge length		Number of cubes occupying a volume of 1 cm ^{3}	Total surface
1 cm		1	6 cm ^{2}
0 1 cm.	.	10^3	60 cm ^{2}
0 01 cm		10^6	600 cm ^{2}
0 001 cm	(The diameter of a human blood corpuscle is about 0 0007 cm)	10^9	6,000 cm ^{2}
1 μ	(= 0 0001 cm , diameter of a small coccus)	10^{12}	6 m ^{2}
0 1 μ		10^{15}	60 m ^{2}
0 01 μ	(Limit of ultramicroscopic visibility)	10^{18}	600 m ^{2}
1 $\mu\mu$	(= 1 millionth of a mm) (The diameter of the finest colloidal particles, limit of ultrafiltration)	10^{21}	6,000 m.^{2}
0 1 $\mu\mu$	(Diameter of elemental molecules)	10^{24}	60,000 m.^{2}

From this, we can understand how small surface forces may, in a dispersed system, become most important, and mask other phenomena We shall proceed to the study of the properties of surfaces in the following pages.

If we compare a point A (Fig 1) in the interior of a phase, e g., a fluid, with one on the surface A', e.g., in contact with air, we notice that the former is surrounded on all sides by an impervious mass, whereas the latter, surrounded on only one side by such a mass, experiences an attraction to the fluid phase The pressure with which the surface layer is drawn inwards is called *inward attraction* (*binnendruck*).

If we imagine a drop of water to be on a surface which it does not moisten, e.g , a leaf, there is a pulling towards the center from all sides, which means that the drop takes a spherical form, in order that it may have the smallest possible surface. The surface acts

13

like an elastic skin which surrounds the drop. If we drop water from a tube, the drop develops in size and is retained by its skin until the increasing weight tears it away.[1] We call this force which determines the tension of the surface, the *surface tension* (σ). A flat surface of water of 1 square cm endeavors to contract with a σ of about 0 075 gm., when it is spread out like a soap bubble with air

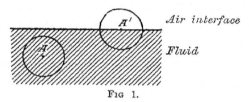

Fig 1.

pressure Every change in shape of the sphere of water, *i.e.*, every increase of the surface, presupposes work, this depends upon the surface area (ω) and the surface tension (σ). Surface energy = $\sigma \cdot \omega$ or $\sigma \dfrac{\text{surface energy}}{\omega}$ expressed in $\dfrac{\text{dynes}}{\text{cm.}}$

There are many methods for determining the surface tension Some of them depend upon the shape (distortion) which the surface of a fluid takes, some, upon the height to which a fluid ascends a capillary; some, upon the determination of the maximum weight attained by a falling drop. Detailed descriptions are to be found in every large treatise on Physics, such as H. Freundlich's " Kapillarchemie."

A number of values of σ are given as examples. The σ of water is determined most frequently; it has the highest σ of all the substances which are fluid at room temperature (mercury excepted). The various methods give quite divergent values The values given here are in each case the *surface tension towards air*.

	(fluid/air) σ		(fluid/air) σ
Water	71 7-76 8	n-Butyric acid	26.3
Mercury	436	Chloroform	26
Benzol	28 8	Olive oil	32 7
Ethyl alcohol	22	Resin (melted and solidified)	37 2-33 1
Ethyl ether	16 5	Glue	48 3
Glycerin	65	Shellac	36 7-30 4
Acetic acid	23 5		

[1] The comparison to an elastic membrane, at best, has only a limited applicability, since it is true that the surfaces are enlarged or diminished, yet they are not stretched The particles in the surface neither separate nor approach each other but more particles are forced into the surface (when the surface enlarges) or removed from it when it diminishes

The gas particles on the surface between fluid/air are affected by different forces than in the center of the gas space, they receive a pull in the direction of the fluid phase, they are *condensed* at the interface, and in the surface film, fluid is constantly changing into gas. Analogous phenomena occur wherever interfaces are formed, that is, at the interface between fluid/gas, fluid/fluid (in the case of non-miscible fluids), gas/solid, fluid/solid, solid/solid. At the fluid/gas and fluid/fluid interfaces we recognize these forces by the shape of the surface of contact (concave or convex), which is formed under the influence of the surface tension. At the interface between solid/gas we recognize the condensation of the gaseous phase at the surface by the fact that it is almost impossible to remove the layer of gas. This is the reason why it is so difficult to create high vacua, and why exhaustion of gas is undertaken in the presence of charcoal which by reason of its still greater surface removes that layer of gas which clings to the glass vessel. Spongy platinum acts as an igniter by condensing on its surface gases which then unite chemically with the liberation of heat

The surface tension at the *interfaces between two fluids* can be determined by the same methods that are employed in the case of fluid/gas. In this case also, a limiting surface develops at the interface of the two phases, which changes with every variation of surface tension

A few values of σ for fluid/fluid are now given:

		σ
Water/benzol	. .	32 6
Water/oil of turpentine	.	12 4
Water/chloroform . .	.	27 7
Water/ethyl ether	.	9 69
Water/isobutyl alcohol . . .		1 76
Water/rosin . .	.	19 8
Water/olive oil . . .		22 9
Alcohol/olive oil	. . .	2 26
Rape seed oil/egg albumen	. . . .	7 10
Olive oil/ox gall (9 per cent) .	. .	7 21
Olive oil/Castile soap (1/4000)	. .	3 65
Olive oil/rubber solution .	. .	14 9–10 2

A method for measuring *the surface tension of the dispersed phase in an emulsion* is here described in some detail, because it is too new to be found as yet in any textbook on Physics, and particularly because on account of its general applicability it promises to be of especially great importance for colloid chemical research

E Hatschek * separated an oil emulsion into water and oil by means of *ultrafiltration* From these experiments Hatschek deduced the diameter of drops of oil and the size of pores of the ultrafilter. The author raised certain objections to these conclusions, as it was not necessary to assume that the drops of oil retained their form in passing through the filter pores, they might have been drawn out into thread-like cylinders, and their diameter thereby reduced. As a result of the correspondence that followed, H BECHHOLD proposed that the pressure necessary to change the shape of a sphere of oil in a fluid be estimated and experimentally verified.

E. HATSCHEK * carried out these calculations and measurements. The method of calculation is in brief the following: Upon entering a capillary, a sphere changes into a cylinder which is bounded above and below by a meniscus, to simplify matters these meniscuses are regarded as hemispheres. Accordingly, let

R = radius of the oil sphere,
r = radius of the capillary,

then $\quad R = nr$,

σ = surface tension in dynes/cm.,
p = pressure per surface unit of the emulsion,
g = 980 (acceleration due to gravity),

then, $\quad p = \dfrac{\sigma n}{Rg}$

n approximately $= C(n-1)$, so that C lies between 1.8 and 1 9, and we have the equation $p = \dfrac{\sigma C(n-1)}{Rg}$; or, if we desire to determine the size of the pores, $n = \dfrac{pRg}{C\sigma} + 1$, or, should we desire to determine the surface tension $\sigma = \dfrac{pRg}{C(n-1)}$.

E HATSCHEK tested the correctness of the formula by determining the pressure necessary to deform a sphere of mercury or oil (nitrobenzol) sufficiently to make it enter a narrow capillary and obtained satisfactory results. To give an idea of the pressures that are involved, let us consider the following example In order to force a drop of mercury with a radius of 0 111 cm in water into a capillary with a radius r, a water column of p centimeters was necessary.

r (in cm)	p per cm of vessel (calculated)	p (observed)
0 0255	21 9	20 5
0 0112	58 65	62 0–63 2

In an emulsion of oil in water in which the diameter of the oil drops was 0.4 μ, a pressure of 20 atmospheres was required to press them through pores having a diameter of 75 $\mu\mu$. According to this theory it should be possible to obtain a clear or a cloudy filtrate from an oil emulsion according to the pressure employed. This assumption was confirmed by an experiment of H BECHHOLD: When an emulsion of oil in water was filtered through a 3 per cent ultrafilter with a pressure of 6 atmospheres a clear filtrate was obtained, and when the pressure was increased to 10 atmospheres the filtrate became turbid; with a decrease in the pressure the filtrate became clear again

In my opinion the greatest importance of the method lies in the ability to measure the surface tension of small fluid or semifluid structures (*e g*, blood corpuscles) and to deduce from such determinations entirely new points of view concerning the passage of fluid or semifluid structures through membranes

Let me point out another idea which forces itself upon me, namely, that the sphere is the form most readily induced by surface tension If a solid substance separates from a fluid as a *crystal* we must recognize that certain forces tending to increase the surface are opposing the surface tension But we know from the microscopic study of crystal formation that spherical structures usually appear first, later, crystalline forms with rounded corners, and only in the later stages true crystals [1] There must be a certain relation between mass and surface in order that the solid phase may be elevated above the surfaces bounded by planes in defiance of the surface tension. If the surface is too great in proportion to the mass, the surface tension overcomes the crystallizing forces. Since it is possible to estimate the increase in surface acquired by the identical substance in changing from a spherical form to a crystal, and further, to observe the smallest quantity of a substance which can become crystalline, it becomes possible to solve many problems, such as, the effective forces of crystallization, the surface tension which solid bodies exert against their solutions, and the decreased capacity to crystallize in the presence of colloids.

A drop of oil spreads out over the surface of water. This occurs because the surface tension of water acting against oil is less than the surface tension of the water acting against air minus the surface tension of the oil acting against air. (The explanation of this is given in all the larger text books on Physics.)

$$\sigma \text{ water/air} \quad > \quad \sigma \text{ water/oil} \quad + \quad \sigma \text{ oil/air}$$
$$75 \quad > \quad 22.9 \quad + \quad 32\,7.$$

[1] Bibliography in Wo OSTWALD, "Handbook of Colloid Chemistry," tran by Fischer, Oesper and Berman, Phila, 1915.

Expressed in general terms, this means that a fluid 2 spreads itse on the free surface of a fluid 1, if

$$\sigma_1 > \sigma_2 + \sigma_{1/2}.$$

σ_1 = surface tension of fluid 1 acting against air

σ_2 = surface tension of fluid 2 acting against air.

$\sigma_{1/2}$ = surface tension of fluid 1 acting against fluid 2.

Similarly, a fluid 3 spreads over the common boundaries of tw fluids 1 and 2, whenever

$$\sigma_{1/2} > \sigma_{2/3} - \sigma_{3/1}.$$

This phenomenon is of the greatest biological interest, because follows that many fluids must spread out on the boundaries of oth fluids or solid bodies and form films, and further, that solid particle suspensions and colloids must collect on surfaces, according to con ditions The diminution of surface tension between two surfaces the forerunner of mixing or solution; there exists no surface tensio between two readily miscible fluids. We shall discuss the distribu tion of dissolved substances on interfaces more fully on page 33 in the discussion of *surface pellicles*. We shall see that numerou organized structures and indeed the movement of protoplasm and of the lower animals are derived from this phenomenon of surfac tension It is the monumental service of G. QUINCKE that he showe the connection between the purely physical processes and the phe nomena of animate nature.

The *surface tension of solids* is deduced from the fact that finely divided particles are more easily and rapidly dissolved than coarse ones; it also explains the fact that artificial hydrophobe colloids ar produced only in a dispersing medium in which they are wholly in soluble (see p 73). The slightest solubility permits them to pas from the dispersed phase into coarser particles. Only to a limited extent is it possible directly to measure the surface tension of soli bodies ROENTGEN measured the σ for rubber/air and rubber/wate and TANGL* tested a new method on the interfaces of rubber/wate and paraffin/water The basis for the method is that a tube of the substance to be tested (rubber or paraffin) undergoes a change in shape when it is plunged from the air into a fluid (water).

Interfaces of Solutions. Whenever substances are dissolved in one or both phases, there is usually a difference between the con centration on the surface and on the interior. *These changes in concentration at the surface are termed adsorption.* A substance be comes concentrated upon the surface if it reduces the surface tension This is the most usual adsorption phenomenon. Only a few ganic salts increase the surface tension of water and they are, accordingly, less concentrated at the surface than in the interior of the solution. This latter occurrence, negative adsorption, is of significance for the distribution of salts in cells, as will be shown on page 25.

"Adsorption," which is of the greatest significance in colloid research, will, in the subsequent paragraphs, be considered from the standpoint of the distribution of a dissolved substance between two phases. In this connection also reference should be made to page 33 (surface pellicles).

CHEMICAL COMBINATION, SOLUTION, ADSORPTION.

We have seen that colloids are diphasic systems, and the question must arise as to *how a third substance will be distributed between the two phases* [1]

Chemical Combination.

If we take as the dispersed phase, a suspension of calcium carbonate (precipitated chalk) in water, this will represent the solution of a hydrophobe colloid. If we add sulphuric acid to the suspension, the acid will be immediately and completely bound. It is impossible to detect free sulphuric acid in the suspension by any reagent if any calcium carbonate still remains in the suspension [2] If we continue with the addition of sulphuric acid, a point *will suddenly occur* when, no matter how much is added, sulphuric acid is no longer bound by the chalk, all the excess remains in the water We are accustomed to say that a *chemical reaction* has occurred between the calcium carbonate and the sulphuric acid and that there is a chemical union of Ca and SO_4. Ca unites firmly with a definite quantity of SO_4 We may add as much water as we want; it cannot abstract any SO_4 from the $CaSO_4$. The process is *irreversible* (cannot be reversed)

Solution.

If we emulsify carbon disulphid in water, and add a little bromin. the entire fluid is colored brown If we allow the carbon disulphid to settle, the water is light brown and the carbon disulphid is colored

---

[1] In this instance "distribution" is used in the most general sense, though in physical chemistry it is employed only to indicate the distribution of a substance between two *solvents*

[2] Although the formation of salts on mixing dissolved acids and bases results with infinite rapidity, it takes an appreciable time in the case of colloid solution (and of course with coarse suspensions). VORLANDER and HABERLE.

dark brown The more bromin we add, the darker both the wat
and the carbon disulphid become; the latter, however, is alwa
more darkly colored than the former If we study the proce
quantitatively, the following becomes evident: if in a given case the
concentration of the bromin in the carbon disulphid is c(carbo
disulphid), in the water c(water), then $\dfrac{c(\text{carbon disulphid})}{c(\text{water})} =$
that is, the relative distribution of the bromin in a given case is n.

If we double the quantity of both carbon disulphid and of wat
and then test the quantity of bromin in the fluids, we shall find th;
in both the concentration has fallen to half and that the distributic
continues to be n. If we double the quantity of water, its color
only slightly less intense, because bromin enters the water from th
carbon disulphid. If we now measure the bromin content of the tw
fluids, we shall find ac(carbon disulphid) and in the water bc(water
that is, $\qquad \dfrac{ac(\text{carbon disulphid})}{bc(\text{water})} = n$

No matter how we vary the quantity of solvent or of bromin, th
apportionment of bromin is always n. We may, therefore, say tha
n is a constant and express it $\dfrac{c}{c_1} = k$.

This equation is characteristic for the *distribution of a substanc
between two phases in which it is soluble. The process is reversible*
it is in labile balance. The law of distribution was formulated b
M Berthelot and Jungfleisch in 1872, though we still frequentl
refer to Henry's *Law of Distribution* Strictly speaking, this ex
pression applies only to the distribution of a gas between a flui
and a gaseous phase (proportionately to the pressure).

The distribution $\dfrac{c}{c_1} = k$ applies only in case the molecular weigh
of the dissolved substance is the same in both solvents. If this i
not the case, the equation becomes $\dfrac{c_a}{c_b} = k$, in which a and b expres
the difference in the molecular weight in the two solvents.[1] W
Nernst has formulated the law of distribution in this way. Fo
example, benzoic acid in water has a simple molecular weight, bu
in benzol it exists mostly in double molecules. In order to ex
press this, the equation of distribution becomes $\dfrac{c(\text{water})}{\sqrt{c(\text{benzol})}} = k$.

---

[1] [Prof J L R. Morgan suggests that a better form would be the following·
$$\frac{c_1{}^x}{c_2} = k,$$
where x is the ratio of the molecular weight in solvent (2) to that in solvent (1)

Adsorption.

With *colloids* in particular there occurs a third possibility of distribution, wherein the *surface* comes into play rather than the total mass of the dispersed phase The condition of distribution which we are about to describe is called *adsorption*. Suppose we suspend in water a substance which we may assume does not dissolve or undergo chemical combination, *e.g.*, pure carbon. We know that bone black may to a greater or less extent decolorize dye solutions; that it is used to bleach dark sugar juices and to decolorize the dark solutions of the organic chemist When suspension of powdered charcoal is added to bromin water, we observe the following If we add very little bromin to the water the latter will become completely decolorized; if we add more, a considerable part is taken up by the charcoal but the water becomes brownish. With further addition of bromin the water is colored more intensely and the charcoal takes up proportionately less bromin This process is *reversible* and the distribution of bromin between charcoal and water follows a certain law We cannot as in the case of a solvent, however, speak of the concentration of the dispersed phase. In experiments, it has become customary to insert the specific gravity of the dispersed phase, and this custom is, as a rule, justified Let us, for example, designate by x the amount in millimols of bromin that is adsorbed from a solution by m grams of charcoal, and by c, the concentration of the bromin in the water after adsorption. If we deal with substances of unknown molecular weight, x indicates the weight in milligrams and c the weight which is present in 1 cc of water after determining the adsorption balance. Empirically we arrive at the equation

$$\frac{\dfrac{x}{m}\,(\text{adsorbed})}{c^{\frac{1}{n}}\,(\text{free})} = k,$$

in which the exponent $\dfrac{1}{n}$ is always < 1. Inspection shows that if $n = 3$ and $k = 20$, the equation is satisfied when $\dfrac{x}{m}$ in the charcoal $= 200$ and c (water) $= 1000$

If we dissolve but very little bromin, then the equation is satisfied when, $e\,q$, $\dfrac{x}{m} = 20$ and $c = 1$ In the first instance only 1/5 of the bromin is adsorbed by the charcoal, but in very great dilutions 20 times as much goes to the adsorbent.

If it is unnecessary to determine constants, the direct graphic representation of results is the simplest method. The concentration in water (the dispersing substance) is made the abscissa. The ordinate is the adsorbed amount of the dispersed phase. (This is the difference between the entire quantity of the substance dissolved and what remains in solution.) The points of intersection are points of the curve experimentally derived. The lines show us at a glance (as is seen in Fig. 2), in simple cases, whether the dis-

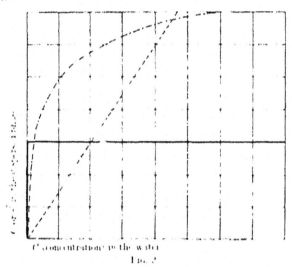

C (concentration) in the water

Fig. 2

tribution and curve is one of chemical combination, solution or adsorption.

The heavy continuous line (———) is the graphic representation of a *chemical reaction*: 3 mols CaCO₃ are suspended in water and H₂SO₄ is added. It is at once seen from the diagram that 3 mols H₂SO₄ are bound, i.e., there is no free H₂SO₄ in the water, but on the addition of more H₂SO₄ the dispersed phase can take up no more acid, so that the acid remains in the dispersing medium.

The broken line (– – –) is the graphic representation of the *distribution* of a substance *between two solvents*. The dot and dash line (– · – · –) is an *adsorption curve*. For the *graphic representation* of such adsorption phenomena the above equation is solved by logarithms; and we obtain

$$\log \frac{t}{m} = \log k + \frac{1}{n} \cdot \log c.$$

This is the equation of a line. If the logarithms of the values found for $\frac{x}{m}$ and for c, of different concentrations of the substances under examination, are carried onto a rectangular system of co-ordinates, these points would lie on a line, provided the substance was subjected only to pure mechanical adsorption.

As the simplest example we shall choose the curves and data which H Freundlich * derived from his studies of the adsorption of certain fatty acids by charcoal. Fig. 3 shows the adsorption curve

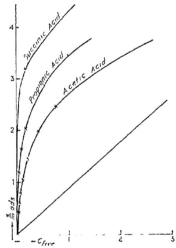

Fig. 3. Adsorption of fatty acids by charcoal. (After H Freundlich)

of acetic acid, propionic acid and succinic acid, in direct graphic representation as we have explained on page 22.

They are derived from the following somewhat abridged data of Freundlich:

Acetic acid		Propionic acid		Succinic acid	
$c\left(\dfrac{\text{millimols}}{\text{cc.}}\right)$	$\dfrac{x}{m}\left(\dfrac{\text{millimols}}{\text{gm. charcoal}}\right)$	$c\left(\dfrac{\text{millimols}}{\text{cc.}}\right)$	$\dfrac{x}{m}\left(\dfrac{\text{millimols}}{\text{gm. charcoal}}\right)$	$c\left(\dfrac{\text{millimols}}{\text{cc.}}\right)$	$\dfrac{x}{m}\left(\dfrac{\text{millimols}}{\text{gm. charcoal}}\right)$
0 0181	0 167	0 0201	0 785	0 0076	1 09
0 0616	0 801	0 0516	1 22	0 0263	1 70
0 2677	1 55	0 2106	2 11	0 0177	1 95
0.8817	2 18	0 6707	2 91	0 2831	3 26
2 785	3 76	1 580	3 78	1 161	4 37

Fig 4 shows the line passing through the logarithms of these data and it should be observed that all logarithms less than unity are *negative*

The tangents to the angle of inclination between the elements of

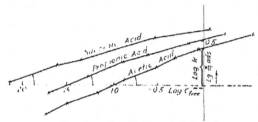

Fig 4 (After H. Freundlich)

the curve (acetic acid, propionic acid and succinic acid) and the abscissa (log c) is the *exponent* $\frac{1}{n}$. The distance on the ordinate $\left(\log \frac{x}{m}\right)$ from the zero point (origin of co-ordinates) to the point intersecting the uniting lines is log k They have these values:

$$\text{Acetic acid } \frac{1}{n} \quad 0\,425, \quad k \quad 2.606.$$

$$\text{Propionic acid } \frac{1}{n} \quad 0\,354, \quad k \quad 3\,163.$$

$$\text{Succinic acid } \frac{1}{n} \quad 0.274, \quad k \quad 1\,426.$$

Since the values observed do not lie all in the same line, as is shown in Fig. 4, a mean value for the angle whose tangent is n may be derived by means of a protractor. In the same way, log k is not derived from the intersection of the last element of the curve, but from the mean value.

The exponent $\frac{1}{n}$ conditions the shape of the curve, and varies within moderate limits. Though marked exceptions have been observed, it fluctuates usually between 0.5 and 0.8 as H. FREUNDLICH has shown in his numerous experiments

The constant k in the adsorption formula is, in an ideal case, a natural constant which may be as characteristic for the adsorbed substance as k is in the distribution between two solvents.

The great difficulty lies in the fact that, in the case of the dispersed adsorbing phase, we do not consider the mass, which may be easily determined by weighing or measuring, but the *surface* which may vary greatly with the selfsame weight   That in fact not the *mass* but the *surface* of the dispersed phase is of importance in adsorption, is evident from the following

FREUNDLICH and SCHUCHT* permitted dyes to be adsorbed by amorphous, *i.e*, *colloidal*, mercuric sulphid flocks. When the HgS became crystallin the dye dissolved again. We have here a counterpart of enzym action in which the adsorbed enzym (*e q.*, pepsin) is liberated when the adsorbing substrate (fibrin) changes its surface as it is split up. W. MECKLENBURG* succeeded in obtaining different curves in the adsorption of phosphoric acid by colloidal stannic acid and of arsenic by ferric hydroxid when, starting with solutions of identical concentration, he precipitated stannic acid and ferric hydroxid at different temperatures; all the other conditions were identical   The lower the temperature at which stannic acid or ferric hydroxid gel were formed the more phosphoric acid or arsenic was adsorbed   The peculiarity of these curves was the similarity in their shape which is described by mathematicians as "affinitive", on this account MECKLENBURG called them *affinitive adsorption curves*   They can not be otherwise explained than that the same mass of adsorbent may have a different surface depending on the temperature at which it was formed

Adsorption is a phenomenon which is *conditioned by the decrease of the surface tension* of the solvent in respect to the dissolved substance, at the interface between the solvent and adsorbent   In 1888, G QUINCKE showed that substances which decrease the surface tension between the solvent and the dispersed phase must collect about the dispersed phase with the formation of a film. H FREUNDLICH has elaborated and experimentally established the theory of adsorption phenomena, basing his ideas on GIBBS' *Theorem.*[1]   The marked diminution of the surface tension of water by fats, fatty acid, soaps, albumin and its cleavage products, and enzymes is characteristic, and it is not surprising that these substances are very easily adsorbed.

From what has been already said, adsorption appears to be a purely physical phenomenon in which the chemical relations between adsorbent and adsorbed substance play no part whatever. [This

---

[1] GIBBS' *Theorem* states: A dissolved substance is positively adsorbed if it depresses the surface tension, negatively adsorbed when it raises it   WILLARD GIBBS deduced these relations for gaseous mixtures and not for fluid solutions. The statement of W. GIBBS, that a small amount of a dissolved substance may powerfully depress surface tension but cannot raise it much, is likewise important (for further proof see H FREUNDLICH's "Kapillarchemie").

statement is too dogmatic; in dealing with colloidal particles which approach molecular dimensions no sharp line can be drawn between physical and chemical forces. Tr.] We shall, therefore, with Wo. Ostwald, call these purely physical phenomena *mechanical adsorption*

Most of the investigations on adsorption have been conducted with pulverized solids, hydrophobe colloids, and gels as adsorbents. From a biological standpoint studies of adsorption by hydrophile sols are of especial importance, when we consider for example what occurs in the blood. The only investigations of this character that I am acquainted with are those of H. Bechhold[*4] on the distribution of methylene blue between water and serum albumin. The volume in solution is directly obtained by *ultrafiltration* and the amount of methylene blue distributed in the aqueous filtrate thus obtained is measured. It was shown that in very dilute solutions of methylene blue the major part is held firmly by the albumin; whereas in greater concentrations the distribution is displaced in the direction of the water. The curve is similar to that of an adsorption curve. [The work of A. B. Macallum, "Surface Tension and Vital Phenomena," University of Toronto Studies. Physiol. Series No. 8 (1912) should be read in this connection as it involves the adsorption of potassium and its concentration at surfaces. Tr.]

Based on what has been said hitherto, we might believe that nothing is easier than to determine by the curves of distribution whether we are dealing with chemical combination, distribution between two solvents or adsorption. If, however, we examine the experimental data, we see that there is rarely close agreement between observation and the calculated results.

These divergences led to the derivation of other formulas determined by the following considerations. According to the formula on page 21 the more concentrated a solution, the more is there adsorbed from it. Actually, saturation limits are reached in many cases. This may be explained as follows: Each interface can adsorb only a layer of a definite thickness, and saturation is reached when this layer is filled with adsorbed molecules. The formulas of Arrhenius,[*] Rob Marc,[*] and C. G. Schmidt[*] were made to be in conformity with the observed facts

The question, whether we are dealing with *adsorption* or *solution*, is frequently difficult to decide when the dissolved substance has a different molecular weight in the dispersed phase than in the solvent (see p. 20). The curve of distribution may then assume the form of an adsorption curve and in solving the problem all the incidental circumstances must be considered; for instance, W. Biltz[*1] found that the distribution of arsenious acid between iron hydroxid gel and water follows the equation

$$\frac{\frac{x}{m}\text{-adsorbed}}{c\ (\text{free})^{\frac{1}{5}}} = 0.631.$$

Were we to believe that the arsenious acid went into solid solution in iron hydroxid gel we should have to conclude that the arsenious acid had a molecular weight one-fifth as large in iron hydroxid gel as in water From other observations, however, we know that arsenious acid in water breaks up into simple molecules so that the assumption that it dissolves in iron hydroxid gel is untenable.

The following statements will show that many conditions may modify the course of the adsorption curve and such cases, according to L Michaelis, are best called *abnormal adsorption*.

A substance may, for instance, as the result of swelling, absorb more water than the substance dissolved and thereby simulate a negative adsorption. Thus, B. Herzog and Adler * found that talcum powder adsorbed from sugar or albumin solution more water than sugar or albumin so that as a result, the solution appeared to be more concentrated at the end than at the beginning of the experiment.

The great *concentration* which adsorbed substances cause in the dispersed phase may be associated with changes in its condition; for instance, it may be thrown down as a solid. It has been observed, that charcoal which has been shaken with a solution of anilin dye shows the greenish metallic shimmer and the dichroism of the *solid* dye; albumin may *coagulate* at interfaces. Profound changes may accompany these variations of condition. This may be shown by the following examples, the so-called basic anilin dyes are salts consisting of a strong acid (usually hydrochloric acid) and a weak color base The aqueous solution undergoes strong hydrolytic dissociation; the free color base shows a more or less colloidal character and is always strongly adsorbed. H. Freund-lich and G. Losev * showed that the color bases adsorbed by charcoal from new fuchsin and crystal violet were changed at the surface of the charcoal, and substances with entirely different properties were formed, probably they were the insoluble substances which A. von Baeyer had previously prepared separately. In the case of the basic dyes, these chemically changed substances form the color on the textile fiber

Now we must recall that pure adsorption is a *condition of equilib-rium* changeable with the concentration of the dissolved substance. There can be no balance if a substance is removed from the solution and thus made insoluble (*irreversible*) as in the above-mentioned example of the basic dyes. As dye stuff becomes insoluble, the charcoal or fibers must adsorb more dye and the process will continue until all the dye is adsorbed from the solution. In the case in question, the process is prematurely ended because of the concentration of the HCl hydrolytically separated, which to a certain degree exercises a solvent action on the colored condensation product. Wilh Ostwald [*] has called attention to the fact that in solutions which are hydrolytically split into fatty acids and free alkali, there is a marked displacement of the adsorption balance. This occurs in washing. The fatty acids are adsorbed by the fabric and the skin; to accomplish this, there must occur in the solution a further hydrolysis, *i.e.*, a splitting off of alkali. In other cases the dissolved substances may be completely removed from solution, *e.g.*, albumin from urine (by charcoal, silicic acid or mastic emulsion, as adsorbents).

If we try to determine the adsorption curves for the phenomena just described (especially the fixation of dyes), we shall find that the curve might be mistaken for that of an irreversible chemical process.

Still more peculiar are the curves which W. Biltz and H. Steiner [*] obtained for the adsorption of night blue and Victoria blue by cotton, and H. Freundlich [*3] for the adsorption of strychnine salts by charcoal or arsenic trisulphid, as well as G. Dreyer and J. Shorto [*] for the adsorption of agglutinins by bacteria. In these cases less substance was taken up by the adsorbent from the concentrated solutions than from those of medium concentration.

The explanation of a phenomenon of this kind was given by A. Lottermoser, [*] who observed with A. Rothe that amorphous silver iodid adsorbed less potassium iodid from highly concentrated solutions than from solutions of medium concentration. The process is influenced by the fact that high concentrations of KI precipitate AgI, and make it partially assume the crystallin form. In this instance the cause is a diminution of surface; in the other cases, above described, there is a strong probability of a diminution of surface, especially with the agglutination of bacteria.

Hitherto it has been tacitly assumed that there is no affinity between adsorbents and dissolved substance. This occurs, though only in a few exceptional cases. Thus B. S. G. Hedin [14] has shown that certain enzymes (trypsin and rennin) are irreversibly adsorbed from water, but they may be displaced by other substances (casein, serum, grape sugar). L. Michaelis demonstrated that acid kaolin could adsorb only basic or amphoteric dyes, while basic clay could adsorb only acid dyes. Similar experiments have been performed by various other experimenters with wool, filter paper, etc. Since the chemical constitution of many of these substances is unknown and others cannot be prepared free of electrolytes, H. BECHHOLD considered it desirable to settle the problem by, using substances possessing definite constitution and which were easily obtained in a pure state. As such adsorbents, he chose naphthalin ($C_{10}H_8$, neutral), naphthol ($C_{10}H_7OH$, acid), naphthylamin ($C_{10}H_7NH_2$, basic), amidonaphthol ($C_{10}H_6OHNH_2$, amphoteric). These substances were freely suspended in water and shaken for several minutes with solutions of various dyes, they were filtered off and washed until the filtrate was practically colorless. The dye solutions employed were those generally used in microscopic technic. The results of my staining experiments are shown in the accompanying table. From these experiments it is evident that in most cases, even with the neutral naphthalin, there is at least a faint staining. The coloration is so slight, that it certainly could not be recognized in a microscopic specimen and it is evidently to be attributed to mechanical adsorption. It may be seen at a glance how remarkably the staining differs, depending on the chemical constitution of the stained substance, neutral naphthalin is not deeply colored by any stain. Naphthylamin and amidonaphthol are always most strongly stained by the acid dyes, and naphthol and amidonaphthol by the color bases. Thus we see that the *chemical constitution of the adsorbent* plays a very important part in the distribution of the dissolved substance between the solvent and the dispersed phase. BERCZELLER and CZÁKI* reached analogous results with the adsorption of alkaloids (cocain, atropin, etc.), by various powders (starches, coagulated albumin, which acted as weak acids and adsorbed most strongly, whereas alkaline $CaCO_3$ adsorbed least). That we are dealing with *electrochemical* phenomena in the above cases is still more evident when we observe how the *addition of electrolytes* affects adsorbability. Wool, which is dyed particularly well by basic dyes in a neutral bath, takes them up still better from an alkaline bath, but it is also dyed in an acid bath with acid colors. Still better evidence lies in the fact that the cations of neutral salts increase the dyeing of acid colors in proportion to the valence of the cation (W. M. BAYLISS).

We must furthermore mention the fact that *supplementary* chemical reactions may occur between adsorbent and adsorbed substances, which may lead to a *fixation* that makes the process irreversible, i.e., a true chemical combination may result. The occurrence of this condition is characterized by the fact that it requires a certain length of time, whereas according to H. FREUNDLICH, the adsorption balance is established in a few minutes. Moreover, such a de-

	Naphthalin	β Naphthol	β Naphthylamin, (freely precipitated)	Amidonaphthol (freely precipitated)
Basic dyes:				
Methylene blue	very faint blue	dark blue	very faint blue	
Loffler's blue [1]	faint blue	dark blue	almost uncolored	blue
Carbol-fuchsin	faint red	reddish	almost uncolored	deep red
Crystal violet	bluish	deep blue	faint blue	deep violet blue
Bismark brown	unstained	brownish	practically unstained	
Gram's Stain:				
Anilin water gentian violet	light violet	deep violet	faint violet	deep violet
Treatment with iodin-potassium iodid solution	almost completely decolorized	dark blue	blue	dark blue
Washing off with alcohol	almost completely decolorized	undetermined because too soluble	completely decolorized	deep violet (in far as could be determined in view of great solubility)
Acid dyes:				
Eosin	unstained	unstained	pink	red
Aurantin	faintly yellow	very faintly yellow	reddish yellow	yellow
Picric acid	unstained	almost unstained	very faint yellow	almost unstained
Alizarin (dissolved in KOH)	brownish violet	brownish	violet	violet
Gallein	unstained	almost unstained	almost unstained	faint brownish red
Chrome violet	almost unstained	almost unstained	almost unstained	red
Amphoteric dyes:				
Benzopurpurin	reddish	reddish (somewhat deeper than the others and mottled blue)	reddish	red
Janus red	reddish	deep red	reddish	deep red
Mixtures:				
Triacid	faint bluish green	deep bluish green	very faint violet	dark bluish green

[1] *Loffler's blue* is a methylene blue solution with a trace of alkali, *Carbol fuchsin* is a fuchsin solution containing phenol. Both of these as well as Gram's stain are employed in staining bacteria.

layed supplementary process may indicate a slow diffusion of the adsorbed substance into the adsorbent, as J. DAVIS has demonstrated in the case of the adsorption of iodin by charcoal. In the fixation of dyes by textile fibers we can assume the probable occurrence of secondary chemical processes. I believe that many misunderstandings in the moot questions of *toxin-antitoxin fixation* might have been avoided, if there had been a clear understanding of the various phenomena which may occur in the course of an adsorption process

Finally, it must be mentioned that *catalyzers* are adsorbed (all organic ferments are colloids). By reason of adsorption, the reaction in a solution may be stopped; or in other cases, the reaction may be accelerated upon the adsorbent. Thus oxidations may be brought about by concentration of oxygen on the adsorbent or reductions by concentration of hydrogen (C. PAALS' reduction of nitrobenzol by colloidal palladium and other chemical reactions)

The fundamental conception of adsorption is so illuminating that the attempt has been made to explain a large series of biological processes as adsorption phenomena (enzym action, union of toxin and antitoxin, etc.). I cannot better express the results of all this work than in the words of W BILTZ,[4] who in another connection, says, "The testing . . . of the material in accordance with an exact method, such as is involved in the use of a formula, offers the worker a rather mingled pleasure, as may be noted from the great difference between the results of experiment and of calculation. If it were not for the novelty of the subject investigated, . . the result which is so frequently accepted for the sake of the principle, would be of very little importance"

I should like to add further· The adsorption formula is a rock which, Lorelei-like, has magically attracted numberless scientific voyagers only to wreck many of them. Every complicated phenomenon of higher organisms, which consists partly of chemical, partly of solution phenomena and perhaps partly of true adsorption, *must* assume the general character of an adsorption and have a formula which seems a cross between a chemical process and a solution. Thus, if a biological phenomenon seems to suit the formula of an adsorption, this may be merely a *sign post*, which, alas, many an investigator may mistake for the goal.

What then is the biological significance of what we have distinguished as chemical combination, solution and adsorption? Here we approach the most important principle governing the processes in the living organism; it is what P. EHRLICH describes as *distribution*. The developing and the fully developed organism are constantly receiving food materials, which are taken up at the places where needed, stored, and when necessary given up again. In other words, the organism, plant as well as animal, is a vessel containing an aqueous solution in which various colloids exist as dispersed phases The balance which rules at each moment is disturbed by food material entering the vessel and by the metabolic products developing in it, and these become distributed between the solvent and the dispersed phase, the organ-colloids. In this entire chapter we have treated the simple case occurring when a *single* dispersed phase exists in a *single* dispersing medium (solvent). We may still assume without serious error, that there is one dispersing medium; but instead of *one* dispersed phase in the organism we have *dozens*, perhaps hundreds, of dispersed phases. Each individual class of cells is a different dispersed phase with different properties Only in this way can we understand how the assimilation products are sorted, stored up and changed into the tissues of the several organs.

To quote a single example, we find (according to a table in E. Abderhalden's Textbook of Physiological Chemistry) that there are the following distributions.

	to 1000 parts by weight	
	Serum of ox.	Blood corpuscles of ox
Sugar..	1 05	.
Cholesterin.	1 238	3 379
Lecithin . . .	1 675	3 748
Soda... .	4 312	2 232
Potash.. .	0 255	0 722
Lime. . .	0.119	
Ferric oxid .	...	1 671

It is difficult to imagine a more unequal distribution. For instance, potassium and sodium salts enter the circulation as electrolytes to the same extent; and there can be no question of any irreversible chemical combination of these salts either with the serum or with the blood corpuscles, since both diffuse away when the serum or blood corpuscles are brought in contact with pure water. There is thus a condition of equilibrium in the blood by which the *blood corpuscles dissolve* or adsorb proportionately *more potassium salts*, while *the serum albumin* dissolves or adsorbs *more sodium salts.* This is not a unique case, for humus adsorbs chiefly the potassium salts from a mixture and permits the sodium salts to pass through. With *iron* the conditions are different; it certainly must enter the organism in some mobile form, yet at the places where blood corpuscles are formed it is *chemically fixed* as hemoglobin We may say *à priori* that the *products of dissimilation* become very soluble in the dispersing medium, being dissolved or adsorbed but slightly by the dispersed phase, in fact they are not chemically fixed at all, so that they leave the body chiefly in the urine, they are, indeed, crystalloids of which only so much is retained in the blood by solution or adsorption as is necessary for a proper balance.

We must here curtail our remarks and refer the reader to the chapter on Distribution of Substances and Metabolism.

What applies to the substances necessary for the maintenance of the organism applies also to such foreign substances as have a toxic or pharmacodynamic effect. It is a principle that such foreign bodies as are *chemically* fixed, *permanently injure the affected cell; narcosis* seems to me, to be a typical example of simple *solution,* a process that is *completely reversible.* [Permanent injury may also be caused by the breaking of an emulsion. See M. H. Fischer and Marian O Hooker, " Fats and Fatty Degeneration," John Wiley & Sons, New York, 1917. Tr] Between these extreme cases there are substances which are adsorbed, and are active even in small doses, though larger doses do not cause materially greater damage Under favorable conditions these processes may be reversible. The details are treated of in the chapter on Toxicology and Pharmacology

Finally, I wish to refer to the chapter on Immunity Reactions where it is an important question whether chemical combination, solution or adsorption obtains.

Surface Skins.

Absolutely pure water has no surface viscidity, which means that a metal or glass disc suspended by a thread at the surface performs as many oscillations after a single turn as it does when immersed. The slightest impurities may, however, suffice to cause a marked retarding effect at the surface. On page 25 we saw that substances which lower the surface tension of a fluid concentrate and spread out at the surface, so it is to be expected that the surface will have a different viscidity from the interior. Poggendorff and Plateau were the first to study the formation of skins on fluids, but we are indebted to M. V. Metcalf,[*] G. Nagel[*] and E Rohde[*] for recent studies that have clarified the subject It was shown as the result of these investigations that colloids and substances at the border line between colloids and crystalloids, especially many dyes, as fuchsin, methyl violet, peptones and several other substances, concentrate at the surface of aqueous solutions and form a layer, which at first is easily movable. In a short time there is a change in this layer. In the case of staining solutions the surface appears dull after an hour and gradually there is formed a *solid* layer which histologists and bacteriologists know to their sorrow. It is, therefore, necessary to filter aqueous solutions of stains each time before using, even though they have been protected from dust. The dye concentrated at the surface undergoes chemical changes which the investigations showed to be independent of the gas upon the surface (it might have been attributed to oxidations with oxygen or to CO_2, etc.). What has been said of dye solutions occurs also in the case of peptone solutions, as METCALF demonstrated.

The thickness of the layer which will just form a solid skin has been measured, and found to be, for peptone 3 $\mu\mu$ (METCALF), for albumin 3 to 7 $\mu\mu$ (DEVAUX). Thus it is probably many times greater than the hypothetical diameter of a molecule, perhaps even equaling the radius of molecular attraction. The process of skin formation may be very much hastened by amplifying the surface, *i.e.*, by shaking the fluid or passing gas through it. Thus W. RAMSDEN * was able to remove by shaking practically all the albumin from an albumin solution. The albumin passed into the foam and there formed solid skins. This phenomenon is of greatest practical importance, since the solidity of meringue, whipped cream and beer foam evidently depends upon it. In the case of beer, the rising bubbles of CO_2 carry foam-forming colloids at their surfaces and conversely the beer foam exerts a tension (pressure) which hinders the escape of CO_2 and thus keeps the beer fresh for a longer time. Everyone who has worked with colloidal solutions knows how high the gas pressure must be in order that a stream of gas may be forced through a solution which has once formed a layer of foam. The formation of a skin on boiling milk is evidently to be classed among these phenomena. The significance of this process for the *coagulation of fibrin* has been indicated on page 299.

To these phenomena belongs "*inactivation* of ferments *by shaking*" described by E. ABDERHALDEN and GUGGENHEIM * and independently by SIGNE and SIGVAL SCHMIDT-NIELSEN.*

The formation of surface skins is so sharply characteristic, that *mixtures of substances*, which diminish the surface tension of water to different degrees, may be separated by shaking. Until now, we have had only the qualitative investigations of W. RAMSDEN,* who determined the predominance of saponin in the foam on shaking a mixture of *saponin* and *albumin*. (Saponin lowers the surface tension of water more than albumin.)

Hitherto we have only regarded the formation of surface skins at the interface fluid/gas. Such skins may be formed, however, at the interface fluid/fluid or fluid/solid, provided only that the substance in question diminishes the surface tension of the water with reference to the other fluid or the solid phase. J. Ziegler has informed me (in a private communication) that on shaking benzol, toluol, etc., with water containing albumin or gelatin, the benzol or toluol forms above the water an emulsion which contains the colloid, and that with repeated shaking, the major part of the colloid may be removed from the aqueous solution. Shortly after this communication, there appeared a publication by Winkelbech * which not only confirmed these facts but called attention to the fact that through the formation of an emulsion mere traces of colloids could be detected. This phenomenon has long been recognized as a very disturbing factor by organic chemists. On shaking reaction mixtures with ether or benzol, such emulsions frequently form and are very difficult to separate. We know now that these emulsions are to be attributed to the formation of colloidal reaction products.

H. Bechhold and J. Ziegler used the method of *shaking out the foam* for the separation of albumoses (Witte's peptone) into their components. They shook a 10 per cent aqueous solution of Witte's peptone with ether, separated the ether foam from the aqueous solution and again shook it out with ether. Then the ether was permitted to evaporate from the foam, and the residue was dissolved in ten times its volume of water, and this solution was again shaken out with ether. After thus treating the solution from three to five times, two substances were obtained, one of which remained in the water in clear solution and became turbid when treated with 24 to 25 per cent of ammonium sulphate. By this procedure a separation of two components was obtained, but it is a question whether the water-insoluble portion was present in the original solutions or was formed by the shaking, like Metcalf's peptone skins. The slight diminution in concentration is in favor of the first view. By "shaking out the foam" a separation of the slightly water-soluble hetero-albumoses and the remaining albumoses was accomplished.

This spreading of colloids and the formation of coiled films at the interface between two fluids is a phenomenon very frequently observed. G. Quincke *2 showed that gum collects at the interface between oil and a gum arabic solution. Pharmaceutical emulsions accordingly consist of oil spheres surrounded by a film of gum. And when oil is emulsified with albumin, oil spheres surrounded by a film of albumin are formed (Ascherson *). I have attributed the so-called "serum films surrounding the globules in milk" to the formation of surface skins, see page 346   Where oil globules occur in aqueous solutions containing colloids, it may be assumed that they are surrounded by a film of colloid which prevents them from running together and forming larger drops of fat   This is exemplified in the emulsion of fats in the intestine and in the milky turbidity of the serum after ingestion of fat as well as in the oleaginous and resinous emulsions in plants, *e.g.*, in the milky sap of the Euphorbiaceæ.

As has been already stated the same conditions obtain for the interfaces between fluid solid as for fluid fluid. H. BECHHOLD [*] explains the action of *protective colloids* (see p. 11) as a manifestation of this phenomenon. Protective colloids form colloidal films about the substance in suspension and thus impede the coalescence (flocculation) of the separate particles. Consequently surface pellicles afford stability to the metal sols, and permit their practical utilization.

On the other hand, suspensions and hydrophobe colloids, depending on circumstances and the surface tension, may either pass from one fluid into another fluid with which it is not miscible, or they may concentrate at the interface (REINDERS). This must be considered in all studies on the distribution of colloids in the body, as in staining with colloidal dyes and the injection of colloidal metals and possibly even infection with micro-organisms.

[According to the views of MARTIN H. FISCHER and MARIAN O. HOOKER,[1] we must distinguish between the making of an emulsion

[1] See MARTIN H. FISCHER and MARIAN O. HOOKER, Fats and Fatty Degeneration, John Wiley and Sons, New York, 1917, where references to their earlier publications may be found.

[*] Both W. D. BANCROFT and G. H. A. CLOWES at the Urbana (1916) meeting of the American Chemical Society, in their discussion of our own views regarding the importance of colloid solvates (colloid hydrates) for the stabilization of emulsions, found in our views something irreconcilable with their notions of the importance of interfacial films and of surface tension changes in these. While we do not wish to insist upon a harmony where such may not be desired, there is, of course, nothing mutually exclusive in the ideas of solvation, of changes in surface tension, and — at times — the formation of a continuous third phase between the two chief substances making up an emulsion. When "water," according to our notion, becomes a "colloid hydrate," the properties of the second liquid are different from those of the first, and these properties include surface tension, viscosity and distribution between two phases. But, we repeat, these factors to which PLATEAU, QUINCKE and PICKERING first directed attention are not by themselves able to explain all the phenomena observed. Where CLOWES holds that an emulsion of oil is stabilized through sodium oleate because the substance reduces the surface tension of water, we would say that stabilization has ensued because the oil has been divided into a highly hydratable sodium soap. When the addition of calcium destroys this emulsion, it is not because of complicated changes in a surface film, but simply because calcium oleate is an only slightly hydratable

and its stabilization The making of an emulsion is essentially a mechanical process concerned with the mere obtaining of the subdivision of one liquid in a second, as oil in water. The problem of the stabilization, after such a subdivision has been brought about, is a totally different matter. In a certain sense the main feature in this stabilization consists of the getting rid of the water as such in the emulsion and substituting for it a hydrated colloid.

An emulsion is stabilized through any so-called emulsifying agent only because this emulsifying agent is a hydrophile (lyophile) colloid. Oil, for example, cannot be permanently emulsified in water in amounts exceeding a fraction of one per cent, but in a medium in which the water is bound to an emulsifying agent as a hydrate (or solvate) the oil content can be carried to a very high figure (50 or 60 per cent). When, for example, acacia is used as an emulsifying agent, it means that the permanent emulsion is made permanent because the acacia unites with the water to form an acacia-hydrate.

After the stabilization of an emulsion has been accomplished through the production of a colloid hydrate, secondary concentration effects may be brought about which lead to a concentration of the colloid material upon or in the surface of the oil droplets but these secondary effects are not to be confused with the primary ones necessary for the stabilization of the emulsion.

W. D. BANCROFT asserts in a review of FISCHER's book that there are no criteria which these alleged compounds (the solvates) could satisfy. J. of Ind. & Eng. Ch., vol. 9, No. 12, Dec., 1917.

BANCROFT observed that while soaps of mono-valent cations used as emulsifying agents for oil and water, promote the formation of emulsions like cream, in which oil is dispersed in a continuous water phase, soaps of di- and tri-valent cations form emulsions of the opposite type like butter, in which water is dispersed in oil. BANCROFT considers that soaps of sodium or potassium, being readily dispersed in water but not in oil, form an interfacial film or membrane, the surface tension on the water side of which is much lower than on the oil, and that consequently an emulsion of oil in water is formed,

---

soap. Free water, in consequence, appears in the mixture, and the oil separates out in gross form, as described above, for only very little oil can be permanently subdivided in "pure" or "free" water. We describe the consequences of such changes from highly hydratable to less hydratable soaps upon the stability of an emulsion on p. 49.

Neither do we wish our statement that an agreement is possible between CLOWES' and our views on simple emulsions to be expanded to include his beliefs regarding the biological behavior of the fat in living cells. We long ago gave up the notion of lipoid membranes about cells and the complex notion of their changing permeability to which CLOWES and many authors still hold."

while soaps of calcium and magnesium, being readily dispersed in oil but not in water, form a film, the surface tension on the oil side of which is lower than on the water, and consequently an emulsion of water in oil is produced.

CLOWES showed that emulsions of oil in water could be converted into emulsions of water in oil and vice versa by varying the proportions of certain electrolytes added to the system. When equal volumes of oil containing fatty acid and water containing NaOH were shaken together sodium soap was produced and an emulsion of oil in water formed. On shaking this emulsion with increasing proportions of calcium chlorid, a critical point at which oil and water separated into two distinct layers was observed when the CaCl₂ was added in sufficient amount to convert half the sodium soap into calcium soap. Further addition of calcium chlorid led to the formation of a stable emulsion of water dispersed in oil. Conversely, the latter emulsion could be reconverted through the critical point into one of oil in water by shaking with the requisite proportions of sodium soap or caustic soda. (See diagram, Fig. 4a.)

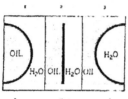

Fig. 4a.   Conversion of oil-water to water-oil emulsion

CLOWES attributes these transformations to variations in the surface tension relations of the water and oil phases, caused by variations in the proportions of the hydrophilic sodium soaps which lowers the surface tension of the water phase, and the lipophilic calcium soap which lowers the surface tension of the oil phase. An emulsion of oil in water is produced when the surface tension is lower on the water than on the oil side of the stabilizing film or membrane formed by concentration of the emulsifying agent at the oil-water interface. A critical point occurs when the surface tension is equal or compensatory on both sides of the film, and an emulsion of water in oil is formed when the surface tension is lower on the oil side than on the water side.

Electrolytes appear to exert a marked effect on emulsion equilibrium, those having a more reactive or more readily adsorbed anion appear to promote the formation of emulsions of oil in water, while those having a more reactive or readily adsorbed cation exert the reverse effect, promoting the formation of emulsions of water in oil.

The antagonistic effects exerted by electrolytes of these two opposing groups appear to correspond sufficiently closely with those observed by OSTERHOUT in experiments on living cells to suggest the possibility that variations in permeability exhibited by protoplasm under the influence of various salts might be attributable at least in part to reversible transformations of the marginal layer of protoplasmic material between systems in which a non-aqueous phase is dispersed in an aqueous, which would be relatively freely permeable to water, and the reverse type of system in which an aqueous phase is more or less surrounded by a non-aqueous film which would be impermeable or relatively less permeable to water.

A Traube capillary pipette was employed to study the influence exerted by given salts individually, and in combination, on the relative degree of dispersion of interfacial soap films in oil and water. Aqueous solutions containing caustic soda or soap and various concentrations of the salts to be tested were allowed to flow from the capillary pipette through neutral oil or oil containing free fatty acid, and the number of drops produced served as an index of the dispersing or protective effect exerted by the electrolytes in question on the interfacial soap film. Those electrolytes which possess a readily adsorbed anion appear to cause an increase in the number of drops, which corresponds with a lowering of the surface tension of the water phase, a destruction of the surface film, and an increased permeability of the system to water. Those electrolytes which possess a readily adsorbed cation exert the reverse effect, diminishing the number of drops, which indicates diminished dispersion or destruction of the film and a diminished permeability of the system to water. For example, a 0.001-m NaOH passed through olive oil gave 44 drops; the addition of NaCl to a concentration of 0.15 m raised the number of drops to 300; the addition of $CaCl_2$ at a concentration of 0.0015 m lowered the number of drops to 24; while a system in which 0.001 m NaOH was employed in conjunction with 0.15-m NaCl and 0.0015-m $CaCl_2$ gave 44 drops, corresponding with the original system and indicating that under the conditions of the experiment NaCl and $CaCl_2$ exert an antagonistic or compensatory effect upon one another in the molecular ratios of $100 : 1$.

In similar experiments with other electrolytes, anesthetics, etc., the ratios in which antagonistic effects were produced corresponded sufficiently with those in which the substances in question exerted antagonistic effects on marine and other organisms as to suggest the possibility that these physical systems may afford a crude model of the mechanism underlying the control of permeability in protoplasm. Salts of magnesium and other substances which exhibit abnormalities in biological systems exerting under varying conditions a protective or destructive effect on the protoplasmic film exhibit similar abnormalities in emulsion and drop systems. Magnesium salts function as protective agents like calcium salts when added to a soap solution which is passed through oil; but as destructive agents like NaOH, NaCl or KCl when added to a dilute solution of NaOH which is passed through an oil containing fatty acid.

Closely parallel results were observed between the drop system described above, the process of blood coagulation, the lethal dose of given electrolytes in mice when injected intravenously, the hemolysis of blood corpuscles by complement and amboceptor, etc., a common critical point being observed in these widely diversified systems. Clowes considers that these experiments lend substantial support to to the view that while protoplasm as a whole consists of a system approximating more nearly to a dispersion of the non-aqueous phase in the aqueous, the extreme marginal layer of protoplasm may be looked upon as an emulsion or gel-like system consisting of two continuous phases in which fluctuations in permeability to water and water-borne substances may be caused by variations in the proportions of metabolic products, electrolytes, etc., a slight change in the system in the direction of water surrounded by the non-aqueous phase leading to a diminution in permeability, while a change in the reverse direction, towards a system in which the non-aqueous phase is more completely dispersed in the aqueous, would lead to an increased permeability.

Substantial support is lent to this point of view by Osterhout's observations that the conductivity of Laminaria tissue is raised by exposure to a solution of NaCl, lowered by $CaCl_2$, but unchanged when exposed to a mixture containing 100 molecules of NaCl and one of $CaCl_2$. Life can only be maintained within certain ranges of electrical resistance or permeability and an increase or decrease in permeability beyond given limiting points is no longer reversible and invariably causes death. Wilder D. Bancroft, Jour. Phys. Chem., 17, 501 (1913). G. H. A. Clowes: Proc. Physiological Section, International Medical Congress, pp. 105-114, London, 1913. Proc. Soc. Exp. Biology and Medicine, 11, pp. 1-3, 4-5, 6-8, 8-10 (1913). Jour. Physical Chemistry, 20, p. 407 (1916). Proc. Soc. Exp. Biology and Medicine, 13, pp. 114-118 (1916). Science, 43, pp. 750-757 (1916). Tr.]

CHAPTER III.

SIZE OF PARTICLES, MOLECULAR WEIGHT. OSMOTIC PRESSURE, CONDUCTIVITY.

For the chemist wishing to discover the constitution of a chemical substance, the determination of the molecular weight is of great importance. Much time has thus been spent on determining the molecular weights of the bio-colloids, such as albumin, starch, hemoglobin, etc., and in the following pages we shall show what probability for success attends these efforts.

A soluble substance, placed in a suitable medium which produces no chemical change, distributes itself uniformly. In the case of crystalloids, it is impossible by either optical or mechanical means to recognize the particles into which it splits up.[1] We shall see that *crystalloids* are frequently broken up into their molecules. Many *colloids* are soluble also. If we examine their solutions in the ultramicroscope which permits a hundred thousand fold magnification,[2] we can recognize numerous particles. In the case of *artificial colloids* (gold and silver hydrosols) in which we are certain that all the dissolved particles are visible, according to R. Zsigmondy we are in a position, as will be shown by the following considerations, to calculate the approximate weight of each individual particle. Let 1 gm. of colloid be dissolved in 1 liter of water, then every 1 cubic millimeter contains 1/1000 milligram of colloid. If by counting under the ultramicroscope, we determine that each cubic millimeter contains 1000 particles, we know that each particle weighs one millionth of a milligram. We can easily calculate the diameter of a particle by supplying the specific gravity and assuming that each particle is a sphere. However, as soon as we become uncertain whether all the particles are visible, which is the case with most *bio-colloids*, the optical method fails us. Under these circumstances, we can determine the size of the particles by *ultrafiltration*. If we sift grains, we know that those which pass through are smaller, and those which are

---

[1] [Optical inhomogeneity of sugar solution has been demonstrated. Van Calcar and L de Bruyn separated sodium sulphate from solution by high speed centrifugation. Tr.]

[2] [The ultramicroscope makes visible otherwise invisible particles but does not magnify beyond the power of its component compound microscope. Tr.]

held back are larger than the meshes of the sieve. If we know the size of the meshes and have several sieves with meshes of different size, it is easy to determine the average size of the grains by letting them pass through the different sieves. H. Bechhold's determination of the size of the particles depends on this principle. *Ultrafilters* (jelly filters) with different sized pores serve as sieves (see pp. 99 *et seq.*). Since there are several methods for measuring the size of the pores (see p. 100), it is possible to determine definite limits for the size of the colloid particles.[1]

Are the particles thus found identical with molecules?

In the case of metal sols we can immediately say, no. We know the molecular weight of metals and understand from it that there is no prospect of directly seeing the molecules of the elements with our present instruments. According to E. Rieke gold particles of 1 $\mu\mu$ diameter have a molecular weight of 300,000, but the molecular weight of gold is probably only 197, and the smallest particles we can see have a diameter of 5 $\mu\mu$. It follows, therefore, that every recognizable ultramicroscopic particle consists of thousands of molecules.

What are the facts in the case of *particles whose size is determinable by ultrafiltration?* Since albumin, starch, etc., have unusually large molecules, it is probable that in them the molecule and particle size, as determined by ultrafiltration, are identical. This is all the more likely since these biocolloids, like crystalloids, are distributed by means of the action of the solvent, whereas the metal hydrosols are brought into such minute divisions only by artificial means.

But what is a molecule? It is the smallest portion of a compound or of an element that may exist alone. If we split a molecule of common salt we no longer have a molecule of NaCl but an atom of Na and an atom of Cl. If we divide an albumin molecule, we still have complicated atom complexes but we have albumin no longer. Molecular *weight* is the weight of a molecule compared to that of an atom of hydrogen which equals unity. Consequently we are measuring not absolute, but relative sizes. The molecular weight is determined by purely chemical means. If, for example, we find in sodium benzoate, that there are 7 atoms of carbon (7 × 12 = 84), 5 atoms of hydrogen (5 × 1 = 5), 2 atoms of oxygen (2 × 16 = 32) and one atom of sodium (1 × 23 = 23), we should know that the molecular weight must be at least 144, because half atoms do not exist. The molecular weight might in fact be two or three times as large, which would have to be determined by other

[1] [J. Alexander has recently proposed measurement of particle size by high speed centrifugation, "ultracentrifugation." Tr.]

chemical investigations and determinations on other chemical compounds of benzoic acid.

From similar considerations the *minimum value* for the molecular weight of certain albumins are obtained. If a protein contains one per cent of sulphur, then its molecular weight must be 3200 times heavier than that of hydrogen. (The atomic weight of S = 32) But there is every reason to believe that there are at least two atoms of sulphur in egg albumen, because one-half of the sulphur is easily split off, whereas the other splits off with difficulty. Thus egg albumen, with one and three-tenths per cent sulphur shows a molecular weight of 4900, and oxyhemoglobin a molecular weight of 14,800. Oxyhemoglobin contains 0.4 to 0.5 per cent of iron; provided it contains but one atom of iron, its molecular weight must be 11,200 to 14,000. The figures obtained approach one another very closely.

Another method of obtaining the molecular weight is based on *Avogadro's law*. This law says: "At the same temperature and equal pressure, different gases contain the same number of molecules per liter." Thus from the weight of a gas or of a vaporized substance, the molecular weight can be determined, if we compare its weight with that of an equal volume of hydrogen gas. *Avogadro's law* was generalized by J. H. van't Hoff and extended to solutions. According to this generalization the "osmotic pressure" of a dissolved substance is proportionate to the number of the dissolved molecules and is as large as if the substance were vaporized. If a sugar solution is placed in a porous clay cell which is so dense that water but not sugar may pass in and out,[1] the sugar tries to expand like a gas and, as a result, water enters the cell and the solution rises in it. If a vertical tube has been attached to the cell, the *osmotic pressure* of the solution may be measured directly from the height to which the fluid rises. There are indirect methods also, the underlying principles of which we cannot discuss here They depend on the fact that in proportion to the osmotic pressure the *boiling point is raised* and the *freezing point lowered*. In ideal cases these changes are strictly proportionate to the concentration of the dissolved substance in just the same way that the original volume of an ideal gas is reduced to one-half by double the pressure and to one-third by three times the pressure. Consequently by determining the freezing or boiling point of a solution, molecular weight may be determined. In the case of crystalloids this method is preferred to the direct reading of the osmotic pressure for the following reasons: It is exceedingly difficult to prepare a cell that really holds back crystal-

[1] Such a chamber is said to be semipermeable.

loids, and, on this account, the danger of considerable error is always present. Moreover, in solutions with ordinary molecular weights, the osmotic pressures are so great that very bulky apparatus would be required. Thus, for example, the osmotic pressure of a 1 per cent aqueous solution of sugar at 15.6° C. is actually 0.685 atmosphere.

The difficulties in the *direct measurement of osmotic pressure* of crystalloids do not exist however, in the case of colloids. Almost any membrane keeps back colloids and the small rises are easily measured. In order to remove the sources of error due to the possible presence of crystalloids, we employ membranes which are permeable for crystalloids instead of semipermeable ones (collodion sacs, animal membranes).

These *physical methods for determining the molecular weight* rest on the assumption that the substance in solution is really broken up into molecules (colloids cannot be vaporized). This condition does not always exist in the case of crystalloids and only exceptionally with colloids. With crystalloids these methods yield figures that are either too low or too high. The former will occur if the substance is incompletely split up, if two, three or more molecules continue to be united in solution. Under these circumstances we obtain one-half, one-third, etc., the osmotic pressure that a molecular subdivision would show. The ultramicroscope and ultrafiltration reveal in many solutions of biocolloids particles of such a size as show no molecular subdivision by other methods; we may assume therefore that colloidal solutions for the most part contain molecular groups, and that there is no prospect of determining the true molecular weight by osmotic methods.

The osmotic method yields a deceptively low molecular weight if, for example, the substance is dissociated further than into molecules. This occurs in the case of electrolytes. A very dilute NaCl solution that has dissociated into Na and Cl ions shows twice the true osmotic pressure, so that the molecular weight might be set at half its real value. In this respect we may also make mistakes with colloids whenever they are ionized. *The osmotic method does us only into how many fragments a molecular complex breaks up in the particular solution.* It may give either *minimum or maximum* values for the molecular weight. Even in the case of crystalloids, the method must be employed with due consideration of all the conditions involved; for colloids it may be exceedingly deceptive. We know at the outset, because of the enormous molecular weight of colloids, that the lowering of the freezing point and the elevation of the boiling point must be very small indeed, requiring most delicate measurements. The matter becomes still further complicated by the fact that crystalloids are adsorbed by colloids and cannot be completely removed by dialysis. Each crystalloid molecule or each crystalloid ion may thus falsely represent the osmotic pressure of a colloid molecule having perhaps a thousand times its mass.

The *coefficient of diffusion* may be employed in the determination of the molecular weight of crystalloids, but in the case of colloids it gives information concerning only the average size of the particles. The method is not much impaired by the increase in the size of the molecule, because it is only the square of the coefficient of diffusion which diminishes proportionately to this increase. The adsorption of crystalloids, on the contrary, is also in this case a source of error because every crystalloid molecule or ion acts as a team-mate of its colloid particle and hastens its rate of diffusion The objection to the principles governing the calculation are mentioned on page 53.

Before we come to concrete examples we shall mention one other method which may enlighten us concerning the particle content of a solution — the *conductivity*. In a solution the electric current is carried only by the electrically charged particles (ions). In an NaCl solution this is done by the Na and Cl ions; in a Na_2SO_4 solution, 2 Na ions and 1 SO_4 ion, that is 3 ions, take part The assumption is that many molecules are completely or almost completely split into ions; this actually occurs in the case of strong electrolytes when in great dilution. The conductivity thus affords us fractions of the molecular weight· minimum figures (values less than actual).

My chief purpose in making these statements is to show what facts may be deduced from the various methods used in determining the molecular weight; they give only *limiting values*, so that no conclusion is to be drawn from any one method.

The following remarks will show what difficulties stand in the way when we try to learn the size of the colloid molecule.

Among the colloids whose chemical composition is best known are the *soaps*.

As was found by F KRAFFT and A. SMITS, very dilute soap solutions showed a well-marked rise in boiling point; but this did not rise in proportion to the concentration of the soap, as may be seen from the following table by A. SMITS for sodium palmitate·

Concentration in mols	Rise in boiling point, °C
0 0282	0 024
0 1128	0 045
0 2941	0 050
0 5721	0 060

Though the concentration is increased twenty fold, the boiling point rises only two and one-half times. In a solution of 19.5 per cent sodium stearate, F. Krafft found absolutely no rise in the boiling point as compared to pure water.

Let us examine the conclusion of W. Biltz and A. v. Vegesack based on their critical study of the osmotic method. True colloids like iron oxid and tungstic acid show a small osmotic pressure, only so long as they contain electrolytes. As the electrolyte vanishes, the colloid particles aggregate to larger complexes which then cease to show any osmotic pressure. For the existence of these colloids, some electrolyte content is an absolute necessity.

When these investigators studied " colloid electrolytes," particularly colloid color salts (congo red, night blue and benzopurparin whose constitution, molecular weight, etc., were determined by chemical methods, they obtained results which especially in the case of congo red must be closely examined. Congo red has the formula $C_{32}H_{22}N_6$ $S_2O_6Na_2$, and being a sodium disulphonate, is a strong electrolyte. Its molecular weight (M) 696. On account of its electrolytic dissociation into 3 ions (2 crystalloid and 1 colloid) we would expect an osmotic pressure three times as much as its molecular weight would indicate. Instead of this W. M. Bayliss and also W. Biltz and A. v. Vegesack as well as Donnan and Harris obtained by dialysis against pure water a pressure which was approximately 5 per cent lower than would have been obtained had the undissociated molecule been active. The explanation is not difficult. Let us designate by R, the acidic color radical of congo red, then congo red has the formula R.Na$_2$. In solution a portion becomes ionized into R and Na Na, of which some, even though possibly only a small fraction, forms with the H and OH ions of the water HH color acid and NaOH. This occurrence would be without much influence in changing osmotic pressure if the measurement was made in a closed vessel in which the equilibrium was undisturbed. As a matter of fact the measurement is made in a membrane permeable for electrolytes. Consequently the NaOH which has been formed diffuses away and some fresh color acid (RH) may be formed. This process continues until practically only color acid remains in the membrane. Consequently in this instance we have not measured the high osmotic pressure of the electrolytically strongly dissociated color salt but that of the practically undissociated color acid. If measured against outer water containing electrolytes, it yields a *very much lower* osmotic pressure, equivalent to a value for M of 2088. We shall thoroughly understand this occurrence when we have become more familiar with the equilibria of membranes. See page 59.

We shall only indicate here, that when the colloid electrolytes (thus Biltz designates salts in which one ion is a colloid) and the electrolyte in the outer water have originally the same osmotic pressure, there is a gradual penetration of the outer electrolytes but the colloid electrolytes cannot escape   Consequently the osmotic pressure in the cell is the resultant of osmotic pressure of the colloid electrolytes plus that of the electrolytes which have entered.   If the latter have an ion in common with the colloid electrolytes, we do *not* find, as might have been expected, that there is an equal division of the true electrolytes (*e g*., NaCl), but on the contrary, outside the osmometer there is proportionately more NaCl the more dilute the NaCl solution is (see page 62)   The osmotic pressure of the colloid electrolytes is consequently depressed.

From this it follows that the values determined by the direct osmotic methods require revision.   E. H. Starling obtained 4 mm Hg osmotic pressure for serum colloid in 1 per cent serum, thus expressing an apparent molecular weight of about 50,000.   E. W. Reid obtained a pressure of 369 mm. Hg for a 1 per cent hemoglobin solution from which is deduced an apparent molecular weight of about 65,000, a figure which approaches the values obtained by the diffusion method by R. O. Herzog and Sv Arrhenius.

These figures are 4 to 10 times greater than those determined for the molecular weight by chemical means

As a matter of fact the theory of the direct measurement of osmotic pressure is so difficult that I do not know any results which are not susceptible of adverse criticism (see F. G. Donnan's theory).   As the result of direct measurement, we know that colloid solutions actually have an osmotic pressure and that it increases with the amount of dispersion. Theoretical considerations, however, show us that this osmotic pressure must be low.   Theoretically, all solutions which contain the same number of particles of the dissolved substance exert the same osmotic pressure.   Thus all normal solutions (leaving out of consideration dissociations, associations and other changes) exert the same osmotic pressure, namely, 22.4 atmospheres.   Normal solutions are such as contain the same number of molecules, namely, one gram molecule per liter.   A normal salt solution is one containing 58 5 gm. NaCl per liter and a normal hydrogen solution is one containing 2 gm. of hydrogen per liter (theoretically).   By various means which yield rather concordant results it has been determined that 2 gm H contain 6.1×10^{23} molecules[1] or fragments of molecules or molecular complexes, *i.e* , particles in solution exerting 22.4 atmospheres of osmotic

[1] This figure ($6 1 \times 10^{23}$) is called Avogadro's figure, and the various methods for deriving it give quite uniform values.

pressure. When we consider that the finest gold particles of a colloidal gold solution have a diameter of only $2\mu\mu$,[1] a dimension one fifth that of ultramicroscopic visibility, according to Svedberg, in order to make a normal colloidal gold solution we should have to cram 50 kilos of gold into a liter, which would have to contain 6.1×10^{25} such gold particles. It is naturally impossible to do this, the most that can be dissolved, experimentally, is one gm. per liter. Under favorable conditions such solutions have an osmotic pressure of 4.5×10^{-4} atmosphere, i.e., they would rise 4.65 mm. in an osmometer, or be in equilibrium with electrolytes which modify the electrolytic or hydrolytic dissociation of colloid electrolytes.

It is unnecessary to catalogue all the dozens of fruitless investigations of the molecular weight of colloids by physical methods. They either gave surprisingly low molecular weights, when it could be shown on testing that the colloid was contaminated with crystalloids, or the values were so small (the molecular weight so large) that they fell within the limits of error of observation which means that it became doubtful whether the colloid studied had any osmotic pressure at all. The *molecular weight is the expression of a chemical point of view which cannot be determined by physical methods for colloids.* What we obtain by these methods are more or less numerous groups of molecules, usually in adsorption balance with irremovable traces of crystalloids which cannot be separated, or which are in equilibrium with electrolytes that influence the electrolytic and hydrolytic dissociation of the colloid electrolytes.

In the present state of the science we may only strive to determine the size of the particles in solutions of colloids having various equilibria.

[1] [According to Zsigmondy particles $5\mu\mu$ in size may be seen with the aid of strong sunlight. — Tr.]

CHAPTER IV.

PHENOMENA OF MOTION.

Brownian-Zsigmondy Movement.

UPON examining a drop of milk under the microscope, we are at once struck by the appearance of the fat droplets on account of their strong refraction (a dark ring with a brilliant center). It is seen that they exhibit a certain oscillation (trembling). This characteristic oscillating movement is more intense with the smaller droplets (Fig. 5), whereas those having a diameter of more than 4 μ do not show it at all. The phenomenon is named after the English botan-

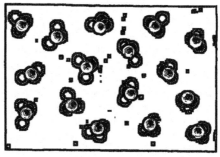

Fig 5   Brownian movement of milk globules.   (From O Lehman)

ist, ROBERT BROWN, who discovered it as early as 1827, in an aqueous suspension of plant pollen. It may be observed in every suspension or emulsion which is sufficiently fine. Particles of 1 μ diameter show a radius of translation of 1 μ The "dance of the motes," the rushing hither and thither of the bright particles observed in the ultra-microscope,[1] is nothing else than an enormously exaggerated *Brownian movement*, due to the fact that the particles are much smaller than those that may be seen under the microscope   Particles of 10 to 50 $\mu\mu$ have a speed of more than 100 μ per second.   These movements

---

[1] R. Lorenz correctly calls attention to the fact that the great advance in our science does not date from Brown who observed the "oscillations" of microscopic particles but from R Zsigmondy who recognized that particles of molecular dimensions are in a similar mobile state   (Frankforter Ztg 4 6.11, I Morgenbl.)

seen under the ultramicroscope are comparable to the dance of the molecules in accordance with the Kinetic Theory of Gases.

The speed of the particles is dependent on the viscosity of the dispersing medium and increases with a rise in temperature. It is very pertinent to enquire at this point whether we have *the movements of the molecules themselves*. In a certain sense this may be answered in the affirmative. Though we cannot yet say that this movement is inherent in the particles, or, that it would be carried out by the particles themselves, we may assert that it is caused by blows from the molecules of the solvent.

A. EINSTEIN and M. VON SMOLUCHOWSKI have independently deduced from the Kinetic Theory of Gases, laws for the Brownian movement (extent of movement, influence of temperature and viscosity). It might be assumed *à priori*, that a particle floating in a fluid would remain at rest, for it simultaneously receives from all sides an equal number of impacts from molecules. The fallacy of this assumption is shown by M. VON SMOLUCHOWSKI in a very pretty comparison. If we play roulette for a long time the chances for gaining and losing are equal (disregarding the banker). If we play only a short time we win one day and lose the next. In other words the law of probabilities shows that the excess of molecular impacts which reach a particle in a given quarter suffice to give it movement one direction or another direction. The smaller the particle the greater is the probability that the impacts will not arrest it and the stronger is its movement.

The formula of VON SMOLUCHOWSKI as well as that of A. EINSTEIN demands that $\frac{A^2\eta}{T}$ be constant for equal sized particles.

A = amplitude, η = viscosity, T = oscillation time

TH. SVEDBERG, by brilliantly devised methods, measured these values on colloid metals, in various dispersing media, and established the constants. It is true that the absolute figures for the measured and for the calculated amplitudes do not exactly agree, but they are of the same order of magnitude, i.e., the values found are on the average three times as large as those calculated. SVEDBERG, also, confirmed the quantitative increase of amplitude accompanying a rise in temperature.

This is a remarkable agreement between the movements of small particles seen with the eyes and the hypothesis of the movements of gas molecules based on scientific imagination, which KRONIG in 1856 and CLAUSIUS in 1857 formulated mathematically (kinetic theory of gases). All investigations that have since been undertaken concerning the laws of gases and the movement of colloidal particles have essentially agreed in showing that the laws of gases proved applicable to very dilute solutions of hydrophobe colloids and conversely, that the laws of gases could be developed from the movements of colloid particles. BOYLE'S law asserts that the volume (v) of a gas is inversely proportional to the pressure (p) exerted upon it: $v \cdot v' = p' \ p$. According to GAY-LUSSAC's law the volume change of a gas having the temperature (t) is $v = v_0 \, (1 + \alpha t)$ in which v_0 is the volume at $0°$ and α is the coefficient of expansion. From the standpoint of molecular kinetics under doubled pressure twice as many moving particles are present in the same space. With increase of temperature (assuming the same pressure) αt times fewer particles are present than in the same gas volume at $0°$. This assumes average values, though in fact, the number of particles in a definite volume varies from moment to moment. If this assumption is correct the average of the "instant values" must give values which satisfy BOYLE-GAY-LUSSAC's law. M. VON SMOLUCHOWSKI developed mathematically the relation between this law and the "instant values" He obtained experimental verification when TH. SVEDBERG counted the number of particles for an "instant value" directly in the ultramicroscope and R. LORENZ counted the particles in cinemetagraphs of the ultramicroscopic field The assumption also bridges the gap between *Thermodynamics*, which studies phenomena on the basis of the involved energy and its transformations, and the *Kinetic Molecular Theory*, which views matter as the smallest possible particles in motion

The impact that our ultramicroscopically visible particles exert against the walls of a vessel is the pressure they exert, and it is measurable for a molecularly dispersed system as the *osmotic pressure*.

The *osmotic pressure*, a function of the mass and motion *of a suspension* whose particles are visible and measurable, was shown by J. PERRIN to coincide with the requirements of the *Kinetic Theory of Gases* and of *Thermodynamics;* that is, with its energy content in the form of heat

The following considerations make this clear. Under the influence of gravity the lower layers of the atmosphere have a greater density than the upper, *i e*, the number of gas particles (molecules) in 1 cc is greater in the immediate vicinity of the earth than at higher altitudes. This applies not only for gases but also for solutions or suspensions.

J. PERRIN prepared a very fine suspension of gamboge which he placed in a tall cylinder Gradually under the influence of gravity an equilibrium developed in which there was dense suspension at the bottom of the cylinder with gradually diminishing concentration of particles in the upper layers — an atmosphere in miniature (Fig. 6). By means of the ultramicroscope the contained particles in each layer of 0.12 mm. The ostinato pressure of a particle was calculated by the following formula applicable to the concentrated gases

$$ln \frac{n_0}{n} = \frac{1}{?} + \ (1 - \ ) .$$

n_0 and n are the number of particles contained in the unit volume at the levels a and b, ... gravity, ... density of particles. The value of ... proved to be $14 \cdot 10^{-5}$.

It thus pressure of a single particle expresses the pressure of a ... ...

a gas, the equation $... \frac{K}{...} ...$ applies.

Here N is the number of the molecules present in a gram molecule ... determined by this method, that is to say ... ... From this we derive the value ... ... 1.98 cal. From this the molecular weight of the gamboge particles was proved to be $4 \cdot 10^9$.

FIG. 6. Mastic suspension showing the effect of gravity. (Perrin.)

Diffusion.

If pure water is layered over a concentrated sugar or salt solution so that there is no mixing it is found that after a certain time (hours or days) the sugar or salt passes into the water — we say that it *diffuses* into the water. If one chooses a colored salt solution, e.g. copper sulphate, the path of the diffusion may be easily observed by the coloration. It is in principle the same process as when one permits a compressed gas to stream into the air — the distinction is only in the difference in speed.

It has been shown that different substances have very different rates of diffusion which are characteristic for these substances. These characteristic constants are called *coefficient of diffusion*. The coefficient of diffusion expresses the amount of substance which passes through an area 1 cm.² per second[1] from a solution containing 1 part per cc.

[1] Because this time is so brief it is usually necessary to multiply the coefficients by a large factor or to choose the day as the unit of time.

It is evident that these values are free from any hypothetical considerations It has, however, been shown that the coefficient of diffusion for crystalloids bears a certain relation to the molecular weight. Small molecules diffuse rapidly, large ones slowly. When suitable formulas are used there is very satisfactory correspondence, provided the molecular weights are not smaller than 50 nor larger than 500 A further advance was made by seeking to calculate from the coefficient of diffusion the molecular weights of colloids whose M was unknown. The results were not concordant because the moving units in colloidal solutions are not "molecules" but "particles," that is, complexes of molecules.

If we connect the fact that the coefficient of diffusion decreases with increase in the size of the molecule, with what we know about the *Brownian-Zsigmondy movement*, the relationship is surprising. We have seen that the movement is smaller as the particles grow larger and it is evident that, when we layer water over a metal hydrosol, the strong translatory movements which we observe under the ultramicroscope must carry the hydrosol into the pure water. In coarser suspensions possessing only vibratory movements, we do not expect diffusion to occur.[1] Svedberg measured the diffusion coefficient in different solutions of colloidal gold and calculated the size of the particles from the very simple relation (particle size inversely proportional to diffusion coefficient). The experiments were carried out with two gold solutions which contained particles of $1-3\mu\mu$ and of $20-30\mu\mu$, directly measured ultramicroscopically. There was a relatively good agreement between the results as calculated and determined. A direct relationship between the *Brownian-Zsigmondy* movement and the coefficient of diffusion cannot be experimentally established by methods free from criticism, because the hydrophobe hydrosols (*e g* , colloidal gold, platinum and the like) which may be counted under the ultramicroscope cannot be prepared entirely free of crystalloids Since every crystalloid molecule which is attached to a colloid particle must greatly accelerate the diffusion of the latter, we are confronted with a source of error that is uncontrollable.

A series of coefficients of diffusion have also been measured for hydrophile colloids, which though they have not the exactitude possessed by those of crystalloids, reveal a remarkable constancy so that they may be considered characteristic for the substance under consideration (Sv Arrhenius, R. O. Herzog, Euler, Öholm)

[1] For the mathematical relations between diffusion coefficient, molecular weight and molecule or particle diameter see R O Herzog and L. W Oholm.

This may be illustrated by the following figures:

Substance	Diffusion coefficient	Molecular weight			
		chemically determined	osmotically		
Urea	110	60	60	0.1	
Glycerin	7.	92	91	0..	
Resorcin	66	110	111	0..	
Cane sugar	38	342	345	0.98	
Inulin	14	975? 3342?	2540	1	66.15
Dextrin	10 .		5153	.	
Soluble starch	7		10000	.	
Pepsin	.		10000	1	
Rennin	6.6		11900	4.88	
Egg albumen	5.9		14380	4.86	
Emulsin	4.6		72000	8.65	
Invertin	3.3		44000	.	

All the facts mentioned above indicate what LINOSSIER emphasized even in 1905, that there is a gradual transition from crystalloid to colloid solutions, and that the translatory movement of the particles of a colloid correspond to the diffusion of crystalloid molecules.

[Sir William Ramsay, in a paper entitled "Modern Matter in Relation to Colloidal Solutions," published in "Chemical News," Vol. 65, p. 90 [1892], stated as follows:

"I am disposed to conclude that solution is nothing but subdivision and admixture, owing to attractions between solvent and dissolved substance accompanied by peristaltic motion; that the true osmotic pressure has, probably, never been measured; and that a continuous passage can be traced between visible particles in suspension, and matter in solution; that, in the words of the old adage Natura nihil fit per saltum." Tr.]

Diffusion in Jellies.

Hitherto we have considered only diffusion in pure aqueous solution; in the organism, however, it occurs in a more or less dense colloidal medium. When the concentration of the colloid is not very great, the diffusion is not much impeded. Until recently it was even believed that diffusion of a crystalloid solution in a jelly, e.g., gelatin or agar, occurred just as rapidly as in pure water. This was the result of employing unsuitable experimental methods. The investigations of H. Bechhold and J. Ziegler,[*] Kurt Meyer,[*] Peter Nell[*] and L. W. Öholm showed definitely that electrolytes and non-electrolytes experience a resistance in jellies which reduced the rate of diffusion by obstructing their paths, and that the interference increased if the gel became more concentrated.

Even the age of the jelly may have an influence. Thus, F. Stoffel * showed (from H. Zangger's laboratory) that the diffusion-path of crystalloids in gelatin which was rapidly solidified is greater than it is in gelatin which was slowly solidified, but that this becomes equalized after several days.

The rate of diffusion may be delayed or hastened through the presence of a *third substance*. This affects the diffusion in jellies to a much greater extent than in liquids. On page 69 *et seq.*, we shall see that chlorin, iodin, nitrate, and other ions, urea, etc., favor swelling, on the other hand, sulphate, citrate, and other ions as well as alcohol, sugar, etc., as compared with pure water, diminish swelling, so that to a certain extent the meshes of the colloid network may be opened or closed   It is easy to understand that diffusion will occur less rapidly through narrow meshes than through wide ones. That such an influence on diffusion actually occurs was experimentally shown by H. Bechhold and J. Ziegler.   They showed that the *permeability* of gelatin and agar jellies for electrolytes and non-electrolytes was *increased by urea*, whereas it was diminished by sodium sulphate, grape sugar, glycerin and alcohol   An increase is also produced by sulpho-groups, according to Bohi *

It is evident that every substance which increases the permeability of other substances, paves the way for its own passage as well.   If a jelly has been saturated with urea, the later coming particles of urea will diffuse more rapidly; conversely, sodium sulphate and grape sugar particles obstruct by their influence on the gel the passage of the subsequent particles.

There are other ways in which diffusion in a gel may be distinguished from that in aqueous solution.   We know from Chapter II that colloids adsorb other substances to a greater or less extent. By this means diffusion may be more or less impeded and under certain circumstances even entirely arrested   This may be observed with ease in the diffusion of dyes.   H. Bechhold and J. Ziegler[2] showed that gelatin was deeply stained with methylene blue and thus the diffusion in the gelatin was impeded;* whereas the juice of red beets is a dye which is not noticeably adsorbed.   Finally, if we observe that adsorption is strongly influenced by the presence of salts and non-electrolytes, and that an effect on diffusion is thus exerted, we shall see what great complications may appear when diffusion occurs in colloid media

Though a diffusion of colloids in aqueous media was long doubted the *diffusion of colloids in jellies* was positively denied.   Thomas Graham held it to be characteristic of colloids that they were arrested by other colloids.   H Bechhold[2] called attention to the

* [Graham recognized the slow diffusion of colloids. Tr.]

ability of true albumins to diffuse into gelatin jellies. The fact was demonstrated by means of the *precipitin reaction*. If goat serum is mixed with rabbit serum nothing noteworthy occurs. If the rabbit has previously been injected with goat serum and the serum of the previously treated rabbit called "goat-rabbit serum" is mixed with goat serum there occurs a *precipitate* of an albuminous substance, called "precipitin." Bechhold mixed a 1 per cent gelatin solution containing 0.85 per cent NaCl with an equal volume of goat-rabbit serum. The jelly was solidified in the ice box and goat serum was layered over it. At the end of 24 hours a fine precipitate formed in the gelatin which in the course of 120 hours penetrated as far as 5 mm. The same phenomena resulted when the gelatin was mixed with goat serum and goat-rabbit serum was layered over it. Thus in both cases actual constituent of the serum had diffused into the gelatin.

Similarly, Sv. Arrhenius[*] and Th. Madsen showed that not only diphtheria toxin and tetanolysin, but the highly colloidal diphtheria antitoxin and antitetanolysin could diffuse into 5 per cent gelatin jellies.

Such a diffusion of colloids into a jelly naturally must be expected if the meshes are quite wide, i.e., if the jelly is quite dilute.

Membranes.

It will be appropriate to introduce the concept of "membrane" in the following way: if we make the colloid medium the jelly thicker and thicker, i.e., poorer in water, diffusion must be increasingly hindered. We very soon reach a point where no colloids are able to diffuse into it and we have reached a special case in our present exposition, the *membrane*. We may describe membranes as *water-sible gels*, whose surface is very great in relation to their thickness. They play an important role in the organism but we shall here discuss their general properties only, as their *biological functions* will be considered in Part III.

An excellent general résumé with a very complete bibliography has been published by H. Zangger ("Membrane and the Functions of Membrane").

On account of the great physical and chemical differences of the membranes of the organisms the employment of *artificial membranes* is preferable for the study of their chief properties.

If a very dilute solution of potassium ferrocyanid is carefully layered over a concentrated solution of copper sulphate there is formed at the layer of contact, by chemical interchange, a very thin brown film of copper ferrocyanid. Naturally this film is very delicate and is torn by the slightest movement. If we add gelatin to each solution and permit the two salts to diffuse towards each other in the jelly, there is formed at the layer of contact a very resistant membrane supported by the jelly. Expressed generally, if we permit two substances which form a precipitate together, to diffuse towards each other within a colloid medium which serves as a support, a membrane is formed at the surface of contact which may have, depending upon the nature of the reacting substances, very different degrees of permeability.

Since the time of MORITZ TRAUBE,* such membranes have been studied, especially by G. TAMMANN,* W. PFEFFER,*[1] ADIE,* P. WALDEN* and N. PRINGSHEIM.* The chief interest, however, centered in the osmotic phenomena of salt solutions which could be investigated with the aid of such precipitation membranes, whereas the properties of the membranes themselves, with few exceptions, received but secondary attention. For investigations of osmosis the following substances are especially suitable: ferrocyanid of copper and ferrocyanid of zinc; indeed all ferrocyanid-metal compounds are suitable since they are completely impermeable to many salts. They are briefly described as *semipermeable membranes*, because they are permeable to water though impermeable to most crystalloids. If we permit a zinc ferrocyanid membrane to develop in a gelatin jelly and by the addition of potassium ferrocyanid exercise a very great osmotic pressure, the membrane will break in spite of the jelly support, but it will not permit any potassium ferrocyanid solution to diffuse through.

Besides this extreme case there are membranes of the most different permeabilities. Following up the work of the botanist N. PRINGSHEIM,* H. BECHHOLD and F. ZIEGLER*[1] exhaustively studied such membranes. They impregnated gelatin with silver nitrate or barium chlorid, and poured the molten solution into test tubes containing sodium chlorid or sodium sulphate. At times a layer of pure gelatin was interposed. At the surface of contact membranes of silver chlorid or barium sulphate were formed, which, however, were permeable for the salt solution on either side, because *the membranes grew in the direction of the greater osmotic pressure, i.e., into the solution with the smaller osmotic pressure.*

If, for example, the silver nitrate solution was more concentrated it diffused through the membrane so that the latter grew into the sodium chlorid gelatin; but if the latter was more concentrated the reverse occurred. If both sides had the *same osmotic pressure* a very thin membrane formed which was sufficient however *to arrest completely* the *diffusion of both salts.* Evidently the meshes of the network were filled with membrane-forming precipitate, for as soon as the membrane was melted, it again became permeable. In the same experiment, it was determined that diffusion was hindered only by *visible* precipitate membranes.

There is no difficulty in forming by diffusion similar precipitate membranes from pure organic materials. We have already, on page 55, mentioned that a membrane may be formed by the diffusion of goat serum into goat-rabbit serum and we shall later refer to the fact that H. Bechhold[*] obtained membranes by the diffusion of metaphosphoric acid into gelatin containing albumin. There is no doubt that they may be obtained in other ways if desired. But it must by no means be assumed that a membrane is something rigid and unchangeable; on the contrary it is constantly affected by the substances which flow through it and bathe it, making it more or less permeable, and in this way under certain conditions may evoke a *self-regulation* or a *valve-like action*.

Hitherto there have been no investigations as to the manner in which the permeability of the precipitated membranes described is influenced by *crystalloids* diffusing through them. A *priori* it is to be assumed that such an influence exists just as in the case of reversible jellies. That membranes may be more or less rapidly occluded by colloids is an observation which has been frequently made during the performance of ultrafiltration.

A number of dried animal and vegetable membranes and parchment paper resemble precipitate membranes, in that they possess the same or but slightly superior swelling capacity. In *dialysis* they are used for the separation of colloids from crystalloids.

Most of the membranes occurring in the organism are more or less *swollen*; on drying they lose this property to a great extent, as they are inelastic gels.

Ultrafilters (see p. 95) formed by impregnating irreversible jellies are similar to natural membranes, since they must be kept in water to preserve their swollen condition.

Membranes may be powerfully *adsorbent*, like reversible gels and in this respect powerfully influence diffusion and filtration. Thus dyes, especially the basic ones, as well as certain groups of enzymes e.g., arachnolysin, staphylolysin and rennin (H. Bechhold[**]) are strongly adsorbed by many membranes. Such adsorbed substances may enter into chemical combination with the membrane, causing either shrinking or loss of swelling capacity, and thus diminish its permeability. This is the effect, e.g., of tannic acid, formaldehyde and chromates.

Alcohol, ether, acetone and sugar increase the permeability in certain low concentrations; stronger solutions work to a certain extent in the opposite direction.

The influence of *electrolytes* on the membranes of the organism and their permeability may depend on different causes. It may, for example, affect the swelling, and thus, the permeability. Alkalis in general increase the swelling, so also do acids in great dilution, but when concentrated they usually cause shrinking. Chemical changes due to chromic acid, etc., diminish the permeability.

The influence of electrolytes is not however limited to this rather indirect action. We shall see on page 77 *et seq.*, that differences of potential may develop at the interface between a solid phase and a fluid. Thus, for example, cellulose and wool are negatively charged with respect to pure water. In the case of the majority of animal membranes, most of which are amphoteric, the difference in potential develops only in faintly alkaline or faintly acid water. The presence of salts likewise raises or lowers the difference in potential. The difference in the adsorbability of ions is accounted for also in this manner. Wherever a difference in potential exists, the diffusion rate of water is lowered. Salts, on the other hand, develop a difference of potential in the course of diffusion; in their passage through a membrane, they raise or lower the existing difference in potential. *Vice versa*, on this account the diffusion rate of salts is affected by the difference in potential existing in the membrane.

A membrane may thus be the seat of an *electromotive force* (F. HABER,[*] GIRARD[*]), provided that it separates two salt solutions, or a salt solution from water, and that one solution be faintly acid or faintly alkaline. In the first instance the diffusion through the membrane will be much impeded, in the latter much accelerated.

The results of R. BURIAN[*1] also indicate differences in potential in the ultrafiltration of albumin-salt mixtures; at reduced pressures, he obtained as filtrate a salt solution isotonic with the liquid filtered. If he filtered under increased pressure, the filtrate contained a lower salt concentration than the original solution F G. DONNAN[*] has made an unusually important and fundamental study of membrane equilibria, based upon the osmotic pressure and membrane potential of electrolytes containing a colloidal ion. I shall try to present DONNAN's ideas without entering upon their mathematical basis. Let R represent an acid colloid, *e g.*, congo red, which forms a salt with Na, and let the line which separates the colloid electrolyte from water in our diagram be a membrane, impermeable to the colloid.

(a) *Membrane hydrolysis.* Let us consider what occurs when the outer water is constantly renewed as described on page 92 *et seq.*, which may be represented in the following diagram:

Initial condition			Terminal condition	
RH NaOH	water		RH	water NaOH

on, there is formed by this... ... does not also which a small diffuse through, although the NaOH ... ... and is a strong acid, the process terminates rapidly provided the NaOH remains in the outer water, and ... ... develop within the cell which is chiefly produced by the R and N constituents of the colloid electrolytes as occurs for instance in the ... ... compared.

If the colloid electrolyte is a weak acid these ... actually more NaOH diffuses outward, and when the equilibrium is established is chiefly by the hydrolytically split colloid acid and the NaOH. Example: soap solution.

If the NaOH is constantly removed by continually renewing the outer water, or by means of a bond which is not at all or slightly dissociated, e.g., carbonic acid, there will finally remain only colloid acid, in fact the weaker the colloid and the more rapidly the process will terminate. What has been stated for an acid colloid applies of course to a basic one also.

It follows from these premises that salts even of strong acids and bases may be completely broken up hydrolytically provided one ion is a colloid which can be held back by a membrane. By *membrane hydrolysis* it is possible to separate from a neutral salt either an alkali (intestinal or pancreatic juice) or an acid—hydrochloric acid in the stomach or acid urine. It requires no special experiment to show that the same process may be brought about by *ultrafiltration*.

The reverse process may occur, however. If there is a colloid acid or base in a cell surrounded by a membrane, e.g., an amphoteric colloid albumin or fibrin, a minimal concentration of H or OH ions in the outer fluids suffices to form a salt with the colloid in the cell which by swelling develops a higher osmotic pressure.

(b) We shall now consider what occurs when the colloid electrolyte within the membrane has an ion in common with the electrolyte outside, e.g., the Na salt of congo red (RNa) and common salt (NaCl). We then have the following formula

Initial condition		Equilibrium	
R	Cl	R	Cl
Na	Na	Na	Na
(1)	(2)	(1)	
			(2)

Na ions cannot pass from space (1) to space (2) since by reason of its colloidal character the anion R cannot follow.[1] However, Cl and with it the same amount of Na will diffuse into (1). The amount of

---

[1] There are always the same number of anions and cations in a solution. It is impossible to separate them by diffusion for then a free electric charge would be liberated.

NaCl which diffuses depends on the concentration of the solutions in space (1) and space (2). If the concentration in space 2 (C_2) is high in proportion to that in space 1 (C_1) much NaCl will pass from (1) to (2) and, if the conditions are reversed, only a little will do so.

Mathematically represented (assuming complete electrolytic dissociation) we have the following equation, where C_1 or C_2 represent the molar ion concentration in the respective spaces and X the fraction of the molar ion concentration which diffuses from (2) to (1):

$$\frac{C_2 - X}{X} = \frac{C_1 + C_2}{C_2}.$$

If C_2 is small in comparison with C_1 we may express it: $\dfrac{X}{C_2} = \dfrac{C_2}{C_1}$

If C_1 is very small the equation becomes $\dfrac{X}{C_2} = \dfrac{1}{2}$.

The following table taken from DONNAN's work illustrates the distribution of NaCl

Original concentration of NaR in (1), C_1	Original concentration of NaCl in (2), C_2	Original relation of NaR to NaCl, $\dfrac{C_1}{C_2}$	Per cent NaCl diffusing from (2) to (1), $\dfrac{100\,X}{C_2}$
0 01	1	0 01	49 7
0 1	1	0 1	47 6
1	1	1	33
1	0 1	10	8.3
1	0 01	100	1

Though we might assume *à priori* that the NaCl would distribute itself equally in both spaces in the presence of a membrane absolutely permeable for it, this table shows that the colloid electrolyte has a remarkable influence as soon as the concentration of NaCl falls. To a certain extent the colloid electrolytes drive the NaCl out of the cell. If $C_1 = 1$ only about 11 per cent of a physiological salt solution ($C_2 = 0.145$) could penetrate the cell, or if it were already in the cell it was reduced to about 11 per cent. Apparently the membrane is permeable only from one side for the readily diffusible NaCl.

(c) Finally we must consider the case when the colloid electrolyte in the membrane is opposed to an electrolyte without an ion in common, as for instance

Initial condition		Equilibrium	
Na	K	Na	K
R	Cl	K	Na

Na will diffuse out, K and Cl will diffuse in ... in ... ... following equation if $C_{Na(1)}$ expresses the mol ... ... Na in space (1).

$$\frac{C_{Na(1)}}{C_{Na(2)}} = \frac{C_{K(1)}}{C_{K(2)}} = \frac{C_{Cl \, 1}}{C_{Cl \, 2}} = \frac{C_1 + C_2}{C_2}$$

If the concentration in the cell (C_1) is large compared with that ... ... solution (C_2), then

$$\frac{C_1 + C_2}{C_2} = \frac{C_1}{C_2}$$

If C_1 is small, then

$$\frac{C_1 + C_2}{C_2} = 1.$$

Let us consider the equation representing a condition that frequently occurs physiologically. If $C_1 = 100$ and $C_2 = 1$ ... know ... ... per cent of the Na originally present in 1 will remain ... 1 ... 1 per cent will diffuse into (2). 99 per cent of the K originally ... cent in (2) will diffuse into (1), only 1 per cent of the Cl originally present in (2) will diffuse into (1).

From this we may understand the hitherto inexplicable behavior of salt in cells, *e.g.*, in red blood corpuscles. ... cells take up in some cases the foreign crystalloid cation and diffuse out the anion ... ... the cations act in the reverse way.

In conclusion DONNAN derived formulas for the difference ... electric potential which must exist after the conditions described have been reached (membrane potentials).

There are already many theories to explain the differences in potential in organs and the electrical currents which occur in ... (muscle, nerve, electric-fish). These theories have the ... that they require conditions which do not exist in the body ... that much greater differences in potential arise in the body than would be possible according to these theories. In this point DONNAN's theory differs much from its predecessors.

We shall not present his formula here but only a general explanation. If there are two equally concentrated solutions of NaCl separated by a membrane, and we insert a piece of platinum in each and connect them with a wire, no current will flow ... ... If the solutions are of different concentrations, the ... ... energy will be evident until the difference has disappeared ... as the result of diffusion. Such systems are called "concentration couples."

A system consisting of colloid electrolyte salt is a "concentration couple which develops a current in passing from "non-equilibrium condition" to "equilibrium." This may be explained by ...

concentration of ions on the two sides of the membrane. Let us consider the simplest illustration of the equilibrium between NaR and NaCl represented in our table on page 60 where the original concentration is NaR : NaCl = 1 : 1 and equilibrium is established when 33 per cent NaCl passes from (2) to (1).

The schematic representation would be:

$$
\begin{array}{c|c}
\multicolumn{2}{c}{\text{Equilibrium}} \\
\text{Na} & \text{Na} \\
\text{Na} & \text{Na} \\
\text{Cl} & \text{Cl} \\
\text{R} & \text{Cl} \\
(1) & (2)
\end{array}
$$

In this instance all charges are mutually satisfied excepting those of Cl and R. The slowly diffusing anion R is opposed to the rapidly diffusing anion Cl so that a difference of potential must arise at the boundary surface. In the cases hitherto described, the membrane itself is the seat of the difference in potential. The conditions are quite different if the membrane acts only as a bounding surface, that is, if it is not equally permeable for all ions. In this case, the universally present "contact potential," existing in two contiguous salt solutions, is modified by the aforementioned property of the membrane.

Finally, we must recall another kind of membrane which does not fall into any of the previous categories. According to W. NERNST, a film of water upon ether forms a semipermeable membrane for benzol. The experiment is carried out in this way: A pig's bladder is soaked in water; the bladder plays no part, other than to hold the water which forms a partition between ether and ether containing benzol. Here the semipermeability of the membrane depends entirely on *selective solubility*. Benzol is insoluble in water; ether on the contrary has a limited solubility, and as a result ether diffuses through the water to the benzol. Subsequently many such combinations were devised. They are very extensively distributed in the organism. It is unnecessary to think of complete semipermeability in every case; scattered deposits (fat, lecithin, etc.) may suffice to bring about a partial permeability.

The membranes of WISTINGHAUSEN depend on this principle of selective permeability. He impregnated with gallic acid salts, animal membranes which then became permeable for fat; by merely washing away the salts the permeability is abolished. Attention should be called to a remarkable observation of ZOTT (cited by H. ZANGGER) which belongs in this chapter. He discovered that a membrane through which sugar has diffused, permitted the passage of gum arabic after it had been moistened with alcohol.

CHAPTER V.

CONSISTENCY OF COLLOIDS.

Internal Friction.

THE various colloids show all possible transitions from fluids to solid substances. A *fluid* may take on any shape, and the work necessary to change its form, *i e.*, to overcome its *internal friction*, is very slight. Solid substances, according to WILHELM OSTWALD, possess a *form-energy* also called elasticity, the energy necessary to change their form, *i e.*, to overcome their internal friction, is very great. If we picture to ourselves a number of colloids and gels we pass from a true fluid, water for instance, through the albumoses and albumin solutions to the semifluid gels (*e.g.*, 1 per cent gelatin), jellies and finally to the firm substances (*e.g.*, horn).

High internal friction, *viscosity*, is a typical property of hydrophile colloids. Since colloids are diphasic systems, the internal friction will depend, above all, upon the size of the free surface of the colloid, *i.e.*, upon the concentration. Changes in temperature are of great importance. The absolute as well as the relative influence of concentration is, indeed, characteristic for colloids. Even traces of colloids (agar, gelatin) may increase the viscosity of water to an extraordinary extent. We may obtain all degrees of internal friction with agar and in fact a 5 per cent solution of agar is a solid body at room temperature.

Usually the viscosity increases with decrease in temperature, inasmuch as substances then approach the solid condition. Gelatinization is analogous to the solidification of a molten fluid, where internal friction rapidly rises within a small temperature range.

J. FRIEDLÄNDER,[*] D. HOLDE[*] and V. ROTHMUND[*] proved that artificial emulsions (gum water, castor oil, so-called solid fats) exhibit a variation in their viscosity curves according to temperature and concentration, similar to that shown by many natural hydrophile colloids. T. B ROBERTSON[*] found that emulsions of oil in water became increasingly more viscous the higher the concentration of the oil, until a critical point was reached when the viscosity decreased; the water then became the dispersed phase.

Internal friction is indeed a very complicated phenomenon. It depends according to W. B. HARDY upon (1) the internal friction of the different phases, (2) the surface friction of the internal surfaces, (3) the surface tension of the internal surfaces and (4) the strength of the electrical charge. To what extent the individual factors influence the internal friction is as yet unknown.

We have, however, received valuable guidance from the study of the effect of electrolytes. Especially remarkable is the *parallelism between swelling and internal friction*. It depends, apparently, on the fact that both phenomena are characterized by an increase, *i e.*, multiplication, of the free surfaces. Thus, for instance, we see that acids and alkalies which favor the swelling of gelatin also increase the internal friction of albumin, because there probably occurs an increase in the free surfaces of the albumin ions (see p. 153 *et seq.*).

Swelling and Shrinking.

If a crystalloid (common salt, sugar) is thrown into water, it subdivides in it until finally it is completely dissolved, the particles of salt or sugar lose their cohesion A colloid (glue, wood) in contact with water increases its volume, it swells, its particles retain their cohesion This property, however, is possessed only by hydrophile colloids

The imbibition of water, that is, swelling, may either go on indefinitely in the case of colloids, so that finally the particles are torn asunder and a solution or sol is formed as in the case of albumin, or the imbibition may reach its limit very rapidly, as in the case of wood. Between these there are all sorts of transitions, *e.g.*, glue. Only in the case of gels is it usual to refer to swelling. In the organism, gels having very slight ability to swell serve as *covering* and *framework* (*e.g*, hide, collagen, shells and wood). They are intended to retain the outward form. The same is true of the supporting tissues of the individual organs and even of the cells, vessel walls, the membranes of the intestinal canal, connective tissues, the vascular bundles of plants, cell membranes, etc. On the other hand, the cell *content* possesses the ability to swell to a high degree.

Every organ has a certain definite normal fluid content. A healthy plant has a definite turgescence and the protoplasm of a healthy animal a given degree of swelling; every abnormal change in this signifies illness or even death. Without doubt swelling plays a very important role in the case of many phenomena which have hitherto been attributed to osmotic pressure. Indeed, the osmotic pressure is only manifested completely in the presence of a semipermeable membrane, whereas the ability to swell does not require the presence of a membrane. Swelling may under some circumstances counterbalance the osmotic pressure or even overcome it and concentrate solutions   An excellent example of the latter is described by C. LUDWIG   He hung a well-dried animal bladder in concentrated salt solution.   The bladder swelled, taking up a dilute salt solution and common salt crystallized out in the remainder.   Amphibia, *e g.*, frogs, may lose one-fourth of their body weight upon drying as has been shown by E. OVERTON [*3]   Although they contain about 80 per cent water, the osmotic pressure of the blood almost doubles. The explanation of this is that only a portion is water of solution, the remainder is water of swelling.   Upon drying the *water of swelling* is more strongly retained than the *water of solution.*

Swelling exhibits manifestations of energy to no less a degree than osmotic pressure   I shall give several examples taken from WOLF-GANG OSTWALD's "Grundriss."   According to the investigations of the plant physiologist, HALES, swelling peas were able to lift the cover of an iron pot weighted with 83 5 kilograms   H. RODEWALD found that it requires 2523 atmospheres pressure to overcome the swelling pressure of starch.   J. REINKE* determined the swelling pressure of laminaria, a sea weed.   Some of his data quoted from H. FREUNDLICH give us an idea of the enormous pressures, changes in volume and amounts of water taken up when swelling occurs and of the pressures required for dehydration   Ten layers of dried laminaria scales each 0.1 mm. thick and 50 mm.² were placed in the apparatus.

Pressures in atmospheres	Elevation in mm due to swelling	Percentage of water by volume in air-dried substance
41 2	0 16	16
21 2	0 35	35
7 2	0 97	97
1	3 30	330

We obtain a fair idea as to the general course of swelling by observing a sheet of gelatin.   Dry gelatin takes up one-third of its weight of water from a moisture-saturated atmosphere at room temperature, in order to reach a condition of equilibrium.   If this sheet is then placed in a dish of cold running water it absorbs from it 10 times its dry weight of water in order again to reach a condition of equilibrium. In dry air the water evaporates and shrinking occurs.   The experiment may be repeated as often as desired with the same result.   On this account substances of this group are termed *elastic gels.*

Coagulated albumin, *e g.*, boiled fibrin, behaves differently.   If it is air-dried a horny residue remains which, though it takes up some water, or swells when it is placed in water, never again approaches its original gelatinous state, such gels are called *inelastic gels*. One of the most important operations of microscopical technic is the hardening of elastic gels. (See Chapter XXIII.) Their ability to swell in water is destroyed by the chemical action of formalin, chromic acid, mercuric chloride, etc. We must consider that in the organism, the inelastic gels, i.e., connective tissue and also the cell pellicle, etc., arise from elastic gels by chemical changes with consequent loss of water or drying, as may be observed at the surface of any wound. In this connection, we may revert to the formation of *surface films* (see p. 35), whose formation is certainly more than merely analogous to that of organized membranes, skin, etc.

Classical studies on the swelling and shrinking of slightly elastic gels were made by J. M. van Bemmelen in the case of silicic acid gel and amplified by O. Bütschli. So many difficulties are unfortunately offered to the application by analogy of these properties to organized inelastic gels, that we must confine our attention to the most important ones. The evaporation of water from a silicic acid gel proceeds at first as it would from a solution. When the gel reaches a certain consistency a turbidity appears, that is, hollow spaces of about 5 μμ form between the supporting walls of the gel which become filled with air. Upon losing still more water, the turbidity disappears and the gel becomes glassy. In this latter respect the inelastic gel of silicic acid differs very materially from the elastic gel of gelatin, which does not become turbid. This is likewise the case in the reabsorption of water. Though gelatin shows a similar curve both on swelling and shrinking, silicic acid gel and indeed we may say all inelastic gels show entirely different curves. That is, the swelling of elastic gels is practically completely reversible, whereas with inelastic gels this is not the case.

The changes a gel undergoes on *freezing* and *thawing* are very similar to those of shrinking and swelling. The crystallization of ice from a gel containing water indicates a withdrawal of water, whereas upon thawing, water becomes again available for swelling (H. W. Fischer, O. Bobertag and C. Feist[*]). There are consequently substances which after freezing and thawing revert almost completely to their original state, e.g., soluble starches, fish glue, whereas others, e.g., silicic acid hydrosol and albumin, undergo changes which are more or less irreversible.

The *influence of electrolytes on the swelling* of gelatin, agar, pigsbladder, cartilage and fibrin, is very considerable. It has been investigated especially by F. Hofmeister,[*] Wo. Pauli,[*] K. Spiro,[*] Wo. Ostwald,[*] and Martin H. Fischer.[*] It may, in general, be stated that *acids* and *alkalis* increase the swelling capacity to an extraordinary degree   This, however, does not depend only upon the electrolytic dissociation of various acids and the concentration of H or OH ions.   In the case of strong acids it reaches a maximum at a certain concentration and then decreases.   Thus MARTIN H. FISCHER found that fibrin, which swelled to 8 mm. in water, in 0 02 normal HCl reached the maximum swelling of 48 mm.; whereas in 0.1 normal HCl the swelling reached only 21 mm.   In the case of H_2SO_4 the maximum swelling was only 11 mm. in 0.024 normal acid Purified glutin (according to the experiments of R. CHIARI in PAULI's

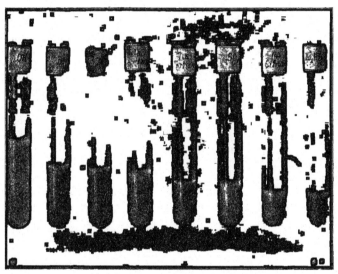

FIG 7.   The swelling of fibrin in solutions of various sodium salts
($\frac{1}{40}$ molecular)   (From M H Fischer)

laboratory) is so , sensitive to acids that it swells less in distilled water than in Vienna Hochquellwasser, because of the CO_2 contained in the latter.   Furthermore, distilled water may even be distinguished from conductivity water by swelling experiments with glutin.   The swelling in alkalis is still greater; in 0.02 normal NaOH it reached 77 mm.   M H. FISCHER believes that the swelling in acids is dependent upon the concentration of the H ions minus the effect of the anions of the acid under consideration.   In this case, there probably exists an antagonism between cation and anion, such as may be demonstrated in the case of neutral salts   A similar rule probably obtains for alkalis.

When such heterogeneous substances as gelatin, fibrin, etc., behave similarly under the influence of electrolytes, we may assume that the same cause determines the behavior, and this cause must be sought in the chemical nature of these substances. Apparently these substances are amphoteric, i.e. at the same time weak acids and weak bases, forming, under the influence of acids and bases, more or less ionized salt. Ionization causes an hydration, i.e., an imbibition of water which is evidenced in the case of these gels by their capacity to swell, and in the case of dissolved albumins, by an increase of the internal friction. We should therefore not expect to see these phenomena in the case of gels of entirely different chemical properties, silicic acid gel, for example.

Neutral salt, to a certain extent, favor the imbibition of water and indeed the swelling is greater in such dilute salt solutions than it is in pure water. At a certain concentration (for NaCl, 13.8 per cent) the amount of fluid taken up reaches a maximum and then falls again. The anions are primarily active in favoring swelling, whereas the cations have a lesser influence in favoring swelling,

$$CNS > I > Br > NO_3 > ClO_3 > Cl,$$

whereas in favoring shrinkage,

$$SO_4 > tartrate > citrate > acetate.$$

Although a dry jelly removes more water from a salt solution than it does salt, so that the concentration of the solution is increased, a wetter jelly takes up more salt than it does water, thus diminishing the concentration of the solution. *The swelling in acid or alkaline solutions is always much decreased by the presence of neutral salt* and anions are much more active than cations. In producing this decrease

$$citrate > tartrate > phosphate > Cl > SO_4 > acetate > I > CNS$$
$$NO_3 > Br > Cl.$$

$$Fe > Cu > Sr > Ba > Ca > Mg > NH_4 > Na > K.$$

Though e.g. 0.78 gm gelatin in 100 cc. of 0.06 n HCl swelled up to 11.61 gm, the swelling reached only 2.84 gm in the presence of $\frac{m}{2}$ pot's ammo citrate and about 7 gm in the presence of $\frac{m}{2}$ KCl.

Protective effect. In addition to the antagonistic action of neutral salt on the swelling due to H and OH ion, there is also an antagonism to a precipitation by polyvalent cations.

Thus it has been determined by the experiments of MARTIN FISCHER on fibrin and of Wo. OSTWALD on gelatin that swelling much more strongly depressed by polyvalent cations than by monovalent ones (Mg < Ca <, Ba <, Sr <, Cu <, Fe) and it seems probable that polyvalent cations counteract the action of monovalent ones favoring swelling. So far as I know there is as yet no colloid chemical confirmation of this assumption in the case of swollen colloids. There are, however, a number of biological experiments concerning the inhibition of the poisonous action of neutral salts by polyvalent cations (see p 378), which in all probability are referable to the inhibition of harmful swelling. According to these biological experiments the antitoxic effect of cations increases with their valence and stands in relation to the ionization pressure or the electrolytic solution tension [1]

Our present knowledge indicates that the *swelling* and the *leaving* of *hydrophil gels* absolutely *parallels the formation of ions in neutral particles in the case of albumin*. This has been more exhaustively discussed on page 163 *et seq*. The same factor which favors the ionization of albumin, namely, acid and alkali, also favors swelling. In this case as in the other the presence of neutral salt depresses the action of acids and alkalis, polyvalent cations, anions acting more powerfully than monovalent ones. We recognize in both ionization and swelling a tendency toward an increase of the free surface, which is associated with the taking up of water. This may go so far that the molecules are split, hydrolysis occurs and cleavage products are formed. Accordingly chemical actions, especially hydrolytic cleavage, occur much more rapidly in swollen than in shrunken colloids. For instance, according to E. KNOEVENAGEL[1], the hydrolysis of swollen metal cellulose potassium hydrate requires only a few minutes, but the same process requires days in the case of the shrunken material.

Non-electrolytes have only a slight influence on swelling. Of the few cases known to us we may mention that urea favors the swelling of *gelatin* even in acid solution, but it has no effect on fibrin. Alcohol and sugar favor the swelling of gelatin in a certain concentration between 1 and 2 per cent.

These data were almost exclusively obtained with *gelatin* and *fibrin*. Both gels behave qualitatively alike in swelling, although there are *quantitative* differences. I determine well in the case

[1] To avoid any misunderstanding it should be stated that salts which are themselves strongly toxic, eg barium, etc in isotonic solution are favorable small doses as antidotes probably by counteracting swelling. In large

than gelatin. Gelatin may absorb about 25 times its weight in water; fibrin 40 times. The order in which neutral salts act on gelatin is different from that in which they act upon fibrin.

It may be assumed that the different gels of the organism vary quantitatively in their behavior under the influence of the same electrolytes and it is obvious that the salt absorption of different gels varies as well as their water absorption. An investigation of the water and salt absorption of different kinds of gels in the presence of *mixtures* of electrolytes is much to be desired. Our knowledge of tissues and secretions forces us to the conclusion that the different tissues possess a very different *specific ability to absorb* certain substances or ions. Only thus can we understand why the blood corpuscles withdraw more potassium salts from the lymph, the cartilages more sodium salts and the bone-building tissues more calcium salts. Only thus can we obtain a conception of the specific crystalloid content of various secretions and of selective resorption.

The Crystallization of Colloids.

Though P. P. von Weimarn describes the crystalline state as the "sole ultimate condition of matter" which is characteristic [1] for all substances (even gases), we shall not attempt here a critical study of this theory nor determine the limits of the crystallization of solids. We shall consider only how crystals occur in colloidal substances and more particularly limit ourselves to the biocolloids. We know only a limited number of crystallizable biocolloids; the most important are egg albumin, horse serum albumin, certain plant albumins (aleuron crystals from Para nuts, cotton, hemp and sunflower seeds), oxyhemoglobins, hemoglobin and methemoglobin. Egg albumin has been obtained in the shape of needles, the albumins of vegetable seeds partly in octahedra and partly in tablet-shaped hexagonal prisms. Oxyhemoglobins crystallize in various ways depending upon the animal species from which they are derived. For example, horse oxyhemoglobin forms rhombic, and squirrel oxyhemoglobin forms hexagonal prisms. These substances may be recrystallized and under the same conditions give the identical crystal form. It may be remarked in passing, that many crystals giving the albumin reaction have frequently been observed in organs, but they have been insufficiently studied. [Crystalline form is markedly influenced by the presence of protective colloids in the crystallizing solution See J. Alexander, Kolloid Zeitschrift, iv, p. 86. Tr.] Crystalline products have been obtained from *starches*, e.g., sphero-crystals from *inulin*.

[1] Bibliography given in Wo. Ostwald's Grundiss der Kolloidchemie (Dresden, 1911).

The crystallization of alkaline salts of the higher *fatty* and *acylic acids* is well known.

The crystals of colloids are distinguishable from those of crystalloids in many respects. That their solution is preceded by a swelling is not surprising in view of the hydrophile colloidal character of the substances under consideration. On the other hand, it is remarkable that *other constituents* may always be demonstrated as inclusions. The crystallized globuline from vegetable seeds always contain common salt. K. A. H. MOERNER[*] showed that only the sulphates of egg and serum albumin were crystallizable. As F. ABDERHALDEN[*] has shown, oxyhemoglobin crystals do not contain their proper proportion of albumin, and although numerous researches on crystallized egg albumin have been undertaken, in different instances the amount of contained carbohydrate varied.

In spite of these facts, we are of the opinion that colloids can actually crystallize, and that their crystal form is not controlled by the crystalloid impurities. We know that crystalloid frequently include mother liquor, that they may form mixed crystals and that it is often impossible to remove impurities by ordinary recrystallization. In view of the persistent salt content of crystallized albumins it is probable that only their salt-like compound possess a definite crystalline shape. Especially favorable to this view is the fact reported by DABROWSKI, that crystallized egg albumin when placed in a 3.6 per cent solution of ammonium sulphate, exhibits a more rapid diffusion than salt free egg albumin, and has about one-sixth of the atomic volume of the latter. The crystallized egg albumin, therefore, is formed of smaller particles.

The Life Curve of Colloids.

Though in the absence of chemical changes crystalloids retain their physical properties, in the case of colloids after a lapse of time changes occur which are commonly called *aging*. For instance, acid gel which has been freshly prepared from water glass solution and HCl is at first dialyzable but loses this property after a few days. Most of the "aging phenomena" of sols are characterized by the fact that the particles of a highly dispersed solution gather together to form larger particles, that their sensitiveness to the reactions increased or that they spontaneously coagulate. In the case of gels their elasticity suffers changes and they become optically inhomogeneous or turbid.

Bearing in mind that colloids are unstable systems it is obvious that in the course of time they must change since they tend to become stable systems. In the examination of a colloid the observer

found, strictly speakmg, are applicable to its momentary condition; previously and subsequently it has different properties. Every point of its *life curve* has a *previous history* and the final portions of this constantly flattening curve are the agmg phenomena In contradistinction to crystalloids every colloid is a particular *individual*.

If solutions of hydrophobe colloids, *e g*, arsenic sulphid, gold solution, etc. (without protective colloid), are permitted to stand for some time, they flocculate after a short time or else after a lapse of years It may be that traces of electrolytes are responsible for the flocculation. In other cases, electrolytes certainly play no part; as I shall show by a number of examples, there is an evident tendency for the unstable colloids to pass over into less dispersed and stable systems (see L. WOHLER's* observation on the aging of colloidal molybdic and tungstic acid). Several years ago H. BFCHHOLD and J ZIEGLER[1] sought to prepare for therapeutic purposes, with the aid of new and especially suitable protective colloids, solutions of such organic substances as are insoluble in water (iodoform, iodochloroxychinolin, camphor, etc.). They succeeded in thus preparing the substances, which, however, kept only a few weeks, when they would separate out in crystals. Obviously these substances are not sufficiently insoluble and they exhibited the adsorption phenomenon described on page 18. P. P. VON WEIMARN made analogous observations on the sol of barium sulphate in which crystals appeared at the end of six months. The inequality of the particles, or more correctly the "specific surface," obviously militates against the stability of such colloid solutions In the majority of cases, it soon leads to the "death" of the colloidal system.

Furthermore, we must emphasize that the changes in the colloidal system need not always consist in a diminution of the dispersion. Occasionally we find that the particles become smaller with the lapse of time, but this has hitherto been observed only in the case of hydrophile colloids (glycogen, benzopurpurin, hemoglobin, lecithin, etc) (W. BILTZ and L. GATIN-GRUSŽEWSKA,* LEMANISSIER,* E. RAHLMANN,*[1] R. ZSIGMONDY*[2]).

Under some circumstances even electrolytes may act disruptively. Thus B. G. MOORE and H. E. ROAF* observed that minutest traces of electrolytes are absolutely necessary for the stability of an albumin solution, as was frequently pointed out by E. JORDIS for hydrophile sols. W. BILTZ and H. VON VEGESACK* observed, however, that in the case of dye solutions, merely with the lapse of time, marked increase in viscosity occurs.

It may be pointed out in connection with the aging of *jellies*, that

[1] As yet unpublished.

freshly poured gelatin cylinders reach a practically constant modulus of elasticity at the end of three to four hours. This accords with the fact observed by F. Stoffel, that crystalloids diffuse more rapidly in quickly chilled than in slowly chilled gelatin, and that this difference disappears after several days (see p. 54).

At the outset we spoke of the "life curve of colloids," of "aging phenomena," "death," "individual properties," etc., and it might appear that these are only similes borrowed from the organized world. In my opinion the relationship is closer, and I believe that we may obtain a more profound understanding of the phenomena of Life (so unintelligible to us) by a study of such phenomena in colloids.

Aging has hitherto been considered, for the most part, a purely biological phenomenon. In my opinion, we may attack the problems with the methods of exact science, if we could but separate two groups: the organs (cell groups), which constantly renew themselves, from those which are lasting. We would, *à priori*, expect changes in the latter similar to those observed as aging phenomena in colloids. We saw that a rapidly chilled gelatin was at first easily penetrable for crystalloids, but that with time its resistance increased. We may, therefore, assume that in young organs (fresh membranes) the exchange of matter by diffusion proceeds more rapidly. The decrease in elasticity, one of the most characteristic phenomena of aging, may be measurably followed in aging gelatin. In fact it has been shown that for the vital staining of nerves with methylene blue, young animals are more suitable than old ones. With aging there occurs *shrinking*, which begins already in intrauterine life. In the third month of human fetal life the water content is 94 per cent, at birth it is 69 to 66 per cent, in adult life 58 per cent. We may say in general that with aging there is a decrease in the swelling capacity of the organ colloids. This holds both for animal organisms, which lose water as they grow older, and for plants (dry leaves — lignification).

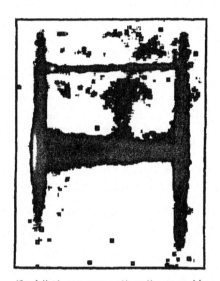

Tyndall Phenomenon. (From Wo. Ostwald.)

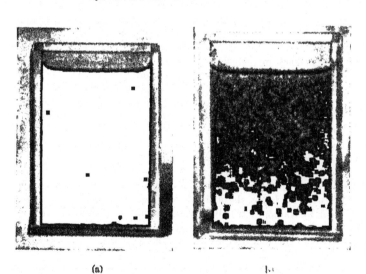

(a)   (b)

Suspensions of Lampblack
(a), uncoagulated, (b), coagulated. (From L. P. Loeb.)

CHAPTER VI.

OPTICAL AND ELECTRICAL PROPERTIES OF COLLOIDS.

Optical Properties.

COLLOIDAL solutions, e.g., albumin, always show a slight turbidity. If a strong ray of light is passed through such a solution, its path may be seen as a bright band. (See Plate I.) The "Tyndall phenomenon," as it is known, is much more distinct if a ray of light is passed through smoke or through a turbid suspension, in which case, the reflected light is polarized. This phenomenon manifests itself if a sunbeam passes into a dark room. The illuminated dust particles (motes) appear bright against the dark background.

MICHAEL FARADAY observed the phenomenon in the case of gold hydrosols and he was led to the opinion that such solutions, which we nowadays call colloids, were nothing but extremely finely divided suspensions (dispersed systems). It was a great service to science, when H. SIEDENTOPF and R. ZSIGMONDY recognized the importance of this phenomenon for the investigation of colloids, and constructed an instrument adapted to this purpose by passing the reflected light into a microscope. In this way they obtained bright pictures of the suspended particles on a dark ground. Since neither of these investigators paid any attention to the representation of the shape of the particles, and devoted their attention only to the reflection of a point of light, it was possible, by utilizing the strongest sources of light (sun, arc lamp), to perceive particles lying below the limit of microscopic visibility. They, therefore, called the apparatus the *ultramicroscope*.

The great number of fundamental observations with the ultramicroscope which we owe to R. ZSIGMONDY [*2] and his followers have been repeatedly mentioned. R. ZSIGMONDY called the particles which he could definitely distinguish against the dark field, but which were far below the limit of microscopic visibility, *submicrons* (from 6 to 250 $\mu\mu$). If only a faint cone of light could be seen, it is to be assumed in many cases, that the smallness of the individual particles precludes the recognition of each one. Such particles (under 6 $\mu\mu$) he called *amicrons*.

Most inorganic hydrosols, especially metals, form characteristically colored solutions, e.g., silver hydrosols are brown, platinum

75

hydrosols are greenish brown, gold hydrosols are red but become blue and finally brown when electrolytes are added. In the ultramicroscope the individual particles are not of a uniform color For instance, collargol has blue, red, violet and green particles, the particles of a red gold solution are chiefly green, those of blue solutions range from yellow to reddish brown.

 Theoretically, submicrons of the same size should have the same color so that the variety of color in the ultramicroscope indicates variation in the size of the particles. As a matter of fact, as we have said, the smaller submicrons of finely divided red gold hydrosol are almost all green though there are very small brown submicrons. There is no entirely acceptable explanation for the color variation of submicrons of identical size.

The number of particles visible in the ultramicroscope is, in the case of hydrophile colloids, usually far less numerous than might have been expected from their other properties This is the result of their inferior reflecting power. If a piece of swollen gelatin is immersed in water it becomes invisible, because no light is reflected to the eye. On this account the ultramicroscope is not suitable for determining the number or size of the particles of hydrophile colloids.

We may here recall an observation of G. QUINCKE *[3] which is perhaps destined to be of great importance for many biological questions but which deserves attention, even from a purely physical standpoint. G. QUINCKE observed that in the induced clarification of mastic, gamboge, kaolin and india ink suspensions, the flocks usually separated on the *dark* side, in spontaneous clarification of kaolin turbidity, however, they settled on the *light* side. A turbid solution of tannate of glue settled out, mostly on the side towards the light. He described this phenomenon as *positive* and *negative photodromy*. This fact is suggestive of many of the phenomena which H. SIEDENTOPF*[1] observed in his *light reactions* in the ultramicroscope.

Jellies, especially those of higher concentration, *on deformation* by compression or traction, show *double refraction* (KUNDT). *Negative* refraction was observed in the case of gum arabic, collodion and gelatin, *positive* in the case of tragacanth and cherry gum. The same kinds of jellies when dried showed respectively the same kinds of refraction. If gelatin poor in water is brought in contact with gelatin rich in water, so that there is a mutual interchange of water, both become doubly refractive. (M. W. BEIJERINCK) On repeated swelling and shrinking of jellies, the positive double refraction passes through an isotropic condition into a negative. (QUINCKE.)

Chlorids and nitrates diminish the double refraction; sulphates are without effect. Phenols change the direction of the refraction.

The phenomenon is important for the understanding of the double refraction of organized structures (plant fibers, muscle, horn, etc.).

Electrical Properties.

If two electrodes are placed in a solution of a hydrosol as free as possible of electrolytes, and a current is allowed to pass through, we immediately notice the movement of the colloid to one of the electrodes. Various suspensions (suspensions of clay, rosin, etc.), as well as most hydrophobe hydrosols migrate to the anode, whereas the colloidal metal hydroxids (iron or aluminium oxid hydrosol, etc.) move to the cathode. Hydrophile colloids (albumin, etc.) exhibit, if almost free from electrolytes, no definite recognizable directive tendency. The zone of H ion concentration in which there is no migration has been named by L. MICHAELIS the *isoelectric zone*. The addition of acids causes migration of these colloids to the cathode, alkalies to the anode; they then behave as if they were salts of the acids or alkalies involved, and this may actually correspond with the facts (see p. 149 *et seq.*).

This movement of suspensions and hydrosols against the water, under the influence of the electric current, is called *cataphoresis*.

The colloid particles behave like ions and their *speed of migration* is similar in rate. ZSIGMONDY calculated from the speed of migration (0.002 mm.) and the diameter ($50 \mu\mu$) of the particles of a colloidal silver solution, that the particles were charged with 297×10^{-10} electrostatic units which is the equivalent of 62 elemental units. Such a particle is in a certain sense an ion of 62 valencies.

If *a protective colloid* (albumin, gelatin, etc.) is added to a suspension, the latter acts as if its entire mass was composed of the protective colloid. The commercial inorganic colloids (collargol, lysargin, etc.) do not behave in an electric current as does pure colloidal silver, but as albumins or albumoses. Their direction may be changed at will by the addition of acids or alkalis.

The process may be reversed, that is, the water may be moved under the influence of electrical difference in potential, provided the suspension is held fixed. The experimental procedure is as follows: Instead of a clay suspension we choose a porous clay wall D (Fig. 8), permeable for water, by means of which a U-shaped tube is divided into two parts. If the tube is filled with water and into each branch an electrode is introduced, the water moves under the influence of the electric current and, in fact, it will rise on the cathode side until it exerts a certain pressure against the anode

This process is called *electro-endosmosis* In principle the two
mena are the same.   For the exact study of electrical migra-
vhich was first investigated by G. WIEDEMANN and G. QUINCKE,
-endosmosis proved to be experimentally more easily avail-
A. COEHN* has shown that it is a general and quantitative law,

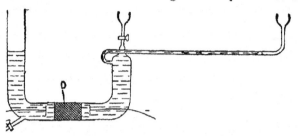

FIG 8   Apparatus for electro-endosmosis. (H Freundlich)

substances possessing higher dielectric constants are positively
d when brought into contact with substances of lower dielectric
nts.

have already seen that numerous substances are negatively
d in respect to water while others are positively charged and
under the influence of the electric current there occurs a move-
of the suspended substance or of the water.   This migration
e influenced by the addition of electrolytes.   J. PERRIN used
agms of porous carborundum and of naphthalin and measured
nount of water which passed through the porous wall by en-
sis, under the influence of an electric current
the following table + indicates passage to the positive, − to
gative pole.

Diaphragm	Solution	Amount of fluid transferred in cmm per minute
undum	0 02 mol HCl	+ 10
undum	0 008 mol HCl	0
undum	0 002 mol HCl	− 15
undum	dist water	− 50
undum	0 0002 mol KOH	− 60
undum	0 002 mol KOH	−105
halin	0 02 mol HCl	+ 38
halin	0 001 mol HCl	+ 28
halin	0 0002 mol HCl	+ 3
halin	0 0002 mol KOH	− 29
halin	0 001 mol KOH	− 60

ed to cause naphthalin suspensions to migrate in strong currents (400 volts) but could not
any cataphoresis either in neutral, in acid or in alkaline solution   Nor could I obtain a
n of suspensions of naphthol and naphthylamin in neutral, very faintly acid or very faintly
solution (hitherto unpublished)

It follows from this that the negative charge of negative diaphragms (as is evident from the table) increased in alkaline solution. With a decrease in the OH ion concentration (with naphthalin) or the increase in the H ion concentration (with carborundum) a point was reached in which there was no difference in potential between water and diaphragm. With further increase in the H ion concentration the diaphragm took on a stronger positive charge.

If a positive diaphragm is chosen, as for instance chromium chlorid, the conditions are reversed.

J. PERRIN studied the influence of salts in the presence of acids and bases. It was shown that they cause a loss of charge with moderate concentrations and, in fact, that the strength of their action depended, in the case of *positively* charged diaphragms, upon the valence of the *anions*, while in the case of negatively charged diaphragms it depended upon the valence of the *cations*. With higher concentration of polyvalent anions or cations a loss of charge may occur.

Upon calculating the concentration of salt which just halves the amount of fluid (v in mm./minutes) transferred, the following figures were obtained.

Diaphragm	Charge	Salt	v	$\frac{1}{v} = 1$ (NaBr or KBr).
Carborundum .	−	NaBr	50	1
Carborundum	−	$Ba(NO_3)_2$	2	25
Carborundum	−	$La(NO_3)_3$	0 1	500
Chromium chlorid	+	KBr	60	1
Chromium chlorid	+	$MgSO_4$	1	60
Chromium chlorid	+	$K_3Fe(CN)_6$	0.1	600

The last column $\frac{1}{v}$ shows us that the discharging effect increases with the valence of the anions as 1 25 : 500 and in the case of cations as 1 : 60 : 600. In the section on "flocculation," we shall see a very remarkable application of this phenomenon

Of the many theories proposed to explain these circumstances, that of H FREUNDLICH and L MICHAELIS, according to which the various ions are adsorbed to different degrees, seems to us most probably correct; in point of fact, the H and OH ion have especially high adsorption coefficients. Since a separation of anion and cation usually cannot occur, there arises a difference in potential at the surface between the dispersed phase and the water. An indifferent substance in a weakly acid solution will adsorb H ions and become

ositively charged in respect to the fluid; in an alkaline fluid it will
ecome negatively charged. If the dispersed phase itself has basic
r acid properties it will behave in pure water like a cation or an
nion respectively. If to an acid suspension, *e g.*, clay, an alkali is
dded, K ions are adsorbed, OH ions are concentrated and held at
he outer film and the negative charge is thereby increased. The
everse occurs upon adding acids; the charge is released and may
ven take the opposite sign. According to this view, colloids wan-
ering to the anode are discharged only by cations, those travelling
o the cathode only by anions. We have seen that polyvalent ions
ave a considerably greater discharging power, which increases with
heir valence   This experimental fact accords, as do all the others,
nth the theory propounded.

In the case of hydrophile colloids, it suffices for us to assume that
re are dealing with very large amphoteric molecules which become
ations in acid solution and anions in alkaline solution.

Salting Out.

If large quantities of a neutral salt, for instance ammonium
ulphate, are added to a solution of a hydrophile colloid (albumin,
lobulin, casein, albumose, silver protected by a protective colloid,
tc.), or certain inorganic hydrosols, *e g.*, sulphur, the colloid is thrown
ut, but it redissolves upon dilution with water. This is the process
f salting out, as practised technically. If, for instance, enough com-
ion salt is added to an aqueous solution of phenol, the phenol
eparates out. We might regard this as a withdrawal of water by
ieans of the electrolyte, since we know from the observations of
cent years that ions form hydrates in aqueous solution, *i.e.*, every
n attracts a greater or smaller number of molecules of water. I
ave, however, been unable to discover any relation between the
alting out process, from the figures for the hydration of a number
f different ions as calculated by E. H. RIESENFELD and B.
EINHOLD*.

The more closely a hydrophile colloid approaches the crystalloid
ondition, the greater is the concentration of salt required for salting
ut   Thus, for instance, the *albumoses* are classified in accordance
nth concentration of salt required for their precipitation (see
. 166.)

As early as 1907, BECHHOLD had already called attention to the
lation between salting out, and particle size and salt concentration.
. ODEN produced the experimental evidence that *reversible* sul-
hur and silver hydrosols could actually be separated in fractions,

distinguishable by the size of their particles, by "fractional coagulation,"[1] i.e., by the addition of salt solutions of progressively increasing strength.

The influence of *neutral salts* exhibits regularities which are of great importance in a number of biological phenomena and which we shall repeatedly encounter The salting out of hydrophile colloids, gelatinization, the irritability of muscle and nerve, the permeability of cell membranes (blood corpuscles, etc.), the swelling of membranes and many other phenomena are thus related to a group of physico-chemical properties of solutions, whose relationship is indubitable even though the true basis is not clear. With H. FREUNDLICH we shall describe these effects of neutral salts as *lyotropic* (solution changing), and we shall study them more closely.

Most inorganic salts increase the surface tension of water and from a table of W. K. RONTGEN and J SCHNEIDER we obtain the following series for the increase in the surface tension by the alkaline iodids:

$$Na > K > Li > NH_4.$$

With the anion of various alkalis.

$$CO_3 > SO_4 > Cl > NO_3 > I.$$

Though the compressibility, the solubility and the viscosity of water are changed in a similar order by neutral salts, the relationship is much more fundamental Neutral salts may accelerate or impede catalytic effects, such as the inversion of cane sugar, the saponification of esters and the changing of acetone into diacetone alcohol. The action in *acid* solutions is usually the reverse of what it is in alkaline solutions as has been shown by R. HOBER. In *acid* media the acceleration by cations is

$$Li > Na > K > Rb > Cs,$$

in *alkaline* media

$$Cs > Rb > K > Na > Li.$$

For *anions* in *acid* solutions the following order holds:

$$I > NO_3 > Br > Cl > CH_3CO_2 > SO_4.$$

In alkaline solution the series is reversed.

In neutral solution also the lyotropic series holds, although small changes in the arrangement may exist for some of the ions.

---

[1] Since reversible hydrosols are considered I might describe the procedure preferably as "fractional salting out "

It is particularly interesting to know, that according to ODEN and OHOLM the particles do not coalesce but retain their identity and when they are redissolved, there are as many particles in solution as before the salting out.

We encounter such lyotropic series regularly in the *salting out* of hydrophil colloids (see Albumin, p 146 *et seq.*, Lecithin, p 140, Gelatin, p. 161) and in many biological phenomena, where they tend to cause either a precipitation or a concentration

However, we must not assume that the action is such that in one case the anion alone is active, and in the other the cation alone. There are many reasons for believing that there is an *antagonism* between anions and cations, and that the action of the cation is more or less powerfully increased or diminished depending upon the anions present. If in a given instance we speak of the cations causing precipitation or dehydration, we always mean the difference between the effect of the cation and the opposed action of the anion present, in which, however, the action of the cation predominates.

The *divalent cations* Mg, Ca, Sr and Ba act more strongly as precipitants than the monovalent cations. Biologically they are important in connection with alkali salts, inasmuch as small quantities of calcium salts are able to replace considerably larger quantities of alkali salts, *e.g.*, Na or K. This greater effect may even lead to an antagonism between the two, it has been thoroughly studied by Wo. PAULI and H HANDOVSKY.[*3] It is sufficient to mention that in the case of alkali albumin, Ca salts form a less ionized Ca albumin combination from a more ionized Na albumin combination. According to the law of mass action small quantities of Ca may be replaced by larger quantities of Na. We may thus understand the significance of the Ca content in all physiological fluids. Mg, Sr and Ba act in a similar manner. They have in addition certain specific properties which obscure the relations.

Large quantities of *alkaline earths* cause irreversible changes in many biocolloids, that is, they produce insoluble compounds with them. Electrolytes may exert another effect on the biocolloids, they may cause "flocculation," a phenomenon we shall now study more closely

Flocculation.

If albumin is boiled, it *coagulates* A coagulation of albumin may also be produced by the addition of ammonium sulphate Though the latter process may be reversed by dilution with water, the boiled albumin cannot again be brought to its fluid condition, by any *physical* means. The hydrophile colloid has been converted into a hydrophobe colloid. For uniformity's sake, we shall consider as *coagulations* only such processes as cause an *irreversible* change

If we heat a very dilute albumin solution, there is apparently no coagulation; at most the fluid becomes slightly opalescent. In reality, coagulation has occurred here, since the addition of a drop of acetic acid or of little ammonium sulphate produces flocks. The process is henceforth called *flocculation*. These albumin flocks are insoluble in water.

Only by the *second process*, by the agglomeration of the smallest particles (see Plate I, 6 and 8) under the influence of the acetic acid or ammonium sulphate, was it possible to separate the two phases (water, albumin). This occurs in a way similar to that in which the drops of a fog are formed under certain conditions by the union of particles of mist. The union is preceded by a slowing of the Brownian-Zsigmondy movement, as has been shown with the ultramicroscope by V. Henri.

Flocculation is an electrical phenomenon. It is brought about by *electrolytes* as well as *by colloids of opposite electric charge*, as well as by *Tyndall* and *Kundsen rays*; the action of rays is much weaker than the action of electrolytes. If we take purified lampblack with water we get a suspension which remains turbid for weeks. If we pour a few drops of an alcoholic mastic solution into water, it remains turbid for weeks and even years. We have seen that the hydrosols are more hydrosol, such as colloidal arsenic sulphid, platinum sol prepared according to Bredig's method, gold sol prepared according to R. Zsigmondy's method, are permanent for months provided the solution is free from electrolytes. Addition of electrolytes causes an irreversible flocculation of these hydrophobe colloid.

This process is to be sharply distinguished from *salting out*, i.e., the reversible precipitation of albumin, albumoses, etc., from solution by large quantities of salt.

The phenomenon of flocculation is encountered especially in the precipitation reactions of albumin, and in Chapter XIII on *Immunity Reactions* where it plays an important role in the agglutination of bacteria by precipitins. Moreover the precipitation of gold by colloid seems to propose that have acquired great significance in the diagnosis of mental diseases (see p. 354).

For any flocculation a certain minimum amount of electrolyte as well as of the dispersed phase is required. Below these limits, which are characteristic for every electrolyte, no flocculation occurs even in a month. If this amount is called the minimum the "*threshold value*" and the "*concentration threshold*."

The *rate of flocculation* is dependent on the concentration of the suspension and of the electrolyte; the more concentrated the more

_____

Note: the recognition of these as truly separate precipitation means, are probably not discussed (p. 107)

pension and the electrolytes within certain limits, the greater is the rapidity of flocculation. The dependence upon the concentration of the electrolytes is especially noticeable in the vicinity of the electrolyte threshold. Further away from the electrolyte threshold the rapidity of flocculation is less dependent upon the concentration of the electrolyte. (H. Bechhold.*1)

Under certain conditions, an excess of electrolytes may lead to re-solution. This phenomenon is called *peptisation*. Graham first observed this occurrence upon treating ferric oxid gel with ferric chlorid and compared it to the formation of water-soluble peptone from coagulated albumin and hydrochloric acid As a matter of fact, peptisation probably depends upon a renewal of electric charge by the excess of electrolytes.

As has been shown by H. Freundlich and his pupils Ishizaka and Schucht *1, these facts furnish an indication that the more sensitive a substance is to flocculation, the more will it be *adsorbed*

The great majority of colloids migrate to the anode, and on flocculation the cation is of much the greatest importance; the anion plays but a subordinate role The conditions are reversed in the case of the few colloids which migrate to the cathode However, R. Burton has shown that with increase of electrolyte concentration the rate of migration of the colloid becomes constantly diminished and finally the direction may change At the stage when the concentration of electrolytes is such that reversal occurs, in other words the isoelectric zone, flocculation is most rapid. The increase in the action of the cations is out of proportion to the increase in their valence. The electrolyte concentration necessary for the flocculation of a mastic suspension is $FeCl_3$: $BaCl_2$: $NaCl$ = 1 : 50 : 1000. There are also certain anomalies (see H. Bechhold,*1 as well as M. Neisser and U. Friedemann *) in connection with the rate of migration of the ions, as well as in the electrolytic dissociation and especially in the ionization pressure of electrolytes. In general the above relation between the action of the cations is maintained. The powerful flocculating action of the H ion without doubt depends upon its high speed of migration while the OH ion has a corresponding action upon colloids which migrate to the anode.

Flocculation by means of trivalent iron and aluminium salts show peculiar *anomalies*. These were discovered by M. Neisser and U. Friedemann* and also by H. Bechhold*1 and called *irregular series*. Later these phenomena of *Inhibition Zones* were followed further by O. Teague and B. H Buxton*2 and also by A Lottermoser.* An example from my published paper will best explain the phenomenon XXX means strong flocculation, XX medium, X none

Concentration of mastic solution	0.01	0.005	0.0025	0.001	0.0005	0.00025	Mol Al$_2$(SO$_4$)$_i$
1/2	×××	×××	×××	××	×××	××	
1/4	×××	×××	××	××	×××	0	
1/8	×××	×××	0	0	×××	×	
1/16	×××	××	0	0	××	×××	
1/32	×××	0	0	0	0	×××	

The discoverers explain the phenomenon by saying that the salts mentioned undergo strong hydrolytic dissociation so that the colloidal iron and aluminum hydroxid present in the solution act as "protective colloids" somewhat like gelatin or albumin

The flocculation hitherto described occurs only with true hydrophobe colloids. If the individual particles possess a film of native albumin, gelatin, an albumose (such as Na lysalbinate), dextrin, etc., the particles act as if they were the "protective colloids" involved (see p. 77); in other words they are salted out only by very large amounts of electrolytes. The colloid precipitate can be redissolved in water providing the protective colloid is not denatured by the electrolytes On this account all the colloidal metal sols used therapeutically such as collargol, bismon, etc., are "stabilized" by hydrophile colloids. Without this protection it would be impossible to preserve them for any length of time and they would be flocculated when they were prepared for intravenous use by dilution with physiological salt solution.

R. Zsigmondy considers as characteristic of hydrophile colloids, the protection they give to his gold hydrosol against flocculation by electrolytes. He designates as the *gold figure*, the amount (in mg.) of the colloid in question, which was just sufficient to prevent the flocculation of 10 c.c of a gold sol. by 1 c.c. $\frac{2}{n}$ NaCl sol. The flocculation is accompanied by a change in color from red to blue, and it is sufficient to observe this change

The following data from R. Zsigmondy illustrate this point:

Colloid	Gold figure in mg.
Gelatin	0.005 0.01
Casein	0.01
Egg albumen	0.06 0.3 (depending upon its origin and ash content.)
Gum arabic	0.15 0.25
Tragacanth	2±
Dextrin	10 20
Potato starch	25
Sodium stearate	10 (added at 60°)
Sodium stearate	0.001 (added boiling hot)
Sodium oleate	0.1

Peptones have no protective action at all [Peptones may cause precipitation E. ZUNZ, Bull. Soc. Roy des Sc., Med , et Nat., June 11, 1906. Tr.], whereas some of the albumoses, especially *sodium lysalbinate* and *sodium protalbinate* have a very powerful protective action which C. PAAL utilized in preparing a large number of inorganic colloids.

Sensitiveness to flocculation may vary considerably with the nature of the protective colloid

The *flocculation* of hydrosols may be brought about not only by electrolytes but also *by hydrosols*, providing they have an opposite electric charge, as has been shown by W. BILTZ. Thus, for instance, arsenic trisulphid, gold and platinum hydrosols, etc , are flocculated by ironoxid, aluminiumoxid, chromiumoxid hydrosols, etc. A proper relative mixture is required, which means the charge of the positive sol must be counterbalanced by the charge of the negative sol. If a sol is in *excess, no flocculation occurs*, and the entire complex consisting of both colloids migrates, when placed between two electrodes, in the direction of the sol (J. BILLITER*) which is in excess. This explains why protective colloids may under some circumstances produce flocculation instead of protection, namely, when they are added in minimal quantities Thus, for instance, mastic emulsions are flocculated by 0.0003 to 0.0001 per cent of gelatin (H. BECHHOLD and also M NEISSER and U. FRIEDEMANN) Hydrochloric acid in a dilution incapable of producing flocculation by itself can coagulate gold hydrosol, mastic or oil emulsion in the presence of one part of gelatin per million.

As has already been mentioned we must not confuse the salting out of hydrophile colloids with flocculation, though there are borderline cases which complicate the phenomenon. If we add for instance a *salt of a heavy metal* to a dilute albumin solution, a more or less irreversible albumin-metal compound will form, dependent on the nature of the salt upon which the excess of albumin acts as a protective colloid. Acids may cause a loss of charge and the metal salt may then exhibit some flocculating and some salting out action. Such a case might occur, for instance, on adding zinc sulphate to albumin (studied by Wo. PAULI). The process is as follows.

$ZnSO_4$ + Albumin.

0 05 n	maximum flocculation (irreversible till 1 n)
1 n	precipitate disappears
2 n	precipitate reappears (reversible)
4 n	maximum precipitate (reversible).

There are *transitions* between hydrophobe and hydrophile colloids which are responsible for the transitions between flocculation and salting out *Cholesterin* and *lecithin* may be regarded as such transitional substances, whose flocculation has been thoroughly studied by O. Porges and E. Neubauer.* Cholesterin closely approaches the hydrophobe colloids, lecithin the hydrophile, and on this account the former is irreversibly precipitated by salts and the latter reversibly. Yet the concentration of alkaline earths required to precipitate lecithin is considerably less than for the more hydrophile albumin, and conversely much greater concentration of salt is required for the flocculation of cholesterin than is the case with true hydrophobe sols. In the case of lecithin, the "irregular series" occurs even with neutral salts (magnesium and ammonium sulphate). As will be seen in Chapter XIII, such transitions from hydrophobe suspensions to hydrophile colloids may be artificially produced with emulsions of bacteria.

Much has been written on the *theory of salting out and flocculation.* No one theory accounts for all the individual facts, yet the following explanation is generally useful Flocculation is brought about by the coming together of small particles to form larger complexes. These agglomerations always occur under the influence of electric forces and in fact the optimum for *reversible salting out* is in the isoelectric zone (see p. 158). The process, must, therefore, be brought about by a discharge of the particles Risdale Ellis has shown by researches on oil emulsions, that the charge at the interface between water and the dispersed phase is probably reduced to a minimum by the addition of precipitating electrolytes. The smaller this charge is at the interfaces (electric double layer), the more readily the double layer is broken down, resulting in a union of the suspended fluid or solid particles

In the case of anodic colloids, cations of an electrolyte, and in the case of cathodic colloids, anions or an oppositely charged colloid, lessen or neutralize the electric charge, so that the particles may unite. (See H. Freundlich's " Kapillarchemie " and Wo. Ostwald's " Grundriss der Kolloidchemie ")

Irreversible precipitation of metal hydrosols frequently occurs outside the isoelectric zone and the electrolyte threshold is not as sharp as with reversible hydrosols.

Radioactive Substances as Colloids.

It has been demonstrated by electric migration and dialysis that radioactive substances occur in colloidal solution. In view of the great biological significance of such substance we shall explain the facts more fully.

GODLEWSKI * found upon electrolysis of the radium emanations and their products that the radioactive substances migrated mostly to the cathode in acid solutions and to the anode in alkaline solutions. PANETH dialyzed a solution of radio-lead nitrate against pure water in a parchment thimble and greatly concentrated the RaE and polonium in the thimble but the relation between RaD to lead was not changed Both phenomena are characteristic of colloids and indicate the colloid properties of radioactive substances; this led them to continue their investigations. GODLEWSKI * successfully adsorbed RaA, RaB and RaC with inorganic colloids and concentrated the radioactive substances by precipitating the latter He was successful not only with radium but with actinium, mesothorium and uranium. The concentration of radioactive substances by adsorption on colloidal silicic acid (EBLER, FELLNER) has attained great practical value in the manufacture of radium preparations. In fact RaA and RaC may be collected from acid solutions simply on filter paper and by burning the paper a highly active ash, free from RaB, may be obtained It is evident that in solution radioactive elements undergo hydrolysis with the formation of a colloidal radio-hydrosol.

CHAPTER VII.

METHODS OF COLLOID RESEARCH.

A FIELD of research extending as does colloid chemistry into so many other branches of science must be served by countless methods. Purely chemical as well as physical and biological methods which the investigator of colloids utilizes in his studies, have been so well developed and so thoroughly described in technical literature, that it is needless to discuss them more fully here.

There are, however, several methods which are peculiar to colloid investigation, and we shall consider them here. Unfortunately, the limits of their usefulness are as yet unestablished, for some one to establish them would be highly desirable.

In discussing the following methods, I have not sought completeness but have considered only those which have proved practical; I have personally tested most of them.

To determine whether a solution of a substance is colloidal in character it must be tested by *dialysis, ultrafiltration* or *diffusion.*

Dialysis is a purely qualitative method which determines whether or not a substance is colloidal in character, *i.e.,* whether or not it consists of large particles.

Ultrafiltration in most cases may be used instead of dialysis; it works much more rapidly and above all permits, in addition, *quantitative* experiments, and consequently has a much broader utility.

Both methods serve to separate colloids from crystalloids. This separation occurs with *dialysis* if the water surrounding the *dialyzer* is frequently renewed, it occurs with ultrafiltration, provided the substance on the funnel is *washed repeatedly,* as in an ordinary filter.

Diffusion is an excellent quantitative method for the investigation of particle size The performance of diffusion experiments is, however, a difficult matter, because even variations in temperature may cause material errors.

Dialysis.[1]

The most varied apparatus and membranes may be used for dialysis. An apparatus described in most textbooks and used in many

---

[1] An exhaustive description of all known methods of dialysis is given by E Zunz in Abderhalden's Handb d. biochem. Arbeitsmethoden **3,** pages 165–189 and Supplement, pages 478–485

teaching laboratories is the one originally described by GRAHAM   A wide-mouthed salt bottle *A* (Fig. 9), with its bottom broken off, has a pig or ox bladder or a piece of parchment bound about the neck; the bottle is placed with the membrane downward, in a vessel of water (*B*)[1].   The solution to be dialyzed is placed in the bottle.

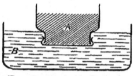

Precautions   Before the membrane is used, it should be tested to see that it can be made wet by water   Greasy animal membranes must be rinsed with fresh water several times, on both sides   To determine whether the membrane leaks, a colored solution (*e g* , a drop of colloidal silver, litmus, or water colored with hemoglobin) is placed in *A* and allowed to remain there several hours, without putting any water in the outer vessel.   Colored drops will pass through at points of leakage (the margin where the membrane is bound should be especially watched)   To make sure that the drops are really colored solution and not pure water, they should be absorbed by filter paper.

FIG 9.   A simple dialyzer

In all dialysis experiments, the substance under examination may simulate colloidal character by being bound or adsorbed by the dialyzing membrane Under these circumstances, if we wish to determine whether the solution under examination contains colloidal substances, it is necessary to use the smallest possible membrane with the largest available amount of substance   If too little substance is used, it may all become bound by the membrane, and in spite of the fact that it is not colloidal, none will be found in the dialyzer   But if so much of the substance under investigation is used, that in spite of any possible adsorption by the membrane, plenty still remains in the dialyzer, then an examination of the water outside will settle the question.

In practice, GRAHAM's dialyzing apparatus is not frequently employed, because it has a small dialyzing surface, and this is a great disadvantage.

In order to bring the largest possible surface into contact with the surrounding water, there are used either whole pig bladders, ox bladders, fish bladders, or the commercial parchment thimbles [2]

I have had very good results with fish bladders (condoms) which are very thin, uniform and elastic, though unfortunately they are expensive.   *Parchment thimbles*, referred to above, are recommended for the dialysis of large quantities of solution.   They may be obtained in all sizes and in all lengths.   The suspension of a fish bladder is conveniently accomplished by pressing it between two glass rods which are held together by rubber bands (cut from gas tubing); the

[1] With organic solvents, instead of water, alcohol, benzol, etc , must of course be employed and the membrane (preferably collodion) is previously soaked in these fluids.

[2] These are on sale at the "Vereinigten Fabriken fur Laboratoriums-bedarf" Berlin, Scharnhorst Str. (The Kny Scherer Co , N Y., are the American agents)

glass rods are laid over a tall narrow beaker, in which the water is placed   Parchment tubes are suspended in a similar manner.   To avoid tying one end of the tube, it is hung up in U-fashion so that both open ends are pressed together by the glass rods (see Fig. 10)

Precautions: In filling and hanging the parchment tubes the air must be entirely pressed out before fastening the ends, for should water dialyze in, considerable pressure will develop, which may burst the membrane   All the precautions given on page 90 must be observed (degreasing, absorption, etc.).

Excellent dialysis membranes may be prepared of *collodion* or *glacial acetic acid-collodion*   Their great advantage is that they may be prepared in any desired size, shape and degree of permeability, and are easily sterilized

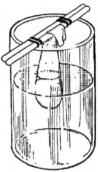

Fig. 10.   A fish bladder (condom) dialyzer

As an example, we shall explain how to make one such membrane.   A test tube is dipped into collodion and then allowed to drip, being twirled meanwhile, and when it has *skinned over*, the whole tube is quickly immersed in water.   In a short time, the tube is circumcised at a height which will give a membrane of the desired length, with a little practice, the membrane can be removed from the tube with ease.   The membrane may be formed inside the tube also by rinsing the test tube with collodion or glacial acetic collodion and then filling it with water   In a similar manner, spherical or cylindrical membranes of 30 to 40 cm. long and 10 cm. diameter may be made (see Fig. 11).   Such sacs may be fastened to a glass tube with thread or collodion so as to form a watertight joint.   The membranes are best preserved in water to which a little chloroform has been added to prevent the growth of moulds.

In making his collodion sacs, G. MALFITANO [1] uses glass tubes of the shape shown in the accompanying diagram, which are rotated by a motor to secure uniform drying.   The spherical swelling affords an easier removal of the rim (see Fig. 12).   After the cut is made through the collodion skin at the equator of the sphere (→), it is carefully loosened from the glass and turned inside out or the rim is fastened to a large glass tube which is exhausted, thus the skin is loosened from the spherical portion.   J. DUCLAUX uses very thin tubes, about 1 cm. in diameter and 1 meter long, so as to get the largest possible surface.

[1] According to a personal communication.

G. MALFITANO and J DUCLAUX use their sacs chiefly for *ultrafiltration* though they are equally useful for dialysis. Biologists frequently use little reed sacks for dialyzing, they are frail though sterilizable, but their capacity is small

SCHLEICHER and SCHULL (DUREN) sell *dialyzing thimbles*. They are tubular, closed at the bottom, moderately firm, made of parch-

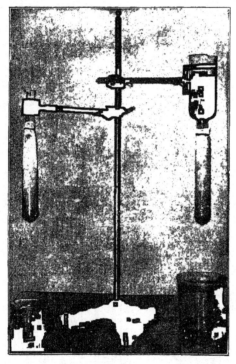

FIG 11. Collodion sacs. (A. Schoef)

ment and, since they maintain their form, they are useful for certain experiments. They are employed in the Abderhalden test.

R. ZSIGMONDY [*][3] constructed a very useful "star dialyzer"[1] The hard rubber ring *B* (see Fig. 13) is covered by a membrane (collodion, parchment or the like) and is placed on a plate *A*, which carries the star-shaped support. Through the central opening in the

---

[1] Obtainable from ROBERT MITTELBACH, Gottingen.

plate, water flows and bathes the extensive dialyzing surface of the dialyzer *A*.

JORDIS has constructed an apparatus resembling a filter press for dialyzing large quantities. A number of wooden rings are soaked in

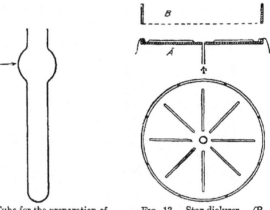

FIG. 12.   Tube for the preparation of   FIG 13   Star dialyzer.   (R.
collodion sacs.   (G Malfitano)   Zsigmondy)

paraffin and then both surfaces are covered with parchment. These rings are placed in an apparatus *G* so that between each ring with parchment there is one without parchment   They are made tight with rubber washers   The individual elements of the filter are

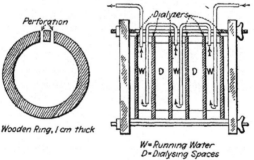

W = Running Water
D = Dialysing Spaces

FIG. 13a   Continuous dialyzing apparatus of E Jordiss
Reproduced from Zeitschrift fur Electrochemie, p 677, Vol VIII, 1902

pressed together with wing nuts so that they are water-tight. The solution to be dialyzed is placed in the rings covered with parchment, the water in the intervening rings circulates through holes made in them for the purpose, see Fig. 13a.

An excellent apparatus[1] for continuous dialysis which also permits a concentration of the dialyzate has been constructed by KOPAC-ZEWSKI. He applies the idea of the Soxhlet extraction apparatus A collodion sac prepared as described on page 91 is placed in the tube A filled with water The dialyzate from the collodion sac may be removed either through the cock C or may pass either at once or drop by drop into the vessel B. If B is heated, the water vaporizes and

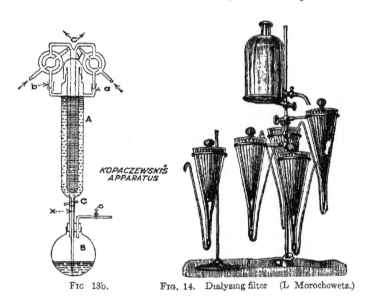

KOPACZEWSKI'S
APPARATUS

FIG 13b.   FIG. 14.   Dialyzing filter   (L Morochowetz.)

passes into the two condensers and drops again through a and b into the tube containing the collodion sac. Since with biological fluids the temperature must remain below 50° C., the heating is done under partial vacuum (reduced pressure) The tube is emptied through the lateral outlet having a cock c. A concentrated dialyzate is finally obtained in the vessel B

Where there is no running water available for dialyzing, the dialy-zing filter of LEO MOROCHOWETZ may be employed. Its arrangement may be seen in Fig 14. The funnels may be obtained from any supply house and the parchment filters from SCHLEICHER and SCHULL (DUREN).

---

[1] The apparatus may be obtained from Poulènc frères, 122 Boulevard St. Germain, Paris, France

Dialysis is considerably hastened by agitating the dialyzing fluid. I have never found it suggested that the contents of the dialyzer should be stirred but this is a useful procedure with non-foaming solutions. F. HOFMEISTER fastens all the dialyzing thimbles to a common rod which he rocks up and down with a motor. R. KOHLER places fish bladders in wide-mouthed bottles which he closes with a rubber cork and a rubber cap, and then places it in a shaking machine; to prevent twisting off the fish bladder at its neck, he inserts several glass rods as shown in Fig. 14a.

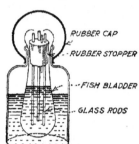

RUBBER CAP
--RUBBER STOPPER
-·FISH BLADDER
--GLASS RODS

FIG. 14a.

Ultrafiltration.

H BECHHOLD defines ultrafiltration as filtration through jelly filters They serve to separate colloid solutions from crystalloids and for the separation of colloid mixtures having particles of different size If we know the size of the pores in an ultrafilter, ultrafiltration affords information as to the size of the particles in the colloid under investigation

Ultrafilter. For ultrafiltration, sac-like membranes may be employed prepared as for diffusion experiments (see p. 91) and mounted as shown in Fig. 11.

A SCHOEP * increased the permeability of membranes by adding glycerin and castor oil to the collodion. This is of great importance in filtering inorganic colloids.

This sort of ultrafiltration is used especially in France (G. MALFITANO, J. DUCLAUX), but it is of limited utility. Filtration occurs very slowly (a few cubic centimeters per hour) and the filters cannot withstand much pressure, so that their usefulness is very limited.

For ultrafiltration, H. BECHHOLD*4 used pieces of filter paper impregnated with jellies. By means of this paper support the filters acquire great strength and may at times sustain in BECHHOLD's ultrafiltration apparatus, pressures of 20 atmospheres or more. Since H. BECHHOLD discovered that the premeability or tightness of the ultrafilters depended on the concentration of the jellies used in preparing them, it is possible to make filters with pores of any desired size. The filters may be purchased ready-made.[1]

¹ Schleicher and Schull, in Duren, market Bechhold's ultrafilters in aluminium boxes which contain 10 filters filled with water and sealed with a rubber ring, (diam 9 cm). This firm keeps in stock six kinds, of different porosity.

Since some may desire to make the filters, brief direction for doing so are given.[1]

The most useful kinds of filter paper are No. 566 and No. 575 of SCHLEICHER and SCHÜLL. These are cut into discs of 9 cm. in diameter and impregnated with the jellies under atmospheric pressure in a glass trough from which the air has previously been exhausted, making a vacuum [2]

The square trough T (see Fig. 15) has its cover ground airtight. On the cross bar B a number of filter papers are suspended The cover C has two openings; through No. 1 pass two tubes, one of which leads to the air pump A and the other to the pressure gauge

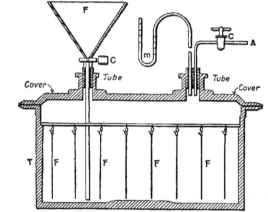

FIG. 15. Trough for the preparation of ultrafilters. (H Bechhold)

m. When the air is exhausted from the trough, the fluid jelly is allowed to enter through the funnel F, which has a cock and a tube leading to the bottom, until sufficient is admitted to cover the filters. Then the valve leading from the funnel is closed and the valve through which the air was exhausted is opened so that the jelly is forced into the filters under atmospheric pressure. After a time (with diluted jellies 10 to 20 min. with concentrated jellies one or two hours) the cover is taken off and the rod with the filters is removed from the fluids. While the filters are draining, they are constantly shaken. Finally the whole filter is rapidly gelatinized by plunging it into a suitable fluid. In the case of *glacial acetic acid*

[1] Given in detail in the original paper of H Bechhold.*[4]

[2] May be obtained from the Vereinigten Fabriken fur Laboratoriumsbedarf, Berlin

collodion, water is used. If *gelatin* is being used, the entire impregnation trough must be placed in a bath of lukewarm water. Gelatin filters are hardened by placing the filters, still moist and gelatinized in the air into a 2 to 4 per cent ice cold formaldehyde solution and keeping them for a time in an ice box.

The filters, however prepared, are washed several days in running water and preserved in water to which a little chloroform has been added to prevent the growth of mould.

II. BECHHOLD generally uses glacial acetic acid collodion, a solution of soluble cotton in glacial acetic acid.[1] By diluting with glacial acetic acid the solution may be reduced to the desired concentration.

If non-aqueous solutions (*e.g.*, benzol, ether, etc.) are to be ultrafiltered, the water must be displaced by a series of solvents. (Water is first displaced by acetone, the latter by benzol, and so on.)

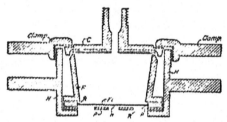

Fig 16. Ultrafilter. (H. Bechhold.)

The Ultrafiltration Apparatus. Very porous filters are permeable under low pressure and can be used like any other filter. In by far the largest number of cases, a pressure of from 1 to 20 atmospheres must be exerted to obtain any filtrate at all. For this purpose H. BECHHOLD prepared an apparatus which in its simplest form is shown in Fig 16[2]; Fig. 17 is more suitable for very high pressures. Fig. 16 consists of a cylindrical vessel *H* into which is inserted the funnel *T*. Between the lower flanges of *T* and *H*, the disc of filter paper is pressed. This is made tight by the two rubber rings *G*, *G*.

To protect it from being torn, the filter lies on a nickel netting or perforated nickeled plate *N* and is further protected from bulging under pressure by the plate *P*, which has several holes in it. The upper part of the funnel *T* is ground conically and is closed by means of

[1] The Chemischer Fabrik auf Aktien (vorm. Schering), Berlin, prepares to order solutions of 10 per cent collodion and 2½ per cent potassium carbonate, which show only slight tendency to contract when they gelatinize.

[2] All this apparatus is manufactured by the Vereinigten Fabriken für Laboratoriumsbedarf, Berlin, Scharnhorst Str.

the cover D with a conical joint and a rubber washer. By turning the screw cap Sch, the cover above as well as the filter below is tightened. A small nipple with a screw thread passes through the cover and to this the pipe from the pressure chamber is attached.

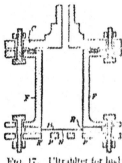

FIG. 17.   Ultrafilter for high pressures.

The apparatus shown in Fig. 17 is chiefly used for pressures above 10 atmospheres, and is closed with clamps. Naturally this is more bulky. The lettering in Fig. 17 corresponds with that of Fig. 16, so that it seems unnecessary to duplicate the description. An apparatus with a stirrer also on the market is already preferable because latex is relatively transparent and the latex is more uniform. The emission of stirrers may detach a gel layer to bring out the ultrafiltrate and thus gel layer may thus act as a filter itself. It is preferable important to have the packing tight against high pressure. In this apparatus the pressure is introduced through a side opening, because the stirrer occupies the central one.

The Pressure. The pressure may be produced by a hand pump. This is especially useful in the quantitative investigation of the action of filters, where fine gradations of pressure are needed and where prolonged pressure is unnecessary. In practical ultrafiltration, it is preferable to use a steel cylinder containing either compressed air, nitrogen or carbonic acid etc. Between the steel cylinder of the ultrafiltration apparatus a reducing pressure valve and two manometers are introduced, one for very high pressure below the pressure in the cylinder, the other beyond that gives the lower pressure in the ultrafiltration apparatus. A second reducing pressure valve near this manometer permits one to observe and reduce a pressure that, in my opinion it is advisable to use arrangement instead of the hand air pump so as to obtain more constants.

The extensive use achieved by ultrafiltration led to some modifications for special purposes. Zsigmondy, Wilke-Dorfurt and Garbsch recommend collodion filters for analytical purposes. They placed collodion disks on a Buchner funnel for this filter or a porcelain funnel with perforated copper plate and filtered off coarse colloids especially in glass apparatus with a tap-water suction pump. This arrangement cannot produce pressures above one atmosphere. J. M. Crispo uses collodion thimbles coated with collodion.

PRIBRAM and KNSCHBACM is the application of compressed air for stirring, the gas which supplies the pressure enters the bottom of the vessel through a perforated spiral and thus agitates the fluid. I have had no occasion to determine whether this has any advantages over the mechanical stirrer

The Gauging of Ultrafilters. It is important in many cases to have a measure for the limits of effectiveness of ultrafilters, as in this way we may obtain information concerning the size of the particles of the colloid under investigation. The following methods given by BECHHOLD are suitable for the purpose:

1 *Hemoglobin Method.* A 1 per cent solution of hemoglobin (hemoglobin scales, Merck) is prepared and the filter is tested to see if it permits the hemoglobin to pass through. If the hemoglobin is retained, the filter is impermeable to most inorganic colloids (with the exception of freshly prepared silicic acid). The degree of permeability of the filter for hemoglobin may be recognized by the intensity of the red color in the filtrate.

II. BECHHOLD has prepared the following table of permeability for ultrafilters, which is arranged in the order of the diminishing size of the particles of the colloids in solution, and was obtained by using ultrafilters having different degrees of porosity.

Suspensions.

Prussian blue.
Platinum-sol, BREDIG.
Ferric oxid hydrosol.
Casein, in milk.
Arsenic sulphid hydrosol.
Gold solution, ZSIGMONDY,
   No. 4, c. 40 $\mu\mu$.
Bismon, colloidal bismuth oxid,
   PAAL.
Lysargin, colloidal silver, PAAL.
Collargol, silver, v. HEYDEN,
   20 $\mu\mu$
Gold, solution, ZSIGMONDY,
   No. 0, c. 1 4 $\mu\mu$.
1 per cent gelatin solution.

1 per cent hemoglobin solution,
   molecular weight c 16,000
Serum, albumin, molecular
   weight 5000 to 15,000.
Diphtheria toxin.
Protalbumoses.
Colloidal silicic acid.
Lysalbinic acid.
Deutero albumoses *A*.
Deutero albumoses *B*, mol. wt.
   c. 2400.
Deutero albumoses *C*.
Litmus.
Dextrin, mol. wt. c. 965.
Crystalloids.

2. *Air Transpiration Method*[1] This method affords approximately absolute values for the *largest* pores of an ultrafilter. It is based on the following principle. In order to force air through a

[1] Before actually undertaking methods 2 and 3 the original paper should be consulted (Bechhold[20]), as the details cannot be abstracted.

capillary completely immersed in and wet with water, a certain
pressure is necessary, which depends upon the surface tension of
water against air which is a constant and the diameter of the
capillary. If D is the diameter of the capillary, p the pressure in
atmospheres and β the capillarity constant, the following formula
applies:

$$ D = \frac{4\beta}{p \cdot 1.033 \cdot 10^6} $$

If $\beta = 7.7$ at 18°, we obtain

$$ D = \frac{30.8}{p \cdot 1.033 \cdot 10^6} $$

With the aid of this formula the smallest diameter of the pores
in question may be calculated from the least pressure necessary to
drive air through the pores of the completely wet filter.

The *practical performance* of the experiment is as follows. The
filtering apparatus is turned upside down, a thin layer of water is

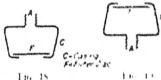

placed on the filter, a certain air
under is applied and the highest
pressure at which air bubbles
begin to appear is determined
(for diagrammatic sketch, Fig.
18, shows the filtering apparatus,
as a thin layer of water; F = filter.

F = ultrafilter. A = air intake. Fig. 19 shows it in the position
necessary for the forcing through of air. Above the filter there is
a thin layer of water.

According to this method the largest pores of a filter which just
permits hemoglobin to pass through have a diameter of 5.9 mμ.

3. *Method Based upon the Rate of Transfusion of Water.*— This
method affords approximately absolute values for the average diameter of the pores of ultrafilters. The method is based upon the
somewhat indefinite *law of Poiseuille for the passing of fluids through
capillary tubes.*

D = diameter of the pores.

Q = amount of water flowing through the surface F under the
constant pressure S.

R is the ratio between the empty space in a given surface and
that filled with solid. This is determined from the weight of solid
material in the jelly of a given filter compared, weight and empty
space in the proportion of 5 to 6.

L is the length of the capillaries (*i.e*, not smaller than the thickness of the wet filter).

k is a constant factor dependent on temperature and kind of fluid. The following formula applies·

$$D = \frac{Q\,(R + I)\,L}{k \cdot S \cdot F \cdot R}.$$

If all the experiments are performed under the same conditions, the formula may be simplified, because $\dfrac{L}{k \cdot S \cdot F}$ becomes a constant.

For the *practical performance* of this experiment two persons are required, one of whom regulates the pressure, while the other determines the amount of water filtered over a certain time, fixed by means of a stop watch.

Under the apparatus is placed a funnel which has a rubber tube with a pinch-cock attached.

The ultrafiltration apparatus is filled with water, and the air pressure is raised to a given point. The pinch-cock is then closed so that all the water filtering at a constant pressure is caught in the funnel. After a given time (*e.g.,* one minute) has elapsed, the entire pressure is instantly released. In this way the amount of water filtered through a given filter in a given time is measured. If we have previously performed the same experiment with a filter paper which has pores of known size, one which, for instance, even partially retains blood corpuscles or bacteria, *i.e* , objects which are measurable microscopically, by means of the above formula, we can estimate the average size of the pores of the ultrafilter.

With this method ultrafilters which just held back hemoglobin showed the average diameter of their pores to be from 33 to 36 $\mu\mu$.

4. *Method of Emulsion Filtration,* described on pp. 15 and 16.

Adsorption by Filters. In ultrafiltration experiments, it is necessary to avoid errors due to adsorption on the part of the filter. Accordingly, as a preliminary experiment, it is advisable to shake a portion of the solution with a shredded filter. If the content of the solution is practically the same afrte as before the shaking, there has been no adsorption. If the adsorption introduces an error into the ultrafiltration experiment, it is necessary to use a different jelly. For instance, arachnolysin is very strongly adsorbed by glacial acetic acid-collodion, but only slightly by formol-gelatin.

In ultrafiltration experiments it is always important to work quantitatively and to test what remains in the filter as well as the filtrate obtained.

[P. A. KOBER has devised a new and valuable form of ultrafilter based on the principle of selective dialysis through collodion and evaporation of the dialysate (per-vaporation). See Jour. Am. Chem. Soc, Vol. XL, No. 8, p. 1226, *et seq.* Tr.]

Applications of Ultrafiltration. Ultrafiltration as previously mentioned serves to separate colloids from crystalloids It can frequently replace *dialysis*, having the advantage of rapidity and permitting separation without the unavoidably great dilution of the dialysate

For this purpose it has been used for the separation of globulin from the electrolytes holding it in solution, and the products of the digestion of casein by pancreatin (H. BECHHOLD[*4])

The most important recent applications of ultrafiltration are, the separation of colloids *with particles of different sizes (fractional ultrafiltration)*, and the determination of the colloid or crystalloid nature of doubtful substances. We refer here to the separation of various albumoses by H BECHHOLD,[*4] the researches concerning the nature of starch solutions by E FOUARD,[*] and those concerning diastase by PŘIBRAM, and the experiment to explain fermentations in the absence of cells by A. VON LEBEDEW,[*] the researches of GROSSER on milk (see pp 174 and 350), the studies of KIRSCHBAUM on dysentery toxin which are still unpublished, as well as those of H. BECHHOLD on the separation of diphtheria toxin from toxon By ultrafiltration, GROSSER was able to distinguish boiled from unboiled milk (see p. 174).

Ultrafiltration is of especial importance in the study of *equilibrium* in solutions, because in this method there is no change in the balance of crystalloid and colloid portions through the dilution of the solution. It is assumed that only small quantities are filtered, that the differential is in some way ascertained so that no changes in concentration occur, and that only moderate pressures are used in the case of solutions containing electrolytes (see p 59). The numerous researches on iron oxid hydrosol by J. DUCLAUX and G. MALFITANO depend on this, as does the work of R. BURIAN[*1] on salt-albumin mixtures.

Ultrafiltration has been variously employed for the solution of purely *biological* questions R BURIAN[*2] has employed it in studying the function of the kidney glomeruli, and H. BECHHOLD[*7] in the question of "internal antisepsis"

Finally, it must be mentioned, that by ultrafiltration *germ-free* fluids may be obtained, as well as *optically pure water* suitable for ultramicroscopic experiments (H. BECHHOLD[*4]). New paths have been opened to the study of filterable infectious agents by ultrafiltration (VON BETEGH).

Diffusion.

Coefficients of diffusion give information concerning the molecular weight and also the size of the particles of a substance in solution. Diffusion in *aqueous solution* is the simplest method for such investigations. The length of time necessary for such experiments introduces so many disturbing factors that, where possible, *diffusion in a jelly* is to be preferred. A jelly offers a means of separating substances having different rates of diffusion. If a mixture of two substances remain for a time in a tube partly filled with a jelly, the more difficultly diffusible substance will, for the most part, remain in solution and can be poured off, whereas the substance easily diffusible will to a greater extent enter the deeper layers of the jelly. Diffusion experiments in jellies teach us the properties of jellies swollen to various degrees, both in the presence of crystalloids and in their absence.

Diffusion in Aqueous Solution. The greatest difficulty lies in avoiding agitation not only when samples are being taken but also during the course of the experiments. The most suitable apparatus is that of L. W. ÒHOLM* (see Fig. 20), with which HERZOG made his experiments, and that of DABROWSKI. The latter (see Fig. 21a) consists of two glass vessels *A* and *B* (a siphon bottle which has been divided in the middle) which are separated by a diaphragm *C*. This diaphragm is a glass ring filled with glass capillary tubes of 1 mm. bore. The interspaces are filled with celluloid.

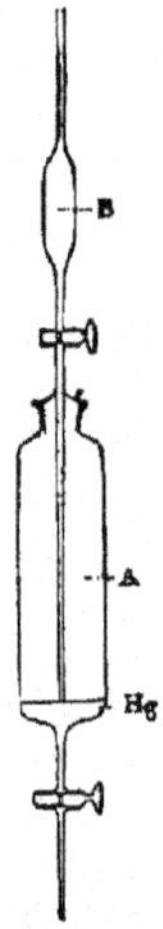

By this arrangement currents are avoided and a very considerable diffusion surface is obtained.

FIG 20. Diffusion apparatus. (L. W. Oholm.)

The solution is placed in *A* and diffuses through *C* and reaches *B* from which samples for analysis are taken from time to time through the tube *F*. The fluid in *A* as well as in *B* is slowly stirred by the stirrer *abd*. We shall return to the consideration of DABROWSKI's experiments on the diffusion of albumin with this apparatus on p. 72.

In the extremely slow diffusion of colloids, which in the case of the experiments of R. O. HERZOG extended over more than two months, absolute sterility is essential. Besides having sterile vessels, the solutions are also sterilized by saturating them with toluol and layering it over them. The addition of 1/2 per cent sodium fluorid solution is useful also. As previously mentioned, the vessels must stand in a perfectly quiet place; instead of portable water baths, incubators should be used, or if these are not placed so as to be free from vibration, the experiments are kept by preference in a cellar.

These diffusion experiments are extremely difficult, but may yield absolutely perfect results, as has been shown by the researches of R. O. HERZOG and H. KASARNOWSKI.[+] These investigators determined the diffusion coefficients for albumin and a number of enzymes (see p. 54 and p 190), from which it could be determined that they were simple substances. On the other hand it could be shown that clupein sulphate, trypsin and pancreatin were mixtures of different substances. Some of them showed various diffusion layers of dissimilar composition (various percentages of N, in clupein), and with other mixtures, products of different origin showed different coefficients of diffusion (trypsin, pancreatin).

Diffusion in a Jelly. A jelly acts like a membrane. It has the advantage over a membrane that its thickness may be varied at will, but the disadvantage that it is usually impossible to obtain the diffused substance in pure form so that the diffused substance must be examined in association with the jelly. Union or adsorption between the jelly and the substance under examination is a more disturbing factor than in the case of a membrane. Diffusion in a jelly has the great advantage over the diffusion in fluids, above described, that it is not disturbed by currents or the almost unavoidable shaking during the experiment, or while samples are being taken.

The experiments are generally performed as follows: A test tube is filled one third to one half full with a very dilute jelly (2 to 5 per cent gelatin). After the jelly solidifies, the solution to be investigated is poured upon it, and the test tube is placed in an ice box. After a longer or shorter time (days, weeks, months) some of the substance will have diffused into the jelly. The supernatant fluid is now poured from the jelly, which is washed with a suitable fluid, water, physiological salt solution or the like. The jelly is now examined to determine the course of diffusion, taking the elapsed time into consideration. *Gelatin* and *agar* are used as jellies. In many cases, inspection shows the extent to which the fluid has diffused into the jelly (*e.g.*, with dyestuffs, indicators or precipitation reactions, the results may be seen). For example, gelatin which has been mixed with red blood corpuscles may have tetanolysin layered above it. By the extent of the hemolysis it is determined how far the tetanolysin has penetrated. H. BECHHOLD[*2] mixed a jelly with goat-rabbit serum and layered above it a solution of goat serum. The appearance of a white ring showed the distance that the precipitin had penetrated.

Precautions For these experiments there should be utilized only absolutely pure gelatin or agar which has been dialyzed at least two or, preferably, four or five days in cold running water Commercial gelatin always contains, besides certain other impurities, sulphurous acid which is used as a bleach in its manufacture, and as a result the gelatin reacts acid to litmus It may be completely freed from the acid by neutralization with NaOH followed by sufficiently prolonged dialyzation in running water The dried gelatin is weighed, wrapped in linen or mull and placed in a trough of running water. After purification the swollen gelatin is very carefully removed from the cloth and weighed to see how much water it has taken up By the addition of, or the evaporation of water, the jelly is brought to the desired concentration and filtered through a jacketed filter This is usually a sufficiently accurate method. For absolutely exact investigation, a measured quantity of the moist gelatin must be weighed before and after it has been dried at 105° C. If working with other than pure aqueous solutions, such as with substances which require physiological salt solution to dissolve them, the gelatin or agar must contain the required amount of salt, if, for instance, the diffusion of globulin solution is desired. Since diffusion experiments with colloids always extend over a considerable time, the test tubes must be closed with paraffined corks or rubber stoppers

In such cases quantitative measurements may be made with a ruler, by placing the zero at the meniscus of the jelly or by means of cathetometer. Tubes with an engraved scale as arranged by

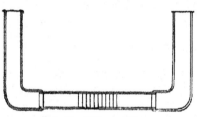

FIG. 21. Diffusion tube.   FIG. 21a Dabrowski's diffusion apparatus.

STOFFEL-PRINGSHEIM* (see Fig. 21) are convenient. The graduated tube is filled with jelly and the solution is poured into the extensions which are ground on water tight. For accurate measurements the same rules are used as in similar physical measurements.

If the diffusion into the jelly is not associated with a visible change, the jelly is removed from the glass by placing it in hot water until the periphery melts, so that the cylinder of jelly may be gently pushed out of the tube The jelly cylinder is then cut into layers of measured thickness which are studied by chemical, biological or animal experiments as to their content of diffused substance In this way SV. ARRHENIUS* and TH. MADSEN have determined the diffusion constants of diphtheria toxin and antitoxin and of tetanolysin and antitetanolysin.

In order to remove the gelatin cylinder easily, H. Bechhold and J. Ziegler coated the interior of the test tube with a lining consisting of parchment, paraffined paper, pergamyn or the like, so that the paper is closed below; on the side, it is closely adherent to the glass, while above it projects about 1 cm. above the rim. This paper lining is filled with gelatin, allowed to cool quickly, and removed with the gelatin at the end of the experiment. The gelatin cylinder is sliced after unwrapping the paper.

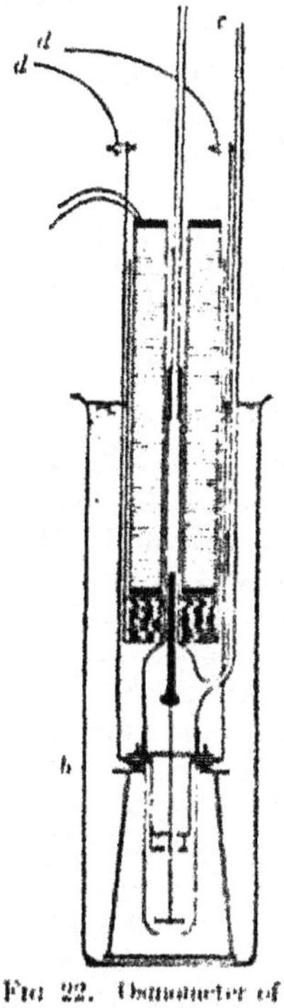

One might imagine that instead of determining the *quantity* of substance which had diffused into the jelly, or the *diffusion path*, the percentage of substance that has been lost by the remaining fluid could be determined. For investigations of colloids this method is not to be recommended because with the slight diffusibility of colloids the loss is also very small and the limits of error approach each other very closely.

The experiments of Voigtländer, placing scales of glass in solutions and determining the amount of the dissolved substance that they took up, are not suitable for use with colloid material.

R. Liesegang [**] has developed a special method. He covers a plate with a jelly and puts on it drops of a solution which diffuse in rings. The method is especially suitable for qualitative studies. If the plate is impregnated with a substance which forms precipitates with the diffusing solution, structures appear whose form and growth may be beautifully studied. In technical processes, a layer of jelly may be placed on the gelatin layer.

Fig. 22. Osmometer of Bültz and Von Vegesack.

Diffusion and capillary ascension in filter paper (which must be absolutely clean) may, under certain circumstances, give useful qualitative information.

Osmotic Pressure.

While in the case of crystalloids, indirect methods of determining the osmotic pressure are used (lowering the freezing point, raising the boiling point), in the case of substances lying at the border line of colloids, the direct osmotic method is most used. W. Bercan and ...

feature consists of a collodion membrane (see Fig. 22) protected by a platinum wire netting. In the case of dextrins which lie on the border line between colloids and crystalloids, W BILTZ decreased the permeability of the membrane by adding cupric ferrocyanid. He filled the collodion sac with 1 per cent potassium ferrocyanid solution and placed it in 1 per cent copper sulphate solution After twenty-four hours he washed the sac for twenty-four hours in running water. The method of procedure recommended by FOUARD, impregnation with tannin and gelatin and subsequent tanning with sublimate, has not proven effective, according to BILTZ. Above the collodion membrane is a glass cap with a vertical tube. The union of netting and cap is at *b*. The fluid is mixed by an electromagnetic stirrer *c*. The electrodes *d* permit the measurement of the conductivity. The entire instrument is placed in a thermostat. Readings of the rise in the tube are made with a cathetometer.

Osmotic Compensation Method

This method determines whether crystalloids present in a colloidal solution are free or in any way bound, *e.g* , adsorbed. L MICHAELIS and P. RONA[*2] have developed this method in their attempt to solve the question whether the grape sugar, always present in the blood and which, strange to say, does not pass through the kidney, is free or bound in any way. For this purpose we place the fluid to be investigated (in this instance blood) in a fish bladder and suspend it in a glass cylinder containing an isotonic fluid (in this case water with 0.95 per cent NaCl) To the surrounding fluid, in a series of experiments, there is added varying quantities of the crystalloids in question. In this instance sugar is added, we shall continue to describe the above experiment as an example. If more sugar has been added than is present in the blood it will diffuse into the blood; the sugar content of the surrounding fluid will decrease. If very little or no sugar is added, the sugar will diffuse from the blood into the surrounding fluid This will occur whether the sugars in the blood are free, osmotically active or even if a portion is adsorbed In the latter case the free sugar will at first diffuse away so that the balance between the adsorbed and the free sugar is disturbed; previously adsorbed sugar may become free and likewise diffuse away. The sugar content of the outer fluid remains constant, only if it accurately expresses the *free* sugar content of the blood. If the total sugar has been determined previously, we may calculate what percentage is adsorbed or otherwise bound, and what proportion is free or osmotically active. With this method, L. MICHAELIS and

P. RONA determined that the entire sugar in the blood serum is in free solution. In analogous ways these authors investigated the conditions of union between calcium and the casein of milk.

Surface Tension.

Because of its sensitiveness, the measurement of surface tension is of the greatest significance for colloid investigation. As far as I know at present, there is no case in which the measurement of these factors has led to the solution of any problem. This is due to the fact that even traces of other substances, especially colloidal substances, markedly influence the surface tension because they are forced to the interfaces. According to J. TRAUBE, $HgCl_2$ in a dilution of one in three million may be detected in dye solutions. For this reason, measurements of surface tension are excessively sensitive and are subject to certain errors.

There are two essentially different groups of methods — a static, (b) dynamic.[1]

(a) Static Methods (the rise of a fluid in a capillary, the deformation of an air bubble in a fluid) show the condition of the developed surface. (b) Dynamic methods (the weight or number of falling drops; the pressure necessary to force air through a capillary dipped in a fluid) show the condition of a nascent surface.

These two methods, especially with colloids, give fundamentally different values because the interior of a fluid has a very different composition from the surface, and a considerable time always elapses before the surface has assumed its normal properties.

As yet, because they are the simplest to perform, only the capillary ascent and the falling drop methods have been used for biological studies.

The measurement of the height ascended in filter paper which has been used especially by GOPPELSROEDER in his numerous investigations on alkaloids, dyestuffs and other organic substances, must be counted a dynamic, rather than a static method, since in the porous material with the ascent and evaporation new surfaces are continually formed. Filter paper offers a very useful method for demonstration purposes. Thus, it shows why alcoholic solutions and soap factures rather than aqueous solutions are adapted to disinfection of the skin (according to BECHHOLD) (see p. 104).

[1] Detailed descriptions of the methods are to be found in OSTWALD's Physico-Chemischen Messungen, Leipzig 1910, and in G. QUINCKE, Poggendorff's Annalen d. Physik, 139, 1 seq. 1870.

[2] Kolloid-Zeit., Vol. 4, pp. 41, 94, 191.

J. TRAUBE has used the falling drop method with his stalagmometer for numerous reseai ches   M. ASCOLI has likewise used it in his *meiostagmin reaction* in cancer.   [CLOWES employed it in his studies. See p. 39.   Tr.]

A given quantity of fluid volume is sucked up into the stalagmometer tube and the number of drops required to empty it, dropping it drop by drop, are counted.

The stalagmometer is an instrument which requires most careful manipulation to obtain reliable results   It is especially important to keep it scrupulously clean, rinsing frequently with distilled water followed by hot potassium hydrate solution   The apparatus is then placed over night in a hot mixture of concentrated sulphuric acid and potassium bichromate   Before use it is again thoroughly rinsed with distilled water   The dropping surface must be absolutely horizontal, this is accomplished by placing it on a stand which can be adjusted in all directions.   There must be no bubbles on the dropping surface or in the tubes   Before each initial measurement the fluid to be measured must be sucked up and allowed to flow out again   The number of drops of the fluid is compared with the number of the same volume of water.   The speed of flow is so gauged that no more than 20 drops fall in a minute   This is best regulated by a screw clamp on a rubber tube slipped over the upper end of the instrument

J. L R. MORGAN has devised a splendid apparatus for determining the weight of falling drops and with it he has measured the surface tension of many substances

There are, however, valuable contributions to the utilization of surface tension (milk investigations by H. ZANGGER; meiostagmin reaction of M. ASCOLI).

The *separation* of colloids and crystalloids *by foaming* as well as the separation of colloids of different surface tension is described on page 35.

Adsorption.

Adsorption experiments may be employed for various purposes. They may be used to determine the distribution of a dissolved colloid between solvent and adsorbent, thus constituting the determination of a physical constant   In such a case an absolutely chemically indifferent substance, e g., charcoal, is chosen as absorbent.   Adsorption presents a suitable means of determining the nature of the electric charge of a dissolved colloid.   Positively charged colloids are adsorbed particularly strongly by electronegative suspensions (*e.g.*, kaolin, mastic suspensions), negatively charged colloids are strongly adsorbed by positive suspensions (*e.g* , iron oxid, clay). Occasionally it is of interest to determine the properties of a gel when it is used as an adsorbent.

If in all cases there occurred pure adsorption, whereby a dissolved substance is taken up by a solid one with which it is shaken, the accurate determination of adsorption constants would be of the greatest value. They would then be natural constants of the same class as the boiling points, melting points, etc , which definitely determine the nature of the substances under examination. Unfortunately this is not the case. Chemical phenomena and unexplained factors complicate the pure adsorption phenomena, so that at present, in biological questions, it is only of value to determine whether adsorption is the predominating force. Investigations in this field are of great importance. Before the advent of physical chemistry and even now, in biological chemistry, it was usual to search for "pure" substances, and to illustrate a phenomenon by a chemical equation. Adsorption experiments have frequently made it clear to us that in a given case such chemical equations do not and could not exist. The studies of H WISLICENUS on *lignin* (see p. 248), and on the *dyeing process* by W. BILTZ and H. FREUNDLICH, are selected from among many other classical examples.

Adsorption experiments for determining distribution are performed by shaking equal quantities by weight, of the most indifferent solid substance obtainable or a gel (charcoal, cellulose) with various dilutions of the dissolved substance. The amount of the substance adsorbed is usually ascertained from the solution. It is first determined how much active substance is contained in a unit volume of the *solution*, which is then examined to see how much has been removed by the adsorbent, the difference gives the quantity adsorbed Thus H. WISLICENUS determined the total solids in the cambial sap of the beech, before and after shaking it with cellulose, and found by taking the difference in weight the amount of colloid that was adsorbed.

In individual instances the quantity adsorbed was determined from the *adsorbent*. B W. ROUX and YERSIN treated diphtheria toxin with freshly precipitated calcium phosphate, they then washed the calcium phosphate well and injected it into guinea pigs A determination by means of the adsorbent instead of the fluid I consider erroneous in principle, because it has been shown repeatedly, in well-controlled experiments, that the adsorbed substance undergoes changes at the surface of the adsorbent.

The fact that a portion of the dissolved substance is removed from the fluid by a solid substance with a large surface does not prove that adsorption has taken place. If, for example, 1 gm. cellulose always removes from a solution the *absolutely identical quantity* of the dissolved substance, irrespective of the concentration of the solution, we would in all probability be dealing with a *chemical* phenomenon. If the proportion between the adsorbed substance and the amount still in solution remains constant over various dilutions, we may assume that the cellulose forms a *solid solution* with the substance in question. Adsorption probably exists only if the cellulose takes up almost everything from a very dilute solution and if the absorbing power of the cellulose is markedly decreased with increased concentration of the solution; this condition is frequently observed with dye solutions. Thus we may make shaking experiments with solutions of the concentration, 0.1, 0.2, 0.3, etc , in which 0 1 denotes any arbitrary standard.

It must be determined first whether an *equilibrium* exists at all. For this purpose a given quantity of adsorbent is shaken with the solution, for example, with 100 c c. In a second experiment an equal quantity of adsorbent is shaken with half the quantity, 50 c.c. of a solution twice the strength. It is then diluted to 100 c.c. and shaken again until an equilibrium is reached. If there is an equilibrium, the final concentration of the solution in the first case is the same as in the second. If there are material differences, the process may nevertheless be considered an adsorption, but it is complicated by other phenomena as explained on page 27 *et seq.*

If it is unnecessary to determine constants, the simplest procedure is to chart the values found on a rectangular system of coordinates (millimeter paper). As ordinate is taken the amount of the material that is being investigated which is taken up by 1 gm. of adsorbent (cellulose, charcoal or the like); as the abscissa, the amount which remains in solution after the adsorption; so that the curve shows the ratio between the amount of substance in the solution and the amount that is adsorbed. It is easy to determine from the characteristic form of the curve whether an adsorption has occurred. (See p. 22.)

The determination of adsorption curves and constants is explained in detail on page 22 *et seq.*

It is of greatest importance that the *adsorbent* be absolutely pure. Many investigators have failed in this and many contradictory results may be attributed to it. The adsorbents are treated with acids, alkalies, alcohol, ether and benzol according as their nature permits (charcoal, diatomaceous earth or kieselguhr, fibrin, etc). In view of the fact that these substances are themselves more or less adsorbed, it is necessary to remove them by prolonged constant treatment with large quantities of the dispersing substance, usually water.

Although *temperature* and *time* do not play as important a role as in other physico-chemical processes it is important to keep temperature and time constant. In most cases the adsorption balance is reached in about one-half hour so that it is always fairly safe to allow an hour

It is usual to shake the adsorbent with the solution, but it must not be overlooked that there are substances which are changed by the mere shaking (see Inactivation by Shaking, p 34)

A second disadvantage of the shaking is that the adsorbent is thereby still further broken up and its surface thus permanently increased. When large quantities of colloid are in solution, there is a counterbalancing error in that the adsorbent becomes coated with a layer of colloid which thus diminishes the active surface. Though these errors are small in the case of adsorbed crystalloids, in the case of true colloids they become quite considerable. To eliminate these two disadvantages, H WISLICENUS and W MUTH* have developed a method which they call the *siphon* (or filter) *process*. In this method a solution of constant strength comes repeatedly in contact with the adsorbent The process is as follows: a tube is filled with washed clay or other adsorbent and in connection with a separatory funnel, forms a siphon The solution to be studied is poured into the funnel and very slowly filters through the adsorbent The apparatus (see Fig. 23) is entirely practical. In the strict scientific sense, however, equilibria are not obtained with it.

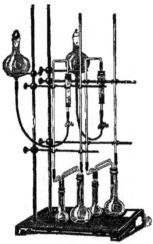

Fig 23   Apparatus for adsorption analysis   (H Wislicenus)

Before determining the content of the solution after adsorption, the *adsorbent must be removed*. Filtration is rarely suitable because the filter-paper itself adsorbs. In any event the filter used should be very small, and the quantity of fluid to be filtered as large as possible. *Centrifugation* is the most practical method. The fluid may be poured or pipetted from the adsorbent which has been deposited.

The determination of the *content of the solution before and after adsorption* varies so much in accordance with the nature of the substance under investigation, that it is hardly possible to formulate general rules. The simplest procedure, when it is possible, is to determine the weight of a given volume after evaporation, or the solutions may be titrated. In other cases suitable physical or biological methods must be employed (animal experiment, hemolysis, agglutination, etc.).

To determine the *electric charge* of a colloid by adsorption, we choose *for adsorbent*, a *suspension* of a substance having the most pronounced electrical charge. Electropositive iron oxid or alumina gel removes electronegative colloids from solution   Electronegative diatomaceous earth (kieselguhr), kaolin or mastic suspensions (obtained by dropping an alcoholic solution of mastic into water) attract electropositive colloids. As has been said, the charge of natural colloids depends chiefly upon their reaction. Experiments are therefore performed with very faintly acid, very faintly alkaline and neutral reactions. Because many substances are destroyed in alkaline or acid solutions, it is necessary to make appropriate preliminary tests. Measurements of the amount contained before and after adsorption determine the character of the particular colloid. In this way L. MICHAELIS investigated a number of ferments (see p. 186).

In the border land between *adsorption* and *chemical combination* belong the studies of *staining*, which open to the histologist a wide field for the application of colloid-chemical knowledge.

Internal Friction.

As has been shown, especially by the investigations of WOLFGANG PAULI on albumin, the internal friction or viscosity serves to give valuable information concerning changes in the condition in colloidal solutions.

In the case of hydrophile colloids an increase of viscosity usually indicates an hydration

The *relative internal friction* is usually determined by taking that of water at the same temperature as equal to 1. This is usually done by allowing a given amount of fluid to flow from a capillary tube, taking the time with a stop watch. If the rate of flow for water has been previously determined, the relation between the two gives the relative internal friction

WILHELM OSTWALD constructed a well-adapted apparatus (described in OSTWALD-LUTHER's "Textbook and Manual for the Performance of Physico-chemical Measurements," which see for details). The colloid investigator should not work with *capillaries that are too fine*, because his fluids are usually very viscous. The maintenance of a *constant temperature* is of especial importance, and therefore it is necessary to employ a transparent thermostat. Furthermore the *specific gravity* must also be taken OSTWALD-SPRENGEL's pyknometer may be used.

In *biological* investigations it is occasionally necessary to work with *very small amounts of fluid*. Special apparatus has therefore been devised so that but one or two drops may suffice for a viscosity determination. The apparatus of HIRSCH and BECK, thoroughly described by P T KORÁNYI and A. v. RICHTER, "Physical Chemistry and Medicine II," p. 27 *et seq.*, is frequently used. The apparatus of H. A. DETERMAN is very simple; as seen from Fig. 24, it resembles an hour glass. The capillary has at either end an enlargement, and

then a constriction as well as markings. This tube is placed in a
large glass shell which can revolve on its axis and has a thermometer
inserted Since the apparatus may be turned upside down like an
hour glass, it is possible to take several successive readings from the
same quantity of fluid. DETERMAN employs it chiefly for the determination of viscosity in uncoagulated blood. For this purpose

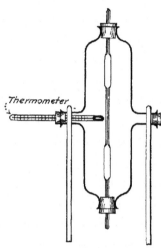

he places a trace of hirudin on
the unbroken skin, preferably on
the lobe of the ear. After punc-
turing the skin he collects the
blood with a pipette directly
connected with the tube of the
viscosimeter.

The apparatus of W. HESS[*]
depends upon a somewhat different principle. He does not compare the *time* of flow, but the
distances fluids may be sucked
up. His apparatus consists of
two capillaries connected with a
T-tube, through which fluids are
sucked with a rubber bulb;
through one capillary water is
sucked, and through the other
blood or some other fluid that is
to be investigated. From the
ratio between the distances to

FIG. 24. Viscosimeter. (H A
Determan.)

which the two fluids are sucked through the capillaries, the viscosity
may be directly determined. The apparatus has certain special
advantages, the horizontal position of the capillaries eliminates the
influence of the specific gravity; and since water and colloid are
simultaneously tested, the errors of temperature are reduced to a
minimum and calculations for correction are unnecessary.

Melting, Coagulation and Solidification Temperatures.

The determination of the melting,[1] coagulation and solidification
temperatures has the same significance for colloids as the measurement of the melting point has for crystalloids.

Coagulation by Heat The fluid to be investigated is placed in
a test tube, in a water bath. The contents of both test tube and

[1] In the case of jellies it is only possible to speak of a " period of liquefaction ";
for the sake of simplicity I employ the expression "melting point."

water bath must be stirred and a thermometer must be placed in each. The test tube must be illuminated by a uniform and protected source of light. It is advisable to make a number of preliminary determinations of the coagulation point before making the final reading.

WOLFGANG PAULI distinguishes the following different appearances in coagulation — clear, opalescent, slightly cloudy, milky translucent, milky opaque, finely, medium or coarsely flocculent in slightly cloudy or clear fluid. These various aspects are strongly dependent on the dilution and the salt content of the solution, and the latter has the greater influence on the temperature of coagulation

Melting and Solidification Temperature. To determine the melting point of gelatin, agar, etc, W PAULI and P. RONA* used an apparatus that is similar to that of E. BECKMANN for determining the freezing point. The melting point is the temperature at which the layer surrounding the thermometer melts.

H. BECHHOLD and J. ZIEGLER*² used an air bath, in which a tube containing the jelly is placed alongside the thermometer. The solid jelly is weighted with 5 gm of mercury¹ The melting point is the temperature at which the mercury breaks through the jelly. Since it is difficult to observe the melting of the jelly and the thermometer at the same time, the authors use an acoustic device (metronome) which is described in the original papers and which is recommended for similar observations.

Swelling.

The methods of measuring swelling, *i.e.*, the water taken up by a gel, are very inexact. *The increase of volume, the gain in weight* or *the pressure of swelling* may be determined.

Volume Increase. Equal quantities of fibrin may be placed in test tubes and covered with different solutions, we then observe how high the fibrin rises upon swelling (M H. FISCHER, see p 68, Fig. 7). The increase in volume consists of the decrease in volume of the swelling gel plus the volume of the water, so that the determination has an error, inasmuch as the contraction of the gel during the swelling is unknown. This error is negligible in comparison with the other experimental errors.

Increase of Weight This method introduced by P. HOFMEISTER is somewhat more accurate The total solids of the swelling substance (gelatin, muscle, etc.) are determined and the substance either in a dry or a swollen state is placed in a solution. The weight deter-

¹ This apparatus is made by C. Gerhard, Bonn, Germany, dealer in chemical utensils

mined before and after the stay in the solution give the amount of
fluid taken up or lost. Before weighing the gel is to be wiped
with filter paper or a cloth in order to free it from the adhering
fluid. Fluid is pressed out in these methods more especially in the case
of very much swollen material by the weight of the gel itself as
well as by its contraction, in tearing the fluid is dried off and must

be taken account of in the
working.

Swelling Pressure. The determination of the factor offers the
greatest practical difficulties. An exact
method proceeds on the appa-
ratus of J. Herbst* may be
adapted for other swelling substances. J. Herbst used his
apparatus Fig. 25 to measure
the swelling pressure. The swelling
is measured. The swelling agar is
placed in the closed end of a metal
cylinder M. The top of the agar
is in the closed end communicated with
the hole b in it. Water was
pressed in the upper end of the
hole. A disc a above which
stresses the gel is in contact the rod
M1M which moves over a various
weight. The lifting power is
measured on the disc. The
theory of the apparatus however
requires further investigation to
establish the relationship between swelling pressure water
absorbed and the gel.

The apparatus of J. Perrin
(see Fig. 26) offers less theoretic difficulties but can be employed
only for pressures up to a atmospheres. The principle employed
follows the substance to be investigated y is placed at the bottom
of a tube G which is closed by a porous partition f. The other
tube dips into a vessel of water. In order to measure the pressure
the whole vessel is filled with pressure, which is measured with a
manometer M. The swelling substance may be placed under a
given pressure by permitting compressed gas to act on the cylinder a. The details of the measurement concern the pressure

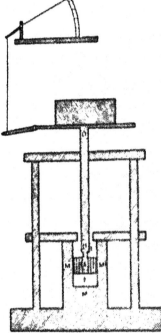

Fig. 25. J. Herbst's apparatus for
measuring swelling pressure.

Flocculation.

Observations of the flocculation of a suspension or colloidal solution determine whether it behaves as a hydrophile or a hydrophobe colloid; furthermore, they show the electric charge and, under certain conditions, the presence of a protective colloid. The method of the experiment is very simple: a suspension or colloidal solution is

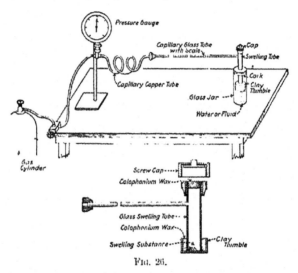

FIG. 26.

divided among a large number of test tubes, diminishing quantities of electrolytes ($NaCl$, $CaCl_2$, $FeCl_3$) are added and the test tubes are filled to equal volumes with a solvent (water, physiological salt solution, etc.). After the test tubes have been exposed at uniform temperature for a given time (1 to 24 hours), they are examined for flocculation.

In comparative experiments it is necessary that suspensions or solutions have the same concentration. On account of the small amount of solid substance little is to be accomplished by determinations of total solids. It is frequently desirable to prepare a large quantity of a standard solution to last a long time, and frequently the determinations may be made colorimetrically. I am accustomed to prepare mastic suspensions by dropping 1 per cent alcoholic mastic solutions into water which is being energetically stirred. The suspension is filtered through rather dense filter paper and tested for transparency in a beaker having parallel sides, to one side of which various printed lines have been glued. The suspension is diluted until, with a definite illumination, a certain size type can just be read.

It is necessary to test especially, ... whether the particles have really gathered at the ... or whether they have only sunk to the bottom under the influence of gravity.

In the case of the measurements ... alkalinity is to be measured, because the leaching out of alkali from the glass ... ...

This method gives information not only concerning the stability, but is at the same time quantitative, it affords, by determining the "*threshold value*," and, under some circumstances, concerning the rate of flocculation.

In order to work with very small quantities ... tubes are used which are narrowed at their lower ends. Is there insufficient fluid even for this determination we must employ a "drop method," in other words, drops are mixed on a cover glass and that is placed up side down on a slide with a depression ground into it so that the drop will hang. The cover glass is ringed with vaseline to hold it to the slide. This method is most quantitative and is especially adapted for the agglutination of bacteria.

It is desirable in all cases to prepare a dilution experiment. It may occur as the result of "*zonegolation*" ... that both small low concentrations result in flocculation whereas those of the mean take and occur in medium concentration.

Electric Migration.

Electric migration reveals the nature of the charge of a colloid. The most primitive arrangement for migration experiments is a

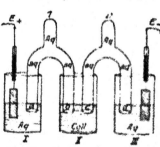

beaker in which are suspended two platinum electrodes that are part of the circuit of a direct current of at least 220 volts. This is to be recommended only for sample demonstrations in the lecture room where migration must be established quickly. Because of the changes to react on the electrodes the results are very uncertain. It is preferable to use an U-shaped tube or an arrangement such as is shown in Fig. 26a. The middle glass jar contains the colloid to be tested and is united by the U-shaped side tubes, filled with water to the two outer beakers which also contain water and into which dip the electrodes EE. For research work I employ

Fig. 26a. Simple apparatus for electric migration.

H BECHHOLD's *"Bell apparatus."*[1] The colloid solution to be tested
is placed in the glass vessels AA (see Fig. 27) which are connected
by a tube. The vessels are closed below by the membranes MM
(best for the purpose is fish bladder or the like). The tube R
allows for the expansion of
the fluid caused by the heat
of the electric current The
bell apparatus is placed in two
separate glass vessels (crystallizing dishes) GG; the membranes are immersed in the
water, into which also dip
the electrodes EE. The advantages of the apparatus are: the

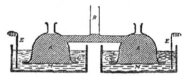

FIG 27   Bell apparatus. (H Bechhold.)

great surface of colloid solution, the products transferred do not
come in contact with the electrodes and each may be conveniently and separately collected and ex-
amined, the current must pass through
the entire colloidal solution; the apparatus may be easily sterilized and the
free surfaces may have toluol layered
over them. The apparatus does not get
out of order very easily. L. MICHAELIS
has avoided the change in reaction due
to electrolysis at the electrodes by using
nonpolarizable electrodes. Fig. 28 amply
explains the apparatus The electrodes,
e.g., zinc or silver wire, are dipped into
the vessels 1 and 5, which are filled
with zinc sulphate and NaCl solution
respectively.

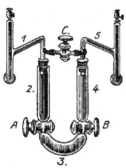

FIG 28 Migration apparatus
with non-polarizable electrodes (L Michaelis.)

Migration experiments are usually very
difficult to perform. Since the nature of the charge may also be
determined by *adsorption*, by employing positive and negative
adsorbents, this latter method is preferable, because it is simpler.

Optical Methods.

There is a certain relation between the cloudiness (Tyndall effect)
of a fluid and its content in suspended particles or colloid. On this
account various authors (KAMERLINGH ONNES and KEESOM, MECK-
LENBURG, WILKE and HANDOVSKY) have constructed instruments to

[1] To be had from the Vereinigten Fabriken für Laboratoriumsbedarf, Berlin N.
Scharnhorst Str.

measure the amount of cloudiness so that they might determine from it, the content of dissolved colloid in the fluid

As yet they have not been applied to biocolloids, and the relation between the clouding of media in a fluid, the intensity of the light and cloudiness yields a complicated curve. On this account it is still impossible to determine the value of these instruments aptly termed by MECKLENBURG, *tyndallmeters*, for the study of biocolloids.

There is need of such an instrument. [P. A. KOBER has devised a very satisfactory nephelometer which has found extensive application in biology, especially by BLOOR. See Journal of Industrial and

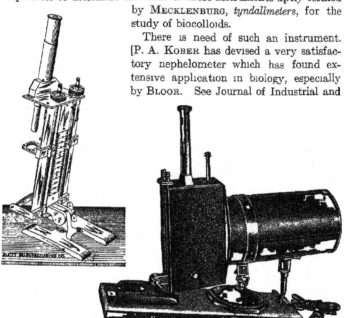

FIG 28a. Kober Nephelometer

Engineering Chem., Vol. VII, p. 843 Tr.] I have always felt the want of being able to determine the exact content of a bacterial suspension by some sort of tyndallmeter. Such an instrument must be very simple to manipulate, which is not the case with the existing instruments

The colloid content of a solution is well measured for certain purposes by

The Fluid Interferometer.

The fluid interferometer[1] was originally devised to determine the concentration or change in concentration of crystalloid solutions. According to MARC it is also available for light or yellowish colloidal

[1] Made by Carl Zeiss, Jena.

solutions, but not for those deeply colored   It depends on the following principle. when parallel beams of light pass through a narrow slit, as the result of refraction a broad band of light with parallel dark bands (interference bands) is seen on the opposite wall.   If light is permitted to fall on the same spot through a second parallel slit, the bands of light will interfere and very fine sharp lines will be obtained which may be greatly magnified.   When a different medium, that is water or a solution of salt or colloid is placed behind one slit the interference bands move to one side depending on the refractive index.   If the process is reversed by a set of glass prisms or something similar, it is possible to read on the adjusting screw of the apparatus the difference of refractive index.

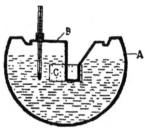

Fig. 28b shows a cross section through the interferometer.   A is the chamber with the standard water, B

Fig. 28b   Fluid Interferometer.

the chamber for the test solution, C the window for viewing the interference bands.   With dilute solutions the concentration increases in proportion to the scale on the graduated drum.   For more concentrated solutions a standard must be set in each case.   Technical details of the readings may be found in Mare's paper (*loc. cit.*)   He has thus far used the interferometer mainly to determine adsorption and for studying the colloid content in drinking water and sewage

Ultramicroscopy.

Ultramicroscopy permits the recognition of certain optical inhomogeneities, and depends upon the use of dark field illumination. Ultramicroscopes magnifying from 750 to 1500 diameters serve in principle the same purpose as the ordinary microscope.   They have the advantage over the latter that without staining or extensive preparation, even living objects, spirilla, etc., become visible to the eye; bright on a dark background.   Ultramicroscopy with a one hundred thousand fold magnification has solved important theoretical questions of colloid chemistry.   By reason of the conditions of light refraction its value is chiefly confined to inorganic colloids.

In the ordinary microscope the field is usually bright, while the object is more or less dark against its surroundings.   In the ultramicroscope, only the rays of light reflected from the object reach the observer's eye and permit the object to stand out bright against the dark background.

In this dark field illumination the form of the objects are not given, but every point appears as a small bright disc which under some circumstances may be surrounded by one or several rings of light. The ultramicroscope is especially suited for the recognition of *inhomogeneities* in a medium.

Apart from the recognition of form, the field of application of the microscope was enormously extended by the invention of the ultramicroscope.

At about seven hundred diameters' magnification, the limit of the available microscopical magnification is reached theoretically and practically, i.e., revelation of new details ceases. The field is to make particles *visible* in the ultramicroscope is almost unlimited, provided only a sufficiently strong source of light is available. Practically, the limits of visibility in our latitude with the best sunlight is about 10 $\mu\mu$ (1 $\mu\mu$ = 1 millionth part of a millimeter). Zsigmondy gives 5 $\mu\mu$. Tr.]

For our purposes, two types must be distinguished of Ultramicroscopes for the study of colloids. They permit the observation of objects or inhomogeneities down to 10 $\mu\mu$ and require very bright sources of light — sunlight reflected from a heliostat, or electric arc lights. (b) Ultramicroscopes for the study of organized material (microörganisms, animal and plant cells) suitable for the study of objects no smaller than 0.1 μ. Weißbach or Nernst light in combination with suitable lenses furnish sufficient illumination.

Ultramicroscopy for the Study of Colloidal Solutions.

The original slit-ultramicroscope constructed by H. Siedentopf and R. Zsigmondy with rectangular arrangement of its optical axes

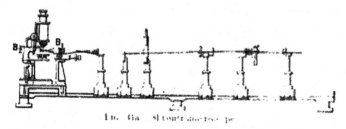

Fig. 6a. Slit ultramicroscope

is nowadays only employed for the study of solid objects (gels?) and on this account may be omitted from consideration in our colloid investigations. Recently Zsigmondy has adapted the original slit-ultramicroscope to immersion. A large proportion of the light

rays in the path of the object examined are lost by refraction. Very
small objects, such as bacteria are too faintly illuminated to be
visible by his "dry system" On this account, a highly refractive
fluid (water or cedar oil) is placed between the object and the objec-

FIG. 29   Illumination of the cardioid ultramicroscope

tive (of wide aperture), which permits many more rays to pass from
the object into the objective. It was impossible to use immersion
in the earlier slit-ultramicroscope because the illuminating (B_1) and

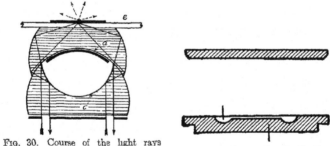

FIG. 30. Course of the light rays
through the cardioid condenser.
(H. Siedentopf.)

FIG 31   Quartz chamber for the
cardioid ultramicroscope

the examining objective (B_2) could not be brought sufficiently close
together (see Fig. 31a). This difficulty was overcome through an
improved method of construction by the optical works of R WINKEL
of GÖTTINGEN (see Fig 30)   A drop of the fluid to be examined is
placed between the two immersion objectives of wide aperture or

they dip into a small trough containing the fluid for examination. The illumination intensity of the "immersion ultramicroscope" is much greater than the original, and particles are made visible which formerly had quite eluded observation; the contrast effect in the intensely dark field is quite perfect. For biologists, the ultramicroscope with a *cardioid condenser* is at present the most important instrument. It permits the use of twenty times as much light as the slit-ultramicroscope, "practically the maximum available from the source of light."

The construction of the apparatus is shown in Fig. 29. *c* contains an electric arc lamp with a perforated sleeve cap *d* to cut out

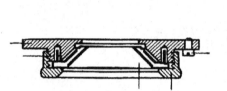
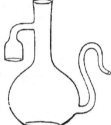

FIG 32   Holder for the quartz chamber em-   FIG. 33   Flasks for storing
ployed with the cardioid ultramicroscope   ultrawater   (A Haak)

interfering light   An illuminating lens *e* passes the light sharply downward, through a glass trough filled with water, to the center of the microscope mirror

The water trough serves to remove the heat rays or when necessary acts as a color filter.   The microscope mirror throws the light perpendicularly through the cardioid condenser, which replaces the ABBE condenser in the microscope.   It is evident from the diagram of the cardioid condenser (Fig. 30) that the various ascending rays strike the slide *e* obliquely by reason of the double reflection from the two spherical surfaces and that thus, all the light is utilized for illumination; only the rays reflected by the object take the usual path through the objective and the ocular to the observer's eye. Water is used for immersion.

With the cardioid ultramicroscope the object is placed between slide and cover glass as in ordinary microscopy.   For reasons we shall revert to later, a slide with a special quartz chamber (Fig. 31) is used, which is held in the holder (Fig. 32).

There are a number of precautions to be observed in working with the ultra-microscope Since every impurity makes a point of light in the field, it is necessary to employ optically clear water. Such water is prepared according to R. ZSIGMONDY by distillation through a silver condensing tube, or according to H. BECHHOLD by ultrafiltration through a very tight ultrafilter (6 to 10 per cent).

FIG. 34 Dark-field illumination for the examination of organisms.

For collecting and storing, only Jena glass vessels should be employed. Ground glass stoppers or corks are to be avoided because they always yield fine dust I have found the suggestion of W BILTZ serviceable, he coated the stoppers with

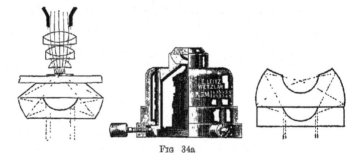

FIG 34a

tin foil I recommend a storage flask for ultrawater manufactured by A. HAAK in Jena (Fig. 33).

Neither water nor alcohol should show microscopically the slightest FARADAY-TYNDALL effect, but wherever illuminated, only a very faint shimmer, whitish in the case of water (ultrawater), bluish in the case of alcohol (ultra-alcohol).

Though a skilled ultramicroscopist usually recognizes impurities from irregular intensity of illumination and color of the submicrons, as well as by differences in motion, the most extreme care is necessary in ultramicroscopic work

Cover glasses for the upper chamber should be of quartz, 3/4 mm thick. The usual methods of cleaning (cloths, brushes, elderpith and Japanese tissue) are to be avoided, as particles, which may cause much trouble, are broken off, scratches, tears, and impurities arising from dry cleaning increase the adsorption of colloids on the chamber walls and reveal their own ultramicroscopic pictures independently of the colloid particles. The chamber and cover slip must always be cleaned in the following fashion· nothing is touched by hand, only forceps with platinum points or with a loop of platinum wire about them may be used. The apparatus is placed in a hot mixture of concentrated H_2SO_4 and sodium bichromate, then washed with tap water and finally conductivity water The water must be removed with ultra-alcohol and finally collodion is poured over the cleaned surface. Before use, the collodion skin may be easily raised at one corner and removed

On forcing the chamber and cover slip in the holder, it is necessary to avoid screwing too tight or tensions will arise which gradually equalize themselves and cause striations which are very disturbing

Ultramicroscopes for the Study of Organized Material.

The apparatus for this purpose may be adjusted to any microscope. Special preparation of the objects is unnecessary.

Objects difficult to make visible by staining or which are too small to see alive with the ordinary microscope are especially suitable for

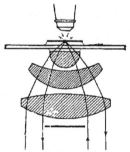

FIG 35   Abbe condenser with central opacity

FIG 36   Paraboloid condenser for the dark-field illumination of organisms (From H Siedentopf)

this method of investigation, *e.g.*, spirilla, protoplasmic structures, etc.   A picture is obtained similar to that with BURRI's India ink method, in which the rest of the field is blackened with India ink, while the objects appear bright.   Oblique illumination reveals inhomogeneities and structures which would be invisible even with staining. In the description of the investigations of N. Gaidukow, E. Raehlmann, etc., we shall return to this topic. The optical system depends on the fact that the central rays of light reflected from the mirror of the microscope are cut out by a disc, whereas the lateral rays which strike the object obliquely are utilized.

The simplest and cheapest arrangement is the one by which a central blind is placed in the diaphragm carrier of the Abbe illuminating apparatus (see Fig. 35), yet this arrangement is not recommended on account of the faint illumination and the difficulty in centering.

Much to be preferred, because of the strong illumination, is Siedentopf's *paraboloid condenser* (see Fig. 36). It is adapted to the study of living bacteria and especially for *thin organized structures.*

The thicker the preparation the weaker must be the objective.

Preparations must be made with greater cleanliness than for bright field illumination, though such scrupulous care is not necessary as for the cardioid condenser.

The slide must have a definite thickness (not less than 1.1 mm or more than 1.4 mm.)

The object to be studied is placed on a slide moistened with a drop of physiological salt solution and a cover glass adjusted so that there are no bubbles. The water pressed out at the sides is absorbed and the rim is sealed tight with wax (1 part wax, 2 parts rosin). A drop of water without bubbles is placed between the slide and the condenser. Neither water nor oil is used between the slide and the objective (dry system).

[Other ultramicroscopes have been devised by Cotton and Mouton, and by Ivanowski (made by E. Leitz). See also L'Ultra-microscope by Paul Gaston, Paris, 1910. Tr.]

PART II.

THE BIOCOLLOIDS.

WITH the exception of water, inorganic salts and a few organic substances as, for instance, urea and sugar, only colloids exist in plant and animal organisms, and if we except water, the colloids quantitatively far exceed the crystalloids. This appears reasonable when we consider the respective roles of crystalloids and colloids in the organism. We may compare living organisms to a city, in which the colloids are the houses and the crystalloids are the people who traverse the streets, disappearing into and emerging from the houses, or who are engaged in demolishing or erecting buildings. The colloids are the *stable* part of the organism; the crystalloids the *mobile* part, which penetrating everywhere may bring weal or woe. Because they have only a transitory use, we find in the organism only a small number and a small quantity of organic crystalloids. In plants we encounter the most important organic crystalloid, sugar, on its way from its place of origin to the place where it is used, or in depots, such as buds, roots, fruits, etc., where it is either changed into an insoluble form of carbohydrate, into starches and related products, or its retreat is cut off by the drying of the stem from which the fruit depends. In its course we may tap great quantities of sugar, as in the birch, maple and palm when they are "in sap." If for any reason it becomes mobilized again in the depots, large quantities of sugar may be formed. In wild plants the amount of sugar is rarely very great, it is otherwise with cultivated plants where as the result of cultivation sugar is stored with no advantage to the plant, *e.g.*, sugar beets, sugar cane and common beets. At times a certain biological purpose may be associated with sugar formation, *e.g.*, the sugar formation in fruits for the purpose of their dissemination. The fruit is always the biological object and serves to perpetuate the species, not the individual. The development of a greater quantity of crystalloid as sugar in fruit is therefore not surprising, since the fruit has completed its service for the *individual plant* Elsewhere, we find the carbohydrates only in colloidal and most often even in insoluble form. I refer to starches, cellulose and gums.

129

Like plants, the animal organism has the power of changing *carbohydrates* into crystalloids Ferments change the starches into sugar, in fact cellulose which is so resistant to chemical attack is made soluble in the intestine of vegetarians, so that it can enter the animal body. As soon as the crystalloid forms of carbohydrate have passed the intestinal wall they are transferred to the main depot, the liver, where they remain in the stable colloidal condition as animal starch, glycogen. We also find glycogen in most of the other organs, whereas the mobile state of carbohydrate, grape sugar, occurs only in minimal quantities (0 08 to 0.12 per cent), in fact only just so much as is necessary for the production of energy.

Fats, too, are found in the truly soluble form (*e.g.*, soaps) in plants, only in the germs of seeds, and in animals, probably only at the moment when they pass through the wall of the intestines They have hardly passed the intestine when they immediately regain their colloidal condition of emulsion, and are carried in that condition to their depots.

The same statements hold for proteins Crystalloid cleavage products are found in germinating seeds and in minimal quantities in the vascular paths; in plants, asparagin, in animals, among others, urea, uric acid and ammonia salts. The organism strives its utmost to retain the colloidal condition Hardly have the crystalloid cleavage products of albumin which have been formed in the stomach and intestines passed through the intestinal wall, than they are straightway changed back into the colloidal form, so that their return may be cut off The crystalloid combustion products are given an avenue of escape through the kidneys.

Physiological chemistry deals with the role of the carbohydrates, fats and proteins apart from *water* and the *inorganic salts* In the study of biocolloids, water and salts cannot be neglected, because water and salts are an indispensable part of the colloids; no colloid can exist in the organism without them, because they condition the *turgescence* which is characteristic of living colloid.

In the case of cells with true membranes, salts may determine at times the balance of osmotic pressure within and without the cell. This general fact does not explain the necessity of the various *kinds* of anions and cations (K, Na, Ca, Mg, Cl, SO_4, PO_4, CO_2); the balance in osmotic pressure may be maintained by any non-electrolyte (*e g*, sugar) and yet a cell cannot be kept alive in an isotonic sugar solution. Inorganic salts have specific relations to certain organs to which we shall refer later: they are the expression of characteristic sharply defined *physical states* assumed in the presence of given quantities of water and salt, by the proteins, carbohydrates, etc., of which the organs consist.

Chemistry in general, and physiological chemistry in particular, aims to investigate the structure of individual chemical substances, and thus explain their properties by splitting them, synthesizing them, and comparing the regenerated (rearticulated) substance with the original, to see if it is the same or different. Unfortunately, so far as the colloidal constituents of the organism are concerned, they are still far from their goal, especially in the case of carbohydrates and proteins. Here colloid chemistry enters and attempts to comprehend and where possible to regulate the behavior of the finished product. Colloid chemistry is not occupied with the parts of the machine, but with the machine itself. The chemist splits the proteins into polypeptids, amino-acids, etc., but the student of biocolloids avoids such profound attacks and strives to keep the molecule intact so far as possible, studying its outward form, the chemical points of attack offered by the unmutilated molecule, its behavior to changes which may occur under normal and pathological conditions, as well as those brought about by drugs.

I wish here to emphasize one other point. Only a few substances occur in the organism that are suitable for study by the physiological chemist. Serum albumin and globulin, the starches and some of the fats, are unquestionably substances which may be separated from the organism without losing some of their essential properties, but they are exceptions. The substances usually studied by physiological chemists are those which have already suffered considerable modification. The organism possesses neither glue, histone nor myosin, and even if we knew the exact chemical constitution of glue, this would throw no light upon the properties and the function of cartilage and the fibrils of connective tissue from which it is derived. But even without knowing the chemical composition of glue, I believe that it would be possible, with the methods of colloid chemistry alone, to collect a series of observations which would afford valuable conclusions concerning the chemical mechanisms of such tissues.

A time will come when the old physiological chemistry and the new chemistry of the biocolloids will meet and the two opposite ends of the tunnel shall be united. We shall first try to learn the properties of the intact colloid molecule of the colloid particle. The following chapters on carbohydrates, lipoids and proteins should be read, bearing this statement in mind.

CHAPTER VIII.

CARBOHYDRATES.

As the name indicates, we classify as carbohydrates a group of substances containing carbon and the elements of water, *i.e*, O and H in the proportion of 1 . 2.

We owe our knowledge of the constitution of the lower members of this group, the crystalloid water-soluble *sugars*, largely to the investigations of EMIL FISCHER. The same difficulties which we encounter in the study of all colloidal substances interfere with determining the constitution of the higher colloidal members of this group, the *saccharocolloids*. There is at present no means of positively recognizing the purity and the individuality of the substance studied or its derivatives. It is true 'that we may crystallize individual colloidal carbohydrates, *e.g.*, inulin, which as a rule naturally occurs in crystals, but all we have said on page 71 concerning the crystallization of colloids in general applies to inulin.

Because of their common occurrence, the most important saccharocolloids are the *starches*, vegetable and animal (glycogen), and also *cellulose*. Next in importance come the various *gums* and *pectinous plant juices*. *Dextrins* which are also usually colloidal are really cleavage products of the starches.

A host of individual facts have been derived from the enormously extensive utilization of starches, as food, cereals and potatoes, for fermented liquors, beer and brandy, as sizing, etc., and of cellulose (in the textile industries and paper manufacture). It is only recently that there has been manifested an effort to reach a general viewpoint such as colloid science has made possible (E. FOUARD.*)

STARCH, obtained from starchy grains, is an amorphous white powder which migrates in the electric current to the anode, it exhibits an acid character chemically, since it adsorbs dissolved alkalis (with the exception of NH_4OH) and hydroxids of the heavy metals, probably thus forming amylates. It does not adsorb acids or salts. (A RAKOWSKI.*) Since phosphoric acid is always present in native starches and in the diastatic cleavage of phosphorus-containing dextrins, we may assume with M. SAMEC that there is a carbohydrate phosphoric acid complex probably an ester (amylophosphate). Starch has a great reversible swelling capacity in water (pore swelling).

133

In swelling there is a great loss of volume, $i\,e$, the volume of the swollen starch is less than that of the dry starch plus the water necessary for swelling, as was shown in exhaustive experiments by H. RODEWALD.[*] This contraction is about 8 per cent, when 20 per cent of water is taken up Swelling is accompanied by the liberation of heat, which, according to E. WIEDEMANN and CHARLES LUDE-KING,[*] amounts to about 6 6 calories per gram H. RODEWALD studied the phenomenon more thoroughly and found a diminution in the amount of heat liberated with increasing water content. The following is an abbreviated table of his results

Per cent of water contained in 100 gm dry starch	Approximate per cent of heat liberated per gm dry starch
0 23	28 11
2 39	22 60
4 58	18 19
9 59	10 28
18 43	3 54

If we add more water to starch, and heat to 55°-70° C, by "solution swelling," we get a jelly-like mass, *starch paste*, which dissolves on continued heating in more water. This solution coagulates when it is frozen. G MALFITANO and A. N. MOSCHKOFF[*] utilize this property of starch solution to obtain a starch free from mineral substances Demineralized starch on being mixed with suitable salts shows all the properties of the different forms of starch. These investigators are therefore of the opinion that the various modifications in the properties of the natural starch granules are due to mineral admixtures.

E. FOUARD,[*] by means of acids, freed starches from their inorganic elements and obtained a substance which formed an unstable colloidal solution in water Heat, alkalis and alkaline salts made the solution more permanent, whereas cold, acids and acid salts favored jelly formation On ultrafiltering his starch solutions, E. FOUARD found that in accordance with their concentration, a given fraction of the solution always passed through collodion membranes. He concluded from this, that for every concentration of the starch solution a balance exists between the coarser particles and the molecularly dissolved (hydrolyzed?) starches Unfortunately, the work of E. FOUARD contains no information relative to the permeability of the collodion membranes, so that it is impossible to arrive at any conclusion in reference to the size of the suspended and the dissolved starch particles.

On account of their great surface development, the adsorptive capacity of starches is very great. As has been said, when they swell they adsorb water, dyes, etc. A very characteristic adsorption compound is formed with iodin. Iodin is the best known reagent for starches, by it they are stained blue. It was formerly believed that iodin and starch united chemically; W. Biltz showed that it is merely an adsorption. According to the degree of dispersion, iodin solution is blue, red, orange or yellow, inasmuch as the starch solution acts as a protective colloid (W. Harrison*). There are, in addition, varieties of starch which give at once a brownish red or a wine red color with iodin. Inulin and lichenin are colored yellow by iodin.

The swelling and pasting of starches, hydration, is analogous to the swelling of proteins, which is a preliminary to their hydrolytic cleavage. The swelling of starches is favored by electrolytes, especially alkalis, so that swelling commences at a much lower temperature in their presence. For this purpose the anions are especially important and in fact, in a lyotropic series, similar to that of acid albumin. See page 152 (M. Samec).*

Starch paste increases the surface tension of water (Zlobicki*). A solution of starch in water, as well as one of *dextrin*, dissolves less CO_2 than pure water (according to A. Findlay*). (A gelatin solution dissolves more CO_2 than pure water!)

Under the influence of dilute acids or diastatic ferments, the starch molecule takes up water and, step by step, breaks into small fragments, *soluble starches*, *amylodextrin*, various *dextrins* some of which crystallize, and finally into grape sugar. The larger the fragments the more marked is their colloidal character.

As the result of osmometric experiments W. Biltz * arrived at the following molecular weights:

Amylodextrin	22,200–20,500
Higher achroodextrin	11,700–8,200
Erythrodextrin	6,800–3,000
Acid dextrin	4,000
Lower achroodextrin	1,800–1,200
Dextrin $(C_6H_{10}O_5)_5$	905
Commercial dextrin	6,200–2,700

"Soluble starch" (according to H. Friedenthal*[1]) produces a definite lowering of the freezing point, which is proportionate to the amount of the substance that is dissolved.

Crystallizable dextrins [amyloses $(C_6H_{10}O_5)_5$] prepared by H Pringsheim* and Eissler combine with iodin to form iodin-addition compounds which dissolve like iodin starches in cold water with a transitory blue color.

Commercial dextrins which are mixtures of starch fragments of different size are almost entirely held back by impermeable ultrafilters (10 per cent) (H BECHHOLD[*4]).

Closely related to the starches is inulin, the reserve carbohydrate in dahlia bulbs and the roots of Inula helenium, etc., as well as lichenin, which occurs in many lichens, especially Iceland moss. Unlike the starches, inulin and lichenin are soluble in water without forming a paste and form yellow adsorption compounds with iodin (see p. 135)

Besides these, a series of starches have been identified, some of which show differences in their final cleavage products, the sugars. As yet they have not been studied colloid-chemically

In its biological function, animal starch, glycogen, resembles the plant starches closely, and in its colloid properties stands midway between these and inulin. It swells in cold water and forms with it an opalescent hydrosol. The electric current carries it to the anode (Z. GATIN-GRUSZEWSKA*) With iodin it forms according to its concentration, a brownish yellow to deep red adsorption compound

The *internal friction* of glycogen solutions have been studied by F. BOTTAZZI and G. D'ERRICO* as well as by J. FRIEDLANDER.*

Glycogen is split up by acids and ferments, and according to the degree of hydrolysis we find all sorts of fragments, from the highly colloidal to the easily diffusible grape sugar. E RAHLMANN[*1] followed this process with the ultramicroscope.

The *glucosides* must be mentioned in this connection. They are compounds of the aliphatic and the aromatic series with sugars, which may be split into their components by acids or ferments. In the vegetable kingdom they include very active pharmacologic and toxic substances, such as digitalis glucoside, phloridzin and saponins Recently several glucosides have been discovered in the animal organism, *e.g.*, cerebron in the human brain. Though some glucosides, *e g.*, amygdalin and myronic acid are unquestionably crystalloids, others, *e.g.*, saponin, are entirely colloidal. Since we know very little of the biological significance of glucosides, it is evident that we do not know what importance may be ascribed to the crystalloid form in one and the colloidal form in the other.

The *gums* are carbohydrates which are widely distributed throughout the vegetable kingdom Some of them play a part, in many respects analogous to that of fibrin in the animal kingdom, since they solidify on issuing from a wound, thus sealing it. Best known of the gums are *gum arabic, carraghen* and *cherry gum*, while *agar*, derived from Japanese sea weed, is of especial importance in bacteriology. Finally, we must mention the pectinous plant juices, which unlike the true gums are slightly or not at all soluble in water.

The gums are typical examples of hydrophile colloids, they swell into jellies in water, and on adding more water pass, at an indefinite point, into solution Rise of temperature shifts this point in favor of solution, though it is by no means immaterial at what condition of swelling the heating occurs. If, for instance, *agar* has been allowed to swell in cold water for a long time, it immediately becomes a homogeneous solution on warming. If solid agar is heated in water, we get a lumpy suspension of agar in water, which only very gradually becomes a homogeneous sol. It is evidently necessary for each particle of agar to have the amount of water necessary for solution in close proximity before it is warmed, otherwise the swelling will occur but slowly from the outside, where there is an excess of water, and proceed inward, since the peripheral particles of agar hold the water until they are dissolved. Indeed, the phenomenon is one which depends on the size of the surface; the large mass with relatively small surface dissolves more slowly than the same mass divided, *i e*, with a relatively increased surface. Solutions of gum do not dialyze. In my opinion little attention need be paid to the determination of their osmotic pressure, since traces of electrolytes which cannot be removed, suffice to simulate it. I know of no studies on the electrical migration or on the diffusion coefficients of gums. [W. M. BAYLISS has recently determined the viscosity and osmotic pressure against water and RINGERS' solution of gum acacia, gelatin and amylopectin. He recommends the use of gum and gelatin in saline infusions as a method of maintaining blood pressure. The more prolonged action of such infusions he attributes to the osmotic pressure of the colloids. Proceedings of the Royal Society of London, Series B, No. 89, pp. 380–393 Tr.]

Gums usually diminish the surface tension of water. The σ of a 20 per cent solution of gum arabic is 9 per cent lower, and a dilute solution of agar 5 per cent lower than that of water (G. QUINCKE). Some kinds of gum increase the surface tension of water (ZLOBICKI[*]).

The general facts, stated on page 66, hold for the swelling and shrinking of gums. On swelling, the heat liberated, according to E WIEDEMANN and CHAS LUDEKING,[*] is 9.0 cal per gm. for gum arabic and 10.3 cal per gm. for gum tragacanth. Wo. PAULI[*1] found that a rise of temperature accompanied the swelling of carraghen.

The significance of crystalloids for swelling and turgor has been studied chiefly in gelatin In the case of the gums, other than agar, no investigations of this point have been made. Though the probability of many similarities exists, an absolute parallelism cannot be assumed. Thus, for instance, the melting point of gelatin is raised by grape sugar and glycerin, whereas that of agar is reduced. NaCl elevates the melting point of agar and depresses that of gelatin. H. BECHHOLD and J. ZIEGLER[52]).

Agar has a very strong tendency to gelatinize, even 1 gm. per liter gelatinizes at 0°. This great gelatinizing capacity led Robert Koch to make his culture media of agar, and permitted him to grow cultures of bacteria on solid media at body temperature. Gelatin media which had been used at first melt at 37°C, and could accordingly, only be used at room temperature.

Electrolytes as well as nonelectrolytes alter the gelatinization time of agar. Nitrates, iodids, sulphocyanids, benzoates, urea and thiourea lengthen it; chlorids, bromids, acetates and salts of poly-basic acids shorten it.

Cellulose is for plants what bones are for animals. It forms the framework which maintains their shape. If it is to fulfill this function it must be insensitive to the chemical influences of the plant juices, and must not be able to swell. Wooden roles are by no means un-common; only in exceptional instances are fats and proteins or gelatinous constituents seen after thousands of years, and then only under very unusually favorable conditions, as in the desert climate of Egypt. Wood, even uncarbonized, is a common object not only for Egyptian archaeologists and travellers in the Turanian deserts but it has frequently been preserved in our own climate and even in water. Oak bridge piles dating from Roman times have been found in the Rhine, wood carvings and wooden buckets in the springs of Salzburg, fragments of boats of the lake dwellers in the Swiss lakes and those of the Vikings in the peat bogs of North Germany and Jutland. Stability of form, in other words, a light swelling capacity makes wood, next to stone, metal and bone, suitable for many pur-poses.

Cellulose, the principal constituent of wood, is extremely inactive and is only split up into soluble sugars (chiefly grape sugar) by strong chemical action (acids concentrated or under pressure) or by specific ferments (bacteria in the intestines of ruminants).

Cellulose not only has a high adsorptive capacity for dyestuff but even true suspensions are fixed at its surface. For this reason cellulose has recently been used like charcoal as a clarifier and as a filter for turbid liquids.

CHAPTER IX

LIPOIDS.

"Lipoids" is the collective name for fatty substances.[1] Many of them are not moistened by water, however, this property is not characteristic of all lipoids.

Fats and *oils* are esters of higher fatty acids, usually with glycerin, which may be substituted by other higher alcohols; for instance, a palmitic acid ester of cetyl alcohol occurs in spermaceti, found in the skull of the sperm whale. Though in other fats all three hydroxyls of glycerin are replaced by fatty acid radicals, in the *lecithins* only two fatty acid radicals occur, and the third hydroxyl group is replaced by a phosphoric acid cholin radical. Cholin is a trimethyl-oxyethylammonium hydroxid.

Formula of Fats	Formula of Lecithin
CH_2O-fatty acid	CH_2O-cholin phosphate
CHO-fatty acid	CHO-fatty acid
CH_2O-fatty acid	CH_2O-fatty acid

Finally, we must consider *cholesterins* and *isocholesterins*, which we may regard as complex terpenes.

The characteristic *fats*, the triglycerides, are universally distributed in the animal body, where they play an important part in maintaining the body heat, while in plants they are of much less importance. *Lecithins* are found distributed throughout the animal organism, not only in the chief depots, the brain, nervous tissue generally and the egg yolk, but in every cell, every organ, even in the lymph, blood corpuscles and muscles. In plants too, lecithin is widely distributed, occurring in the seeds.

The fact that lecithins occur in all parts of the body is an evidence of their great biological importance. So far as may be gathered from previous researches, they play an important role in the life

[1] Various investigators give different definitions of the term "lipoids." BANG at it most inclusively and regard everything in the body soluble in organic solvents as lipoids. But we gives it the narrowest scope, and include only substances which form colloidal solution in organic solvents (e.g., cephalin, cerebrosid).

processes of the cells and in the adjustment of the metabolism between cells and their surrounding media. The same is true of *cholesterin* which is frequently associated with them.

Fats and oils are not soluble in water and aqueous solutions, but instead they are easily emulsified by a great variety of substances A few drops of lye suffice to make the finest sort of subdivision of oil in water. It is still an open question, whether this is accomplished by the lye itself, or whether it is due primarily to soaps, which are formed from the free fatty acids always present in fats and oils, and which themselves act as emulsifiers. Soluble soaps, *i e*, the fatty acid salts of the alkalis, possess remarkable fat-emulsifying properties; this property is also shared by the intestinal juice, the pancreatic juice and the bile. Emulsions of fat and oil usually occur in alkaline solution, while on the other hand acids produce flocculation. There are exceptions to this, *e g*, the lipase of the castor bean emulsifies fat in acid solution, and milk curded by rennet yields a stable acid emulsion on digestion in pepsin-hydrochloric acid In general, fat emulsions behave like hydrophile colloids; they are not as easily coagulated by neutral salts as are hydrophobe colloids or other suspensions.

Milk is a natural emulsion of fat (see p 345 *et seq*).

Though in the examples given so far, fat has been the dispersed phase and water or the aqueous solution the dispersing medium, conversely, water and aqueous solutions may be incorporated in fats In this case fat is the dispersing medium and the aqueous solution the dispersed phase. Instances of this condition are *butter, cold cream*, which is cooling because of the water it contains, *lanolin*, as well as many *salves* and *liniments*. Structures like *cream* and *whipped cream* occupy a characteristic intermediate position.

Lecithin behaves in a very peculiar way. It forms an emulsion with water of its own accord; indeed like a protein it swells up in water into a turbid colloidal solution, without dissolving. It may be said that it occupies a place, in respect to its colloidal properties, between the emulsifiable fats and the hydrophile colloids, closely approaching the latter.

O. PORGES and E. NEUBAUER[*] studied its properties by experimenting upon the coagulation of lecithin emulsions

The precipitating action of neutral salts is in a lyotropic series similar to that for acid albumin, in which the greatest effect is produced by the *anions*. Salts of the alkaline earths and the heavy metals frequently yield "zones of inhibition" as described on page 84. It is remarkable that neither $HgCl_2$ nor $Hg(CN)_2$ even in $\frac{n}{5}$

concentration cause precipitation. This is in thorough accord with the solubility of such substances in fats.

Lecithin acts towards colloids and suspensions (ferric hydroxid, mastic suspension) like any other colloid which migrates to the anode. Similarly charged colloids cause no precipitation (and lecithin may even act as a protective colloid for mastic); oppositely charged colloids produce flocculation in suitable mixtures (ferric-oxid hydrosol). Saponin clears lecithin suspensions.

Alcoholic lecithin solutions are much more *stable* in the presence of salts than aqueous solutions. Mercuric chlorid is an exception. Alcoholic lecithin solutions protect some other colloids, *e.g.*, albumoses, from the precipitating action of alcohol. (L. MICHAELIS and P. ROSA[61].)

Ethereal lecithin solutions cause some otherwise insoluble substances to dissolve in ether (*e. g.*, NaCl and grape sugar). This property is evidently due to the fact that in ethereal solution, lecithin has a great capacity for taking up water.

Cholesterin, according to the investigations of O. PORGES and E. NEUBAUER,* is a hydrophobe colloid. Its aqueous emulsion behaves like a mastic suspension in the presence of a large variety of salts. The same is true for its behavior with other colloids. In neutral solution it is precipitated by certain proportions of albumin and saponin. Lecithin may act as a protective colloid for cholesterin. Cholesterin forms a true solution in alcohol and ether, and in such solutions exhibits no colloid precipitation reactions.

CHAPTER X.

PROTEINS.

WE designate as proteins a group of nitrogenous colloids which are the chief constituents of animals and plants. They consist entirely or chiefly of substances which contain quantitatively

	Per cent
C	50–55
H . .	6 5– 7 3
N . . .	15–17 6
O . . .	19–24
S	0 3– 2 4

One of the chief characteristics of most of the dissolved albumins is their coagulability when heated. The effect of heat on undissolved proteins is shown by the loss of their capacity to swell, they are "denatured." Hydrophile colloids become hydrophobe.

A host of the most diverse substances are included under the generic term "albumin." It includes water-soluble substances such as egg and serum albumin, and substances soluble in saline solutions, as globulin, vitellin, myosin and, finally, such substances as are soluble neither in aqueous nor in saline solution, for example, fibrin. We know that there exists in each plant and in each animal a distinct serum albumin and a distinct serum globulin, etc. In the chapter on "Immunity Reactions," we shall return to the species-native characteristics (Artspezifität) of proteins (see p. 194). We shall not speak of these distinctions here, but we shall dwell, rather, upon the properties that the different proteins possess in common.

Colloid research, in a *negative* way, by destroying a large number of false conceptions, has been of great service to the chemistry of proteins; and it is in a position to establish new principles, since only a few proteins crystallize and, with others, common methods of purification are unavailable. Absolutely misleading methods have been relied upon to separate and distinguish proteins. It was formerly believed, *e.g* , that the *coagulation* temperature of different proteins varied, but colloid investigations demonstrated that small quantities of electrolytes could raise or depress it to a great extent. By precipitation with copper sulphate, E. HARNACK believed that he had obtained characteristic copper albuminates, and other observers that they had obtained characteristic silver or calcium albuminates. Colloid chemistry has shown that the different amounts of copper,

142

silver, etc., contained in such precipitates depend upon the concentrations of the solutions of albumin and of electrolyte, and that precipitates of constant constitution are always obtained under the same conditions. Fr. N. Schulz and R. Zsigmondy showed that *crystallized* egg albumin which had adsorbed colloidal metallic gold, recrystallized *with* it.

As the result of such observations we become very sceptical concerning the "purity" of proteins. However, it is just such explanation of earlier errors which shows us upon what facts we may really depend, and gives to science a new method and, in part, a new course.

Before we describe the few proteins which have been studied colloid-chemically, we shall consider briefly some of their general properties.

One of the most characteristic properties of many proteins is *coagulation*. It may be brought about, either by a rise of temperature (heat coagulation) or by chemical means.

Most of the coagulations due to the salts of the light metals and some of those due to the alkaline earths are reversible, *i.e.*, the coagulations reverse themselves by the addition of more water. *Heat coagulation* and coagulation due to many of the *salts of the heavy metals* are irreversible. The coagulations due to alcohol, acetone and ether are intermediate, that is, the coagulation produced is at first soluble in water but becomes insoluble after a while. Globulin which has been preserved for a time in pure water behaves in a similar way, for it then becomes less soluble in salt solutions.

Though reversible coagulation may be viewed as a purely physical *salting out* (see under this heading) a chemical change must be assumed in the cases of irreversible coagulation. Many heavy metals form insoluble complexes with albumin (see p. 157).[1] Irreversible coagulation by heat, alcohol, etc., may be explained, possibly, by a chemical transformation. The fact that the H ion concentration diminishes after heat coagulation is in favor of this view (Sörensen and Jürgensen,[*] H. Chick and C. J. Martin,[*] Guagliarmito[*]). In the case of heat coagulation, water appears to enter the albumin molecule, because absolutely dry hemoglobin and egg albumin may be heated to 120° C. without losing their solubility in water (H. Chick and C. J. Martin[*]). Possibly this is the initial stage of hydrolysis, since according to Berezeller[*] the surface tension of salt-poor albumin solutions is temporarily depressed upon boiling, just as occurs upon hydrolysis by pepsin, trypsin, etc. Irreversibly coagulated albuminous pellicles may be formed merely by shaking with air (see p. 341).

---

[1] [Sassum has shown that after the absorption of a lethal dose of the soluble of mercuric chlorid, no treatment avails. Jour. Am. Med. Association, vol 70, p 824. Tr.]

Though native albumins are usually hydrophile, they become hydrophobe upon *heat coagulation* Traces of acids and salts cause precipitation. The *precipitate* of albumin *induced by freezing* is irreversible.

Albumin may be partly changed to globulins, and ultimately coagulated and precipitated by light, particularly light of short wave length (G. DREYER and HAUSEN, CHALUPECKY), ultraviolet rays are particularly intense in their action (BOVIE) This is especially significant for some future explanation of the action of sunlight on the organism. SCHANZ attributes to it the clouding of the crystalline lens in cataract. The rays of shortest wave length, the Roentgen rays, coagulate albumin

A number of proteins have been *crystallized* (*e g*, egg albumin, horse serum albumin, hemoglobin, aleuron) and though the shape of the crystal is characteristic for the kind of albumin, nevertheless it is impossible to obtain the crystals absolutely chemically pure as in the case of crystalloids (see p. 71).

Albumin solutions have been studied *ultramicroscopically* by E RÁHLMANN,[*2] E von BEHRING, H. MUCH, ROMER and C. SIEBERT,[*] by L. MICHAELIS,[*1] L. PINKUSSOHN[*] and J. LEMANISSIER [*] The results expected at the outset were not realized, so that, in recent years, there has been little heard on the subject In my opinion this is unfortunate; I am inclined to believe that valuable data might be gleaned from a properly controlled ultramicroscopic study of proteins. It is evident that a large part of albumin solutions is amicroscopic, so that only such portions are seen as show a different refraction than water or physiological salt solution. An albuminous solution shows a different number of ultramicrons, entirely depending upon whether it has been prepared in water or in physiological salt solution (MICHAELIS); and with different dilutions depending upon the salt content, a different number of small particles become visible (RÁHLMANN). On this account L MICHAELIS and J. LEMANISSIER do not share the opinion of E. RAHLMANN and the school of E. VON BEHRING as to the suitability of ultramicroscopic observation for the quantitative determination of albumin, *e g*, in the urine. Great interest must attach to ultramicroscopic observations of the cleavage of albumin by pepsin,[1] the influence of therapeutically active substances (ferric chlorid, alum, tannic acid, silver nitrate, copper sulphate, collargol, etc), as well as the effect of dyes on solution of albumin (RÁHLMANN) A few submicrons were found by J. LEMANISSIER in albumin solution and many in hemoglobin, but they disappeared in 24 hours

Ultrafiltration of albumin solution is still in its infancy. H. BECHHOLD has shown that the particles of serum albumin are some-

---

[1] [Already observed by J. ALEXANDER. Jour Am. Chem. Soc, Vol. XXXII.

what smaller than those of hemoglobin. Unlike ferments, proteins are not strongly adsorbed by filter material.

All albumins are *amphoteric electrolytes, i.e.,* they yield H and OH ions; otherwise expressed, they have at the same time the character of weak acids and of weak bases, with the acid character more or less in excess. The consequences resulting in the case of albumin have been discussed more extensively on p. 154.

The *isoelectric* point is that where the sum of the H and OH ions is least. This point acquired especial significance from the studies of L. MICHAELIS who showed that the isoelectric point was characteristic for each albumin. That albumins are most easily precipitated at this point was also demonstrated (by HARDY, TR.). In this respect they behave like crystalloid electrolytes. Neutral molecules are much more difficult to dissolve than their ions. Acids slightly dissociated electrically, *e.g.,* uric acid, salicylic acid, quinine, are much more difficult to dissolve than their strongly dissociated salts.

Adsorption phenomena are of great importance. Proteins may be strongly adsorbed or, on the other hand, exert a powerful adsorption. The purely physical phenomena are complicated by the intermingling of specific chemical properties and thus very decided differences between the various groups of albumins are brought to light.

Proteins as Adsorbed Substances. Adsorption has been most carefully studied in the case of *albumin.* As a result of its faint acidity it is completely adsorbed by ferric oxid hydrogel, but mastic and kaolin suspensions on the contrary adsorb it only in faintly acid solution (L. MICHAELIS and P. RONA*). On this account, any suspension may be employed *to remove* albumin from *acid* solutions, *e.g.,* urine, whereas an electropositive adsorbent (*e.g.* ferric oxid gel) must be chosen in the case of *neutral* fluids. Although the distribution between solvent and adsorbent has the shape of an adsorption curve, it must nevertheless be emphasized that the process (adsorption by iron-oxid, cellulose and kaolin) is only incompletely reversible, thus resembling the phenomena of dyeing (W. BILTZ*). The adsorption of euglobulin by kaolin (K. LANDSTEINER and PRIBRAM*) is to be explained in a similar way.

Proteins as Adsorbents. Proteins are frequently used as adsorbent both in a solid and in a denatured condition. They take up acids, alkalis, salts, dyes, etc., from solution, in accordance with the formula of an adsorption curve. In my opinion it is best to regard the compound as an adsorption whenever the chemical constitution of the adsorbed substance is unknown or when it, itself, possesses colloid properties. To view the facts from the standpoint of chemical constitution (see p. 154), a viewpoint which presupposes a more exact knowledge of the mechanism of the reaction, seems to me to be a still more advanced step.

Adsorption by protein in solution is more important than adsorption by solid proteins. By *ultrafiltration* it might be possible to investigate the distribution between a dissolved colloid and a crystalloid. In this connection I am acquainted only with the investigations of H BECHHOLD on the distribution of methylene blue between water and serum albumin (see p. 26).

THOMAS GRAHAM and R. O. HERZOG*[6] determined the *coefficient of diffusion* of egg albumin and ovomucoid to be $\dfrac{D \text{ cm}^2}{\text{seconds}} \cdot 10^5$. Its values are in the case of

Egg albumin　　　　0 063 (at 13° C) measured by GRAHAM, calculated by
　　　　　　　　　　　　　　STEFAN.
Egg albumin　.　　0 054 (at 15 3° C) according to HERZOG
Egg albumin　　　　0 046 (at 7 75° C) according to HERZOG
Egg albumin [crystallized with 3 6%　　0 081 (at 16° C) according to DABROWSKI* (NH₄)₂SO₄]
Ovomucoid　　　　　0 034 (at 7 75° C) according to HERZOG
Glucose
　(for comparison)　0 57 (at 18° C)

From these figures the radius r of albumin particles has been calculated for

Salt-free egg albumin　　　　　　　　　　　　　2,43 $\mu\mu$
Crystallized egg albumin　.　　　　　.　　　　1,37 $\mu\mu$
　[with 3 6% (NH₄)₂SO₄]

This diminution in the size of the albumin particles in the presence of $(NH_4)_2SO_4$ coincides with what we shall learn of the other effects of neutral salts on albumin (see p. 151)

When solid albumins go into solution there occurs a diminution in volume amounting to about 5–8 per cent, as is the case with starches　(H. CHICK and C. J. MARTIN.*)

Egg albumin and *serum albumin, globulin, casein* and *fibrin* have been most carefully studied colloid chemically.

ALBUMINS.

Albumins are soluble in water, and in *dilute* neutral salt, and in acid and in alkaline solutions. They are usually found in the company of globulins and there are reasons for believing that they may be converted into globulins by moderate heating　Albumins occur almost exclusively in serum, in eggs and in milk; the existence of plant albumins is not yet definitely established.

In the organism proteins may occur accompanied by electrolytes which greatly modify their properties. On this account we shall try to get an idea of *albumin unassociated with electrolytes* in order to understand the influence of the addition of electrolytes.

Electrolyte-Free Albumin.[1]

WOLFGANG PAULI obtained an albumin free from electrolytes by dialysing ox serum in closed vessels for eight weeks. After standing undisturbed for several weeks, the serum was filtered and was found to furnish a stable crystal clear fluid. Boiling and the addition of alcohol completely coagulated the solution. Such albumin is amphoteric with a weakly electronegative charge, so that it consists chiefly of neutral and very slightly ionized particles[2] which migrate to both electrodes in an electric field (L. MICHAELIS[3]). According to L. Michaelis and P. Rona, the isoelectric point for serum albumin, at which there is the greatest tendency to precipitation, occurs with an H ion concentration of $2 \cdot 10^{-5}$, for boiled, denatured serum albumin when the H-ion concentration is $4 \cdot 10^{-5}$. It increases the internal friction of water considerably. If the friction coefficient of water is represented by 1000, a 1 per cent amphoteric albumin solution at the same temperature will be 1068. An equimolecular 1 per cent salt solution causes no demonstrable change in the coefficient of friction of water.

Solubility in Albumin Sol.

We shall see in the following pages that albumin usually has a powerful influence on the solubility of substances. It is a remarkable fact that the solubility of carbonic acid is the same in an albumin sol as it is in water (A. FINDLAY[4]). This is all the more remarkable since starches and gelatins, in contradistinction to albumin, are very active in affecting the solubility of carbonic acid. This is physiologically important, since serum consequently plays no part.

---

[1] The colloid-chemical study of proteins was inaugurated by F. Hofmeister and his pupils; in recent times they have been studied chiefly by Wo. Pauli and his co-workers in numerous experimental investigations. We wish especially to call attention to Wo. Pauli and H. Handovsky, Hofmeister's *Beitr. z. Chem. Phys. u. Pathol.*, **11**, H. 415; *Biochem. Zeitschr.*, **18**, pp. 340-171. *L. c.*, **24**, 239-262. Further references in the text-book of H. Freundlich and Wo. Ostwald, as well as H. Handovsky, *Koll.-Zeitschr.*, **4** and **5**, 1910.

Since an absolutely ash-free albumin cannot be prepared by dialysis, as shown by the investigation of Pauli and the unpublished experiments of H. Handovsky and F. Zuckermann, it is apparent that the question of the electric charge of pure albumin is not yet definitely determined.

in respiration. I have no knowledge of researches as to whether the H-ion concentration of water containing CO_2 is affected by ash-free albumin.

WOLFGANG PAULI and M. SAMEC* have commenced exhaustive studies into the influence of albumins on the solubility of electrolytes. They employed a serum albumin solution which had been dialyzed eight weeks and contained 2 23 per cent of albumin. All the *readily soluble electrolytes* investigated showed a *slight decrease in solubility* as compared with pure water. The solubilities were as follows.

	In 100 gm water	In 100 gm serum solution
Ammonium chlorid . .	28 49	27 9
Magnesium chlorid . .	35 94	35 51
Ammonium suphocyanate	62 46	62 06

Contrariwise, the solubility of *difficultly soluble electrolytes* was decidedly *increased* by the presence of albumin.

The solubilities were as follows:

	In 100 gm water	In 100 gm serum solution.
Calcium sulphate	0 223	0 226
Calcium phosphate $Ca_3(PO_4)_2$.	0 011	0 021
Calcium carbonate .	0 004	0 023
Silicic acid . . .	0 023	0 030
Uric acid .	0 040	0 057

Having in view the *deposition of urates in gout*, H. BECHHOLD and J. ZIEGLER[43] undertook exhaustive studies of the solubility of uric acid and urates in electrolyte-free serum. Since even traces of $NaHCO_3$ (in the case of uric acid) and Na salts (in the case of Na-urate) may greatly influence the solubility, before dialysing the serum, HCl was added until the $NaHCO_3$ was completely neutralized, and the last traces of Na salts were removed by repeated additions of KCl Each addition was followed by dialysis. In this way the following solubilities of Na-urate and uric acid were obtained in electrolyte-free serum albumin solution containing 7.6 per cent albumin (expressing the percentage in relation to the entire quantity of protein in defibrinated blood serum) at 37° C

In 1000 gm. serum albumin solution (in 1000 gm water):

Uric acid, 549 to 668 mg . . . . 64.9 mg.
Monosodium urate, 476 to 568 mg . . . . 1200 to 1500 mg.

The ability to decrease the solubility of easily soluble electrolytes and to increase the solubility of difficultly soluble electrolytes is not a specific property of albumins but is common to colloids in general, *e.g.*, gelatin.

Albumin and Hydrosols. The exhaustive studies of U. Friedemann[*] show that electrolyte free serum and egg albumin are precipitated both by positive and negative inorganic hydrosols. An optimum precipitation zone exists here, as it does in other colloidal precipitations. Excess of albumin or inorganic hydrosol hinders the precipitation. Addition of NaCl shifts the zone of precipitation without, however, conforming to any definite law. As an example I might mention the precipitation (see ---) of albumin by diminishing quantities of molybdic acid, with and without added NaCl.

Molybdic acid	Albumin about 1 per cent	Degree of precipitate in salt free solution	Degree of precipitation after addition of 10 per cent NaCl
	c.c.		
0.5	1	. . .	. . .
0.25	1	0	. . .
0.1	1	0	. . .
0.05	1	0	. . .
0.025	1	. . .	0
0.001	1	. . .	0
0.005	1	. . .	0

As the result of cataphoretic experiments, U. Friedemann believes that the charge of proteins towards water is *not* determinative of their precipitation by inorganic hydrosols. Albumin which travels to the anode notwithstanding this fact gives heavy precipitates with inorganic hydrosols (arsenic trisulphid, silicic acid, molybdic acid). There is much to justify the assumption of U. Friedemann that a given hydrosol, according to its charge, collects at the + or – charge of the amphoteric albumin, thus permitting its aggregation to larger complexes.

The albumins appear to act with proteins *of definite basic* (histones) or *acid character* just as they do with inorganic hydrosols (U. Friedemann and H. Friedenthal[*]).

Influence of Electrolytes

If an electrolyte is added to an amphoteric albumin, the properties of the albumin undergo considerable modification. Salts, even in very small quantities (hundredth normal), *raise the coagulation temperature*, as is shown in the subsequent coagulation temperatures taken from a table compiled by Wo. Pauli and H. Handovsky[*]

Salt	0	0 01 n	0 02 n	0 03 n	0 04 n	0 05 n
NaSCN . .	60 3° C	68	69 7	70 6	71 6	72 5
Na_2SO_4 . .	60 3° C.	66 7	68	68 5	69 1	69 7
NaCl . .	60 3° C.	63 16	65 7	66 4	67 2	67 9
$NaC_2H_3O_2$.	60 3° C.	66 9	69 2	70 6	71 5	72 1
KSCN . . .	64 6° C	68 3	.	69 5		70 3

This table shows the remarkable fact that the first traces of salt have a much greater influence than somewhat greater concentrations. 0.01 normal Na_2SO_4 added to salt-free albumin raises the coagulation temperature about 6 4° C while a similar addition to albumin already containing 0.04 normal Na_2SO_4 raises the coagulation temperature only 0 6° C. We shall show the significance of this fact later.

If the salt is more concentrated, coagulation by heat varies; the coagulation temperature rises continuously in the presence of K, Na and NH_4. Thus for

3 normal KCl, coagulation occurs at 75 6° C
3 normal NaCl, coagulation occurs at 73 6° C
3 normal $MgCl_2$, coagulation occurs at 75 4° C

The coagulation temperature reaches a maximum at a certain salt concentration and then falls again in the case of other salts, especially alkaline earths and the allied lithium

Maximum coagulation temperature,° C
6 normal NH_4Cl 72 8
2 normal $(NH_4)_2SO_4$ 74 3
1 normal LiCl 73 8
0 5 normal $CaCl_2$ 71 4
0 5 normal $BaCl_2$ 72 2
0 5 normal $SrCl_2$ 72

Some of the magnesium salts may completely inhibit heat coagulation; $MgCl_2$ below 6 normal. $Mg(NO_3)_2$ below 4 normal.

Cations also may be divided into different groups, according to their influence:

In the case of SO_4, Cl, Br and NO_3, there is a greater rise with lower concentrations (up to 0.5 to about 1 normal) then a smaller rise up to 1 normal. In the case of SCN and I the inhibition from 1 to 2 normal is so complete that no coagulation occurs even at the highest concentration of the salt. In the case of citrate, acetate and oxalate the coagulation temperature rises sharply from 0.05 to 0.1 normal, whereupon the curve again falls. Obviously this is associated with the strong hydrolytic cleavage of these weak acids in the presence of strong alkalis, whereby there is formed more or less alkali albumin which is not coagulated by heat.

We have discussed these questions separately in order that we may obtain a picture of the complicated relations which also reappear in the other properties of albumin.

Heat coagulation involves two overlapping processes; albumin becomes *insoluble* and it *flocculates*. WOLFGANG PAULI and H. HANDOVSKY demonstrated this very simply. a mixture of albumin with 2 normal KSCN was boiled and a portion of it dialyzed against running water. The control portion remained clear, but the portion from which the KSCN was removed by dialysis showed marked flocculation.

A further influence exerted by neutral salt upon amphoteric albumin is the change in *viscosity*, the *internal friction*. Although NaCl, NaSCN, Na₂SO₄, CaCl₂ and KSCN in concentrations of 0.01 to 0.05 normal raise the viscosity of water, they depress that of amphoteric albumin solution. If the salt concentration rises, the diminution in the viscosity of albumin may finally be exceeded by the increase in the viscosity of the water, as occurs in fact at 0.1 normal NaCl and (NH₄)₂SO₄. Closer observation reveals a far-reaching *parallelism between* the influence of neutral salts on *heat coagulation* and *viscosity*.

If non-neutral salts, or salts strongly dissociated hydrolytically, (Na₃PO₄, NaHCO₃, AlCl₃) are allowed to act on amphoteric albumin, the result is quite different since even minute traces of acid or alkali form acid or alkali albumins, which behave quite differently, as we shall see. *With higher salt concentration* the albumin is salted out or flocculated. Neutral salts of the *alkalis* as well as *magnesium* cause a reversible salting out such as occurs also with salts of the alkaline earths, though after a very short time an irreversible coagulation sets in. Some of the salts of the heavy metals cause an immediate irreversible coagulation. With the alkali salts, the cations (Li, K, Na, NH₄) do not materially differ in their salting out action, but the anions do, as may be seen from the following table of F. HOFMEISTER. The figures refer to the onset of turbidity in egg albumen containing globulin but according to LEWITH apply also to ox serum.

	Mols per liter at 30-40°C.
Sodium citrate	0 56
Sodium tartrate	0 78
Sodium sulphate	0 80
Sodium acetate	1.69
Sodium chloride	3 62
Sodium nitrate	5 12
Sodium chlorate	5.52

Iodid and sulphocyanate do not cause precipitation.

Acid Albumin.

There is a marked change in the properties of amphoteric albumin when acid is added to it. It migrates to the cathode as though it were the basic portion of a salt, it loses its coagulability by heat and alcohol, its internal friction is greatly increased and its surface tension diminished. If an excess of acid is added, coagulability by acids and alcohol is restored and its viscosity diminishes.

SJOQUIST* was of the opinion that albumin formed with acids strongly hydrated (swollen) ionized salts. This assumption was confirmed by the researches of ST. BUGARSZKY and L. LIEBERMANN* and of K. SPIRO and PEMSEL.* It was finally established by MAUABE and J. MATUTA by extremely accurate measurements on the ionization constants of acid albumin   W. PAULI and M. HIRSCHFELD then established that albumin was polybasic, *i e.*, behaved like a tri- or tetra-amino acid, and that the salts were subject to the normal hydrolytic dissociation, characteristic of weak bases   S ODEN and W. PAULI conclude from the rise in migration velocity with increasing fixation of acid that polyvalent protein ions are formed [1]

In a solution containing about 1 per cent albumin, the maximum internal friction is reached at 0 016 normal HCl, and falls with greater concentrations of acid. Such a maximum is also found with other acids (oxalic acid, sulphuric acid), while with others (acetic acid, citric acid) a continual rise in internal friction accompanies the concentration of the acid.

Precipitability by alcohol runs parallel with the increase or decrease in the internal friction (K. SCHORR).

When amphoteric albumin has been made incoagulable by acids, the addition of *neutral salts* restores the coagulability by heat and alcohol   All the salts investigated ($NaSO_4$, $NaNO_3$, Na_2PO_4, Na-acetate, Na-formate, etc.) depress the internal friction   In this respect, the cations are of lesser importance, the anions being *decisive* in the following order:

$$Cl < NO_3 < SCN < SO_4 < C_2H_3O_2.$$

Nonelectrolytes (cane sugar, urea) have, on the contrary, little influence in this respect.

Caffein and its salts are an exception, as they increase the internal friction of acid albumin (H. HANDOVSKY*[2]).

An excess of acid alone or the addition of neutral salt to an amount of acid which is insufficient to cause precipitation causes at first a

[1] See also W. E Ringer, Acid Fixation by Albumin and Viscosity, Van Bemmelen-Festschrift (Helder 1 H u. Dresden, 1910), 243–60

reversible flocculation of albumin in the cold, but with greater concentration (from about 0.03 normal up) an irreversible flocculation. Here also the *anions* have an unequal influence, which is arranged in an order the reverse of that obtaining for neutral albumin, namely,

$$SO_4 < Cl < NO_3, Br < SCN$$

This series, accordingly, does not agree with the other one in all respects.

It is quite evident in the case of the acid salts that their action is the combined result of the acid albumin formed and the action of the salt itself. The process is, therefore, quite complicated.

Alkali Albumin.

There is a far-reaching parallelism between alkali albumin and acid albumin. Alkali albumin like acid albumin is not coagulable by heat or alcohol (even 0.003 normal NaOH inhibits the heat coagulation of amphoteric albumin); its viscosity is greatly increased, its surface tension diminished; excess of alkali restores the precipitability by alcohol and again decreases the internal friction; it migrates to the anode. St Bugarszky and L. Liebermann[*] showed that NaOH was bound by albumin, and that albumin depressed the freezing point of soda-lye. *Neutral salts* arrest the action of alkalis, in contradistinction to acid albumin it is the *cations* to which the greatest significance attaches, and, in fact, the effect of the divalent earth alkalis (Ca, Sr and Ba) and the divalent magnesium very greatly exceeds that of the monovalent alkalis. Though heat coagulation does not occur at all or advances only to a milky turbidity e. g., the effect of 1.2 normal KCl was doubtful, in alkali albumin containing large quantities of alkaline salts the ability of alkali albumin to coagulate with 0.003 normal NaOH is demonstrable upon the addition of 0.0002 normal CaCl_2.

Additions of *neutral salt* bring about a decrease of internal friction in a manner analogous to their influence on heat coagulation, and, in fact, a small addition of salt has a proportionately greater effect than a large one. Moreover, the earth alkalis greatly exceed the alkali salts in their ability to diminish internal friction.

The salting out of alkali albumin requires a greater concentration of alkali salts than is required for neutral albumin; the product is reversible and the anions are effective in the same order as for neutral albumin.

In general, the relations are simpler for alkali albumin than for acid albumin. In the former, they depend upon the electrolytic dissociation of the base, while in the latter, certain electrochemical factors which may not be disregarded play a part.

If dilute *soda-lye* (0.025 normal NaOH) acts for a *long time* on serum albumin, the internal friction reaches a maximum, remains constant for a while and then diminishes (K. Schorr) Evidently there occurs fixation of water, swelling. The cleavage of the albumin molecule is accompanied by the formation of less colloidal disintegration products, and is characterized by a diminution of the viscosity

If from these results we try to obtain an idea of the processes involved, we shall find a useful guide in the theory of the *amphoteric nature of genuine albumin* proposed by G. Bredig* and extended by Wo. Pauli. Let us think of albumin as built according to the structure of a cyclic ammonium salt:

$$R \diagdown \begin{matrix} NH_3 \\ | \\ COO \end{matrix}$$

in which R represents a complicated organic complex and the absorption of water follows according to the scheme.

$$R \diagdown \begin{matrix} NH_3 \\ COO \end{matrix} \quad + H_2O + R \diagdown \begin{matrix} NH_4OH \\ COOH \end{matrix}$$

This is an amphoteric electrolyte which unites with bases and acid, which splits off H as well as OH ions and in which the

$$K_A \text{ (acid dissociation)} > K_B \text{ (base dissociation)}$$

in other words, it behaves like a very weak acid Pure albumin consists principally of electrically neutral particles but forms acid and alkali salts which are strongly ionized.

There exist

$$R \diagdown \begin{matrix} NH_4OH \\ COOH \end{matrix} \qquad R \diagdown \begin{matrix} NH_4Cl \\ COOH \end{matrix} \qquad R \diagdown \begin{matrix} NH_4OH \\ COONa \end{matrix}$$
$$\text{neutral albumin} \qquad \text{acid albumin} \qquad \text{alkali albumin}$$

That the *albumin ions* are responsible for *the great internal friction* is to be assumed from the investigations of E. Laqueur and O. Sackur* on alkali-caseinates. The cause of this phenomenon is found in the strong hydration (water fixation, swelling) of the albumin ions. According to Wo. Pauli and M. Samec the existence of polyvalent ions must be assumed in the case of acid and alkali albu-

min. Even assuming the smallest values for the molecular weight
of albumin, the quantities of acid or alkali found are so large that they
indicate the fixation of several acid or alkali molecules. This offers
a further explanation of the marked increase in hydration produced
by acids and alkalis. The stability of an albumin solution and its
precipitability, *e.g.*, by alcohol, are directly proportional to the number of albumin *ions* it contains. The circumstances here are quite
analogous to those with crystalloids. Ions tend to go into solution
and to form hydrates, the saturation concentration of neutral particles is always less than that of ions.

In this way, we may explain the properties of strongly ionized
pure acid and alkali albumin as contrasted with the slightly dissociated neutral albumin. How does this theory agree with the effect
of *neutral salts?* Wo. Pauli explains it in the following way

$$R \underset{\searrow COOH}{\overset{\nearrow NH_4Cl}{}} + NaNO_3, \rightleftarrows R \underset{\searrow COONa}{\overset{\nearrow NH_4Cl}{}} + HNO_3$$

Acid albumin + neutral salt   Na salt of acid albumin + free acid

In this way was explained not only the increased number of free
H ions, which he demonstrated, but also the marked diminution in
internal friction; because an amphoteric salt, in which both anions
and cations tend to ionize about equally, is but slightly dissociated.

The action of neutral salts in *alkali albumin* is different, it follows
the following scheme:

$$R \underset{\searrow COONa}{\overset{\nearrow NH_4OH}{}} + KCl \rightleftarrows R \underset{\searrow COONa}{\overset{\nearrow NH_2KCl}{}} + H_2O$$

Alkali albumin + neutral salt   complex albumin salt + water

Accordingly, a complex albumin salt was formed to which a less
amount of ionization may be ascribed than to alkali albumin. The
action of salts of the alkaline earth follows this scheme

$$R \underset{\searrow COONa}{\overset{\nearrow NH_4OH}{}} + \frac{Ca}{2}NO_3, \rightleftarrows R \underset{\searrow COO\frac{Ca}{2}}{\overset{\nearrow NH_4NaNO_3}{}} + H_2O$$

The replacement of the alkali ion in the carboxyl of the amino
group results in a weakly ionized complex salt. The effect on albumin of organic bases, which are often highly toxic, and of amphoteric
electrolytes, have also been studied by H. Handovsky, and the results agree with the above scheme.

The conditions governing the action of neutral salts upon acid albumin are not sufficiently understood to warrant proposing a simple scheme.[1]

The *optical rotation* of albumin runs parallel with the changes in its internal friction and coagulability (Wo. PAULI,[*5] M. SAMEC, E. STRAUSS). In fact, the albumin ions rotate light more powerfully than neutral albumin.

Let us summarize briefly: *neutral albumin has a low internal friction, coagulates easily and shows little optical rotation; ionized albumin has high internal friction, coagulates with difficulty and rotates light powerfully; neutral salts diminish ionization.*

This chemical point of view is additionally supported by the investigations of P. PFEIFFER and J. W. MODELSKI as well as of P PFEIFFER and WITTKA. These authors have shown that amino acids and polypeptids of known chemical structure form with neutral salts of the alkalis and earth alkalis, crystalline addition compounds constructed on simple stoichiometric principles Some of these molecular compounds are much more readily soluble in water than the aminoacids or polypeptids and some much less soluble, so that, as in the case of albuminous substances, it is possible to salt some of them out (analogous to globulins).

Albumin and Inorganic Hydrosols

According to U. FRIEDEMANN[*1] electrolyte-free albumin is precipitated both by positive and by negative inorganic hydrosols *Hydrophobe hydrosols* such as As_2S_3, Au, etc , regularly form precipitates, which, according to W. PAULI and HECKER, are not inhibited by an excess either of hydrosol or of albumin. *Neutral salts*, acids and alkalis exert a protective action, but nonelectrolytes, such as urea and sugar, are inactive

In the case of *positive hydrophile* inorganic hydrosols such as $Fe(OH)_3$ there is an optimum precipitation zone that lies somewhere between one part by weight of $Fe(OH)_3$ and three parts by weight of the *electrolyte-free* albumin. With an excess of $Fe(OH)_3$ there is increasing solution which is complete in about the proportion of two to three, there is no complete solution with an excess of albumin. *Neutral salt* exerts a protective action when albumin is in excess but on the contrary favors precipitation when $Fe(OH)_3$ is in excess. Acids inhibit precipitation; alkalis precipitate when $Fe(OH)_3$ is in

[1] From the formula it should not be assumed that only free terminal NH_2 groups are considered As the result of the work of BLASEL and J MATUTA on deaminized glutin (glutin whose free NH_2 groups are satisfied) it is more probable that its interior NH groups are involved in the formation of salts with acids

excess, otherwise they exert a protective action. Hydrophile *negative* inorganic hydrosols, *e.g.*, silicic acid, differ from positive hydrosols only by the presence of H and OH ions which act oppositely to those in the positive hydrosols.

Only a small fraction of the albumin is precipitated by hydrophobe inorganic colloids, but the greater portion, and at times all the albumin, is precipitated by hydrophile hydrosols.

Albumins appear to react with proteins of *pronounced basic* (histones) or *acid* character (U. FRIEDEMANN and H. FRIEDENTHAL[*]) just as do inorganic hydrophile hydrosols.

Albumin, Heavy Metals and Salts of Heavy Metals.

On shaking salt free albumin solutions with metallic iron, cobalt, copper, lead, nickel or aluminium, portions of these metals go into solution and are bound by albumin in a hitherto unrecognized "masked" form, according to BENEDICENTI and REXELLO-ALVES.

Electrolyte-free albumin yields no precipitate with zinc, copper, mercury or lead salts. In the presence of salts, however, albumin forms with *salts of the heavy metals* precipitates whose chemical composition is not constant, but depends on the concentration of the components at the time of precipitation. By precipitating albumin with solutions of heavy metal salts of varying concentrations we get "irregular series," which frequently show *two zones of precipitation*: one with very dilute solutions of the metal salt (one ten thousandth normal and under) and another with high concentration, between these there is always a zone with no precipitation. The precipitation zone with great dilutions of the metal salt is due according to H. BECHHOLD[*] to metal hydroxid split off hydrolytically, which precipitates with albumin, forming an insoluble heavy metal albumin compound. The resolution of this precipitate at somewhat greater concentration of metal salt results from ionization. W. PAULI and HEXKER have shown by very convincing experiments upon the action of $FeCl_3$ on albumin that a soluble ferric ion-albumin complex occurs somewhat in accordance with the following scheme

$$[xFe(OH)_4 \cdot protein] + yFeCl_3 \quad [xFe(OH)_4 \cdot protein \cdot yCl] + 3yCl$$

Upon addition of more $FeCl_3$, just as when acid is added to acid albumin, partial neutralization occurs and there is further precipitation. CrO_2Cl_2 behaves like $FeCl_3$, as do also, to a certain extent, $AgNO_3$, $ZnSO_4$ and $PbNO_3$. On the other hand, the precipitate disappears with higher concentration of $CuCl_2$ and $HgCl_2$, and, absolutely no precipitate is formed with electrolyte-free albumin and the chlorides of Fe'', Cr'', Mn'', Cd''.

Globulin.

Those proteins which are insoluble in pure water and soluble in salt solutions are called globulins. They are constituents of the blood serum, eggs and milk of animals. They occur in other organs in traces, thus, *e.g.*, thyreo-globulin, the iodin-containing protein of the thyroid, is a globulin. Large quantities of globulin are found stored in the seeds of plants. A seed globulin, edestin, has been obtained in crystalline form.

If serum is dialyzed against pure water, globulin will be precipitated as the content of the dialyzer cell (globulin) parts with salt. By *ultrafiltration*, H Bechhold[*4] was able to separate globulin from the common salt holding it in solution Globulins are also soluble in acids and alkalis. If globulins are kept undissolved (*e.g.*, dried or suspended in distilled water) a change occurs; they lose more and more of their solubility in dilute solutions of neutral salts. Like the albumins, globulins are amphoteric without the presence of salt they have no definite direction of migration; in the presence of traces of alkali they pass to the anode and in the presence of acids they pass to the cathode. According to L Michaelis, an H ion concentration of $4\ 10^{-6}$ is the isoelectric point for serum albumin. According to W. B Hardy,[*1] a given quantity of salt-free globulin is dissolved by an equimolecular quantity of strong monobasic *acids* (HCl, HNO₃, monochloracetic acid). The weaker the acid the more of it is necessary to dissolve the globulin. About twice as much sulphuric acid, tartaric acid and oxalic acid, and three times as much phosphoric acid and citric acid. is required than of HCl W. B. Hardy concludes from this that globulins form salts with acids which in the case of weak acids are greatly hydrolyzed.

Bases act in a manner similar to the acids, with the exception that NH₃ dissolves as much globulin as NaOH

Rise of temperature increases the hydrolysis, *i.e* , globulin, dissolved in an amount of weak acid or weak alkali just sufficient to give a clear solution, becomes turbid when it is warmed; however, the process is not completely reversible.

It was deduced from the conductivity values of alkali globulin that globulin is a pentavalent acid, and from its saponification with methyl acetate as well as its action in the inversion of cane sugar, that it is of a more strongly acid than basic character. This is also evident from the fact that the conductivity of its acid salts increases progressively more, when diluted, than the conductivity of its alkali salts. The preponderant acid character is also evident from the fact that litmus is reddened by globulin.

As in the case of albumin the *globulin ions* are responsible for the *internal friction*. Though the internal friction of globulin in neutral salts is low, it is considerably higher in the ionized solutions occurring in acids or alkalis, the viscosity is highest in the case of alkali salts of globulins which are ionized most strongly and least hydrolyzed. The viscosity rises disproportionately with concentration and, in fact, the increase for alkali globulin > for acid globulin > for neutral salt globulin (W. B. Hardy[*]).

W. B. Hardy gives the following viscosity values for 7.50 gm. globulin per liter.

Water	1
MgSO₄-globulin	4.05
HCl globulin	45.5
NaOH globulin	67.9

He derived these velocities for globulin ions:

Acetic acid globulin	$21 \cdot 10^{-5}$ cm per second
HCl globulin	$40 \cdot 10^{-5}$ " "
NaOH-globulin	$72 \cdot 10^{-5}$ " "

W. B. Hardy regards solutions of globulin in *neutral salts* as molecular combinations, since, in contrast to solutions in alkalies or acids, they are thrown down upon dilution. It can be understood from the dominant acid character of globulins that a neutral salt solution of globulins is precipitated by acid. Though alkali globulin solutions are permanent in the presence of neutral salts, acid globulins are precipitated by them.

According to W. B. Hardy, *serum* contains no globulin ion.

If serum is kept warm for a long time (e.g., 2 hours) below its coagulation temperature, the amount of globulin is increased at the expense of the albuminous portion (Moll[*]). This formation of globulin is either impeded or entirely stopped by salts.

"Artificial globulins" is the designation of the salt-free precipitates prepared from egg albumin by André Mayer.[*] He found that when he added to egg albumen a certain quantity of a solution of a salt of a heavy metal ZnSO₄, Zn(NO₃)₂ or a positive colloid colloidal Fe(OH)₃, the resulting precipitate was insoluble in water and in solutions of nonelectrolytes, but on the contrary, it was soluble in solutions of salts (e.g., NaCl, Ca(NO₃)₂, etc.). With these facts in mind we must consider the suggestion made by A. Mayer that globulins are complexes of albumins (possibly with other positive colloids).

Fibrin.

Fibrin is the substance of blood plasma, which coagulates shortly after the blood has left the vessels. Upon the clotting of plasma, which contains no blood corpuscles, no jelly is formed, but characteristic fibrous masses. Formerly it was thought that uncoagulated fibrin, called fibrinogen (see p. 200), was something quite different from fibrin. As a result of the investigations of HUXLEY it is possible that fibrinogen is the hydrosol of alkali fibrin. If fibrin is dissolved in extremely dilute alkali we obtain a fluid having all the properties of fibrinogen. *Normal coagulation* outside the blood vessels as well as the resulting product must be sharply differentiated from *fibrin coagulated by heat*. Fibrin coagulated by heat ceases to show the swelling phenomena it possessed before it was heated; it has become hydrophobe. When coagulated, fibrin is an irreversible gel. In weak acid and alkalis it swells and gradually goes into solution following, as it does so, the same laws as does gelatin (see p. 68, *et seq.*). MARTIN H. FISCHER* has studied its swelling under the influence of acids, bases and salts, and utilized his results for his theory of *edema* (see p. 223, *et seq.*)

Muscle albumin or *myosin*, the coagulation of which at death causes *rigor mortis*, belongs to the same group as fibrin.

Nucleins.

Basic substances have been prepared from cell nuclei, *histone* from the leucocytes of the thymus, fish roes, etc., as well as *protamine*, so thoroughly studied by A. KOSSEL, and usually obtained from the spermatozoa of several different kinds of fish. They do not exist as such in these organs but occur in combination with acid nucleins as *nucleo-proteins* and *nucleo-histones.*

Neutral solutions of histone yield a precipitate containing very little salt with solutions of egg albumin, casein and serum globulin. When we recall that casein and globulin are of decided acid reaction, their union with basic histone is quite easily understood. A priori, it is improbable that the precipitate should contain 1 part histone, 2 parts casein and globulin and 1 part egg albumin, as has been claimed. It has been shown by C. FRIEDEMANN and H. FRIEDENTHAL* that according to the relative concentration in which solutions of histone and albumin are mixed, the precipitate will vary in composition; that the addition of NaCl changes the precipitation limits and that fresh solutions have different precipitation limits than older ones. All these facts point with certainty to the fact that nuclein is not a definite chemical combination but that nucleins are colloid compounds consisting of a negative and a positive colloid.

Albuminoids. (Scleroproteins)

Though the organic framework of plants consists of cellulose, that of animals is formed of nitrogenous substances classified as *albuminoids*. Like cellulose, they are very resistant chemically to foreign influences, water, salt solutions, acids and bases.

The most important of the albuminoids is *collagen*, derived from bone, cartilage and the fibrils of connective tissue On boiling with water, it swells and gradually dissolves, undergoing hydrolytic cleavage and forming *glue* or *gelatin* Gelatin, which has been the subject of the most important investigations concerning hydrophile gels and from which the whole class of gels take their name, does not occur in the organism at all The most important data concerning it have been given on page 68, *et seq*. What has been said, especially in reference to the preparation of a solution of *agar* (p. 137) holds for gelatin as well. It should be recalled that acids and alkalis greatly increase the swelling of gelatin. The swelling capacity reaches a maximum with increasing concentration of HCl (0.025 n) and KOH (0.028 n) (Wo Ostwald). We thus find an absolute parallelism between the swelling of gelatin and the ionization of albumin (see pp. 152 to 156). In excellent agreement with this is the fact that the minimal swelling occurs at the isoelectric point of gelatin, namely, with an H ion concentration of 2.10^{-5} (L. Michaelis, R. Chiari) It must be emphasized especially, that a very dilute solution of gelatin depresses (according to G Quincke) the surface tension of water 12 per cent. The solubility of CO_2 is very considerably greater in gelatin sols than in water (in contrast to other hydrophile sols).

Compared with other colloids (serum albumin), gelatin lowers the solubility of easily soluble electrolytes and increases that of those soluble with difficulty. The following are the figures from the investigations of Wo. Pauli and M Samec:[*]

There dissolves in	100 gm water	+ 4 per cent gelatin	+ 10 per cent gelatin
Ammonium chlorid . ..	28 49	27 55	26 48
Magnesium chlorid . . .	. 35 94	35.22	35.13
Ammonium sulphocyanate. .	62 46	61.46	58 92

		1 5 per cent gelatin
Calcium sulphate	. 0 223	0.295
Tertiary calcium phosphate		
$Ca_3(PO_4)_2$.	. 0 011	0 018
Calcium carbonate. . .	0 004	0 015
Silicic acid. .	0 023	0 027

The *solidification* and the *melting points* depend greatly upon the previous history of the gelatin, the longer gelatin is warmed the less it tends to solidify. Upon heating a 2 per cent gelatin solution

to 100° C., the relative internal friction (according to P. von Schroe-
der) falls from 1.75 (at the end of one-half hour) to 1.22 (at the end
of 16 hours). Possibly this is due to the increasing hydrolytic cleavage. The following figures give some idea of the relations:

Content per liter	Solidification temperature, °C	Melting temperature, °C
Grams		
1 8	<10 (Rohloff and Schinja)	
2 5	0 (S J Levites)	
50	17 8 (Pauli and Rona)	26 1 (Pauli and Rona)*
100	21 (Pauli and Rona)	29 6 (Pauli and Rona)
150	25 5 (Pauli and Rona)	29 4 (Pauli and Rona)

These solidification temperatures are markedly shifted by *electrolytes* and, in fact, the anions have the greatest influence, whereas
the cations are of less moment.

The solidification temperature is raised by $\big\}$ $SO_4 > CH_3CO_2 >$
The solidification time is shortened by $\big\}$ tartrates.

The solidification temperature is lowered by $\left.\begin{array}{l}\end{array}\right\}$ benzoates and salicy-
The solidification time is lengthened by $\left.\begin{array}{l}\end{array}\right\}$ lates $> SCN > I > Br$ $> NO_3 > Cl.$

The following data (from H. Bechhold and J. Ziegler[*2]) serve
as an example

	Melting point
10 per cent gelatin .	31 6
10 per cent gelatin + 1 mol NaCl	28 5
10 per cent gelatin + 2 mol Na$_2$SO$_4$.	34 2
10 per cent gelatin + 1 mol NaI	10 0

Nonelectrolytes also influence the melting point of gelatin.
Glycerin and sugar (mannit, cane sugar, etc.), in contradistinction
to agar, raise the temperature and increase the rate of gelatinization,
while furfurol, urea, alcohols, resorcin, hydrochinon and pyrogallol
lower them. Nongelatinizing colloids have no influence on gelatinization.

The following figures from H Bechhold and J. Ziegler[*2] serve
to make this clear.

	Melting point.
10 per cent gelatin	31 66
10 per cent gelatin + 1 mol grape sugar	32 25
10 per cent gelatin + 2 mol glycerin	32 17
10 per cent gelatin + 2 mol alcohol . . .	30 0
10 per cent gelatin + 1 mol urea	26 3

Precipitation of the gelatin sol must be sharply differentiated from
gelatinization. Precipitation is induced by electrolytes, whereas
nonelectrolytes usually interfere with it. Precipitation corresponds

rather to salting out, which, we may assume, occurs also in the case of crystalloids, it may be induced not only by electrolytes which raise the melting point of the gel, but also by those which depress it.

Precipitation becomes evident at first through a turbidity which may be sufficiently marked to give a tenacious gelatin phase and a more limpid aqueous phase. In precipitations, also, the *anions* have the determining influence, their precipitating effect being arranged in the following order:

$$SO_4 > Citrate > Tartrate > Acetate > Chlorid.$$

Inorganic hydrosols behave quantitatively toward gelatin the same as toward albumin (see p. 156).

The *swelling* and *shrinking* of gelatin referred to on page 68, *et seq.*, are characteristic for all elastic gels.

According to J. Traube and F. Köhler there exists a parallelism between the swelling, shrinking, solidification and melting point of gelatin when it is mixed with other substances.

The tinctorial properties of *elastic fibers* and their chief constituent *elastin*, are better known than their other colloidal properties.

To the investigations of P. G. Unna and L. Golodetz, we owe our knowledge of the *keratins*, the *horny substances* composing skin, hair, nails, hoofs, horns, feathers, etc. Chemical studies of these substances are very difficult because they resist chemical attack.

We shall merely mention the remaining albuminoids, *spongin*, the structural support of ordinary sponge, *chondrin*, the framework of mussels and snails and further, the *albumoids*, a group into which almost all unclassified proteins are thrown.

Nucleoalbumins.

These proteins, like the albumins, are digested by pepsin hydrochloric acid; they dissolve almost entirely, but at the same time split off an almost insoluble phosphorus-containing complex. The *casein* of milk, the *vitellin* of egg yolk and perhaps also *legumin* and *vegetable casein* are nucleoalbumins. It is remarkable that among the phosphorus-containing proteins obtained from seeds, there should be several that are soluble in alcohol (*gliadin* from cereal grains and *zein* from corn). Because of this, it is a question however, whether they are related to casein.

On account of its importance, *casein* has been most extensively investigated. In milk, casein exists as a salt (united to lime and alkali) and, being dissolved, exhibits profound hydrolytic dissociation. Casein may be thrown out of solution by the addition of acid, or connin, yet the casein obtained by the addition of acid and that obtained by rennin are not identical. Furthermore, casein may be separated from the crystalloid portions of milk by ultrafiltration H. Brinnora and by centrifugation (H. Emden staal). We are indebted to E. Laqueur and O. Sackur as well as T. B. Robertson (who gives a bibliography) for the exhaustive chemical studies of casein upon which we base our remarks. In water casein is completely insoluble and decidedly acid. A piece of casein stains damp blue litmus paper red. According to L. Michaelis the isoelectric point occurs when the H ion concentration is 2.10⁻³. Casein forms salts soluble in water with alkalis and alkaline earths. One gram of casein binds 8.81 c.c. 1 10 normal alkali (using phenolphthalein as an indicator). From this the combining weight of casein is 1135, and a constant multiple of this is its molecular weight. E. Laqueur and O. Sackur deduced from the conductivity of sodium casein solution with increasing dilution, that casein was a tetra or hexavalent acid and that, therefore, its molecular weight lay between 1540 and 6840. T. B. Robertson, as a result of his investigations, comes to the contrary conclusion, that only a *single* carboxyl group is available for union with a base. W. van Dam has investigated the diminution in H ion concentration of lactic acid solution upon adding casein and concludes from it, that a basic group unites with four replaceable H atoms in a casein molecule.

In solution, casein salts are hydrolytically dissociated and, in fact, it follows from the following experiment that casein acid forms a hydrosol. A neutral solution of casein sodium solution is slightly opalescent and becomes clear upon the addition of an alkali. The solution of casein-lime salts are still more opalescent as the alkaline earth salts are weaker bases. Casein sodium does not diffuse through parchment; the membrane must have a decided difference in potential since the sodium ion has a strong tendency to diffuse.

E. Laqueur and O. Sackur showed that the internal friction of casein salt solutions increased proportionately to the electrolytic dissociation, and that every diminution of electrolytic dissociation was accompanied by a diminution of internal friction. The casein ions are thus responsible for high internal friction.

Hemoglobin.

Hemoglobin, the coloring matter of blood, has only recently been studied by P. Bottazzi. It is preeminently not a fit colloidal chemical investigation on account of its color, ease of crystallization and pronounced colloid character. Chemically, it is composed of the protein *globin*, a histone, and the iron-containing component, *heustin*, which is apparently a pyrrol derivative.

Bechhold used 1 per cent hemoglobin solutions to gauge his ultrafilters (see p. 99).

After dialyzing three to four months, hemoglobin solutions have a conductivity of K 20° $= 1 \times 10^{-4}$. After dialyzing five and a half months, the hemoglobin was completely precipitated though the precipitate did not have the amorphous flocculent character of other proteins but was more granular although no crystalline formations could be recognized. If the granules were removed by filtration during the dialysis, there was obtained a reddish, optically inactive solution which showed no particles in the ultramicroscope. Such a solution does not pass through the dialyzing membrane and contains particles which are somewhat larger than those of serum albumin as determined by ultrafiltration.

Regarding the absorption of O and CO, by hemoglobin see page 308, *et seq.*

During dialysis, hemoglobin changes to methemoglobin. Methemoglobin, which is insoluble in water and neutral salts, redissolves upon the addition of traces of alkalis or acids.

Purified hemoglobin migrates to the anode. In view of this fact and the relatively high conductivity of a dialyzed hemoglobin solution P. Bottazzi assumes that hemoglobin is an *hemoglobinic acid* insoluble in water, but which exists in solution as an *alkali hemoglobinate* Being an amphoteric electrolyte it is also soluble in acids and then migrates to the cathode, if H ion dissociation far exceeds its OH ion dissociation. According to L. Michaelis, on the contrary, hemoglobin is less acid than serum albumin, its isoelectric point occurs with an H ion concentration of $1.8 \cdot 10^{-7}$. The viscosity curves which P. Bottazzi[*] obtained on dissolving it in alkalis and acids indicate the occurrence of methemoglobin ions; they resemble the viscosity curves of alkali and acid albumin. Completely dialyzed methemoglobin coagulates at 47°-53° C; in the presence of traces of alkalis or acids, and in the absence of neutral salts coagulation fails to occur even at 100° C.

In conclusion we shall mention the *mucins* and *mucoid*. They are the excretory products of many glands and may be briefly described as animal *mucus*. The possession of a carbohydrate in addition to the protein component distinguishes them chemically. Colloid-chemically they also occupy an intermediate position, since they are not coagulated by heat but are precipitated by salts and alcohol. Because of their acid character they are precipitated by acids and dissolved by alkalis.

The Colloid Cleavage Products of Proteins.

Proteins undergo hydrolytic cleavage by acids, alkalis, and enzymes. From the viscosity curve resulting from the prolonged action of NaOH on albumin it is observed that the disintegration of albumin depends upon the albumin ion (W. M. Bayliss, K. Schorr). T. B. Robertson arrived at a similar conclusion from his studies of the tryptic digestion of casein. Under these circumstances, it is obvious that, in general, the digestion of albumin by enzymes occurs more readily in acid or alkaline solution than in neutral solution where there are but few albumin ions.

With increasing subdivision of the molecule the diffusibility, etc., increases, and the precipitability by neutral salts decreases. The group of cleavage products, known as *albumoses*, diffuse slowly through animal membranes, where the *peptones* are not to be distinguished in this respect from true crystalloids. That they are still to a certain extent colloids is proved by fact forming films on the surface of water described on p. 44 which place them in the class of those dyes which lie midway between colloid and crystalloids. H. Bechhold arrived at a similar result by separating albumoses from the remaining fluid by means of *ultrafilter* whereas peptones and the closely related deuteroalbumoses C were not held back even by 10 per cent filters.

The albumoses and perhaps also the peptones are evidently mixtures of numerous different substances which have not yet been chemically identified. They are differentiated and classified according to their precipitability by electrolytes and alcohol which doubtless stands in a certain relationship to the size of their molecules and particles and to their ionization, see page 152. By means of ultrafilters of different permeability, H. Bechhold separated albumoses into various groups which corresponded to their precipitability.

Subjoined is the classification of F. Hofmeister's results of the results by ultrafiltration:

	Substances per cent of an equal weight ammonium sulphate required to precipitate	Dialysis	Ultrafilter
Hetero- and protoalbumoses	34.9	3	Precipitated
Deuteroalbumoses A	54.62		Retained
Deuteroalbumoses B	70.03		Already to some
Deuteroalbumoses C	100 + acid	10 th.	Back to some extent and filters well through
Peptones	Not salted out		Goes through filter

These experiments were undertaken and largely carried out by Edgard Zunz.[2] They lead to a multitude of valuable results. It suffices to mention that by ultrafiltration of thioalbumose,[1] there were shown to be two components of obviously different chemical constitution; and that in hetero- and protoalbumose at least two and in the latter probably even three "proteoses" should be assumed.

[1] Deuteroalbumose—A, on account of its large content of easily split-off sulphur, is termed "Thioalbumose," by Pick.

CHAPTER XI.

FOODS AND CONDIMENTS.

FORMERLY the preparation of food was one of the most important tasks assigned to the housewife, nowadays among the middle and better classes this duty is almost entirely surrendered to servants, while among the working classes the women can give it but little attention as they must increase the family income by work away from home. These conditions have brought with them the steady deterioration of the *Art of Cookery*. The raw materials nowadays supplied to the kitchen from wholesale establishments, *e.g.*, the bread, fruit, vegetables, beer, and perhaps even meat, etc., are, it is true, of a much superior quality than formerly This is due to competition, easier means of communication, improvement in methods of cultivation and all the advantages consequent upon production on a large scale. The conversion of this raw material into palatable meals requires a large measure of experience, loving care, and great interest — which one can expect from neither a twenty-year-old cook nor the tired working woman.

Nutrition is undoubtedly the most important factor in our whole social life, if we place the yearly expense for nourishment in the German Empire at ten milliards of marks, it is surely underestimated. Only a one per cent increase of the successful utilization of food would show a yearly profit of at least one hundred million marks ($25,000,000).

It is hardly to be expected that we shall accomplish this by returning to former conditions, but rather, in a different way, namely, the development of the *art* into the *science* of cookery. The kitchen will probably adapt itself more and more to wholesale preparation, and then there will be men and women who will choose cooking as a profession because of their scientific training for the work:

Colloid Chemistry furnishes us the rules for the selection and preparation of our foodstuffs; because cooking is nothing but practical colloid chemistry. Our foodstuffs consist entirely of colloids and their nutritive value is to be judged mainly from a colloid-chemical point of view.

168

Very little truly scientific work[1] has as yet been accomplished in this field, so that we must content ourselves with indicating the problem.[2]

Meat. What we consume as "meat" consists for the most part of muscle fibers and connective tissue with the interspersed fat. In judging the meat of healthy animals its source is the chief criterion, young, well-nourished animals possess a juicy meat and tender connective tissue, whereas old worn out animals are less juicy and their connective tissue shows a firmer structure. From these few premises it is evident that it is a question of *turgor* and *swelling capacity*, which change with age, this is an important colloid-chemical problem. It is still an open question whether the toughening of connective tissue may be compared to the lignification of the vascular bundles of plants, which according to H. Wisselingh[*] (see pp. 249 and 250) is due to the adsorption of colloids from the cambial sap

Fresh killed meat is tender, it becomes soft again only upon the disappearance of rigor mortis. This is conditioned by phenomena of swelling and shrinking, an interesting method for studying meat adopted by O. von Fürth and E. Jirak. After death lactic acid accumulates in the muscular tissue, and greatly increases the swelling capacity of the muscles (see p. 290). If such a muscle is placed in a dilute salt solution, it swells up and after about 25 hours has taken up a maximum amount of water of swelling. Then shrinking occurs as the result of the progressive coagulation of the muscle albumin. The curve obtained in this manner has a quite characteristic shape depending on what has happened to the meat. Fig. *A* shows the curve of swelling of horse heart three or four hours after slaughter; Fig. *B*, after it has been kept 3 days in the ice

---

[1] In this connection Dr. J. G. M. Bullowa mentions favorably "The Chemistry of Cookery," by Mattieu Williams, London, Chatto & Windus, 1892. H. C. Sherman has included in his book, *Food Products* "Macmillan Co. 1917, the important recent data. By reason of the war the preservation of perishable foodstuffs has assumed great importance. Dehydrating processes make possible the transportation of large quantities of vegetables in limited cargo space. Cf. also N. Ekberg has presented an excellent account of the method and literature of drying and dehydrating foods in Allen Rogers' "Manual of Industrial Chemistry," Van Nostrand 1918. The products dried by Ekberg's "G. H." Evaporator in the Mrs. Olivia Heckman's Food Research Laboratory are of excellent quality, are said to retain the important food substances. The "G. H." Dehydrator dries its product in moist air at a moderate temperature. Humidity and temperature are controlled. A fan blower is provided for recirculation of the air so that volatile substances are kept in contact with the product and only a small percentage is lost. The process is quite the reverse of ordinary cooking which in effort is made to retain moisture and volatile substances by rapidly closing the surface of the food by quick heat coagulation. Tr.]

box. In the first instance it absorbs approximately 10 per cent of its weight in the first 25 hours, then shrinking occurs. The ice box heart, on the contrary, immediately begins to lose water, and at the

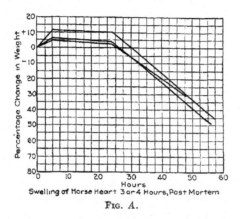

Swelling of Horse Heart 3 or 4 Hours, Post Mortem

Fig. *A.*

end of 45 hours has lost by shrinkage about 55–75 per cent of its water.

Typical are curves, Figs. *C, D, E,* which show comparatively

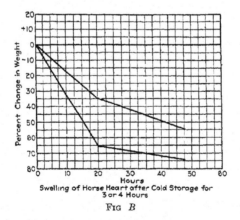

Swelling of Horse Heart after Cold Storage for 3 or 4 Hours

Fig *B*

butcher's meat, cold storage meat and hare, which have been kept a year at − 10°. In actual practice the method is to weigh morsels of meat of as nearly the same size as possible, and after placing them in salt solution, at hourly intervals, to determine the changes in weight.

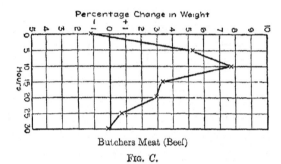

Butchers Meat (Beef)

FIG. *C.*

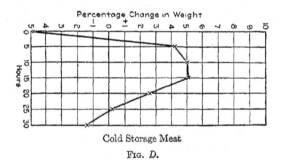

Cold Storage Meat

FIG. *D.*

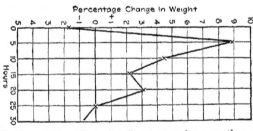

Swelling of Hare Flesh after Preservation for more than a
Year at −10° C

FIG. *E.*

Naturally a salt solution of the same concentration (5–10 per cent) is always employed. In pure water, shrinking occurs immediately, since muscle albumin coagulates in it spontaneously. High concentrations of salt, 25–30 per cent, likewise depress the curve.

New problems arise in cooking meat. If meat is boiled in pure water we obtain a "weak" broth. Muscle albumin coagulates in water before heat coagulation occurs and this impedes the exit of the crystalloid. Salt is therefore added immediately if good soup is to be expected. With *boiling*, heat coagulation occurs whereby the meat loses from 20 to 30 per cent of its water. The mechanism of this loss is still unknown. We can understand why there should be a loss of from 20 to 35 per cent in *roasting*, and it would be still greater if the surface were not constantly protected by pouring over or dipping into fat (basting).

Preserved meats are less perishable because they contain less water and because the muscle albumin has been converted into a characteristic gel condition. This end is attained in various ways: In *pickling*, water is removed from the meat by the salts of the brine, while at the same time there is an exchange of crystalloids, whereby salts enter from without which change the albumin as regards its coagulability and swelling capacity: and extractives leave it and are removed with the brine. Of course very important changes occur during storage, so that according to A. GARTNER, with increasing age pickled meat becomes more difficult of digestion and loses 30 per cent of its nutritive value. *Smoking* of meat is usually preceded by a short pickling process. The abstraction of water in this case is accomplished by means of a strong current of air, and in the dried meat (pemmican) which is much relished in some regions, in the Arctics (for instance), there is no loss other than water.

Naturally, the properties of every gel, materially, depend upon its history. To quote a single example F. STOFFEL* (in the laboratory of PROF. H. ZANGGER) found, that the diffusibility of one and the same substance through the identical gelatin differed, depending upon whether the gelatin was rapidly solidified with ice or slowly cooled at room temperature. Accordingly, we may assume in the case of meat, that the properties of the coagulated albumin will vary with the conditions maintained during coagulation, and that upon these depends its food value.

An essential question in the investigation of sound meat, preserved meats and food preparations must be their *available* food *value*, which can be answered only by complicated and expensive metabolism investigations. From my point of view this ought to be a fruitful field for the colloid chemist, who ought certainly to be in a position to replace with simpler methods some protracted metabolism experiments I might incidentally mention the methods of adsorption and staining which hitherto have not been sufficiently considered. In the various *food preparations* (whose names need not be mentioned), it is quite unessential whether they contain a few per cent more or less of carbohydrate or nitrogen, a fact which is always especially emphasized in the advertisements; whereas it is quite important to know their swelling capacity, and whether this permits their complete and *rapid* utilization in the alimentary canal.

Milk and Dairy Products. Milk, as a physiological excretion will be considered on pages 345, *et seq.*, and there also much is said which pertains to its properties as a food material. Here we shall concern ourselves merely with the *examination of milk*. The present-day methods of milk examination are limited to certain characteristics which are especially easy to determine and, therefore, are easily simulated by adulterators. Pure food officials lay most stress on the water and the fat content Sometimes, in addition, they determine the protein percentage, preservatives, and the possible existence of disease organisms. Inasmuch as milk is by far the most valuable food-stuff, it is of the greatest importance not only to determine variations produced under the normal circumstances by adulteration, but also those occurring under normal conditions of production, change of fodder dependent upon change of season, natural and artificial fodder, boiling, pasteurization, etc. Accordingly, H. Zangger[*2] and his pupils undertook to discover new methods; in them he regarded milk as a solution of colloids and electrolytes Of the colloid methods, Zangger and his pupil, Kobler, have chosen the determination of *surface tension*, which proved to be one of the "most complicated but perhaps the most delicate and flexible method " Among the various procedures, the *bubble method*, in which bubbles are allowed to form in the fluid, gave the most constant results

Normal milk gave quite constant figures. Inasmuch as by this method only such substances have an influence as are forced to the surface, these can make themselves evident in the minutest quantities Adulteration with water is not easily detected by this method. *Fermentation*, on the contrary, causes great departures from the *normal*, which are explained by the development of fatty acids. The addition of alkalis also changes the surface tension.

By the study of the *viscosity*, abnormal *protein* and *fat content* could be shown and likewise additions (adulterations) which influenced the amount of swelling (especially alkaline additions) The viscosity is also diminished by violent shaking, though milk regains through quiet its original viscosity (to within 1 per cent) provided it has not been shaken long enough for curds to form.

This observation was of great practical importance because milk suffers violent shaking during transportation. Experiments in which milk was carried by wagon, train and post more than three hundred (300) kilometers showed that there was no evident irreversible loss of viscosity.

Dr. GROSSER, according to a personal unpublished communication, has made a very noteworthy observation in the *ultrafiltration of milk* [1] It was shown that raw milk gave an ultrafiltrate much *richer in lime* than did boiled milk. In boiling, the calcium is bound to the milk colloid and remains with the latter on the ultra-filter. Thus, a simple means is furnished for distinguishing raw from cooked milk. Definite differences exist between human and cow's milk which offer a new basis for the difference these two kinds of milk exhibit in respect to their assimilibility (available food value)

The classification of the milk colloids to which J. ALEXANDER and J G. M. BULLOWA have drawn attention must be considered in future tests of milk (see p 349)

Since the water and the crystalloid content of milk are almost constant, many adulterants can be detected by the departure of the water and the milk content from the normal For this purpose it is necessary to remove the fat and colloid constituents without changing the content in water and salts. To determine the *addition of water*, J. MAI and S ROTHENFUSSER* coagulate the milk colloids with calcium chlorid and then measure the water content by refraction. KURT OPPENHEIMER determines the *milk sugar* polarimetrically, after he has removed the milk colloids with colloidal ferric hydroxid. According to S. ROTHENFUSSER, by treating milk with lead acetate in strong ammoniacal solution at 85° C., the milk sugar is adsorbed when the colloids are coagulated, while saccharose remains in solution. According to ROTHENFUSSER,* the smallest adulteration with foreign sugar (saccharated lime) may thus be detected.

Among dairy products, condensed milk must be considered as of great importance. This is milk which is evaporated with the addition of 25 to 50 per cent cane sugar. All who are forced to use it, especially colonists, know how ill it satisfies the demand for a milk substitute. One of the essential properties of colloids is that their condition is not reversible to the same extent as crystalloids This may be, in addition to the destruction of certain flavoring substances, an important reason for the lessened value of condensed milk The various dried milk products when stirred with cold or warm water

[1] In a private communication, as yet unpublished.

give an incomplete emulsion and there always remains a sediment. The older the preparation the more incomplete is the solution. We here approach once more a phenomenon which was touched upon under "Aging of Colloids" (p. 74). J. G. M. BULLOWA informs me that JUST and HATMAKER have invented a process which avoids these disadvantages and which is already in use on a large scale.[1]

Cream is a fat emulsion which contains at least 10 per cent fat. Cream for whipping contains as much as 30 per cent This emulsion has the property of building thick foam walls which possess considerable consistency. In order to simulate a high fat content, potato flour, gelatin or whipped white of egg are added as adulterants to cream deficient in fat. Calcium saccharate may also raise the viscosity. S. M. BABCOCK and H. L. RUSSEL* recommended its addition to milk or cream which has become thin from being heated. The food industry has adopted this and, nowadays, calcium saccharate solutions enter commerce under various names (grossin, etc.) as thickeners. According to FR. ELSNER, their effect is quite marvelous. Their detection is easy by the method of ROTHENFUSSER, described on page 174. An *artificial cream* may be obtained by emulsifying warm margarine with skim-milk and adding egg yolk

It is evident from what was said on pages 15 and 34, why an emulsion such as whipped cream or the like is so stiff, because we know how great a force is necessary to deform spheres of such small size.

In milk and cream, the aqueous colloid solution is the dispersing medium and the fat is the dispersed phase, in the case of *butter* this relation is reversed.[2] According to law, butter may not contain more than 16 per cent water, though it is possible to impregnate it with water to more than 30 per cent.* According to POSNJAK, the addition of alkalis and glucose increases, whereas increase of acidity diminishes the capacity of butter to absorb water. (W. MEIJERINGH *) The kneading in of water is always reckoned to be an adulteration, because water is cheaper than butter From the standpoint of the colloid chemist, it has always been a question whether the amount of water in butter or rather the content of skim-milk does not increase its digestibility and whether it is not the dispersion by means of the albumin or rather casein-containing aqueous solution which makes butter so much superior in digestibility to other fats of high melting point, and whether, if the above assumption should be proved correct, it would not be possible to find a legal way to permit butter to have a greater water (*i.e.*, skim-milk) content. In the manufacture of *margarine*, skim-milk is

[1] [MERRALL and SOULE of Rochester, N. Y., spray milk into heated air to dry it. Tr]

[2] [See work of MARTIN H FISCHER and G F. L CLOWES. Tr.]

added to the fat in order, we are accustomed to assume, to give it the taste of butter. It is yet to be determined whether it is not just this addition, which gives the fat the dispersion characteristic of butter, and thereby its greater digestibility. The darkening of margarine in heating is undoubtedly to be attributed to the added skim-milk.

By changing the colloidally dissolved albuminous substances of milk into the gel form, we obtain *cheese*. Coagulation can be brought about by means of rennet (sweet milk cheese) or through acidification (sour milk cheese). In cheese we have an emulsion of fat in a protein gel, whereas in *skim* or *sour milk cheese* (kummel, Harz and hand-käse), the amount of fat is only the small amount afforded by skim-milk; it is quite high in the *fatty cheeses* (cream, Swiss, Camembert and Roquefort).

A process of great interest, as yet uninvestigated from the colloid-chemical standpoint is the *ripening of cheese*. Through the action of bacteria there occur changes in the structure of the cheese which are specific for every variety and which cause the spotted appearance found in the various kinds of cheese.

For cheese, chemical tests are limited to the determination of the water, fat, albumin and salt content and the possible adulterants. The most important, namely, the swelling capacity in the presence of the digestive ferments, is nowadays entirely ignored, although this would furnish the simplest method of deciding the important question of the digestibility of cheese

Honey should in the main be composed of sugar, it is nevertheless frequently adulterated with glucose and dextrin. My opinion is that tests of the surface tension of dilute solutions would lead to the detection of such colloidal adulterants.

Flour, Dough and Baking Products.

The examination of flour, in addition to the microscopic histologic study, extends to its *doughing* and *baking properties*. These two questions belong entirely to the province of colloid chemistry.

Art is in advance of science in this matter. There exist the most diverse methods for discovering the presence of foreign substances in flour and for distinguishing its various varieties by determining the temperature at which it becomes pasty. The baking capacity in particular, which is intimately bound up with the swelling capacity of the gluten, is applied colloid chemistry. The more glutenous the flour, the more water it binds (38 to 60 per cent) and the greater is its capacity to be kneaded.

The apparatus for this determination, especially that of Leo Liebermann, measures the expansion of the "doughed up" flour under the influence of heat

I must not omit to state here, that flour whose baking capacity has suffered (for instance by over-heating the gluten in grinding) may be restored by the addition of common salt, plaster of paris, water and alum.

What has been said of flour applies also to *prepared flours* and *infant foods*. In the latter, in addition to the proper composition, ease of digestion and the property of preventing curdly coagulation of milk in the stomach must be considered. It should be determined whether a part of the difficult and complicated metabolism experiments could not be substituted by simple testing according to suitable colloid-chemical methods (swelling, etc.)

In the investigation of *dough, egg-dough* and *prepared products* (bread, noodles and macaroni), there occurs a phenomenon which is very suggestive of a similar occurrence in the case of milk (see p. 345), namely, that one cannot recover the quantity of fat present in the original flour by means of ether extraction, and indeed, it would be interesting to determine how the adsorption of the fat occurs if there is any adsorption. In this connection we may consider that in the case of products made of egg-dough, we distinguish between *free* lecithin (extractible with ether) and *bound* lecithin (extractible with alcohol). Perhaps here, too, it is a question of adsorption.

Next to milk, *bread* is our most important foodstuff. *Bread making* may be briefly mentioned here. Bread is prepared from flour, which, if it were consumed directly or made into a paste, would be badly digested because the flour grains possess only a small swelling capacity and the surface development of the entire mass is very small. The making of bread renders the individual parts easily accessible to the digestive juices. For this purpose, the dough (flour mixed with water) is caused to ferment by the addition of yeast or sour dough. As a result, the starch grains swell, burst and take up water, a portion is converted into dextrin, part of which is still further broken down into sugar, alcohol and carbonic acid gas. By foam formation the carbonic acid gas causes an enormous increase in the surface of the mass. Incidental fermentative processes give the gluten, the plant albumin, the power to swell up. This condition is completed and to a certain extent fixed by baking. The dextrinization of the starch is thus completed, the development of surface is increased by the conversion of the water into steam and the expansion of the carbonic acid gas, the gluten is coagulated and further changes are stopped by the killing of the fermenting agents.

Ultimately we obtain a framework of coagulated gluten whose pores are filled with shattered starch grains.

The crust, which does not swell much, acts as a protection both against the absorption of water and its loss from the interior. A good bread should contain from 35 to 45 per cent of water. Upon keeping, it loses about 1 per cent daily until the loss reaches 15 per cent After that, the water content is dependent on the humidity of the atmosphere; this corresponds to the behavior of an elastic gel. It is interesting to note that the *salt* content plays a role in the condition of swelling, because unsalted bread dries much more readily than salted bread.

There is a widespread error that *stale bread* has lost water and is dessicated. This is not true; the crumbling consistence of stale bread is due to a shifting of the water within the loaf; the starch grains transfer water to the albuminous framework   J R. KATZ studied this problem and found that bread kept fresh longer at 50° to 100° C. as well as below −10° (best in a current of air), in other words, there is a balance of swelling in starch and gluten which corresponds to that of fresh bread. At from 0°-25° C. stale bread is the stable form.   Staling is a particularly reversible process, dry rolls are made fresh by heating them. This is an old expedient frequently employed. The results of KATZ' research on keeping bread fresh at low temperatures deserves the attention of the trade

The digestibility and available food value of bread depend particularly upon its "dispersibility" and swelling capacity

A perfect wheat bread may be utilized to the extent of 94 per cent — a rye bread to 90 per cent   For this purpose, the flour used must be as fine as possible, otherwise the utilization is imperfect. It must also be properly swollen up, fresh bread which is too wet is digestible with difficulty   It packs together and the changes induced by the incorporation with the saliva and other digestive juices are different from those with old or dry bread   Most difficult to absorb are the proteins (55 to 85 per cent)   The great heat (in the inner parts amounting to 110°), acting in the presence of a small quantity of water, produces a coagulation which greatly reduces their swelling capacity.

The grain shortage during the war caused the attempt to make bread from potatoes. Potato flour yields a heavy, indigestible mass when heated in the way usual for ordinary flour   Different attempts were made to overcome this. According to A FORNET, the *Experimental Station for the Utilization of Grain* mixes in an unknown gluten substitute. WILHELM OSTWALD recommended blood or casein dissolved in ammonium carbonate as a substitute for gluten.

Walter Ostwald and A. Riedel made a porous starch bread by adding a starch paste to the starch dough before baking. A "pseudo-coagulation" occurred during the baking, the unburst starch grains abstracting water from the burst ones. The internal friction of the paste becomes so great that the air bubbles cannot escape during the baking process, the dough does not fall but is fixed as a foam.

[In discussing the physical chemistry of bread making, E. J. Cohn and L. J. Henderson (Science, Nov. 22, 1918, p. 501, *et seq.*) conclude that "the acidity of the dough, at the time of baking, seems to be the most important variable factor in bread making." Soluble serum protein is an acceptable physical substitute for gluten. Tr.]

Beer.

The fermentation industry so highly developed scientifically and technically has already paid attention to colloid chemistry and produced a not inconsiderable literature (see F. Emslander[*1]) which in part, however, is not altogether free from dilettantism.

It would take us too far afield, were we to consider the whole process of beer brewing[1] from the colloid-chemical viewpoint; we must restrict ourselves to the finished product.

Beer is a fermented beverage with an alcohol content of from 2 to 5 per cent, some acetic acid and from 4 to 8 per cent extractives.

The extractives consist in greatest part of carbohydrates (maltose, dextrin and gums) to a lesser extent of proteins (about 0.6 per cent), and in addition, salts, hop bitters, hop resin and several alkaloidal substances, besides small quantities of fermentation products such as glycerin, lactic acid and succinic acid.

The persistent fine foam which a fresh beer should show is brought about by its colloidal content. It is a sign that the colloids have not yet been broken down too far, and has at the same time the more important purpose of retaining the carbonic acid gas. In a solution supersaturated with gases, the formation of bubbles is either increased or diminished by the colloids present at the moment. We know further, from page 34, that a certain pressure is necessary to overcome the surface tension and burst the bubble, *e.g.*, a soap bubble, so that the carbonic acid gas of beer is under a certain pressure beneath the foam.

The condition rather than the amount of the foam-forming albumins is more important for the foam-keeping quality of beer. There are beers rich in albumin which remain foamless and beers poor in albumin which foam well. According to F. Emslander[*] it is mainly the soft hop resin, in addition to the acidity of the beer, which makes the albumins foam.

[1] Rich. Emslander calls attention to an interesting relation between beer brewing and inactivation of ferment (by shaking, see p. 189. Brewers have long

A perfect beer should be absolutely clear; turbid beers are unreliable, but no objection can be raised to a dusty or net-like appearance. In the latter case the disperse phase consists of protein particles, dextrins or precipitates of hop resin. Some yeast may also be suspended.

Occasionally in very cold beers cloudiness develops which may be ascribed to precipitated albumins, which disappear when the beer is warmed. In the United States where iced drinks are in great demand, especial pains have been taken to master the difficulty

The alkalinity of the wash water, the carbonic acid, and the atmospheric oxygen during the brew, play an important role in the resistance of beer to cold. According to R. Emslander* the surest means is the addition of some pepsin. [Wallerstein has patented the addition of a proteolytic enzyme to beers, to prevent cold-cloudiness. Tr.]

What is designated as "vollmundigkeit" or body in beer is caused by the colloid content This property is almost identical with the viscosity, and is determined by the viscosimeter. If, for instance, the time required for water to run from a 50-c c pipette = 1, and that of an equal quantity of beer = 1.43, we say that the "viscosity" is 1.43. It follows from what has been said on pages 152 and 153, that we may assume à priori, that the "vollmundigkeit" is largely dependent on the electrolytes, that is, on the content of acids and the kinds of salts. Even though the larger part of the salts is derived from barley, yet some are derived from the brewing water, and the hitherto partly unrecognized influence of the water may be attributed to this fact.

E. Moufang determined empirically the relation between optimum keeping quality, "full" and "palatable" taste, sediment and acidity. I refer to F. Emslander *[1] for the colloid-chemical effect of the brewing water on lagered beer

Among the proteins, in addition to the gluten which flocculates out on boiling with acetic acid, peptone may be mentioned. H Bechhold *[2] was able to demonstrate only albumoses, upon examining a beer by ultrafiltration. Before *generalizing*, a large number of beers would have to be investigated in this way. It seems that E. Fouard has carried on such ultrafiltration experiments with starch solutions, worts and beer (cited by Emslander). W. H. van Laer has also made noteworthy experiments on the relationship between the ultra-filtrates of beer and musts, and their transparency. F. Emslander and H. Freundlich * have performed cataphoretic experiments and found that the colloids migrate to the cathode. In consideration of the acid content of beer, this finding is theoretically correct.

R. Marc * has worked out a simple method for quantitatively determining beer colloids by means of the fluid interferometer.

A study should be made of the usefulness of several other colloid-chemical methods for the testing of beer, especially the determination of surface tension, which might serve to distinguish the amount of various colloids contained, coagulation methods, etc. The mere suggestion should suffice.

It must be mentioned in addition, that F. EMSLANDER[*2] has attributed to the "protective colloids" of beer a significance for the more easy adsorption of milk and other foodstuffs. Even earlier experiments, especially those of ROSS VAN LENNEP indicate that the presence of colloids and suspensions have an influence on the growth of microorganisms S HNGEN thoroughly investigated this matter in connection with alcoholic fermentation and obtained interesting results. He found that colloidal iron, albumin, silicic oxid and humic acid had no influence on alcoholic fermentation, but that, on the contrary, it was greatly hastened by turf, filter paper, blood charcoal and garden earth He succeeded in proving the cause of this; the carbonic acid which is developed during alcoholic fermentation impedes fermentation and all substances which favor the disappearance of the carbonic acid favor fermentation. The action of the colloids mentioned is purely mechanical, somewhat like that of powdered glass, threads, wood chips or platinum shavings which hinder boiling. In the fermentation industry it is generally known that brewers grains and spun glass increase alcoholic fermentation, and these phenomena have now been explained by SOHNGEN's investigation.

S ROTHENFUSSER * has employed his colloid-adsorption method for detecting *saccharose* in the most diverse kinds of foods and condiments (wine, weissbier, café parfait, kilned malt, pastry, etc.).

In practice naturally many other questions will appeal to food chemists. It might be determined whether the availability of vegetable protein, which on digestion is only from 60 to 70 per cent, could not be increased by a suitable method of preparation. Colloid-chemical methods must unquestionably be utilized in the investigation of fruit juices, jellies and marmalades. We must remember that these are frequently mixed with glucose, which, when undeclared, should be regarded as an adulteration Glucose contains in addition to dextrose, dextrin and unfermentable substances which may be determined by colloid-chemical analysis. Marmalades are adulterated with gelatin, agar-agar and isinglass.

We trust that the mere mention of these facts may cause food chemists to give greater attention to colloid-chemical methods.

CHAPTER XII.

ENZYMES.

For more detailed study we recommend the following books of reference: "The Nature of Enzyme Action," by W M Bayliss, "Allgem Chemie der Enzyme," by H Euler (J F. Bergmann, Wiesbaden, 1910), "Die Fermente und ihre Wirkungen," by C Oppenheimer (F C W Vogel, Leipzig, 1913); ["Biochemical Catalysis in Life and Industry," by Jean Effront. Translated by Samuel Prescott. John Wiley & Sons, Inc , 1917 Tr]

List of the best known enzymes.

Amylase hydrolyzes starches and glycogen into dextrin and maltose.
Catalase decomposes peroxid of hydrogen
Chymosin is rennin.
Diastase fluidifies starches and hydrolyzes them to maltose.
Emulsin hydrolyzes glucosides.
Erepsin hydrolyzes albumoses and peptones to amino-acids
Fibrin-ferment an hypothetical ferment which coagulates fibrin.
Invertase hydrolyzes cane sugar.
Lipase hydrolyzes fats into fatty acids and glycerin.
Maltase cleaves glucosides.
Oxidase an oxygen carrier
Pancreatin from the pancreatic juice is a mixture of several enzymes.
Papain hydrolyzes albumin
Pepsin hydrolyzes albumin in acid solution.
Ptyalin is the amylase of the saliva.
Rennin coagulates milk.
Steapsin is lipase.
Trypsin hydrolyzes albumin in alkaline solution.
Tyrosinase oxidizes tyrosin and some of its derivatives.
Zymase splits sugar into alcohol and CO_2

To split complex molecules, chemists have to employ powerful reagents, such as acids, alkalis, etc They smash, as it were, the clockwork with a hammer and then pick out the undamaged particles. Just as a watchmaker employs for each screw a suitable tool or a specially made pliers, so nature has constructed delicate instruments for this purpose. *Enzymes* are such tools for the chemical breaking down or building up of molecules. Albumin, carbohydrates and fats may all be split up by acids. For each purpose nature has a special enzyme, or even several; for the cleavage of albumin, pepsin and trypsin; for starches, diastase; for fats, lipase.

We shall see that some enzymes are fashioned exactly for their use, so that the simile of Emil Fischer, which compares the enzyme to a key and the substance split up to a lock, is a very happy one. The simile can be extended still further, since the key may unlock thousands of similar locks and fails only when the key is worn out. Moreover, only very small quantities of enzymes are needed which are utilized over and over again. This conception of enzymes corresponds with our present-day chemical conception of *catalyzers*. These latter are substances which either bring about or accelerate chemical reactions, without themselves figuring in the end products. For instance, platinum hastens the combination of O and SO_2 into SO_3, or the union of H_2 and O into H_2O.

It is the nature of catalyzers that they split up compound substances and build up the same substances from the cleavage products until a definite equilibrium is obtained. Thus, ricin, the enzyme of the castor bean, not only splits fat into glycerin and fatty acid but also unites glycerin and fatty acids into fats. The equilibrium is frequently one in which the synthetic action is very subordinate. Thus, amylase under certain circumstances splits up 99 per cent of starch, yet it forms possibly but 1 per cent of starch from maltose. This, being a colloid, precipitates from the solution, and thus permits the formation of another 1 per cent of starch which gradually appears as starch grains or glycogen and thus permits the further formation of starch.

Hitherto, it has been impossible to obtain an enzyme in pure form and only by its stronger or weaker activity was it known whether a dilute or a concentrated preparation of enzyme existed. W. M. Bayliss rightly calls attention to the fact that, on account of their colloidal nature, enzymes always carry down by adsorption portions of the solutions from which they are obtained. It is, therefore, not surprising that albumin reactions are obtained from pepsin and trypsin and a carbohydrate reaction from amylase and invertase. In many cases it is possible to decide by means of diffusion whether mixtures are present (see R. O. Herzog and Kasarnowski[*]). According to L. Rosenthaler [*] the presence of albuminous substances is of biological importance, protecting the enzyme from many destructive influences, especially from H and OH ions. As the result of the constant presence of adsorbed impurities, we know almost nothing concerning the chemical nature of enzymes. However, we do know that all enzymes are colloids.

S. Fränkel assumes that pure diastase is very greatly dispersed but as yet no sufficient evidence has been adduced; neither observation in the ultramicroscope nor filtration through a 1 per cent ultra filter is conclusive. To us it merely seems probable that such diastase is more highly dispersed than hemoglobin.

Even the colloidal state itself, *i e* , great surface development, under certain circumstances, may be responsible for work similar to that performed by certain of the enzymes.   For instance, G. BREDIG catalyzed hydrogen peroxid by means of metal sols, particularly platinum sol, which he prepared by electric pulverization; that is, he obtained a result, the splitting off of oxygen, which in all appearances resembles that brought about by catalase, a ferment which occurs in blood, in milk, and in many plant and animal tissues.   On this account G. BREDIG called his metal sols "inorganic ferments," although with enzymes (or ferments), they share other properties to which we shall return.   The action of enzymes is explained in part by their colloidal nature   In the organism they act chiefly on colloid substances (*e.g.*, foods) with very extensively developed surfaces, so that under certain circumstances enzymes may be merely mechanically adsorbed. They consequently act upon the substrate in the greatest concentration.

It was shown by numerous adsorption experiments with indifferent suspensions (charcoal, kaolin, cellulose) that enzymes have a strong tendency to *concentrate on surfaces*.   It is possible to remove the rennin or pepsin (M. JACOBY*), and trypsin (G. BUCHNER and KLATTE*) from solution by means of fibrin flakes or other coagulated albumin, or diastase by means of starch (H VAN LAER).   The reagents and sometimes also the *products of the reaction* are adsorbed by the colloidal enzymes   If the former accumulate, in accordance with recognized laws, the progress of the reaction is slowed.   An example is the breaking down of hydrogen peroxid by catalase   The oxygen formed by the breaking down of H_2O_2 into H_2O and O is adsorbed by catalase and the reaction is slowed (WAENTIG and STECHE). Some enzymes, especially pepsin and papagotin, according to ROHONGI, give *reversible* precipitates in salt-free, neutral solutions of different albumins on which they act.   The inhibition of the action of an enzyme by a suspension or a colloid may be removed again under certain conditions by another indifferent colloid   If the activity of rennet has been destroyed by charcoal or normal serum so that the mixture no longer produces curdling of milk, the activity of the rennet may be restored by the addition of saponin.   Somewhat different modifications are obtained by the addition of cholesterin or by combinations of trypsin with charcoal, saponin or cholesterin (JOHNSON, BLOM*).   In this way, the numerous possibilities which result from the interaction of enzyme and antienzyme (*q.v.*) rest on a physical basis

The essential difference between an indigestible adsorbent and one which is dissolved by the enzyme is that the combination, *e.g.*, between animal charcoal and trypsin, is primarily irreversible. The trypsin is *fixed*, water is unable to tear the trypsin from the charcoal though casein is able to do so (S. G. Hedin). It is seen accordingly, that trypsin undergoes a change on the surface of charcoal similar to that undergone by dyes on fibers and if the process were to occur in the organism as it does on charcoal, the trypsin would be permanently withdrawn from the mixture. If, however, the substrate is digested and crystalloid cleavage products result, *e.g.*, in the cleavage of fibrin by trypsin, the adsorption ceases of its own accord and the enzyme becomes free for further use, acting like a true catalyzer.

This serves to explain the significance of the *surfaces* of the substrate on enzyme action. The action increases in speed in accordance with extent of surface per unit of weight. E. Abderhalden and Pettibone,* demonstrated this in the digestion with pancreatic juice of albumen coagulated in different ways.

In the case of enzymes their *electrochemical* nature is more important than in the case of other colloids, and influences their adsorption.

We frequently observe that if the proper H or OH ion concentration is absent, an enzyme acts feebly on its substrate. Many neutral salts favor enzyme action; others inhibit it. For instance, pepsin acts strongly in acid solution only, trypsin in alkaline solution only.

The investigations of L. Michaelis* and his co-workers show that the electric charge of different enzymes varies (see H. Iscovesco*) and that, proportionately to the charge, they are unequally adsorbed by various substrates.

We have previously mentioned that electropositive gels or suspensions, *e.g.*, ferric oxid, completely adsorb electronegative solutions, *e.g.*, serum albumin. An electronegatively-charged mastic or kaolin suspension completely attracts to itself serum albumin, only when it has become electropositive by acidification.

These investigations gave the following results for a group of enzymes. In the table (see p. 186) ⚹ signifies a pronounced electric migration (to cathode or anode), *i.e.*, complete adsorption; 0 signifies no migration or no adsorption: ✕, 0, 0 − ✕, respectively, more or less migration or adsorption.

Ferment	Migration towards		Adsorbents		
	Anode ÷	Cathode −	+ Iron oxid, clay, etc	− Kaolin, mastic, arsenious sulphid, etc	neutral charcoal
Invertase					
in neutral solution	×	0	×	0	×
in acid, solution	×	0	×	0	×
in alkaline solution			×	0	×
Plant diastase					
in neutral solution	0 − ×	×	0 − ×	0	×
in acid solution	0	× − 0	0 − ×	×	×
in alkaline solution	×	0	×	0	0
Salivary diastase					
in neutral solution	·		×	×	×
in acid solution		·	×	×	×
in alkaline solution		·	×	×	×
Trypsin:					
in neutral solution..	×	0	×	×	× − 0
in acid solution	0	×	×	×	×
in alkaline solution	×	0	× − 0	0 − ×	0 − ×
Pepsin.					
in neutral solution.	×	0	×	0	×
in acid solution . .	×	0	×	×	×
in alkaline solution	destroyed	destroyed	destroyed	destroyed	destroyed
Rennin (from pepsin)					
in neutral solution				0	
in acid solution				0	
in alkaline solution		· ·		destroyed	
Rennin (Grubler)					
in neutral solution		· ·		×	
in acid solution				destroyed	
in alkaline solution					

We learn from this table that analysis by simple adsorption may replace the more difficult and complicated electric migration   It is very instructive for our knowledge of enzymes, that their action is strongest with the reaction which expresses their own charges as may be seen from the following table (from L. MICHAELIS):

	Optimum Activity Occurs with an H-ion Concentration of
Water . .	$.1 \ 10^{-7}$
Invertase .	$2 \ 10^{-5}$
Maltase . .	$2 \ 5 \ 10^{-7}$
Trypsin . .	$2 \ 10^{-8}$
Erepsin	$2 \ 10^{-8}$
Pancreatic lipase	$2 \ 10^{-6}$
Pepsin . . .	$2 \ 10^{-2}$

Electronegative (acid) pepsin digests best in an acid; and amphoteric (almost neutral) trypsin in an alkaline reaction. We may think of enzymes as being amphoteric substances, in some of which the positive charge predominates, in others, the negative, as a corollary of this, pepsin dissolves in alkaline solution; in other words, the pepsin is dissolved away from the substrate it would digest and is thus inactivated, the reverse of this holds true for trypsin. Salivary diastase seems entirely neutral, since saliva must fluidify as readily in acid as in alkaline reaction. In some cases we observe a relationship between the reaction of the substrate upon which a ferment is to act and the ferment, thus, pepsin-rennin has a pronounced basic character, casein an acid character, albumin in acid solution has a basic character, and as such combines with acid pepsin; in alkaline solution it has an acid character and so can unite with basic trypsin. Consequently, we find here phenomena which I pointed out in my experiments on the adsorption of dyestuffs, page 29.

This difference in adsorbability is utilized in many cases for the *purification of enzymes* Thus L. MICHAELIS removed albumin from mixtures of serum albumin and invertin by shaking them in acid solution with kaolin; the invertin remained without loss of strength in the albumin-free solution. E. ABDERHALDEN and F. W. STRAUCH extracted pepsin from the stomach content of animals by means of elastin and then recovered it from the elastin by means of water.

Depending upon the reaction, decided differences were found when enzymes were filtered through Chamberland filters. According to HOLDERER most of those studied by him passed through the filter when they were neutral to phenolphthalein but they were held back when neutral to methyl orange. HOLDERER attributes this principally to the effect of adsorption by the filter mass.

For a number of enzymes the course of the reactions was studied and proved to be quite complicated I refer to the investigations of *platinum sol* by G. BREDIG and his pupils, of *invertase* and *amylase* by V. HENRI; of *lipase* by M BODENSTEIN and DIETZ and of *emulsin* by P JACOBSON, which are described by H FREUNDLICH in his "Kapillarchemie." It is conclusively shown in the publication of W. S. DENHAM* from BREDIG's Institute that among all the complicated factors, it is the surface concentration which is of the greatest importance for the acceleration of the reaction

In the case of gels, the greater the surface concentration becomes, or in other words, the more swollen the substrate is, the better is the opportunity offered an enzyme to enter the substrate. This observation can be made over and over again in the cases of enzyme cleavage E. KNOEVENAGEL* offers convincing proof of this fact.

He says "The degree to which acetyl cellulose swells, runs parallel with its speed of saponification by aqueous alkalis, so that with greatly swollen acetyl celluloses the saponification by $1/2\,n$ KOH is completed quantitatively in a few hours, at room temperature."

We have not yet answered the question. What property is to be ascribed to the *specific action* of enzymes? We may regard this query as being answered by G. BREDIG and FAJANS* as far as the principle involved is concerned. They demonstrated that right and left campho- and bromo-campho-carbonic acid (which resemble one another like a picture and its reflection in a mirror) may be split into camphor and carbonic acid by bases acting as catalyzers. The speed with which these two opposites are broken down differs considerably if optically active bases (quinine, quinidine, nicotine and cinchonine) are employed, and may amount to 50 per cent. This is analogous to the *specific action of enzymes* upon chemically known substances with catalyzers which have definite chemical characteristics. It has been shown for most enzyme actions, with certain exceptions among the sugars, that of two optically active isomers both are attacked by a given enzyme, but one is always affected more quickly. We thus have a complete analogy for natural enzymes, but beyond this point the "lock and key" idea fails, since under no circumstances could "an asymmetric key fit the mirror image of its proper lock."

But the analogy extends further. G. BREDIG and FISKE effected asymmetric *synthesis* by a catalyzer of known composition. According to L ROSENTHALER, the enzyme action of emulsin accelerates the following reaction:

$$\underset{\text{Benzaldehyde}}{C_6H_5 \cdot CHO} + \underset{\substack{\text{hydrocyanic,} \\ \text{acid}}}{HCN} = \underset{\text{nitromandelic acid.}}{C_6H_5 \cdot CH(OH) \cdot CN.}$$

G. BREDIG and FISKE replaced emulsin with quinine, but if they employed chinidin as a catalyzer they obtained *laevo* rotary nitromandelic acid in addition to the inactive product

We may summarize our present understanding of enzyme action thus As a result of their colloidal properties, under favorable external circumstances, enzyme and substrate are greatly concentrated at their interfaces, so that the course of the reaction is very much accelerated; the reaction between enzyme and substrate is purely chemical, conditioned by their mutual chemical constitution or configuration. [Ultramicroscopic observations suggest that possibly physical action is also involved. J. ALEXANDER, Jour. Am. Chem. Soc., 1910, vol. 32, p. 680. Tr.]

Enzymes, perhaps, exhibit the property of *aging* to a greater extent than all other colloids. Some, *e.g.*, trypsin, if dried, lose their activity after a time; in solution they all deteriorate more or less rapidly. We do not know whether this depends upon purely mechanical variations, or whether it is associated with a chemical change. For the former view we have the fact that many enzyme solutions may be *inactivated by mere shaking,* a rennet solution, for instance, need be violently shaken only two minutes in a test tube in order largely to deprive it of its capacity to coagulate milk. Even E. ABDERHALDEN and M. GUGGENHEIM* had observed that tyrosinase, expressed yeast juice, and pancreatic juice had their activity partially inhibited by shaking them for 24 hours. A. O. SHAKLEE and S. J MELTZER* found the same true for pepsin and M M HARLOW and P. G. STILES* for ptyalin.

Quite independently in 1908, SIGNE and SIGVAL SCHMIDT-NIELSEN* observed the *inactivation of rennet by shaking,* and subjected the phenomenon to a thorough study. It was deduced from this that inactivation by shaking is a *surface phenomenon;* the inactivation increases with the length of time and the violence of the shaking, the volume of air present, the concentration of the enzyme, and the temperature are all influencing factors The enzyme becomes concentrated in the foam and on the surface of the vessel employed The foam is more active than the fluid and the procedure offers a possible method of concentrating enzymes. If a rennet solution that has been shaken is allowed to stand, it recovers some, but never all of its original activity; a portion remains irreversible. If saponin is added to a rennet solution, no inactivation results from shaking because saponin drives the rennet from the surface.

Subsequently M JACOBY and A. SCHUTZE* published an analogous observation They found that *hemolytic complement* (see p 196) of guinea-pig serum was inactivated by shaking it at 37° C. Reactivation, in other words the reversibility of the process, depends on the duration of the shaking. At first, only a definite fraction of the complement is irreversibly inactivated by the shaking since it may be reactivated by "end piece" and also incompletely by "middle piece." When the shaking has been sufficiently prolonged the complement is irreversibly inactivated according to RITZ. The inactivation depends, according to P SCHMIDT and LIEBER, on the fact that the serum is made turbid by shaking, a foam is formed into which the globulin separates, and this globulin adsorbs the complement. The reactivation by "end piece" results from the solution of the flocculated globulin thus liberating the complement (see p 196). To what extent the action of the alkali (from the glass) assists in the inactivation has not been determined with certainty. On the contrary, it seems from the data, that only a portion of the complement is inactivated, since it may be reactivated by addition of "end piece" and of "middle piece." Serum becomes turbid on shaking, and it is the author's opinion that this is evidently due to a coagulation of the albumin by shaking.

In many investigations, especially in "immunity studies," it is customary to shake the test tubes, and I believe that some of the disagreements in the results of experiments by different investigators are due to a disregard of such surface phenomena. [R. OTTENBERG does not consider this factor in his exhaustive study. Arch. of Int. Medicine, vol. xix, pp. 457–492. Tr.]

The *diffusion coefficient* of several enzymes was measured[1] by R. O. HERZOG and H. KASARNOWSKI * They are for

Pepsin				0 062 (at 12° C.)
Pepsin				0 066 (at 16° C)
Rennin				0 062 (at 16° C.)
Invertin				0 032 (at 16° C.)
Emulsin				0 033 (at 15 3° C)

From these figures the following molecular weights were calculated.

Pepsin.				13,000
Invertin.				54,000
Emulsin.				45,000 [1]

In studies on the *filtration, ultrafiltration* and *diffusion of enzymes through membranes* it must be determined beforehand, whether the filter absorbs too strongly. Thus, e g , a Chamberland filter permits no pepsin, trypsin, lipase or zymase to pass through, though the pores are of ample size. By choosing suitable membranes, these methods of separation have given valuable results. It has been possible by diffusion and ultrafiltration to separate a number of enzymes, which were formerly regarded as individual, into two constituents having different properties. Thus, according to S FRAENKEL and M. HAMBURG,* diastase prepared from malt may be divided into two enzymes. The one which diffuses changes starch into sugar, whereas the other merely fluidifies the starch. A. VON LEBEDEW* ultrafiltered expressed yeast juice and thus succeeded in demonstrating, that in fermenting sugar the disappearance of the sugar and the formation of carbonic acid are two distinct processes.

In the course of such experiments it has been shown frequently, that the components are inactive individually and only exert their enzyme action in combination. The first observation of this kind was that of R. MAGNUS,* who dialyzed liver extract. The extract which originally split up fat thus became inactive; when MAGNUS

---

[1] The figures are the mean of several determinations.

united re able and of distate, the mixture recovered its lypolytic properties. A. Harden and W. J. Young[*] made a similar observation when they attempted expressed yeast juice. The filter residue lost its ability to cause fermentation but regained it when mixed with the filtrate. It is evident from this, that some enzymes consist of a second and crystalloid constituent, the latter following the suggestion of G. Bertrand is called *coenzyme* or *co-ferment*. In still other ways the coenzyme show crystalloid properties; unlike the colloid portions it is insensitive to boiling and frequently consists of a substance whose composition is well known. Thus, e.g., according to A. von Fürth and J. Schütz,[*] sodium cholate and sodium glycocholate as coenzymes of lipase; and according to Bierry and V. Henri[*] the chlorin and bromin ions of alkaline salts are the coenzymes for the action of ptyalin the juice upon starches.

In contradistinction to the coenzymes the *antienzymes* are usually colloids. Antitoxins are defenses which interfere with the action of enzymes, such as the *antitoxin*, which detoxicate toxins, and also the *antitoxins*; they occur to some extent in normal serum or may be produced in it by the injection of enzymes. For instance, horse serum contains a large amount of *anti-rennin* which inhibit the coagulation of milk by rennin. By injecting the proper enzyme, antienzymes for lipase, emulsin, amylase, pepsin, papain and others have been obtained. An exception to this is *antitrypsin* which seems to be a crystalloid one, it diffuses readily. It is the antienzyme which protects intestinal parasites from digestion by the pancreatic juice.

According to S. G. Hedin[*] the relationship between enzyme and antienzyme is an adsorption which probably results in a fixation.

A certain amount between enzyme and coenzyme is possessed by proenzyme and its activation. Most enzymes are *formed* in an inactive state called the *proenzyme*, *proferment*, or *zymogen*, which becomes active only after the addition of some crystalloid, usually a simple substance. The proenzyme of pepsin may be extracted from the gastric mucous membrane but cannot digest albumin; only after the addition of acids. Little acid does it become pepsin and acquire its ability to digest. The trypsin of pancreatic juice is excreted into the duodenum as an inactive proenzyme, it is activated by calcium salts. This is of the greatest biological significance, since otherwise, secreting glands would not be safe from their own secretions.

According to L. Pincussen,[*] the formation of proenzymes occurs in this manner the protoplasm of the glandular cells retains a certain portion of the food by adsorption. Acids, calcium salts, etc., affect the adsorption, and the active ferment becomes free. In support of this view, E. PŘIBRAM and E. STEIN injected through a tube into the stomach of one rabbit an active solution of rennin, and into the other, one inactivated by boiling. After four hours the rabbits were killed and the amounts of pro-ferment contained in their gastric mucous membranes were measured. The gastric mucous membrane of the rabbit treated with active rennin contained much more pro-enzyme than the other. From this, the authors deduced that the colloidal gastric mucous membrane adsorbed the rennin and changed it into pro-enzyme. S G. HEDIN* also views zymogen as the combination of an enzyme (rennet) with an inhibiting substance. In the condition studied especially by him, rennet is freed by hydrochloric acid, the inhibiting substance is let free by ammonia, with the destruction of the rennet.

CHAPTER XIII.

IMMUNITY REACTIONS.

THAT the organism is overwhelmed by a *large* dose of poison but recovers from a *small* one should not particularly surprise us. Ever since the recognition of the nature of infectious diseases, it must have amazed biologists that every infected organism did not succumb to the slightest infection. Microörganisms multiply indefinitely, and, theoretically, it is only a question of hours before the number present shall be overwhelming whether the infection is with a large or a small dose. Were this assumption, to which we might be led from the observation of culture media, correct, no living thing, plant or animal, could exist. There must be inherent forces in the *living* organism which protect it against pathogenic germs, which make it *immune* to such injuries, and which are called, accordingly, *immune bodies* (immune substances).

L. PASTEUR was the pioneer in the systematic study of immunity. He produced experimental proof that immunity might be artificially produced by previous treatment with attenuated infective agents (chicken cholera) just as had been done previously, in the case of vaccination against smallpox. These investigations received a mighty impulse when ROBERT KOCH succeeded in growing disease germs in pure culture. The doctrines of *immunity* and *predisposition* were developed into a special branch of science which at present holds the chief interest of scientific medicine.

It was recognized that the body could overcome its invaders in various ways: substances occur which make bacteria harmless by dissolving them, *bacteriolysins* (acting against vibrios, *e.g.*, of cholera, and against typhoid), and others which clump them together and precipitate them, the *agglutinins* (against typhoid, paratyphoid, dysentery, etc.). In other cases, the protection is directed principally against the poisons, *toxins*, which the organized germs develop (diphtheria toxin, tetanotoxin, etc.) The organism possesses a peculiar protective mechanism in the leucocytes, which take up and digest the bacteria and cocci, devouring them like free living amebæ in search of food. This phenomenon, which was recognized and studied chiefly by E. METSCHNIKOFF, is called *phagocytosis*.

The bacteria are previously prepared for phagocytosis by certain immune substances in the serum called *opsonins.*

The study of these phenomena was very much simplified, when it became possible to transfer many of them from the living organism to test tubes. They were thus freed from disturbing epiphenomena and made susceptible to quantitative investigations By these methods of study, we have learned a number of properties of the blood and cells, which have no direct influence on the natural *protection* of the organism against the attacks of microörganisms, or which may be regarded merely as epiphenomena. They lead to the knowledge that the weapons of the organism against disease germs are not teleologically forged for this sole purpose, but that they are the product of a universal biologic law, according to which the organism produces antisubstances against all kinds of substances foreign to the species (art-fremde)

In accordance with their historic recognition, and the method of their investigation, it is customary to class them with immunity phenomena I am referring to the substances which dissolve and flocculate blood corpuscles, the *hemolysins* and *hemagglutinins* and the albumin-precipitating substances, the *precipitins:* and finally the *Wassermann reaction* in syphilis, and *anaphylaxis.*

If the sera of two animals, *e.g.,* cattle serum and rabbit serum, are mixed, the solution remains clear If an animal, *e.g* , a rabbit is injected with the serum from a different species of animal, *e.g* , cattle serum, substances are formed in the rabbit, *precipitins.*[1] If we then mix the serum of such an animal, "cattle-rabbit," with ox serum, a precipitate forms. *Agglutinins* and *hemolysins* develop in a similar way. If a rabbit has cattle blood corpuscles injected into its veins, substances develop in the rabbit serum which agglutinate and dissolve the cattle blood corpuscles. Hemolysin consists of two substances, one heat resisting (thermostable) and specific, the *amboceptor,* and another, heat sensitive (thermolabile, destroyed at 55° C.) and nonspecific, the *complement.* Only the amboceptor develops as a result of injecting the red blood corpuscles, the complement is always present in every serum. However, both are required for hemolysis We have now explained the formation of precipitins for cattle serum or blood corpuscles in rabbits, but the principle is of general application for the injection of blood into a different species of animals. To

---

[1] The so-called "precipitin reaction" is of great medico-legal importance. It serves for the differentiation of human and animal blood, for which a small drop suffices It is also employed in detecting adulterations (horse-meat in sausage, etc) In the study of phylogenesis it is a valuable aid particularly in teaching the natural relationships of animals.

make the application general, if an animal is injected with substances foreign to its species (*antigen*), *e. g.*, albumin, animal cells, bacteria, toxin, *antibodies* or *immune substances* (precipitins, hemolysins, agglutinins, antitoxins) are formed in the injected animal.

Binding of antigens (toxin, bacteria, etc.) by the immune substances (antitoxin, bacteriolysin, etc.) results from combination or a sort of neutralization which may be compared to the neutralization of an acid by a base. P. Ehrlich* was the first to study this neutralization quantitatively and showed in the case of diphtheria toxin and its antitoxin, that the saturation did not occur as in the case of a strong acid, *e.g.*, HCl, and a strong base, *e.g.*, KOH, but that the diphtheria toxin must consist of a mixture of more or less acid toxins. We reach this conclusion, not only from the course of the saturation curve, but also from a study of the different poisonous actions possessed by the individual saturation fractions. Though, *e.g.*, the largest part of the diphtheria toxin has an acute toxic action, there is a particular fraction, the toxon, which, after two or three weeks, produces paralysis of the extremities that are quite foreign to the toxin. In different cases various indicators are used as a *sign* of the *union between antigen* and *immune substances*. In the case of *toxin-antitoxin* [1] we are reduced to the biological proof by animal experiments; the reduction in the toxicity of the mixtures is determined from the toxic action remaining in them. In the case of *hemolysins*, the ability to dissolve red blood cells more or less completely is used as a sign. *Precipitins* are recognized by testing the antigen against various dilutions and determining the greatest dilution at which turbidity can still be recognized. If, *e.g.*, a rabbit has been injected with goat serum a substance develops in the rabbit which precipitates goat serum. If we add to goat-rabbit serum which has been placed in a row of test tubes goat serum in a dilution 1/100, 1/1000, 1/10000, etc., we shall find a dilution at which merely turbidity occurs. In a similar manner *agglutinins* are tested (in this instance the immune serum is diluted).

Since the nomenclature is not uniform, a table of the terms in common use is given here.

Agglutinins change bacteria so that they may even be precipitated by alkali salts (see antigen).

Amboceptor, see hemolysin.

Antigens, foreign substances (bacteria, proteins, toxins, etc.) against which specific antisubstances (antibodies) are developed by an animal injected with them (agglutinins, precipitins, antitoxins, etc.)

Antibodies, immune bodies.

Antitoxin, specific antibodies which neutralize toxins.

End piece, see hemolysin.

[1] [Jerome Alexander observed in the ultramicroscope the mutual coagulation of diphtheria toxin and antitoxin and tetanus toxin and antitoxin. Diphtheria

Hemolysins dissolve red blood corpuscles. Two substances are usually required for hemolysis. One is specific, the real antibody, and is called *amboceptor*. The other occurs in every serum and is *complement*. Complement consists of two parts, one of which, the *middle piece*, is precipitated with the globulin, the *end piece* remains with the albumin of the serum. Only when both are united does complement act According to H SACHS, OMORYKOW and RITZ there is an additional "*third component*," quite heat stable. According to P. SCHMIDT complement is a single substance of which a portion is adsorbed by globulin when it is precipitated.

Complement, see hemolysin.

Lysins cause solution. Bacteriolysins dissolve bacteria, hemolysins dissolve red blood corpuscles.

Precipitins flocculate albumin.

Toxins, poisons which produce antitoxins when injected.

The Nature of Antigens and Immune Bodies.

The substances involved in immunity reactions are all dissolved or suspended *colloids*. There is, therefore, a particular reason for studying these questions from the standpoint of colloid investigation [1]

So far it has been impossible to produce immune bodies by means of a crystalloid, a foreign colloid (antigen) has always been required

The proof of the *colloid character* of antigens and immune bodies has been demonstrated in numerous cases. Upon dialysis, they do not pass through a dialyzing membrane; the diffusibility of diphtheria toxin and tetanolysin and their antitoxin are indicative of a particle magnitude of the same order as hemoglobin (Sv. ARRHENIUS) Ultrafiltration of diphtheria toxin, toxon and antitoxin and anti-rennin gave similar results (H. BECHHOLD). The hemolytic complement of guinea-pig serum is inactivated by shaking with the formation of a precipitate (M. JACOBY and A. SCHUTZE). This indicates a concentration at the boundary of fluid/air, as in the case of albumin and other colloids. The observation of W. BILTZ, H. MUCH and C. SIEBERT that a bactericidal horse serum loses its bactericidal activity upon shaking is to be ascribed to a similar phenomenon.[2]

---

[1] We may mention the following papers which treat Immunity with particular reference to the standpoint of colloid chemistry:

K. LANDSTEINER, Die Theorien der Antikorperbildung, Wiener Klin Wochenschr. **22**, Nr. 47 (1909).

Idem., Kolloide u Lipoide in d. Immunitätslehre im Handbuch d. Pathogenen microorganism VON KOLLE u Wassermann, Bd II (1913).

O. PORGES, im Handb. d. Technik u Methodik d Immunitätsforschung, Bd. II, Lief. 2 (Jena, 1909).

H. ZANGGER, Vierteljahrsschr. d Naturf-Ges. in Zurich, 1908, 408-455.

[2] It might be claimed that these substances, which it is impossible to prepare in pure form, are not in themselves colloids, but that they are adsorbed by the proteins simultaneously present in the solution and thus simulate what colloid character they exhibit. For the correctness of this view no evidence has hitherto been presented

It is held by one small group of investigators that *antigens* are lipoids or lipoid-albumin compounds. Since the part taken by lipoids in many immunity reactions is not definitely settled, it is impossible as yet to determine the general correctness of this view. At any rate it has not as yet been possible to immunize with the lipoids chemically known.

Since our knowledge concerning the chemical composition of normal proteins is still meager, what we know about the proteins of immune bodies cannot be more ample. According to Kraschnax *dysentery toxin* is acid. By ultrafiltration, he prepared water insoluble acid dysentery-toxin which was nearly atoxic, though the salt obtained by dissolving the acid in an alkaline carbonate possessed the poisonous properties of the toxin. The experiments of Fr. Obermayer and E. P. Pick* indicate that the aromatic nucleus in the antigen is of great importance for the development and character of the antibodies.

Antibodies are universally regarded as albuminous.

Before we discuss *details*, let us indicate a great misunderstanding which at the time gave rise to heated discussions and clouded the issues. The quantitative relations in which the substance in question enters into reaction (toxins with their antitoxins, bacteria with their agglutinins, etc.) have great similarity to *adsorption curves* (W. Biltz) and to the *neutralization curves* of certain weak acids and bases (Sv. Arrhenius). These investigators laid great stress on this fact and believed that they had thus discovered the nature and the course of the immunity reactions in question. P. Ehrlich raised the weighty objection, that the reaction is *specific*, and that the poisons are very *complex:* diphtheria toxin is detoxicated *only* by diphtheria antitoxin; typhoid bacilli are precipitated only by typhoid agglutinin. There is no doubt that these specific processes cannot be explained by what we call colloid-chemical reactions (see H. Bechhold*). We must conceive of the process as occurring in two stages, and we must emphasize that this sharp distinction does not obtain in every case.

First Stage: The two colloids, toxin and antitoxin, bacterium and agglutinin, unite in accordance with the laws *governing other colloids,* *e.g.,* fiber and dye, and the *specific* substances react on one another and it is still an open question whether we must represent these reactions as chemical or catalytic.

Second Stage. The colloidal product of the reaction shows physical properties which distinguishes it from the reacting substances, *e.g.,* it precipitates.

We cannot enter here into the question of specific combination.

A. The Distribution of Immune Substances Between Suspensions and Solvent.

Bacteria and blood corpuscles form suspensions which to a greater or less extent are able to attract to themselves immune substances. It is fortunate for the study of these phenomena that many experiments have been preformed upon the adsorption of inorganic suspensions (kaolin, charcoal, ferric hydroxid gel, etc) from solutions of known composition. For comparison many investigators have performed appropriate experiments on toxins and immune substances.

Adsorption by Means of Inorganic Suspensions and Hydrogels. A sign of adsorption is a strong withdrawal of a dissolved substance from dilute solutions and a *relatively smaller* withdrawal from such as are more concentrated. This requires extensive *quantitative* investigation with solutions of different concentration Unfortunately, there are but few such experiments published. It may, however, be deduced from the results of some of these experiments that an adsorption curve is actually involved

Even W Roux and Yersin* found that calcium phosphate, aluminum hydroxid and bone ·black removed some poison from a solution of diphtheria toxin, but that the solution was never entirely detoxicated. W. Biltz, H. Much and C Siebert* shook gels of iron oxid, chromium oxid and zirconium oxid, among others, with tetanus and diphtheria toxin, tetanolysin and a bactericidal horse serum. They determined a diminution in the activity of the respective solutions, and that for the same quantity of hydrogel, the diminution by activity was frequently more marked for dilute than for concentrated solutions. Occasionally complete fixation or destruction occurred, e.g., in the case of typhoid agglutinin. H Bechhold*[4] found that arachnolysin and staphylolysin were never completely removed from solution by formol-gelatin or cellulose. K. Landsteiner and his pupils shook tetanus toxin with kaolin, protagon, cholesterin, palmitic acid, stearic acid and lecithin, a poisonous residuum was always discovered in the solution

Since *complement* may be removed from a solution by various suspensions (for literature see H. Sachs), a mechanical adsorption is probable.

Specific Adsorption.

Glancing at the entire literature on this question, we are confronted with the great difference in adsorption capacity of the adsorbents as well as of the adsorbed substances Although tetanus toxin is well adsorbed by kaolin, protagon, cholesterin, palmitic acid, stearic acid, and lecithin, only very little of it is taken up by cetyl alcohol, casein, coagulated serum albumin, and starches (K. LAND-STEINER and A BOTTERI*). Arachnolysin is adsorbed more strongly by glacial acetic acid collodion than by formol-gelatin, glacial acetic acid collodion adsorbs rennin very strongly, but adsorbs practically none of a serum containing anti-rennin (H. BECHHOLD*4) Silicic acid and barium sulphate fix complement which, however, is also fixed by kaolin to a lesser extent (E HAILER*).

In view of these specific influences, L. JACQUÉ and E. ZUNZ* undertook extensive experiments upon the adsorption of antigens and antibodies by inorganic suspensions They concluded, as had previously been shown by E. ZUNZ* that differences in surface tension were not alone determinative for adsorption. They found, e.g., that bone black strongly adsorbed diphtheria toxin as well as antitoxin, though neither was adsorbed by wood charcoal, diatomaceous earth, talc, kaolin or clay. Nevertheless kaolin and clay adsorb tetanolysin. Bone black, a good adsorbent for diphtheria antitoxin, does not adsorb the antitoxin of tetanolysin or cobra hemolysin.

Reversibility. A purely mechanical adsorption demands that the process be completely reversible. This occurs in the case of the slightest adsorptions of immune bodies by unorganized suspensions. W. BILTZ, H MUCH and C SIEBERT* have already called attention to the fact that the adsorption of their antigens by hydrogels was only slightly reversible. Only to this extent was J. BORDET's* comparison of immune reactions to the dyeing of fiber with dyes appropriate This irreversibility has its analogies in the adsorption of numerous other known substances in which we assume that secondary changes occur as a result of the concentration at the surface; some of these changes are chemical, e.g., the adsorption of crystal violet and of rennin by bone black.

Of great interest are the observations of L. JACQUÉ and E ZUNZ* illustrating the competing action of several adsorbents for a single substance. They found that the adsorption of diphtheria toxin by bone black was reversible in the body but irreversible in vitro [probably because of protective substances. Tr.]. The adsorption of diphtheria *antitoxin* is, on the contrary, irreversible in the body and reversible in vitro. Serum albumin may prevent the adsorption of diphtheria toxin and antitoxin by bone black.

Adsorption by Organized Suspensions.

If agglutinin is added to bacteria, or hemolysin to blood corpuscles with the same quantity of the suspension, proportionately more agglutinin or hemolysin will be combined from a dilute solution than from a solution that is concentrated. EISENBERG and VOLK* demonstrated this for typhoid bacilli and cholera vibrios and Sv. ARRHENIUS* and his co-workers for hemolysins (see also G. DREYER, J SHOLTO and C DOUGLAS*).

This is illustrated by a table (after EISENBERG and VOLK) showing the combination of agglutinin with a uniform quantity of typhoid bacilli and increasingly concentrated agglutinin solutions.

Agglutinin fixed by the bacteria	Agglutinin free in the solution
2	0
20	0
40	0
180	20
340	60
1,500	500
6,500	3500
11,000	9000

The course is entirely that of an adsorption curve.

Cases also occur, according to the investigations of G. DREYER, J. SHOLTO and C DOUGLAS* in which, after exceeding a certain maximum, less and less agglutinin is taken up by the bacteria, in spite of greater concentration of the agglutinin, typical "abnormal adsorption."

It may be mentioned, moreover, concentrated salt solutions interfere with the fixation of agglutinin (until now this had been demonstrated only for blood corpuscles). (K. LANDSTEINER and St. WELECK.) Analogous to this is an observation of W. BILTZ,*[3] according to which the addition of salt interferes with the adsorption of proteins by inorganic colloids [1]

As has been stated elsewhere, *hemolysis* with immune sera occurs through the interaction of two components; *amboceptor* is bound by the blood corpuscles and it causes the fixation of the *complement* which accomplishes the hemolysis. This is obviously very similar to what occurs with mordant and dye, the dye is fixed to the fiber by means of the mordant. K LANDSTEINER and N. JAGIČ* have to a certain extent devised a model for the process, as amboceptor they use silicic acid hydrosol, as complement active serum or lecithin

Silicic acid precipitates with blood corpuscles as well as with lecithin; it thus links together blood corpuscles and lecithin, concentrating

---

[1] In my opinion it is chiefly *globulin* which has been strongly adsorbed in these experiments, since the final portion of globulin is separated very slowly from dialyzed serum.

the lecithin on the surface of the blood corpuscles. It is very probable, as assumed by the investigators mentioned, that lecithin in this instance acts as a solvent for the lipoid membrane of the blood corpuscles. Numerous similar models in which complement was replaced by lipoid were subsequently devised.

Reversibility. The combination of agglutinin with bacteria and red blood corpuscles is partially reversible; it may be partially removed at a higher temperature by washing with physiological salt solution (K. LANDSTEINER, EISENBERG and VOLK).

This is deduced from an experiment of J. Joos.[*] He mixed typhoid bacilli bearing agglutinin with untreated typhoid bacilli, and all the bacilli became agglutinated. There must have been a withdrawal of agglutinin from the typhoid bacilli which had been treated. In a similar way, J. MORGENROTH[*1] demonstrated that the combination of *amboceptor* and red blood corpuscle is partially reversible. Reversibility within the organism, where numerous varieties of cells occur, is of great practical importance.

B. The Distribution of Immune Substances Between Dissolved Colloids and Solvent.

The colloid-chemical theories regarding the combination of toxin and antitoxin are tacitly based upon the assumption that toxin and antitoxin behave like a suspension or a hydrogel; they premise that surfaces occur, upon which, for instance, the toxin may concentrate in accordance with the laws of adsorption. Theoretical basis for this assumption is lacking. Very little is known concerning the fixation of crystalloids and of hydrosols by *hydrosols*, when no precipitate occurs. There are, at present, two methods of attacking the problem. By means of ultrafiltration, H. BECHHOLD[*] has shown that the combination of methylene-blue with serum albumin satisfies the conditions of an adsorption (see p. 25). L. MICHAELIS and P. ROSA have used the osmotic compensation method in order to determine the kind of combination in which sugar, Ca, etc., are fixed in the blood. Both methods are recent and had not previously been utilized in the solution of this problem. On this account I consider it unprofitable to discuss at present the manner in which toxin and antitoxin are combined.

It may be mentioned that the toxin-antitoxin combination is incompletely reversible in part and in part irreversible. P. EHRLICH and his pupils demonstrated by numerous biological investigations, that the combination between diphtheria toxin and its antitoxin rapidly became irreversible.

The relations between *precipitin* and *precipitable substance* is somewhat more obvious   Inasmuch as the two dissolved colloids yield a precipitate when mixed in suitable proportion, we can form a judgment concerning the proportionate quantities that combine. However, this has regard for the composition *after* precipitation.   According to E. von Dungern* the precipitate binds much more precipitin than is required to cause complete precipitation.   It is still a question whether this combination existed in the solution.

C. Precipitation of Dissolved Colloids and Organized Suspensions,

Serum containing *precipitin*, for instance, goat-rabbit serum, gives a precipitate with its antigen (goat serum)   The serum is precipitated by the *precipitin* just as it would be *by an inorganic hydrosol or an acid protein* (histone), U. Friedemann and H. Friedenthal* (see p. 157)   The precipitation occurs best in the presence of an optimum mass proportion between precipitin and precipitable substance; excess of precipitable substance interferes with the precipitation.   A precipitation, according to M Neisser,* occurs also in salt-free solution (which contains no globulin) but the precipitation zone differs from that in a solution containing salt.

Though the mutual precipitation of two amphoteric colloids depends on the hydrogen ion concentration (see p. 147), *specific* precipitations (this applies to precipitins and agglutinins) are largely independent of it (L Michaelis and Davidsohn).   The electric charge of the components plays a very subordinate part in these precipitations.

The plant toxins, ricin (from the seeds of varieties of castor bean) and abrin (from jequirity seeds) have a similar precipitating effect upon albumin.

The conditions in the case of organized bacterial albumin are similar to (but not identical with) those of serum albumin.   If an animal (*e.g.*, a rabbit) is injected with bacteria (for instance, typhoid bacilli) there develops in its blood an agglutinin which causes typhoid bacilli in a test tube to precipitate.[1]   Agglutinin forms a compound, with the (actual) albuminous capsule of the bacteria, so that these behave as though they were changed from a hydrophile to a hydrophobe suspension.   Precipitation occurs only in water containing salt.[2]   Though a suspension of bacteria is unchanged by

---

[1] This phenomenon was first observed by Gruber and Durham.   Widal was the first to use it for diagnosis, and since, as the *Gruber-Widal Reaction*, it is employed in the diagnosis of typhoid, paratyphoid, dysentery, etc.

[2] According to U. Friedemann it is possible to obtain agglutination in a salt-free solution, though this has nothing in common with *specific* agglutination   The resemblance to the precipitins is, in this respect, only a superficial one.

dilute alkali salts, these salts cause a precipitation of agglutinated bacteria as they would a suspension of kaolin or mastic. This was demonstrated by H. Bechhold[3] as well as M. Neisser and U. Friedemann[4], and practically confirmed by B. H. Buxton P. Shaffer and O. Teague[5], as well as by B. H. Buxton and A. H. Rahe[6].

Capsulated bacteria possess, in their mucous capsules, a natural protective colloid and accordingly, they are not agglutinated by immune serum even in suspensions containing salt. O. Porges showed that if the mucous capsules were removed by gently heating them with dilute hydrochloric acid, even capsulated bacteria were agglutinated by immune sera.

As in the case of the precipitins, a certain quantitative relationship between bacteria and agglutinating serum is required for precipitation. But in this instance, there are certain irregularities as regards native and heated sera.

This phenomenon also has its analogue in the precipitation of unorganized suspensions in the presence of protective colloid. Table I (see below) illustrates the agglutination of bacteria by diluted immune serum. Table II illustrates the precipitation of a mastic suspension by $Al_2(SO_4)_3$ in the presence of leech extract as a protective colloid.

These "irregular series" (see p. 84) frequently occur in the precipitation of suspensions by ferric chloride, aluminium chloride and certain dyes. They are explained by the fact that the hydrolytically split iron oxid hydrosol, etc., functions as a "protective colloid," and in certain proportions interferes with the precipitation. If still another protective colloid (gelatin, leech extract, etc.) is added, the circumstances are still further complicated as shown by Table II.

TABLE I	TABLE II.
Agglutination of typhoid bacilli with very dilute immune serum. (After Eisenberg and Volk.)	Precipitation of mastic suspension by 0.0002 cc. $\frac{n}{1}$ $Al_2(SO_4)_3$ in the presence of leech extract as protective colloid. (After M. Neisser and U. Friedemann, and H. Bechhold.)

Dilution of the serum	Appearance after 2 hours.	Dilution of leech extract.	Appearance after 24 hours.
		c.c.	
1/100	No agglutination	0.1	No precipitation
1/1000	Almost complete agglutination	0.03	Almost complete precipitation
1/25000	Trace	0.01	No precipitation
1/30000	Heavy flocks	0.001	No precipitation
1/15000	No agglutination	0.001	Complete precipitation

Since bacteria, like other proteins, may be precipitated by acids without previous treatment with agglutinating serum, L. MICHAELIS and BENIASCH tested different groups of bacteria (typhoid, paratyphoid, colon, etc.) to determine whether the result depended on the H ion concentration. They found that different concentrations of H ions were necessary for the precipitation of different groups of bacteria. The discoverers based on this fact, a method for distinguishing certain bacterial groups. It is still a question whether the procedure is practical either alone or in combination with agglutinating serum (see S GALITZER).

Blood corpuscles, resembling bacteria, behave like a hydrophile suspension whose surface is so changed by various agglutinins that they flock out. I am inclined to believe that a true *glueing* together occurs more frequently with blood corpuscles than with bacteria

From our previous experiments, we see that colloids and suspensions are precipitated not only by electrolytes but also *by colloids of opposite charge*. It must therefore be possible to agglutinate organized suspensions as bacteria and blood corpuscles by suitable hydrosols. Experiments with hydrosols of iron, zirconium, thorium oxid and silicic acid [1] (W BILTZ, H. MUCH and C. SIEBERT*, also K. LANDSTEINER and N JAGIČ*, GIRARD-MANGIN and V. HENRI*) confirm this assumption and show that as with other colloid precipitations in salt solutions, an optimum proportion between the two colloids must exist, or no precipitation will occur.

It should be emphasized that the combination of bacteria or blood corpuscles and inorganic hydrosols is *irreversible* (in contradistinction to the agglutinin combination).

Blood corpuscles differ very greatly in one respect from bacteria. Though the latter migrate to the anode showing their negative charge, blood corpuscles are more amphoteric. As a result of this, they are precipitated by negative hydrosols (arsenic tri-sulphid, silicic acid, etc.) L. HIRSHFELD*[2]. A very important observation is that of L. HIRSHFELD, that the agglutination of blood corpuscles of different animals by zinc nitrate follows the same order of precipitability as their agglutination by agglutinating sera and abrin.

Ricin and *abrin* also agglutinate blood corpuscles, obviously, because they precipitate their albumin.

From our entire exposition, it is evident, that the adsorption of the agglutinating substance and the agglutination are two separate processes which, in their principle, have nothing in common. The agglutinin changes the bacteria or erythrocytes, making them agglutinable;

[1] Colloidal silicic acid agglutinates in much greater dilution than the crystalloidal.

the electrolyte, which itself is not adsorbed, agglutinates or flocks them out.[1] It is therefore obvious that an electrolyte which changes the cells may, nevertheless, without being adsorbed, agglutinate them. According to J. DUNIN-BORKOWSKI*, red blood corpuscles are agglutinated by FeCl₃, though it is not combined with them.

Electric Charge, H and OH Ions.

Numerous attempts have been made to determine the electric charge of antigens and immune substances by cataphoresis (K LANDSTEINER and Wo. PAULI*, C. N FIELD and O. TEAGUE*. It is so small, however, that in my opinion it cannot be definitely recognized since traces of H or OH ions may cause a reversal of charge (see BECHHOLD*[10])

This also applies to the results of exhaustive adsorption experiments with adsorbents of opposite electric charge, namely, the experiments carried out by EDGAR ZUNZ with electro-osmotically purified silicic acid, aluminium hydroxid, kaolin, diatomaceous earth, talc, and clay upon toxins and antitoxins. With K. LANDSTEINER and W. PAULI it is well to regard antigens and antibodies as amphoteric electrolytes

The difference between bacteria and bacteria bearing agglutinin is clearly demonstrated (H BECHHOLD*[1], M. NEISSER and U. FRIEDEMANN*). Though the former (typhoid, dysentery) migrate to the anode, the latter lose their charge on account of the agglutinin and precipitate between the electrodes.

More characteristic than electrical migration is the behavior of toxins, antigens and immune bodies to acids and alkalis.[2] From our standpoint, only very weak dilutions of H and OH are considered from such as cause no irreversible destruction in the substances affected. Acidity diminishes the toxicity of some toxins, but it is restored by neutralizing them. KIRSCHBAUM isolated a nontoxic dysentery toxin by ultrafiltration and precipitation with acids, it dissolved in alkalis and forms a toxic salt-like combination. An observation made by J. MORGENROTH *[2] points to the occurrence of a salt-like combination of cobra hemolysin and also of cobra neurotoxin; these neutral toxins, although colloids, diffuse through an animal membrane into a solution containing hydrochloric acid. Cobra venom may be recovered from crystalloid cobra venom salt by neutralizing it, yet it gradually goes into the colloidal state as I

---

[1] P. SCHMIDT assumes an additional phase, modification of the bacteria by agglutinin, adsorption of globulin by modified bacteria, flocculation by electrolytes.

[2] Only great dilutions of H and OH are here considered, such as do not cause an irreversible change in the material.

have inferred from the following experiments of J. MORGENROTH and D. PANE *[6]

I wish to call attention to one other property which is strongly suggestive of colloids. J. MORGENROTH and D PANE* heated cobra venom in $n/20$ HCl solution and determined its hemolytic action immediately after cooling and neutralization. The hemolytic activity induced by lecithin was greatly diminished but gradually (after hours or days) resumed its original strength. It seems reasonable to regard the gradual restoration of toxicity as phenomena of "maturation" since the particles of the molecular dispersed cobra hemolysin, gradually unite to larger agglomerations and thus acquire greater adsorptive capacity.

Colloid chemistry offers numerous similar examples; to mention only the *aging* of dye solutions (hemotoxylin) which must occur previous to its utilization in histological stains. The same interpretation applies to the anologous observation upon the *neurotoxin* of cobra venom.

As a rule the union of antigen and immune substances is inhibited both by H and by OH ions   Just as H and OH ions may break down the union of toxin and antitoxin so may they dissolve the bonds holding agglutinin to its substrate (HAHN and R. TROMMSDORF), or either abrin or amboceptor to blood corpuscles.

The influence of reaction on the action of hemolytic sera is told in the researches of S ABRAMOW, HECKER, L. VON LIEBERMANN, P. RONDONI, H. SACHS and ALTMANN, L. MICHAELIS and SKWIRSKY (see P. RONDONI* for bibliography).

Under certain conditions hemolysis is hastened by slight acidity and retarded by larger quantities of acids or by alkalis.

The inhibiting action of alkali and to a less definite degree, of acid, is evident in antigen-antibody combinations, as is revealed by *complement deviation* (see p. 207). Its significance is also evident in the WASSERMANN reaction.

Addition of 1/1000 to 1/3200 normal NaOH may inhibit the reaction in a strongly positive serum; similarly, a negatively reacting (luetic serum) may give a strongly positive reaction after the addition of 1/1000 to 1/2000 HCl (H. SACHS and ALTMANN)

The following findings favor the view that the physical fixation of *amboceptor* by blood corpuscles is influenced by the reaction. By means of alkali, the blood corpuscles may be prevented from combining with the amboceptor, on the other hand amboceptor-laden blood corpuscles may be deprived of amboceptor by alkalis, and the amboceptor may be recovered in an active condition. The facts for acids are not so obvious.

Complement Fixation and the Wassermann Reaction.

A mixture of antigen and immune substance (*e.g.*, goat serum + goat-rabbit serum) has the property of binding complement. This is recognized by the following: if complement is added to a suspension of red blood corpuscles + amboceptor, hemolysis occurs. If the complement has previously been mixed with antigen + immune substance and we then add the entire mixture to the blood corpuscles + amboceptor, no hemolysis occurs.

Complement			Complement
+			+
Amboceptor	Amboceptor	Amboceptor +	Antigen
+	+	+	+
Erythrocytes	Erythrocytes	Erythrocytes	Immune substance
Hemolysis	No Hemolysis	No Hemolysis	

This phenomenon, which is called *complement fixation* or *complement deviation*, was discovered by O. Gengou and Bordet. It has acquired great practical significance by its utilization for the recognition of antigen by M. Neisser and H. Sachs (one billionth c.c. of human blood may be recognized by complement deviation) and also indirectly, through a reaction analogous to the Wassermann reaction for the recognition of luetic infection.

A mixture of antigen and immune serum may give a precipitate, though only when mixed in definite proportions, otherwise this does not occur. Complement fixation occurs regardless of the occurrence of a precipitation. Since complement is easily adsorbed by many colloids and suspensions, it was natural to suppose that the precipitate of antigen and immune substances was the fixing agent. This view is held especially by G. Friedemann who attributes to euglobulin the complement binding power of the immune serum. The investigations of Dean are of great interest to students of colloid chemistry. According to these investigations, much complement is bound when there is a slowly developing turbidity and but little when turbidity develops rapidly. From this aspect a definite development of surface tension favors binding of the complement. Though it is probable that binding of complement depends on a physical adsorption of the visible or invisible precipitate, its mechanism requires further elucidation. The objection that the fixation may occur even without the appearance of a precipitate cannot definitely be proven. We know that albumin particles may aggregate into larger particles without a precipitation, provided the excess of one of the precipitate-forming colloids acts as a protective colloid. On the other hand, it has not yet really been demonstrated that a physical fixation and not an irreversible chemical change occurs in complement fixation. Therefore, in what category complement fixation by means of antigen plus immune substance is to be placed, is still an open question.

Wassermann Reaction.

Complement fixation is much more obvious in the Wassermann reaction. When A. WASSERMANN began his studies, he started with the assumption that extract of spirochæte (as antigen) + luetic serum (as immune substance) must fix complement. It was very soon evident, that spirochæte extract could be replaced by numerous lipoid suspensions:—by lecithin (O. PORGES and MAIER), by sodium glycocholate (LEVADITI and YAMANOUCHI), vaseline (FLEISCHMANN), by sodium oleate (H SACHS and ALTMANN), sodium palmitate and stearate (P. HESSBERG), potato extract and emulsion of shellac (MUNK) As ELIAS, O. NEUBAUER, O. PORGES and SALOMON showed, these hydrophile lipoids give precipitates with the globulin of luetic sera which fix complement.[1]

The parallelism between precipitation reaction and complement fixation is very suggestive of a colloid phenomenon It would be a convincing proof that complement fixation in the Wassermann reaction was a surface phenomenon, if it could be demonstrated that the reaction did not occur in the absence of a precipitation. This proof I gather from an observation of H SACHS and P RONDONI. They found that complement fixation by an alcoholic extract of syphilitic livers[2] depended upon the manner of dilution with saline solution, diluting drop by drop, they obtained a fluid which bound complement strongly. If the extract is added rapidly to the saline solution, there occurs a weak complement fixation or none at all. By slowly adding drop by drop we obtain a *turbid* fluid, by rapid mixing a *clear* fluid. We have here two fluids, which in their ability to fix complement can be *distinguished only by the surfaces of the suspended lipoids* The observation of F MUNK also confirms this view that only *alcoholic* or *acetone* and not *ethereal* extracts or solutions of the above-mentioned lipoids are suitable for binding of complement

---

[1] The observations of these authors are very interesting They observed that even normal sera give precipitates with the lipoids, but that the range of precipitation is much broader with luetic sera and that the complement fixation presupposes an optimum mass relationship of lipoid and serum.

[2] Before it was discovered that the above-mentioned lipoids were suitable for the Wassermann reaction, extracts of syphilitic livers were employed.

P. HESSBERG observed that freshly prepared solution of sodium palmitate bound complement, but it *lost this property by repeated heating*. This change by means of repeated heating is a characteristic colloid property, which evidently is associated with a fragmentation of the particles, the more frequently gelatin, agar-agar, etc., are heated, the more difficult it is to solidify them. Unfortunately P. HESSBERG did not determine whether the repeatedly heated solution of sodium palmitate recovered, on long standing, its ability to fix complement.

ANAPHYLAXIS, DEFENSIVE FERMENTS, AND MEIO-STAGMIN REACTION.

Anaphylaxis.

If an animal (*e.g.*, a guinea pig) is injected with antigen (*e.g.*, horse serum) there are no sequelæ. If the injection is repeated after an interval of about 10 to 14 days there occur serious symptoms of poisoning (convulsions, rise of temperature and respiratory distress) which frequently terminate fatally in a few minutes (anaphylactic shock). This condition induced by the first injection of serum or bacteria is called anaphylaxis (induced defenselessness— the reverse of immunity). Human "serum sickness" is also a phenomenon of anaphylaxis which appears after the repeated injection of curative sera and manifests itself in erythemata, swelling of the lymph nodes and joints and moderate rises of temperature. Anaphylaxis is strongly specific, which means that it occurs only upon repeated injections of the same protein or the same strain of bacteria. The specificity is so absolute and the quantities required so minute, that like precipitin reactions, anaphylactic phenomena may be employed in distinguishing traces of human from animal blood or in detecting adulterations.

FRIEDBERGER and his coworkers were successful in preparing the anaphylactic poison (anaphylatoxin) outside the body, in vitro. If an animal (*e.g.*, a guinea pig) is injected with antigen (*e.g.*, horse serum) antibody appears in the blood after a time. FRIEDBERGER proceeded from this fact; he mixed antigen and antibody in a test tube and obtained a precipitate from the mixture. By digesting the precipitate with guinea-pig serum (which always contains complement) he obtained what he designated as *anaphylatoxin*.

Since peptones produce phenomena resembling anaphylactic shock it was thought that peptone-like products were split off, perhaps by fermentation in the interaction between antibodies and antigen.

This view, still held by FRIEDBERGER, regards the appearance of the anaphylactic poison as the result of a fermentation of antigen by the degradation action of complement resulting from antibody fixation.

It was a surprise to find that the anaphylatoxin might be prepared even without antibodies as when guinea-pig serum was digested with bacteria; and even by digestion with colloidal carbohydrates (agar, starches, starch paste, pectin and inulin).[1] [The work of VAUGHAN and NOVY on the protein poisoning should be mentioned as well as that of R. WEIL on the mechanism of anaphylaxis.   Tr.]

H SACHS and E. NATHAN demonstrated that the physical state of the poison-producing substances was a determining factor   They employed inulin as absorbent. This carbohydrate is practically insoluble in cold water though it forms a clear solution without pasting in warm water   Upon mixing guinea-pig serum with a 5 per cent *suspension* of inulin, a serum was obtained which produced the severest anaphylactic shock when injected into guinea pigs, though no toxic substance resulted from the mixture with inulin *solution.* Pastes have a very extensive surface development, consequently, anaphylatoxin is formed best with starch paste. H. SACHS and E. NATHAN find in these experiments decisive confirmation of the physical theory of anaphylaxis first proposed by H. SACHS and RITZ. According to them, antigen is not the mother substance of anaphylatoxin, which is not newly formed, but which exists preformed in normal serum. This poison becomes active by the adsorption (separation) of a substance as yet undetermined. In the case of artificial anaphylatoxins, bacteria and carbohydrates serve, in true anaphylaxis, the products of antigen and immune body act as adsorbents. The specificity of anaphylaxis is thus explained since only the specific antibody formed causes a precipitate with the antigen.

Protective Ferment.

The remarkable relation between immunity reactions and protective ferments should be mentioned here. E ABDERHALDEN considers under this term the ferments which destroy and render innocuous species-foreign proteins, entering the organism parentally. Since the connection between protective ferments and colloid research is still unestablished we shall merely refer to the work of E. ABDERHALDEN.[2]

[1] It is not yet definitely established that anaphylatoxin may be made by shaking inorganic suspension with normal guinea-pig serum.

[2] [D VAN SLYKE has thoroughly discredited the Abderhalden reaction with his nitrous acid method for the quantitative determination of amino acids. Harvey Lectures, 1915–16, p. 170, Lippincott, N Y. Tr.]

The Meiostagmin Reaction.

M. Ascoli and G. Izar found that substances which lower surface tension of the solution are formed in the reaction between antigens and immune bodies. He determined this with Traube's stalagmometer by counting the drops which formed from a measured quantity of fluid.[1] When, for instance, he mixed an extract of typhus bacilli with normal serum and with the serum of typhoid patients, 10 c.c. gave 58 drops in the former instance and 61 drops in the latter. M. Ascoli considers it to be a general reaction and has employed it in the serum diagnosis of various conditions (syphilis, tuberculosis, anchylostomiasis and echinococcus infection). It has not been generally introduced as a means clinical diagnosis of infectious disease since the technic is so precise that the differences are within the limit of error, but it has been more frequently employed in the detection of malignant growths. Two dilutions of the serum are prepared, one with water and the other with an equal quantity of tumor extract (recently Ascoli employed ricinoleic acid or linoleic acid, etc.). If the number of drops are larger in the latter mixture than in the former, there is a presumption that the serum is from a cancer patient.[2]

[1] Meiostagmin reaction = reaction of smaller sized drops.

[2] [E. P. Bernstein and Irving F. Simons, after critically reviewing the literature and their personal experience, have discarded th Meiostagmin reaction as useless clinically. Amer. Jour. Med. Sci., vol. 142, p. 862, *et seq.* Tr.]

An asterisk (*) after an author's name refers to a reference in the index of names.

PART III.

THE ORGANISM AS A COLLOID SYSTEM.

The Significance of the Colloidal Condition for the Organism.

RECENTLY, I read in a French magazine, a fantastic description of a visit to the Martians. They were pictured as men with iron faces, with a great bill replacing the nose; three glass eyes and joints and limbs of iron. Why did not the artist construct his people of a material actually found on that planet? If we assume that life exists on other planets and disregard the theory of panspermogenesis [1] accepted as probable by Sv. ARRHENIUS, *a priori* it is probable that life is associated with substances similar to those with which it is associated on our earth. One thing I can assert, *that whatever the material composition of such living beings may be, it must be colloidal in nature.*

Those iron Martians could no more exist than could crystallized life. What condition of matter, other than the colloidal, could adopt such changeable, such plastic shapes, and yet, when necessary, be in a position to maintain them.

An exchange of substance may occur in jellies as well as in a fluid; in the latter the least touch, an unintentioned movement, disturbs the result of diffusion and brings about the death of the system; the changes in a jelly are fixed as in a solid mass. Colloids may form permeable walls or membranes, whose permeability is regulated by the substances which pass through them; thus, for instance, the sulphates which are less important to the organism close the passages on themselves; the chlorids facilitate their own entrance.

Foods enter our digestive tract in colloidal condition, as albumin and starches. Made fluid and easily diffusible by the enzymes, they penetrate the organism in order to be fixed and again transformed into colloids. In that condition only are they retained by the organism and prevented from flowing away. Colloids, because of their

---

[1] According to this theory, it is conceivable that germs of life travel from one planet to another and that they develop there under favorable circumstances, so that, to a certain extent, one star infects another one with life.

surface development, unite the advantages of the solid condition with that of the fluid; observe for a moment a mountain climber, a fever patient, or a tree in the springtime, which is decked with leaves in four or five days. What enormous amounts of chemical energy are expended by the mountain climber in a few hours, what large quantities of protein are in a short time consumed by the fever patient, what large quantities of material are carried to and from the periphery of the tree. With the least loss of time the reserves must be mobilized and carried to the seat of war, the places where they are consumed. Such a rapid mobilization is unthinkable in the case of a solid crystalloid, with its small surface, a chemical process in a swollen colloid may only occupy minutes, whereas the same reaction in a shrunken colloid requires days.

How wonderful by means of *adsorption* is the action of *surface development as a regulative mechanism*. Luxus consumption of foods, salts, oxygen, etc., are excreted as quickly as possible by the colloid components of the body, but when the supply ceases, the amount given off becomes less and when there is a deficiency the organism tenaciously retains the last traces for its time of need.

Quantitatively, the substance most important for the organism is *water*; colloid and water are one in the organism, an organism without water is lifeless. We can imagine such an intimate and varying relation to water only in a colloid system, the process of *swelling*, the adsorption of water, and *shrinking* to complete dryness exhibit no leaps or sudden changes in condition. If we compare crystalloids with colloids, we shall see that something entirely new with very changed properties, a solid crystalloid precipitate, appears from a solution upon losing water. Such a system would be unable to maintain correctly the constantly oscillating water balance and the normal condition of swelling in the organism, or to act as an *accumulator* of large quantities of water, like muscle, and release it for use when necessary. Such a system could not, like a pen, *smooth out the irregular chemical impulses*, which the organism experiences as the result of physiological and pathological life processes, and which, after absorption, constantly restores its state of swelling to normal by means of secretion (kidney, skin, etc.).

We thus see that the processes which cause us to marvel at the wonderful adaptability of Nature rest upon the simple laws applicable to colloids. Thus it is that I am unable to imagine that the complicated and adaptive phenomena of Life could possibly be associated with any other than a colloidal system.

CHAPTER XIV.

METABOLISM AND THE DISTRIBUTION OF MATERIAL.

The Distribution of Water in the Normal Organism.

The earliest stages in the development of life are accompanied by powerful processes of swelling which soon reach a maximum, and then pass over into a shrinking, which becomes progressively greater, until death occurs. In the cases of plants, the struggle for water between seed and soil starts with germination (A. Müntz*). Growing and full-grown plants show a certain turgor, i.e., a fulness or tension like a distended rubber balloon, while a dying plant is withered and poor in water.

A three months' *human* fetus contains 94 per cent water; at birth the water content is from 69 to 66 per cent, in adult life 58 per cent.[1] I am not acquainted with any figures of the water content of the aged, but it is generally and with justice assumed, that in old age, the water content decreases; turgescence in general, and of the skin in particular, is obviously lost. The organism, taken as a whole, during its life evidently passes through the curves of swelling and shrinking of an inelastic gel. In individuals of the same species, the water content is probably fairly constant for the same period of life.

The water content of the individual portions of plants and of similar organs of different plants varies remarkably. Though jelly-like protoplasm contains from 60 to 90 per cent of water, the dry wall of ligneous cells takes up from 48 to 51 per cent, while the jelly-like membranes of nostocaceæ and palmellaceæ absorb as much as 200 per cent of water, according to Nägeli; on the other hand, cork membranes have hardly any swelling capacity at all.

The resistance offered to loss of water is exceptionally variable. It may be said, with certain exceptions, that plants are much more resistant than animals. Especially the lower forms of life, particularly the spores of bacteria, yeasts, algæ, mosses and seeds may bear almost complete dehydration without dying. Loss of water is often of great biological significance for plants. It makes spores and seeds less sensitive to changes of temperature; and in the case of some

---

[1] The greater water content of the individual organs of the *newborn* as contrasted with those of *adults* is especially evident from the tables of E. Bischoff.*

215

highei plants, the spreading of the seed pods upon drying leads to movements which serve to distribute the seeds   Best known is the "blooming," or the swelling of the "Jericho-rose."   Higher animals on the other hand are very sensitive to losses of water: frogs, according to KUNDE, may withstand a gradual loss of water up to 30 per cent, but, if they are rapidly dried, they perish when the loss is only 18 per cent.   In the latter case, there is evidently no time for an equalization in the distribution of the water.   Thirsting human beings also show great losses of water, though of course, there are no data as to the *lethal* point.   A. DURIG informs me that, after a forced march in hot weather, he lost 5 kg. of water.   The investigations of N. ZUNTZ and SCHUMBERG on marching soldiers, as well as those of N. ZUNTZ on mountain climbers, showed that exercising men lost water. Roughly measured, the water ingested after forced marches does not replace the water lost   We may say here, anticipating somewhat, what animal experiments of H. GERHARTZ* show, that the loss of water affected primarily the musculature and then the fluids circulating in the organs

Freezing (gefrieren)[1] has an effect on the organism similar to the withdrawal of water.   It was formerly believed that the formation of ice burst the cell walls or tore the protoplasm, and the damage from freezing was ascribed to these gross mechanical influences.   It was shown by the investigations of A. E. NAGELI, W. SACHS, H. MOLISCH, and MULLER-THURGAU that these views were false, that usually there was no formation of ice in the cell, but that the ice crystals grew between the cells in the intercellular spaces.   P. MATRUCHOT and MOLLIARD* studied plant cells and found that the phenomena observed in drying or plasmolysis resembled those induced by freezing (erfrieren).   H. W. FISCHER,*[1] as the result of exhaustive studies, reached the conclusion that the damage done to animals and plants by freezing them (gefrieren) was analogous to the partially irreversible changes produced in gels by glaciation.   He believes that the adsorption of electrolytes in particular is thus affected unfavorably.   If a solution of potato starch is frozen and then thawed out, the electrolytes may entirely dissolve again but the starch has become insoluble.   Frozen leaves present an analogous condition in that the chlorophyl is no longer retained.   In this valuable work he

---

[1] Freezing (erfrieren) and glaciation (gefrieren) must not be confused. A plant or an animal *freezes* if life processes cease by reason of the low temperature. This temperature depends upon the nature of the organisms involved, and in the case of warm-blooded individuals is usually far above zero, in the case of other organisms (seeds and spores), however, it may be far below zero (−200). *Glaciation* always means ice formation.

ows that the condition and age of protoplasm when frozen, *i.e.*, at
le lethal point, is similar to that observed by VAN BEMMELEN in the
ying of colloids, when the latter are frozen, they become optically
homogeneous, and their staining capacity changes.

For normal *functioning* there is an indispensable normal water
)ntent for every individual or-
inism and organ

The total water content of an
ganism gives us an idea of its
ater requirements; the water
)ntent of the individual organs
forms us about the *distribution*
water in the organism.

A clearer idea is obtained by
)serving the distribution of
ater in animals especially in
iammals. In Table III (see p.
[9), I have compiled the *water*
ntent of the different adult organs
om available data. Table II
). 218) shows the distribution
' the *total water content* (100
er cent) in the various organs.
have placed the proportionate
eights of the organs to the
)tal weight alongside for com-
arison. The data in Tables I
nd II show far-reaching differ-
nces (see especially Skin in
'able II), for which age and nu-
'itive condition are responsible.

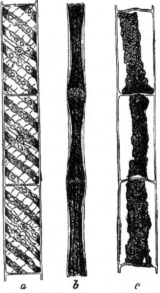

a   *b*   *c*

FIG 37 Spirogyra: *a*, before the experiment, *b*, frozen, *c*, after thawing
(From H Molisch.)

In healthy animals and men, there is a definite *swelling ratio* for
he individual organs, a dynamic equilibrium. The maximal varia-
on of normal *swelling*, more or less, is called *the swelling range* [1] It

---

[1] Definitions

Swelling capacity is the maximal capacity for absorbing water, expressed in
$$\frac{W \text{ (weight of water)}}{D \text{ (dry weight)}}.$$

Swelling is the water content of a gel or an organ expressed in
$$\frac{W}{D}.$$

Swelling range is the greatest variation in the capacity of an organ to absorb
ater under different conditions
$$\frac{\cdot\ W \text{ (maximal weight of water)} - W \text{ (minimal weight of water)}}{D}$$

A normal swelling range and an abnormal swelling range exist.

TABLE II

PERCENTAGE DISTRIBUTION OF WATER IN THE INDIVIDUAL ORGANS.

(Entire water in the organism = 100 per cent)

(After A Albu and C Neuberg,* Bischoff,* Engels * and A W Volkmann *)

	Human		Dog.	
	Distribution of total water in each organ	Weight of organs in per cent of body weight	Distribution of water in each organ	Weight of organs in per cent of body weight
Blood .	4 7—9	4 9	8 27	7
Fat ..	2 3	Newborn 13 5		
		Man 18 2		
		Woman 28 2		
Skin .	6 6—11 0	Newborn 11 3	11 58	16 11
		Man 6 9		
		Woman 5 7		
Viscera.				
Intestines .	3 2	Man 4 1	9 68	8 18
Liver	2 8	Woman 5 4	3 86	3 60
Lungs	2 4		2 83	2 36
Spleen	0 4			
Kidneys	0 6		1 01	0 85
Bony skeleton	9—12 5	Newborn 15 7-17 7	9 08	17 39
		Adult 15 9		
Muscles..	47 74—50 8	Newborn 22 9-23 5	47 74	42 84
		Man 41 8		
		Woman 35 8		
Nerve substance.				
Brain .	2 7	Newborn 12 2-15 8		
Spinal cord		Man 2 6	1 59	1 37
		Woman 2 7		
Remainder	11 0			

is very small for the skeleton, the blood, and the intestines, has a middle value for the viscera, and becomes higher for skin, muscles, and kidneys.

This was deduced especially from the experiments of ENGELS.* He kept dogs without food four days and determined the water content of various organs (normal animals).   Another series of dogs, after the same preliminary treatment, received an infusion into their jugular veins of 1160 gm. physiological salt solution (on the average). Three hours after the termination of the infusion, the animals were killed and the water content of the organs determined (water treated animals).

In the following table, the percentage of the water infused, that is, recovered from the individual organs, is shown in column A, and in column B is the percentage increase in weight of the several organs in terms of their own weight:

(Basis of the swelling range)

	A	B
Muscles	67 89	17 1
Skin	17 75	11 9
Liver	2 96	8 9
Intestine	2 25	3 0
Lungs	1 97	9 0
Blood	1 55	2 4
Kidneys	1 41	17 9
Brain	1 13	8 9
Uterus	0 28	10 0
Lost in bleeding	2 82	
	100 01	

TABLE III

WATER CONTENT OF VARIOUS HUMAN ORGANS IN PER CENT [1]

(After Albu-Neuberg,* Bischoff,* Halliburton,* Pribram,*1 Rumpf.*)

	Adult (normal).	Child (normal) N — New born 2 M — 2 months old	Adult (pathological)
Blood.	77 9—83	N 85	90 and more (Anemia) 75 5—83 9 (Nephritis) 73 2—66 5 (Diabetes)
Fat	29 9		
Viscera			
Intestines..	73 3—77	N 83 1 2 M 75 5	
Heart	79 2—80 2	N 83 3—93 1 2 M 80	79 2—80 4 (Nephritis)
Liver	68 3—79 8	N 80 5 2 M 73	68 5—87 3 (Nephritis)
Lung	78—79	N 82 6 2 M 79 4	
Spleen	75 8—86 1	N 78 4 2 M 77 7	90 6 (Nephritis)
Kidneys	77—83 7	N 85 7 2 M 81	84 8—88 2 (Nephritis)
Bony skeleton	22—34	N 32 3 2 M 62 3	
Muscles	73—75 7	N 81 8 2 M 71 7	
Nerve substance.			
Brain	75—82	N 89 3 2 M 89	80 9—83 (Nephritis)

[1] I have omitted the figures for skin, they vary for different authors between 31 9 and 73.9, because some have given the water content of skin deprived of fat and others that with the fat attached.

Since, in the dog, muscles constitute 42 82 per cent and skin 16.11 per cent of the total body weight, these organs under normal conditions actually store up, respectively, 47.74 per cent and 11 58 per cent of all the water in the body. As a result of their great swelling range, the two chief water excreting organs, the skin and kidneys, the *muscles*, most of all, are able to accumulate large quantities of water. In ENGEL's experiment they took up 2/3 of the water supplied.

If water is supplied to the organism, the blood, on account of its low swelling range, gives off the excess chiefly to the muscles and skin, it parts with some to the glands, chiefly the kidneys On this account, saline infusions after a severe loss of blood have usually only a temporary effect.[1] Muscles and skin behave like a reservoir, the blood, like a rigid pipe system, from which, if the pressure is sufficient, excess of water constantly flows through a small vent. In carrying out this wise arrangement, the organism utilizes the various swelling ranges of the organ colloids.

Though I have used the above picture of a rigid pipe system for the blood, it is not strictly accurate, for the blood has a small swelling range of its own, as we see from ENGEL's table. This may be attributed to the *fibrinogen*, as we learn from the following facts. The required data I have taken from E. ABDERHALDEN (pp. 592–593).[*1]

The water content of various animals is:

		Per mil
In the entire blood	.	749–824
Serum	..	. 902–926
Blood corpuscles	.	.. 604–633

From this we see that when the water content of serum increases 2.6 per cent (from the minimum), it reaches its maximum, and the blood corpuscles reach their maximum with an increase of 5 per cent. The entire blood on the contrary has a swelling range of 10 per cent There must therefore be something in the blood that swells especially well and the only possible substance is the fibrinogen.

Let us compare the maximal and minimal content of water distributed between serum, blood corpuscles, and the whole blood in the *identical animals*.

Max. = maximum water content among the various species of animals.

Min = minimum water content among the various species of animals.

---

[1] Attempts to hold the fluid in the vessels by the addition of colloids have been unsatisfactory. A more favorable result is obtained when 14 grams of salt and 10 grams of crystalline sodium carbonate are administered either intravenously or by rectum (J. J. HOGAN and M. H. FISCHER). It was accomplished through reducing the swelling of the other tissues by hypertonic saline and neutralization of acid by the alkali Cholera collapse, which results from the water deprivation by reason of diarrhœa, may be successfully combated by hypertonic saline infusions (ROGER). [W M Bayliss and M H Fischer have recommended the use of gum arabic solution, and it is being successfully employed at the front in the present war, see p 137. Tr.]

	Serum	Corpuscles	Entire blood
Cat	926⁰⁰ oo (max.)	624⁰ oo	795⁰ oo
Horse I.	902⁰⁰ oo (min.)	618⁰ oo	749⁰ oo (min.)
Sheep I	917⁰ oo	601⁰ oo (min.)	821⁰ oo
Rabbit . . .	925⁰ oo	633⁰ oo (max.)	817⁰ oo

The serum of the cat had a higher water content than that of the other animals experimented upon; the corpuscles also had a high water content, even though not the highest, the entire blood, however, is only a little above the average. For Horse I, serum and entire blood have minimum values and the corpuscles a low but by no means the lowest value. In the case of Sheep I, the entire blood reaches a maximum, whereas the blood corpuscles show a minimum, and the serum possesses a water content a little above the average. With the rabbit, there is a high water content in all portions. From this we learn that a substance possessing a great range of swelling exists in the whole blood, namely, the *fibrinogen*. We recognize further, that the elements of the blood possess a certain elasticity, which smoothes out the fluctuations in the water content, and which shows itself by a "*lag*" of the water plenitude or poverty in the various elements of the blood, depending on whether there is a supply or a withdrawal of water, a swelling or a shrinking.

The following swelling ranges are found for the various elements of the blood: fibrin > whole blood > corpuscles > serum. It would be desirable to have investigations of the water content of the different elements of the blood in the same animal before and after water has been given.

What is it then, that determines the water content or swelling of an organ? Undoubtedly each organ colloid has a definite *swelling capacity* and a definite *swelling range*. A priori, we may assume that the colloids of muscles swell more than those of the epidermis. Without doubt, the *structure* of the given colloid is also a factor. W. PFEFFER[*] (*loc. cit.* I, p 613) justly emphasizes the distinction between *water of swelling*, consequent upon the hydrophile state of the swelling substances and the *water of imbibition*, which is drawn up into the capillary interstices as into a sponge.[1]

E. PFLÜGER[*] believes that the swelling of protoplasm in its true sense, *i.e.*, of the assimilated (species-native) colloids of the cell is con-

---

[1] W. PFEFFER speaks it is true, of "molecular" water of imbibition or adherent water, and of "capillary" water of imbibition, yet he intends the same distinction that I have indicated above

stant. Only the swelling of the nonassimilated reserve substance is variable. This view, it seems to me, receives its chief support from the findings of H. W. FISCHER and P. JENSEN* on muscle, which is treated more thoroughly on page 291. According to their findings, water occurs in muscle in two phases. One has a constant value and is closely associated with the viability of muscle (conditioned by the integral muscle protoplasm). The other phase varies in the exercising muscle and is only loosely bound (water of swelling of the reserve material)

Besides these factors of swelling which are *inherent* in the organ colloids under consideration, there are others which are to a certain extent *impressed from without*. The natural salt content as well as the products of metabolism, especially the acids, are determinative of the swelling of a tissue. Acid formation in an organ (*e.g.*, CO_2 or lactic acid in active muscle, CO_2 in blood corpuscles) increases its swelling capacity If we observe that the potassium salts predominate in one organ, and in others, the sodium salts, or even that there is an accumulation of salts in a certain portion of a single cell, we may conclude from that alone, that the water content also depends upon such concentration Potassium salts increase swelling, Ca salts deplete (E. WIDMARK*), and according to R. CHIARI and JANUSCHKE inhibit exudation.

When the loss of water is very great (cholera, infant diarrhœas), there is an increase of potassium salts and phosphates in the urine. From this it may be assumed that Na salts replace the K salts of the muscles, and at the same time water is given off. According to E. PŘIBRAM,*[2] this occurs in order to protect more vital organs, especially the brain, from loss of water

Little is known concerning swelling from a biological point of view. On this account, an observation of H. PAUL* seems especially noteworthy. He pointed out in the case of *peat mosses* that the high moor sphagnum is able to absorb much more water than the low moor sphagnum. For example, sphagnum molluscum absorbs 27 times, and sphagnum platyphyllum absorbs 16 times its dry weight of water. In the same paper we find that the high moor sphagnum contains much more acid than the low moor sphagnum, and that the former are much more sensitive than the latter to the action of alkalis, lime and salt. From this it seems to me we may certainly infer that swelling of high moor sphagnum is greater than that of low moor sphagnum because of its greater acidity, and that the damage it suffers from salts, etc., may be attributed to the alteration in its normal condition of swelling.

We shall see that abnormal accumulation of acid in the tissues results in their swelling or edema. We recognize from this, that the dynamic balance of the swelling is dependent upon the normal course of the processes of assimilation and dissimilation. Conversely, pathological processes are always followed by an abnormal condition of swelling.

Pathology of Water Distribution.

In *pathological* conditions, the water content may have values very different from normal. The water in the blood rises to 90 per cent and more in severe anemias, and may fall to from 73.2 to 66.5 per cent in diabetes (see p. 219). Under other pathological conditions, organs may show abnormal swelling (see last column in Table III, p. 219).

With the active metabolism and formation of crystalloids, which occur in *fever*, there are alterations in swelling (thirst, dryness of the skin), the exact nature of which we do not as yet understand.

As a rule, there has been less attention paid to the study of the conditions in which the swelling of an organ is below normal. The injection of protoplasmic poisons (some heavy metal salts, strong acids) causes a coagulation of the organ albumen, which reduces to a greater or less extent its swelling capacity. I am still occupied with more exhaustive studies of these questions which are also touched upon in the chapter on *Necrosis*. It is too early to report the results.

Edema.

By *edema* we understand an abnormal collection of fluid in tissue or tissue spaces; if the fluid collects abnormally in a body cavity, we call it an *exudate* or hydrops

The view most generally accepted up to a few years ago was that edema occurred whenever the venous blood pressure, or more correctly, the difference between arterial and venous pressure was generally or locally raised, and the resistance of the vessel walls was diminished (JULIUS COHNHEIM, 1877). It is known that in heart disease and in nephritis, when the circulation is disturbed, that large portions of the body, especially the lower extremities, swell and become edematous The local inflammatory edema accompanying inflammation, insect bites or the injection of an irritating fluid (*e.g.*, diphtheria toxin) must also be considered.

The above explanation has some fascination, and it cannot be denied that it will continue to be invoked in explanation of certain points, especially since the observation of increase in the permeability of vessel walls cannot be avoided, when we see that even corpuscles

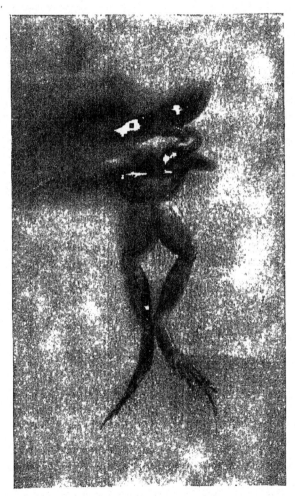

FIG 38.   The ligated leg (right) of the frog is edematous.
(From M. H Fischer)

Reproduced from Fischer's "Oedema and Nephritis," second edition, by permission of Messrs.
John Wiley & Sons, Inc.

pass through the walls. In general, however, it may be asserted that the above explanation has brought no advance to our understanding of edema. Histologists and physiologists have contributed an interminable amount of work without making any progress

A fundamental departure in the understanding of edema and its associated questions was made in 1907 by the investigations of an American, MARTIN H. FISCHER[1], who sought the cause of edema, not in the vessels, but in the tissues themselves, he attributes to the *edematous tissues* an increased swelling capacity. M. H. FISCHER's views were immediately contradicted and led to more experimental studies and scientific discussions than most biological theories. However, though we must now admit that M. H. FISCHER's views are too far reaching, it cannot be denied that he set up a very productive working hypothesis. We shall first state his theory and then discuss his opponents' views.

The most important experiment of M. H. FISCHER is the following: he ligatures the hind limb of a frog so that its circulation is cut

FIG. 39   Rabbit's kidneys: left normal, right experimentally edematous

off (Fig. 38) and places it in water so that the limbs are covered. The ligatured limb swells up and at the end of 2 or 3 days may be 2 or 3 times its original weight. If the frog is kept in a dry vessel, the ligatured limb dries up completely, and if it is cut off and placed in water, it swells up. Under these conditions the blood pressure or the increased permeability of the vessel walls cannot play any part in the development of the edema, but it is only the tissues, which swell more strongly under the circumstances mentioned. In the same manner, M. H. FISCHER was able to demonstrate the occurrence of edema in rabbits' *kidneys* (Fig. 39), and in the *liver* and *lungs* of

He was led to this by experiments of JACQUES LOEB, which showed that frogs muscles swelled more in acid and alkaline fluids than in neutral ones

sheep. These became edematous, not only if the veins were ligatured, but also if the artery was tied. Under the circumstances, an increased blood pressure as the result of congestion need not be considered. Indeed, all dead bodies or portions of them which certainly are without blood pressure swell up when immersed in water.

It was thus demonstrated that the development of edema depended upon the increased capacity of the tissues to swell, and the question then presented itself, *What change in the tissues permits the development of edema?*

An explanation was provided by the studies of F. HOFMEISTER, his pupils and successors, upon the swelling capacity of gelatin and related substances (see pp 67–68). We learned in that chapter that acids and alkalies increase swelling capacity, that other electrolytes in the order there mentioned, either favor or diminish swelling, while nonelectrolytes, as far as appropriate studies as yet show, have only slight influence. MARTIN H. FISCHER* (in collaboration with GERTRUDE MOORE) was able to demonstrate that the same laws governed the swelling capacity of fibrin, the swelling of frogs' muscles and the extirpated eyes of oxen and sheep This explanation presupposes no membrane or osmotic pressure; it permits an unstrained interpretation of processes which otherwise are explained with great difficulty in the case of animal cells unprovided with membranes.

The further question now presents itself, *What electrolytes are responsible for the altered swelling capacity of the tissues in edema?* We can no longer offer a single explanation, and we must study individual cases.

Edema fluid, the CO_2 of which has been removed, is acid to phenolphthalein; F. HOPPE-SEYLER found in it valeric, succinic, butyric and lactic acids. STRASSBURG and R. EWALD found that the CO_2 content of edema fluid was greatly in excess of that of venous blood[1] Of especial value is the discovery by F. ARAKI and H. ZILLESSEN that any lack of oxygen is followed by an excessive production of acid, though this fact may not be demonstrable by indicators.

One answer is thus given to the question asked above. Increased acid production, one of the results of deficient oxygen, may cause the development of edema. Such a condition occurs in *circulatory disturbances* and in *cardiac insufficiency*, where edema is especially fre-

[1] I wish to point out that a certain contradiction is contained in the simultaneous presence of organic acids and increased CO_2. Possibly this may be attributed to the fact that various edema fluids have been examined and unjustified generalizations deduced. (The author.)

quent, it occurs also in *severe anemias* and in certain *cachexias*, starvation and scurvy. In *nephritics*, some substances recently discovered in the blood, may perhaps contribute to the inhibition of oxidation. *Cadaveric edema* is well known, as is the bloated appearance of drowned bodies. In the case of living animals, only the injection of excessive quantities of water or physiological salt solution are able to bring about edema. According to R. Magnus, this is readily accomplished by injecting salt solution into the blood vessels of dead animals. A dead frog may double its weight in from 36 to 48 hours if immersed in water.

The injection of certain *poisons* (especially lactic acid) results in an oxygen deficiency and thus brings about an excessive acid production. M. H. Fischer injected morphin, strychnin, cocain, arsenic and uranium nitrate into the dorsal lymph sac of frogs and thus produced an edema which disappeared if the frog was given an opportunity to excrete the poison.

Edema in the case of metal intoxications, especially in the case of arsenic, is well known to clinicians, and the great thirst and the diminution in the excretion of urine which occurs after morphin, ether and chloroform administration, may also be attributed to the deficiency of oxygen in the tissues, with concomitant absorption of water.

We have only referred to the development of edema by acids, and I wish to call attention to the fact that intense edema may be produced by alkalies. Subcutaneous injection of n 10 sodium hydrate results in severe edema.

If such substances produce edema as favor the swelling of gelatin, fibrin, etc., edema must be counteracted by electrolytes which reduce swelling. The correctness of this assumption was demonstrated by M. H. Fischer on the amputated leg of a frog. The addition of neutral salts diminished the swelling and acted in the same order that the cations and anions did in diminishing the swelling of fibrin. Nonelectrolytes, on the other hand, had no influence.

M. H. Fischer regards *glaucoma* as a typical example of a local edema. This is a disease of the eyes, of which the most characteristic symptom is very greatly increased tension, which produces hardness of the eyeball. The excruciating pains and loss of vision are mere consequences. The various explanations given in ophthalmological textbooks are quite unsatisfactory, whereas the experiments of M. H. Fischer are quite convincing. M. H. Fischer placed extirpated ox eyes[1] in water, to which so little acid had been added that it was imperceptible to taste. These eyes became stony

---

[1] The investigations of P. Bottazzi[2] and his pupils on the swelling and shrinking of lenses in solutions of acids, bases and salts should be mentioned.

have ...das in the most aggravated glaucoma. On the other hand, by the injection of a few drops of 1.8 to 1.0 (molecular at 0.5 to 5.41 per cent) sodium citrate solution under the conjunctiva it was possible to cause the ... pressure in human glaucomas and in artificially glaucomatous eyes to become normal or even subnormal in less than five minutes. [The observation of RIESMAN on the lowered ocular tension of diabetics and the ... lowering of ocular tension by intravenous injection of glucose by WOODYATT's method are important in this connection. Tr.]

Cloudiness of the cornea occurs without reference to the absorption of water by the eye. It probably depends on the precipitation of a protein, since all acids, bases, salts and non-electrolytes which cause a precipitation of proteins cause a corneal turbidity. What is true of the cornea may be supposed to apply also to the other transparent media of the eye, the lens and the vitreous humor. Here, too, therapeutic results have been obtained already, by injecting sodium citrate.

HAYWARD G. THOMAS obtained an improvement in vision in cases showing a cloudiness of the cornea, the haze in the vitreous humor. It is natural to assume that the turbidity is due to a reversible precipitation of albumin. Similar results were obtained in an edema of the tissues surrounding the knees.

The tiny swellings which result from mosquito bites are regarded by M. H. FISCHER as local edemas produced by a drop of acid or some substance which interferes with the normal oxidative processes of the tissues. The biochemical action of ammonia customarily employed on insect bites, favors this view. M. H. FISCHER ... produced "artificial flea bites" on gelatin plates by ... stroking them with needles dipped in formic acid and then placing them in water with ammonia he was also able to make the swellings vanish.

One of M. H. FISCHER's observations was of great significance to me in explaining the phenomena of some skin diseases. He observed in gelatin plates upon which moulds had been sown, an elevation in the centre of each colony a few ... It we recall that many skin diseases are caused by true fungi planted in the moulds and that in many, the most characteristic symptoms are wheals (swellings), papules and vesicles the analogy cannot be neglected. Moreover, we must think of analogous processes in two cases of other local edemas occurring after inoculation with ... microorganisms or the injection of diphtheria antitoxin.

In a later work, M. H. FISCHER elaborated his fundamental ideas of cellular pathology and attached ... body swelling. Cloudy swelling is found in the liver, kidneys, spleen, and muscle cells of

Studies in Intermediate Carbohydrate Metabolism. R. T. Woodyatt ...

persons dying as the result of acute infectious diseases. The cells involved are enlarged and more or less cloudy; macroscopically, the organ involved appears at times as if it had been boiled; microscopically, granular deposits are seen.

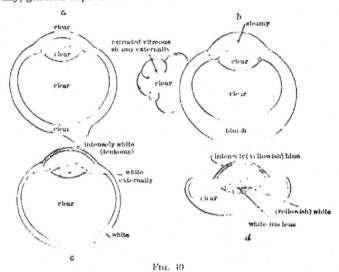

Fig. 40

Reproduced from Fischer's " Oedema and Nephritis," second edition, by permission of Messrs. John Wiley & Sons, Inc.

M. H. Fischer experimentally produced cloudy swelling in the livers and kidneys of rabbits by placing them in distilled water or dilute acids. Addition of various salts delayed or hastened the development of cloudy swelling. According to M. H. Fischer, whether the *swelling* occurs pathologically or experimentally, it is explained just as is edema; as the result of the production of acid in the injured tissues, they swell. The cloudiness runs parallel with the precipitation of proteins, especially that of casein by acids. The production and disappearance of granules in parenchymatous cells in the presence of additional acid occurs exactly like the precipitation and re-solution of casein upon increasing the concentration of acid. The "cloudy swelling" is, therefore, the result of acid production in the tissues, though the swelling and the clouding are two processes entirely independent of each other.

As has been stated already, M. H. Fischer's theory was actively discussed and contradicted. Before approaching this discussion we shall present a brief résumé. Fischer maintains that edema results

from the swelling of organ colloids, which is induced by acids that are
produced by a disturbance in the oxidative processes of an organ

The first objection is directed against the assumption that processes
which occur in dead colloids may be transferred to the living organism. It was raised by G. BENTNER, JACQUES LOEB and A R.
MOORE. They admit that FISCHER'S experiments apply to dead
tissue, especially muscle, but that they fail in the living organ where
osmotic processes are active and satisfy all the conditions. The objection of R. HÓLER is especially searching, that if only electrolytes may
inhibit acid swelling, a piece of muscle would swell in sugar solution.
As a matter of fact the muscle volume is unchanged in an isotonic sugar
solution. M. H FISCHER [*1] combats this by stating that the existence
of osmotic membranes in living cells is quite readily conceivable (see
p. 290), and points to his experiments which reproduced the contraction
of living muscle by means of catgut, a dead colloid material   Osmotic
attraction of water is inconceivable nor does it assist the explanation.

The second objection is directed against the very development of
acids in tissues and was raised by A. R. MOORE, who was unable to
detect acids by acid fuchsin or neutral red in muscles made edematous
according to FISCHER'S technic nor in the lymph or kidneys of rabbits
injected with acid salts, and who maintained that consequently the
acid content of such tissues is not responsible for the edema or albuminuria. FISCHER meets this objection by stating that acidity of tissues is not to be detected by color indicators since the acids combine
with proteins and that even traces of acids induce swelling and that
there is no more delicate indicator of acidity than the swelling of
proteins. [FISCHER insists that p_H swelling in protein nowhere parallels p_H concentration. The degree of swelling follows the order,
HCl > lactic > sulphuric acid. Tr.]

The third objection is directed against the generalization of FISCH-
ER's hypothesis. FISCHER performed his experiments principally on
muscles which behaved by swelling in the presence of acids like fibrin
or other dead colloid but this would not apply to *all kinds of tissue*
Connective tissue and cartilage apparently behave the same way.
L. PINCUSSOHN, however, found that kidney, spleen, liver and lung
usually became less swollen in acid than in pure water. Kidney cortex
and kidney medulla showed a difference in that the former became
more swollen in acid and water than the latter   These experiments do
not impress me as decisive because physiological salts were absent.

The behavior of nerve tissue is especially interesting. REICHARDT
called attention to a clinical condition which occasionally occurs in
dementia præcox and causes sudden death. He noted an increase of
weight and volume in such brains without other detectable macro- or

microscopic changes. He designated this condition *swelling of the brain* in contrast with *edema of the brain;* it is possible to demonstrate the fluid transudate from the blood. In swelling of the brain, it is dry, solid and gelatinous. REICHARDT's observation was made about the time FISCHER published his theory so that it seems apropos to mention it. J. BAUER and BAUER and AMES tested slices of brain and cord and found that swelling was observed occasionally with a one thousandth normal acidity, but with greater concentration (even of carbonic acid), a shrinking always occurred. On this account they reject FISCHER's acid theory.

Contradicting J. BAUER, FISCHER in experiments (with HOOKER) found that nervous tissue behaved toward salts and acids like fibrin and other tissue. He explains the disagreement by the fact that BAUER chose tissue which had been dead 6 to 24 hours. The optimal concentration for swelling had already been exceeded by the post mortem development of acid.

The fourth objection was raised by pathologists who maintained that what FISCHER described *was not edema at all*. The main location of edema, *connective tissue*, exhibits apparently, like fibrin, the swelling and shrinking phenomena with acids and salts but is essentially dissimilar from edematous tissue and more like hyaline or amyloid degeneration. (MARCHAND, KLEMENSIEWICZ, H. SCHADE.) The fibers show the chief swelling in acids but in edema the main swelling is extrafibrillar. FISCHER fails to distinguish between *swelling* of the protoplasmic substance and *turgor* of the entire tissue. Against this view that in edema the aqueous fluids accumulate in the tissue spaces and not merely in the protoplasma and that increased inhibition of water by the cell is not the criterion of edema, M. H. FISCHER argues that the tissue spaces are not filled with air but by colloid material which may very well contribute to the edema by acid swelling.

LUBARSCH noted marked swelling of the tissue in his histological studies but determined a difference in kidney edemas due to clamping the renal artery or renal vein. The changes are similar; those produced by clamping the vein are reversible but those due to clamping the artery are irreversible if the artery is clamped off for three hours. The sensitive cells are killed. This contradicts FISCHER's theory which requires the damage to be the same in either case. KURT ZIEGLER made the important observation that chlorid metabolism as well as water metabolism play an important part in edema. Chlorid and water retention alternate as primary factors in edema, but in all cases, there are nutritive disturbances which affect chiefly muscles and connective tissue. P. TACHAU offered experimental verification by feeding mice excessive amounts of sodium salts. There occurred edema about the head, neck and attachment of front limbs resembling that observed in human nurslings when they are given too much salt. In TACHAU's experiments it is noteworthy that there was no increase in average amount of water in the animal but the edema was the expression of *abnormal distribution* of water. These observations lend some support to FISCHER's theory. FISCHER observed that when fibrin and gelatin swelled up they accumulated salt from an acid table salt solution and, consequently, he regarded the salt retention as resulting from the edema.

When we consider the controversy concerning FISCHER's theory of edema, it is evident that as yet he has offered no experimental proof for his hypothesis. Except in a few special instances his opponents have likewise failed to show its invalidity since, in my opinion, their experimental methods failed to produce a local accumulation of acid in living organs as required by FISCHER's theory. No matter what value may be set on FISCHER's theory in the future, it has been of enduring service in that it has transferred the emphasis in the study of edema from the circulation to the tissues; it is not hydrostatic differences in pressure but chemical damage to the tissue which occasions edema.[1]

Inflammation.

Though healthy cells are impermeable for blood plasma inflamed tissue permits a selective passage of plasma elements

A. OSWALD[2] found that the frequency of passage stood in the following order:

Albumin > Globulin (Euglobulin) > Pseudoglobulin > Fibrinogen.

This occurs in an order inversely to their susceptibility to salting out by salts and to the viscosity of the various solutions the less viscous a plasma element is, the more easily does it pass through the inflamed tissue. Albumin alone may be found in an exudate, but never fibrinogen without the simultaneous presence of albumin and globulin. In the acute stages all kinds of albumins are found in the exudate, whereas, with the lapse of time, fibrinogen and then globulin diminish.

The normal cell membrane evidently behaves like an impermeable ultrafilter, which has become more permeable by reason of the inflammatory process. We do not know the factors which bring this about. [The tissue may be "coagulated" allowing freer diffusion because of larger diffusion paths, or they may be more dispersed and accumulate more "water of swelling." Either condition would explain some of the phenomena. TR.]

[1] [The most recent discussion of the question by LAWRENCE J. HENDERSON and MARTIN H. FISCHER is contained in the Journal of the Am. Chem. Society, Vol. XL, No 5 (May, 1918) Tr.]

It is to be hoped that an extension of the viewpoint of M. H. FISCHER, together with that of A. OSWALD will explain the problem of *inflammation*, which has been so long kept at a dead center

We thus see that the science of colloids throws new light on the most difficult portions of pathology, and that even therapy may gaze with hope upon the young science

Salt Distribution.

Just as the water content of a normal organ is relatively constant and may undergo *reversible* changes due to changes in the condition of the organ colloids, this is also true in the case of the *salt content*.

Unfortunately the basis for the comprehensive explanation of these questions is lacking (bibliography, see ALBU-NEUBERG *) The values that have been obtained cannot be used for comparison. Some have been derived from healthy and some (especially the determinations on man) from sick individuals, moreover, age is a very important factor In the first place, it is essential to determine accurately the limits within which the salt content in the separate organs of normal individuals may vary. We know that muscle, liver, blood corpuscles and brain are rich in potassium salts, while in the blood serum and spleen, sodium salts predominate.

In man the muscles contain 0 743 per cent of NaCl, the lungs, kidneys and skin 2.5 per cent Sodium chlorid and water content do not run parallel The salt content varies within wide limits in different species of animals. For instance, there is present in the ash of

Ox blood	. .	7 4 per cent K_2O
Calf blood	.	11 2 per cent K_4O
Sheep blood.	.	7.1 per cent K_2O
Pig blood	. .	20.4 per cent K_2O
Chicken blood	.	18 4 per cent K_2O

We should assume from our colloid-chemical knowledge, that a given electrolyte content must correspond to each organ's condition of swelling, though as yet this assumption offers but little towards elucidating the problem Pathological retention of common salt in edema, see page 232, invites experimental study of the question.

What has been said of animals is also true of *plants* But here, too, the salt content varies greatly with organ and sex, and we have no basis for its true significance. For instance, it is merely necessary to mention that the ash of wheat flour contains 0.76 per cent Na_2O, whereas that of buckwheat flour has 5.87 per cent Na_2O

The *distribution of salts* occurs similar to that of water; if they are *artifically introduced* into the organism, they are stored up and again released. If a dog received an intravenous injection of table salt, 28–77 per cent of the saline retained by the body accummulates in the skin (PADTBERG). In salt starvation the skin acts conversely, suffering 60–90 per cent of the chlorid loss. [The ancient name for eczema was "salt rheum"; see also "Karell Treatment," J. G. M. BULLOWA, Amer. Medicine, June, 1918. Tr.]

For animals, an intravenous injection of potassium salts acts as a poison (especially for cardiac muscle and peripheral vessels); thus, according to HELD, even solutions with 0.08 per cent KCl affect frogs and rabbits. By way of the intestinal tract, potassium salts are relatively harmless. HELD * showed that when thus introduced, the K was stored in the tissues and only slowly given up to the blood. Here we observe the same phenomena as with water, of which an excess is also taken up by the tissues

For the maintenance of the osmotic pressure, a definite concentration of any crystalloid suffices. Observations of the most different kind teach us that exactly *that electrolyte* which is normally found, is necessary for function and development. If in a suspension of blood corpuscles the NaCl is replaced by sugar, hemolysis becomes more difficult, even though the osmotic pressure is identical. Experiments on excised hearts prove that the action of the heart is retained much longer if it is perfused with a fluid containing a proper quantity of K, Ca, Mg, PO_4, than if only physiological salt solution is used. Na, K, Mg and Ca salts are individually poisonous for plants, but mixed in the proper proportions they are absolutely necessary. In Chapter XXII, there are further examples

Evidently the condition of swelling required for normal function is afforded by a proper balance in the mixture of electrolytes.

A. B. MACALLUM[1] investigated microchemically the distribution of K, Fe, Ca, Cl and PO_4 in many animal and plant cells, and from his investigation made deductions concerning their functional significance, to which we shall again return (see p. 292) TH. WEEVERS has elaborated them with far reaching studies of the distribution of potassium in plant cells.

[W. BURRIDGE, Quarterly Journal of Medicine, 10, No. 39, p. 172, aptly remarks that analyses of the blood ash give little information concerning the balance of its salts by reason of the fact that the proportions of them which are in "sorption" or in solution may vary. Tr.]

---

[1] A. B. MACALLUM proceeds in part from the fact that inorganic salts increase the surface tension of an aqueous solution, and as a result the surface contains a more dilute solution Conversely the author concludes that the surface tension is diminished at the points of the cells which are approached by the salts in question We cannot agree with this conclusion at present, because not only mechanical but chemical influences may determine the adsorption of salts For instance, L. MICHAELIS and P RONA (as the author has mentioned) demonstrated that certain kinds of sugar have no influence on the surface tension and yet may be adsorbed.

There are, moreover, the interesting observations of P. Rona and D. Takahasui,[*] Hollinger[*] and E. Frank[*] concerning the distribution of *sugar* between blood corpuscles and plasma.

If we go further and observe the distribution of the other elements of the organism, the albumins, nucleins, elastin, the lipoids, etc., we approach the greatest problems of anatomy and histology and set out upon a boundless and uncharted sea. Possibly we shall learn more of these things in the not too distant future.

The Circulation of Material.

Both the plant and the animal organism are surrounded by membranes or pellicles, which separate them from the outer world. These membranes are more or less permeable to water and crystalloids, but normally, they are impermeable to colloids. Even though this last fact were not experimentally demonstrated, we should assume it *a priori*, because if the dissolved colloids could leave the organism, the loss of material would mean death. To demonstrate the correctness of our conclusion, we need but mention a pathological condition, *albuminuria*. In this condition the kidney becomes permeable for serum-albumin, and it is one of the physician's most important duties to compensate for the continuous loss of substance by proper dieting, so that no impoverishment of the tissues as regards albumin occurs.

Within the organism also, there are many such partitions; they serve to organize activity, to guide the food along certain paths (arteries, veins, vascular bundles of plants) and to collect secretions (urinary bladder, gall bladder).

The substances necessary to support life must accordingly enter the organism as *gases* or *crystalloids*. In the case of *plants*, CO_2 enters through the leaves; other foodstuffs, water and most of the inorganic salts (nitrates, phosphates, potassium and lime salts, etc.), enter through the roots. These substances are at the outset very diffusible and need no preparation. It is otherwise in the case of animals, which require outside of water but few crystalloids (sugar, salts) and are chiefly sustained by colloids (vegetables and meat). In order to enter the organism at all, these substances must first be changed to a crystalloidal condition. This is accomplished by enzymes; the diastatic ferments split starches; pepsin and trypsin split protein; and herbivora have ferments which are able to change even cellulose into a crystalloidal condition, etc.

In like manner only gases or crystalloids can leave the organism (expired CO_2, urine, perspiration).[1]

[1] Feces, etc., do not, strictly speaking, leave the organism any more than diatoms which have been surrounded by an ameba and then cast out (they are evacuated from a tube which passes through the animal).

The forces which accomplish the entrance of food into the organism and keep up the *circulation of matter* are in part purely mechanical, as performed by the lungs, the heart, the peristalsis of the intestines, etc   In addition to these, there are forces which accomplish chiefly the metabolism of the cells; the most important of these are diffusion, osmotic pressure, swelling and shrinking.[1]

Circulation of Water.

Until a few years ago the circulation of water in the organism was chiefly attributed to osmosis.   The vital processes constantly produce from the colloids osmotically active crystalloids, which both retain the water formed by oxidation and, in addition, attract water into the cells, thus maintaining the *turgor* or normal tissue tension.   This presupposes that an almost semipermeable membrane surrounds every cell   In the case of plants, this hypothesis offers certain difficulties, and in the case of animals, it is impossible to maintain it,

We shall present only a few examples which show that osmotic conditions alone do not satisfactorily explain the distribution of water in animal cells.

Through the investigations of H. J. HAMBURGER, H. KOEPPE and E. OVERTON, it is known that in the presence of alterations of osmotic pressure, blood corpuscles and muscles change their volume to much less an extent than would be expected of cells with fluid contents and a semi-permeable membrane.   Blood corpuscles contain about 60 per cent water.   In his experiment with osmosis, HAMBURGER showed that only from 40 to 50 per cent of their volume could consist of an aqueous solution, so that from 10 to 20 per cent of the water arises in some other way   According to OVERTON the same thing holds for frog's muscle

Water is also retained by swelling.   *Swelling* and *shrinking* are the most powerful factors governing the circulation of water in the organism.   They may even act against osmotic pressure; nor are we forced to explain their activity by any hypothetical membranes. Changes in the reaction of the cells, especially the constantly recognizable acid production during vital processes, give rise to the conditions necessary for swelling or the circulation of water.   With the removal of the acids shrinking must occur again.

M. H FISCHER properly calls attention to the fact that a semipermeable membrane permitting the entry and exit of water from the

---

[1] J. TRAUBE*[1] regards the "surface pressure" as the force which causes the movement of matter in the organism   Since there exists a certain parallelism between the ability of many substances to lower surface tension and their capacity to penetrate the cells, TRAUBE disregards the osmotic forces and lipoid solubility.

cell is a monstrosity, for how does it explain the entry of food and the exit of metabolic products (metabolites) from the cell? If the membrane is permeable for these, the osmotically active crystalloids cannot induce transfer of water. All variations in volume of blood corpuscles, spermatozoa, plant cells, etc., produced by electrolytes and attributed to osmotic pressure up to now, are just as well explained by swelling and shrinking. Gels swell up in water, acids and alkalies; salts on the other hand, hinder swelling and cause shrinkage.

Moreover, new, purely physico-chemical observations likewise warn us to employ great caution in our consideration of osmotic processes in the organism. Much more substance may be dissolved in the interior of the cell than in its surrounding fluid without the osmotic pressure making this evident. We saw on pages 46 and 47 that with decrease in the surrounding osmotic pressure, the osmotic pressure in a cell with a permeable membrane containing colloid, falls, although if reckoned according to the salt content, the osmotic pressure should have increased. These findings of W. Biltz and A. von Vegesack* necessitate a revision of all former conclusions derived from the observation of osmosis in cells.

Circulation of Water in Animals.

A movement of water results when conditions arise which change the relative swelling of the organs. When subjected to high temperature or after violent exercise, etc., the skin loses water, the blood loses water through the lungs, which causes a flow of water from the other organs. Conversely, an excess of water from the intestines, or in the case of frogs and certain other animals from the skin, is transferred to other organs and re-excreted by the kidneys. Other circumstances may arise, however, which determine the circulation of water: concentration of acid in a tissue increases its swelling capacity, attracting water, e.g., in venous blood or an edema, whereas simultaneous salt formation leads to a shrinking or loss of water.[1] In circumstances in which osmotic pressure may become active, as when a membrane is interposed, the change of a colloidal substance into a crystalloid under the influence of enzymes may effect a transfer of water; the water flows to the place where the osmotic pressure is higher. We shall return to the details of this question when we consider the individual organs.

[1] From this it results that the presence of colloids regulates the movement of water in an entirely different and at times in a direction opposite to that of the osmotic pressure. Acid + salt, as a result of the higher osmotic pressure, should increase the amount of water attracted; in the case of colloid structures, however, they decrease it, since salts abolish to a greater or less extent the swelling action of acids.

The Movement of Water in Plants.

The evaporation of water in plants proceeds more rapidly than in animals. The enormous development of surface in the shape of leaves and needles underlies a great transpiration which requires replacement, so that a stream of water moves upward through the roots and vascular bundles to the leaves. On bright summer days (see W. Pfeffer*² *loc. cit.* I, p. 233) 1 to 10 gm. water are evaporated from 1 cm ² of leaf surface. On very hot days the loss by transpiration from big trees exceeds 400 kilos, on rainy days, however, it may be reduced to a few kilos. To explain the upward movement of the water, the most varied theories have been advanced, and usually abandoned. Explanation by means of osmotic pressure has proved thoroughly unsatisfactory, and mere capillary imbibition is of no greater use We may well understand that the colloids of leaves suffer a loss of water by evaporation, and that, in swelling, they are able to lift a great column of water from the ground to the tree top. Experiments of E. Strassburger showed that in poisoned trees, water may rise to a height of 22 meters, so that pure capillary forces do not suffice for the explanation of the phenomena. More recent experiments (P. A. Roshardt,* E. Reinders*) show that in the *living* plant, *living* elements assist in *pumping* up the water. Since no previous explanation of this has been given, I believe that I am justified in formulating the following hypothesis. In my opinion, the living cells of *plants assist in the elevation of the sap by their respiration.* With respiration, not only does CO_2 develop, but also great quantities of organic acids. Both cause a swelling or attraction of water, which is liberated to the extent that CO_2 disappears, and the other acids are removed in any one of the many possible ways. This would fit in with the fact that the breathing in fully developed leaves and branches, in which the need for water is also diminished, is less than in the developing shoots. The dead leaf, whose breathing has ceased, withers.

Circulation of Crystalloids.

The *circulation of crystalloids* is also largely governed by the factors of diffusion and osmotic pressure, with certain limitations due to the colloid media. Although between two aqueous solutions, separated by an easily permeable membrane, unrestricted mixing occurs as a result of diffusion, this does not hold for a jelly-like medium (see H. Bechhold and J. Ziegler*¹). In order to bring about a mixture in such a case an excess of osmotic pressure is required (see p. 57). It even seems that with equal osmotic pressure, acid and alkaline reacting substances may be side by side in colloidal (amphoteric) media for a long time without neutralizing each other (R. E. Liesegang). In the case of phagocytes, that is, in living cells, the existence of acid areas in alkaline protoplasm has been shown by staining with neutral red (E. Metschnikoff). We thus see that in different portions of the organism, the most various crystalloids are present, and may functionate specifically without being accompanied by any exchange or mixture; this only occurs when a crystalloid substance accumulates and becomes osmotically active. Swelling and shrinking may also be of importance for the circulation of crystalloids, since dissolved substances are soaked up with the water of swelling or are expressed during shrinking.

If these crystalloids are at the same time electrolytes, they may increase or diminish the swelling according to their nature (acid or salt), and in this way, either aid or impede the entrance of crystalloids.

Circulation of Colloids.

Compared with crystalloids, the osmotic pressures in the case of colloids are extremely small. To be sure, we know (see p. 55) that proteins may diffuse through gels, so that they also are independently motile. Of great significance is the discovery of H. Iscovesco to the effect that colloid diffusion is dependent on the electric charge. In general, however, the colloids, as opposed to the crystalloids, furnish the *stable* element of the organism.

The Influence of Membranes Upon the Interchange of Substances.

The physico-chemical conditions for the interchange of substances through cell membranes was for a long time completely ruled by the *theory* of Overton, which is somewhat as follows. Protoplasm is surrounded by a fatty lipoid membrane; an exchange of substances can only occur if the given substance is soluble in such a membrane. Overton's theory has not proven universally applicable; it is ever becoming better recognized that the problem will probably be solved when we cease to look entirely to the *osmotic conditions* and *membranes* for the factors governing the interchange of substance. The fact that both cell content and cell membrane consist of *colloids capable of swelling* must be taken into consideration.

The earliest fundamental investigations of the physical interchange of matter in individual cells were made on plant cells. I refer particularly to the investigations of W. Pfeffer and H. de Vries. In plants, especially, we find that the cell content is very frequently surrounded by a *visible and solid membrane* which is usually regarded as semipermeable.

The basis of this view is. if such a cell is placed in hypertonic salt solution, the protoplasm retracts from the cell wall and water is lost. This phenomena is called plasmolysis. If the cell is immersed in pure water, the protoplasm swells up again. The phenomenon was formerly explained by saying that the membrane was impermeable for salts.[1] In a hypertonic salt solution, water may indeed leave the cell but salt cannot enter; in pure water the process is reversed.

Nowadays discussion is focussed on the nature of the plasma pellicle and two main tendencies may be recognized.

Among the adherents to the *lipoid theory* in addition to E. OVERTON, is VERNON, who considers it probable that the lipoid membrane penetrates the interior of the cell. J. LOEB and R. BEUTNER in view of their investigations of bio-electric phenomena may be regarded as adherents of the lipoid theory Those investigators (J. TRAUBE and F. CZAPEK) who regard changes in surface tension as the means of penetrating surfaces may be regarded as adherents of a modified lipoid membrane theory. They arrive at this conclusion because their experiments have been chiefly concerned with the action of lipoid soluble substances on the cell.

According to F. CZAPEK all substances whose surface tension is less than 0 68 (water/air = 1) are toxic for the higher plant cells and CZAPEK's pupil KISCH determined 0.5 to be the limit of toxic surface tension for yeast cells and fungi Since lecithin and cholesterin, that is, the lipoids and their emulsions, have a surface tension of 0.5, F. CZAPEK agrees with NATHANSON and regards the cell membrane as a concentrated fat-emulsion which is permeable for either fat or for water soluble substance depending on the conditions of surface tension. Similar views (loose union of albumin and lipoid) are entertained by W. W. LEPESCHKIN with the difference that he regards the entire protoplasm as such an emulsion possessing properties in the center similar to those on the surfaces.

The "emulsion theory" obtained very definite support from the following observation of CLOWES (see p. 38). He prepared an oil-water emulsion by shaking equal quantities of water and olive oil and sufficient $n/10$ NaOH that the outer phase (the water) was just alkaline to phenolphthalein. If he now added a small excess of $CaCl_2$ solution the emulsion changed into a water-oil emulsion; in other words, water became the dispersed phase in a continuous layer of oil. We

---

[1] The *visible* cell membrane is quite permeable for most crystalloids, serving only to a certain extent as a support for the protoplasm.

observe that by this chemical attack the layer which had been permeable for hydrophile substance became impermeable for them and was made permeable for substances soluble in fat. However, we know from the investigations of J. LOEB and W. J. V. OSTERHOUT (see p 378, *et seq*) that small amounts of divalent cations detoxicate neutral salts by inhibiting, according to the view of J. LOEB, the free exchange of ions through the plasma pellicle. CLOWES extended his observations to other polyvalent cations and the quantitative relations are in excellent agreement.

The other tendency is to assume a *pure albuminous* membrane; W. J. V. OSTERHOUT assumes this, as the result of the following remarkable observation: he placed spyrogyra cells in common salt solution of such concentration that no plasmolysis[1] occurred; when he added very dilute calcium chlorid solution so as to depress the osmotic pressure, plasmolysis occurred. The plasma pellicle must have been permeable for NaCl and its passage is only impeded by the CaCl₂. In contrast to OVERTON's view, OSTERHOUT regards the plasma pellicle as permeable for most ions of the light metals and consequently it must be albuminous.

The action of the Ca-ion possibly depends on its antagonistic action (see p 69) though it may be due to a variety of tannage of the plasma pellicle. With the death of the cell, the pellicle becomes generally permeable.

RUHLAND also, discards the lipoid theory. He considers only the thickness of the membrane to be responsible for permeability or impermeability; the membrane acts like an *ultrafilter* in the sense of BECHHOLD. He studied a large number of dyes, enzymes, alkaloids and other substances which occur in plants and found that their ability to penetrate the plasma cells was in proportion to their ability to spread out in thick jellies, in other words, it depended on their particle size (see p. 56).

In view of the known facts we must admit that at present we can arrive at no conclusion concerning the nature and structure of the plasma pellicle. Of one thing we can be certain, that OVERTON's original theory of a continuous lipoid membrane must be abandoned. I am of the opinion, however, that it is possible to conciliate the theories which have been elucidated here and which seem to be mutually exclusive.

In the first place, the assumption of a pellicle of emulsified fat does

---

[1] Osterhout distinguished between true and false plasmolysis. The latter may occur in dilute solutions even in pure water most usually in marine plant. It is probably due to the coagulation of the protoplasm from the penetration of the water.

not exclude RUHLAND's ultrafilter theory. If we have an emulsion
in which the lipoid is the dispersed phase we have an ultra filter which
is permeable for water soluble substances and impermeable for lipoid
soluble substances. The size of the pores of the ultra filter depends
on the relation of the lipoid to the aqueous phase. If the amount of
lipoid is small, the pores of the ultra filter are large and vice versa.
When the lipoid content is large we have a narrow pored ultra filter
which absolutely satisfies the conditions found by RUHLAND in his
dye investigations. Further, we have seen from CLOWES' experiment,
that an oil water emulsion is easily changed to a water oil emulsion,
and in that case the layer is open for fat soluble substances and closed
for water soluble substances. In my opinion such a layer satisfies
all the conditions demanded by the various investigators.

I wish, however, to emphasize that there is no justification for too
wide a generalization, for different cells behave very differently.
Observations on plant cells cannot be applied without modification
to animal cells; a cell in a plant root cannot be compared to nerve
cells which are surrounded by a dense isolating layer of fat. It seems
possible to conclude from R. HÖBER's and RUHLAND's experiments
on the penetration of dyes into cells that the animal cells which they
studied contain larger pores than the plant cells.

Let us consider the simplest instance, one in which the cell protoplasm is a colloid capable of swelling, with surfaces limited by a
pellicle which can also swell and offering certain exterior boundaries.
Any injury to this pellicle will be repaired of its own accord somewhat
like rubber. We can thus (pp. 284-285) readily understand how
amœbæ or phagocytes send out protoplasmal prolongations, envelop
foreign bodies or bacteria and incorporate them without their margin
being broken. As a matter of fact, it must immediately repair itself
just as does an oily film on water broken by a stone. Let us see how
this view agrees with former theories, and to what extent this view is
an improvement upon them.

To begin with, it must be noted that OVERTON assumes that a substance is taken up by the plasma pellicle in accordance with its
coefficient of solubility, in agreement with the laws of solutions
(HENRY's distribution). This may be the fact in many cases, only we
must recall that adsorption fulfills similar conditions for the passage
of a substance through the plasma pellicle into the interior of the
cell. The only condition which need be assumed in order that a
substance may enter the interior of a cell from outside, is that there
shall be a reversible absorption by the plasma film. What curve of
distribution this follows, is immaterial for the present. That, as a
matter of fact, in numerous cases an adsorption certainly does exist

but not a distribution according to HENRY's law, has been determined by H. BECHHOLD in the action of disinfectants (see p. 399), and STRAUB-FREUNDLICH on the distribution of veratrin between heart muscle and pericardial blood. G. LOEWE has shown by simple physico-chemical experiments that lipoids adsorb dyes, narcotics, nicotin and tetanus toxin. The substance interchange in animal cells has been studied most thoroughly in the case of *red blood corpuscles*. In my opinion (see p. 304) the latter have a very peculiar structure, conditioned by their special function; their lipoid pellicle is quite strong. In spite of this, we shall find phenomena in the case of the erythrocytes which cannot be brought into accord with the idea of a salt solution surrounded by a semipermeable membrane.

The theory of osmotic pressure demands that various isotonic salt solutions shall have equal influence upon the volume of the blood corpuscles. S. G. HEDIN[1] showed, however, that this is not the case, for instance, in isotonic solutions of $NaCl$ and KNO_3; in the case of lower concentrations, the volume is smaller, in the case of higher concentrations it is larger than with the corresponding $NaCl$ solution; we must recall that the NO_3 ion favors swelling or the deflocculation of colloids and lecithin; if the outer pressure is low, crystalloids leave the blood corpuscles, and the osmotic pressure, and consequently the volume of the corpuscles, will be less than with the corresponding $NaCl$ solution. The reverse occurs if the outer solution is hypertonic.

We find in the literature, repeated references to the permeability of the cell membrane, especially of plants, for *potassium nitrate*. B. VAN RYSSELBERGHE[*] has demonstrated the entrance of diphenylamin into tradescantia cells. If fungi, such as aspergillus niger or penicillium glaucum, are grown upon a concentrated solution of saltpeter, they will take up so much of the electrolyte that in the end they will have an osmotic pressure of 200 atmospheres. Such cultures actually explode when placed in pure water.

The ability to take up such substances as favor swelling is much greater in the case of young cells with membranes that can swell than in the case of old inelastic cells. On this account, an older aspergillus cell may plasmolyze with a 20 per cent $NaNO_3$ solution which possesses an osmotic pressure of only 102 atmospheres. In this difference between old and young cell membranes, may lie a partial explanation why bacteria and fungus cultures, namely organisms which multiply rapidly, readily *adapt* themselves to changed conditions. Young and old cells differ in their turgidity.

R. HOBER[6] prepared suspensions of blood corpuscles in dilute isotonic solutions of various alkali salts and observed the order in which they *favour* hemolysis. He established the following series:

$$SO_4 \cdot Cl \cdot Br \cdot NO_3 \cdot I \quad \text{and} \quad Li \cdot Na \cdot Ca \cdot Rb \cdot K.$$

The anion series corresponds fairly well with the action of the anions upon lecithin, so that we may safely assume that alkali salts may bring about an increase or a diminution in the porosity of the plasma pellicle. Other examples of this action on the part of neutral salts are given in Chapter XXII (salts).

Substances which favor swelling in a diluted condition (p. 88) may prevent it when they are more concentrated. It must also be borne in mind, that beside hydrophile lecithin and albumin, hydrophobe cholesterin must also exist in the lipoid membrane. This latter is, however, precipitated by electrolytes which causes the former to swell. Thus there exists in the cell membrane a self-regulating system something like a compensation pendulum: when the temperature rises, the center of gravity of the pendulum falls but by a combination of metallic rod. The center of gravity is raised and the fall is compensated. Thus compensatory actions of hydrophile and hydrophobe colloids appear to be an essential factor in the *automatic regulation of cell metabolism*.

The following considerations afford an explanation for some particular kinds of cells. If Hamsun[*] in particular, his attention to the fact that, "the plasma skin is really impermeable for everything the cell needs or produces." It is impermeable for amino acids, for the various kinds of sugar and soluble carbohydrates which are formed in the interior of a cell from the undissolved carbohydrate reserves and for inorganic salts and alkalis of organic acids. The interchange of these substances, which naturally takes place, is on this account, somewhat of a riddle. In my opinion these phenomena are less mysterious if we recall that with equal osmotic pressure without and within, even the thinnest membranes interfere with diffusion as has been shown by H. Bechhold and J. Ziegler (see p. 57). The most recent investigations of H. J. Hamburger on blood corpuscles indicate that their transitory membrane is not as impermeable as was formerly believed. It will be understood thus how the cells are sharply cut off in cases of isotonicity, while if there be hypertonicity, some substances may penetrate through the membrane. This seems to me to be the meaning of the following experiment of J. Hamo[*]: if red blood corpuscles are placed in an 8 per cent cane sugar solution and the solution is immediately diluted, hemolysis occurs when the cane sugar concentration is 1 per cent. If, however, the red blood corpuscles are brought into the same sugar solution

tion for several hours and the dilution is then undertaken, the hemolysis will occur only when the cane sugar concentration reaches 2 per cent. Sufficient time has thus been given for salts to leave the blood corpuscles and enter the cane sugar as was shown by A. GURBER.

Experiments of JAQUES LOEB[*4] upon the *parthenogenesis* of *sea urchin's eggs* are in accord with this. If the eggs are placed for a short time in hypertonic salt solution and then returned to sea water (which corresponds with their normal osmotic pressure) segmentation takes place. J. LOEB[*4] found that a cane sugar solution acts like a *hypertonic* salt solution even if, as regards concentration, it be *isotonic* with the eggs. J. LOEB explains the action by saying that the egg pellicle is permeable for sugar and salts, and that the salts diffuse out more rapidly than the cane sugar diffuses in, so that the outer fluid becomes hypertonic. We must, moreover, recall that substances exist which to a certain extent close the pathways automatically, as for instance the SO_4 ion, whereas others, especially urea, open a passage, not only for themselves but for other substances (see p. 55) The permeability of red blood corpuscles and muscles for urea is then no longer surprising, any more than the changes in permeability (observed by M FLÜRI[k] and R MEURER[*]) in the plasma pellicle of plants under the influence of certain salts.

This may be accomplished not only by chemical agencies, but purely physical factors may have an influence It might be expected *a priori* from change in temperature; the influence of *light* is surprising, as experiments of W W LEPESCHKIN and by A. TRONDLE have shown. The latter's experiments indicate that plant cells (foliage) are more permeable, not only for NaCl but even for glucose, in a bright light than in the dark.

One of the most remarkable and still unexplained phenomena is that when death occurs, the permeability of the cell membrane changes into that of an ordinary membrane which retains only colloids.

Assimilation and Dissimilation.

After a crystalloid foodstuff has entered the organism, it is the organism's most important task to retain it for use, this is accomplished by changing it into a colloid, inasmuch as complicated combinations are formed from more or less simply constructed crystalloids From the CO_2, which enters the leaf, starch is formed under the influence of chlorophyl granules and daylight; and from nitrates which have entered through the roots, with the assistance of carbohydrates, proteins develop. In the animal organism, the

pp 283 to 286), which, in spite of their considerable diameter, change their shape so that they pass through the finest vessel walls. If to the leucocytes is to be attributed a share in the resorption of fat, they must journey into the intestines and return laden with fat It has not been possible as yet to decide microchemically whether fat passes the intestinal epithelium unchanged. [In the presence of protective colloids, colloidal gold will pass through Pukall filters which otherwise hold them back. ZSIGMONDY-ALEXANDER, Colloids and the Ultramicroscope, p. 153, *et seq.* Tr.]

One fact, at least to me, seems very much to favor the idea that fat may be resorbed unchanged from the intestines, namely, linseed oil, sesame oil, cottonseed oil, etc., may occur unchanged in the milk, and foreign fats (rapeseed oil) may be deposited in the body. Absorption occurs almost exclusively in the small intestines (NAKA-SHIMA) Within the intestinal wall, neutral fat may be synthesized from the absorbed fatty acid alkali and glycerin, so that neutral fat is carried to the body in very fine emulsion through the chyle ducts, and in fact fat may enter the blood stream directly.

The milky turbid lymph collects in the thoracic duct and empties into the subclavian vein. It is especially easy after the ingestion of fat to recognize ultramicroscopically, in the blood, numerous granules (hemoconia), which may be considered fat droplets (A NEU-MANN,* K. REICHER*).

It is possible, therefore, to follow visually the path of fat by means of dark field illumination. S. BONDI and A. NEUMANN* experimented as follows· at times, they caused hemoconia to appear in the blood by a liberal fat diet, and at others they injected a very fine emulsion of fat into the veins. Large fat droplets suspended in blood are evidently unable to change their form, and as a result cause emboli in the lungs, which may prove fatal. These investigators experimented thus with emulsions of lanolin, cholesterin, lecithin, butter and olive oil, whose particles were only recognizable in the dark field. They dissolved the fat they were using in alcohol and poured the alcoholic solution slowly into water with constant stirring. The alcohol was removed from the filtrate of this emulsion by gently warming it on a water bath.

S. BONDI and A NEUMANN then established that the fat droplets were not dissolved by lipolytic ferments during their sojourn in the blood [1] They are emulsified by the venous blood in the right heart, and after they have passed the capillaries of the lesser circulation, they enter those of the greater circulation. Their goal, like that of

[1] In my opinion such emulsions of uniform particle size could serve in measuring the exact dimensions of the smallest capillaries under *normal* conditions.

1. Formation of cellulose hydrogel in the youngest plant tissues as a chemically indifferent surface or framework. This primary stage will be explained more fully.

2. The colloidal constituents of cambial juice become layered upon the cellulose surface by adsorption and gel-formation, and thus increase the thickness of the surfaces.

3. Chemical reactions occur between the adsorbed hydrogels which lead to lignin formation.

The following facts indicate the truth of these assumptions·

(a) Colloidal constituents can be extracted by adsorption from the cambial juice.

(b) The colloids adsorbable from the cambial juice and the running sap are indicative of their lignin content, which means their wood-forming properties.

(c) The quantity of adsorbable colloidal constituents in the cambial juice varies with the season of the year — (shown in the annular rings as early summer and late summer wood)

Certain trees give such large quantities of spring sap on tapping, that it is easy at times to collect a liter or more in a day. In North America the sugar maple has this property. In Norway, Sweden and Russia people drink the sap of the birch either fresh or fermented The trees are bored about 10 cm deep, 30 to 40 cm above the ground and a glass tube is inserted and sealed in with tree-wax. The sap drops through the bent tube into a bottle.

To obtain the *cambial sap*, trunks of birch, pine and gray ash are sawed into pieces, 15 to 20 cm. long. The bark from 7 to 15 kilos of this is taken and then split vertically. The smooth inner layer of the bark and the outer cambial mass of the smooth surface of wood are well shaved off with glass. The shavings are placed in from 1 to 2 liters of water and allowed to remain several hours, a few drops of thymol solution being added. The water is poured off, the residue squeezed in a fruit press and the combined turbid fluids are filtered.

The *adsorption experiments* were performed partly by shaking with finely divided cellulose (filter paper) and partly by siphoning through "washed clay." (See p. 110.) In both cases the quantity of material adsorbed was estimated by determining the weight of the dried residue of (a) a measured quantity of fluid *before* adsorption, (b) the same volume *after* adsorption.

H. WISLICENUS was able to prove in the case of the rising sap obtained by tapping the hornbeam and in the cambial juice of the birch, that the abstraction of colloidal substances followed an adsorption curve, because the more dilute the solutions the more colloida' substance relatively was extracted from them by "filtrous clay" or filter paper

It appeared rather more that the ... soluble of the birch contains only a small quantity ... about the opening of the leaves ... of Apra there is no new formation of colloids, but there is ... the dissing of everything that is soluble (partial reversal of wood formation)

The *cambial juice* on the other hand contains, at the time of most active wood formation (end of May to end of July) large quantities of adsorbable colloids (24 to 57 per cent. ... Towards the end of July or beginning of August, when wood formation quickly ceases, the colloid content of cambial sap also decreases rapidly.

Pine	beginning of July	57 per cent. adsorbed colloids
	beginning of August	6.11 per cent.
Gray ash	beginning of July	24.14 per cent.
	beginning of August	8.11 per cent.

Thus H. WISTINGER has convincingly demonstrated that wood formation is a colloid-chemical process.

Enzymes without doubt play a most important part in the development of organs. We know that enzymes ... the body by changing colloids into crystalloids. They split albumen into poly-peptids and amino acids, starch into sugar and etc. ... Reduction or synthesis is also brought about by enzymes. Reactions which are hastened by enzymes are reversible and it depends entirely upon surrounding conditions, whether the balance of the process weighs more in one direction than in another. Thus, for instance, A. CROFT HILL was the first to show that the same ferment which splits maltose into glucose actually forms maltose in a concentrated solution of glucose. Since then, similar reversals have been frequently observed. POTTE-VIN split fats by means of pancreatic lipase and with the same enzyme he also prepared fats from glycerine and oleic acid. The well-known cleavage of fats with the enzyme of the castor bean was as successfully reversed by WELTER that he obtained synthetically almost 30 per cent of neutral fat with the ... of same.

In general the cleavage process proceeds best in the presence of much water, whereas synthesis is most favored by the absence of water. By the swelling or shrinking of the colloids present during the reaction, the organism is able to permit the process to proceed in one or the other direction. Swelling and shrinking are in turn dependent upon the formation and removal of acids by oxidative processes. The concentration of the products of a reaction in the solution brings the reaction to a standstill. If we are dealing with cleavages the crystalloid products may be readily removed by diffusion. This does not occur in the case of synthetic colloid products. Nor is it so essential because from the point of view of the law of mass action they are not to be regarded as dissolved.

We know enzymes to be the excreta of the stomach and intestines, but we also know that cells themselves contain enzymes, we may mention the uricolytic enzyme of the liver and zymase of yeast which ferments sugar

We must also recall that *enzymes* are the most strongly adsorbed of all the colloids of the body, and that the ability to be adsorbed is largely dependent on the acid or alkaline character of the medium. An enzyme may be so fixed (*e.g.*, rennet by charcoal) that its very existence is no longer determinable; a change of reaction recalls it to life. It may also be released by the approach of another colloid (in our example casein) by which it is adsorbed still more strongly. We thus get an inkling of the great importance enzymes have for the life of the cell, without as yet understanding the details.

The conditions governing *dissimilation* are much more readily understood. Through enzymatic cleavage of colloids, there are formed crystalloid products which pass into the circulating fluids of the organism by diffusion and leave as excreta, or, after oxidation to CO_2, are expired.

We must not conclude that in every instance the entire colloid molecule breaks down into crystalloid cleavage products. In this way, by the splitting off of individual "side chains" (P. EHRLICH) there is permitted great variation in cell life, which we might assume from our previous experiences.

CHAPTER XV

GROWTH, METAMORPHOSIS AND DEVELOPMENT.

Growth.

Of all the problems in biology, one of the most difficult and most engrossing is the development to constant type. From cells, which externally can hardly be distinguished we see develop a spiral, an oak tree, a butterfly or a man. In their evolution they always pass through the same stages to the same ultimate forms which, after a progressive senescence, return to the eternal process of evolution.

If we try to reduce these developmental processes to their simplest terms, we find diffusion and swelling phenomena with the formation of precipitate-membranes.

E. F. Runge, who discovered aniline and in coal tar, and who made the first aniline color, published a book in 1855 which is one of the most original scientific diversions I have ever seen. It is called

"*Der Bildungstrieb der Stoffe*"
(*The formative impulse of matter
viewed as automatically developing figures*)
By Dr. F. F. Runge
(Oranienburg. Printed by the Author)

The book consists of a collection of blotting paper leaves, upon which various inorganic salt solutions were stabbed. they interacted and gave colors by which the most remarkable figures were produced. At first glance these seem to be lower forms of animal life, amœba or rhizopoda, and the collection, just as Haeckel's "Kunstformen der Natur," might well serve as a text for designers because it offers such a multitude of suggestions with respect to color and shape. All the pages of the collection were prepared by the author himself (not printed) and are accompanied by a small amount of text which explains the method of preparation.

The explanation of these creations is one to the author who uses in one of his conclusions.

[1] [Chas Lowig is regarded as his wife of phosphorus. But Joseph and Sir Wm Henry Perkin is generally acknowledged even in Germany as the discoverer of the first aniline color, mauve. Tr.]

269

"After all, I believe I may make the assertion that the creation of these pictures is due to a *new* and hitherto *unrecognized* force. It has nothing in common with magnetism, electricity or galvanism. It is not stimulated or created by any external force but is innate in substances and becomes active when their chemical affinities neutralize themselves, that is, they undergo selective attractions or repulsions, and thus combine or separate I call this force 'Formative Instinct' and regard it as the prototype of the 'vital force' of plants and animals."

Of course, no special "Force" need be invoked for the explanation of RUNGE's pictures. They are the result of very complicated *diffusion* and *capillary* phenomena associated with chemical transformations.

What is especially interesting in RUNGE's pictures, on the one hand, is the *constancy* of the forms obtained by employing similar substances, and on the other hand, the extraordinary *multiplicity* brought about by the diverse action of different substances.

If we let a drop of copper sulphate solution fall on a piece of filter paper moistened with potassium hydrate, at the surfaces of contact a membrane of copper hydroxid forms, which changes rapidly but always in the same way If we always employ the potassium hydrate and copper sulphate in the same concentration, the copper hydroxid boundary will always have the identical form, provided the same filter paper is used. A change in the concentration of one or the other ingredients, however, gives a membrane of different shape. If, instead of copper sulphate, we place a drop of copper nitrate on the paper, we obtain forms entirely different, and a drop of nickel sulphate changes the picture completely. We thus see that small variations in the concentration of the solutions and in their chemical composition possess numerous possibilities for the formation of new shapes

In the living organism variations in *concentration* perpetually occur. We know from biological reactions that not only different animals, as, for instance, sheep and lions, have *chemically* different tissues, but that even the ass and the horse, and indeed different races of men, may be chemically differentiated, consequently the second condition for variation in form is also given, namely, the difference in *chemical* composition. The processes of the body (organism) are *regulated by* its colloidal state, and this very colloidal state also permits the *retention* of shapes.

If we seek to leave this far too general point of view and study details of the question more closely, we encounter almost insurmountable difficulties.

If a small lump of copper sulphate is thrown into a dilute solution

of potassium ferrocyanid, there will soon develop a brown envelope
which throws out upward-growing runners, and in half an hour's
time the fluid is filled with figures which vividly recall both the
shape and the color of seaweed. If a small amount (0.5 per cent) of
gelatin has been added to the water, the figures have some stability.
Their development is easily explained: the copper sulphate dissolves and immediately forms a semipermeable membrane of copper
ferrocyanid, through which no copper sulphate can escape, but water
may enter. Since a concentrated solution of copper sulphate is
formed within, water will be absorbed until the membrane bursts,
whereupon the copper sulphate solution is brought into contact
with the potassium ferrocyanid again and forms a new pellicle of
copper ferrocyanid, and thus the process goes on.

STÉPHANE LEDUC has studied these figures most industriously
and has discussed their significance in numerous publications.[1]

Some of his directions are here given: Prepare granules of 1 part
sugar and 1 or 2 parts copper sulphate. This is scattered in a fluid
consisting of 100 parts of water and from 10 to 20 parts 10 per cent
gelatin, 5 to 10 parts saturated potassium ferrocyanid solution and
5 to 10 parts saturated sodium chlorid solution, which mixture has
been heated to 40 degrees Centigrade. In this way we obtain figures
like that in Fig. 44, which may attain a height of 40 cm. The gelatin
is solidified by cooling and the figures may be preserved. Other figures are obtained by throwing granules of fused calcium chlorid or
barium chlorid into a concentrated solution of soda.

Another recipe is:

Water	1 liter
33 per cent potassium water glass solution	40 gm
Saturated soda solution	40 gm
Saturated sodium phosphate solution	60 gm

Beautiful branching figures are given by scattering calcium chlorid
granules in this mixture.

The more concentrated the solutions, the more rapid is the growth
and the more branching and delicate are the shapes. If the outer
water is diluted while the growth is in progress, we may produce
figures with stems and tops, like fungi (mushrooms and toad-stools,
etc.). These figures react to small changes in osmotic pressures by
changing their shape.

[1] I shall mention only his latest publications. St. Leduc, Biochem. Ztschr.
(Festband f. H. J. Hamburger), 1908, 280 u. ff. Les croissances osmotiques et
l'origine des êtres vivants (Bar-le-Duc, 1909). Les bases physiques de la vie et
la biogenèse (Presse Médicale, 7, 12, 1909). Théorie physico-chimique de la vie
(Paris, 1910). La dynamique de la vie (A. Poinat, Paris, 1913, and many others.

Sr. Leduc calculated that a granule of potassium ferrocyanid acquired 150 times its original weight when it grew, and that calcium structures acquired many hundred times their original weight

The *internal structure*, also, has some similarity to natural forms. They have a cellular structure as Sr. Leduc showed by microphoto-

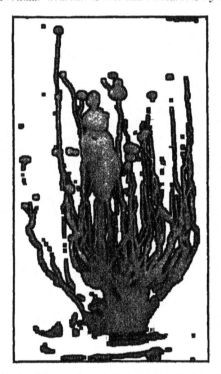

Fig. 41.   Artificially prepared osmotic seaweed   (Made by St. Leduc.)

graphs, Fig. 42, and as could be inferred from the way in which they are formed. The solution, e.g., of copper sulphate, which is surrounded by a membrane of copper ferrocyanid, imbibes water until the membrane bursts, and some copper sulphate solution is exuded, which straightway surrounds itself with a film of copper ferrocyanid, and thus a new cell is formed. The process repeats itself and one cell is added to another.

It cannot be denied that the pictures reproduced have a marked external resemblance to natural algæ, fungi, etc., and that it is

possible to imitate nucleus and cell division, growth and all sorts of
phenomena, and that even their internal structure is in many respects suggestive of a cellular structure. Doubtless structures do
occur in nature which develop in the same way as these artificial
osmotic products. In fruit wines after fermentation, H. Müller-

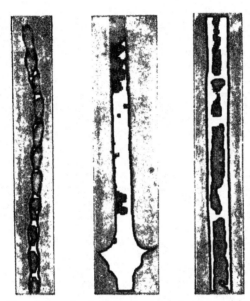

FIG. 42. Microphotographs of osmotic structures, showing a cellular structure.
Magnified x 60.   From St. Leduc.

THÜRGAU* found vesicles which were filled with bacteria (Fig. 43)
on the yeast sediment. These "bacteria vesicles" were developed
because the colloid substances eliminated by the bacteria, in conjunction with the fruit wine, which contains tannin, form a semipermeable membrane, a vesicle, that grows and sends out tubules.

*Is there really an analogy in the development of these structures to
the development of natural organisms?* The fact that there is not the
slightest chemical resemblance to organisms may be completely
disregarded since Sr. Leduc and all who share his views speak only
of the similarity of the physical force at work in both.

---

* W. Roux has treated the entire question in a very instructive essay on the
"Angebliche Künstliche Erzeugung von Lebewesen" in the "Umschau" (Frankfort a. M.), 1906, Nr. 8.

It is a detriment to the scientific treatment of the entire question that the outward resemblance (form and color) is so strikingly like the natural structures. Involuntarily, we are reminded of wax figures which move their arms and legs. Though the internal structure has some slight resemblance to some natural organisms, the analogy completely fails if we consider such details as cell division and cell multiplication The figures of St. Leduc absorb no nourishment, other than water; their increased weight, as far as solid substances go, consists only in pellicle formation, and in spite of a shape suggestive of higher organisms, they have no differentiated internal structure, and the cell division has not the remotest resemblance to natural cell division, but occurs intermittently by bursting, etc We might, if it did not seem fruitless, multiply the dissimilarities indefinitely and we might show that metabolism and the development of germ cells is out of the question in such formations. We must not overlook, in the presence of all these dissimilarities, that the physical forces which produce these inorganic formations are the same as those *which produce the growth and configuration of organized material: membranes, osmotic pressure, diffusion.*

Fig 43   Vesicles of Bacterium manitopoem from a pure culture in sterile peai juice The vesicle has developed a long transparent tube Magnification 200 1. (After H Muller-Thurgau)

In one point, at least, Leduc's analogies fail completely. excepting the membranes, they are devoid of *colloid material.* We have already seen that *swelling* frequently replaces osmotic pressure If we could imagine the crystalloid material of St. Leduc replaced by colloids capable of swelling, we would have the essential physical and chemical conditions for growth and structure of organisms.

A serious study of these problems, one which extends beyond external resemblances, is still in its earliest beginnings; see R. E. Liesegang, *Nachahmung von Lebensvorgangen* Formations resembling the creations of St. Leduc have been independently noticed by others. B. D. Uhlenhuth* produced beautiful growths by putting iron objects into antiformin. Antiformin is a mixture of sodium hypochlorite with sodium hydrate. The formations consist of iron oxid, and their development is easily understood from the explanations that have been already given. Since a small amount of a water-soluble iron salt must be formed first by the action of the hypochlorite of soda on the iron, the growth is slower, the figures are more beautiful and possibly more natural. In two weeks the structures attain a height of from 5 to 10 cm.

The growths described above offer analogies to organisms which are completely surrounded by water only, yet there are those which offer a resemblance to the growth of terrestrial plants. We might mention the "blossoms" of many crystalloid substances, especially the ammonia salts. H. Wislicenus[1] has thoroughly studied the growth and structure of *fibrous alumina*. If granules of aluminium which have been activated by contact with traces of mercury sublimate, for example, are permitted to lie in a moist place, very soon

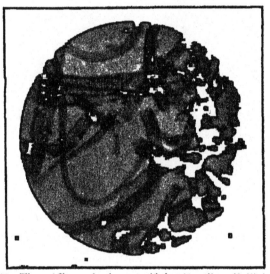

Fig. 44.   Fibers of fibrous alumina, magnified × 40.   (From H. Wislicenus.)

fibrous structures grow from the metal, which in a few hours may reach more than 1 cm. in length.   Under the influence of the mercury as a catalyzer, aluminium oxid is formed from the aluminium according to the formula:

$$Al + 3 H_2O = Al(OH)_3 + 3 H.$$

In this instance it is not the osmotic pressure of entering water which bursts the films, thus bringing a fresh metal surface to the reaction, but the pressure of the hydrogen gas.

Though in this case, as well, there are many gaps in the resemblance to natural organisms, nevertheless the fibers formed show certain

In the first place they resemble most organic fibers by being doubly refractive (L. Jost*) even though this double refraction is caused by different conditions than in organized structures. In contradistinction to natural fibers, the substance is isotropic; it is only its lamellated structure which produces that type of double refraction (H. Ambronn*) which is found in the siliceous envelopes of

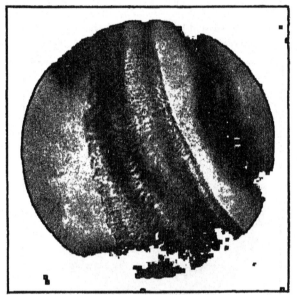

Fig. 45. Piece of doubly diffracting fibrous alumina. Magnified × 440.
(After H. Wisliccnus)

diatoms (*e.g.*, pleurosigma and amphipleura) and probably also in tabasheer, the colloidal silicic acid which occurs in the internodes of some species of bamboo.

The Genesis of Structures.

What *phase* is for the physical chemist, *cells* and *tissues* are for the biologist. Like phases, cells and tissues are "portions of a structure separated from one another by physical interfaces" (Wilhelm Ostwald's definition of phase). The interface may consist of an *invisible transition layer* (see p. 280). The interface is most evident when it consists of a *visible membrane*. Such a membrane whether visible or invisible is always a structure poor in water. At the interface against air it may be created by desiccation. Within the organism, we must assume that membranes develop similar to chemical *precipitation-membranes*. If we add silver nitrate to a solution of common salt, a precipitate of silver chlorid is formed. If we permit common salt and silver nitrate to diffuse together in a jelly, at the point of contact a *membrane of AgCl* develops. We considered the results of this more thoroughly in the introduction to this chapter. It is now, therefore, merely necessary to recall that not only may crystalloids form such membranes in a jelly, but that with albuminous material H. BECHHOLD*[2] produced such membranes in jellies (phosphoric acid, goat serum and goat-rabbit serum). Theoretically, therefore, the development of membranes offers no difficulties

The *development of a precipitate in a jelly gives a certain direction to the further evolution* of the process   The sense in which this is intended will be elucidated by some examples; by membrane formation, to begin with. Substances which form *no* membrane by precipitation, diffuse together unhindered, and in time become completely mixed. If a *semipermeable* membrane has formed, it behaves like a solid wall that arrests any further mixture. If two solutions of *equal osmotic pressure* diffuse together in a jelly till they form a permeable membrane, no matter how thin, e.g., sodium chlorid and silver nitrate, diffusion ceases as soon as the membrane has a very slight thickness. If, however, the osmotic pressure on one side is greater, the membrane continues to grow until the osmotic pressure is equal on both sides (N. PRINGSHEIM,* H. BECHHOLD and J. ZIEGLER*[1])

The phenomena are exceedingly interesting when *precipitates develop simultaneously in several places*   These phenomena have been studied by R. LIESEGANG.*[3]   If we place on a plate which is covered with sodium chlorid jelly, a drop of silver nitrate, there forms a disc-shaped precipitate of silver chlorid, whose circumference increases equally in all directions (a circle) according as the silver nitrate diffuses into the sodium chlorid jelly   If, however, two drops are placed on the sodium chlorid jelly several centimeters apart, there develops a picture like Fig 46, the two silver chlorid precipitates grow towards each other, that is, an "apparent chemical attraction" is observed. The reason for this is as follows: immediately upon applying the silver nitrate, the jelly loses sodium chlorid because of the precipitation of AgCl, and this causes a *movement in the entire mass of sodium chlorid:* the spot where the precipitate forms is deprived of chlorin ions, which then diffuse in afresh from the periphery   If two neighboring drops of silver nitrate have been placed on the sodium chlorid jelly, there forms between them a region poor in chlorin, which thus permits a more rapid

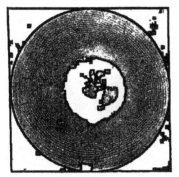

FIG 50   Liesegang's rings   (From
R. Liesegang)

FIG 51.   Laminated   urinary   calculus
(urates)   (Drawing by H   Schadde,
from von Frisch and E   Zuckerkandl)

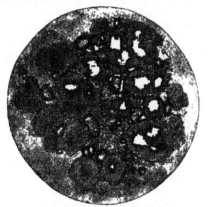

FIG. 53.   Oil-droplets super-saturated with cholesterin.   Crystalline separation of cholesterin
may be recognized in several droplets

FIG. 52.   Primitive gall-stone
pattern   (Myelin clump)
Magnified × 62.

FIG. 54.   Laminated
calcium   bilirubin
stone.

PLATE II.

advance of the silver nitrate. What is shown here in the case of the silver chlorid holds for every other precipitate, and for every osmotic disturbance, provided only that diffusible substances are present in a jelly

If such disturbances (precipitates, membranes) occur simultaneously in various places, it is possible for the most complicated figures to form.

Fig 16   Apparent chemical attraction   (R Liesegang)

In addition, we must consider the changes which occur in the ordinary course of swelling and shrinking of the colloidal material.

As far as I know, it has hitherto not been possible to explain such a phenomenon in vivo. I wish to refer to only one analogy C U. Ariens-Kappers* described as *neurobiotaxis* a phenomenon of nerve fibers· if *two* nerve cells, a certain distance apart, are injured simultaneously or in close succession, the growth of the chief dendron of both injured ganglion cells occurs in the direction of the other stimulated or injured cell. We thus have a growth towards each other, analogous to the apparent chemical attraction just described.

[C. A. Elsberg concludes from his experiments that hyperneurotization of a normal muscle is impossible. A normal muscle cannot be made to take on additional nerve supply. The implanted nerve cannot make neuro-motor connections   If the muscle is permanently separated from its original nerve, the implanted nerve will then establish such connections. Science N S., Vol XLV, p 319 *et. seq.*   Tr.]

Naturally, cells mutually modify each other's shape   A structure which would develop spherically if uninfluenced, under the pressure of neighboring cells acquires a reticulated, fibrous or pavement shape.

Layered Structures.

We saw that if two solutions which form a precipitate meet in a jelly, a precipitation membrane develops at the point of contact. Provided this is sufficiently permeable and *one* solution has a higher osmotic pressure, the membrane continues to grow *uninterruptedly*, becoming constantly thicker until the osmotic pressure is the same on both sides.   In 1898, R E. Liesegang*[1] published an observation which does not accord with the continuous growth mentioned above.

If, for instance, ammonium bichromate is dissolved in melted gelatin, which is then solidified in shallow dishes, and upon it a drop of silver nitrate is placed, then there does not develop upon diffusion a constantly thicker precipitation membrane of silver chromate but concentric rings called Liesegang's *rings* (see Plate II, Fig. 50).   The experiment may be performed by solidifying the ammonium bichromate gelatin in a test tube and layering some silver nitrate over it. We thus get instead of rings true precipitation membranes, which are separated from one another by layers containing no silver chromate (see Fig. 47). Subsequently, WILHELM OSTWALD,[*2] J. HAUSMANN,[*] H. W. MORSE and G W. PIERCE,[*] H BECHHOLD[*2] and E. HATSCHEK studied the development of these rings. It may be assumed as a result of these investigations that the formation of such layers is the result of a very complicated combination of events whose further elucidation at this point would carry us too far afield.

It should be definitely stated that the development of rhythmic structures is in no way dependent on the interdiffusion of two solutions. Similar structures may be produced in jellies also by crystallization (e.g , tri-sodium phosphate) or by freezing water.

The ring formation occurs especially when ammonium chromate and silver nitrate come in contact; at times there may be produced as many as twenty or more parallel membranes, which, according to the concentration of the solution, may be separated from a fraction of a millimeter up to 1/2 centimeter. They have also been produced by numerous other precipitation reactions.

H. BECHHOLD prepared similar stratified membranes with *organic material*. This occurs readily if serum mixed with gelatin is permitted to solidify in a test tube and metaphosphoric acid is layered over it. The number and beauty of the membranes depend very much on the relative concentrations of the solutions employed. Most advantageous is a mixture of 2.5 per cent serum and of 5 per cent gelatin, upon which is placed 2 per cent metaphosphoric acid; this gives as many as five concentric rings The author obtained two parallel membranes by the diffusion of goat serum into gelatin, containing goat-rabbit serum.

FIG. 47. Stratifications in a test tube (F Stoffel)

It is evident in the formation of this kind of layered membranes that the phenomenon noted on page 85 *et seq.* plays an important role colloids only precipitate in definite mixture relations, and solution occurs in the presence of an excess of either one. This phenomenon can be followed visually in the above-described membrane formation.

It is easy to imagine that layered membranes develop by the *removal* of a substance which holds another substance in solution. I have experimented with this end in view by dissolving *globulin* in gelatin containing sodium chlorid and layering water over it; when the sodium chlorid diffused away, then the globulin precipitated out. As a matter of fact no layered structures developed in the gelatin but only turbidities uniformly distributed. This does not by any means mean that, with a different arrangement of the experiment, regular layered membranes might not be obtained.

In organisms we frequently encounter *stratified structures* which, in most cases, occur as the result of rhythmic deposition. The *annual rings of trees*, the various layers in the otoliths of young and of old fishes cannot be explained in any other way than that periods of

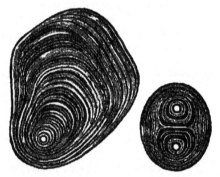

Fig. 18. Starch granules. (Külnitz-Gerloff.)

rest follow periods of strong accretion. In contrast to these "external rhythms" which obviously are induced by changing conditions affecting an organ, there are also layered structures with "internal rhythms" which suggest LIESEGANG's *rings*. As such, we must regard *starch grains* (Fig. 18), the silicious, spongious and calcareous structure of sponges, and the perforated calcareous shells of the foraminifera and many fish scales. R. LIESEGANG[5] mentions in addition the concentric lamellæ about the HAVERSIAN canals in the bones of vertebrates, the rods of the retina and the spiral cross striæ of muscle fibers. W. GEBHARDT compares the rhythmic markings on butterflies' wings to LIESEGANG structures. The coarse layers of the otoliths of fishes, the annual rings of trees, the concentric structure of pearls are penetrated by still finer layers, whose formation R. LIESEGANG thinks is analogous to the formation of the rings he described.

E. KÜSTER has called attention to numerous rythmic phenomena among plants in which the influence of external forces cannot be recognized and which consequently he attributes to LIESEGANG's law. Among others we may mention the thickening of membranes in vessels and tracheæ, the bands in striated portions of plants (herbs, pinus Thunbergii Parl), and the rhythmic changes in many blossoms Doubtless the number of instances where we may entertain the idea of internal rhythms may be increased at will and it will be the task of future investigators to determine the essential causes.

A valuable contribution in this connection was made by M. MUNK who studied the formation of fairy rings. When moulds are grown on bread, nutrient agar, etc., we frequently observe growth in concentric rings which suggest LIESEGANG's layers and are popularly called fairy rings.

M MUNK demonstrated that the accumulation of metabolic products interfered with growth, causing a zone where there was but little mould In the case of some strong acid producing moulds the distance between the individual rings may be regulated by the addition of alkali to the nutrient medium   If litmus agar is used the blue and red rings make visible the cause of the ring formation.

It is interesting that layered structures in the ends of the peripheral nerves, which were looked upon as real, have been proved to be *artefacts*. GOLGI stained nerves by saturating them with potassium bichromate and then treating them with silver nitrate. He obtained stratified structures whose appearance, as H. RABL showed, changed with the concentration of the solutions, and they could be nothing other than Liesegang's rings.

Biological Growth.

The *fertilization* of the egg is evidently the cause of the powerful *swelling processes*, which are possibly induced by the formation of acids   According to JACQUES LOEB,[3] oxidation processes accompany the development of the egg (whether fertilized or parthogenetic), without oxygen no development of the ovum occurs. The increase in the volume of the ovum of Echinoderma, until it reaches the pluteus stage, is entirely conditioned by the absorption of water (C. HERBST[*]) Before the larvæ reach the pluteus stage they cannot assimilate any organic nourishment. DAVENPORT[*] in the case of frog embryos has shown that their dried weight remains the same or diminishes till the moment when they commence to eat Their water content on the other hand was enormously increased. This absorption of water is *not* due to an increase in the osmotic pressure, since the fertilized and the nonfertilized frog's egg shows, according to L. BACKMANN and J. RÜNNSTROM,* only 1/10 of the osmotic pressure of the egg in the ovary, or of the adult frog. In the course of development, the osmotic pressure increases so that in the tadpole of 25 or 30 days, the osmotic pressure is almost the same as in the metamorphosed animal. L. BACKMANN and J. RÜNNSTROM agree that the decrease in osmotic pressure is due to the fertilization, which results in a gel formation by means of which crystalloids are adsorbed.

After a certain time, which varies for different animals, but not as yet definitely established for individual ones, a *shrinking* begins again, as may be seen from the following data, taken in part from the tables of H. GERHARTZ*[1]:

MAN

	Water, per cent	Dry substances, per cent.
3d fetal month	94 0	6 0
6th fetal month (Rubner)	90 0	9 7
7th fetal month (Rubner)	86 0	14 0
8th fetal month (Rubner)	83 3	16.7
Newborn (Camerer, Jr)	71 7	28 3
Adult (Moleschott)	67 6	32 4
Adult (Bouchard)	66 0	34 0

DOG

	Water, per cent	Dry substances, per cent.
6 days old (Gerhartz)	80 3	19 7
15 days old (Gerhartz)	77 0	23 0

SHEEP.

	Water, per cent	Dry substances, per cent.
6 months old (Lawes and Gilbert)	47 8	52 2
15 months old	43 4	56 6

MOUSE

	Water, per cent	Dry substances, per cent.
Fetus (½ inch long) (A v Bezold)	87 2	12 8
Newborn (A v Bezold)	82 8	17 2
8 days old (A v Bezold)	76 8	23 2
Full grown (A v Bezold)	73 3	28 7

CHICKEN EMBRYO (without yolk)

	Water, per cent	Dry substances, per cent.
7th day (L v. Liebermann)	92 8	7 2
14th day (L v. Liebermann)	87 3	12 7
21st day (L v. Liebermann)	80 35	19 65

What constituents are especially deprived of water cannot be properly determined from the limited material at hand, yet, according to H. Gerhartz, there seems to be a very great shrinking even of the albumin. For man he calculates the proportion of albumin to water to be:

Newborn. ...   . 1 albumin, 5 6 water
Adult .   .   .. 1 albumin, 4 3 water

J. A. Kubowitsch has shown that the water content of a mammalian embryo's muscle sinks from 99.4 per cent to 8 per cent at the termination of fetal life and finally to 75–80 per cent in adults. According to L. B. Mendel and Leavenworth, pig's liver has a quite constant water content of about 80 per cent during fetal life but diminishes to 67.3 per cent in the adult.

From this we understand that in the earliest stages, growth only results by means of the water taken up through swelling, though a time comes when growth is induced by the entrance of solid substances, by assimilation. This assimilated substance meanwhile binds less water, with further growth there is associated a *relative shrinking* which after reaching its maximum (growth) passes with further age into an *absolute shrinking*

According to Mühlmann, aging of different organs does not proceed equally. The weight of human intestines increases up to the fiftieth year, but the heart and lungs never cease gaining weight; the brain, on the other hand, has achieved its maximum weight at about the end of the second decade and from then on it gradually declines. The brain also shows definite microscopic aging phenomena, even in the earliest years Lipoid pigment granules appear in the nerve cells which continually increase and at an advanced age fill the entire cell According to Marinesco it is much easier to destroy with solvents suspensions of ganglion cells of a newborn puppy than an old dog As the result of his studies of pigment granules in nerve cells he also arrives at the conclusion that aging is due to the coagulation of physiological elements, a diminution of surface tension, such as we know occurs in the aging of colloids (see p. 73).

H. Schade determined that the subcutaneous connective tissue dissolved much more rapidly in NaOH when it was derived from a month old child than when it was taken from a thirty-two year old woman.

F. Tangl* is of the opinion that the shrinking of the animal organism during embryonal development is a duplication of the same phylogenetic process and shows by numerous tables that the lower invertebrates, even those which do not live in water, are usually more rich in water than the higher vertebrates

By what chemism increase of water and substance are conditioned, how *cell division* results, what are the relations between nucleus and cell protoplasm, are questions which are not yet ripe for colloid research.

To be sure we know that such swelling and shrinking processes occur, not only for the entire cell, but also in the *nucleus*. Before each cell division the nucleus swells up very much, and after division shrinks again, decidedly.

BOROWIKOW* made interesting observations on *plant growth*. All who are familiar with plants know that even in summer, periods of apparent rest alternate with periods of active growth (sprouting). The latter phase is associated with considerable entrance of water. It is impossible to explain this inbibition of water by osmotic forces since the increased rate of growth was usually associated with a *diminution* in the concentration of the cell juices instead of the reverse, and a growing plant absorbed unequal quantities of water from solutions osmotically identical. There was, on the contrary, some evidence that swelling processes were active. MARTIN H. FISCHER had already called attention to the fact that the tips of buds are always acid in reaction. It was quite natural, therefore, to test the influence of acids, bases and salts on the sprouting of plants and to compare it with the swelling of colloids. For this purpose BORO-WIKOW placed six-day old sunflower seedlings (Helianthus annus) in sieves and dipped them in various solutions, using distilled water as a control.

Dilute acids (1/100 normal) accelerated growth while salts simultaneously present acted against the acids. Acids and salts were active in a series which was analogous to that for the swelling and shrinking of dead colloids.

That bases caused no acceleration of sprouting seems to militate against the original assumption. BOROWIKOW explains this by the fact that the cell juice in the growth zone is essentially acid and constantly forms carbonic acid; the bases neutralize the acid, forming neutral unhydrated albumin and in higher concentrations damage the plants. In this way he explains the stimulating action of dilute solutions of organic bases (0 001 n urea nitrate, 0.0015 n caffein sulphate, 0.0025 n phenylene diamine chlorid) which, according to BOROWIKOW, act like their respective acids since they are hydrolyzed in solution.

BOROWIKOW expects especially to bring *growth* into relationship with *turgor* (tissue distention) Unnoticed, great turgor may be diminished by the growth process According to BOROWIKOW growth is ionization of the plasma protein by H ions in the growth zone, causing the protein to pass from the gel to the sol condition.

Ossification Processes.

One of the most interesting of colloid chemical problems is bone formation. We shall see on page 302 that from an aqueous solution containing blood salts, calcium carbonate and calcium phosphate precipitate. The precipitation is hindered by the presence of the blood colloids, though two-thirds of Ca salts, at least in the serum of higher animals, occur in the crystalloid state. This interference must stop during the formation of bone. To account for this there are several theoretical possibilities. It may be assumed that changes in the serum colloids are brought about at or from the bone cells, which remove their protective action and results in the precipitation of the calcium salts. This agrees with the views of Wo. Pauli and Samec,* which we shall consider more closely. It was shown that it is stated that the increase in the solubility of calcium carbonate by serum albumin was 175 per cent, and of calcium phosphate 90 per cent. We would consequently expect to find a very much more extensive precipitation of calcium phosphate than of calcium carbonate when the protective action was removed. But in the case of bone, the proportions are just the reverse. The bone ash of man contains about 850 parts Ca₃PO₄ and 90 parts CaCO₃ per 1000.

But in the case of a cleavage product of albumin Wo. Pauli and Samec found that the solvent action upon calcium salts was the reverse. Witte's peptone, consisting almost entirely of albumoses, holds in solution only the calcium carbonate, whereas the calcium phosphate exhibits a diminution in solubility. Based on these results, ossification might occur in the following way. In the bone or cartilage cells, there occurs a concentration of colloids in which a large quantity of calcium salts are piled up. When these bone colloids are broken down, a precipitation occurs, the precipitate consisting chiefly of calcium phosphate with smaller amounts of calcium carbonate. This corresponds with the histological evidence, by means of which a tissue destruction may be seen to accompany ossification.

A further possibility, which does not in the least contradict the above explanation but possibly coincides with it, is that phosphates are set free and come into contact with the calcium always present when the tissues, especially the cell nuclei, break down. In accordance with well-known physico-chemical laws, an increase in the concentration of an ion, in this case the phosphate ion, results in an increase in the calcium phosphate molecules, and this changed albumin must, accordingly, favor the precipitation of calcium phosphate.

Finally we may think of a kind of specific adsorption by certain cell organs. In fact, M. ...

calcium when he placed pieces of cartilage in chlorid of lime solution. This suggests the method by which lime is deposited in damaged tissues (vessel walls or tubercles). We must also consider the simultaneous precipitation of positively and negatively charged albumin with the breaking down of calcium salts as we shall describe later when we discuss concrement formation at greater length (see p. 271 *et seq.*).

Finally, we may consider some kind of specific *adsorption* by definite cell groups. We might also consider the mutual precipitation of positively and negatively charged albumin which carry salts down with them in the same way as is more fully described in the case of concrement formation (p. 271 *et seq.*)

What has been said here of bones also holds, of course, equally well in principle for the shells of molluscs and snails, for the armor of crustaceans, as well as for other ossification phenomena. Morphologists distinguish, primarily, between calcification and ossification (see GRÜNWALD. In lower animals (shells of snails and mussels, carapace of crabs, spicules of sponges, etc.), the lime salt occurs chiefly in microcrystalline form, as line granules in the calcifying tissues. In contrast with this ossification, lime forms an optically completely homogeneous deposit in bone and never occurs as a formed or crystalline precipitate. Possibly this essential difference depends on the fact that particular cells, osteophytes, take part in bone formation. It is still impossible for colloid research as yet, to offer even an hypothesis in explanation of this difference.

If I am correct (his correctness in doing so, I shall not discuss) critici an explanation of ossification which involves the presence of special cells the osteoblasts. He calls attention to the fact that deposit of lime occur in places where there are no osteoblasts, as in the arterial wall in arteriosclerosis, or in brain cells. He evidently concludes that under some circumstances, even without a special storing up, it is possible to have a precipitation from blood serum supersaturated with calcium salts, in which action the formation of centers might possibly take part (similar to the theory of H. BURIAN and ZUCKER[11] for the deposition of urates).

The very marked *decay* and the poverty of the bony framework in organic substance is deserving of special consideration. For this, the investigations of R. LIESEGANG[11] offer valuable experimental support. He showed that when calcium phosphate membranes were allowed to form in gelatin jellies (by the diffusion of disodium phosphate and calcium chlorid towards each other), that they were almost free from gelatin, to a certain extent the organic supporting substance had been forced away.

This investigator has simulated the formation and growth of the *long bones*. He filled test tubes half full of gelatin which was made alkaline, with tricalcium phosphate, for instance, this layer represented the periphery of the bone. After solidification there was placed on top a thin coating of gelatin containing a suspension of tricalcium phosphate, this was to represent the bone. Upon this was poured some acid solution, for instance, lactic acid, representing the center of the bone. The acid diffuses through the tricalcium phosphate layer, dissolves the calcium, reaching the lower periphery, where the calcium is precipitated again in layers as a phosphate. If a suitable calcium salt is added with the lactic acid, the layer becomes stronger and less porous; in a successful experiment, it shows, inside, the characteristic worm-eaten appearance of the long bones, and outside, a smooth firm and sharply defined structure. As material sources of acids, R. LIESEGANG mentions the accumulation of CO_2, lactic acid and glycerophosphoric acid derived from lecithin. [BARTEL] found that tricalcium phosphate was dissolved by water containing CO_2 under pressure, forming an unstable compound tribasic calcium phosphate, $Ca_3P_2O_8 + 4 H_2CO_3 = H_2O + P_2O_5Ca_3 \cdot 2CO \cdot CO_2H_2Ca$.

In discussing calcification and ossification in his Harvey Lecture, 1910-11, H. GIDEON WELLS concludes that "there seem to be no essential differences between the processes involved in normal ossification and in most instances of pathological calcification. Areas of calcification may be changed to true bone in the course of time," and that "calcium deposition seems to depend rather on physico-chemical processes than on chemical reactions." [JEROME ALEXANDER] suggests the importance of the removal of or alteration of protective substances resulting in the deposition of calcium salts. *Cf.* also HOFMEISTER's observation on the difference between solubility of calcium phosphate dissolved in serum and the dissolving of calcium phosphate by serum. Tr.]

Diseases of the Bone.

Of the noninfectious bone diseases, *rickets* and *osteomalacia* attract our special attention.

Rickets is characterized by lime-poor, so-called osteoid tissue, instead of the solid calcareous structure. In this way a pliable mass takes the place of the rigid framework. This lack of lime might readily be attributed to a lack of lime in the food, but it has been shown that this is certainly not the cause, since such a lack of lime can be produced only by artificial preparation of the food. In my opinion PAULI's theory of bone formation offers a good explanation for rickets. He supposes, as indicated on page 268, a preliminary tissue degeneration, in rickets we find quite the reverse, namely, an over-production of the osteoplastic tissue, so that we lack the conditions necessary to the precipitation of calcium phosphate and carbonate, or, in other words, bone formation.

Osteomalacia, bone consumption, is in certain respects the reverse of rickets. If in rickets we find a deficient precipitation of insoluble lime salts, in osteomalacia we have the eating away of existing bone. Osteomalacia occurs most frequently during pregnancy, during which even under normal conditions the teeth may suffer. *Osteoporosis*, the bone consumption of the aged, which is especially noticeable in the skull, belongs to this group Here, too, we must reject the theory of the deficient introduction of lime salts, as it is contradicted by all metabolism researches. We are much more inclined to accept a dissolving away of calcium phosphate and carbonate, especially by acids Since the oxidizing processes are deficient and the circulation functionates less perfectly, an accumulation of acids is not surprising. Magnus Levy has raised the objection to this "acid theory" that the proportion of the calcium phosphate to calcium carbonate is the same in osteomalacic as in normal bones. He placed normal bones in lactic acid and found that much more carbonate than phosphate is dissolved away, and from this he concluded that the "acid theory" was useless. This objection cannot be allowed. If acid diffuses from any direction into a mixture of calcium carbonate and phosphate imbedded in a *jelly*, the acid advances only to the extent that it has previously dissolved away all the carbonate and phosphate, this was shown experimentally by R. Liesegang[*2] (assuming, of course, that an acid stronger than phosphoric acid is employed). As may be readily seen, the result of the experiment depends entirely upon the conditions; at any rate the contribution of Magnus Levy cannot count *against* the "acid theory."

Concrements.

In various pathological processes we find in the body cavities of animals and men, structures varying in size from that of a grain of sand to that of a fist, and which have developed without the help of cells. Such precipitates are called concrements. We find them as renal gravel, urinary calculi, gallstones, brain sand (in the lymph spaces of the brain), rice bodies in the exudate of diseased joints; as the pearl of the pearl oyster; and similar formations which are found at times in cocoanuts, in view of their structure, can be considered nothing else.

The common characteristic of all concrements is that in addition to the special characteristic ingredients (urates and cholesterin) they always contain albuminous elements and they usually show a scaly and radial structure. These formations have been studied with especial care by H. Schade, as well as by L. Lichtwitz.

In the following pages, we shall consider the origin of urinary and biliary calculi from the standpoint of these studies.

Urinary Calculi. H. Schade mixed ox plasma which had been made uncoagulable by the addition of potassium oxalate, with an emulsion of calcium phosphate and calcium carbonate. When he coagulated the mass by the addition of CaCl₂ a hard cake formed, which, when preserved in salt solution at 40° shrank and after eight weeks had approximately the hardness of a true urinary calculus. Fibrin was absolutely necessary, yet from 0.07 to 0.1 per cent in plasma diluted ten times sufficed to produce a coagulation, and the phenomenon was the same if neutral urine was used for dilution instead of physiological salt solution.

By changing the composition of the sediment mineral ingredients it is not difficult to produce stratified structure resembling urinary calculi. This similarity is not a mere superficial one. Renal calculi have been repeatedly found which were still soft and plastic like the initial stages of these artificial stones. Whether the one membranous layered framework of natural urinary calculi (see Plate II, Fig. 4) consists of fibrin is still an open question though there is much in favor of this view. According to H. Schade the formation of urinary calculi is somewhat as follows: coagulum and mineral sediment simultaneously or in close succession shrink and harden. By the repetition of such processes layers form the stone grows, and after a while becomes stony hard, because the crystalloid ingredients grow into large crystal aggregates and take on a radial structure. The lesson for therapeutists is, that not only must the formation of crystalloid sediments be prevented but also the passage of fibrin or similar colloids into the urine. Alone urinary sediments form a crumbling mass. Calculus formation is possible only by means of colloidal "mortar."

Gallstones (biliary calculi): Gallstones differ very widely in their chemical composition. We recognize those which merely consist of *cholesterin* and others which contain only *calcium bilirubin*; between these extreme forms occur all sorts, consisting of mixtures of the two chief constituents with albuminous material.

Without going into the individual reasons it may be said that according to H. Schade, cholesterin appears to be dissolved in the bile as a hydrophile, and calcium bilirubin as a hydrophobe colloid. It must also be noted that, besides the cholates, the bile contains salts of the fatty acids, lecithin and mucinous substances which must partly be regarded as solvents for the gallstone material. *Cholesterin* precipitates in individual crystals from a supersaturated aqueous solution of cholates; however a few drops of an oil suffice to cause precipitation in an amorphous clump very similar to the "myelin clump" which NAUNYN described as the (uranlage) "*precursor* of gallstones" (Plate II, Fig. 52). After a few days, radiating crystallization starts from the center (Plate II, Fig. 53), oil droplets are released and may again give rise to oil-cholesterin precipitates. In this way may be prepared, artificially, hard or more or less plastic cholesterin stones, such as rarely occur, however, in the gall bladder. The presence of fats or fatty acids is, therefore, a requisite for their formation. For the precipitation of cholesterin it is only necessary that the substances which hold it in solution, the cholates and salts of the fatty acids, be destroyed. *A priori*, a supersaturation with cholesterin is brought about in all processes that interfere with the normal alkaline reaction of the bile, especially infection with B. coli, B. typhosus, B pyocyaneus and B proteus. I am inclined to accept the view of L. LICHTWITZ[1] that the acid formation of these bacteria is chiefly responsible for the breaking down of cholates and *soaps*, since staphylococcus aureus, which does not form acid, causes no separation of cholesterin. The precipitation of cholesterin can also be caused by sterile autolysis as well as by rendering less favorable the conditions requisite to solution, since cholates are absorbed by the walls of the gall bladder if the bile stagnates there (congestion).

Bilirubin forms amorphous precipitates with lime salts which normally do not sediment out in the bile. In the presence of albumin and fibrin, under conditions as yet not accurately studied, calcium bilirubin may precipitate and include the albuminous ingredients, giving rise to clumps which in their cheesy structures are very like natural calcium bilirubin stones (Plate II, Fig 54). In my opinion the neutral or faintly alkaline reaction of the bile is essential for the development of a calcium bilirubin stone as opposed to the cholesterin stones, which require acidity. H. SCHADE[*] considers that catarrhs, inflammatory and strongly exudative processes in which much lime enters the bile are responsible for the formation of calcium bilirubin stones; this view explains the occurrence in them of albuminous ingredients.

In some of the so-called mixed forms there may be an alternation of processes which condition the separation of cholesterin and of calcium bilirubin.

An answer to the question whether a *simultaneous precipitation* of cholesterin and calcium bilirubin may occur would be very interesting.

It follows from this in contradiction to previous views that the blood in gout is frequently supersaturated with monosodium urate According to the analysis of G KLEMPERER, MAGNUS-LEVY and SALOMON, the uric acid content of the blood in gout varies between 30 and 80 mg per liter, whereas in normal blood at most only traces of uric acid can be demonstrated When the content reaches 25 mg. of sodium urate per liter of blood serum, every further addition must be associated with a deposition of sodium urate, provided urate nuclei are present. We thus see that the serum colloids are of great importance for the solution of sodium urate in the blood and in preventing its deposition in gouty processes. [STANLEY R. BENEDICT in his Harvey Lecture, 1915 1916, p 362, discusses the presence of two forms of uric acid in blood. He determined ten times the amount of uric acid originally obtained by the preliminary boiling of the protein free filtrate with hydrochloric acid. The probable destruction of a "protective" substance is quite apparent. This aspect has an important bearing on uric acid determinations in nephritis and out. Tr.]

The influence on these processes exerted by *radium emanations* which inhibit the deposition of sodium urate from supersaturated serum (H. BECHHOLD and J ZIEGLER*)) deserves the attention of students of colloids.

In order to grasp these figures F. HOFMEISTER shows how a structure might be erected whose molecules are bricks, not to exceed in number 200,000 milliards, of which 200 milliards colloid molecules with a portion of the salt molecules form the walls, roof, ceilings, etc , whereas the water molecules with the remaining crystalloid molecules fill the rooms, halls and corridors. If such a structure had the enormous average height of 50 meters it would cover a ground space 7000 square kilometers or one-half the area of Alsace-Lorraine. It is evident that the compexity of the molecular structure of a cell baffles our powers of description.

A cube with edges 0.1μ which is much smaller than the limits of microscopic visibility contains 25 million molecules of water, 25 thousand molecules of colloidal, and 250 thousand molecules of crystalloidal substance, which under the same conditions would correspond to a building 100 meters front, 20 meters high and 20 meters deep.

Protoplasm.

Until recently there was little definite knowledge concerning the colloidal nature of *protoplasm*, that is, whether it was *fluid* or *gelatinized*. It was known that after the fragmentation of yeast cells it was possible to press out a juice containing various enzymes, and that meat juice obtained in a similar manner contained albumin. In the case of yeast it may be inferred that the protoplasm contains sols, but in the case of muscle such an inference is met by the objection that the albuminous substance may have arisen from the blood serum which bathes the muscle fibers The facts that portions of cells form drops and that foreign fluids in protoplasm assume spherical shapes likewise point to the fluid nature of many protoplasms

Most of the numerous investigations concerning the physical nature of protoplasm are at present of mere historical interest, since the *ultramicroscope* has solved many of the main questions or has placed us in a position to do so in the future. One of the most important criteria for differentiating between a sol and a gel[1] is the presence of *Brownian movement* If it is possible to observe an oscillatory movement in the granules of a cell, such granules must be in a fluid medium; if they are motionless the medium must be either a gel or very viscous. If we observe that the oscillating movement has ceased, it means that the fluid has gelatinized.

Numerous ultramicroscopic observations of cells have been published *Plant cells* have been studied most carefully by N GAIDUKOV.* He studied the pollen hairs of tradescantia, myxomycetes (slime fungi), the cells of various algæ (spirogyra, cladophora, œdogo-

[1] There is no sharp line between sol and gel. The more viscous the medium

nium, desmids, diatoms, oscillaria etc. as well the common frog-
bit, valisneria, and several others.

GAIDUKOV comes to the following conclusions as the result of
these investigations. Protoplasm is to be classed as colloids because
everywhere in living protoplasm he saw particles with Brownian
movement. Frequently he observed that the particles combined
or separated and that their motion increased or diminished, phenomena which in no sense are related and are the changes. In
some, usually in very well grown leaf cells, there were no movements,
which may be attributed to the fact that the distance between the
numerous particles was too small.

A transition from sol to gel or vice versa, the cessation of Brownian
movement, was not observed in normal protoplasm. The colloids of
plant protoplasm evidently consist of a ... sol and a reversible
portion. If a cell is opened a few protoplasm expands a portion
will expand in the water and becomes liquid ... in it, whereas
other portions remain as precipitate. The same observed in living
and in dead protoplasm. The observations of NAEGELI are analogous.
If we crush a root hair of hyacinth in water under a cover glass,
clumps of protoplasm pass the cut. Moreover these are immediately
surrounded by a membrane which ... and tends ... so that they
are coagulated on the surface. There is formed at the site of the
wound an irreversible layer of hydrogel similar to the fibrin formation of higher animals. The other observations quoted
entirely confirm what was earlier observed when plant cells absorbed
water. For instance if we place tissue cells in water they swell
and in spite of the increase in surface the outer layer plasma retains
its thickness. Evidently the entering water causes a gelatinization
of the granular plasma at the surface of contact so that the hyalo-
plasm layer spontaneously complements itself.

W. W. LEPESCHKIN regards protoplasm as a loose combination of
proteins and lipoids which breaks down under lethal conditions
(coagulation). If I understand him correctly he does not assume
the existence of a plasma pellicle except at the best I believe that all
the properties ascribed by other investigators to this membrane as
a limiting surface should be attributed to the protoplasm as a whole.

It must be remembered that all these observations experience
certain limitations depending on the kind and the part of the plant
involved. As a result of his experiments with sunflower seedlings,
BORODOWKOW assumes that plasma exists in seeds and spores as a
solid phase which changes to the gel condition in resting plants
(evidently jellies are meant).

In the growth period, the plasma as the result of hydration exists in the gel condition, the one in which we usually find it in cells according to BOROWIKOW.

With the occurrence of death protoplasm gelatinizes, Brownian movement of the smaller particles ceases, and the structure of the gel appears in the ultramicroscope as a conglomeration of many reflecting platelets. It makes a substantial difference whether the protoplasm slowly dies or is suddenly killed by a fixative (alcohol, formalin, etc.). In the first instance there is a precipitation (flocculation), whereas, in the latter there is a *stiffening*; this difference may be readily recognized under the ultramicroscope.

From this we may understand why a dead plant cell simply bursts in water, for the defects are no longer repaired from within. The cell contents have been already gelatinized. *Chloroblasts* (chlorophyl granules) may be assumed to possess colloidal properties similar to protoplasm; only it seems the latter are more delicate (PONOMAREW). The living protoplasm of many *animal cells*, however, seems to exist as a *gel*. At least in monocellular organisms, blood cells, etc., A. MAYER and G. SCHAEFFER* could not discover any Brownian movement of certain granules.

On account of the great differentiation of animal cells, more comprehensive investigations must be awaited; thus it appears to me probable that red blood cells have viscous contents (see p. 305).

The Nucleus.

We know even less about the colloidal nature of the nucleus than of protoplasm. Ultramicroscopically, the nucleus appears to be a complex of hydrosols containing larger particles and to be quite poor in water. This corresponds well with the picture produced by staining.

The colloids of cell protoplasm seem to be rather indifferent chemically, they are poorly stained by both acid and basic dyes. The nucleus, or more properly the chromatin substance, seems to possess pronounced acid properties, which are manifested by its intense staining with basic dyes (see A. KOSSEL*).

The Cell Membrane and the Plasma Pellicle.

The *cell* pellicle imparts its shape to the fluid protoplasm which otherwise would be spherical as the result of surface tension. The cell pellicle occurs in plants especially. In animals an interior skeleton or a spongy framework may determine shape. Theory requires an additional invisible *plasma pellicle* as bounding the protoplasm. Formerly from an interpretation of the experimental facts as pure osmosis, the pellicle was considered semipermeable, that is, permeable for water but impermeable for everything else. This view is theoretically untenable since the cell requires numerous substances and there must also be an exit for excreta. As a matter of fact, the studies of recent years have shown that the plasma pellicle is by no means as impermeable for many substances as was assumed. The attempt has been made to decide its chemical and physical condition from the nature of the substances which pass through it.

The statements on page 281 show that there is no uniform opinion as to whether the plasma pellicle consists of albuminous or lipoid substance or a mixture of both. In my opinion it differs in each instance depending on the contents of the cell. However, colloid research offers at least a foundation for a conception of the plasma pellicle.

In *animal cells*, with few exceptions, we can discover no membrane, yet many of their properties indicate that they also possess some sort of a pellicle. Colloid chemistry gives us a basis for the explanation of such phenomena. The conditions are most simple when the cells are surrounded by air. We know from page 33 that colloids concentrate and unite into a firm skin at an interface fluid-air. The process is much more complicated in the case of cells in a fluid or semifluid medium. Let us recall the following experiment: If ether is shaken with water containing albumin or albumose, there will form a foam consisting of drops of ether surrounded by albumin or albumose films. Certain other colloids and fluids permit the formation of fluid foams, which have unmistakable similarities to agglomerations of cells.

Although this analogy may at first sight seem entirely superficial, we must remember that the interface between two immiscible fluids and between a fluid containing solid or semisolid bodies, gel, possesses other properties than does the interior (see pp. 14 17, *et seq.*). The surface of a cell *must* have special properties, such substances as shall lower the surface tension must collect there. These substances are probably lipoid, lecithin and cholesterin, which have been demonstrated in every cell, animal as well as vegetable. The thickness of the transition layer varies according to different observers of different substances, from 1 to 2.5 $\mu\mu$, whereas the thickness of the material *coherent pellicle*, lecithin, etc., does not need to be thicker than from 0.3 to 7 $\mu\mu$. These are minimal figures which show that a membrane may be entirely invisible with the microscope and yet fulfil all the conditions of a true membrane as far as the transfer of material is concerned.

In brief our conclusions so far are: Every cell at its surface possesses a membrane which is dependent upon the composition of the interior of the cell. This membrane may be visible and may have been formed through the *gelatinization* of the cell protoplasm at the periphery. It may, on the other hand, be so thin as to be invisible, being formed by the *concentration* and *spreading out of such* albuminous and fatty *colloids as diminish the surface tension* of the cell content *at the interface*. The cell *membranes*, developing *as a result of the gelatinization* of cell protoplasm, are at first, in *youth*, expansile and elastic, with increasing *age* these membrane colloids, depending upon their environment and upon chemical influences, or as a result of mere colloid aging phenomena, become *poor in water and lose their elasticity*.

[In his " Growth and Form," Cambridge, 1917, D'Arcy W. Thompson invokes the aid of colloid phenomena in discussing the dynamics of cell life. Tr.]

CHAPTER XVII.

THE MOVEMENTS OF ORGANISMS.

The Movements of Lower Organisms.

FREEDOM of the will is still a problem in philosophy, and even the investigation of the purely reflex phenomena and actions of higher organisms is still entirely in the stage of observation and measurement. In any case, it is still impossible to connect the external stimulus and the resultant action by a series of obvious physical and chemical processes

It is otherwise in the case of the movements of certain portions of plants and of the lowest organisms, especially certain amebæ and their relatives, our symbiotic blood fellows, the leucocytes In this case, opportunities are offered for an exact explanation of their movements and actions; but even here analogies must frequently carry us over gaps.

It is customary to refer to such regulated movements of lower organisms and portions of plants as tropisms. [In this connection reference should be made to the discussion on "Animal Instincts and Tropisms in the Organism as a Whole," by JACQUES LOEB. G. P. PUTNAM'S SONS, 1916. JOHN HAYS HAMMOND, JR., has constructed heliotropic machines which follow a lantern in the dark The "retina" consists of selenium wire which changes its galvanic resistance when illuminated Tr.] We speak of *heliotropism* when certain plankton organisms swim toward the light or when a tree or a flower grows toward the light We speak of *positive thermotropism* if a root grows in the direction of a heat stimulus, of *negative thermotropism* when it grows away from it Every fact in this connection is not only valuable in explaining the subject but serves as well to enrich the meaning of the term "stimulus." "Stimulus" is an expression employed in biology wherever the more profound causes are not evident.

MARTIN H FISCHER has already indicated how tropisms may be explained in analogy to curling sheets of gelatin.

TH. PARODKO contributed extremely valuable studies on plant tropisms. He stimulated growing roots from one side and they became crooked The stimuli were chemicals, heat and traumata. He concluded that all these tropisms might be explained by protein coagulation in the affected cells. All substances and concentrations which salt out or precipitate protein proved to be chemotropic In connection with positive and negative chemotropism, salts of the alkalis and earth alkalis could be arranged in a lyotropic series similar to that we have repeatedly found in the precipitation of albumin and the swelling of gelatin, fibrin, etc. The salts of the heavy metals act still more strongly and always negatively chemotropic

Those movements which are manifest as general effects are still the most accessible to investigation

When placed between electrodes, bacteria, spermatozoa, yeast cells and red and white blood corpuscles migrate to the anode, amebæ pass to the cathode. Although organized suspensions and colloids migrate either to the anode or a few (*e g ,* iron oxid hydrosol and aluminium oxid hydrosol) to the cathode, hydrophile organic colloids such as thoroughly dialyzed albumin and gelatin pass in no definite direction when placed in an electric field, they acquire a definite direction only by the addition of electrolytes. OH ions cause an anodal and H ions a cathodal migration Since the organisms mentioned, considered as a whole, are hydrophile organic colloids, we must assume that their direction of migration in the electric field is determined by the ions clinging to them Normal albumin with a content up to 0.01 normal $NaHCO_3$ still migrates to the anode. We need not be surprised, therefore, that the majority of micro-organs and microorganisms also migrate to the anode The problem reduces itself to determining the direction taken by pure albumin

The cathodal migration of amebæ is remarkable and requires more thorough study. Equally remarkable is the fact observed by H. BECHHOLD,[*] as well as by M. NEISSER and U FRIEDEMANN,[*] that agglutinated bacteria lose their direction of migration (p. 205), agglutinin having produced a neutralization.

Following the ideas of G. BERTHOLD,[1] we are nowadays tempted to explain by a simple formula certain individual movements of the lower organisms and of leucocytes, that is, by changes in *surface tension* [1] A fluid or semifluid structure which is constantly under the stress of surface tension assumes a spherical form, as, for instance, oil in a mixture of alcohol and water. If such a drop is placed between two other phases, a change in form occurs, and with it a *movement*. A drop of oil on the surface of water spreads out, every moistening brings about an enlargement of the surface, a spreading out upon the moistened body (see p. 17) A structure may suffer a change of surface tension *in some single spot*, locally, so that a movement

---

[1] A full bibliography is given in L RHUMBLER's "Zur Theorie der oberflachen krafte der Amoben" Zeitschr. f wissensch Zoologie, **83**.

occurs; this may be induced for instance by an electric charge, chemical reactions and the like Thus a structure may retain its general spherical form yet increase its surface at some single point, flattening out, putting out limbs, pulsating, making slight movements which may be explained purely by physical chemistry. The vital phenomena of amebæ and of leucocytes which are evidenced especially by movements of the plasma may be regarded as changes in surface tension Portions of plasma (pseudopodia) are far extended and the remainder of the body follows them. so that movements of progression arise. Sometimes the pseudopodia surround foreign bodies, a starch granule, a bacterium or the like and draw it into the ameba or leucocyte; ingestion of food thus takes place.

The migrations of an ameba, according to L. RHUMBLER, may be deceptively imitated with a drop of chloroform in the following way A Petri dish is covered with an alcoholic solution of shellac and the excess is poured off, so that after a few minutes the shellac layer is superficially hardened. Boiled water is then poured into the dish and a drop of chloroform dropped on the shellac with a pipette. Immediately the drop begins its characteristic migration, especially if it is pushed with a glass rod inserted between the chloroform and the shellac layer The phenomenon is explained as follows a marked surface tension develops between the chloroform, the water and the moist shellac layer, soon chloroform and shellac commence to be moistened at some point and at this point the surface tension of the chloroform is lowered and it seeks to spread itself out. In this way the chloroform drop progresses in a way similar to the flattening of the advancing margin of an ameba The thin shellac layer is dissolved by the chloroform flowing over it, so that the path traversed by the drop "appears as if cut out of the shellac." Still more deceptive is the similarity of movement if one does not take a surface entirely covered with shellac, but prescribes the path of the drop by a fine shellac line and retards the movements by the addition of Canada balsam or neat's-foot oil to the chloroform. According to the proportions of chloroform, size of drop, thickness of the shellac layer and the degree of its dryness, the movements may imitate the most diverse kinds of amebæ If a drop of chloroform is placed on a spot of shellac which branches in various directions, an imitation of the spreading of pseudopodia is obtained. The taking up of nourishment (taking up of oscillaria threads by ameba verrucosa) may, according to L. RHUMBLER, be imitated when a drop of chloroform in water comes into contact with a thread of shellac; the drop completely envelops the thread of shellac and rolls it up into itself.

At times small amebæ are pursued by larger ones, the former change their direction and their speed, the pursuer continues its journey and catches its prey, which may again escape, and the pursuit continues. All these processes are explained according to L. Rhumbler, without invoking a conscious intelligence and purposeful movements, by the trail left behind by the pursued ameba, just as the chloroform drop pursues the track of shellac mentioned above.

Though the movements are so similar and the explanation by changing surface tension is so clear, we are still forced to enquire how the surface tension of amebæ and leucocytes is changed. Analogy is quite absent in the character of the substances whose surfaces are in contact and in the physical process (solution of the shellac) that takes place. It was assumed that substances which diminish surface tension (for instance, soaps, albuminates, L. Michaelis) form at the point of motion and then break up again. Though a definite demonstration has not been possible, I shall discuss an hypothesis of L. Hirschfeld* which has much to recommend it in certain cases. We know that an electric charge depresses the surface tension (see p. 87) but the question is whether the development of an electrical charge at any point of a mass of protoplasm is conceivable. Let us consider the circumstances under which a bacterium approaches an ameba that puts out a pseudopodium, envelops the bacterium and draws it in. Between two electrodes, amebæ migrate to the cathode and bacteria to the anode. H ions diminish surface tension, causing the extension of pseudopodia as demonstrated by the plentiful formation of pseudopodia upon fixation with osmic acid; OH ions cause an increase of surface tension and a retraction of pseudopodia. If we imagine a bacterium to be a negatively charged particle which gives off H ions, by dissociation it will lower the surface tension at the presenting point of the ameba and occasion the appearance of pseudopodia. When the bacterium is surrounded, there is an equalization of charge, the surface tension is raised and the pseudopodium is retracted with the bacterium. L. Hirschfeld attributes the positive charge of amebæ to the excretion of CO_2. If the metabolism of the ameba is impaired, the formation of CO_2, and with it the mobility of the ameba, are diminished. What occurs in the case of amebæ may be applied to the special case of *phagocytosis*. It was the phenomena occurring in amebæ that led Elie Metchnikoff to his fundamental studies on phagocytes, scavenger cells. Thus he names such white blood corpuscles as attack by taking up and digesting microörganisms entering the blood stream. They are the defending army of the organism, and according to E. Metchnikoff, the most important weapon in the fight against disease germs.

L. HIRSCHFELD is supported in his theory by the statement of H. BECHHOLD* that lactic acid (H ions) increase the phagocytic activity of leucocytes, whereas alkalis (OH ions) are without such effect.

This introduces us to one of the most important fields as yet [almost] untouched by colloid investigation, *chemotaxis*, the experimental study of which from modern viewpoints ought to prove most promising.

In 1884, E. STAHL and DE BARY on the one hand, and W. PFEFFER on the other, simultaneously gave their attention to the nature of *chemotaxis*. They studied the lower monera, plasmodia of myxomycetes (slime fungi) bacteria, flagellates, wheel animalcules, the clustered spores of algæ, the spores of ferns, mosses, etc. The essence of chemotaxis lies in the attraction of these unicellular organisms by certain substances (*positive chemotaxis*) and their repulsion by others (*negative chemotaxis*), while other substances do not affect them at all. If for instance a cane sugar solution is placed in a very narrow test tube, and the open end is dipped into a drop of moss spores, the latter will pass into the tube, attracted by the cane sugar. It is necessary to assume some such chemotactic relation between eggs and spermatozoa, especially of aquatic animals, as the spermatazoa discharged into the water are attracted by the eggs. We owe our knowledge of the chemotactic action of *leucocytes* of the higher animals to C A PEKELHARING and especially to TH LEBER who gives in his classical work, "Die Entstehung der Entzündung," a wealth of experiments in which the most varied substances were introduced into the eyes of rabbits In the same field, but it is quite obvious independently, he was followed by MASSART and J. BORDET.

We reproduce the following series of substances with a chemotactic action (after A. GABRITSCHEWSKY) to show how difficult it is to explain the existence of chemotaxis on a *single* principle.

SUBSTANCES SHOWING CHEMOTAXIS.

Negative	Absent	Positive
10% K and Na salts	Distilled water	1% papayotin (for rabbits)
1–10% glycerin	Carmin powder	Living and killed cultures of:
Bile	0 1 to 1% K and	Bacillus pyocyaneus
10% alcohol	Na salts	Bacillus prodigiosus
Chloroform in aqueous	Phenol	Bacillus of anthrax
solution	1% antipyrin	Bacillus of typhoid
0 5% quinine solution	1% phloridzin	Bacillus of hog erysipelas
0 1 to 10% lactic acid	1% papayotin (for	All the bacteria that have
Jequirity	frogs)	been studied excepting the
Sterile culture of chicken	1% glycogen	bacilli of chicken cholera
cholera bacilli	1% peptone	
	Bouillon	
	Aqueous humor	
	Blood	

It may be concluded from this that a substance may be neutral for certain leucocytes and positively chemotactic for others (papayotin), and that the chemotactic relation may vary with concentration (K and Na salts; with reference to lactic acid and quinine solutions see pp 286–288)

What relation does all this bear to the theory of changing surface tension? Some data are in its favor. The very first observation of E. STAHL on the plasmodia of æthalium septicum of tanner's bark gives a decided impression that a surface phenomenon is involved. When he brought such a plasmodium clinging to the internal surface of a glass in contact with pure water by introducing the water from below, the plasmodium spread out uniformly, if he introduced tannic acid, it traveled downwards; and on the addition of from 1/4 to 1/2 per cent sugar solution, it traveled upwards. It is just this action of tannic acid which tans the surface of protoplasmic mucus and the phenomenon of spreading out in pure water that point to surface forces   They are also suggested by the observation of RANVIER, according to whom leucocytes spread out more, the larger the surface development of the given body (better on rough than on smooth surfaces and especially well upon elder pith)   On the other hand, we recognize from what has been said that the theory which attributes the decrease in surface tension to an electrical charge does not suffice for the explanation of all phenomena. An intensely positive chemotactic action is possessed not only by bacteria, but also by extracts and proteins obtained from them.   The chemotactic experiments undertaken on the bodies of higher animals (eye, pleura, etc.) do not justify a physico-chemical explanation, because in this instance two factors coexist   The substance itself may act chemotactically; on the other hand, it may be inactive yet cause a necrosis of the adjoining tissue, which then becomes chemotactic and simulates activity on the part of the substances under investigation. [Elsewhere (p. 234) reference has been made to the observations of A B MACALLUM   His monograph "Surface Tension and Vital Phenomena," No. 8 Physiological Series, University of Toronto Studies, 1912, includes a bibliography   Tr]

Possibly the very original "Quantitative Studies on Phagocytosis" of H. J. HAMBURGER and HEKMA* will permit conclusions concerning the causes of the protoplasmic movements of leucocytes, when a method shall have been discovered for measuring the surface tension of protoplasm against water and salt solution.   Even now it may be recognized from these studies that the causes of movement are quite complicated since it has been shown that the *calcium* ion has an entirely *specific* action in stimulating phagocytosis.   If such action were due merely to the electric charge possessed by Ca as a divalent ion, we would expect the same effect from barium, strontium and magnesium; this however is not the case.

Especially noteworthy is the fact, only recently studied by G. DENYS and LECLEF, WRIGHT and his pupils, and NEUFELD among others, that leucocytes are stimulated to the phagocytosis of certain bacteria only by the presence of *serum*, and that, on the one hand, the intensity of the phagocytosis is dependent upon the virulence of the bacteria, and, on the other, upon certain properties of the serum, closely related to those which determine immunity

To the colloid chemist, it is of importance to determine whether the general colloid properties of serum play a rôle in phagocytosis, and whether the serum may be replaced by other colloids. H. BECHHOLD* showed that egg albumen, which stands nearest to serum in respect to its colloid properties, caused no phagocytosis, whereas Witte's peptone, a markedly broken down protein, has such an action.

In the case of chemotaxis, as in the case of phagocytosis under the influence of *opsonins* (or certain hypothetical irritants which increase the appetite of leucocytes) only comprehensive quantitative experiments will yield material utilizable for the development of a physico-chemical theory by the colloid chemist. Although, for instance, quinine is regarded as a substance which inhibits phagocytosis, M. NEISSER and GUERRINI* have shown that in minimal doses it increased the appetite of leucocytes.

It may be said in conclusion that the surface tension of leucocytes in relation to the surrounding medium (serum) must be very low. On page 16, we saw what force is necessary to change the form of such small bodies (leucocytes have an average diameter of from 6 to 8 μ). If we recall what changes in surface tension a leucocyte may undergo in phagocytosis, and the very great changes in shape suffered in traversing the tissues, we are forced to ascribe to them a very low surface tension, much lower than that possessed, *e.g* , by red blood corpuscles.

The Movements of Higher Organisms.

The movements of higher organisms are controlled by the nerves and accomplished by the muscles. In the present state of our knowledge and in the limits of this book we can only consider this question: From what physical and chemical processes does muscle contraction result? For this purpose we shall first consider the muscle as a colloid system and endeavor to gain an idea how a contraction occurs.

Muscle as a Colloid System.

In the case of higher mammals, muscles constitute approximately 43 per cent of the entire body. Since they have a greater range of swelling than all the other organs (see p 219), besides their usual function as a water reservoir, they are of great importance.

As regards swelling, they behave very much like fibrin or gelatin. It was formerly believed that the circumstances of swelling in muscle, which were at first chiefly studied in the case of frog muscle, could be explained by osmosis, but the quantitative studies of J. LOEB,* followed later by A. DURIG, C. E OVERTON* and R W WEBSTER, showed that no satisfactory solution could be thus obtained. If the osmotic conditions alone were determinative, the muscle should retain its water in isotonic solutions, shrinking in hypertonic and swelling in hypotonic solutions. But this is not by any means the case, since there is a material difference between solutions of electrolytes and of nonelectrolytes. Whereas neutral salts greatly diminish the swelling produced by acids and alkalis, this property is not possessed by nonelectrolytes (cane sugar, ethyl alcohol, methyl alcohol, urea and glycerin) Even the supposition of a lipoid membrane does not explain the phenomena, since cane sugar is as insoluble in lipoids as are most of the neutral salts.

As early as 1901, A. DURIG concluded from his investigations with whole frogs that the laws which are invoked in osmotic processes alone are inadequate, in this case muscles are chiefly concerned in the absorption and relinquishment of water. MARTIN H. FISCHER* was the first to direct attention to the fact that for *dead muscle*, qualitatively and to some extent quantitatively, similar laws governed the taking up and the relinquishment of water as governed unorganized colloids capable of swelling.

To summarize his results briefly: muscles swell more in acids and in alkalis than in water, and indeed, in hydrochloric acid, nitric acid > acetic acid > sulphuric acid. The maximum amount of water that a muscle can absorb under the circumstances is about 246 per cent of the original muscle weight, or 13 times the dried muscle substance. It therefore possesses, it is true, a smaller swelling capacity than gelatin which can take up from 15 to 25 times, or fibrin which takes up upon solution 30 to 40 times, its dried weight

The absorption and relinquishment of water by muscle is a reversible process, yet M. H. FISCHER emphasizes the fact that during the time of his experiments *no complete reversibility* was observed, that "every change of condition left its permanent results."

Salts diminish the swelling of muscle in acids and alkalis in a way similar to the case of fibrin and gelatin, though not so obviously.

There is, indeed, a very important difference between *dead* and *living* muscle. the swelling of dead muscle in distilled water, for instance, is brought about by the formation of lactic acid, which sets in within a few minutes. If this were not the case, a living frog would swell up as much in fresh water as a dead one [1] According to M. H. FISCHER, a dead muscle retains its form in a 0.7 per cent NaCl solution, not because the same osmotic pressure exists inside and outside the cell, but because the concentration of the NaCl solution is just sufficient to overcome the action of the acids formed in the excised muscle. We must again point out here that the experiments of W. BILTZ and A. VON VEGESACK * show that if colloids are present in a medium, the presence of isotonicity does not by any means permit us to infer that equal osmotic pressures exist

Against M. H FISCHER's experiments, the objection has been raised that *dead* muscle possesses no semipermeable membrane, so that its swelling follows laws similar to those of fibrin, etc. In living muscle, however, semipermeability exists; on this account the results of M. H FISCHER cannot be transferred to living muscle. There are also certain discrepancies in respect to some nonelectrolytes; thus, for instance, dead muscle does not swell up in isotonic sugar solution; this does not accord with FISCHER's theory. [Sugar has a specific dehydrating action   Tr]

The studies of E. B. MEIGS * have illuminated these discrepancies; they showed a definite difference between *smooth* and *striated* muscles. Smooth muscles are involuntary and occur in automatically acting organs (intestines, urinary bladder, iris, etc.), and especially widely distributed among the lower animals. They contract much more slowly than striated muscles   E B. MEIGS concludes that *smooth* muscle is not surrounded by a semipermeable membrane, in other words, osmosis is not a factor, but that they behave toward electrolytes like any hydrophile colloid, fibrin or gelatin, with reference to change in volume.

The behavior of *striated muscles* is quite different. To understand it we must briefly recall their *histology*. Muscles consist of bundles of *fibrils*, longitudinal fibers which are surrounded by a connective tissue sheath. Each fibril, that is, every minute fiber, is surrounded by a membrane, the *sarcolemma*, and is bathed in a fluid substance, the *sarcoplasm*. The individual fibrils are striated at right angles to their axes. The striations appear microscropically as alternating dark and bright zones; while the latter are isotropic, the dark striations are doubly diffractive, anisotropic (see Fig 49).

[1] [If the circulation of a living frog is impeded so that local acidosis develops,

E. B. MEIGS * studied the rate at which fresh muscles increased their weight in water and in salt solutions. He concluded from his study that the weight increase is the result of *two* processes: At first, water is osmotically taken up by the sarcoplasm of the fresh (still irritable) muscle; after the muscle is dead, lactic acid forms, the semipermeable membrane of the fibrils (the sarcolemma) becomes permeable and now the fibrils *swell up* at the expense of the sarcoplasm fluid and are thus shortened; this is evidenced by rigor mortis (O. VON FÜRTH and LENK). The proteins become coagulated through the accumulation of acid, this especially induces a shrinking and thus a relaxation of rigor mortis. By this experimentally established explanation O. VON FÜRTH and LENK have cleared away an old fallacy that the onset of coagulation induced rigor mortis. By artificial *fatigue* (e.g., electrical stimulation of an excised frog's muscle) the accumulation of acid and the consequent swelling of muscle in dilute

FIG. 49 Striated muscle fiber. (Stohr.)

salt solution is much hastened (C. SCHWARZ *). It is a well-known fact, moreover, that after great muscular exertion (forced marches, convulsions, hunted prey), rigor mortis sets in sooner than when death overtakes a rested organism.

When rigor mortis disappears striated muscle behaves like an hydrophile colloid, whose swelling and shrinking are unhindered by semipermeable membranes.

A further study of E. B. MEIGS * is concerned with the nature of the semipermeable membrane of a fibril. It tends to show that the latter consists of calcium phosphate. Collodion membranes impregnated with calcium phosphate proved impermeable for salts, sugar and amino acids, but were somewhat permeable for glycerin and urea and easily permeable for ethyl alcohol. They were moderately permeable for potassium chlorid as was to be expected. The predication of a semipermeable layer of calcium phosphate explains two facts very well: 1. The suspension of the semipermeability of muscle after death (the accumulation of lactic acid destroys the membranes) and 2. the importance of calcium for the maintenance of semipermeability in living muscle; since the layer of calcium phosphate is destroyed in a neutral lime-free solution.

A unique observation was made by M. H. FISCHER and P. JENSEN * upon the *water in muscle.* They put the gastrocnemius of frogs into narrow glass tubes, cooled them down to $-76°$ in a mixture of ether and solid CO_2, and followed the curve of cooling with a needle-shaped thermocouple. With a torch of average size, the phenomena are about as follows. Within about 1 minute there is a very slight cooling; within another 5 or 10 minutes the water freezes in the muscle and further cooling occurs. This part of the curve is quite characteristic for the fixation of water. It should fall more steeply than the curve of control water or of physiologic salt solution. If it is less steep, it is "a sign that there is some process in the colloid structures which liberates heat." In H. W. Fischer and P. Jensen's investigations, it was shown that it is necessary to distinguish two kinds of water fixation in freezing, namely . . . After or during death by freezing, there occurs a phenomenon by which water is fixed in some unknown way and by which it is again liberated at lower temperatures," and indeed the amount of water fixed in a muscle increases with the amount of disturbance, whether frozen once, twice heated to 100° or boiled. In this case also it is essential two kinds of water fixation exist.

The relation between cooling and the death of muscle by freezing is very interesting. The degree of . . . fidity . . . was measured by the biting capacity of a muscle in response to stimulation. It was shown that cooling the muscle to the point of freezing and even freezing out the water to a certain extent did no harm, but if the muscle was cooled 1.5° C more it died. The difference or the margin between life and death of muscle is therefore only 1.5° C wide.

The normal state of swelling in muscle is conditioned by a normal content of electrolytes. This may vary greatly for different classes of animals, for instance, according to J. Katz the striated muscle fibers of the dog contain 35 times as much K and those of the pike 44 times as much K as Na. For the same species it appears to be uniform at the same age.

A remarkable fact regarding muscle is their *high potassium content*, which is closely associated with their capacity to functionate. (See Macallum, also Beutner.) In . . . for a normal swelling, the isotonicity of the surrounding solution appears to be of much less importance than a definite electrolyte content. This follows from experiments of E. M. Widmark,[*] according to which even 10 millimols $CaCl_2$ in the surrounding solution produced a loss of weight amounting to 36 per cent in the split muscle plate.

Muscle Function.

Every stimulus, whether of thermal, mechanical, electrical or chemical nature causes an irritation in the living muscle which is manifested by a contraction. R. Hober,[*] whose investigations we . . .

[†] The mathematical laws for this phenomenon are . . .

shall now consider, is primarily responsible for the electrochemical theory of this *irritability*

For our consideration, two electrical phenomena of muscle are important: In activity, that is during the contraction of muscle, electric currents (action currents) develop, the stimulated point in the muscle becomes negative in relation to the remaining fibers which are at rest. The same thing holds true for *nerves* in which no external sign of activity is discoverable.

If, in an excised mollusc muscle, an injured point is united to an uninjured point of the mantle by a wire having a galvanometer in its circuit, the cut surface is negative and the mantle surface is positive. The same electrical phenomena are observed in a *resting nerve* This is called the *current of rest*, or, according to H HERMAN, the *demarcation current* (HERMAN calls the *demarcation surfaces* the interface between the injured, dead, and the uninjured, living, substance)

Evidently action current and current of rest are due to the same cause. In his textbook, R. A. A. TIGERSTEDT states the phenomenon as follows: In muscle as in nerve, a stimulated point, or one which is injured in any way, is negative electrically to every other point which at that time happens to be at rest or uninjured.

Let us consider how we may explain the direction and magnitude of different potentials which occur when muscle contracts. Electrical differences in potential arise on every interface between an electrolyte and a pure solvent or one containing less electrolytes. The simplest case is when an acid, *e.g* , HCl, is limited by pure water — then the more mobile positive H ion will rapidly advance and give a positive charge to the water while the acid is negatively charged by the more slowly moving negative Cl ion This applies to muscle, for lactic acid arises at the point stimulated or injured.

The electromotive forces which are derived from a circuit of acids and water or crystalloid electrolytes are much smaller than we observe in muscle.

Wo. PAULI invokes the colloidal properties of the protein ions in explaining the high electric tension which we obtain in muscle or even in the electric organ of the torpedo

Protein in general contains an amino acid with many NH_2 and COOH groups. Let us illustrate the development of electromotive forces by the following diagram in which R represents the protein radicle and L the lactic acid radicle·

$$\begin{array}{l} \text{OHCO} \cdot \\ \text{OHCO} \cdot \\ \text{OHCO} \cdot \end{array} \mathbf{R} \begin{array}{l} \cdot \text{NH}_2 + \text{LH} \\ \cdot \text{NH}_2 + \text{LH} = \\ \cdot \text{NH}_2 + \text{LH} \end{array} \begin{array}{l} \text{OHCO} \cdot \\ \text{OHCO} \cdot \\ \text{OHCO} \cdot \end{array} \mathbf{R} \begin{array}{ll} \cdot \overset{+}{\text{NH}}_3 & \overset{-}{\text{L}} \\ \cdot \overset{+}{\text{NH}}_3 + \overset{-}{\text{L}} \\ \cdot \overset{+}{\text{NH}}_3 & \overset{-}{\text{L}} \end{array}$$

The difficultly mobile colloidal acid-protein ion immediately becomes positively charged at the surface of a neutral medium, and should it touch an acid medium its positive charge is raised and at the same time the acid field becomes more negative as the following diagram indicates·

$$\begin{matrix} OH\cdot CO\cdot \\ OH\cdot CO\cdot \\ OH\cdot CO\cdot \end{matrix} R \begin{matrix} \cdot \overset{+}{N}H_2 \\ \cdot \overset{+}{N}H_2 \\ \cdot \overset{+}{N}H_2 \end{matrix} + LH = \begin{matrix} OH\cdot CO\cdot \\ OH\cdot CO\cdot \\ OH\cdot CO\cdot \end{matrix} R \begin{matrix} \cdot \overset{+}{N}H_2 \\ \cdot \overset{+}{N}H_2 \overset{+}{H} + \bar{L} \\ \cdot \overset{+}{N}H_2 \end{matrix}$$

for the H ion moves faster than the L ion. Measurements of series consisting of acids and acid albumin couples yielded potentials quite large enough to account for action currents

The development of such diffusion potentials in muscle would not be possible if the *fibrils* were not quite *poor in salt* and the sarcoplasm quite *rich in salt.* Since both the fluid and the fibrillar portions contain protein (see BOTTOZZI and his school) a couple consisting of acid albumin/acid/acid albumin yields no current. The current is reestablished through electrolytic dissociation of the acid albumin due to the salt in the sarcoplasm (see p 292). If such couples are placed in series considerable electric tension (voltage) may be obtained.

These results are in agreement with the fact that the normal properties of muscle are conditioned by definite states of swelling and electrolyte content

If frogs' muscles are placed in an isotonic solution of cane sugar or other nonelectrolyte (mannit, asparagin, etc), they lose their irritability (*e.g*, for the induced current) but retain their volume, they do not swell as in distilled water in which the irritability is likewise suspended. The ability to contract is restored by Na ions (about 0.07 per cent NaCl) (C. E. OVERTON) as well as by Li ions, but it is not restored at all by K ions. The irritability is also suspended by isotonic potassium and rubidium salts If the anions and cations are arranged in accordance to the extent with which they interfere with irritability, we obtain lyotropic series similar to those which we discovered for the salting out of colloids (see pp. 80 to 83); according to R. HOBER,* C. E. OVERTON * and SCHWARZ,* they are as follows

inhibitory· K > Rb > Cs > Na, Li
inhibitory: tartrate, SO₄ > acetate > Cl > Br,NO₃ > I > SCN.

If an uninjured frog's muscle is dipped into an isotonic solution of a neutral salt and the part so treated is united with another part of

scle by a wire, we obtain a current of rest whose strength and direc-
n depends on the nature of the neutral salt. [The study of these cur-
its of action in the heart muscle has been elaborated into the science
electrocardiography. I know of no attempt to associate electro-
rdiographic curves with changes in the colloids of the heart muscle
response to salts. Tr.] If the anions and cations are arranged
rording to their action on this current of rest (see R. Hober and
aldenberg [*]), we obtain series similar to the above Since we
ve previously seen that the salting out of protein, the swelling and
nking of gelatin and fibrin (which means the ionization) occur in
ilar lyotropic series, R Hober concludes that the normal irrita-
ity of muscle is dependent upon a definite condition of solution or
elling of its protoplasmic colloids; increased solution or precipitation
the colloids leads to loss of irritability. J. Loeb and R. Beutner
e of the opinion that the current of inactive muscle due to salt
s well as the currents rising in plants because of an injury to some
rt) bears no direct relation to the condition of swelling of the
smn colloids,[1] but is due to a lipoid membrane on the surface of
e muscle or its constituent elements The variation in activity of
e salts chosen (NaCl, KCl, etc) is due to their different threshold
solubility in the lipoid membrane

R. Hober correctly emphasized that for such questions of physio-
gical function we need consider only those influences which are
versible. Substances causing a more or less irreversible change by
eans of aromatic anions require no further consideration here.
The dependence of the irritability of muscle upon, and its relation
, the condition of the organ colloids are not unique. Examples of
her organ functions were studied by R. S. Lillie [*2] (movement of
e cilia of the larvae of marine annelids) and by R. Hober [*3] (the
ovement of the ciliated epithelium of the frog).
The movements of cilia above mentioned cease upon the addition
various salts: in fact, of the alkali salts, Li salts are the most
rmful. In hemolysis and in the diminution of the movement of
lin, the anion series shows an order the reverse of that for the
minution of muscle irritability, which means that the swelling of
ood corpuscles and muscle are affected in an opposite way. Such
ell-known hemolytic agents as saponin, solanin, taurocholic acid,
ycocholic acid and sodium oleate diminish the irritability of muscle
an irreversible manner; they evidently damage the lipoid plasma
embrane (R Hober [*21]).

---

[1] We must forego further discussion of the extremely interesting results of
Loeb and R Beutner since they have no direct bearing on colloids.

The accompanying table (in part after R. Hober) gives at a glance the action of the various alkaline salts, and parallel with it the extent to which such salts salt out hydrophile colloids.

The question now arises, *What are the colloid-chemical changes which occur as the result of stimulation and bring about the change in the shape of the muscle ?*

We know from the investigations of G. Jappelli and D'Errico as well as of G. Buglia, that muscle absorbs water when it contracts (fatigue) This is not surprising, since acids are formed which favor swelling (see p. 267). According to the conception of E. Přibram, the formation of acids and the contraction of muscle are closely associated. Even Th W. Engelmann had already drawn the conclusion that during contraction, water passes from the iso-tropic water-rich layer of the striated muscle into the anisotropic water-poor layer, which swells. This is due to the transfer of acids from the sarcoplasm where lactic acid is created by stimulation Water flows from the blood and the lymph into the isotropic layer, so that as a result of the contraction, the entire muscle is richer in water We must picture of the shifting of fluid within the fibrils as occurring in such a way that the anisotropic layer, which, according to Munch, is spirally arranged, can expand only from side to side when it swells (at the expense of the isotropic layer). This causes a trans-verse thickening of the muscle fibers and a shortening in length, a contraction If the lactic acid in the living muscle is consumed or otherwise neutralized the process is reversed and the muscle regains repose.

Streitmann and M. H. Fischer constructed from catgut a working model of muscular contraction. The catgut strands represented the anisotropic substance and the sarcoplasm was replaced by water, acids, and salt solutions.

For the sake of completeness, we shall refer to one other theory which is by no means as well established experimentally as the one described. Bernstein first suggested the idea that muscular con-traction was associated with changes in *surface tension.* As has been mentioned previously, muscle is characterized by an especially high content of *potassium.* From the researches of A. B Macallum we are compelled to assume that it has a most important function dur-ing contraction.

In contractile tissues (muscles of frogs, lobsters, beetles, etc.), according to A. B. Macallum * and his pupils, the potassium seems to be localized in the dark zones of the resting muscle fibrils, especially at their surfaces. From this, A B. Macallum concludes that the surface tension must be lowered in these zones. With the contrac-

Action	Cations	Anions
Diminution of muscle irritability	$K > Rb > Cs > Na, Li$	$SCN < I < Br, NO_3 < Cl < acetate < SO_4$
Production of current of rest in muscle	$K > Rb > Cs > Na > Li$	$I, NO_3 < Br < Cl < SO_4$
Paralysis of ciliary movement (in arenicola larvæ)	$K < Rb < Cs < Na < Li$	$SCN > I > Br, NO_3, SO_4 > Cl, acetate$
Decrease of ciliary movement (ciliated epithelium of the frog)	$K < Rb < Na < Cs < Li$	$I, Br > NO_3 > Cl, SO_4$
Diminution in the irritability of nerves	$K > Rb > Cs > Li > Na$	
Promotion of hemolysis	$K > Rb > Cs > Na, Li$	$I > NO_3, Br > Cl > SO_4$
Precipitation of albumin in neutral solution	$K > Rb > Na > Cs > Li$	$I < Br, NO_3 < Cl < SO_4$
Precipitation of albumin in acid solution	$Cs < Rb < K < Na < Li$	$SCN > I > Br > NO_2 > Cl > acetate$
Precipitation of globulin		$Bi < NO_3 < Cl < acetate < SO_4$
Precipitation of myogen		$SCN > NO_3, Cl > SO_4$
Swelling of gelatin		$I > Br > NO_3 > Cl > acetate > SO_4$
Precipitation of lecithin	$K < Rb < Li < Cs < Na$	$I < SCN < Br, NO_3 < Cl < acetate < SO_4$

tion there occurs a change in the distribution of potassium. There is thus associated with each contraction and return to rest a shifting of potassium, a shifting of the swelling and a change in the surface tension. We may leave undecided which phenomena are primary and which are secondary. A B. MACALLUM calls attention to the fact that next to hydrogen, the potassium ion has a greater mobility than any other cation, and attributes to this the rapidity of the change in surface tension, and the rapid contractility of muscle.

The efficiency of muscle depends to a marked extent upon its content of water (see J. DEMOOR and PHILIPPSON *) and may be influenced by extreme dehydration (shrinking). Such extreme shrinking may be brought about by the introduction of concentrated salt solutions or glycerin as well as of numerous poisons (especially veratrin) (see SANTESSOW * and GREGOR *). Under these circumstances the muscle is shortened, as when it is very much fatigued, by tetanic contractions.

Likewise, by unsuitable nutrition, which results in a greatly swollen state, the efficiency of the muscle may be depressed TSUBOI brought about such a swelling in rabbits which were fed entirely on potatoes. The water content of their muscles was from 2 to 7 per cent higher than normal. Potatoes are especially rich in potassium, and in this connection it is natural to think of the swelling which potassium salts also cause in gelatin and fibrin, and of the influence of the K ion on the depression of muscle irritability, discovered by R. HOBER.

[W. BURRIDGE associates the occurrence of fatigue phenomena with the accumulation of K ions in muscle and in blood   Adrenin antagonizes K salts.

In their Crooman Lecture on "The Respiratory Process in Muscle and the Nature of Muscular Motion," W. M FLETCHER and F G. HOPKINS come to the conclusion that lactic acid is not a toxic product but an essential agent in the muscular contractions   Its free H ions in the presence of colloidal fibrils cause an increase in tension in the fiber, either by increasing the muscular tension along the longitudinal surfaces or by the process of imbibition. They studied the effect of oxygen on muscle and found that it not only delays the stiffening of muscle but may altogether inhibit its onset   A muscle forced by stimulation to stiffening may be recalled again by oxygen to its previous flaccidity. It was shown that immersion of a fatigued muscle in oxygen restored the osmotic properties to those of resting muscle. Fatigued muscle contains more lactic acid than resting muscle, and a fatigued muscle, after resting in an oxygen atmosphere, subsequently contained less lactic acid   A. V. HILL and PARNAS from studies of heat production in contracting muscle conclude that the combustion of the lactic acid to CO_2 furnishes the heat which restores some of the lactic acid to its metabolic source, thus removing the acid ions from the colloidal fibrils, so that they may return to their former tension — the tension of rest or relaxation — and possessed of their inherent potential   Proceedings of the Royal Society of London, Series B 69, Vol. LXXXIX, p. 444 *et seq.*

Contraction of the heart is a special instance of muscular function upon which considerable light has been thrown by the studies of W. BURRIDGE.

He views excitation as a coagulative change induced through the formation of a calcium compound. According to MacDonald this coagulative change is accompanied by a release into aqueous solution of previously adsorbed K salts which now confer a positive charge on the colloids whence they came. This electric charge in its turn reverses the coagulative change in the colloids and so brings conditions back towards the original state. BURRIDGE has shown that the positive charge renders cardiac colloids incapable of combining with Ca and can decalcify them just as well as does oxalate, and that Na ions may be a factor in determining a finer state of subdivision of these colloids   Inhibition resides in the inability of the colloids of the inhibited tissue to combine with Ca.

BURRIDGE found two modes of reaction of the heart when exposed to the influence of drugs. One effect, immediate in appearance on application and in disappearance on withdrawal, he ascribes to "surface" phenomena involving the muscular colloids   The other he calls "deep" changes on the assumption that they involve changes in aggregation or of chemical composition in the same colloidal bodies in which changes of the first type take place.

Calcium has a surface and a deep action on the heart. BURRIDGE measured the response of the perfused heart to solutions containing different concentrations of calcium in the presence of different substances. He found that digitalis caused the heart to act as well with a weaker solution of calcium, as it did with a stronger solution of calcium in the absence of digitalis. Barium was an imperfect substitute for calcium. Adrenin and pituitary extract act like digitalis in improving Ca utilization. Alcohol, chloroform and ether have a two-fold action. (a) A depressing or surface action associated with poor utilization of calcium; (b) a favoring or deep action associated with an improved utilization of calcium.

Strychnine improves Ca utilization thus diminishing inhibition. Dibasic potassium phosphate increased the result from a given percentage concentration of Ca. This latter is evidently an adsorption phenomenon as it is maintained by adding a smaller percentage of the dibasic potassium phosphate to the perfusing solution. Burridge suggests that loss of phosphates may occasionally be a factor determining cardiac failure. The antagonism between chlorids and phosphates is evidently of importance in cardiac weakness or nephritis with salt retention. W. Burridge. Quarterly Journal of Medicine, Vol. 9, Nos. 33 and 36; Vol. 10, No. 39 for bibliography. See also Nerves, p. 352. Tr.]

CHAPTER XVIII.

BLOOD, RESPIRATION, CIRCULATION AND ITS DISTURBANCES.

Blood.

(See also Chapter XIV, The Distribution of Water in the Organism.)

THE blood consists of a fluid, the *plasma*, and the formed elements, the *blood corpuscles*.

Plasma.

In a short time after the blood leaves the body it coagulates spontaneously. It separates into two components, one a yellowish fluid, the *serum*, and the jelly-like clot, the *fibrin*, which has enmeshed the blood corpuscles and has undergone shrinking during coagulation. If the blood is beaten or shaken with a rough surface (wood or steel shavings) after it has left the vein, it clots at once and the fibrin separates immediately as an irreversible fibrous mass which may be completely cleansed of the adherent constituents of the blood by washing it with water. Recently colloid-chemical explanations associated with the names K. SPIRO and ELLINGER, NOLF, RETTGER, and HEKMA have received more support. Fibrin occurs in the blood as fluid fibrinalbuminate (fibrinogen) which is normally characterized by being coagulated by dilute salt solutions and serum, so that something must exist in the blood which prevents coagulation in the vessels. We possess no knowledge as to what this "something" is [HOWELL has recently separated this substance antiprothrombin. See HARVEY Lectures, 1916-1917 to be published. Tr.] Certain aspects may be indicated which help the solution of the problem. Coagulation occurs when the blood leaves the closed vascular system, and comes into contact with other surfaces which it *moistens* If blood is collected in oil or vaseline, it remains fluid many hours and may even be beaten with a thoroughly greased glass rod without clotting. Shed blood may be centrifuged in paraffined vessels and a plasma may be thus obtained which remains fluid, provided the suggested precautions are employed. Such plasma clots when a glass rod which it moistens is introduced. It is not known whether or not the interface blood gas plays any part in clotting

H ISCOVESCO is of the opinion that the electric charge of the vessel wall plays an important part in the coagulation of fibrin; in life it differs from what it is in death and pathological conditions. Blood does not clot in a paraffined vessel because the paraffin is negatively[1] charged. [The spontaneous and immediate development of vasoconstrictor substances in shed blood have made necessary the development of special technique " caval pockets " for the study of the influence of the nerves on the adrenal glands   J. M. ROGOFF, Journ. Lab and Clin. Medicine, Vol. III, No. 4, Jan , 1918, p 209 *et seq.* Tr.] He arrives at this view, because he regards clotted fibrin as a complex which results from the combination of all the electropositive globulins of the blood with some of the negative ones   He assumes that plasma contains two kinds of globulins, one of which coagulates at 72° and the other at 55°.

At any rate it follows from what has been said that the determinative factor in coagulation is a surface tension phenomenon which offers a profitable field for more thorough study   It must not be forgotten that the blood moistens the vessel walls, the intima, so that it is not the mere moistening which is important   Injuries to the intima may bring about local blood coagulation (*thrombosis*). If such thrombi are dislodged into the vessels the resulting phenomena are called *embolism*.   It is well known that the chief danger of any extensive surgical operation is the development of such emboli. Air emboli are especially dangerous, they may occur from injuries to the veins, or air may be injected during intravenous infusions. Sometimes in air embolism, coagulation may occur at the interface blood/air as I have been informed in a personal letter from Geheimrat Prof. QUINCKE, the clinician.

The serum is a solution of proteins in salt solution   We must at present assume that these proteins are different, not only for every animal, but even for every race   They consist chiefly of *serum albumin* and *serum globulin*, which were described in Chapter X (see also ISCOVESCO [k2])   It is quite possible to remove a considerable portion of the proteins from the blood without immediate destruction of the organism, as is well known, common salt infusions are employed in severe hemorrhages, *i e*, the blood that is lost is replaced by a 0 85 per cent salt solution   It would be impossible to keep an organism alive permanently without serum   Aside from the fact that nourishment would cease, the serum plays a most important rôle as "buffer" in order that the acid and alkali content of the organism may be kept at a uniform level, it is of little importance, however, in maintaining the level of the water content

---

[1] French authors frequently use a terminology the reverse of this; they call whatever migrates to the anode electropositive, and vice versa   I have translated their mode of expression so as to conform with ours

The organism is carefully provided with mechanisms to maintain the neutral state. [This is not in accordance with present views In American clinical literature this is at present usually expressed H7, $p_H 7$ or $p_H^{+} 7$ = neutral. In normal blood $p_H = 7.4$, while in advanced acid intoxication, $p_H 7.2$. Tr.] Every abnormal excess of H or OH ions influences the condition of swelling in the tissues and may thus give rise to grave disturbances. Although 0.37×10^{-7} represents the normal H-ion concentration of the blood, $1.00 \times 10^{-7} nH$ indicates an advanced acid intoxication. $1.00 \times 10^{-6} nH$ damages the red blood corpuscles according to L. MICHAELIS and D. TAKABASHI just as do traces of NaOH. We know from the investigations of H. J. HAMBURGER and HEKMA that the functional activity of the leucocytes depends on the normal concentration of H and OH ions. To maintain this condition, nature has provided a double safeguard and surrounded neutralization with a double line of defense. The outer wall is the serum salts, which are so skillfully combined that the concentration of the H or OH ions is unchanged by the moderate addition of acids or bases. This property of the serum salts is of great importance in the metabolism, formation and removal of CO_2, in the formation of lactic acid, of ammonia, etc.; it is even to a certain extent increased by the artificial introduction of acids and bases. Circumstances may arise when these outworks are overcome and the inner line trenches have to bear the defense.

Severe poisoning with acids or alkalis are dangerous not only because of the burns they cause, but especially because of the danger of disturbing the balance between the H and OH ions. We must especially consider the acid intoxication in certain diseases, as in the fever of many of the infectious diseases and in diabetes, associated with the over-production of oxybutyric acid. Under these circumstances the inner though weaker line of defense must be the proteins, which, because of their amphoteric character, are able to bind acids as well as bases. It is not a matter of little consequence when the proteins have to be invoked for neutralization. We have seen from pages 152 and 153 that the addition of alkali or acid increases the *internal friction* of albumin; that albumin ions have a much higher viscosity than the albumin molecule; and further that in media that are not neutral the blood corpuscles swell. Therefore, under circumstances where there is a higher ionization of serum albumin and parallel with it a swelling of the formed elements, we may expect that the blood will show a higher viscosity and that greater demands will be made on the organ of circulation, the *heart* (see p. 310 *et seq.*).

There are no exhaustive investigations on the influence of *salts* upon the *internal friction* of proteins in normal serum   Yet it seems possible to conclude from the figures of Wo. PAULI and H HANDOVSKY that the *friction in serum* in the presence of salts is approximately the same as in a salt-free albumin solution, however, it must not be forgotten that the solutions investigated possessed a much smaller amount of albumin than does serum.

Albumin + NaCl	Internal friction	Albumin + $(NH_4)_2SO_4$	Internal friction
Normal		Normal.	
0 00	1 0783	0 00	1 0783
0 05	1 0592	0 05	1 0582
0 1	1 0681	0 1	1 0725
0 5	1 1064	0 5	1 1020

We see that when the solution of salt is very dilute, the internal friction may even sink, but that between 0.1 and 0.5 n which is in the neighborhood of the physiological concentration (physiological salt solution 0.85 per cent NaCl = 0 14 normal), the original internal friction of the salt-free albumin solution is again reached and exceeded.

A matter formerly very much discussed was whether some electrolytes and nonelectrolytes, especially sugar, chlorin, phosphate, sodium and calcium, exist in the blood free or fixed.   In the light of the facts this does not seem to be a correct statement of the problem. It is more important to determine what percentage of the ions involved are diffusible.   B. P RONA and GYORGY by ultrafiltration of CO_2-sera have demonstrated that 10 to 15 per cent of the Na in some sera was not diffusible   P. RONA and D. TAKAHASHI * determined that 25 to 35 per cent of the calcium in the serum is not diffusible and probably exists as a calcium protein compound.   The Cl ion, on the contrary, was found to be completely diffusible.

We know from pages 147 and 161 that the solubility of salts in solutions of hydrophile colloids is very different from what it is in pure water.   As a matter of fact, the solubility of easily soluble electrolytes is somewhat diminished and that of the difficultly soluble ones is markedly increased.   If we make a solution of salts of the same strength and proportion per liter as occurs in natural serum (see H. M. ADLER *)

```
KCl . .    ...     ..      . . . . . . . . .   0 40
CaCl2 + 6 aq ......  .   .  ...... ..     .... . 0 62
MgCl2 + 6 aq.  .    .. .  .        . ... .... .. ..  0 37
NaCl ...   ..  ....   ...  ..     .   .......  ... .  5 90
NaH2PO4 + 1 aq ..........    ....   ... .... .. ...  0 236
NaHCO3...............................................  3.51
```

a precipitation takes place immediately, the precipitate consisting of a mixture of calcium carbonate and phosphate. It is only because of the presence of the serum colloids that this precipitation does *not* occur. Accordingly, the serum colloids serve the purpose of keeping soluble substances in solution and of releasing them at the proper time. This phenomenon is of great physiological importance in the formation of bone (see p. 268), and it is of great pathological significance in gouty deposits (see p. 274).

The *surface tension* of serum has been frequently studied in recent years. The incentive was afforded by the observation of M. Ascoli and G. Izar that the surface tension of immune serum was depressed when it was united with its specific antigen (see meiostagmin reaction). Morgan and Woodward recorded especially exact determinations. They found that the surface tension of healthy men did not vary much, on the average (from 44.3 to 46.4), but that the diet might cause marked variation. The surface tension is especially high in some patients, especially nephritics (reaching to 51.4). Mammalian serum does not differ much from human serum.

Lymph.

We can think of the lymph as a *filtrate* derived from the blood. It does not by any means have a composition identical with blood plasma; on the contrary, we find in it many metabolic products which have entered it by diffusion from the cells it bathes. It is generally assumed that the blood pressure affords the increased pressure necessary for filtration; but I wish to call attention to the fact that it may possibly be the *pulsation* which is of prime importance in this instance, just as I have established for the glomerular filtration in the kidney (p. 332).

The Blood Corpuscles.

The red blood corpuscles or erythrocytes present under the microscope the well-known round or elliptical shape with a thickened rim, like a biconcave circular or elliptical plate. In reality, according to the investigations of F. Weidenreich, they seem to approach the shape of a spinning top (a cone with a convex base); so that under the microscope their appearance is distorted. When they leave the blood vessels we frequently encounter erythrocytes in rouleau. Schwyzer attributes this to the fact that the normal OH charge is disturbed by the glass slide. In the blood vessels, however, the similar and equal charge of the vessel wall opposes the corpuscles and they never form rouleau. In view of what follows, we should recall that, on swelling, they swell up symmetrically and have the shape of a pea,

and on shrinking they take the shape of a thorn apple, and have
character the pointed outgrowth

Then constructs on what remarks according to the process a
beet's red blood corpuscles, beads with contents according to F.
AMBLANARDUS [?]

Water	....	24 6
Hemoglobin	...	56 7
Albumin	..	64 2
Cholesterin	.	1 4
Lecithin	.	3 7

In an electric field they migrate to the anode (R. Höber) and
though as a matter of fact the form changes are according to the
species (Kozawa set H. Lawrence considers that only the corpuscles, and the stroma are electronegative because red blood corpuscles, and stroma are precipitate the electronegative an hydrosol
sol. The content on the corpuscles electronegative two corpuscles
dissolved in water are precipitated by a cathodical hydrosol.

The investigations on the lowering of the freezing point induced
by the contents of red blood corpuscles etc. are exceptionally
numerous. The old data will however as those values of certain data
concerning the osmotic pressure of the corpuscles solution require a
revision in accordance with the investigation of W. Pauli and A.
von Vogelaar out put too who have shown that the presence of
colloids greatly influence the osmotic pressure of sol solutions, as
H. J. Hamburger and J. Brinkman [?]. It is established by the
investigation of R. Höber that erythrocytes have a high internal
conductivity, this indicates that a considerable fraction of the salts
they contain are freely dissolved and do not occur in any organic
combination.

As numerous as have been the studies on erythrocytes yet as
divergent are the ideas concerning their structure. Hitherto it has
been difficult to reconcile the demands of physico-chemistry with
their other properties. Its alternate freezing and thawing acid,
hemolysis, &c., exit of colouring matter may be induced, this be-
tokens a capsule which may be burst by a purely mechanical
effort exerted on the blood corpuscle in its entirety, thus giving exit
to the dissolved hemoglobin. This capsule must for the most part
consist of fatty colloidal particles (lecithin, cholesterin or both
since it may be removed by ether and alcohol acetone, and may
even be melted at a temperature of from 60 to 65° C. thus allowing the hemoglobin to escape. It can't certainly contain lecithin
since pure cholesterin cannot be moistened by water and is totally
impermeable to it. Unfortunately, the properties of mixtures of

lecithin and cholesterin in relation to water and salt solution are entirely uninvestigated. Investigation of the swelling capacities of such mixtures would greatly advance our knowledge of plasma membranes.

It is evident that the lipoids can form only very thin surface pellicles if we consider how small, in view of the analysis on page 304, is the amount of cholesterin and lecithin they contain.

A question remains Is the membrane of uniform composition and consistence? Against this view is the fact that on shrinking, thorn-apple forms appear. This shape might also occur if there were an inner framework, the interstices of which are filled at the periphery with compressible elements Such a theory best fits in with physico-chemical observations The pellicle of red blood corpuscles is permeable for water, fat-soluble substances and to a certain extent for cations and anions of the salts occurring in the body

The existence of a fatty pellicle does not eliminate the probability that the blood corpuscles may also form a fatty layer at an injured *point*, which impedes the exit of hemoglobin (see p. 243). GRUNS* discovered that red blood corpuscles could be cut up without the subsequent exit of hemoglobin, and E. ALBRECHT* showed that blood corpuscles divided by crushing or by gentle heating, to a certain extent resumed their spherical form by reason of surface tension, and retained their coloring matter It must be borne in mind that red blood corpuscles contain only 591 parts water to 316 parts hemoglobin If the hemoglobin were to appropriate all the water, which is certainly not the case, we should obtain only a very viscous mass,[1] which would require a considerable time to swell or undergo other changes, thus giving an opportunity for the formation of a surface membrane (see p. 35)

Based on my own hitherto unpublished studies on hemolysis and on those of others accessible to me, I have formulated the following hypothesis for the structure of red blood cells: they possess a sponge-like framework consisting of a fibrinous mass, the stroma (to what extent lipoids are involved in this framework is an open question entirely immaterial to our discussion). The sponge is entirely soaked with a salt-containing albumin solution, chiefly hemoglobin, and has a very thin lipoid pellicle as a capsule. On the basis of such a structure all the known properties of red blood cells find an unstrained explanation They would swell and burst in hypotonic solution and shrink in hypertonic solution. Such salt solutions as

---

[1] It is easy to convince oneself of this by observing a pure suspension of blood corpuscles becomes hemolyzed by a drop of arachnolysin

dehydrate (shrink) the stroma without causing coagulation of the hemoglobin hemolyze red blood cells.   In fact, concentrated sodium chlorid solution causes hemolysis.   The blood coloring matter is pressed out just as in the case of the salts[1] of heavy metals mentioned later.   By carefully cutting, crushing or warming. the blood corpuscles do not lose their coloring matter, provided sufficient time is allowed for the lipoid membrane to close before the coloring matter diffuses out.   If the lipoid membrane be destroyed by warming or solvents (ether, saponin, etc.), hemolysis occurs   The salts of the heavy metals which coagulate albumin harden red blood corpuscles also, and if red blood corpuscles are placed in such weak solutions of heavy metals that no coagulation of the dissolved albumin occurs, there are two possibilities: the salt of the heavy metal causes no shrinking of the stroma (*e.g.*, $CuCl_2$) and the blood corpuscles are left unchanged, or the heavy metal causes shrinking of the stroma (*e.g* , $HgCl_2$ and many others) so that hemolysis occurs, for the blood coloring is pressed out as water is from a sponge.[2]   The spongy framework with its largest outgrowths reaches to the surface of the blood corpuscles, so that there is at the surface if there is no stress a mosaic of lipoids and albumins which can assume, in hypertonic neutral salt solu-

---

[1] With a few special exceptions, it is entirely immaterial to our point of view whether we regard behavior towards hypotonic and hypertonic solutions as the result of osmotic pressure or as the result of swelling and shrinkage of the corpuscular colloids

MARTIN H FISCHER * has developed an entirely revolutionary conception of the constitution of the red blood corpuscles and the phenomenon of hemolysis He starts out with the idea that hemolysis may occur as two phenomena: (*a*) with swelling of the blood corpuscles (in water, acids, alkalis. etc), (*b*) without swelling (alcohol, saponin, hemolysins, etc)   On this account M H FISCHER regards the increase of volume and the exit of the hemoglobin as two phenomena which frequently run parallel and yet have nothing to do with each other   He assumes that the proteins (not the hemoglobin) swell under the influence of water, acids, alkalis and hypotonic salt solution   The hemoglobin, however, which he considers to be an hydrophobe colloid, he regards as being *adsorbed* by the remaining protein constituents of the blood corpuscles   To demonstrate his conception M H FISCHER stained fibrin with carmine and observed a loss of color with acids, alkalis, hypotonic salt solutions, urea, etc , just as in the case of hemolysis.   In this way M H FISCHER injects a new point of view into the discussion, since he replaces the influence of osmotic pressure by the force of swelling and the salts by the colloids, yet many of his points seem untenable to me.   If we consider that a blood corpuscle contains almost five times as much hemoglobin as other proteins, we must cease talking of an adsorption of the hemoglobin by the albumin, adsorption is a reversible process, a term applicable to only very few hemolytic phenomena.   I cannot subscribe to the view, that hemoglobin is an hydrophobe (suspension colloid).   This, however, is not vital to the main question

[2] From experiments still unpublished.

tion, a thorn apple shape. On the basis of this hypothesis, whenever we exert an influence on red blood corpuscles, we must consider the effect upon each of the three colloidal constituents (stroma, hemoglobin solution and lipoids) as well as its distribution among them, from this the behavior of the blood corpuscles may be deduced (hemolysis, swelling, shrinking, hardening, etc.)

There is an extensive literature on the changes in the volume of erythrocytes in neutral isotonic salt solutions,[1] I shall mention only the names of GURBER, H. J. HAMBURGER, S G. HEDIN, R. HOBER, H KOEPPE and M. OKER-BLOM. In these studies, the blood corpuscles were usually regarded as vesicles with a more or less permeable membrane filled with a solution of electrolytes This conception does not permit a general satisfactory explanation of all the observations that have been made: There are already evidences of a revision which shall ascribe due influence to the colloidal character of the corpuscular constituents. R. HOBER [*7] immersed blood corpuscles in neutral salt solution, which possessed the same osmotic pressure, but in relation to the blood corpuscles, were somewhat hypotonic, so that hemoglobin gradually escaped. This escape took place more or less slowly in accordance with the salt employed and in the following order:

$$SO_4 < Cl < Br, NO_3 < I$$
$$Li, Na < Cs, Rb < K.$$

This is the recognized lyotropic arrangement for colloidal precipitation, or what seems more likely to me, for swelling and shrinking (see M MICULICICH *). An investigation by EISENBERG contains much important data which ought to yield valuable conclusions, in connection with the theory outlined above. [NOTE. J. TAIT has just published a paper—Capillary Phenomena observed in Blood Cells: Thigmocytes Phagocytosis, Ameboid Movement, Differential Adhesiveness of Corpuscles, Emigration of Leucocytes. Quarterly Journal of Experimental Physiology, Vol. XII, No. 1. Tr.]

Leucocytes have a special significance which we have considered in Chapter XVII.

As has been frequently emphasized, the normal organism establishes a *dynamic balance* in the swelling of the organ colloids (see p. 217 *et seq.*). The tissues, the blood plasma, the blood corpuscles possess a certain swelling range, which is specific for each tissue. If certain component colloid groups suffer disturbances in this respect, in order to restore equilibrium all the other components modify their state of swelling. This may occur in severe diarrhœas

---

[1] Numerous investigations have been performed to determine the behavior of blood corpuscles towards neutral salt solutions From them it may be deduced that *iso-osmotic* solutions are not necessarily *isotonic* to blood corpuscles.

(cholera), which result in dehydration of the entire organism. This is combated by an injection of physiological salt solution into the blood vessels. If, on account of abnormal conditions, there is an increased swelling of tissue (edema, exudates), the balance may be restored by withdrawing water from the blood (by sweating, diuretics or cathartics). [Reference should be made to the influence exerted by increasing the colloids of the blood either by transfusion of blood or by injection of colloidal substances. Tr.]

Respiration (Gas Exchange).

The supply of oxygen to the cells is probably the most important condition for the life of the organism, whether animal or plant. For the latter, quantitative estimations are not as convenient, and on this account they have been less studied than in animals, especially mammals.

In the case of higher animals, the provision of oxygen is assigned to the red blood corpuscles which take up oxygen in the lungs or gills, transport it to the places where it is needed, and return laden with CO_2. Ability to take up and relinquish oxygen or carbon dioxid is a characteristic of *hemoglobin* Formerly, the combination of oxygen or carbon dioxid and hemoglobin was considered to be a purely chemical one In favor of this view is the fact that it is possible to crystallize both hemoglobin and also oxygen-laden oxyhemoglobin The union must be a very loose one, since it is possible to remove with an exhaust pump almost all the oxygen from an oxyhemoglobin solution or even from oxyhemoglobin crystals, so that the absorption of oxygen and carbon dioxid follows the gas pressure. It would be natural to think of a solution of O or CO_2 in the hemoglobin, but quantitative investigations show in contradiction that the absorption of O or CO_2 is not proportional to the outer gas pressure as would occur for the solution of a gas in a fluid in accordance with Henry's law. It has been found on the contrary, that with low gas pressures relatively much O or CO_2 is taken up, but that with higher pressures the amount diminishes, the following table of A. Loewy [*2] shows this.

Oxygen tension in mm	Oxygen saturation in per cent with a CO_2 tension of 5 mm
5	11
10	28 5
15	51
20	67 5
30	82
40	89
50	92 5

Since DONDER's time it has been assumed, therefore, that a dissociation occurs much as in the case of calcium carbonate which is dissociated into CaO and CO_2 at high temperatures, the degree of dissociation is dependent upon the CO_2 pressure. CHR. BOHR especially followed up this idea and on the basis of rather complicated premises reached an approximate agreement between theoretical and experimental values. H. W. FISCHER and E. BRIEGER think that iron exists in hemoglobin " protected " by the organic complex. In alkaline solution it occurs as a ferrate, *i.e.*, a superoxid (analogous to manganate), but in a solution made acid by CO_2 it is unstable and parts with oxygen. Another explanation offered by the assumption of Wo. OSTWALD [*] is that the taking up and release of O or CO_2 by hemoglobin and blood is an *adsorption*. He compares the process to the absorption of gases by charcoal, spongy platinum, etc. In both cases there exists a *reversible balance*, in both cases one gas may be replaced by the other (O by CO_2 and *vice versa*). The curves obtained in the adsorption of O or CO_2 by hemoglobin or blood in the presence of increasing gas pressures correspond to the recognized adsorption curves. On comparing the differences between theory and experiment in the case of BOHR's dissociation formula, on the one hand, and Wo. OSTWALD's adsorption formula, on the other, it is evident that for the latter they are much smaller.

Hitherto we have spoken of the adsorption of O and CO_2 by *hemoglobin, blood corpuscles* and blood as identical, but in reality the phenomena in the blood are very complicated.

The absorption and the release of *oxygen by hemoglobin* may be considered a relatively simple phenomenon. But even in the case of blood corpuscles and blood, observation and calculation do not agree so well. Wo. OSTWALD says (*loc. cit.*, p. 296), "These variations are characterized by the fact that in the case of *low* oxygen pressures (somewhat below 25 mm. Hg) the observed oxygen absorption is considerably less than would be expected in accordance with the adsorption formula." In my opinion this variation is sufficiently explained if we consider the *lipoids* of blood corpuscles; O is more soluble in them than in water and there is no objection to the assumption that the distribution in the lipoids with changing gas pressure follows Henry's law. Under these circumstances the curve of oxygen absorption in the blood must waver between that of the adsorption curve and the straight line of distribution in accordance with Henry's law. By observation of the curve elaborated by Wo. OSTWALD (in accordance with A. LOEWY), I find this view substantiated (*loc. cit.*, p. 297).

The *absorption* and *release* of CO_2 by the blood and blood corpuscles is further complicated by the *blood salts*. By their presence the serum is able to take up more CO_2 than the blood corpuscles, but it is impossible at present to formulate in detail the steps in the absorption and release of CO_2 by the blood. The adsorption theory of WO, OSTWALD naturally does not help us over these difficulties, but under the complicated conditions mentioned it formally establishes the *adsorption character* of the absorption and release of CO_2 in the blood. If we view teleologically the manner of gas exchange, we recognize that adsorption serves this purpose best   Excess of oxygen (up to 100 per cent) in the respired air has no effect either in the O used or on the general metabolism; when oxygen is deficient small quantities are taken up with avidity and tenaciously held   The inhalation of oxygen recently recommended for clinical use may be explained only by considering the *plasma* [1]   From a mixture rich in oxygen, hemoglobin will take up only a given maximum quantity, but the ability of the plasma to take up oxygen follows the gas pressure.   Finally, it must be recalled that with higher pressure the lipoids of the blood corpuscles take up more oxygen   [No discussion of the gas exchange in the blood would be complete without mention of the work of BARCROFT, "Respiratory Function of the Blood," Cambridge, 1914, and of HENDERSON, and of DONALD VAN SLYKE, who have supplied methods and data of great value   Tr]

The Circulation and Its Disturbances.

A normal circulation can exist only when the *internal friction of the blood*, the viscosity, remains within normal limits.   This varies considerably, and in man, measured for uncoagulated blood, is from 4.05 to 6 8 (water= 1)   In cardiac patients, besides normal values, values from above 14 to 23.8 have been found   Muscular exercise, heat and chemical stimuli influence the viscosity (H. A. DETERMANN *)   Salivation, lack of water, perspiration increase, whereas ingestion of fluids or nourishment as well as increased frequency of respiration lower the viscosity (M. SCHEITLIN *).   According to H. BLUNSCHLY the viscosity of the blood falls with every intake of nourishment, reaching a minimum after the midday meal, and then rises with fluctuations   The differences in the same person on one day were 11.8 per cent; yet the figures vary much on different days. Moderate muscular work according to H. A DETERMANN lowers the viscosity of the blood, hard work raises it as do alcohol and coffee.

The viscosity of the blood may be influenced by certain substances, according to W SCHEITLIN,* a *gelatin* injection of 0.15 per cent of the

[1] Naturally this does hold in the case of CO poisoning

·d volume increases the viscosity temporarily 15 per cent, *are-* ι (0 1 grm., subcutaneously) up to 36 per cent; cutaneous appli- on of spiritus sinapis, up to 12 per cent; a *phlebotomy* (up to ʒer cent) and the action of other derivatives, for a few hours ʒr the viscosity (these results were obtained on horses). Changes ·iscosity were observed by W. SCHEITLIN in various diseases ncipally of horses), and by W. FREI* on dying horses. In dis- ·s of the lungs and pleura associated with fever, especially high ·es were found, and in anemias they were especially low (as low ?.3). The viscosity usually reaches its highest point with the ·s and then falls.

ll these observations furnish valuable material for future knowl- ·e of the relationship between the viscosity of the blood and ·hology. Already it may be said that the viscosity of the blood a certain prognostic value.

·he viscosity of the blood is conditioned by the internal friction ·he *plasma* and by the *blood cells.* We shall see later that the ·l amount of the former plays a far less important part than latter, and that, as a matter of fact, an important part in the nges in viscosity of the plasma must also be ascribed to the ·rface tissue/plasma.

·larked changes in the viscosity of the plasma may also be indu ced the inclusion of some foreign substances. P. ADAM found that it ·owered markedly by iodids, and to a less extent by bromids. s possible that some of the therapeutic effects from the adminis- ·ion of potassium iodid (especially in arteriosclerosis) may be ·ibuted to the diminution of the internal friction. Investigations ·man have not as yet given uniform results (P. ADAM, H. A. ·TERMANN,* O MULLER and R. INADA).

·he concentrations of urea possible in the organism can have no ·uence on the internal friction of the plasma (as far as I can gather n G. MORUZZI's * figures).

·o the extent that the data furnished by Wo. PAULI and H. ·NDOVSKY warrant it, an increased *ionization of the serum albumin* ·st also result in an increase of viscosity. Such an increased ·zation of albumin may be brought about by an increase in con- ·tration of H or OH ions. An increase of the latter is impossible, ·ve shall see. On the other hand, the following tables of R. HOBER ·w that an increase of CO_2 may produce an increase of the con- ·tration of H ions in the blood.

·t HOBER *[2] measured the concentration of H ions in the blood ·n the addition of carbonic acid mixed with hydrogen I have ·roduced only the percentage of CO_2.

Volume per cent CO_2	Concentration of H ions $\times 10^7$
3 18	0 37
4 15	0 49
6 51	0 79
9 19	0 89
15 50	0 94
29 05	2 37
57 86	2 98

Within the physiological limit of 3 to 6 volume per cent CO_2, the concentration of H ions in the blood varied only from about 0.35 to 0.75×10^{-7} When the content of CO_2 is greater, we shall see that the H ion concentration may rise   According to H. LOEWY,[*1] the normal CO_2 content in the alveoli on closure of the air passages may increase from 5 per cent to 13.4 per cent, which produces approximately 50 per cent increase in the concentration of H ions.

A SZILI* injected rabbits and dogs intravenously with hydrochloric acid and found shortly before death an H ion concentration of 9×10^{-7}; in diabetic coma H. BENEDICT* observed a p_H value of 1.5×10^{-7}.

This increase in the H ions is doubtless associated with an increased viscosity of the plasma.   We shall see that this is vanishingly small, hardly measurable in proportion to the increase of the viscosity of the blood which an equal concentration of H ions produces through a *swelling of the red blood corpuscles*.

The viscosity of the *total* plasma does not teach us anything about its *viscosity at the interface between tissue and blood*. The friction at this surface is absolutely determinative for the circulation of the blood.

What are the conditions at these surfaces? The blood is neutral, the tissues are acid.   In the cells there is an oxidation which passes by way of the most diverse fatty acids to carbonic acid.   The fatty acids involved are without exception stronger acids than carbonic acid.   Accordingly, at the interface tissue/blood, an ionization of the albumin must occur and with it an increase of the friction.   The friction *must be greater in proportion to the disturbances of the oxidizing processes in the cells; i e.*, the less oxidation to CO_2, the faintly acid end product, the more acids with high dissociation constants are formed.   The friction at the boundary, i e., the *albumin ionization*, *becomes great* also when the *blood itself is saturated with* CO_2, that is, when the products which diffuse into the blood from the tissues have less alkali to combine with than normally.

Let us test the correctness of this view with the facts at our disposal [1]

It follows from the evidence to be given (p. 315) that the accumulation of CO_2 increases the viscosity of the blood, but we do not learn from this how the swelling of the blood corpuscles and to what extent the *H ion concentration* at the interface tissue/blood may be involved. Indirectly we obtain a certain insight from the studies of *acid intoxications*. A. LOEWY and E MUNZER * determined the ability of the blood to absorb CO_2 in normal animals and in those poisoned with hydrochloric acid, with the following results.

NORMAL BLOOD

CO_2 tension	CO_2 fixation
Per cent	Volume per cent
2 196	28 43
3 290	34 75

BLOOD OF AN ANIMAL POISONED WITH ACID

CO_2 tension	CO_2 fixation
Per cent	Volume per cent
3 630	7 37
6 143	17 88
7 530	22 26

Accordingly, the CO_2 tension must be greater in the animal poisoned with acid for the same absorption by the blood to occur as in a normal animal; which means that there is less alkali for use in combining with the acid products diffusing from the tissues than in the normal one.

Similar conditions occur when there is an abnormal acid production in the tissues; namely, after great muscular exertion with overproduction of lactic acid, in fever, where, measuring the alkalinity of the blood (by the CO_2 exhausted), KRAUS found it reduced to one-half or one-third of the normal, as in typhoid, erysipelas, scarlatina or continued fever of tuberculosis, in starvation, in coma, especially diabetic coma with over production of oxybutyric acid, and frequently in diabetes mellitus. KRAUS found in a severe case instead of a vol-

[1] It is only possible to indicate here that the difference in the reaction between blood and tissue necessitates a difference in potential which offers resistance to the movements of the blood. It is greater in proportion to the relative difference in the concentration of H ions. Unfortunately, we lack the experimental basis to establish my assumption mathematically.

ume per cent from 30 to 36 CO₂ only 12.4 and 9.8, and O. MINKOWSKI once found only 3.3 per cent. [Mention should be made of the work of JOSLIN, VAN SLYKE, MARRIOT and HOWLAND in America. Tr.]

On these grounds we must realize that in all respiratory disturbances not only the accumulation of CO₂ in the blood, but also that the incomplete oxidation in the tissue resulting from insufficient O, leads to circulatory disturbances

The following line of proof seems especially interesting to me. We know that in obesity, the oxidizing forces in the tissues are reduced, so that the fat is no longer attacked, and, as a matter of fact, it is in the obese especially that circulatory disturbances regularly appear.

Clinicians know that the circulatory disturbances from diminished alkalescence in such cases are benefited by giving large doses of alkalis.

I am fully convinced that the facts heretofore mentioned may be explained by the increased viscosity of the blood due to the swelling of the blood corpuscles, and also that we have no experimental evidence to separate the two phenomena. My sole object is to introduce into the organic development of existing ideas a new viewpoint based on colloid-chemical facts. *At the interface, tissue blood, increased H ion concentration may develop, and as a result of the ionization of the albumin, a greater friction may be produced.* The increase in the concentration of H ions may be produced by *diminution in the alkalinity of the blood or through a disturbance of the oxidizing processes in the tissues,* so that many circulatory disturbances may be viewed as errors of metabolism. The possibility of an increased friction as the result of a change in the difference in potential between blood and tissue has thus been indicated.

The mere disturbance in the oxidation processes in the tissues also causes them to swell, resulting in an abstraction of water from the blood and a consequent increase in its viscosity. We must thus recognize a relationship between the viscosity of the blood and the questions considered in the chapter on Edema (see p 223 et seq).

The influence of the blood cells on the internal friction of the blood. As was shown by A. GÜRBER, the red blood corpuscles swell when carbonic acid is introduced. H. J. HAMBURGER and VON LIMBECK have confirmed and thoroughly analyzed this observation in the case of carbonic acid and other acids. The increase in the volume of the red blood corpuscles, which is 15 per cent more in venous than in arterial blood, in pathological conditions, e.g., in asphyxiation, may rise to 30 per cent.

The most exhaustive investigations in this direction were undertaken by A. VON KORÁNYI and J. BENCE It is to the credit of A. VON KORÁNYI that he applied these results to the disturbances of the circulation. We have to thank him for a truly illuminating discussion of the pathological physiology of the circulation (A. VON KORÁNYI and O RICHTER,* Vol. II, p. 51 *et seq*).

Finally, we may conclude that increase in the CO_2 content causes a swelling of the blood corpuscles which may be considered the chief factor in the increased viscosity of the blood. By introducing oxygen the process is reversed.

Circulatory disturbances may be conditioned by failure of the motor, the *heart*, by changes in the *pipe system*, the arteries, veins or capillaries, or finally by increased *viscosity of the blood* Every change in the internal friction of the blood must in the first place have an effect upon the heart, and in the second place upon the tubular system. It follows then that a deficient cardiac function may primarily produce an increased viscosity of the blood (through insufficient supply of oxygen), or an increased viscosity of the blood, due primarily to a disturbance in tissue metabolism, may secondarily result in a disturbance of the heart We have recognized that an accumulation of acids, especially an accumulation of CO_2, may be responsible for an increase in the viscosity of the blood It would indeed be a grave error were we to believe that the course of events in the body, during circulatory disturbances, has the simple formula we have given. A further presentation of the complicated circumstances and the therapeutic influences would take us far beyond the limits of this book, although most of the phenomena have not as yet been considered from the colloid-chemical standpoint. The increase in the number of red blood corpuscles, the increase in their Cl content, etc., the entire course of circulatory decompensation and compensation are questions which in the present state of knowledge are solved better by the practised eye of clinicians than by the calculations of research.

Secretion and Absorption.

Water and food enter the gastrointestinal canal in normal nutrition. The food is changed from a colloidal to a crystalloidal condition and is thus able to pass through the intestinal membrane with the water and so reach the interior of the body it is *absorbed*. Excess of water and useless crystalloids are eliminated by the glands (*secretion*) If we accept this rough sketch, *secretion* becomes, as M. H. FISCHER has defined it, *the mirror image of absorption*. There are organs which take up solutions and those that eliminate them. We know from previous chapters that the organism strives its utmost to maintain its normal condition of swelling, so that there must be phenomena in the absorptive organs which oppose those in the secreting glands   M. H FISCHER recognized these, both in the oxidation processes of the cells and in the circulation.   The functionating cell producing acid, like venous blood rich in CO_2, has an increased swelling capacity — it absorbs water; the resting cell, being well supplied with oxygen like the arterial blood, has an excess of water — it secretes.   Thus we see that in the fluctuating supply of oxygen to an organ are furnished the conditions for the occurrence of absorption and secretion.

CHAPTER XIX.

ABSORPTION.

(See also p. 409 *et seq*, section on Purgatives)

THE absorption of food materials or alien substances is accomplished by a dissolving current which originates *in the intestines* and flows through the body There it parts with some substances and takes up others, finally excreting through the various glands, but especially the kidneys, such crystalloids as have become superfluous

Substances may be absorbed from other places, through the skin and mucous membranes, from peritoneum and pleura. This may occur when exudates have collected and have been absorbed, or when the substances have been injected. In some animals, as in the frog, absorption of water occurs only through the skin Subcutaneous, intramuscular and intravenous injections are made in order to introduce substance into the body without their passage through the intestines. The absorption of substances thus introduced into the organism is termed *parenteral absorption*.

Alimentary Absorption.

Besides the fluids which are taken with food, there is daily poured into the intestines of adult men 700 to 1000 c.c of saliva, 600 to 900 c.c. of bile, 600 to 800 c.c. of pancreatic juice, 1000 to 2000 c.c. of gastric juice, 200 c.c. of succus entericus; in all 3.1 to 4.9 liters. Inasmuch as in healthy men hardly 400 to 500 c.c of this fluid are evacuated with the feces, there must normally occur a reabsorption of 2.7 to 4.5 liters. To this must be added 1 to 1.5 liters of liquid food, so that the alimentary tract absorbs about 6 liters daily quite a considerable task.

With the water, dissolved substances are also absorbed. Inasmuch as the intestinal membrane is impassable for colloids (with the exception of very finely emulsified fats), it is the function of the alimentary tract with the help of the ferments to convert the foodstuffs into an easily diffusible condition.

The intestinal tube is a membrane which separates the interior of the body from the foods introduced and the digestive juices. It is the function of research to discover what forces drive these solutions

317

of crystalloids through the intestinal membrane. For many years it was believed that osmotic forces were concerned. This conception proved to be a serious obstacle to further progress since it diverted attention in a direction offering no prospect of results. It was only when swelling and shrinking were recognized as the dominant factors in absorption that it became possible to understand many experimental data which previously had been inexplicable.

The recognition of the importance of swelling for absorption dates from F. Hofmeister. He said, "The essentially absorbing apparatus, the intestinal epithelium, is possessed of the power to swell."[1]

Water and Crystalloids

If water or dilute salt solution is introduced into a loop of intestines, it is absorbed more or less rapidly. If the intestine behaved like a parchment membrane and the absorption of the fluids was brought about by the osmotic pressure of the body juices, water would be most rapidly absorbed. This is, however, not the case. According to G. O. Grützner,* pure water is less rapidly absorbed than 0.25 per cent NaCl solution. Accordingly, the intestine behaves like gelatin which swells more in salt solution than in pure water.

The matter becomes more complicated if we consider quantitatively the absorption of water and salt in hypotonic and hypertonic salt solutions. We shall study the experimental figures of M. Heidenhain, who placed sodium chloride solutions of various concentrations in loops of small intestine of a dog and permitted them to remain there for 15 minutes.

Experiment.	Introduced			Recovered		
	c.c.	Per cent NaCl	Total gram NaCl	c.c.	Per cent NaCl	Total gram NaCl
			grams			grams
1	120	0.3	0.36	14	0.64	0.08
2	120	0.5	0.6	34	0.68	0.23
3	117	1.0	1.17	75	0.80	0.62
4	120	1.46	1.75	108	1.30	1.4

A glance suffices to show that this experiment cannot be explained by the osmotic relations; with a parchment tube having slight swelling capacity surrounded by physiological salt solution the amount of water recovered would have to be more than 117 and 120 c.c.

* I would venture the suggestion that many poisons which are supposed to lose their "physiological components" by absorption through the intestines, ...

respectively (instead of 75 and 109 c.c.) in experiments 3 and 4. The process becomes clear immediately if we regard absorption as actually a *swelling* phenomenon. We know from page 67 that according to F. Hofmeister, a swollen gelatin absorbs more salt than water from a dilute salt solution, and that in the presence of NaCl the absorption of water is stronger than in the case of pure water.

Further light is thrown on this discovery by the researches of M. Oker-Blom,* who showed that serum takes up a hypertonic common salt solution more readily than an isotonic one.

From the table on page 318 we see that a *concentrated* salt solution which causes shrinking is but slowly absorbed.

If we consider the absorption of other salts, we find that those which as a rule promote the *swelling* of fibrin, gelatin, etc., also as a rule promote the *absorption of water* in the intestines. Therefore, there is a further *parallelism between rapidity of diffusion and furtherance of swelling.*

From the researches of R. Hober *[1] as well as those of G. B. Wallace and A. R. Cushny,* we obtain the following series

Rate of diffusion [1] HPO_4, $SO_4 < Fl < NO_3 < I < Br < Cl$,
Rate of absorption. $Fl < HPO_4$, $SO_4 < NO_3 < I < Br < Cl$,
Rate of diffusion: $Mg < Ca < Ba < Na < K$,
Rate of absorption: $Ba < Mg$, $Ca < Na$, K.

From this series we see that there is in general a **parallelism between** the rates of diffusion and of absorption.

Fl and Ba being powerful protoplasmic poisons, it does not surprise us that they form an exception and inhibit absorption.

Similar relationships between the rates of diffusion and of absorption were determined for a series of organic salts and nonelectrolytes.

It may be said, then, that *slowly diffusing* substances are slowly absorbed, and that electrolytes causing shrinking may impede not only their own absorption but also that of others, and that substances *rapidly diffusible and favoring swelling* act contrariwise. This follows from the investigations of F. Hofmeister and his pupils as well as those of H. Bechhold and J. Ziegler.

The importance of swelling is especially evident when two different substances are absorbed simultaneously. Let us take for example an experiment of Katzenellenbogen.* Simultaneously with sodium chlorid, there were introduced glycocol and acetone, which surely do not favor swelling, but the latter rather the reverse, and urea which induces swelling to a high degree.

[1] For I, Br and Cl there have been substituted the diffusion *path* in jellies instead of rapidity of diffusion.

Experiment	Introduced		c c	c c of menstruum (average)	Per cent NaCl.
1	Glycocol + 0 45% NaCl		50	36	0 332
2	Acetone + 0 45% NaCl		50	15 5	0 631
3	Urea + 0 45% NaCl		50	17	0 496

From this we see that sodium chlorid absorption is greatest in the presence of urea, because, in spite of the great shrinkage in the quantity of fluid, the concentration of sodium chlorid is but slightly increased. This coincides with the results of the experiments of H. BECHHOLD and J. ZIEGLER [*2] in which urea in the main favors diffusion in gelatin and in jellies. If we assign to acetone properties similar to alcohol, we may explain the surprisingly rapid absorption of water in the above experiment, because, as has been said on page 70, a certain proportion of alcohol increases the ability of glue to swell. From these observations we gather new points of view in regard to the ready absorption of protein cleavage products, which I shall elaborate on page 411

We may make still further deductions from the above observations, since in experiment 1 we have seen that the NaCl content of the blood is higher (about 0.6 per cent), so that it has been absorbed against the *osmotic pressure of* NaCl in the intestines This is explained on pages 318 and 319. In experiment 2, the contrary is the case: the osmotic pressure is higher than in the blood, apparently the structures capable of swelling absorb less NaCl in the presence of acetone.

Nor need we be surprised by the fact discovered by OTTO COHN-HEIM, that a hypotonic grape sugar solution introduced into a loop of the small intestine becomes more concentrated. From the same experiments we know that grape sugar, which of itself diffuses slowly, decreases the permeability of the swollen jelly, and thus blocks its own passage.

Substances which themselves possess great capacity to swell, e.g., agar, hinder the absorption of water to a high degree.

It still remains a question, how the intestine maintains its ability to take up water, since water is constantly being removed from the intestine by diffusion or swelling The theory proposed by MARTIN H FISCHER * seems to offer valuable assistance

He starts with the idea that venous blood containing carbonic acid has a tendency to swell, i e , to take up water; arterial blood, on the other hand, has a tendency to shrink or become dehydrated He showed that the arteries of the mesentery spread out into a capillary network which lies *directly under the intestinal epithelium* and empties into the portal vein as blood containing much carbonic acid According to V. LIMBECK, A. GURBER and H. J. HAMBURGER red and white blood corpuscles undergo an increase in volume of from 5 to 10 per cent when they enter the venous blood from the arteries. According to this, one liter of blood which passes through the intestine would take up 17 5 c.c of water even if we were to ascribe the abstraction of water to the blood corpuscles alone From this fact, M. H. FISCHER assumes that venous blood, so long as it is present as such, absorbs water from the intestinal mucous membrane.[1]

Though the facts so far discovered seem so clearly to explain the processes of absorption, we must not overlook the fact that they are the result of experiments which have nothing in common with natural taking of food, etc., by mouth On this account, certain objections have been raised. The living intestinal wall is not a closed tube but one traversed by solutions, so that it is therefore a question whether many phenomena are not quite different in the *living* animal. The important discovery of LOEPER[*] must be mentioned. if salt solutions of a given concentration are given by mouth, they are either concentrated or diluted so that they *reach the intestines in approximately isotonic condition*. From a practical standpoint, all those conclusions must be ignored which are based on the presence of hypotonic or hypertonic salt solutions.[2] For the pharmacologic deductions see page 411.

Within the intestine the osmotic pressure must vary greatly with the enzymatic cleavage of the food, and it is impossible to understand why at low osmotic pressures, salts of the blood, or crystalloid cleavage products of albumin might not diffuse back into the intestine from the interior of the body. Based on the investigations of F. ABDERHALDEN, it is almost certain that colloidal albumin is reconstructed from its cleavage products in the intestinal wall. The intestinal wall functionates as a suction pump for the crystalloid cleavage products of albumin which draws a stream of crystalloids from the intestinal lumen in the direction of the interior of the body. We may dismiss from consideration the absorption of albumins.

[1] In my opinion, FISCHER's theory offers valuable aid in explaining *nervous influences* upon processes of secretion and resorption. I might suggest that *nervous diarrhea* may be attributed to increased arterial blood supply to the mesentery. It is quite natural to regard diarrheas accompanying inflammatory processes in the intestines as a consequence of the increased supply of arterial blood.

[2] In my opinion this does not exclude the fact that when introduced into the intestines, the intestinal contents are usually hypertonic since crystalloids are uninterruptedly formed as a result of digestion in the intestines.

There are two important facts established by H. J. Hamburger[*] and Girard.[*] The former showed that it was possible to prepare membranes that were more permeable from one side than from the other. As a result of this experiment of H. J. Hamburger we may state that crystalloids pass from the lumen of the intestine toward the periphery and yet no crystalloids of the blood may diffuse back into the lumen of the intestine. It remains an open question, whether the small quantities of NaCl found in the intestine in absorption experiments come from the secretion of the intestinal glands, or whether the semipermeability of the intestinal membrane is limited in the direction of the lumen of the intestine.

Of the greatest general importance are the investigations of Girard. The exhaustive theoretical discussion of their basis would lead us too far afield. The following experiment is suggested: if a salt solution is suspended in a pig's bladder in water, the rate of diffusion depends on whether the salt solution is neutral slightly alkaline or slightly acid. The cause of this is found in the fact that the membrane is the seat of an electromotive force. We conclude from this that by changing the reaction on both sides of the intestinal membrane the rate of diffusion may be changed or regulated, so that, e.g., with an alkaline reaction which occurs in the intestines, the diffusion is very strongly increased.

Hitherto we have started from the assumption that the intestinal wall is of uniform texture. This is not the case, as a view of a microscopic section and simple consideration shows; the intestine is composed of cells as is every other organ, and we know that cells are only permeable for crystalloids to a limited extent. Accordingly, there must exist an easier way for the absorption of crystalloids than through the cells; *it must occur intercellularly*. It is different in the case of *lipoid-soluble substances*; they are absorbed *intracellularly*, e.g., ethyl alcohol is absorbed much more rapidly than salt solution. Numerous experiments of R. Höber have established in general the correctness of this view.

The colloid-chemical study of intestinal absorption has already yielded results for pathology.

E. Mayerhofer and P. Pŕibram,[*] in a series of valuable investigations, have tested the condition of swelling and the ability to swell of the normal and the pathologically changed intestine. They found that the *normal* and especially the *acutely inflamed intestine* were much swollen and the latter possessed an increased permeability for crystalloids. The *chronically inflamed intestine*, which already showed a connective-tissue atrophy, had a very small swelling capacity, so that a much more limited passage was afforded to dissolved substances. Outside the body, excised pieces of intestine, when artificially swollen, showed an increased permeability for KCl, NaCl and dextrose such as is possessed by acutely inflamed intestine. The reverse occurred on partial drying (shrinking); a diminished permeability of the pieces of intestine was obtained corresponding to chronic enteritis. By means of dehydrating substances (alcohol, tannin) it was possible to remove the great difference in permeability between the acutely swollen and the chronically swollen intestine. Sugar (dextrose), especially, markedly increases the permeability of the intestinal wall.

Thus, the clinical discoveries of H. FINKELSTEIN, concerning intoxication with sugar-rich mixtures in children, find colloid-chemical confirmation. [An interesting colloid-chemical application is the treatment of diarrheas, especially in children, by adjusting the diet with a view to the formation of insoluble calcium soaps in the intestine. It has also been pointed out by BOSWORTH *et al*, Am. Jour. Diseases of Children, Vol. XV, No. 6, p. 397 *et seq.*, that the formation of Ca soaps may interfere with the absorption of fats and account for certain types of malnutrition and milk intolerance. Tr.]

We must refrain here from a more exhaustive investigation of *absorption by the stomach*. The number of experimental observations is still not large and from a colloid-chemical standpoint they do not assist.

It is established, *e.g.*, that the stomach absorbs no water (VON MERING); on the contrary dissolved substances (salts, carbohydrates and albumins) above a "certain level of concentration" are absorbed (for bibliography see H. STRAUSS [*1] and W. ROTH and H. STRAUSS [*]).

Parenteral Absorption.

Like those concerning intestinal absorption, the studies of parenteral absorption have been based almost exclusively on the laws of osmotic pressure in relation to the permeability of membranes (see C. FRIEDEMANN [*]).

The countless difficulties were only successfully met with the entrance of the colloid-chemical views of swelling and shrinking, for which the researches of MARTIN H. FISCHER [*] paved the way

Researches on the absorption from *serous cavities* have been most numerous. As regards the absorption of *exudates*, the question should be, under what circumstances do exudates form? Normally the organism allows no fluid to collect in the serous cavities. We must, therefore, assume a change in the permeability of the living membrane or a shrinking of the surrounding tissue.[1]

[1] See also M. H. FISCHER, "Nephritis"

On the basis of M. H. Fischer's investigations, the latter view must be regarded as correct If a dilute salt solution is placed in the peritoneal cavity of a normal living or a dead guinea pig, it will soon be absorbed. More concentrated salt solutions as well as solutions of the salts which cause loss of water in the case of fibrin, gelatin, etc. (*e.g* , sodium sulphate, citrate and tartrate) are either not absorbed at all or even increase their volume inasmuch as fluid enters the peritoneal cavity from the body. If albumin solution is injected into the peritoneal cavity, very little will be absorbed within an hour. The tissues about the peritoneal cavity behave in this case just as does every dead colloid that is capable of swelling, and there is no difference between intestine and peritoneal cavity. The results are not so uniform when glycerin or sugar solution are injected into the peritoneal cavity. Though these have a very slight influence on the swelling of fibrin, they cause an entrance of fluid into the peritoneal cavity. Evidently they cause, as they do in the intestine, an irritation (see p. 323).

The investigations of this question are not completed as the researches of L. Asher * have shown

A great number of *marine animals* have a body surface which is permeable for water though not for salts. Corals, echinoderms, holothurians, etc., swell in dilute, and shrink in concentrated sea water. [A practical application is the " ripening " of oysters." Tr] The same fact obtains for many *fresh-water* animals, especially amphibia, worms and snails. Frogs never take water through their mouths, they "drink through their skins " In the case of these fresh water animals there occurs no swelling during life for the kidney excretes the excess of water. The skin is also permeable for lipoid-soluble substances. The skin of *warm-blooded animals* is different from that of *cold-blooded animals* in that it is almost impermeable for water and allows only lipoid-soluble substances to pass through (W. Filehne * and A. Schwenkenbecher *).

From what has been said, it is evident that a whole group of factors such as rate of diffusion, swelling, osmotic pressure, play a part in absorption — and we shall observe the same for secretion — and that there are many gaps in the experimental data which support these views

The undoubtedly active rôle of *adsorption* has not been touched upon, and it is possible that the negative phase of the blood pulsations may have certain importance through its suction Some phenomena regarded as filtrations, for which the pressure in the intestines seems somewhat too slight, may be explained by a pulsating loss of swelling (dehydration). The *alcohol question* received a new light from colloid studies   We saw on page 70, that gelatin swelled more in weak alcohol solutions, and we know, on the other hand, that strong alcohol causes shrinking.   Thus we may possibly explain the favorable action that small doses of alcohol have on the absorption of nourishment.   Some day, *chronic alcoholism* may possibly receive a physico-chemical explanation from the change in the condition of the body colloids, whether albuminous or lipoid.

[W BURRIDGE has offered what seems an adequate physico-chemical explanation of chronic alcoholism.   Quarterly Jour. of Medicine, Vol. X, No. 39.   In the alcoholic who "takes a little, often," the adrenin-like action of alcohol predominates, and there is an improved utilization of Ca.   To accommodate for this the Ca tension of the blood is diminished so that when deprived of his drug the circulation of the chronic alcoholic is like one using a perfusion solution containing an inadequate supply of Ca.   This accounts for the acute circulatory symptoms upon the withdrawal and possibly for the tremor.   It also accounts for the increased anesthetic risk, if the accustomed Ca tension in the blood is below that which is adequate to maintain the circulation in the presence of a percentage concentration of anesthetic usual for anesthesia.   A similar colloid-chemical explanation based on this work of W. BURRIDGE may be offered for other drug addictions.   Tr.]

CHAPTER XX.

SECRETION AND EXCRETION.

(See also Chapter XIII, The Enzymes.)

The Glands.

THE lymph and the blood current discharge into the glands, where they are modified in a specific manner. The result of this selective action is the secretion which pours from the ducts of the various glands.

The cause of secretion is one of the most debated of physiological questions. None of the blood colloids are found in the secretions, but the crystalloids, which are also contained in the blood, occur in abundance. The freezing point depression gives us an idea of the total crystalloid content. This shows that the crystalloid content (expressed in osmotic pressure) of the *saliva* is always lower than that of the blood; the osmotic pressure of *gastric juice* and *bile* may equal that of the blood, *milk* has approximately the same osmotic pressure as blood and fluctuates with it in this respect. *Sweat* and especially *urine*, on the contrary, may either have a lower osmotic pressure than the blood or exceed it. If secretion were *only* an ultrafiltration of the blood through the gland filters, it would be incomprehensible how an excretion could occur with a lower osmotic pressure than the blood, or with one that is higher, as sweat and urine. The conditions are especially complicated by reason of the fact that the relative crystalloid content of various secretions may be absolutely different from what they are in the blood plasma. Thus, for instance, milk contains from 4 to 5 per cent milk sugar, whereas the blood shows only from 0.08 to 0.12 per cent grape sugar, urine contains disproportionately more urea than other salts, whereas the amount of urea in the blood is entirely insignificant. We thus find, besides producing specific substances (bile, pepsin, ptyalin, etc.) that the individual glands have a *specific activity* in relation to the lymph crystalloids, which some biologists even to-day prefer to assign to the inexplicable physiological functions and thus to remove it from physical and chemical study. As yet colloid chemistry has no better explanation to offer. However, it seems probable to me that we shall, with its help, come to a solution of these questions.

We may assume that various colloid-tissue elements differ in their ability to absorb different crystalloids which they remove from solution, just as fibers remove dyes, and that thus a different composition is given to the ultrafiltrate. There is ample reason to believe that certain crystalloids (*e.g.*, urea, nitrates, etc.) open the paths through the colloid membrane, while others (*e.g.*, sulphates) close them just as was shown in their diffusion experiments with jellies by H. Bechhold and J. Ziegler (see p. 55) Side by side with this occur the specific chemical activities of the gland elements which give them their particular character, the formation of ptyalin in the salivary glands, and of bile in the liver, etc.

E. Přibram [1] has formulated a theory according to which there first occurs a coagulation of nutritive material (granule formation) in the gland cells, which is followed by swelling, *i.e.*, secretion.[1]

With the above *systematization* of glandular function, we may obtain an explanation of a number of processes, and we may learn how to study the remainder We shall, therefore, *regard every secretion as an ultrafiltrate whose composition is changed by reabsorption and specific adsorption*, and to which, in the case of most glands[2] (*e q*, salivary, pancreas, liver, etc.), specified chemical products of glandular activity are added. In what order the change by adsorption and ultrafiltration occurs remains for the present an open question.

The presence of *free* water is an essential condition for the ultrafiltration of the blood This applies only to the glands. As was mentioned in more detail elsewhere, we may assume with Martin H. Fischer that venous blood, rich in CO_2, abstracts water, whereas arterial blood can release it We now know that all glands are plentifully supplied with arterial blood so that the free water necessary for ultrafiltration is supplied. The influence of the pulsations of blood pressure, noted by H. Bechhold, is considered on page 332.

---

[1] Many authors distinguish between *secretion* and *excretion* (urine, sweat, etc.); whereas the former contain colloidal ingredients, they are more or less completely absent from the latter. Since there is no essential difference we shall not strictly enforce this classification.

[2] It cannot be denied, that the consideration of the *digestive glands* from this viewpoint offers very considerable difficulties, since their function is controlled to a very great extent by *nervous* influences The glands which are not directly under the control of the nervous system, *e.g.*, the kidneys, give clearer pictures. Since we know that there is an excess of water in arterial blood and that venous blood fixes water, the nervous control of secretion becomes a working hypothesis or at least the question becomes shifted, and we must investigate the effect of nervous influences on the supply of blood to the glands.

The Saliva.

Under normal circumstances, 700 to 1000 c.c. of saliva are secreted daily. The amount of salivary secretion is largely influenced by the amount of water contained in the body   If large amounts of water are taken, the salivary secretion is plentiful, whereas, with diarrhea, profuse sweating and fever, it diminishes greatly (dry mouth).

Of all the secretions, the saliva has on the average the lowest osmotic pressure; its freezing-point depression is from $0.11°$ to $0.27°$ in man, in contrast to blood with from $0.58°$ to $0.60°$.   If the excretion of saliva increases, there is an increase in the crystalloids contained and to such an extent that when the secretion is greatest it almost reaches that of blood plasma; it then contains 0 58 per cent NaCl.   The fact that with increased salivation the carbonates are proportionately increased in the saliva, strongly supports in my opinion the rôle of ultrafiltration of the blood plasma in the secretion of the saliva.   If the NaCl content of the blood is increased, that of the saliva also increases, and conversely (J. NOVY, J. N. LANGLEY and FLETCHER). If potassium iodid or lithium citrate are introduced into the circulation (J. N LANGLEY and FLETCHER), iodin or lithium may be demonstrated in the saliva immediately; whereas, after introducing grape sugar and potassium ferrocyanid they do not appear in the saliva at all or only after a long time.   All these facts support the view that the chief process is an ultrafiltration.   The last-mentioned experiments, especially, show that potassium iodid and lithium citrate, which diffuse rapidly and open paths, appear in the saliva promptly, whereas grape sugar and potassium ferrocyanid, as a result of their slowness in diffusion, penetrate the filter membrane slowly, so that meanwhile they may be excreted in other ways   For the two remaining elements in the function of the salivary glands, the change in the composition of the ultrafiltrate and the addition of the colloid constituents, we have as yet no experimental data.

The Bronchial Glands.[1]

An analysis of the individual functions of the secretion of the bronchial mucous membrane has proved hitherto entirely impossible. It is an indication of ultrafiltration that with an increase in the

---

[1] MARTIN H. FISHER with justice questions why the secretion of superfluous water commences in the kidneys instead of in the lungs, since by the change of the venous blood rich in carbonic acid into arterial blood, water is actually liberated.   He thinks that water is not secreted in the lungs because of the impermeability of the membrane, or because there is insufficient time.

secretion, there is an increase of the alkali carbonates in the mucus, which like all alkaline substances fluidify the mucus colloids, especially the mucin The utilization of potassium iodid as an expectorant may be similarly interpreted; possibly it also favors ultrafiltration in the sense of H. Bechhold and J. Ziegler. Moreover, R. Höber upon applying iodin found an increase in the ciliary movements in the ciliated epithelium of frogs; this increased activity may assist in the discharge of mucus.

Gastric Juice.

The daily excretions of the stomach amount from 1000 to 2000 c.c.

As has been mentioned, the osmotic pressure of the gastric juice usually is *less* than that of the blood, and according to H. Strauss[*2] it normally has a freezing-point depression of from 0.36° to 0 48°. Pathologically it may rise to 0.58, which is the freezing-point depression of the blood It is of especial interest to know that in those cases where osmotic pressure approaches that of the blood, according to H. Strauss, *free HCl is usually absent* These observations have been confirmed by others (Winter, S. Schönborn). This fact of itself would indicate that in a stomach where the second glandular function, the modification of the ultrafiltrate, is arrested, the composition of the gastric juice is more like that of the blood crystalloids. We cannot omit to mention that another fact is opposed to this: in normal gastric juice, the NaCl content is nearer that of the blood (0 59 per cent) than in subacidity. Unfortunately, I know of no adequate data upon pure gastric juice from a subacid stomach, so that for the present the interpretation must remain indefinite.

The secretion of a juice with *free* hydrochloric acid from a neutral fluid, the blood, is one of the problems which offers especial difficulties to physiologists. An attempt has been made to explain the phenomenon by the law of mass action with the help of carbonic acid. In my opinion colloid chemistry offers analogies which permit an unforced explanation. We know that *neutral salts may be split into acids and bases by adsorption* (see p. 28), thus, for instance, an acid fluid with *free sulphuric acid* remains after shaking a solution of potassium sulphate with hydrated manganese dioxid (J. M. Van Bemmelen). With this in mind we need not be surprised at the splitting off of free HCl from a solution of chlorids.

The secretion of gastric juice is analogous to the secretion of acid by plant roots, which, according to Baumann Gully, likewise occurs by decomposition of salts through the adsorption of bases by the pellicle of plant cells.

Investigations of gastric secretion, as far as they relate to physical chemistry, have hitherto almost exclusively consisted of observation of the osmotic condition and the electrolyte concentration; the material for review is consequently as yet far too limited for a colloid-chemical consideration.

The Secretions Which Pour Into the Intestines.

There are 200 c.c. of succus entericus daily secreted by the intestinal glands.

The *Succus Entericus* is usually hypertonic. If we inject into an animal (D'ERRICO, chickens, D'ERRICO and SAVARESE, dogs) a hypertonic common salt solution, the osmotic pressure of the succus entericus becomes still higher so that its freezing-point depression may increase to from $0.89°$ to $0.99°$ (blood $= 0.59°$) This corresponds to our conception that an ultrafiltrate may be concentrated by the absorptive activity of the intestinal wall. The succus entericus, like the pancreatic juice which pours into the intestine, is almost neutral. The OH ion concentration is about 10^{-8} at $18°$ according to AUERBACH and PICK. Its alkalinity is approximately that of a sodium bicarbonate solution. On account of its higher sodium bicarbonate content, pancreatic juice has a greater capacity to combine with acid than has succus entericus.

According to H. ISCOVESCO [*2] the colloids of the *pancreatic juice* are electropositive; they form with the electronegative colloids of the succus entericus complexes soluble in a neutral environment.

The Bile: 600 to 900 c.c. of bile are secreted per day.

The osmotic pressure of the bile is approximately that of the blood; its conductivity is somewhat higher. According to H. ISCOVESCO,[*2] the colloid constituents of the bile probably have an electronegative charge.

The Kidneys and the Secretion of Urine.

(See also p 409 *et seq*, on "Diuretics.")

We shall briefly review the structure of the kidneys of vertebrates. the renal artery branches and in the cortex or outer portion of the kidney develops by the formation of numerous glomeruli an enormous surface (Fig. 50) These are knotted ball-like branches of the smaller arterial vessels placed in a vesicle (*Bowman's* capsule). The artery leaves *Bowman's* capsule, subdivides into capillaries which collect together and form the renal veins. *Bowman's* capsule has an outlet into the urinary tubules which have, at first, a convoluted course covered with a thick layer of cells and collect into larger and larger tubules (Fig. 51), which ultimately discharge the urine into the pelvis of the kidney.

The phenomenon of *urine secretion* consists in separating water and crystalloids from a solution containing colloids and crystalloids (blood), though, usually, in a much *higher concentration* and with a different proportion of crystalloid constituents than occurs in the blood.

Without going into the various theories of urine secretion, we shall here sketch those which, from physiological and pathological investigations, seem most probable. According to this the glomeruli are a *filtration apparatus* in which water and crystalloids are filtered off while the colloids are held back. From this ultra-

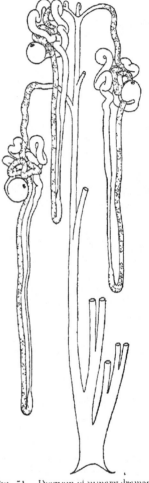

Fig. 51. Diagram of urinary drainage from Bowman's capsule. (From G. Ludwig.)

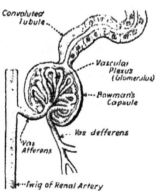

Convoluted Tubule

Vascular Plexus (Glomerulus)

Bowman's Capsule

Vas defferens

Vas Afferens

Twig of Renal Artery

Fig. 50. Glomerular structure.

filtrate which contains the crystalloids in no higher concentration than blood, later, possibly in the first portion of the urinary tubules, *water and some of the crystalloids* are absorbed, so that a *concentrated* solution, the urine, passes off.

In order to give an idea of the quantities of fluid which are involved, the figures of H. MEYER and R. GOTTLIEB * are reproduced. The blood contains about 0.6 per cent urea, the daily urine about 30 gm. There must thus be about 50 liters filtered through the glomeruli and about 48 5 liters reabsorbed by the tubules. Since in 24 hours from 500 to 600 liters of blood flow through the kidneys, 10 per cent of the water of the blood must be filtered off This is not at all improbable when we recollect that the afferent vessels (*vas afferens*) have a much larger lumen than the efferent (*vas deferens*).

The *filtration processes* are relatively the least difficult to explain. The criticism until recently offered that no filtration could occur through homogeneous colloid layers has been disposed of by the ultra-filtration experiments of H. BECHHOLD.*41 It must not be insisted too strongly that the phenomenon in the glomeruli is a "filtration" since it is evidently a process midway between filtration and diffusion.

As in the case of every other ultrafiltration, that in the kidney is dependent upon the pressure. According to E. H. STARLING, it begins with an arterial pressure of at least 40 mm mercury; below this the secretion of urine ceases. In blood artificially diluted with water, a minimal blood pressure which just maintains the circulation suffices for the secretion of urine [1] R GOTTLIEB and R. MAGNUS showed this by permitting normal saline to flow continuously into an animal's vein. According to GOLL the urinary secretion rises and falls almost proportionately to the blood pressure. The experiment of D. R HOOKER * furnishes a result in point. He found in the isolated dog's kidney, that with a *constant* perfusion pressure the quantity of urine formed was directly proportional to the size of the (artificial) pulse pressure. The *pulsation of the blood pressure* plays an important part in the rate of filtration H BECHHOLD *12 compared the amount of fluid which flowed through an ultrafilter under constant and under pulsating pressure, and found that in the latter case the filtrate was considerably more than in the former. We may imagine that with the lower pressure the filter absorbs the fluid completely and it is pressed out again with the increased pressure. This depends very much on the *elasticity of the ultrafilter*, if it can follow the variations in pressure very rapidly, the rate of filtration is higher than for an inelastic filter. Perhaps this will

---

[1] I cannot agree here with MARTIN H FISCHER (Oedema, p. 209) He says, "Enormous pressures are necessary to filter fluids through thin colloidal membranes." This is not correct With suitably prepared thin collodion membranes, a few centimeters of pressure suffice for ultrafiltration.

give us the basis for an understanding of certain changes in the function of the kidney in pathological and senile conditions, in which the filtering membrane is inelastic. From what has been said it cannot be ruled out, that even in glomerular filtration a change in the salt content of the filtrate from the blood may occur, since salts and water are not taken up equally during swelling (see p 69). We can thus more readily understand how a salt solution *hypotonic* towards blood may flow from the glomeruli, although according to R. BURIAN an *isotonic* filtrate is always obtained upon ultrafiltration through an artificial ultrafilter. Moreover, the difference in the reaction of blood and of glomerular filtrate may contribute to the dilution

R. A. GESELL made a remarkable observation Repeating BECH-HOLD's experiment he employed more rapid pulsation and lower pressure and obtained from defibrinated dog's blood a filtrate richer in globulin with the steady than with the pulsating pressure.

Obviously, the glomerular membrane is just at the limit of permeability for serum albumin; albumoses pass over into the urine. We do not know whether the normal urinary colloids such as urochrome are derived from the glomeruli or secondarily from the urinary tubules.

This explanation receives valuable support from the investigation of MARTIN H. FISCHER.* As we saw on page 215 *et seq.*, there is in the body a dynamic swelling equilibrium for the organ colloids which may be regarded as constant for a brief period in thirsting individuals, in them the secretion reaches a minimum. With excessive ingestion of water, edema does not by any means occur, but the excess of water is excreted by the excretory glands, especially the kidneys. As we have seen on page 220, there is a very narrow range of swelling for the blood; as the result of this all water (free water in contrast to water of swelling) which is in excess of what is needed for the normal condition of hydration of the blood is filtered off by the kidneys, especially if the muscles, the main reservoir, are already saturated with water. A most convincing proof that it is not the absolute quantity of water but the swollen condition of the blood colloids which is of significance for the secretion of urine may be found in the older experiments of E PONFICK and the more recent ones of R MAGNUS.*[1] These investigators transfused a rabbit with the blood of another rabbit so that its blood was increased from 30 to 70 per cent In spite of this there was no increase or hardly any increase in the excretion of urine. The same results were obtained for dogs and rats.

The novel conception introduced by M. H. FISCHER* is the following blood rich in CO_2 (venous) *has a tendency to swell, or absorb water; blood poor in CO_2* (arterial) *has a tendency to shrink or give up water.* The blood passing to the intestines is very rich in CO_2

and, consequently, abstracts water from the intestinal mucous membrane, causing absorption from the intestinal lumen. The reverse process occurs in the kidneys. These are traversed by great streams of arterial blood which can give up water. If this assumption is correct, every increase in the supply of oxygen to the kidneys increases urine secretion, and every interference decreases it. Now, every elevation of blood pressure and everything favoring the circulation in the kidneys signifies an improvement in the supply of oxygen and *vice versa*. We might, however, wherever this occurs, just as well attribute the change in the secretion of urine to the changed filtration pressure or rate of filtration. On this account we must select the circumstances which M. H. Fischer mentions, which always indicate an improvement or impairment in the supply of oxygen. Among them is, "that blood poor in oxygen or rich in carbonic acid supplied to the kidneys for the briefest period and without even the slightest disturbance of the circulation otherwise, is inadequate to maintain even for the briefest period a normal secretion of urine by the kidneys." On the other hand there are diuretics which cause an increased secretion of urine though accompanied by no change in blood pressure. M. H. Fischer injected hypertonic solutions of various sodium salts chlorid, bromid, iodid sulphate, tartrate, phosphate and citrate and obtained with them an increased kidney secretion, which stood in a certain relation to the lyotrope action of the salts involved. M. H. Fischer explains his results by the fact that the salts involved act by shrinking or dehydrating the body colloids, and thus increasing the quantity of the free or filterable water (see also E. Pick[*]). Sugars especially dextose, act similarly. M. H. Fischer and A. Sykes thus explain the thirst and diuresis of diabetes.

Some diuretics, for instance, *urea*, cause no increased circulation of blood, yet they still increase the kidney secretion as J. Ranstorm and Bromig showed. This has been urged as an argument against the theory of filtration. In my opinion the explanation is as follows urea obviously causes deflocculation of the colloids included in the kidney filter. We know from pages 55 and 162 that urea lowers the melting point of gelatin decreases its rate of solidification and facilitates diffusion through gelatin. All these factors produce a readier filterability of the water of the blood and a greater permeability of the renal filter; to what extent the reabsorption of water is influenced cannot be decided.

The experiments of E. Lamy and A. Mayer[*] seem an additional factor in favor of the filtration theory. They tested the relationship between the *viscosity* of the blood and diuresis. The following tables definitely show that with the diminution of friction the

retion of urine increases and conversely. Though the relationship
not as evident in the second experiment as in the first, it is still quite
finite

Amount of urine secreted in ten minutes	Coefficient of friction
c c 1 5	12 5

Injection of 20 gm. cane sugar in 40 c.c water:

Amount of urine secreted in ten minutes.	Coefficient of friction
c c 16	8 96
10	12.14
2 5	14.89
1	14.71

Injection of 50 gm. cane sugar in 100 c.c. water.

Amount of urine secreted in ten minutes	Coefficient of friction
c c. 8	11 39
3 5	10.17
1 5	11.75
0 5	13.92

[The choice of sucrose for these experiments is unfortunate since, as
. H Fischer and Woodyatt have shown, sucrose dehydrates and
ers free water to the kidney. Gelatin and gum arabic raise the
efficient of friction without increasing urine as Starling has shown.
u re is consequently no foundation for the conclusions of Lamy and
Ayer. Tr.]

The Concentration of the Glomerular Filtrate.

The filtrate through the glomerular filter probably shows a concen-
tion of crystalloid constituents not much different from that of the
ood plasma, although a certain selection and redistribution in the rel-
ive proportion of the crystalloids by the renal filter is conceivable.
ae blood shows a depression of the freezing point of about 0.56°,
ereas the urine of man in health may vary between 0 07° to 3.5°.
For a urine of higher osmotic pressure than the blood, the filtration
ory must look for support to the assumption that water must be sub-
quently withdrawn from the diluted filtrate in the first portion of the
inary tubules. The investigations of J. Demoor seem to me to be of
pecial importance for the assumption of a subsequent change in con-
ntration in the urinary tubules. This author perfused hypotonic
id hypertonic salt solutions through the renal artery and while he

measured the variations of renal volume in a plethysmograph, he analyzed the fluid coming from the renal passages for the same time.

The kidney perfused with a hypotonic solution is firm and pale, no fluid is expressed with pressure, the cells are so swollen that the lumina of the urinary tubules are almost occluded — typical swelling. The kidney perfused with hypertonic solution is large and soft, much fluid is expressed by pressure, the cells are shrunken and the tubules patent — typical shrinking. (See also R. Siebeck.)

In the light of Martin H. Fischer's theory, the explanation of the concentration of the urine and the tubules becomes simple. We need only recall that the tubules are interwoven with capillaries containing venous blood which reabsorb water. This conception is supported by the experiments of R. Gottlieb and R. Magnus[*] as well as of E. H. Starling,[*] who found a diminished swelling of the organ when the supply of blood to the kidneys was diminished.

The greater concentration of the urine is not the only fact requiring an explanation, but also the fact that the relative proportion of the individual crystalloid ingredients is different in the urine than in the blood plasma. [A. R. Cushny in his monograph on "The Secretion of Urine," 1917, divides the constituents of the plasma into *threshold* bodies and *nonthreshold* bodies. Dextrose, chlorids and sodium are excreted only when their concentration in the blood exceeds a certain definite or threshold percentage. Urea is an instance of a substance with no threshold. According to Ambard (Presse Médicale, April 25, 1918), threshold substances are necessary for cell life. He quotes Chabanier's research showing that nonthreshold substances have a common secretory constant for each individual and that they all seem to be solvents for fats. Tr.]

Though in the blood, 75 per cent of all crystalloids are inorganic molecules according to J. Bugarszky and K. Tangl, in the urine they comprise only from 47 to 66 per cent according to J. Bugarszky, Roth and Steyrer. In the blood plasma, 0.58 per cent are NaCl, 0.05 per cent urea; in the urine, on the contrary, the average amount of NaCl is 1 per cent in the presence of more than 2 per cent of urea. In the blood there is from 0.08 to 0.12 per cent grape sugar, but only traces occur in the urine. As has been said, it is entirely possible that even during filtration certain changes occur so that the relative proportion of crystalloids even in the glomerular filtrate differs from that in the blood plasma though the most important change results from the reabsorption of water in the first portion of the tubules.

That concentration may be brought about by swelling has already been shown in the classical example of C. Ludwig, mentioned on page 66. So much water may be withdrawn from a concentrated common salt solution by a fish bladder that salt crystallizes out. From the investigations of F HOFMEISTER and Wo. OSTWALD it may be concluded that the swelling of gelatin-jellies is favored by some salts in accordance with their lyotropic action, while other salts diminish the swelling (see pp. 69 and 70), in other words, according to the nature of the dissolved salts, more or less water may be removed from a solution by the swelling of jellies. The extent to which the individual ions in mixtures of electrolytes may be more or less concentrated in the solution which remains after the swelling has received as yet no satisfactory experimental study But even LUDWIG sought such an interpretation and sought by its aid to explain the proportionately greater excretion of phosphates than of chlorids in the urine

LAGERGREEN found a negative adsorption with charcoal and kaolin in solutions of chlorids of Na, K, NH₄ and Mg; in other words, there resulted a concentration of the solution, whereas nitrates show a positive adsorption, in the case of sulphates the adsorption was partly positive and partly negative F. HOFMEISTER in the case of gelatin found that the absorption of water and of dissolved substance proceeded independently of each other, that the absorption of water from an NaCl solution increased until the concentration reached 13 to 14 per cent, and that when the concentration was higher than this, the absorption of water fell again J M. VAN BEMMELEN demonstrated that potassium sulphate is split up by manganese dioxid, because K is adsorbed while SO_4 remains in solution (the solution has an acid reaction). Subsequently, similar cleavages were demonstrated by M MASIUS and L MICHAELIS. It is thus evident that there exists the possibility of a varying adsorption of salts (and other substances) during swelling, so that an acid fluid (urine reacts acid) may result from a neutral filtrate. If we now attempt to apply these general facts to the special instances of the concentration of the glomerular filtrate, we shall see that the most important scientific support is lacking. Adsorption experiments with renal substance are especially necessary. The experiments of TORALD SOLLMANN may be explained on the basis of our hypothesis. He found that the percentage of chlorids in the urine was increased by nitrates, iodids and sulphocyanids, and, on the other hand, that it is decreased by acetates, phosphates and sulphates.

No facts contradict the colloid-chemical conception of urine excretion, but we still lack the special experimental data that should support it. If we recall that none of the other explanations of diuresis are in any better position but that they must cling to vitalistic assumptions, we are compelled to accept the filtration theory as the most advantageous until a better one shall replace it.

Pathology of Urine Secretion.

As our preceding statements show, two different functions of the kidney may suffer the filtration of the glomeruli and the concentrating activity of the tubules.

Filtration is deficient whenever the glomerular filter is damaged; it will also be abnormal if there is nothing to be filtered, which happens when an insufficient quantity of arterial blood containing free water is supplied to the glomeruli

MARTIN H. FISCHER[*1] finds the chief cause of *nephritis* is an *abnormal increase in the acidity* of the kidney cells It is the cause of *albuminuria*. According to him, the acid dissolves kidney protein so that the urine contains albumin, it dissolves away the formed elements (epithelial cells), which are then washed into the urine as *casts* Depending upon the (experimental) conditions, epithelial, granular or hyaline casts are formed "The first change to the second, and these to the third variety if the acid concentration is progressively increased. Hyaline may be changed back to granular casts if a little salt is added to the acid solution " (M H. FISCHER) M. H. FISCHER supports this theory with numerous experiments

The *increase in acidity* may *result from a deficient supply of oxygen* to the kidneys which may be due to a number of different causes It may be caused by deficient cardiac activity of any kind, hemorrhages or irritation of the vasomotor nerves, as well as compression of the renal artery by a tumor, or interference with the flow of blood resulting from arteriosclerosis or embolism Congestion of the renal vein must of course have a similar effect. [Lack of exercise with insufficient breathing may induce acidosis Tr]

Disturbances of renal function may result directly or indirectly as a result of *toxic* influences, such as chemical poisons and toxins from infections In such case the oxidation processes of the renal cells suffer so that renal edema results, and this causes a compression of the blood vessels, so that the supply of arterial blood to the kidneys is deficient, a vicious circle is thus established.

M. H. FISCHER also explains the action of *alcohol* and *anesthetics* in a very plausible way. Small doses increase the excretion of urine by increasing and strengthening the heart's action, and the respiratory frequency by vasodilatation; these are all factors which favor the supply of oxygen to the blood, and in that way the formation of free filterable water. *Caffein* and *digitalis* act in a similar way. Large doses of *alcohol, ether, chloroform, chloral, morphine*, etc., on the contrary, bring about a deficiency of oxygen, causing a binding of water by the body colloids and thus a diminution of the secreted urine (see E. FREY).

As the result of these colloid-chemical views, Martin H. Fischer successfully treated experimental anuria (of rabbits) by introducing salts which counteracted the development of edema. Upon ligating the renal arteries of rabbits diminished secretion of urine occurs, and the kidney may be so damaged that the anuria persists. M. H. Fischer injected solutions of sodium phosphate, sodium sulphate, sodium chlorid, after which the edema receded and the secretion of urine recommenced. He also obtained gratifying results clinically by administering hypertonic solutions of sodium carbonate and sodium chlorid which is a treatment quite opposite to the customary one. His purpose is to hinder the accumulation of acid in the kidneys. The prohibition of violent exercise, the substitution of a vegetarian diet rich in alkalis for a meat diet and the drinking of alkaline mineral waters is the customary treatment for nephritics and is explained by Fischer on the basis of his acid theory of albuminuria. We have discussed on page 239 the criticism Fischer's theory received. Fischer has offered a new working hypothesis whose experimental discussion will be very productive, no matter which side ultimately wins. [A. A. Epstein has recently successfully treated edema in certain types of chronic parenchymatous nephritis by transfusion and, adopting the practice of Fernand Widal and of Hermann Strauss, feeding large quantities of protein, 120–240 gm. per day, in an endeavor to increase the blood proteins which he had found were diminished The increase in the osmotic pressure of the blood due to the added protein restored the normal relations between tissues and blood. The fluid which exudes in response to osmotic pressure of proteins should be salt and water. Epstein found that such was the composition of edema and effusion fluids in chronic parenchymatous nephritis. Am. Jour. Med. Sc., No. 548, Nov. 1917, p. 638 et seq.]

A functional incapacity of the *concentrating activity of the upper uriniferous tubules* becomes evident whenever the glomerular filtrate is not materially altered, and the composition of the urine approaches that of an ultrafiltrate of the blood. As a matter of fact, this may be observed in many cases. [The antidiuretic action of the extract of pituitary posterior lobe and pars intermedia extract has not yet been satisfactorily explained. Molzfeld * concluded, as the result of experiments on rabbits, that it is due to a stimulation of the renal vasomotor system. Tr.]

We saw that the freezing point depression of the blood was remarkably constant about $0.56°$ but that for the urine it varies between $0.07°$ and $3.5°$.

A. von Korányi * showed that the "limits of accommodation" of renal function were diminished in proportion to the severity of the renal disease, and that the *molecular concentration of the urine of nephritics approaches the molecular concentration of the blood.* A table from the paper of A. VON KORÁNYI, KOVESI and ROTH-SCHULTZ* explains this:

FREEZING POINT DEPRESSION.

	Maximal	Minimal.
	Deg	Deg
Healthy	3 5	0 08
Chronic interstitial nephritis	0 63-2	0 12-0 38
Chronic parenchymatous nephritis	0 68-1 11	0 36-0 47
Subacute parenchymatous nephritis .	0 75-1 27	0 53-0 83

A. GALLEOTTI* obtained from dogs suffering from phosphorus and sublimate nephritis, a urine with a freezing point depression practically identical with that of the blood, PH BOTTAZZI and ONORATO* obtained it likewise from dogs poisoned with sodium fluorid. An experiment by these authors with a dog suffering from *cantharides nephritis* is, however, especially instructive; in this case the uriniferous tubules are practically unchanged and, accordingly, their activity in concentrating the urine is practically uninfluenced

If a healthy person drinks water freely, there results a markedly increased flow of urine, which in the case of nephritics does not occur   KOVESI and G. ILLYÉS examined the urine obtained through ureteral catheters from persons who had a healthy and a diseased kidney.   When a great deal of water had been drunk, there was secreted from the healthy kidney a large quantity of very dilute urine, while from the diseased kidney, urine of average concentration was obtained.   Since both kidneys received the same blood, the blood could not have been responsible for the more dilute filtrate, but the subsequent dilution must have been omitted by the kidney with the impaired function.   In a diseased kidney, not only does the concentration of the urine approach that of the blood, but even the amount of the individual crystalloids contained becomes similar to that of an ultrafiltrate from the blood.   There are very few investigations on this subject and they are chiefly limited to the chlorids   Some data supplied by ALBARRAN warrant our conclusion.   We saw on page 335 that there is approximately twelve times as much NaCl as urea in the blood, whereas in the urine there is about one-half as much NaCl as urea   Whenever the kidney parenchyma is much diseased, the urea content of the urine falls, and there is a rise in the amount of chlorids in proportion to the amount of urea.   However, the absolute quantity of NaCl in the urine diminishes   In health there is approximately double the amount of NaCl in the urine as in the plasma, the NaCl content of the urine of nephritics approaches that of the plasma. The same fact seems to obtain for the other crystalloids, including water.

Inasmuch as the functionally inadequate kidney continues to *ultrafilter* but ceases to regulate the ultrafiltrate, it likewise loses its function as a regulator of the entire organism; it is no longer able to maintain the "milieu intérieur" The diminished excretion of crystalloids by insufficient kidneys causes an increase in the crystalloidal content of the blood as was first shown by A. von Korányi by measuring the freezing point depression (cryoscopy).

The Result of Deficient Kidney Function Upon the Organism.

If in animal experiments both kidneys are removed, an *hydremia* develops even though no water is given, or if the water removed by respiration and through the skin is just replaced. If a nephritic is given¹ water *ad libitum*, the hydremia does not increase at all, or when it has reached a given grade only to an insignificant extent, the tissues which have been deprived of water take it up again.

There thus develops between blood and tissues an equilibrium in which more water enters the blood than normally. This is not surprising since there is in functionating kidneys a *dynamic* equilibrium inasmuch as there is a current of water from the tissues into the blood and from the blood into the bladder. When the kidneys and water maintenance are both deficient, a *static* equilibrium occurs, which (to the extent that we may speak of it in a living system) represents the true water equilibrium between blood and tissues. The question now presents itself: is this equilibrium conditioned by *osmotic* relations or by the *condition of swelling* of the colloids in the blood and the tissues?

The investigations of A. von Korányi, P F. Richter and W. Roth, H. Strauss, Kovesi and Surányi show that the Cl content of the blood serum of nephrectomized animals and nephritic men is *not* materially *increased,* nor has the electrolyte content increased, but on the contrary the freezing point depression of nephrectomized rabbits rises from 0 56° to 0 60° (normal) to from 0 65° to 0 75° (A. von Korányi). In spite of the increased concentration of the nonelectrolyte crystalloids, the content of water has been increased

Let us imagine what would happen if matters were under the sole influence of osmotic conditions Ever since Pfluger's observations, we know that metabolic processes occur in cells. Consequently, an increased osmotic pressure would have to be present in the tissues, and this would at first result in an impoverishment of the blood in water and a proportional increase in molecular concentration. Gradually to the extent that the metabolic products enter the blood, there would occur a water equilibrium so that finally the molecular concentration of the blood would be increased, but there would be no change in the content of water. If, however, we do find an increase of the water, it must follow from this that the *osmotic relations offer no satisfied explanation of these phenomena, and in order to understand them we are compelled to invoke the condition of swelling in the cell and blood colloids.*

The Urine.

A. Normal Urine.

Normally the urine contains no serum albumin, this does not by any means mean that it is free from colloids. Even the fact that urine gives a moderately permanent foam when it is shaken, shows that it contains colloids. According to H. Bechhold these colloids have an electronegative charge.

Exhaustive investigations on the total quantity of nondialyzable substances in the urine have been undertaken in the laboratory of F. HOFMEISTER (KUMGE SASAKI, M. SACCIA, W. LINTCKE). In the normal urine these substances are

In men, 0.87 2.356 gm   average 1.14 gm per day.
In women, 0.24 0.70 gm   average 0.44 gm per day.

Their quantity is strongly influenced by the diet, and increases after the ingestion of albumin, it is especially high on a purely meat diet. Of less importance is the work of TAMIKA, who tried to determine from the viscosity the quantity of hydrophile colloids. Since this was done in undialyzed urine which contains very inconstant quantities of urinary salts, that influence the viscosity of colloidal solutions in some unknown way, the method proposed cannot be utilized.

L. LICHTWITZ and F. J. ROSENBACH showed that colloids could be removed by three equally useful methods: by dialysis, by shaking out in the foam made with benzine, and by alcohol precipitation. The urine colloids exert a protective action upon colloidal gold (gold figure 0.69 to 0.81 mg.), and in this regard they are between gum arabic and gum tragacanth (table of R. ZSIGMONDY). Obviously they are hydrophile colloids whose activity is not diminished by boiling, evaporation or freezing. By heating them their protective action is raised inasmuch as a finer distribution results, just as occurs in the case of gelatin (L. LICHTWITZ).

Other studies seek to explain the nature of the colloid constituents. These may be mucin (MÖRNER [2]), chondroitin-sulphuric acid and nucleic acid, which, according to the studies from F. HOFMEISTER'S Institute, do not pass through dialyzing membranes. Moreover, animal gum (LANDWEHR and BAISCH) and a nitrogen-containing complex carbohydrate (SALKOWSKI) probably belong to the urine colloids. That the yellow coloring matter of the urine, *urochrome* of G. KLEMPERER, is not a colloid has been shown by DETERMEYER and WAGNER * as well as by L. LICHTWITZ and ROSENBACH *

The fact that the surface tension of normal urine is about 10 per cent lower than that of water may also be attributed to certain colloid constituents (see W. D. DONNAN and F. G. DONNAN * as well as J. AMANN *).

If we approach the question teleologically, *the purpose of the colloids in normal urine* is obviously that the urine be excreted clear. They prevent the formation of sediments within the body. WOLF-GANG PAULI as well as H. BECHHOLD and J. ZIEGLER have shown that the presence of albumin decidedly increases the solubility of uric acid; and J. LICHTWITZ showed that the same property was possessed by the urine colloids [1] He writes of a case (*loc. cit*, p. 154) of myelogenous leukemia in a woman.

"It (the urine) was clear, strongly acid, free from albumin and albumoses It always had a sediment of well-developed uric acid crystals, etc. The urine was clear only on October 27, the undialyzed urine had no protective action until the urine of October 27 was examined, then the gold figure was about 0 1 c c."

Though the protective action of the colloids has been demonstrated only for uric acid, in my opinion it is probably of significance also for other substances which tend to sediment

A *normal* amount of colloid in the urine is essential, if it is deficient it may lead to the formation of *urinary calculi*, as has been shown by H. SCHADE (see p. 272).

B. Pathological Urine.

The kidney behaves like a very sensitive membrane A slight rise in blood pressure, even venous congestion, suffices to permit the appearance of proteins in the urine. If the kidney has been damaged so as to change the kidney parenchyma, we are not surprised to find constituents of the blood mixed to a greater or less extent with the urine.

[1] As early as 1902, G. KLEMPERER called attention to the action of colloids such as soaps, gelatin and starch paste in interfering with the precipitation of uric acid (G. KLEMPERER, Verh. d. Kongresses f. inn. Medizin, Wiesbaden, 1902)

Clinicians have paid more attention to the serum albumin and globulin than to the other colloidal constituents. All the usual methods of detecting them depend upon the fact that albumin is made *irreversible* by boiling or by the addition of a substance with which it combines (sublimate, picric acid, potassium ferrocyanid. etc.), and by a second process (addition of nitric acid or other electrolyte) it is flocked out. If the urine is to be examined further, especially for sugar, every trace of albumin must be removed first. It is frequently impossible to remove the final traces of albumin by coagulation and flocculation. In these cases an adsorptive substance must be employed, the urine is shaken with animal charcoal or diatomaceous earth or a precipitate is formed in the urine (lead acetate is added, filtered and the lead removed with sodium phosphate).

The other nondialyzable constituents also show quantitative changes, especially in pathological urine. They are much increased in lobar pneumonia (122 to 488 gm. per day) and to an enormous extent in eclampsia (as high as 13.84 gm. per liter).

The determination of the *surface tension* of the urine which points to certain constituents may in the future become of great importance for diagnostic purposes. Though the surface tension of normal urine is about 10 per cent. less than that of water and is not much changed by either albumin or sugar, the salts of the bile acids (sodium taurocholate and sodium glycocholate) produce a very definite lowering (as much as 40 per cent below that of water). W. D. DONNAN and F. G. DONNAN * found that the degree of *icterus* ran parallel with changes in the surface tension of the urine.

Fibrin, nucleoalbumins, blood and blood pigments, as well as all the other organized constituents coming from the organism, are the result of local disease of the kidneys or urinary passages and at this point they cannot be discussed at greater length. More thorough studies of albumosuria and peptonuria from a colloid-chemical standpoint are much needed.

Casts occupy an entirely distinct place. To a certain extent, these are actually casts of the uriniferous tubules; they are spiral or cylindrical structures which occur in inflammation of the kidneys (nephritis), whose form and properties are of diagnostic importance (hyaline, fine and coarsely granular, etc.). Casts, according to M. H. FISCHER,[81] are epithelial cells of the kidney dissolved away as the result of the formation of acid. By changing the concentration of acid, he was able to change hyaline casts into granular casts and the reverse.

Urinary calculi have been exhaustively studied by H. SCHADE.* (see p. 272).

He finds that they are caused by the clotting of fibrin when insoluble or difficultly soluble salts are simultaneously excreted   The lamellation is caused by the repeated precipitation of fibrin with the inclusion of crystalloid sediments. As many various experiments showed, fibrin has a tendency to separate on surfaces. so that under the conditions given, layers are formed.

Sweat Glands.

The daily excretion of sweat varies very widely. With the average intake of water, average atmospheric temperature and at rest, it is about 700 c.c in 24 hours, in a man weighing 70 kilos (according to A. Schwenckenbecher). Cramer found an excretion of 3 liters during a summer march. and H. Strauss was able to establish a loss of 1/2 to 1 liter of sweat in a half hour under the influence of diaphoretic procedures

The sweat glands are more dependent on the influence of the nerves than are any other glands, yet it cannot be doubted that here, too, ultrafiltration of the blood plasma plays an important part, since the sweat glands have a knotted structure similar to that of the glomeruli of the kidneys.   In support of this we have the following facts. sweat contains only the solid constituents most easily permeable, NaCl and urea, whereas the difficultly diffusible salts, phosphates and sulphates occur only in traces. The fact that nitrogenous products of metabolism also occur, agrees with my assumption that the NH_2 and NH_4 groups facilitate diffusion (see page 411)   The acid reaction is probably due to the sebaceous glands; when the secretion is artificially increased, the sweat becomes alkaline (corresponding to the blood plasma).

Milk.

Of all foods, milk is the most important; on this account it has been investigated by food chemists and physicians. Its specific gravity, fat content, dried fat-free residue, and even the casein and albumin content and the quantity of milk, sugar and salts (ash) have been determined, but it is only in the last few years that the important part played by the *condition* of the colloidal constituents has been pointed out.

Milk is an aqueous solution of crystalloids (salts and milk sugar) which contains the colloids, casein and albumin, and also an emulsion of fat.

Though the colloid constituents and the fat of milk vary within wide limits according to food, season, age, etc. (from 5 to 8 585 per cent), the water and the crystalloid content is practically uniform. G. CORN-ALBA* showed this by extensive investigations upon large dairy herds. The widest limits for the content of dissolved substances was only from 5 9 to 6.6 per cent, whereas the variations were usually from 6.05 to 6.25 per cent. From this we must conclude that milk is the product of at least two processes. One is the result of an ultrafiltration of the blood which yields an ultrafiltrate of uniform water and crystalloid content. The colloids and fat are mixed with this solution by a second process.

The fat globules of the milk (milk globules) have a diameter of from 0.1 to 22 μ averaging about 3 μ, yet it is possible mechanically so to break them up, that they are no longer visible microscopically; according to WIEGNER their average diameter is 0 27 μ Such so-called *homogenized* milk is recommended as being very easily digested and it has the advantage that the cream cannot be removed either by gravity or by centrifuging.

It is known by dairymen that milk may separate spontaneously to a certain extent, on standing, the cream rises to the top. The result is produced more rapidly and completely by centrifugation, though a complete separation is not obtained even in this way, we have an opaque milk which contains the finest globules. Nor can a separation be obtained by filtering through the least porous Chamberland filter. All the fat globules can be held back by an *ultra-filter* which still permits the complete passage of albumin.

If we wish to make *butter* from cream, in other words to make the milk globules unite, the cream must be churned, since between the individual globules aqueous and water-soluble constituents of the milk occur as partitions, and these partitioning walls must be broken down. It is a remarkable fact that milk globules do not dissolve in ether if milk is shaken with it [1] If milk fat were an ordinary emulsion such as oil in water, the fat would be completely removed by shaking it with ether. From this we conclude that the fat globules in the milk are surrounded by a pellicle impermeable for ether. If potassium hydrate or acetic acid are added, this interference is removed, moreover, the fat may be removed from the dried milk globules by treatment with ether, and the pellicles will be left behind. It is absolutely impossible to extract the fat completely from homogenized milk by shaking with ether.

There is quite an extensive but at present practically useless bibliography (see VOELTZ*) on the *pellicles of fat globules*. Especially erroneous were the experiments directed to splitting off the pellicles

---

[1] The fat of *human milk*, with its much larger quantity of albumin, is readily shaken out with ether.

chemically, since the equilibrium of the milk was thus changed.
The experimental arrangements by which VOELTZ, at least qualitatively, established the existence of serum pellicles, are the most
fortunate. No value is to be attributed in my opinion to the quantitative results, since the composition of the pellicles must change
while they pass through the layer of water. VOELTZ layered a
column of milk about 10 cm. high *under* a column of water 50 cm.
high. The milk globules mounted through the water and were thus
freed of all water-soluble ingredients. The cream thus formed was
then taken up, freed from fat and the residue determined. The
composition proved very variable and qualitatively contained the
ash and organized constituents of the milk as far as that could be
deduced from the mere determination of ash, organic substance,
Mg, Ca and P.

By emulsifying butter fat in skimmed milk, VOELTZ produced
artificial pellicles and compared them with the natural ones.

In the light of our knowledge of the spreading out of colloidally
dissolved substances on surfaces, it ought not to be very difficult to
explain the phenomenon of the pellicles of milk fat (incorrectly called
serum pellicles). According to G. QUINCKE, a substance spreads out
at the interface between two fluids (or a gas and a fluid) if by this
means the surface tension of the surface possessed in common is
diminished. Oil spreads out, for instance, at the interface between
water and air. We know from W. RAMSDEN* and METCALF* (see p.
34) that albumin and peptone separate out at the interface between
water and air as a *solid*. G. QUINCKE *² showed that a film of gum
solution surrounded each globule in the pharmacopeal emulsions.
H. BECHHOLD *¹ bases his explanation of protective colloids which
prevent the flocculation of organic colloids and suspensions on this
phenomenon.

Simple consideration shows that a fat globule in an albumin
solution must surround itself with a layer of albumin. Since the
surface tension at the boundary surface of albumin or serum and fat
(0.1 to 1.6) is smaller than that of water and fat (1.6 to 2.4) the
albumin of milk must collect on the surface of the fat globules.
An experiment of ASCHERSON* shows the correctness of this *a priori*
assumption. ASCHERSON emulsified olive oil in an alkaline solution
of egg albumin and observed that the oil droplets were surrounded
by an albuminous membrane. The strength and composition of
the pellicles of the milk globules vary, of course, not only with the
colloidal, but also with the crystalloid constituents, especially the
salts. In passing through the aqueous layer (in VOELTZ' experiment) the pellicles are again changed, and from the investigation

above mentioned (RAMSDEN and METCALF), we need not be surprised that most authors (including VOELTZ) are convinced that the pellicles surrounding the milk globules are solid membranes. There is certainly not the slightest indication that this is actually the case, while the globules remain in the milk. In addition, it must be granted that the composition of the pellicles vary with the size of the milk globules. VOELTZ believes that the pellicles of the individual fat globules are individually distinct as a result of their origin (in the mammary gland). But his own data convince me that this individual difference results from purely physical causes, namely, the extraordinary variations in composition according as they mounted quickly or slowly and according to the size of the fat globule pellicle examined.

G. WIEGNER developed an idea which appeared in the first edition of this book. He compared the various physical properties of ordinary and homogenized milk and found that with increasing subdivision of the fat globules (a fat globule is subdivided 1200 times during homogenization) there is an increasing internal friction which is explained by the increased adsorption of casein by the expanded surface of the fat globules. G. WIEGNER reckoned, that, on the basis of HATSCHEK's formula (see p. 16), the thickness of the adsorption skins were 6 to 7 $\mu\mu$, so that in normal milk 2 per cent and in homogenized, 25 per cent of the entire casein was adsorbed by the fat.

Casein of milk is itself insoluble in water; it is a fairly strong acid which reddens litmus and displaces CO_2 from its salts. For instance, casein may be dissolved with the liberation of CO_2 if it is shaken with a suspension of calcium carbonate in water. In the milk the casein is kept in solution by lime salts, and it is an old and still incompletely solved problem, what sort of solution exists. If milk is filtered through clay filters or shaken with pulverized clay filters the casein is separated out (HERMANN and FR. DUPRÉ *). According to some authors only 26 to 40 per cent of the lime remains in the whey after this treatment. If milk is filtered through an *ultrafilter* (BECHHOLD *4) without being stirred, the casein separates out upon the filter, undissolved. In the case of the powdered clay filter there is obviously an adsorption and flocculation of the casein by means of which part of the casein-calcium combination is split up just as the salts of basic dyes are split by textile fibers or wood charcoal.

P. RONA and L. MICHAELIS * have investigated the influence of actually dissolved and of colloidally dissolved lime by means of the "osmotic compensation method" (see pp. 107 and 108) They dialyzed whole milk against iron-milk (milk from which the proteins were removed by means of colloidal iron oxid), against whey (the casein was removed by rennin) and against distilled water. Whole milk contained approximately about 0 15 per cent CaO; iron-milk about 0 12 per cent CaO, and whey only from 0.04 to 0.06 per cent CaO. The amount of diffusible lime is accordingly only about 0.06 to 0.07 per cent CaO and consists thus of about 40 to 50 per cent of the entire lime contained.

It is remarkable that the iron-milk contains more lime than is really diffusible, so that when casein is flocked out by colloidal iron oxid, calcium goes into true solution. But the iron-whey contains much less phosphoric acid than the milk so that it must have been precipitated by the iron oxid. From this it is evident that no considerable quantity of calcium phosphate is in colloidal solution or the lime would be retained with the phosphoric acid by colloidal iron oxid. Evidently the lime exists to a considerable extent in solution as a slightly dissociated casein salt. In favor of this view are the other properties of milk, which are manifested when the equilibrium is shifted (depression of freezing point, conductivity).

Albumin. The milk of various animals varies much in the proportionate amounts of the chief constituents; especially contrasted is the relation between casein and albumin, as the following data show:

	Casein.	Albumin.
	Per cent.	Per cent.
Cow	3 02	0 53
Human.	1 03	1.26
Goat.	3 20	1.09
Sheep.	4.97	1.55
Ass	0.67	1.55

The significance of these differences upon the structure of the different organisms cannot be determined at present, though according to the investigations of J. ALEXANDER and J. G. M. BULLOWA,* the *digestibility* is influenced by this ratio. These investigators are of the opinion that the reversible albumin serves as a protective colloid for the irreversible casein. They base this on the fact that woman's milk, which is rich in albumin, is difficult to coagulate by acids or rennet, and that the same condition obtains for cow's milk if it is protected by gelatin, gum arabic, albumin or the like.

In the dark field, too, human milk shows a finer division than cows' milk, as was shown by the investigations of J. LEMANISSIER,* A. KREIDL and NEUMANN,* as well as G. WIEGNER.* Two distinct elements in cows' milk (casein and fat) may be definitely recognized in the dark field though only the fat globules can be recognized in human milk   The submicrons are larger in asses' and cows' milk but largest in ewes' milk.   In boiled milk the submicrons are larger and disappear more slowly under treatment with solvents (potash, gastric juice) than in unboiled milk, which is an indication that unboiled milk is more easily digestible than boiled milk.

Human and cows' milk may be distinguished by their ascent or rise in strips of filter paper and their diffusion on blotting paper.   For instance, according to A. KREIDL and LENK * in 150 minutes cows' milk ascends only 2 5 cm., while human milk ascends 10.8 cm. According to LENK * this is chiefly due to the viscosity which in turn depends on the amount of albumin and casein contained.   If a drop or two of cows' milk is placed on blotting paper, three zones (fat, casein and solution of crystalloids) are observed, whereas human milk exhibits but two (fat and other ingredients).

I refer to page 173 *et seq.* for the *methods of examining milk* and *dairy products.*

It is necessary for completeness to mention the *formation of skin* on boiled milk.   The phenomenon is obviously analogous to the formation of solid skins on dyes and peptone solution (see p. 33 *et seq.*).

Referring to the changed condition of the surface, it might well be worth finding out whether the unavoidable shaking during prolonged transportation damages milk.   We learn from clinical experience that *raw milk* is more easily digested than boiled milk. [From the fact that boiled milk forms smaller curds, it offers a larger surface and on this account may be more readily passed through the pylorus.   It may even remove acid from the stomach by adsorption. Tr.]   This has been attributed to the presence of enzymes, which are destroyed on heating, though no one has ever been able to give any proof of the action of these enzymes   The most recent results of research indicate that considerable changes in condition are associated with boiling.

O. GROSSER [1] found by *ultrafiltration* that the lime was attached more firmly to the milk colloids in boiled milk than in unboiled milk.   The ultrafiltrates of boiled milk contained less lime than those of unboiled milk.   The nitrogen and phosphorus content were diminished in human milk, by boiling, but in cows' milk it remains approximately the same.   For instance, GROSSER found the following quantities of CaO in ultrafiltrates

---

[1] According to a private communication (as yet unpublished).

	Ultrafiltrate of raw milk.	Milk boiled 5 minutes
	Per cent CaO	Per cent CaO
Woman's milk...	0 017	0 007
Cow's milk.	0 011	0 031

The length of time the milk was boiled, influenced the results. The ultrafiltrate of *woman's milk* after 5 minutes' boiling still contained about one-third, after 15 minutes one-tenth, of the original amount of CaO. After boiling 30 minutes there were only traces of CaO.

That there is hardly any difference between the freezing point depression of raw and of boiled milk is, therefore, very remarkable.

[McCollum has shown by his feeding experiments on rats that dried milk contains both of the essential food accessories, fat soluble A and water soluble B. Tr.]

CHAPTER XXI.

THE NERVES.

THE nervous system began to be investigated colloid-chemically when the problem of brain swelling and edema of the brain was formulated through FISCHER's theory of edema (see p. 223). Various attempts were made to determine whether the swelling induced by acids and in the presence of salts was analogous to the swelling of fibrin. From the start it was not very probable that nervous tissue was like the latter, an individual protein substance. Though the nerve cell consists mainly of protein material, the neurolemma which serves as insulation for nerve conduction is largely formed from lipoids which behave quite differently towards acids and salts

MARTIN H. FISCHER and M. O. HOOKER conducted experiments upon the swelling of brain and cord in acids and salt solutions and discovered that their behavior quite paralleled the behavior of fibrin.[1]

For reliable data it is important to employ absolutely fresh nervous tissue from normal animals; results of no comparative value were obtained from diseased rabbits or animals which had been chased about before they were killed FISCHER justly criticizes the experiments of J. BAUER and of J. BAUER and AMES who used material 6 to 24 hours post mortem; the post mortem accumulation of acids rendered these experiments useless for the purpose of comparison.

The experimental attempts of BARBIERI and CARBONE to produce swelling by injection of acids into living animals we must regard as naïve. The authors evidently overlook the fact that the acids are distributed in the organisms and that various organs compete for the available water, we may expect swelling only from local accumulation of acid. On this account the interesting experiments of KLOSE and VOGT deserve elaboration in the direction of colloid research. The authors found in thymectomized dogs an acid preponderance localized among other places in the nervous system (gray matter); the brain of a thymectomized dog completely filled the skull, the ganglion cells were swollen. R. E LIESEGANG justly cautions anthropologists against attributing too great significance to the weight of brains (PETTEN-

---

[1] This parallelism must not be applied too generally, there are important differences in behavior with the salts of the heavy metals as hitherto unpublished experiments of H. BECHHOLD show.

KOFER'S brain weighed 1320 gm. — HELMHOLTZ'S, 1900 gm.); for sickness, age, etc., may produce considerable changes in a brain's capacity to hold water, so that the brains of men offer no basis for post mortem comparison.

MASUDA supplied the following figures:

		1st Man	2nd Man
Weight of brain	... . ..	1,291 gm.	1,133 gm
Dried substance	. ...	176,36 "	260,30 "
1 gm of dried substance contains water. .		6,14 "	3,55 "

With the same aqueous content as Brain II, Brain I would have weighed 767 gm. With the same aqueous content as Brain I, Brain II would have weighed 1858 gm. There are increasing indications that colloid investigation is destined to carry nearer to solution the old problem of nerve irritability

Nerve Irritability and Swelling.

In considering muscle function we have seen that it is associated with a certain condition of swelling (see p 294). The like is also true of nerves. The nerves lose their irritability when placed in isotonic solutions of cane sugar or other nonconductors and recover it again when they are placed in physiological salt solution (MATHEWS,[*] E. OVERTON [*4]). Various other neutral salt solutions also injuriously affect the irritability of nerves in accordance with a lyotropic series The arrangement given by various authors (MATHEWS, P. VON GRUTZNER) is not as unequivocal as for muscle. We must remember that the methods of investigation were not the same as for muscle, and that the penetration of the salt solution to the axis cylinder through the lipoid insulating layer was not as uniform. R. HOBER [*la] (p. 307) summarizes the depressant action of ions on nerve irritability in the following series:

$$Na < Li < Cs < NH_4 < Rb < K$$
$$SO_4 < Cl < Br < I$$

The anion series is the reverse of that for muscle irritability. We know that in the precipitation of acid albumin, the lyotropic series is the opposite of that for alkali albumin, we know further that contracting muscle has an acid reaction; on this account we may with some probability infer that nerve albumin is more or less alkaline (negative).

HOBER succeeded in rendering visible the changes which reveal irritability or the absence of irritability of nerves. The sciatics of frogs still connected to their gastrocnemii were placed in isotonic salt solution until they lost their characteristic irritability to the

Faradic current. Teased preparations of the nerves were then suitably stained. The difference in the turgescence of the axis cylinder was not only indicated by the different intensity of the stain, but also by the fact that according to the salts employed, the axis cylinder remained as thin threads or were swollen to broad bands, and that the order in which the swelling was affected agreed with the lyotropic series characteristic of the loss of irritability. [W. Burridge, *loc. cit.*, has adopted MacDonald's view that " in the excited nerve the protein aggregates are agglutinated to form aggregates of greater individual size; this change is due to the reception of a negative electric charge   As a result of this (K) salts are liberated which charge the next segment of nerve negatively, and so excite it and leave the original segment a positive charge. This positive charge determines the return of the colloid of the original segment towards their former state of aggregation." Burridge considers that it is calcium plus the negative charge which determines the coagulative change, and sodium plus the positive charge which brings the colloids back to the original state. Inhibition, according to this view, " is essentially a decalcifying process." See also page 361. R. Lillie, Science N. S., Vol. XLVIII, No 1229, has offered an electromotor working model of nerve conduction in the transmission of the active state along a " passivated " iron wire. Tr.]

Cerebrospinal Fluid.

Our most sensitive instrument, the brain and spinal cord, is protected by a solid casing, the skull and spinal column   These latter do not fit the nerve organ closely, but have a certain amount of dead space which is filled with the cerebrospinal fluid. We may add that both the bony case and the central marrow are covered with membranes which are connected by a delicate mesh work   This network is filled with fluid in which, to a certain extent, the brain and cord float. It is a clear, colorless, aqueous fluid amounting to from 60 to 200 cc. in adults. Besides a very few formed elements it contains 1/2 per cent of albumen.

Several cc. may be withdrawn, by lumbar puncture, from patients, without injury — a procedure introduced by Quincke. This procedure has yielded valuable physiological and pathological data of scientific and diagnostic importance. The fluid circulates constantly and slowly. Under pathological conditions the fluid may be quickly formed so that at times several liters may be lost through a fistula in a day.

There are two opposing theories of cerebrospinal fluid formation. The one assuming a secretion has most supporters, whereas Mestrezat, who asserts an "elective filtration," has fewer followers. Mes-

THEZAT's "diffusion governed by osmosis" expressed in our terminology is nothing other than ultrafiltration.

GOLDMANN's experimental data, subsequently to be mentioned, support this view, that the choroid plexus, the exceedingly vascular membrane in the ventricles of the brain, serves as an ultrafilter. [J. McCLENDON has recently offered additional experimental support for this view. Tr.]

Under pathological conditions the albumen content of the cerebrospinal fluid suffers very striking changes in which the globulin seems particularly affected. On account of the minute amount of albumen (0.5 per cent) the usual tests for albumen have been refined though none have acquired the significance which has been won by "the colloidal gold test" of LANGE. It rests on a modified clinical determination of the "gold number" (see p. 85), in other words upon a measurement of the protective action on the gold hydrosol by cerebrospinal fluid. Normal cerebrospinal fluid diluted with 4 per cent saline has no effect in any dilution upon the red color of the gold sol. If precipitation occurs at any dilution it indicates a pathological change. By this reaction, luetic affections of the central nervous system are detected when the WASSERMANN reaction is still negative and there are as yet no subjective changes. The reaction also weighs in favor of diagnosing luetic disease (tabes, paresis, cerebrospinal syphilis), when other diseases of the brain and cord are in question. Meningitis, tumors, apoplexies are distinguished from lues by a *shifting* of the precipitation zone. [Recently mastic solutions have been employed for the same purpose. Tr.]

Observations of KISCH and RUNERTZ indicate that under certain pathological conditions (cirrhosis of the liver) the surface tension of the cerebrospinal fluid varies from the normal.

The Integument.

Though other portions of the organism have greater or less capacity to swell, this property is very much limited in the skin, epidermis, hair, feathers, scales, etc. It is also evident that this limitation is essential for maintaining shape and for retaining water within the body. If the epidermis had unlimited swelling capacity like gelatin, the fluids inside the organism would suffice to stretch the skin and to enlarge it until all shape was lost, and finally the interior parts desiccated. Conversely, every natural atmospheric dampness and every rainstorm still more would cause an almost unlimited addition of water from the outside; a steady stream of water would flow through the skin and the organs, and would be poured out through the kidneys. If these opposing forces could still establish an equilibrium it would vary so much in accordance with meteorological conditions that it is hard to believe that the body would have any definite shape

When we think of aquatic animals the idea of an integument which can swell leads only to caricature.

This does not mean that hair, feathers, etc., cannot take up any water. We all know that wool and feathers absorb water from the air and that in very moist air they feel damp; in making hygrometers, human hair, which expands with a certain degree of moisture and contracts with dryness, is used.

The skin may be preserved thousands of years on account of its slight swelling capacity. In fact, we find the framework of plants, cellulose and wood, in graves of animals or men in addition to bones, and usually hair, hide and leather articles.

The evaporation of water from the skin occurs not only as the result of the secretory activity of the sweat glands, but there is also an "insensible perspiration." As P. G. Unna[*] has shown in convincing experiments, this may be either inhibited by fats or on the other hand increased by enlarging the surface, as with powders, coating with gelatin, collodion, etc. (see p. 110).

As in the case of other cell membranes the saturation of the skin with lipoids, especially with lanolin, is of the greatest importance. W. Filehne and J. Biberfeld[*] investigated the absorption capacity of clean keratin structures (wool fibers, leather film and human hair) as well as such as were saturated with lipoids. As was to be expected, substances soluble in fat (phenol, chloroform, etc.) were easily absorbed, whereas water and salts penetrated but slightly. This corresponds with the animal experiments of E. Overton on amphibia and of A. Schwenkenbecher[*] on doves and mice. The almost complete impenetrability of the lipoid-saturated skin for salts is of the greatest importance to the organism in maintaining its electrolyte content.

[Internal Secretions. W. Brünings, by his perfusion experiments with calcium solutions of varying strength, has offered an explanation of some of the activities of several hormones. Pituitary substance apparently increases the response of the uterus and the heart to calcium. Adrenalin has a two-fold activity on the heart, a primary depressing or surface action and a secondary or deep augmenting action. During the period of exalted cardiac activity the heart is more responsive to calcium than previously. The factors involved are the concentration of adrenin, the concentration of calcium in the perfusing solution, and the state of the heart induced respectively by adrenin and by calcium. Excitation is viewed as a coagulative change produced by calcium in certain colloids.

The effect of thyroid secretion is similar to that of alcohol, causing the circulation to be maintained on what otherwise would be an inadequate calcium tension in the perfusing solution. Tr.]

PART IV.

PART IV.

CHAPTER XXII.

TOXICOLOGY AND PHARMACOLOGY.

In the following chapter we shall chiefly consider the action of foreign chemical substances and organisms. If only monera (bacteria, protozoa and yeasts) were involved, the matter would be relatively simple; we might regard them as suspensions and approach their investigation with exact physico-chemical methods. It may be seen from the chapter on "Disinfection and Agglutination" that these viewpoints have been successfully employed.

Some of the substances which are injurious to monera (bacteria, protozoa, etc.) we call *disinfectants*, and some *preservatives*. One of the ways by which they are tested is to add the solution under examination to a suspension of bacteria in water or bouillon and observing in what concentration growth is inhibited. It is obvious that this action is dependent upon the concentration and distribution of the disinfectant between bacteria and solvent. Similar experiments may be performed on higher aquatic animals.

The problem becomes much more complex in the case of multi-cellular organisms, especially the higher terrestrial animals, where the action may be affected by the portal of entry. Water, so essential to life, becomes a poison when injected intravenously.

Depending on their point of entrance, substances must pass through membranes, filters or places with digestive ferments (stomach, intestines, etc.). This may either determine the action and the course taken by the poison or drug, or it may even entirely block its entrance. Since small intestines and colon send their blood through the portal vein to the liver, substances which are taken by mouth may have no effect in spite of being well absorbed if they are strongly adsorbed by the liver, as happens in the case of potassium salts, curare, etc. Only such substances are absorbed through the skin as are soluble in its fats.

The action of diphtheria antitoxin when injected intravenously is 500 times stronger than when it is injected subcutaneously (W. Berghaus). [This has been shown by Park to be due to its slow absorption from the tissues. Tr.]

359

In common parlance *poisons* are such substances as are harmful to
warm-blooded animals if they are taken by mouth or are inspired even
in minute quantities. With few exceptions "poisons," popularly
so-called, are acids, alkalis, various metallic poisons, CO and similar
substances, nerve poisons which even in minimal quantities may
depress essential functions, e.g., strychnine, atropine, etc.

The actual poisonous effect, the death of the organism, is only the
closing act of a complicated drama which is enacted before our eyes.
The introductory scenes are for us no less important since they
teach us what phenomena may lead to a tragic termination. The
drama may end happily if the concentration of the drug is kept
sufficiently low or suitable antidotes are employed. From our point
of view it is impossible to separate Toxicology and Pharmacology.

Next in importance to the concentration, the most important
influence upon toxicological or pharmacological action is the *distribution*. The fundamental and essentially chemical idea of distribution was transferred by PAUL EHRLICH to the processes in
multicellular organisms. Minimal quantities of alkaloids have such
intense action because, in conformity with this view, they are concentrated in definite groups of nerves. In the treatment of infectious
diseases, it is necessary to find substances which will be so distributed between the infected organisms and the infection producers
that the largest possible quantity becomes attached to the microorganisms and the least possible is attached to the man, domestic
animal or plant. It is readily seen that the distribution may be
either a chemical combination, a distribution between two solvents
or a variety of adsorption. In but few cases has it been possible to
determine the kind of distribution adopted. If FÜRTH NÄGELI has calculated from the researches of W. STRAUB * that an adsorption equilibrium obtains for the distribution of veratrine between the heart
muscle of a marine snail (*aplysia limacina*) and the bath containing
it. In the special section we shall give other examples.

To cause damage, the substance taken up must also change the
affected organ of the multicellular organism and under certain conditions it may be immaterial whether the change is reversible or
irreversible. A poison which renders the respiratory muscles func-
tionless for only a few minutes as, for instance, curare, causes death
in warm-blooded animals, though the absorption is reversible.
Cold-blooded animals, for instance the frog, may, on the contrary,
live for days or even recover since they are able to breathe through
the skin. We must assume that the organs most essential to life
have special protection against many, especially autogenous toxins.
This may be a physical protection, in a partially isolating channel

about the cell or cell group, or a chemical defense in the sense of P. EHRLICH, who believes that in these cases there is no "receptor" for the poison. Probably both methods are involved.

Although "distribution" is a very difficult and as yet scarcely investigated field, in the study of the organic changes due to drugs we are met largely by unsurmounted difficulties, since in many cases no external or even histological change may be recognized. It is our hope that colloid research may also prove of great value here, since it is not only profound changes in chemical constitution which interfere with the function of an organ, but harm may be done even by changes in turgescence, flocculation, reversible precipitation and in fact even changes in the size of the particles. [This is the basis of the explanation of changes of muscular activity in response to drugs, offered by W. BURRIDGE, to which reference has been made Tr] More particularly than heretofore, we must observe the *course* of an injury, we shall have to observe whether a permanent local change occurs as in the toxic action of most metals, or whether the process is reversible as in the case of the narcotics, or whether after a severe effect occurs, a moderately prolonged after-effect takes place in the organs involved, suggesting an adsorption.

Valuable suggestions for such a viewpoint are offered by the classical observations of PAUL EHRLICH on the "Oxygen requirements of the body" and by his study of the histology of the blood (P. G USNA*), and W. STRAUB'S * researches on the distribution of various alkaloids (veratrine, strychnine, curarine) between heart muscle (of a sea snail) and the surrounding solution. [W. BURRIDGE has shown that digitalis and strychnine increase the utilization of calcium by the heart. The action of strychnine on nerves is explained by a relative calcification of the synapse, facilitating the passage of the nerve impulse (see p. 354). Tr.]

Coöperation of Indifferent Substances.

On pages 55 and 334, we saw that the presence of many substances might either increase or diminish the permeability of membranes; from this fact we are justified in concluding that the addition of an essentially indifferent substance may increase or diminish the toxic or pharmacologic action of a substance by aiding or impeding its arrival at the spot where it is active. We may in general assume from this that such other substance is also stored in the same organ.

We may exemplify this by several observations (see G STOFFEL*), which must be viewed from this standpoint. VON SCHRÖDER found that the diuretic action of caffein was increased by chloral hydrate, and yet that this effect did not depend on the ability of the chloral to paralyze the vessels (*i.e.*, increased blood supply to the kidneys). According to CERVELLO and LO MONACO, chloroform checks caffeine diuresis when simultaneously administered, but it has no influence if the chloroform effect precedes the caffein. According to THOMPSON and WALTI, atropine checks renal secretion and at the same time decreases the amount of urea. According to H. LOWE the amount of urine secreted was not increased by the injection of pilocarpine, the sugar remained unchanged, the uric acid was somewhat increased, phosphoric acid was diminished greatly and the total nitrogen to some extent.

It must be emphasized that we are here dealing with pure secretory activity. The action of CO_2 on glycosuria may possibly be attributed, according to STOFFEL,* to changes in permeability, whereas phloridzin diuresis is much more probably accounted for by a hindrance to the reabsorption of the sugar formed in the kidneys

Since our colloid-chemical knowledge in the realm of pharmacology and toxicology is extremely restricted, we are limited to the few short chapters which follow   It must be especially emphasized that the most important territory, the specific nerve actions [1] (see note on p 352) is colloid-chemically still almost completely *terra incognita*.

Toxicology and pharmacology study the action of chemical and physical influences upon *organisms*, *i e.*, *colloid structures*. Aside from general considerations, the action of suspensions and colloids upon the body deserves our special attention In the following pages, these questions though apparently separated are to a certain extent systematically handled, yet this is upon superficial and not upon essentially scientific grounds.

Colloids.

Pharmacy and therapeutics ever since the classic age have made considerable use of colloids and suspensions, that is of the general colloidal properties of substances which have absolutely no specific chemical action. I do not refer to the containers for medicines, such as gelatin capsules or wafers, but to the strongly adsorptive properties of colloids and suspensions which guarantee a rapid action by reason of their enormous development of surface. Colloids may serve to correct the action of substances such as morphine, chloral, aloes, etc.,

---

[1] We cannot always assume that it is a nervous effect when, among its other actions, the substance involved acts upon the nerves For instance, strong coffee aids digestion An investigation of Handovsky,*[2] based upon observations of A Pick, makes it probable that the cause may be found in a specific property of *caffeine*, which raises the internal friction, *i e*, the ionization of albumin But we know from page 156 that the disintegration of albumin starts with the formation of albumin ions, and we can consequently understand why caffeine and theobromine, which is related to it, favor the digestion of albumin by pepsin.

or diminish their irritation of the stomach or intestines. Upon this action rests the utility of mucilages (decoctions of salep, marshmallow and gum arabic), of talcum, etc., in diarrheas as well as the addition of gelatin and vegetable mucilages to acid foods and fruit juices. In cases of poisoning with acids, alkalis or caustic salts, we are accustomed to employ as our most important antidotes, milk, egg albumen, gruel (oatmeal gruel, quince mucilage or gum arabic) or emulsions of fat and of oil. Gastric hypersecretion also is favorably influenced by such substances (mucilage of gums, starches, bismuth subnitrate, talcum, etc.). TAPPEINER demonstrated the protective action of such substances by the following experiment. A "reflex frog" which is suspended with the hind legs in an acid solution withdraws the legs after a few seconds. If a solution with the identical amount of acid also contains gelatin, gum arabic, starch paste or the like, there will be no reflex movements. The action of adsorbents in protecting against other poisons has long been known.

In 1830, the apothecary THOUÉRY, experimenting on himself, took without harm 1 gm. of strychnine (ten times the fatal dose) with 15 gms. of charcoal. The use of charcoal as an antidote against poisoning though neglected in practice has been mentioned in several textbooks. Only *freshly* precipitated iron hydroxid (ferric hydroxid in water, *antidotum arsenici*) is in general use as an antidote for arsenic poisoning, thanks to the authority of BUNSEN. From the earliest times greater usefulness has been accorded to the hydrophile colloids as gruel (against aloes, cantharides, colchicum, croton oil), milk or white of eggs against mercury weed, glue solution against alum.

Scientifically exact study of the adsorptive action of suspensions on poisons was undertaken only in recent years. W. MECHOWSKI, ADLER, E. ZUNZ and L. LICHTWITZ have contributed valuable researches on the adsorption of poisons (phenol, strychnine and various poisons, arachnolysin) by animal charcoal which proved to be in some ways equivalent to kaolin (bolus alba), silicic acid, chalk, diatomaceous earth and bismuth subnitrate. In practical toxicology the results did not meet expectations. Consequently, as a matter of course, colloidal carbon was tested. SABBATANI actually inhibited the toxic action of strychnine intravenously by injecting simultaneously 6 times the quantity of colloidal carbon.

Adsorption Therapy.

The happy results from adsorption of acids and poisons by charcoal, clay, etc., led to their use even when the acids and poisons arose in the body itself. "Adsorption therapy," so-called by LICHTWITZ, was accordingly introduced as a therapeutic procedure. It

can, indeed, look back upon an honorable and ancient past. Dios-
corides recommended kaolin (bolus alba) as a dressing for erysipelas,
poisonings and many other conditions. Throughout antiquity and
the middle ages adsorption therapy retained its reputation until
modern chemistry, which could not explain its action, delivered its
quietus and looked derisively on some nature-therapeutists who employed it (Claypastor, Father Kneipp). Stumpf deserves credit for
having retested the clinical advantages from the use of kaolin, which
as a therapeutic measure had been forgotten.

The scientific clinical application of adsorption is the product of
the past year. During the war with its severe enteric infections
(cholera, dysentery, typhoid) it has triumphed unexpectedly.

In addition to kaolin and silicic acid (prepared by the Gesell-
schaft für Electroösmose) charcoal has been employed most. Charcoal has yielded good results in stomach conditions (hyperchorhydria
and fermentation), and also in obesity cures it has been employed by
Lichtwitz who removes by it the important ingredients of the
chyme (acids and enzymes, see p. 329), and fills the stomach so as to
satisfy the distressing pangs of hunger Gastric hypersecretion is
also treated by gum arabic, starches, bismuth subnitrate and talcum.

In the serious infectious intestinal diseases, cholera, dysentery and
typhoid, as well as in the gastrointestinal diseases of infants, kaolin
and charcoal act not only by adsorption of toxins produced by the infectious agents but also by the adsorption of the bacteria themselves.

Finally we must mention the original use of kaolin and charcoal,
in purulent and dissection wounds as well as in catarrhs (vagina and
nose) and in exuberant carcinomata. The action is the same here as
in the intestinal infections. Naturally, only sterile preparations are
employed in modern surgery.

A further advance has been to impregnate charcoal with drugs which
are then gradually yielded. A good effect was obtained in typhoid with
iodine and thymol. A preparation of charcoal impregnated with sulphur (eucarbon) is used as a mild laxative which at the same time re-
lieves flatulence by adsorption of bacteria and putrefactive material

Dermatologists employ powders extensively for a cooling effect.
Obviously the powders absorb the water which emerges from the
skin and as a result of their surface development accelerate evaporation, to a certain extent they amplify the skin surface. Good
results may be obtained on burns and inflammatory edemas with
thick layers of kaolin. A cooling (febrifuge) effect may be obtained
according to P. G. Unna [*1] by painting the entire body with a thin
layer of gelatin or collodion, this effect is explained by the magnification of the body surface (see p 355).

The *intravenous introduction* of colloids has achieved great importance through therapeutic use of colloidal metals (see below). Other apparently quite indifferent suspension colloids have a very powerful action when introduced into the blood vessels. One or two ccm. of a kaolin suspension injected intravenously into a guinea-pig induce a violent reaction with more or less rapidly fatal termination. FRIEDBERGER and ISUNEOKA demonstrated that this could not be attributed to emboli but that the toxic action depends on the adsorption of vitally important constituents of cells (analogous to the destruction of blood corpuscles and bacteria in vitro, see p. 200). "Sizing" the feet against chilblains and severe freezing is an ancient household remedy which received renewed attention in the winter campaign of 1914–1915. At present, there is no satisfactory explanation of its action. [BAYLISS has recommended intravenous administration of gum arabic solutions in shock to increase the blood pressure after hemorrhage. DELAUNAY reports favorably on its use. Tr.]

The peculiar effect of gelatin on the coagulation of blood is still unexplained. In severe hemorrhages, purpura haemorrhagica and hemophilia, gelatin is given internally (15 to 20 gm. daily) as well as subcutaneously. Whether a colloid reaction occurs, or whether the clotting of fibrin is favored by the calcium contained in the gelatin is still an open question.

Colloidal Metals.[1]

If we except the use of finely emulsified mercury in the form of blue ointment, the introduction of colloidal silver by CREDÉ * in 1896 was the first instance of the employment of a colloidal metal because of its colloidal nature. It was quite natural then to test other colloidal metals, mercury, gold, platinum, etc. The French have been especially industrious in the study of the biological action of colloidal metals (bibliography given by STODEL.*), but the comprehensive investigations of the Italians, M. ASCOLI and G. IZAR* as well as E. PHILIPPI * and PRETI,* anticipated them in showing that in all probability the action of inorganic hydrosols in their main features was the same as that of the corresponding salts or of complex metal salts. Salts with the cations concerned have in suitable, usually very small, dosage, an effect similar to the action of the hydrosols. This conclusion was demonstrated by the experiments of P. PORTIG * as well as O. GROS and J. M. O'CONNOR,* but it was first placed on a

[1] A useful résumé of the methods of preparation and of the properties of colloidal metals may be found in TH. SVEDBERG, Die Methoden z. Herstellung Kolloider Lösungen anorganischer Stoffe (Th. Steinkopff, Dresden, 1910). The older methods are contained in the little work of A. LOTTERMOSER, Anorganische Kolloide (Ferd. Enke, Stuttgart, 1901).

scientific foundation by TH. PAUL. He demonstrated that colloidal preparations of silver split off silver ions in aqueous solution and in such quantity that the blood is saturated with silver ions because it can take up very few of them by reason of the NaCl it contains. In these investigations the interesting fact was disclosed that the various colloidal silver preparation behaved differently when diluted in aqueous solution. The Ag ion concentration diminished when *protargol* is diluted, it remains constant with *sophol* and increases with *lysargin* and *collargol*. This explains the difference in their therapeutic application. The remarkable fact that the concentration of Ag ions increases with dilution is paralleled in complex substances as well as in mixtures of the weaker acids and their salts (increase of H ion concentration). According to O. Goos the action of silver nitrate and silver iodid is to be attributed to the silver ions and complex compounds.

Heretofore colloidal metals and their compounds were employed solely in aqueous solutions; recently, however, metal organosols have achieved therapeutic recognition. Employing *lanolin* as a protective colloid, C. AMBERGER has prepared many colloidal metal solutions. We have interesting publications concerning lanolin solutions of palladium hydroxyd sol (trademarked *leptynol*). M. KAUFFMANN employed it successfully in obesity cures. It acts as a carrier of hydrogen, increasing oxidative processes which are deficient in the obese Certain psychoses which may be traced to similar causes seem also at times to be favorably influenced (W. GOM).

Silver hydrosol of all the metal hydrosols has been the most carefully studied, the other hydrosols show great variations in some respects.

According to G. IZAR,[*3] even the Macedonians covered wounds with silver plates, and in parts of Italy erysipelas is still treated in the same way. In the United States, silver foil is employed in some hospitals to seal open wounds (R. HUNT, Washington). CREDÉ at first employed CAREY LEA's colloidal silver. Manufacturers soon began to make colloidal silver preparations which are sold under a great variety of names. Among the best known are Argentum Colloidale Credé, which is sold as Collargol (von Heyden) It is prepared by the reduction of silver nitrate with ferric citrate; a dextrin probably serves as the protective colloid. In the case of Lysargin (Kalle) a sodium lysalbinate serves as protective colloid. Electrargol and Argoferment are made by electric pulverization in the presence of a stabilizer (probably gelatin). According to J. VOIGT the linear diameter of the particles in various commercial preparations varies between 14 and 26 $\mu\mu$.

M. ASCOLI and G IZAR prepare their hydrosols according to the method of G. BREDIG (pulverization of silver, gold or platinum electrodes by electric arcs under water) They stabilized some of their solutions with pure gelatin

Since CREDÉ's publication the literature on the action of colloidal silver has become extremely extensive, and the results are very contradictory It was at first employed in septicemias, by some, with professedly good results, and by others without any apparent influence. I have personally interviewed many practitioners of medicine on the action of colloidal silver and have found among them similar contradictions. Some were enthusiastic advocates of colloidal silver therapy at first, but after several failures dropped the use of colloidal silver entirely. E. FILIPPI is possibly correct in attributing a therapeutic result only to a single dose [A similar observation has been made in connection with non-specific therapy by intravenous injection of typhoid vaccine in rheumatism. Tr] He emphasizes the decided difference in the hydrosols of different metals, so that the hydrosol of the one most suitable must be selected for each individual case. Colloid silver is not only said to be active in general infections, but it has been praised also in local processes. VON OETTINGEN, who served in the Russo-Japanese war, recommends it heartily as a disinfectant for wounds [MACDONAGH has used colloidal manganese. Tr.]

Action on Microörganisms.

The action of colloidal metals on protozoa (paramecium, vorticella, opalina) has been studied by E. FILIPPI.

There are killed	Paramecium	Vorticella
	Diluted approximately.	
By Colloidal:		
Silver	1 : 450,000	1 . 170 000
Mercury	1 : 390,000	1 . 92,000
Copper	1 : 70 000	1 : 36,000
Nickel	1 . 24,000	1 . 9,500
Palladium	1 . 6,500	1 : 5,200
Gold	1 : >1,000	1 : >4,000
Platinum	1 : >1,000	1 : > 400

It is noteworthy that the lethal threshold for salts of the same metals are very similar for the same dilution and for the same content of metal.

Colloidal silver has absolutely no effect on moulds I found that a 1 per cent collargol solution which had been left unstoppered was covered after a time with a species of mould. Similar observations were made by FILIPPI* with penicillium and aspergillus in the case of different colloid metals R. ZSIGMONDY*[1] mentions that moulds grew on his gold hydrosol and that the solutions were gradually decolorized by them as the gold precipitated on the mycelia and stained them black.

Earlier investigators (CREDÉ, COHN, BRUNNER, NETTER) observed only a moderate inhibition of growth (1 : 2000 to 1 : 6000 in the case of staphylococcus aureus) but no destruction of the germs by colloidal silver. Recent studies of CERNOVODEANU and V. HENRI * on anthrax bacilli, B. coli, staphylococcus pyogenes aureus and albus, B. dysenteria, etc., show a strong bactericidal action of silver hydrosol in test tubes; researches of CHARRIN, V. HENRI and MONNIER-VINARD * show the same effect in the case of B. pyocyaneus. The size of the particles in a hydrosol is of very great importance, and in fact the finely granular red solutions are much more active than the coarser green ones; the former completely inhibited growth in dilutions of 1 : 50,000 to 1 : 100,000. [JEROME ALEXANDER has produced especially fine dispersion by a new principle. Tr.]

Similar results were obtained for pneumococci by CHIRIÉ and MONNIER VINARD.*

According to G. STODEL,* colloidal mercury in a dilution 1 : 132,000 inhibits the development of B. typhi and of staphylococci.

On account of the results obtained with colloidal silver,[1] as well as because of the lack of irritating effect and of toxicity (it was possible to employ it in large doses subcutaneously and intravenously), the hopes for its therapeutic action were justified It is remarkable that, instead of extensive especially planned animal experiments, clinical experiments which were at times favorable and at times unfavorable have occupied the stage The number of times it has been employed clinically compared with animal experiments is comparatively small, and it was tried on many hopeless cases.

The judgment of the results depends largely on the experience of the clinician and is much influenced by the subjects; in short, the results hitherto obtained lead to nothing definite. On this account the indications for use are very inadequate. It is from the above-mentioned exhaustive researches of M. ASCOLI and G. IZAR[1] that an idea of the mechanism of the action of metal hydrosols has been obtained [HARRY CULVER (Jour. Lab. & Clin. Med., May, 1918) found that the gonococcidal action of colloidal silver (argyrol, protargol, silvol and nargol) was diminished in vitro by aging the solution by light and by heat. He also found that the gonococci became resistant or adapted to a particular preparation by growth in its presence. This was not a resistance to the other colloidal silver preparations but specific. The importance of the " protecting " substance is evident from this experiment. Tr.]

[1] According to STODEL also, colloidal mercury is less toxic than mercury salts.

Ferments.

Ferments are much reduced in activity by the salts of heavy metals. Since a parallelism has been shown to exist between the toxicity of colloidal metals and that of their salts, it was expected that the colloidal metals would exert a powerful action on ferments. It is a remarkable fact that the colloidal metals proved to be more or less indifferent.

The digestion of albumin by *pepsin,* the digestion of gelatin by *trypsin,* the coagulation of milk by *rennin,* the cleavage of fat by *pancreatic steapsin* and *lipase,* the fluidification of starch by *pancreatin* and *takadiastase* were uninfluenced by colloidal silver (see M. Ascoli and G Izar *).

L. Pincussohn * examined the following substances for their influence on digestion with pepsin· chemically prepared hydrosols of silver, selenium, gold, copper, bismuth, mercury (Hyrgolum) and arsenic, and electrically pulverized preparations of silver, gold, platinum, mercury and bismuth. In no case was the activity of pepsin increased, but it was diminished by large doses, and least in the case of hydrosols obtained by electrical pulverization.

E. Filippi * was unable to obtain any effect with colloidal metals (Au, Hg, Cu, Ni, Pd) upon fermentation in the case of yeast, pepsin, trypsin or rennin.

Small quantities of silver hydrosols, on the contrary, activate the *diastatic ferment* of the liver and of the blood serum.

According to H. J. Hamburger, the action of staphylolysin, the hemolytic excretion of staphylococci, is inhibited by collargol According to W Weichardt, colloidal platinum and palladium neutralize fatigue poisons.

In vitro, C Foa and A. Aggazzotti were unable to demonstrate any action of silver hydrosol upon toxins, but they could if it was injected into the circulation immediately after the toxin.

O. Gros and J. M O'Connor obtained divergent results for the decrease in the strength of tetanus and diphtheria toxin produced by collargol.

Autolysis.

In marked contradiction to the inactivity of silver hydrosol on most ferments is the very considerable influence of metal hydrosols on the enzymes of autolysis. If any organ, the stomach, liver, spleen, etc , is kept, especially if kept at body temperature, changes occur in it which finally lead to a softening and decomposition characterized by a more or less extensive cleavage of the albumins, nucleins, etc., involved.

This decomposition occurs even though the organ is absolutely sterile, so that incidental bacterial growths are not the cause; it is brought on by a series of different enzymes each of which has a definite function, and the process is called autolysis or autodigestion.

All the hydrosols investigated, namely, those of silver, gold, platinum, mercury, palladium, iridium, copper, lead, ferric hydroxid and aluminium hydroxid have the ability to assist autolysis; M. Ascoli and his coworkers, by separately investigating the resulting products, were able to determine the action of the individual enzymes. For instance, the liver of a recently killed animal was cut up into small pieces and passed through a sieve; it was then diluted with water and distributed in a number of sterile vessels with 1 per cent toluol to prevent putrefaction. In one sample the albumins were immediately coagulated, and the total nitrogen, as well as the individual nitrogen fractions, determined. Varying quantities of metal hydrosol were added to the remaining vessels and they were kept for 72 hours at 37° C.

Each portion was then tested for

1. Total nitrogen (according to KJELDAHL).
2. Nitrogen (as monamino acids).
3. Purin-bases (according to SALKOWSKI).
4. Albumose-nitrogen (according to BAUMANN and BÖMER).

The difference between the total nitrogen and the sum of the other values gave the quantity of nitrogen present as diamino acids, peptone and ammonia.

In general, there is an accelerating action on the total autolysis as well as on the cleavage of the nucleins, and the formation of monamino acids, though there are considerable quantitative differences between the different hydrosols   For instance, minimal quantities of Ir, Hg, Cu and Ag favor the *autolytic process in general*, yet decidedly larger quantities of Pb, Au, Pt and Pd are required for this purpose   The same facts hold for the formation of monamino acids. Small doses increase, while larger quantities of hydrosols interfere with the cleavage of nucleins, however this does not hold true for silver, platinum and gold hydrosols   Under ordinary circumstances the uric acid formed during autolysis is broken down still further by a uricolytic ferment; the action of this ferment is inhibited by silver hydrosol

Though there is no difference between the action of *stabilized* and *unstabilized* silver upon autolysis, such a difference was noticeable after the addition of defibrinated blood.   Defibrinated blood interferes with the acceleration of autolysis due to unstabilized silver hydrosol, but it does not do so in the case of the stabilized hydrosol.

This observation is also of great interest in connection with the theory of *protective colloids.* A *priori* we would be justified in believing that no difference exists between stabilized and unstabilized metal hydrosol, but that a stabilization could be produced by the dissolved albumins of the hashed organ or of the added blood. The above example indicates the delicate adjustments in the mechanism of colloid protection. [Different substances may compete for the protector, thus establishing " preferential " protection   Tr.]

It is interesting to note in addition, that the above investigators found that minimal traces of prussic acid, mercuric chlorid and cyanid, arsenious acid and carbonic oxid had as toxic an effect on the autolytic action of silver hydrosol as upon its ability to split hydrogen peroxide. This process which was exhaustively studied by G. Bredig may be made to regress so that the metal hydrosols may "recover." The identical observation was made by M Ascoli and G. Izar in respect to the autolysis by poisoned silver hydrosol

Blood. Hydrosols of silver, lead and mercury have the ability to dissolve red blood corpuscles, whether the hydrosols are stabilized by gelatin or not (M Ascoli *). It is also interesting to learn that pure powdered silver causes hemolysis, though this proceeds very slowly.

The same silver powder when repeatedly used for hemolysis becomes inactive, serum inhibits hemolysis by silver. H. Bechhold[1] observed that a drop of mercury causes strong hemolysis, which serum did not inhibit. He also observed hemolysis with metallic lead, though this was much weaker than in the case of mercury. Metallic copper hardens the erythrocytes.

Poisons do not interfere with the action of silver hydrosol

It is necessary in these effects to distinguish between the specific activity of the metal involved and the generic activity due to the development of surface   Hemolysis is induced by quite indifferent suspensions, by kaolin (Friedberger and his pupils) as well as by barium sulphate and calcium fluorid (O. Gengou)   Such hemolysis is inhibited by serum.

After Achard and E Weill, as well as A. Robin and E. Weill, had studied the influence of colloidal silver, and G. Stodel[2] had studied the influence of colloidal mercury upon erythrocyte production, E. Filippi, and later Le Fèvre de Arric, carried these investigations further and extended them to other metal hydrosols. The results in brief show that the red blood corpuscles are at first diminished to a greater extent than the white. Later there is a considerable increase of both red and white blood corpuscles. After the

[1] As yet unpublished
[2] The fact that G Stodel did not observe hemolysis of dog's blood with electrically pulverized colloidal mercury is remarkable, and deserves further investigation

prolonged injection of hydrosols the red blood corpuscles and the hemoglobin are somewhat increased, but there is no noticeable increase of leucocytes. Silver, copper, manganese and mercury prove most active; platinum, palladium, gold and nickel are much weaker. *Identical results are obtained with small doses of the salts of these metals.*

This does not completely accord with the results of O GROS and J. M. O'CONNOR,* who observed an immediate increase of the polynuclear leucocytes just as occurs after the introduction of any other foreign substances.

Very noteworthy is the observation of FILIPPI, that colloidal silver, copper and mercury introduced into the circulation markedly increase phagocytosis.

The following table obtained with slightly different experimental conditions on rabbits illustrates this

PHAGOCYTOSIS OF ALEURON AND CARMINE

Normal	Ag	Cu	Hg	Pt
Per cent	Per cent	Per cent	Per cent	Per cent
3 12	27 50	17 80	38 00	
5 20	37 80	40 16	16 10	8 20

LE FÉVRE DE ARRIC found, on the contrary, that this assumption could not be generalized. In experiments with silver hydrosol (electrargol) he found in guinea-pigs an increase in the phagocytic activity for colon and typhoid bacilli; in rabbits there was a diminution for typhoid bacilli. In both guinea-pigs and rabbits there was an unfavorable effect on the phagocytosis of pyocyaneus and staphylococci.

Metabolism.

Naturally, the processes occurring in the living organism are far more complicated than in the individual organ elements or in the dead organ. However, since there were obtained from the study of autolysis viewpoints for the action of hydrosols on the disintegration of nitrogenous constituents, the investigation of the nitrogen change in the living organism offered a prospect of profitable study (M. ASCOLI * and G. IZAR,*1 FILIPPI and RODOLICO).

For this purpose bitches were fed entirely on bread made from wheat or rye flour. The total nitrogen in the feces was determined, and in the urine the total nitrogen, the urea nitrogen and the uric acid. In a previous series of experiments with men, like determinations were made (excepting of the N of the feces) as in the experiments undertaken on rabbits by E FILIPPI and RODOLICO Metal hydrosols were administered intravenously. The results were concordant.

The result of the experiment was as follows: unstabilized silver hydrosol (prepared according to G. BREDIG) as well as collargol had no action in small doses. Silver hydrosol (prepared according to G. BREDIG), stabilized with gelatin, increased the nitrogen metabolism; the nuclein metabolism was chiefly affected since there resulted a decided increase in the elimination of uric acid in the urine. Silver hydrosol stabilized by gelatin has a more powerful action than the corresponding quantity of silver nitrate, silver thiosulphate or silver albuminate, which exert a qualitatively analogous action. On the other hand, the N elimination in the feces is decreased. Mercury and lead hydrosols have a similar effect, differing only in the time curve. Large quantities of collargol also increase the uric acid excretion.

Temperature Curve.

The injection of a few cubic centimeters of silver hydrosol causes a rise of temperature of varying but usually brief duration (M. ASCOLI and G IZAR*); on the other hand, the unstabilized hydrosols have no observable effect on temperature (BOURGOUGNON*). This corresponds with the observations on autolysis described above.

Distribution.

Finally, we must inquire, what becomes of the injected silver hydrosol. This has already been investigated, at least as far as concerns collargol injected intravenously. G. PATIN and L. ROBLIN* found it chiefly in the liver but to a less extent in the kidney They contend that there occurs a concentration and gradual excretion through the kidneys. S. BONDI and A. NEUMANN showed that collargol as well as other indifferent suspensions (india ink, fat) disappear from the circulation within 1/2 to 1 hour after intravenous injection and are temporarily deposited in the liver, bone marrow and spleen. It is the star cells of VON KUPFFER which chiefly take up these suspensions.

J. VOIGT contributed especially accurate researches. He traced the fate of the stored silver in the more important organs by examining microscopic sections in the ultramicroscope Of his findings let us emphasize particularly that it made a difference in the distribution of the silver in the individual organs whether the animal was overwhelmed by a single large quantity of silver solution or smaller repeated doses were injected. There were definite differences in the pictures obtained with different colloidal metals and metallic compounds. According to personal, hitherto unpublished communications from J. Voigt the silver is precipitated at the site of injection after intramuscular injections and in the peritoneum after intraperitoneal injections, whence it is gradually transported to the internal organs   It is still an open question whether the transportation is purely mechanical or results from solution and reprecipitation.

Therapeutics.

It is obvious from the preceding statements that metal hydrosols may, from very different causes, exert a therapeutic action.   In infectious processes we may imagine that there is a direct action on the excitants of infection; although this may be due to an indirect action inasmuch as the hydrosol stimulates the formation of antibodies and phagocytosis, or it may injure the infecting organisms by intensifying metabolic changes in some way

In view of G Bredig's experiments on the catalytic action of colloidal metals, a catalytic action of metal hydrosols which produces effects similar to the ferments in the living organisms has been frequently suggested   Personally, I prefer to leave undecided whether such an expression as "catalytic action" has any real meaning in this connection or whether it is nothing but an empty word.

We shall merely mention here the experiments with colloidal mercury, which has been chiefly used in syphilis and shows a specific action similar to that of other mercury preparations.

Animal Experiments.

In the case of silver hydrosol there exist many experiments of C Foa and A. Aggazzotti * They infected rabbits with staphylococci and after an hour injected 30 cc of a red silver hydrosol, repeating this several times   In this way they delayed the death of the animal from 1 to 3 days but recovery was not brought about

In infections with diplococci and typhoid (in dogs) the animals could be kept alive with injections of silver hydrosols.   In the latter instance this was even possible when the silver-hydrosol injection was given in doses of 5 cc. intraperitoneally as late as 12 to 24 hours after the injection of the microörganisms.

The same authors found that silver hydrosol has no effect on toxins in vitro, whereas it inhibits the toxicity if it is injected immediately after the toxin.   From this they concluded that silver hydrosol activates the oxidizing ferments of the body

Charrin, V. Henri and Monnier-Vinnard * speak very guardedly concerning their therapeutic results, and characterize them as "very promising." Chirié and Monnier-Vinnard * experimented with pneumococci on white rats and mice. They obtained at times a retardation of the disease process and in individual instances they allege a cure by means of silver injections

Clinical Experiments.

I shall pass over the majority of experiments which, because of their limited scope, are without significance and frequently contradictory, and shall only regard such results as are unimpeachable. To all appearances, only experiments performed with a stabilized silver hydrosol have practical value

The use of silver hydrosol, as collargol, in septicemia and pyemia is most frequent and best known. It is usually used as an intravenous injection, at times as an ointment or an enema. If the numerous case histories[1] are reviewed, two phenomena are prominent: the fall in temperature and the subjective improvement of the patient which follow several hours after the application is given. In contrast to this it is hardly possible to determine to what extent the disease process is influenced. The effect of silver hydrosol on pneumonia has been studied most thoroughly. G. Etienne[*] and J. Cavadias obtained good results, the rapid defervescence is also the most significant fact here. G Izar[82] treated 28 cases of pneumonia with silver hydrosol and several with platinum and iridium hydrosol; no difference was noted between the Ag, Pt and Ir. These thoroughly studied cases gave the following results: the course of the pneumonia process seems in general to have been favorably influenced though it was hardly possible to attribute this to a specific action upon the infectious process, but rather to the amelioration of the symptoms. As in the case of healthy individuals, in a pneumonia patient a rise of temperature, which reaches its maximum in about 4 hours, follows the injection and this is followed by a severe rigor, which is succeeded by profuse sweating and a rapid temperature fall, "critical in character, however, it cannot be termed a crisis." The subjective improvement of the patient is characteristic of the action of silver hydrosol

The brief period of oppression and anxiety which accompanies the rigor is succeeded when the temperature falls by a feeling of well-being or euphoria. Cardiac and renal functioning are not affected, nor is there any action on the course of the pneumonia process as far as may be determined from a change in the excretion of chlorids.

[1] A very complete bibliography is given by WEISSMANN, Über Kollargol. Therapeut Monatsh Aug, 1905

Mentioned by ISCOVESCO, Presse Médicale, May 8, 1907.

G. Izar reaches the conclusion that "the regular use of the injections shortens the course of the infection and seems to make it more favorable."

It was mentioned at the outset that the number of infectious diseases in which silver hydrosols as well as other metal hydrosols were employed is very great, and the opinions of the results very divergent; silver hydrosol, and at times platinum-hydrosol, have been employed in inflammatory rheumatism and erysipelas, in typhoid and para-typhoid, in appendicitis, furunculosis, phlegmons, anthrax, cerebrospinal meningitis, and scarlatina, dysentery and diphtheria, etc. As in the case of the diseases previously described, it affects the temperature curve though at times only temporarily, and there is frequently no influence on the patients subjectively.

I have not as yet discovered in the literature any published cases of the use of silver hydrosols in tuberculosis; if they exist they are probably isolated instances. The reader may well get the impression that there do not exist for most diseases such thorough studies as G. Izar's [*3] in pneumonia, and that on this account the records of metal hydrosol therapy are incomplete.

Mercury.

Mercury has been used for centuries in syphilis. Since metallic mercury as such, as well as in the very finely emulsified form of blue ointment, is absorbed by the organism, there is no reason for expecting a very marked difference to result from the colloidal solution.

The chemical firm of von Heyden manufacture a mercury hydrosol called Hyrgolum and a mercurous chlorid hydrosol called Calomelol, which may also be employed for inunctions.

Sulphur.

For some time a water-soluble sulphur hydrosol has been introduced into medicine and employed in skin diseases. Its action depends on the method of introduction since sulphur is reduced to the highly toxic hydrogen sulphid in the organism. The lethal dose for a rabbit weighing 1 kilo, according to L. Sabbatani, is 0.0066 gm. of colloidal sulphur intravenously (death is immediate), whereas death occurs only after several hours when 0.25 gm. is introduced into the alimentary tract. The action also depends on the kind of animal; dogs are much less sensitive to sulphur than other experimental animals

The reduction and consequently the toxicity depends on the physical condition; it is most intense in colloidal, less in amorphous, and least in crystalline sulphur. Moreover the toxicity is directly proportional to the dispersion. JOSEPH recommends sulphur hydrosol in diseases of the skin.

Phosphorus, Arsenic, Antimony.

Of all the complicated phenomena caused by these three substances in different doses, there is only one which can be considered colloid-chemically. Phosphorus, arsenic and antimony greatly influence metabolism. Whereas arsenic and arsenic salts inhibit liver autolysis even in small doses, minimal doses of arsenic trisulphid hydrosol favor it. Small quantities of the latter preparation activate and larger ones inhibit the uric acid forming ferments in liver autolysis (M. ASCOLI and G. IZAR *).

Phosphorus, arsenic and antimony inhibit oxidation processes. In minute doses this results in an increased constructive activity, its effect may be compared with slight oxygen need, such as occurs at high altitudes. In larger doses the toxic action comes to the foreground The metabolism does not reach its end product, weak carbonic acid, but there are formed the intermediary stronger acids (lactic acid, glycuronic acid, etc.); the difficultly oxidizable fats are no longer normally attacked; there is a fatty degeneration of the glands (liver, kidneys), subcutaneous tissue and in the peritoneum and all the organs successively. [It is more probable that there is a change in the aggregation of the fat globules as the result of these poisons (breaking of emulsions). T. BRAILSFORD ROBERTSON has recently presented this view, and he refers to the fact that GAY and SOUTHARD observed the loading of the gastric epithelium with visible fat globules in animals which have experienced anaphylactic shock. Science N. S., Vol. XLV, No. 1170, p 568 *et seq.* Tr.] It is upon this very retention of fat that the therapeutic employment of arsenic depends. It has been recognized a long time by the arsenic eaters of Steiermark and by breeders. [This may be due to the destruction of the protective action of an emulsostatic substance. Tr]

With toxic doses, when the formation of stronger acids instead of weak carbonic acid occurs, there must results an increased friction of the blood in the capillaries. As a matter of fact circulatory disturbances are among the most characteristic phenomena of phosphorus, arsenic, antimony and lead poisoning. "Generalized dropsy" (edema resulting from acid formation in the tissues, see p 208 *et seq*) is a symptom of chronic arsenic poisoning.

We must also regard the "capillary paralysis" due to arsenic as caused by an increase of the viscosity of the blood at the interfaces It must be specially emphasized that these statements are only working hypotheses.

Salts.

The neutral salts of alkalis may cause injuries[1] to organs or organ groups by reversible changes in the condition of the organ colloids; strictly speaking, they are not poisons. We are unable to produce a poisoning, for instance by the oral ingestion of moderate doses of potassium salts, though this may be accomplished with intravenous injections, under such circumstances, disturbances of the heart muscle and the peripheral vessels are observed. It would be worth determining whether these phenomena are not to a great extent caused by changes in the viscosity of the blood. Hitherto, potassium salts have not been purposely employed therapeutically with this in view H. BECHHOLD and J. ZIEGLER[*3] attribute the favorable action of a vegetarian diet in gout to the generous supply of potassium salts which hinders the precipitation of urates.

The biological action of neutral salts has been studied chiefly by biologists and physiologists. We owe to them valuable contributions concerning the inhibition of irritability (see p. 274 *et seq*), the death of lower salt and fresh water organisms in changed media, and the inhibition of the development of the eggs of marine creatures

It follows from all these investigations that for the normal functioning of the organisms, no matter whether animal or plant, high or low, a definite combination of electrolytes is necessary, upon this the normal state of swelling for the organ colloids depends The cations are especially important. The monovalent cations (Na, K) are held in check by small quantities of divalent ones (Ca, Mg) [See CLOWES, p 38. Tr] Several examples may serve to explain this For animal organisms a given content of Na ions is necessary, which may at best be replaced by Li ions. K ions are especially poisonous because they change the state of turgescence of the organ colloids Pure sodium chlorid solution of physiological osmotic pressure behaves as a poison; this was shown by JACQUES LOEB on the fertilized eggs of *fundulus heteroclitus*, a small sea anemone He also showed that this poisonous action was arrested by the addition of a small amount of any salt containing polyvalent cations. Substances which were themselves very poisonous, such as barium, zinc, lead and uranium salts, under these circumstances detoxicate sodium chlorid, but copper and mercury salts and ferric ions showed no detoxicating action. K. G. LILLIE[*1] observed a similar antitoxic action of polyvalent cations in the poisoning of the larval forms of *arenicola*, a sea annelid. Its ciliary movement is stopped by pure Na and Li salts

[1] These questions are treated in Chapter XVII.

since the cilia dissolve. This injurious action is stopped by poly valent cations

Interesting in this connection are the experiments of Wo. OST WALD *[1] on the vitality of the sand flea (*gammarus pulex*) which lives in fresh water. It survives in sea water three or four days but in : mixture of four-fifths sea water and one-fifth distilled water, it live almost as long as in fresh water. If each constituent of the sea wate is successively removed, the toxicity of the remainder rises, that i the duration of life diminishes in the following order:

$$NaCl + KCl + CaCl_2 + MgSO_4 + MgCl_2$$
$$NaCl + KCl + CaCl_2 + MgSO_4$$
$$NaCl + KCl + CaCl_2$$
$$NaCl + KCl$$
$$NaCl.$$

According to W. J. V OSTERHOUT what has been demonstrate for animals is equally true for plants (algae, grains, liverwort an moulds) The fresh water alga, *vaucheria sessilis*, is killed in $\frac{3n}{32}$ NaCl solution but continues to grow if a trace of calcium chlorid i added According to CHAS B. LIPMAN the dry weight of rip barley was increased if $CaSO_4$ was added to a culture containin sufficient sodium sulphate to be harmful. In this case as with cul tures of bacteria, the antagonistic action of the cations play a important part.

Though we employ physiological sodium chlorid solution in man experiments for the maintenance of isotonicity, it is merely a make shift, and on this account there have recently been introduced solu tions which, as well as being isotonic, have a composition similar t the blood (RINGER's and ADLER's solution) and thus maintain it normal state of swelling. [More recently McCLENDON's. Tr.]

All these solutions contain the divalent Ca ion. We have indi cated on page 70 how we believe its detoxicating effect is brough about; it opposes the swelling due to monovalent ions (Na, K And it is usually assumed that the "tanning" is limited to the plasm pellicle

Though the cations are of major importance in "balanced combinations of salts, the anions are not without significanc (J LOEB)

As was mentioned previously, the toxic action of the neutral salt is, in general, reversible. On this account the question arise whether their action is due to a solution or an adsorption phenomeno by the organ colloids. Wo. OSTWALD decided the question in fave of the latter view. In the adsorption equation (see p. 21) ir stead of $\frac{x}{m}$ (concentration of the salt in the dispersed phase) he

placed $\frac{1}{t}$, in which t = length of life, $\frac{1}{t}$ is accordingly the toxicity

The equation becomes $\dfrac{\frac{1}{t}}{\frac{1}{p}} = k$. Wo. OSTWALD experimented with the

sand flea mentioned (gammarus pulex) and with another small crustacean (*daphnia magna*). He placed a given number of them, *e g*, twenty-five, in a definite quantity of water (100 cc.) of different salt concentration and every two minutes he observed how many had meanwhile died   It was evident that the zero point of the adsorption curve must be placed to coincide with the normal salt content of the organism, and that either a dilution or a concentration of the surrounding water is toxic   This must be expressed in the adsorption equation. Accordingly, the toxicity formula for neutral

salts, when their concentration is increased, is $\dfrac{\frac{1}{t}}{(c - n)\frac{1}{p}} = k;$ in

this case n is the quantity of salt normally adsorbed in the tissues.

For the toxicity of subnormal salt solutions, the adsorption formula becomes $\frac{1}{t} \cdot C\frac{1}{p} = k.$ Wo OSTWALD [4] calls the latter the "formula of leaching" Observed and calculated results agree quite well

A peculiar place is occupied by potassium iodid and iodin compounds With all of them, the "iodin action" is the most important; we may even assume that the iodin of nonelectrolytes finally becomes an iodin ion. The emaciation caused by its prolonged internal use and the atrophy of certain glands are the most characteristic iodin effects upon higher animals   Prolonged use of iodin preparations, according to H MEYER and R. GOTTLIEB,[*] among others, causes an excessive secretion from mucous membranes, which is an inflammatory reaction   Even though metabolism experiments have not revealed any constant variations from the normal, it may be recalled that according to the experiments of H. BECHHOLD and J. ZIEGLER (see p. 54) potassium iodid facilitates the diffusion of a third substance through a jelly. All the phenomena mentioned above indicate a facilitation of metabolism. As was to be expected potassium iodid (according to E. ROMBERG) lowers the viscosity of the blood, and according to O MÜLLER and R INADA[*]

improves its circulation. The action of iodin in the functional disturbances of arteriosclerosis may be explained by this property since such disturbances may be attributed to a faulty blood supply to the organs. The analysis of the individual features of the process has not yet been completed.

E. BERNOULLI explains the action of bromin salts as a colloidal action. Bromids, which are given as sedatives, induce in both man and beast apathy and slumber as their most marked effect. It may be demonstrated that a portion of the chlorin in the body is displaced by bromin and that administration of NaCl induces recovery. E. BERNOULLI has shown that the brain is more swollen in equimolecular solutions of NaBr than of NaCl. In addition he was able to restore rabbits poisoned with NaBr by injecting, instead of NaCl, other salts which inhibit swelling (sodium sulphate and nitrate). Thus it is highly probable that change in the function of the nerve cells induced by bromids may be attributed to a swelling.

In the case of the alkaline earths there occur actual specific actions and we find transitions to irreversible conditions which are induced by the salts of heavy metals on albumin and lipoid colloids. For instance, barium has a very intense action on the heart and the vascular musculature. Of all the anions sulphocyanid inhibits precipitation least, so that Wo. PAULI [1] asserted, *a priori*, that a combination of sulphocyanid and barium would exert an especially severe effect. He maintained animals under the influence of a moderate sulphocyanid intoxication which, though the heart was strong and regular, stimulated the vagus and the vascular centers. In a moderate-sized dog 5 mg. of barium chlorid sufficed to cause an immediate stoppage of the heart. Calcium and strontium salts acted in a similar way, but much larger doses were required since with these there is much less specific affinity for heart muscle.

C. NEUBERG * and his pupils were able to prepare in methyl alcohol colloidal solutions and jellies of compounds of calcium, strontium, barium and magnesium, which are insoluble in water, as for instance CaO, $CaSO_4$, $CaCO_3$, the oxalate and phosphate of Ca, $MgHPO_4$, $BaCO_3$, etc. Since they are lipoid-soluble, it is possible they are of importance in the animal organism. C. NEUBERG believes that possibly they may develop in the cells in the presence of sugar, glycerin or even in the presence of ethyl alcohol in an aërobic respiration; in my opinion the presence of the body colloids should suffice to permit them to develop. The blood pressure elevating properties of barium salts may eventually be utilized in the form of colloid solutions inasmuch as such solutions do not possess the undesirable by-effects of barium salts.

Aluminium is the bond between the earth alkalis and the heavy metals   It coagulates albumin in "irregular series" and under certain conditions the albumin-aluminium precipitates are reversible.   In this connection, thallium coagulates the protoplasm of aquatic plants (spirogyra, elodea, etc.), but they recover when replaced in their original medium (J. Szücs).

The soluble salts of heavy metals form irreversible metal albumin precipitates with albumin which either flock out immediately or, depending on the concentration of the salt solution, persist in the colloidal condition

For this property of the salts of the heavy metals, besides the valence, the electrolytic solution pressure (see H. Bechhold [*1]) is determinative, colloid precipitation depends upon these two factors. The toxicity threshold of the various salts of the heavy metals has been arranged in series.   Mathews * tested it on the motor nerves of frogs   Kahlenberg and True, as well as F. D Heald, tested them on plant seedlings.   I reproduce (from R. Höber) the series determined by Mathews for the inhibition of the development of the fertilized eggs of the sea anemone, *fundulus heteroclitus*.

Salts	Solution pressure in volts	Threshold of toxicity
$MnCl_2$	$+0$ 798	$1/4\,n$
$ZnCl_2$	$+0$ 493	$1/800\,n$
$CdCl_2$.	$+0$ 143	$1/12,500\,n$
$FeCl_2$	$+0$ 063	$1/10\,n$
$CaCl_2$	-0 045	$1/12\,n$
$NiCl_2$	-0 049	$1/15\,n$
$Pb\,(CH_3COO)_2$	-0 129	$1/5,000\,n$
$CuCl_2$	-0 606	$1/15,000\,n$
$HgCl_2$	-1 027	$1/50,000\,n$
$AgNO_3$	-1 048	$1/90,000\,n$
$AuCl_3$	-1 356	$1/20,000\,n$

The exceptions which $ZnCl_2$ and $CdCl_2$ show (according to R. Höber) may depend in the first instance upon strong hydrolysis (acid reaction) and in the latter on the smaller amount of electrolytic dissociation together with greater lipoid solubility.

For the antagonistic action of ions of the heavy metals see pages 70 and 378.

The intravenous injection of the salts of the heavy metals, which is associated with precipitation of protein, causes in suitable doses *anaphylactic* phenomena which may be explained by what has been said on page 210.

The salts of the heavy metals in respect to their toxicity appear to me to have powerful specific influences.   For instance, copper salts are powerful poisons to algae, infusoria and fungi. According to Bokorny they are effective even in dilutions of 1 . 100,000,000. Vertebrates can stand them in relatively higher doses, but even among these there is considerable variation; cats, for instance, are said to be very sensitive to copper salts

Some of the heavy metal cations in spite of always precipitating albumin appear to be able to enter the circulation and to be definitely stopped only when they reach the filter membranes of the glands (liver, spleen, kidneys). On this account we frequently encounter kidney irritation from the toxic heavy metal cations (mercury, lead, etc.). Doubtless their solubilities in the lipoids are an important factor.

The formation of irreversible albumin compounds kills the cell which is involved. [Hg, when absorbed to the extent of 4 mg per kilo, slays relentlessly. It forms an irreversible compound, unaffected by antidotes or by washing with water as has been shown by Sansum. Tr.] On this account besides the acids and the alkalis, salts of the heavy metals, e g., copper sulphate, silver nitrate and zinc chlorid, are used as caustics. Astringents act by causing a coagulation of the topmost layers of mucous membranes or inflamed surfaces. Therefore they include salts of the heavy metals, as silver nitrate, copper sulphate and acetate, zinc sulphate and acetate and bismuth subnitrate. Besides these, ferric chlorid and the various aluminium salts (aluminium acetate, alum, etc) of whose powerful flocculating action, resulting from the trivalence of Fe and Al we have already learned (see p 84), the flocculating action in fact depends on the colloidal ferric hydroxid and aluminium hydroxid contained (see below). Similar results may be obtained with tannin, formaldehyd, and in short from all the hardening agents discussed in Chapter XXIII, provided their employment is not precluded by undesirable properties (e.g., picric acid and osmic acid).

Iron Salts and Iron Oxid Hydrosol.

Recent researches have shown that only ionizable iron compounds have a pharmacologic action (upon the formation of red blood corpuscles in chlorosis), but they show,[1] on the contrary, that preparations with iron firmly bound (hemoglobin preparations in particular) have no specific action. The numerous preparations in which iron is administered as a colloidal iron oxid (*ferri oxidat. saccharatum solubile, liq. ferri oxid. dialys*, and in some of the chalybeate mineral

---

[1] It may be mentioned in contradiction to this, that colloidal Fe(OH)₃, according to M. Ascoli and G. Izar, favors the total autolysis of the liver as well as its individual factors (see p. 369 et seq.) and that the ferments taking part in the formation of uric acid are activated by the addition of colloidal ferric hydroxid; larger quantities, however, inhibit uric acid formation.

waters) are active only to the extent that they are dissolved in the hydrochloric acid of the gastric juice. I cannot form any idea as to the process of absorption since in the alkaline content of the small intestine where absorption occurs, the iron is thrown down again as a colloidal gel   Those colloidal iron preparations from which the iron ion slowly splits off (*e.g , liquor ferri albuminati, ferratin,* etc.) are preferable since they exert a less injurious effect on stomach and intestine (indigestion and constipation)   After intravenous or subcutaneous injection of iron salts colloidal ferric albuminate compounds are formed which may cause severe anaphylactic-like symptoms of poisoning (see p 382)   When iron salts are taken by mouth this action does not occur, since the iron is arrested in the liver.   The cathodal-migrating positive iron oxid hydrosol precipitates with the anodal-migrating blood colloids as an irreversible gel.   This is the reason why ferric chlorid is so suitable for hemostasis   The greater part of the Fe in $FeCl_3$ exists as iron oxid hydrosol as the result of hydrolytic cleavage. When blood coagulates, the excess of HCl is bound by the blood salts.

R. Bunsen, in his first scientific paper, showed that "freshly precipitated ferric hydroxid" is able to take up considerable quantities of arsenious acid and recommended it on this account as an antidote for arsenic poisoning.   W Biltz [*2] showed that the distribution of arsenious acid between iron oxid hydrogel and water has the characteristic of an adsorption curve and not that of a chemical combination.   The protective action against arsenious acid depends moreover upon the method of preparing the ferric oxid hydrogel   Works on materia medica prescribe that it be freshly prepared.   Perhaps, the inhibiting action which, according to L. Pincussohn,[*] ferric oxid hydrosol exerts on pepsin digestion depends upon adsorption

Although colloidal ferric hydroxid serves as the typical positive colloid H W Fischer [*2] succeeded in preparing a negative ferric oxid hydrosol, as well   He did this by pouring ferric chlorid solution into sodium hydrate solution which contained glycerin as a protector. Glycerin and the excess of alkali were then removed by diffusion. Instead of glycerin other polyvalent alcohols, *e g.,* mannit, erythrit and cane sugar, may be employed   The object of his experiments was to obtain ferric oxid hydrosol which might be injected intravenously.   Positive ferric oxid precipitates with the negative serum colloids; on this account the intravenous injection of positive ferric oxid is immediately fatal to animals, on account of embolism.   A remarkable exception to this was found by C Foa and A Aggazzotti [*] in dogs; they are insensitive to positive ferric oxid, no explanation for this exists   Negative ferric oxid may be mixed with serum in any proportion.   It forms a deep ruby red solution which may at times take up much more than its own volume of oxygen. Since it has some other properties of hemoglobin H. W. FISCHER calls this preparation "synthetic active hemoglobin" (*Effectsynthese des Hamoglobins*) Properly prepared ferric oxid may be injected intravenously into rabbits; yet depending upon how it was prepared it proved to be more or less toxic even though no embolism could be discovered

Negative ferric oxid seems to store itself up in the glandular organs (liver, kidneys) just as do other hydrophobe, mostly negative colloids. No change of charge occurs since it is only after HCl is added that a blue coloration occurs with potassium ferrocyanid. Although positive ferric oxid hydrosol strongly adsorbs arsenious acid, its protective action is almost completely lost if such a mixture of the ferric oxid hydrosol and the adsorbed arsenious acid is injected subcutaneously Negative ferric oxid hydrosol, under the same circumstances, exerts a very considerable protective action, but fails completely when such a mixture is injected intravenously. H W. FISCHER attributes this to the presence of hemoglobin which tears the arsenious acid from the ferric oxid hydrosol.

Narcotics and Anesthetics.

We class as narcotics such substances as temporarily suspend cerebral function, and the activity of the reflex centers. Narcosis is, therefore, a reversible process

According to the theory of HANS MEYER and E OVERTON, narcosis is produced by such substances as dissolve especially easily in the lipoids of the plasma pellicle but are not entirely insoluble in the plasma.[1] They determined the distribution coefficient between oil and water for a large number of substances and found that those substances in which the distribution coefficient (oil . water) is high are good narcotics, *e.g* , chloroform, ether, acetone, chloral hydrate, urethan, etc. The coincidence is not only qualitative but it was possible by determining the "critical concentration" to show that it was quantitative By "critical concentration" is meant the concentration of a narcotic in water which just suffices to maintain the narcosis of an organism (animal or plant) With over 100 substances, a surprising parallelism was shown to exist between "critical narcotic concentration" and coefficient of diffusion between oil and water, so that a causative connection between narcosis and fat solubility seems obvious.

[1] There exists a certain parallelism between the physiological action of narcotics and their ability to depress the surface tension of water. Upon this is based J TRAUBE's * theory of narcosis The depression of surface tension favors the penetration of the narcotic into the cell.

In recent years we have become acquainted with a number of facts which cannot be reconciled with the MEYER-OVERTON theory For instance, S. J. MELTZER showed that magnesium salts possess powerful narcotic properties G. MANSFELD and BOSÀNYI then showed that during profound magnesium narcosis there was absolutely no change from the normal magnesium content of the brain. No increase in Mg was demonstrable either in the lipoid or the lipoid free brain substance. Furthermore, it developed, that the lipoid solubility of the narcotics was to a certain extent merely accidental which paralleled other physico-chemical properties. According to J. TRAUBE and J CZAPEK diminution of surface tension parallels the narcotic properties. We must emphasize, however, that in TRAUBE's experiments only the diminution of the surface tension to air was determined, whereas in the organism we are concerned with surface tensions arising between two fluids or between a fluid and a gel phase The observations of BATTELLI and STERN have less connection with fat solubility, according to them there is a parallelism between the precipitation of certain proteins, the inhibition of oxidations in the tissues and the narcotizing activity of narcotics WARBURG and WIESEL showed that narcotics inhibit the ferment activity of the pressed juice of yeast as well as of the yeast cells Without discussing the hypothetical basis of these processes we may conclude from them that lipoid solubility does not constitute the sole physico-chemical basis for narcosis.

At present the tendency is to believe that the essential factor in narcosis is a modification of the plasma pellicle which reversibly changes its normal permeability for electrolytes, so that it is an open question whether this membrane is pure protein (see p. 239 *et seq* , membrane) or a mixture of lipoid and protein (see also S. LOEWE).

An interesting support for this view was supplied by R HOBER and his pupil A JOEL when they measured the electric conductivity of blood corpuscles under the influence of narcotics Although it is true that blood corpuscles are not nerve cells there are such similarities as justify us in applying to nerve cells, observations made on blood corpuscles. R HOBER found that narcotics inhibited the exit of electrolytes when dilute, and increased it when concentrated. Narcotics when dilute produce quite the opposite effect they do when they are concentrated. This is analogous to the conductivity determinations of OSTERHOUT on plant cells and the observations of Sv. ARRHENIUS and BUBANOVIC as well as J. TRAUBE that small amounts of many hemolytic agents inhibit homolysis.

Obviously, every substance which dissolves in fat is not a narcotic; it is such only if it can be again removed from the lipoid without leaving permanent changes. We thus arrive at the chief point in the problem. The MEYER-OVERTON theory explains the conditions under which a substance may act as a narcotic, but it does not show why it narcotizes; in other words, what the essence of narcosis is. Recent investigations, especially those of R. HÖBER, have shown that narcosis is brought about by a change in the state of swelling of the nerve colloids by which the changes which would otherwise be induced by the cell electrolytes upon stimulation are arrested. Experimentally we consider an organ narcotized if its irritability is temporarily arrested or definitely changed. If we pass the impulse of an electric current through a muscle it contracts. If the ends of a muscle are attached to a galvanometer and we stimulate the muscle the needle of the galvanometer makes a short excursion; this is called the current of action. This is associated in no way with the muscular contraction, for we may produce an electric impulse in the nerve the same way and nerves do not contract. The excursion of the galvanometer needle is the only evidence that the nerve is stimulated. All these phenomena are temporarily arrested as soon as the organ is narcotized.

If we now see that normal irritability is manifest as the result of an electrolytic process in which transitory changes in turgescence occur, and that the turgescence of nerves and muscle colloids are changed by salts, by which the irritability is consequently influenced, we shall not doubt that there is a connection between turgescence and irritability. When we find that the influence of salts upon the swelling capacity of cell colloids, especially the lipoids, is placed in abeyance or suspended by narcotics, the mass of evidence is conclusive.

The connection between irritability and colloid turgor was discussed in Chapters XVII and XXI; the following passages will show that narcotics arrest changes in turgescence. R. HÖBER[*4] has shown that the axis cylinders of nerve fibers swelled up in some portions under the influence of neutral salts and shrank in others, as is beautifully shown by staining with methylene blue. The phenomenon is reversible. Swelling under the influence of neutral salts does not occur when ethyl urethan narcosis is produced simultaneously. Accordingly, in this case the narcosis may be demonstrated in the stained sections (see p. 336). A. R. MOORE and H. E. ROAF[*] found that lipoid suspensions are precipitated by small quantities of chloroform, alcohol, ether, etc., instead of being dissolved by them. R. GOLDSCHMIDT and E. PŘÍBRAM[*] found a similar action of chloral hydrate and urethan in lecithin suspensions.

According to S. J. MELTZER magnesium salts produce narcosis if subcutaneously or intravenously injected   I wish to call attention to the fact that according to O. Porges and E. Neubauer [*] MgSO$_4$ and MgCl$_2$ in $\frac{n}{100}$ solution, unlike other electrolytes, have very narrow precipitation limits for lecithin suspensions; with this fact their narcotic action possibly stands in some relation.   Lower animals are also narcotized by magnesium salts.   On this account it is used by zoologists to fix objects in their natural state, because Mg narcosis is not preceded by irritation.   There is still not very much evidence that change in swelling is inhibited by narcotics; the evidence must be reinforced, especially by simple test-tube experiments on the relative influence of salts and narcotics in changing the turgor of lipoids. We see here a promising field for experiment.   It may be possible to combine this theory with that of Verworn's school.   According to their view, the oxidation processes in the cell are arrested during narcosis, a hypothesis supported by numerous experiments.   [A R. C. Haas has recently shown that when *Laminaria* is exposed to anesthetics (in sufficient concentration to produce any result) there is an increase in respiration, which may be followed by a decrease if the reagent is sufficiently toxic   Science N. S , No 1193, p. 46 *et seq.*   Tr.] In this connection it must be recalled, especially, that oxygen and carbonic acid are much more soluble in lipoids than in water and that narcotics diminish the absorption capacity of the cell lipoids for oxygen (G. Mansfeld [*]).   It would be interesting to determine the extent to which this solubility is influenced by the turgor of the lipoids.

Elsewhere I have already stated that the Meyer-Overton theory of narcosis demands a reversible distribution of the narcotic between lipoids and plasma.   Whether this distribution occurs as a Henry's distribution or as an adsorption is immaterial in principle (but not for the action [']).   According to a table of M. Nicloux [*] the distribution of chloroform seems to me to approach that of adsorption.   After the termination of narcosis, the blood of a dog contained the following content of chloroform (in per cent).

CHLOROFORM CONTENT IN PER CENT.

After	First experiment	Second experiment
0 minutes	0 054	0 0595
5 minutes	0 0255	. ....
15 minutes	0 0205	...
30 minutes	0 018	0 023
1 hour	0 0135	0 018
3 hours		0 0075
7 hours		0 0015

The action of narcotics on the permeability of electrolytes is reversible according to R. HOBER, and may be reversed by washing them out provided the amount of added narcotic is not too great. R. HÓBER is of the opinion that narcosis is characterized by a change in the plasma pellicle in which the *increase of permeability* to normal stimuli is inhibited

A physico-chemical study by S. LOEWE actually showed that chloroform was adsorbed by the white matter of the brain and that sulphonal, trional and tetronal were adsorbed by lipoids.

We see from the table that, at first, chloroform disappears very rapidly but that the final portions are tenaciously held A similar table for ether reveals an approximately proportional disappearance of ether from the blood in given units of time, which would approximately answer the demands of HENRY's law. The slower recovery from chloroform than from ether narcosis is thus explained

It is evident from what has been previously said that narcosis merely represents a given segment of the curve which different concentrations of the narcotic cause in the turgor of the cell lipoids. The commencement of the curve with low narcotic concentration indicates the condition of irritability before narcosis, the terminal limb with high narcotic concentration means death.

What has been said here of benumbing the entire body *mutatis mutandis*, applies, for the individual organs, in the case of local anesthesia. Local anesthesia may be produced by all sorts of substances — by very dilute caustics (acids, phenol), by distilled water, by anisotonic salt solutions, in short, by all substances which change the turgor of the cell lipoids. Practically most of them are useless because the first portion of the curve, the state of irritation which is expressed by pain in subcutaneous injections, is too prolonged; in the case of others, because the segment which signifies local anesthesia and which lies between the "irritation limb" and that of permanent damage is too short; still in others, because an irreversible change in the cell colloids may occur even with the smallest doses, or other cell colloids suffer too much in sympathy Practically only such anesthetics are utilizable as produce only a reversible change in the turgor of the nerve lipoids, as is exemplified by cocain, novocain and anesthesin

It is not difficult to range the other methods of anesthesia, such as cold and the production of anemia in this scheme, but experimental confirmation is still lacking

Colloid research also offers an explanation of certain by-effects of narcotics. [EVARTS A GRAHAM has shown that the toxic action of many anesthetics is due in part to mineral acids formed by their decomposition   He believes that delayed chloroform poisoning results entirely from the destructive action of HCl formed in the tissues and he attributes the protective action of glycogen to the fact that the glucose resulting therefrom inhibits the diffusion of HCl into gels. The toxic action of anesthetics has been shown by J. A. NEF to be due to an unsaturated carbon atom   The effect of such atoms has not yet been discussed colloid-chemically. (Jour. Amer. Med. Assoc , Vol LXIX, No 20, p 1066 *et seq.*, quoted by GRAHAM, *loc. cit.*)

BURGE attributes the anesthetic action of anesthetics to the decrease in oxidation processes produced by the destruction of catalase. The specific action on the nervous system is due to the greater solubility of the lipoids of nervous tissue facilitating the entrance of the narcotic into the nerve cell. Science N. S., Vol XLVI, No. 1199, p. 618 *et seq*   Tr] With large doses of morphine, chloroform and ether we observe more or less intense phenomena of irritation, especially in the kidneys, before the general circulation is much disturbed, albuminuria and hematuria may thus occur   MARTIN H. FISCHER * (see p 333) explains this by the disturbance in the oxidation processes of the body which suffers from such substances and by the fact that as the result of the accumulation of CO_2 and ultimately of other acids, a fixation of water occurs in the body so that no excess of water remains for excretion by the kidneys   Besides the anuria, we may thus explain the thirst which such patients frequently show. Secretion of urine occurs again and the thirst disappears when the effect of the narcotic wears off, even though the patient takes no water. Small doses of ether, alcohol, etc , cause the reverse phenomenon, since by increasing the activity of the heart they bring on an improvement in the supply of oxygen   By this means not only a stronger flow of blood is supplied to the kidneys but the "free" filterable water in the blood is increased, provided the oxidation processes are still uninjured

Colloid research seems to me to have raised new questions regarding investigations of the effects from the prolonged use of alcohol. Though the larger part of the alcohol ingested is seized by the lipoids, we cannot neglect the effect upon the albuminous colloids   At present we can only assume that it causes a diminution of swelling. The extent of the relationship between the degenerative changes of the cells, arteriosclerosis, etc., and of this action of alcohol remains for future investigations to determine. [W. BURRIDGE has shown that alcohol increases the utilization of calcium by certain cells.   Tr.]

Disinfection.

By disinfection we understand the killing or rendering harmless of dangerous germs outside of or within the body. Substances which destroy germs living on foods, without being very harmful to higher organisms, are called *preservatives*

For simplicity we shall first consider *external disinfection* by chemical means. In the process of disinfection a distribution *of the disinfectant between the organism and the medium first takes place* This distribution may occur either in the manner of chemical combination, adsorption or in accordance with HENRY's law. In the two former cases it is conceivable that even traces of the poison are active, whereas this would be possible in HENRY's distribution only if the substance is very much more soluble in the bacillus than in its medium. It follows from the ease with which they are stained that surface attraction is of great importance in the case of bacteria. And in fact staining and disinfection are distinguished only by the fact that in the latter instance the absorbed substance exerts a particular poisonous action on the microorganism

If for the present we consider a microorganism only as a small particle without special chemical properties and add to such a hypothetical emulsion of bacteria, a dissolved substance, this substance would by reason of the mere surface attraction have a tendency to concentrate on the surface of the bacteria to a greater or less extent, depending upon the nature of the dissolved substance, i e., the more strongly the given substance diminishes the surface tension of the water, the greater is the concentration at the surface[1] Most bacteria act like a suspension which has been protected by a protective colloid, before being flocculated by neutral salts; they are so changed by boiling or by agglutination that they change from hydrophile to hydrophobe suspensions, which cannot be differentiated physically from kaolin suspensions or the like. The electric charge is that of an inorganic suspension, *i.e.*, negative, it is discharged by agglutinin All these questions are taken up in detail in the chapter on "Immunity Reactions"

As the dispersed phase, microorganisms are strongly adsorbed by substances with great surface development. (See Fig. 52) Because of this adsorption, they are readily held back in fine-pored filters such as Chamberland candles (unglazed porcelain), Berkefeld filters (Kieselguhr), asbestos, wadding or carbon filters.

[1] This conception was originally developed and established by H BECHHOLD in the "International Congress for Applied Chemistry," London (May to June, 1909) (see Kolloid Zeitschr., 5, 22, 1909)

Besides the microorganisms directly visible in the microscope, there are others so small as to be microscopically invisible, and only recognizable by their pathogenic effects.   They are, therefore, called *ultravisible*   Among these are about forty pathogenic germs, among others, smallpox, rabies, measles, scarlet fever and the mosaic disease

DISINFECTING ACTION OF HALOGEN NAPHTHOLS

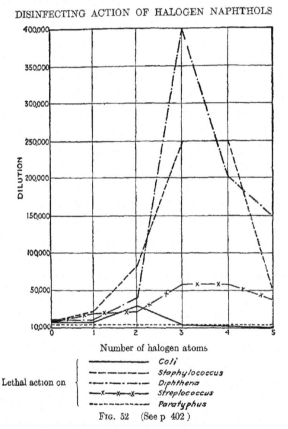

FIG. 52   (See p 402)

of tobacco.   The name ultravisible is not a happy one, since recently by dark-field illumination there have been recognized, in the case of many infections, minute organisms, which we are justified in believing to be the cause of the diseases.   The ultravisible viruses are not held back by ordinary bacteria filters; recently they have been called *filterable* microorganisms.

The study of these forms of life is difficult because of the lack of technical methods for their investigation. Besides dark-field illumination, colloid research has provided two methods which have already led to important advances· these are *ultrafiltration* and *adsorption* By means of the Chamberland filter the solution of virus may be freed from visible bacteria. In order to concentrate the filterable germs and make quantitative tests with them, they may be concentrated on an *ultrafilter*, as was done by BETEGH with hog cholera virus, PROWAZEK and GIEMSA with variola; or they may be adsorbed on charcoal or clay (as did GINS with smallpox).

I believe the colloid investigation of filterable microorganisms will yield valuable results, since they form a transition group to true colloids. A beginning has already been made. Thus ANDRIEWSKY has shown by ultrafiltration that the virus of chicken cholera is smaller than the hemoglobin molecule.

It has been repeatedly observed that the *development* of microorganisms is facilitated by the presence of suspensions or hydrogels. Thus KRZEMIENIEWSKI found that a pure culture of nitrifying bacteria grew more luxuriantly and bound more nitrogen if earth or humus was added to the culture medium and KASSERER found a similar effect from the addition of colloidal silicates and phosphates of iron and aluminum According to ROSS VAN LENNEP pieces of kidney, meat, cellulose, etc , improve the growth of aneorobic bacteria, yeast and B. coli. We thus see that these microorganisms on purely physical grounds find much more favorable conditions for growth in their natural habitat than in artificial media. In some instances it was possible to determine the reason for this phenomenon. Thus SOHNGEN * and also ROSS VAN LENNEP showed that charcoal and some other solids favor the dissipation of carbonic acid which inhibits the growth of yeast. In other instances the suspensions or colloids adsorb oxygen for aerobic bacteria, nitrogen for nitrifying bacteria, or other nutritive ingredients which are then available for growth at the surfaces of the respective substances (literature given by SOHNGEN *) [1] H FREUNDLICH *[1] mentions the following substances which show slight adsorptive affinity salts (especially of the baser metals), highly dissociated substances (such as strong acids and bases), aggregations of OH groups (sugar) and the sulpho group. As a

[1] Though it is shown on page 396 that the distribution of phenol between the bodies of the bacteria and their environment occurs as it would in two solvents, it does not by any means contradict what has been said here, since a disinfectant action does not result from adsorption Disinfection occurs when the disinfectant penetrates the microorganism; the portion which has penetrated may very well comply with HENRY's law (distribution).

matter of fact but few disinfectants are furnished by the inorganic acids and bases and by the salts of the baser metals Of course we do not include such concentrations of the acids and bases as produce a direct destruction of the organized substance As a matter of fact, substances containing the phenyl group are our most useful disinfectants, such as carbolic acid, cresol, naphthol, anilin water, etc. H. BECHHOLD and P. EHRLICH * by combining phenyl groups (derivatives of dioxydiphenylmethan and o-diphenol) obtained substances of hitherto unequalled disinfectant action (with the exception of sublimate, etc.) and even this action was greatly increased by the introduction of halogens The work of H. BECHHOLD,[*9] which introduced into practice the halogen derivatives of naphthol and dicresol, disinfectants of great activity, establishes the breadth of this assumption

A dilute solution of alkalis or acids is the normal environment for the majority of microorganisms. Although the majority of microorganisms prefer a more alkaline nutriment corresponding to the dearth of H ions in the animal organism, there are other bacteria and moulds, for instance, lactic acid bacteria, which require or prefer an acid medium, e.g., the moulds which grow on acid fruit From this it follows that when acids or alkalis injuriously affect a microorganism, the specific vital conditions of the microorganism in question have been unfavorably disturbed and accordingly it is impossible to speak of a general injurious action of H or OH ions.

Many salts of the heavy metals (e.g , silver, mercury and copper salts) are disinfectants. Their strong adsorptive power, in which sublimate excels all others, was demonstrated by P MORAWITZ *

Adsorptive capacity is only a condition preliminary to the exercise of specific toxic action It is generally accepted in the case of salts of the heavy metals that this toxic action depends on the formation of albuminates.   I am at present engaged in the explanation of these phenomena and I am already in a position to state that adsorption is by no means the most important factor

Finally, there are among the inorganic salts, substances with specific activity, e.g , the fluorids, thallium carbonate, sulphurous acid salts, boric acid, etc. We know of no disinfectants among the sugars or their related substances (e g , glycerin).   P EHRLICH and H. BECHHOLD * as well as H. BECHHOLD [*9] have shown in the case of a large number of aromatic compounds that the introduction of sulpho groups into a disinfectant considerably diminishes its activity.

Adsorption in water according to H FREUNDLICH [*1] is favorably influenced by the phenyl group and the halogens This author mentions as an example chlorbenzoic acid ($\lambda = 154$), benzoic acid ($\lambda = 140$).

Microörganisms.

Microorganisms occur more or less densely in their media as millions of minute dots, rods or threads. They constitute a dispersed phase and as such obey the physical laws to which all *suspensions* are subject Collectively they possess an enormous development of surface, and, consequently, surface attraction especially influences those substances that are dissolved by them (in other words, more as the substance diminishes the surface tension of water).

Should our assumption that adsorption plays an essential part in disinfection be correct, then the same substance will be a much better disinfectant in aqueous solution than when dissolved in alcohol or in acetone.[1] This assumption is sustained by such investigations as have been undertaken According to ROBERT KOCH, *anthrax spores* were not destroyed by the application for 100 days of 5 per cent carbolic acid in oil nor by 5 per cent carbolic acid in alcohol for 70 days, whereas they were destroyed after 48 hours' exposure to 5 per cent aqueous solution of carbolic acid *Anthrax bacilli* were of undiminished virulence after 2 days' treatment with 5 per cent carbolic acid in oil, whereas 1 per cent aqueous solution killed them in 2 minutes. Moreover, according to REICHEL,* the distribution of the phenol between albumin and the oil (as compared with water) is in favor of the oil.

According to the researches of PAUL and KRONIG, as well as those of SHEURLEN and K. SPIRO, phenol acts in disinfecting as a molecule and not as an ion. Sodium carbolate which is strongly dissociated has a much weaker action than phenol. Phenol is less dissociated in alcohol than in water, so that if it were merely a question of dissociation, phenol should be a better disinfectant in alcoholic than in aqueous solutions As is shown by the following data taken from PAUL and KRONIG's paper, the facts are quite the reverse Anthrax spores were treated with the disinfectant, according to the marble method, and then sown on agar, the resulting colonies were counted.

	Number of colonies
4 per cent carbolic acid in water	1505
4 per cent carbolic acid in alcohol	∞

We thus see that in disinfection adsorbability from water is more important than solubility.

[1] In disinfecting the hands and skin, alcohol and alcoholic solutions and even acetone are almost exclusively used, though entirely different factors are of importance in determining their use (better capacity to wet the fatty epidermis, the shrinking action of alcohol and deeper penetration into the capillary spaces of the skin (BECHHOLD)).

Cresol is less soluble than phenol and is a stronger disinfectant than the latter. Its solubility in water is so limited that it must be dissolved with the aid of soaps and similar substances. These are not true solutions; they are manifest emulsions in the dark field (FÜRTH and MARGADANT). It is still an open question whether the effect on bacteria is exerted by an envelopment by the individual cresol soap droplets, thus forming about them a highly concentrated disinfectant film. Another possibility is that the bacteria withdraw dissolved cresol from their environment, and that cresol diffuses from the droplets to an equal extent into the water.

A group of disinfectants are active even in a dilution in which the substance is no longer chemically demonstrable. According to R. Koch, interference with the growth of anthrax bacilli is caused by sublimate even in a dilution of 1 : 600,000. According to H. BECHHOLD and P. EHRLICH * tetrachlor-o-diphenol interferes with the growth of diphtheria bacilli in a dilution of 1 : 400,000 to 1 : 640,000. According to H. BECHHOLD,* tribrom-naphthol inhibits the growth of staphylococci in a dilution of 1 : 250,000. We can understand the effect of such traces of substances if we consider the course of the adsorption curve (see p. 20) in which the distribution between adsorbent and solvent occurs in such a way, that the dissolved substance is practically completely adsorbed in the weaker concentration, whereas in higher concentrations the distribution approaches that required by HENRY's law (between two solvents).

The objection may be raised that the same conditions are fulfilled in a purely chemical combination, to which we may reply that in many instances such a chemical combination must be considered to occur.

In favor of *adsorption*, there are two distinct phenomena, *inhibition* and *death*. By choosing a suitable disinfectant in sufficient concentration and exposure, microorganisms may be completely *killed;* that is, they cannot under any circumstances be brought back to life. In other cases, it is only necessary to remove the disinfectant, to dilute it or to transfer the germs to another environment, for the germs to start multiplying again; such action is called *inhibition*. In such a case, we must assume that the reaction between microorganism and disinfectant is *reversible*. In killing, the process *may be irreversible.*[1]

[1] I can readily imagine that death may occur in a reversible process if the action of the disinfectant persists for a sufficient length of time to nullify other vital processes. To give a very crude comparison, if a man is drowned, the water cannot be regarded as a poison though it depresses necessary vital processes. A man who cannot be resuscitated after a submersion lasting 5 minutes has fixed no more water in his body than one who has been resuscitated after 2 minutes' submersion.

If the disinfectant were a firm combination with the microorganism it would be difficult to explain how the germ could multiply again when removed from the disinfectant solution   This is readily understood if we assume that the union between microorganism and disinfectant is an adsorption   In that case the disinfectant will pass into the absolutely indifferent solvent so that the microorganism having become free again (from the disinfectant) is in a condition to continue its development

A few examples will explain the foregoing   R. Koch performed certain experiments in the following way: he dried germs on silk threads and subjected them for a given time to a disinfectant solution; after this he placed them in nutrient bouillon or in gelatin; if the germs developed, he considered that the disinfectant was active; if they did not, that it was inactive.   In this way R. Koch subjected anthrax spores for two days to 5 per cent carbolic acid and found that afterwards they did not develop in gelatin.   B. Riedel, in the Imperial Health Office, found that, even after 14 days of immersion in 5 per cent carbolic acid, the germination of anthrax spores was not inhibited if the silk threads were first washed with water and then placed in fluid gelatin; the gelatin and silk threads were thoroughly mixed by prolonged agitation of the test tube

According to R. Koch, a single immersion of anthrax spores in 1 : 5000 sublimate solution suffices to destroy them   J Geppert * found that the same concentration acting four seconds longer, on one trial, produced their death and on another did not   Among countless experiments on this point we shall mention those of Eisenberg and Okolska because of the method they employed

They mixed uniform quantities of disinfectant and bacteria, sometimes adding the entire quantity of bacteria at once, and sometimes in fractions.   If the phenomenon is reversible, the results in both cases should be the same, if it is irreversible there should be a point in the fractioning experiment when the disinfection should prove less satisfactory.   As was to be expected from other considerations, the action of phenol proved to be reversible and that of $KMnO_4$ and $HgCl_2$ to be partly irreversible (in these instances the time of action was an important factor).

Numerous experiments have been performed in an attempt to test *quantitatively* the views given here; the results actually satisfy the hypothesis in some instances   An exact agreement between observation and calculation is not to be expected because in disinfection adsorption is not the only factor, though it is chiefly accountable for the action of the disinfectant on the microorganism (lipoid solubility, modification of protoplasm, etc.).

The question of adsorption may be solved in one of two ways which I shall call respectively the *chemical* and the *biological methods*

The *chemical* method regards the microorganisms as a lifeless suspension   Suspensions are shaken with various known dilutions of the disinfectant, and after the suspension is removed the amount of disinfectant remaining in the fluid is chemically determined   From this we learn how much has been absorbed by the microorganism in the various dilutions.   It is the same method that is usually employed in chemical adsorption experiments   It may be criticized because it determines the amount of disinfectant absorbed by the microorganism but not the result of the adsorptive action, the disinfection.   From a concentrated solution much more disinfectant is removed than is necessary for killing or inhibition.

R O Herzog and Betzel * employed the chemical method, with yeast as the microorganism.   They obtained an adsorption curve for *chloroform* and *silver nitrate* and a chemical combination for *formaldehyd.*   The results are interesting inasmuch as chloroform obviously acts by reason of its lipoid solubility, I question whether the precipitation of albumin by silver nitrate is the only factor which determines its disinfectant action   The result for formaldehyd is especially surprising; its powerful inhibitive action on development is well known, however its lethal action was discovered to be much weaker.   We shall await with great interest the further prosecution of Herzog's experiments which promise an explanation of some of the questions proposed.   The results with *phenol* are quite complicated.   According to Reichel,* in an aqueous solution of phenol there is a distribution in accordance with Henry's law, *i e*, as if it were distributed between two solvents.   This was demonstrated by Reichel * in the distribution of phenol between water and oil, albumin, cholesterin and the bodies of bacteria.   This explains why phenol is active only in relatively high concentration.   Increasing NaCl content shifts the relative distribution in the direction of the nonaqueous phase.   According to Reichel the disinfectant action depends on the fact that phenol causes a shrinking of the albumin phase; this is strengthened by the NaCl   In this way, the views developed by K. Spiro and J. Bruns * are revived in modified form.

R. O Herzog and Betzel obtained an *adsorption* curve on treating yeast with a phenol solution weaker than one per cent.   These contradictory results may probably be explained by the primary *adsorption* of the phenol at the surface of the bacterial cell which then in some way *absorbs* it until the body of the bacterium is filled.   This I infer from the experiments of E. Küster and Rothaub who show that upon the death of the bacteria a part of the phenol is liberated.

The *biological method* regards the rapidity of death (measured by the number of surviving bacteria) in known concentrations of the disinfectant and during a known time for action. In this case, the changes in concentration by means of the adsorbing microorganism are not considered, as in the chemical method, but only the damage to the microorganism. The method assumes that "the rate at which the solution of a substance acts as a disinfectant is proportional to the amount adsorbed from this solution" (MORAWITZ *). This method also is open to the objection that microorganisms are not a single mass with uniform vitality but a mixture in various stages of growth and with varying resistance; so that it is possible that the curves obtained do not represent the course of an adsorption in various concentrations, but express the resistance at various stages of growth.

These criticisms are offered to show the difficulties encountered in an experimental test.

We may count in this group, also, the experiments in which an insight into the mechanism of disinfection may be obtained, by varying the number of bacteria with known changes in the concentration of the disinfectant acting for a constant time (EISENBERG, OKOLSKA).

As a result of *biological methods*, PAUL, BIRSTEIN and REUSS * came to the conclusion that the death of dried adherent staphylococci in oxygen or in mixtures of oxygen and nitrogen is due to the adsorption of oxygen by the cocci.

P. MORAWITZ[1] (*loc. cit.*) found a good agreement between the figures obtained by KRÖNIG and PAUL, upon killing anthrax spores with sublimate and the formula for adsorption.

Accordingly, we learn from the quantitative tests that the distribution of a disinfectant between microorganism and solution may possess the *formula* of a chemical combination (formaldehyd) of adsorption (chloroform, silver nitrate) and of distribution in solvents in accordance with HENRY'S law (phenol). In the following pages we shall see that transitions between these different kinds of distribution occur.

It would certainly be an error to regard *distribution* as the essential factor in disinfection. As a result of adsorption the germ is surrounded by a highly concentrated film of disinfectant whose action

---

- This calculation is referred to in the communication of H. FREUNDLICH which is mentioned in the paper of H. BECHHOLD * on Disinfection and Colloid Chemistry, page 23.

destroys it much sooner than would be expected from the extremely dilute solutions employed, the germ retains the disinfectant in other media or in an infected organism and may subsequently succumbs to the damage the disinfectant inflicts. We must seek the *real activity of the disinfectant* in a modification of the living substance with which the disinfectant combines or changes, so that its vital function is suspended.

I know of no experimental investigations which show *what part of the disinfectant is combined (fixed) and what part is adsorbed* although such studies are very desirable, as they would afford a clearer insight into the nature of disinfection and they would also be of great practical significance. For the present we must be satisfied with analogies which without question can be applied correctly to the principle of disinfection. Chemically the microorganisms have so much similarity to textile fibers, especially to wool and silk, we mention only the great similarity in structure of all such properly employ in argument the results of W. Suida[?]. He took 1 gm. of fiber with 50 cc. of a sublimate solution containing 1 per cent Hg and found

	Per cent	Hg as acetate	Hg as cyanid (?)
From sublimate containing 1% Hg			
Fruit hairs of eriodendron			11
Jute	1.49	4.48	4.22
Silk	1.41	3.14	4.54
Wool		1.46	18.30
From mercuric cyanid containing 1% Hg			
Fruit hairs of eriodendron		1.14	1.14
Jute		1.4	1.4
Silk			
Wool			
From mercuric acetate containing 1% Hg			
Fruit hairs of eriodendron			
Jute			12.0
Silk			12.1
Wool			

1 The adsorption figures were calculated [...]

These figures are interesting from various points of view. We see that in the case of sublimate of 3 parts of Hg approximately 2 parts are absorbed and only one is fixed. Mercuric cyanid is the one substance which is only adsorbed and offers practically no evidence

weak destructive action. According to K. Spiro and J. Bruns,* as well as Paul and Krönig, the figures show that mercuric cyanid is far inferior to sublimate as a disinfectant

We see from the table, moreover, in the case of mercuric acetate, which is more strongly fixed and more strongly adsorbed than HgCl₂, that fixation and adsorption are not in themselves alone sufficient for strong disinfection; the disinfectant must be offered in a suitable form. Mercuric actetate is less ionized than HgCl₂, and since, according to Paul and Krönig, as well as Scheurlen and Spiro, the Hg ion is responsible for the disinfectant action, mercuric acetate is weaker than sublimate.

An especially convincing proof of the specific chemical action of the disinfectant on the living substance seems to me to be that there is a difference in the resistance of various groups of bacteria to disinfectants. Whereas anthrax spores, tubercle bacilli, etc., show an enormous resistance, cholera vibrios, gonococci and streptococci succumb to even slight chemical attacks The other groups of bacteria are ranged between these two extremes — typhoid, B. coli, staphylococci, diptheria bacilli, etc.

Were merely the strength of adsorption responsible for the disinfectant action, we could readily understand that substances of different disinfectant power would exist, we would understand for instance that cresol has a stronger action than naphthol, but in that case cresol would *always possess a stronger action than naphthol*, both on B. coli and on typhoid bacilli, as well as on streptococci If we found, however, that lysol was more active against one microorganism and that β-naphthol was more active against others, we could attribute the action to general physical properties among which we might include adsorption, but we would then have to ascribe it to the difference in behavior caused by specific inherent chemical differences in the bacteria affected This might be either a variation in the solubility of the bacterial pellicle or a variation in the grouping of the atoms in the body of the bacteria so as to manifest a greater or less affinity to the disinfectant, in either case the important factor is the chemical difference in the microorganism. *Such cases actually exist* as has been demonstrated by H. Bechhold.*⁹ He showed that the minimal lethal dose in 24 hours is·

	Diphtheria bacilli	B. coli.
For lysol (the cresol content being compared)	1 20,000	1 800
For β-naphthol .	1 : 10,000	1 · 8000

In accordance with this, lysol acts twice as powerfully against diphtheria bacilli as does β-naphthol, whereas it has only one-tenth the effect of the latter on B. coli.   He showed further that a mixture of tri- and tetrabrom-β-naphthol in one per cent solution killed staphylococci in from two to three minutes, whereas lysol dilutions containing one per cent cresol took more than ten minutes to do so   Conversely, a 5 per cent lysol solution containing 2.5 per cent cresol is lethal for tubercle bacilli within four and a half hours, whereas a solution of tri- and tetrabrom-β-naphthol of corresponding strength had no effect even at the end of twenty-four hours.   We see, therefore, that tri- and tetrabrom-β-naphthol surpass cresol in its action upon streptococci, while upon tubercle bacilli the cresol acts more powerfully   H. BECHHOLD [*9] examined naphthols containing 1, 2, 3 or more bromin or chlorin atoms with reference to their effect on various bacteria.   He found, that with the admission of the halogens the effect upon various bacteria sometimes increased, that at times it decreased, and that certain optima could be obtained (see Fig 52 on page 392).   Thus the maximum disinfectant action against staphylococci is obtained with tri- and tetrabrom-β-naphthol,[1] while for B. paratyphoid it is obtained with dibrom-β-naphthol and so on.   EISENBERG has recently determined partly specific activities for a large number of coal-tar dyes.

It follows from this that to test an antiseptic on only one kind of bacteria is an absolutely inadequate method for testing disinfectants, it is necessary to subject a number of different types of bacteria to investigation

The presence of a third substance is a factor in the action of a disinfectant that cannot be neglected.   We have already called attention on page 383 to the influence of the solvent.   To PAUL and KRÖNIG, as well as to SCHEURLEN and SPIRO, belongs the credit of having made clear the significance of electrolytic dissociation for disinfectant action.   Dissociation may be increased or diminished by adding certain substances to the disinfectants.   The ionization of $HgCl_2$ is decreased by the addition of NaCl, and since it is the Hg ion which is of importance in disinfection, the addition of common salt diminishes the disinfectant action of sublimate.   On the other hand, the disinfectant action of carbolic acid, cresol and the other phenols is decidedly increased by common salt.   Since NaCl can have no effect on the electrolytic dissociation of phenols, we must seek some other explanation.   Again, the nearest comparison must

---

[1] Tribrom-β-naphthol is sold under the trade name "providoform" by the Providogesellschaft (Berlin) and has proven useful in connection with the pus cocci and diphtheria bacilli.

be drawn from the process of dyeing; common salt or sodium sulphate is frequently added in dyeing cotton in order to get a more rapid and complete utilization of the bath. The simplest explanation of this is that there has been diminution in the solubility of the dye by means of the added salt (i e , the dye is made more colloidal) and as a result of this a stimulation of adsorption occurs. This idea guided SPIRO and BRUNS* in their experiments. They found that salts and other substances which did not "salt out" phenol from aqueous solutions, such as sodium benzoate, urea, glycerin, etc., had no effect in strengthening the disinfectant action of phenol. Pyrocatechin may be precipitated by ammonium sulphate but not by common salt, the former increases the disinfectant action of pyrocatechin, while the latter does not It is also interesting that according to PAUL and KRÓNIG equimolecular quantities of salts added to a 4 per cent carbolic solution increases its action in the following order. NaCl > KCl > NaBr > NaI > NaNO₃ > C₂H₅ONa. According to SPIRO and BRUNS,* the same order obtains for the precipitating action of these salts on phenol; however, the sulphates exert a much more powerful effect The close relationship of this series of salts to albumin precipitation and to many other biological processes is quite obvious (see pp 81 and 272). FREI and MARGADANT have determined similar relations between both the increased activity of cresol soap solutions by salts of the light and of the heavy metals as well as the decreased surface tension induced by such salts.

We may imagine that there is yet another possible way for salts or other substances to exert an influence by their mere presence H BECHHOLD and ZIEGLER *² showed that the permeability of jellies was influenced by certain substances, and from this we may assume that the permeability of the bacterial plasma pellicle for a disinfectant may be changed by the presence of a third substance.

This assumption is reinforced by experiments of EISENBERG and OKOLSKA which showed that alcohol, alkalis, urea and some other substances, which increase the permeability of jellies, also increase the disinfectant activity of many antiseptics

In practice the conditions are complicated enormously. We are no longer concerned with the distribution of the disinfectant between solvent and microorganisms but organic substances are added (sputum, albumin, feces) so that we have the sums of unknown factors which can only occasionally be resolved. The action of a disinfectant is usually much depressed by organic matter This is also the reason why disinfection of the organism, an internal disinfection or antisepsis, has so seldom been accomplished by chemical means There are, indeed, substances so slightly toxic, that men or animals may take the dose theoretically necessary to disinfect the body, for instance, tetrabrom-o-cresol and hexabromdioxydiphenylcarbinol which, according to H. BECHHOLD and EHRLICH, stop the development of diphtheria bacilli in bouillon at a dilution of 1 . 200,000. In the organism they have no effect at all, in spite of the fact that there may be introduced into the body without harm, doses which are one hundred times that necessary to inhibit the development of the bacteria in vitro or to kill them within twenty-four hours. Tetrachlor-o-diphenol behaves similarly, it inhibits development of diphtheria bacilli in dilutions of 1 · 400,000 to 1 : 640,000. Individual colonies still grew in a serum culture in the presence of the chemical at a dilution of 1 : 10,000 We might question whether the result was due to favorable vital conditions in serum removed from a living organism or to other causes. Experiment proved the latter view correct. By *ultrafiltration* the free tetrachlor-o-diphenol was separated from the fraction bound to serum colloids and it was found that 87.5 per cent of the disinfectant had been fixed by the serum colloids

The relatively simple conditions in the disinfection of skin and hands are especially instructive. The hands adsorb solid particles from the air and particles of dirt and bacteria from dirty water (H BECHHOLD). Upon washing with soap these particles are surrounded by fatty acids or fatty acid alkali hydrolytically split off and cease to cling to the hands A *priori* we might conclude that there would be a diminution in germs or disinfection associated with the cleaning of the hands; indeed, it was shown by earlier investigators and recently by H. REICHENBACH that soaps possess considerable germ-killing action. I was able to prove that there exists *absolute parallelism between the detergent and the disinfecting action of soaps.* It is impossible to disinfect the hands with soap in any practicable time (10 minutes), though this can be readily accomplished with alcohol and alcoholic solutions. According to H. BECHHOLD, the reason is that alcohol with its low dynamic surface tension readily enters the capillary interspaces of the bare hand where the bacteria are lodged, but aqueous solutions, on the contrary, enter them very slowly. This can be readily discovered by the difference in the distance they ascend in strips of filter paper.

[As the result of trench warfare the study of antiseptics in the treatment of wounds has received intensive study. Antiseptic surgery has been revived. CARREL and DEHELLY have elaborated a valuable system for the treatment of wounds by irrigation with antiseptics of the chlorin group. The whole subject of wound irrigation has been restudied and new antiseptics discovered.

J. F. McCLENDON, in the Journal of Laboratory and Clinical Medicine, August, 1917, discusses "The Relation of Physical Chemistry to the Irrigation of Wounds.' He emphasizes the importance of protecting the tissues from the effects of prolonged diffusion The action of the antiseptics employed is oxidative. "Oxidizing substances are, however, reduced by cells and an ideal local antiseptic would be one whose reduction product is indifferent. Hydrogen peroxide falls in this class but is not a powerful oxidizing agent and is decomposed by catalase so rapidly as to render a large percentage of it ineffective. It acts as a mechanical cleanser. If infusoria are placed in a solution of H_2O_2, the latter penetrates their protoplasm and is decomposed on the inside with the liberation of bubbles of oxygen which burst and destroy the cells. More useful agents are iodin and chlorin, especially the latter since HCl formed on its reduction may be neutralized by $NaHCO_3$ that has been added, and thus rendered indifferent. According to DAKIN and his collaborators, chlorin forms chloramines when it acts on protoplasm, and these chloramines have an antiseptic action. It is true, however, that chlorin oxidizes many organic compounds with the liberation of HCl. Chlorin gas escapes rapidly from its solution in water, but this may be retarded by the addition of a base transforming it into hypochlorite. Its oxidizing power is impaired, however, if the reaction is very alkaline, but may be restored by bubbling CO_2 through the solution."

McCLENDON emphasizes the importance of having the irrigating fluid physiologically normal. It is not enough in his opinion that the solution should contain the salts in the proper proportion but it must have the correct hydrogen ion concentration (p_H). This may be provided by bubbling CO_2 through the fluid and measuring the p_H with indicators

The most important new antiseptics are chloramine T or sodium toluene sulphonchloramide soluble in water, and dichloramine T or toluene-p-sulphone dichloramine soluble in organic solvents, and a paraffin saturated with chlorin, called chlorocozane. See Handbook of Antiseptics (DAKIN and DUNHAM). Tr.]

The Method of Testing Disinfectants Considered in the Light of Colloid Research.

For testing disinfectants bacteria are usually dried on silk threads or marbles. These are dipped in the disinfectant solution, and after the solution is removed they are placed in bouillon or fluidified agar. If the bacteria have been killed by the immersion, no germs develop.

From the length of time required to kill the germs and from the concentration of the disinfectant solution we may judge the strength of the disinfectant action

From the standpoint of the colloid chemist the silk thread procedure contains a serious error of method. Even at present on account of its apparent simplicity this method is frequently employed. We know from practical experience that silk is a very powerful adsorbent. The investigations of W Schellens * on the relation of silk to sublimate is of interest in this connection. He shook 1 gm silk with 50 c.c. of 1 per cent sublimate solution and then determined how much mercury was present both in the remaining fluid, and in the silk after it had been washed many times. He found that the silk had taken up 6.04 per cent of its weight of metallic mercury but had fixed only 1 9 per cent. We thus see that silk retains very considerable quantities of sublimate. Similar results were obtained by W. Schellens for ferric chlorid, ferric acetate, several mercuric salts, lead nitrate, etc. From this we must conclude that silk is not a suitable germ carrier for disinfection experiments, since as the result of adsorption (no action can be ascribed to the "fixed" mercury, etc) it retains too much disinfectant, on this account the germ cannot escape from the disinfectant, and accordingly we are only given information relative to inhibition of development and not concerning the lethal action Paul and Kronig chose, as germ carriers, marbles because the disinfectant can barely adhere to them by adsorption H Bechhold and P Ehrlich,* as well as H. Bechhold,*9 in their experiments on lethal action completely discarded germ carriers, they prepared bacterial cultures on agar, which they covered with the disinfectant fluid After removing the disinfectant, they washed the culture twice with physiological salt solution (which is finally made very faintly alkaline) and then transplanted the culture to a new medium (agar) On account of the thickness of the culture, very great demands are made upon the disinfectant by this method, but no germ carrier whatever is transferred to the new culture medium, and the method thus completely avoids the source of error mentioned above.

The experiments on the disinfectant action of *formaldehyd* gave such contradictory results, because the great adsorption of *formaldehyd* by silk was ignored, as was pointed out, especially by Schumberg.*

In order to annul the adsorptive action of germs and germ carriers in disinfection experiments, an attempt was made to render the disinfectant inactive by chemical means, as it was found impossible to accomplish this by washing. J. GEPPERT* inactivated sublimate by means of the action of ammonium sulphid; the sublimate is thus changed to the innocuous mercuric sulphid In the case of formaldehyd, ammonia is employed, for by means of ammonia, formaldehyd is changed to hexamethylentetramin. There is no chemical agent destructive for phenol and phenol-like compounds to which objections cannot be raised

From the colloid-chemical standpoint, I regard the principle of chemically removing the disinfectant as erroneous in many cases. The idea which guided GEPPERT and his successors was evidently that if a germ which had been immersed in a disinfectant is placed on a suitable culture medium, the medium abstracts the last traces of the adherent disinfectant; it is thus washed just as a chemist washes a crystalline precipitate on a filter In this way we consider the effect only *for the time during which the germ remained in the disinfectant,* and J GEPPERT and his followers seek to imitate this limited time by chemical destruction of the disinfectant when the germ is removed. As a matter of fact the process proceeds differently: when the germ is removed from the disinfectant and is placed on a fresh culture medium, it releases the disinfectant only slowly and incompletely in accordance with the laws of adsorption. We may compare the process to the "bleeding" of dyed fabric; especially the bleeding of cotton which has been dyed with a dye that is chemically insufficiently fixed by the fiber and which for days gives up color when washed with water; the dyer says it "bleeds." Thus for a long time by a pure adsorptive action the germ retains the disinfectant and is injured by it That this assumption is correct is shown by some experimental results taken from the literature, throughout which the expression is employed that the germs are "weakened." This expression appears to me to be the transfer to organisms to which it no longer applies of a conception applicable to men and higher animals.

According to J GEPPERT, anthrax spores are weakened but not killed by the action of 0.1 per cent sublimate solution for 15 minutes. They are unable to develop even in a culture medium which contains as little as 1 2,000,000 sublimate, whereas normal anthrax bacilli thrive quite well in this medium. Our interpretation of this is that anthrax spores previously treated with 1:1000 sublimate adsorbs so much sublimate that they are in adsorption equilibrium with a nutrient medium that contains 1:2,000,000 sublimate.

HEINZ says, "Sublimate acts in animal infections just the same as when transplanted upon artificial media and the minutest traces suffice to prevent multiplication or the infection of animals on the part of the germs weakened by the antiseptic "

"Anthrax bacilli (HEINZ) like anthrax spores prior to the lethal action show a stage of weakness in which the bacilli are unable to grow in a nutritive medium containing a minimal amount of disinfectant Thus anthrax bacilli which had been immersed in 1 per cent carbolic acid (and had not been killed) did not grow in a culture medium which contained a small amount of carbolic acid," whereas fresh anthrax bacilli grew luxuriantly.

I find a very instructive example in OTTOLENGHI's * paper. He says, "The fact is very interesting, that occasionally certain paper strips (he soaked blotting paper strips with an emulsion of anthrax spores, dried them and then placed them in sublimate solution) after they have been subjected for 24 hours to a sublimate solution (up to 2.712 per cent) and were inoculated into guinea pigs, may yield a *luxuriant development of anthrax bacilli* if they are removed from the thoroughly healthy animal after one week and are placed on media after a thorough treatment with H₂S." The results of H REICHEN-BACH[1] are to be judged from the same standpoint   After treating anthrax spores with sublimate, they first lost their activity in the bodies of animals, then their ability to grow in bouillon (without ammonium sulphid treatment) and only after a much longer time did they cease to grow, even after treatment with ammonium sulphid.

Unquestionably numerous analogous examples would be found were the literature carefully studied.

It may be seen from this that in disinfection experiments, the chemical removal of the disinfectant may lead to false results, that it may simulate a weaker action of the disinfectant than it actually has, i.e., a weaker action than it possesses in practice under natural conditions.   On this account I regard repeated washing of the germs with indifferent solvents (water or physiological salt solution which is finally made faintly alkaline with soda) as the proper method for the removal of the disinfectant.   Whatever is retained by the germ after such a washing would also be retained under natural conditions.   The BECHHOLD-EHRLICH method of killing germs (see p. 406) meets all these conditions correctly.

This criticism relates to the testing of disinfectants against germs which can directly enter the organism (disinfection of the hands, antiseptics, etc.). It is otherwise with substances which serve for the disinfection of stools. sputum, etc.   Under these circumstances we must consider that the disinfectants penetrate an environ-

[1] According to personal letter See also H REICHENBACH, Zeitschr. f. Hygiene und. Infectionskrankh , 50, 455, u 460–462 (1905)

ment which contains hydrogen sulphid, ammonia, etc. The testing of a disinfectant must always take its use into consideration and be accordingly varied in different cases. [The criterion of CARREL and DEHELLY is the bacterial count per field in smears taken from the wound Tr.]

Diuretics and Purgatives.

Diuresis and defecation may be influenced in the most varied ways, for instance by increased blood pressure or by increased peristalsis — in brief, by such factors as chiefly exert a more or less specific nervous action, similar effects may be obtained by a purely mechanical facilitation of secretion or by hindrance of absorption.

We have repeatedly referred to the lyotropic series of the alkaline salts (see pp. 80 and 296) and have shown among other things, that there exists a remarkable parallelism between the swelling of gelatin and fibrin, the precipitation of albumin and lecithin and the irritability of frog's muscle and ciliated epithelium. Also for diuresis and defecation there exist such evident relationships which we shall here elucidate. We give the classification of F. HOFMEISTER. The figures above the columns I, II, etc , indicate the concentration of the salt solutions which are necessary to salt out globulin.

I	II	III	IV	V.
1 51-1 66	2-2 03	2 51-2 72	3 53-3 63	5 42-5 52
Li sulphate	NH₄ sulphate	Mg sulphate	NaCl	Na nitrate
Na sulphate		NH₄ phosphate	KCl	Na chlorate
Na phosphate		NH₄ citrate		
K phosphate		NH₄ tartrate		
K acetate		Na carbonate		
Na acetate				
K citrate				
Na citrate				
K tartrate				
Na tartrate				

The various members of Group I are purgatives; those of IV and V are diuretics, while the action of those in II and III with the exception of magnesium sulphate are not sufficiently definite to be of any service

Obviously, the anion is of the greatest importance for the action of the above salts: we observe that Cl and NO₃ have the highest rate of diffusion and are most rapidly absorbed NaCl, KCl and NaNO₃ aid swelling so that a gel swells more rapidly in such a salt solution than in pure water From this it follows that the intestine will take up such solutions more rapidly than pure water. Accordingly, all the conditions necessary to give the body a large quantity of dilute salt solution are fulfilled. We know from Chapter XIV that there is a strong effort on the part of the mammalian organism to keep constant the swollen condition of the blood and tissues, as well as the osmotic pressure For this purpose, the kidney is most important, since it is able to remove excess of water and salts. We may even at present recognize thus the qualitative relationship between physical properties and the diuretic action of Groups IV and V Unfortunately, we are not in a position to pursue the process quantitatively, but we may assume that there would not be a simple relationship The above-mentioned physical properties of Groups IV and V are to be classified not only in reference to the intestinal membranes and the kidney function, but they also pay a rôle in the irritation of nerves and the contraction of muscle (see p. 289 *et seq* and p. 354). According to Wo Pauli [*3] the majority of cations raise the blood pressure, whereas Br depresses it. This explains why bromids are of no use as diuretics in spite of the fact that they might be classified as such from their behavior with colloids, the depression of blood pressure they cause opposes their diuretic action. Hypotonic common salt solution and potassium nitrate solutions remain therefore the chief diuretics among the alkali salts. In fact, it is the solution of common salt which plays, in the Spa "mineral water cures," the chief part in increasing the urinary excretion.

The result is quite different when solutions are introduced directly into the blood stream A physiological salt solution is excreted practically quantitatively If we inject a hypertonic salt solution, then more water will be excreted than was introduced, and (within certain limits) proportionately more will be excreted the greater the concentration. This is not surprising, because the salt withdraws the water of swelling, especially from the blood corpuscles and the muscles The water thus set "free" is then filtered away by the kidneys Sulphates, phosphates, tartrates and citrates, etc , of sodium impede diuresis when taken by mouth; however, when directly injected into the blood stream, they are even more strongly diuretic than common salt This depends on their strong dehydrating action and their low diffusibility. Martin H. Fischer by introducing such salts was able to make a kidney, which had been edematous by ligating the renal artery, function again. On injecting an appropriate salt into the renal artery or even into the kidney itself the swelling subsided and the anuria ceased.

According to E Frey,* if we inject the salts mentioned along with narcotics (morphine, chloral, ether, urethan), no diuresis develops, and on the other hand the absorption of water from the intestines is unimpaired This is explained by the fact mentioned (p. 338), that such narcotics inhibit the oxidizing processes in the organism, which results in a greater fixation of water ("acid swelling").

What holds for electrolytes is also true for nonelectrolytes. We have recognized in urea a substance which greatly aids diffusion through jellies (see p 55) and which opens through the hydrogel paths for itself and other substances, as a matter of fact it acts as a diuretic. I wish to mention some additional facts concerning ammonium salts and the cleavage products of protein. All the evidence (see pp. 80 to 82) is in favor of the view that the action of the cations and of the anions of an electrolyte is antagonistic and that they mutually counteract a portion of their own activity. Thus NH_4 seems to oppose the precipitating and dehydrating action of SO_4, citrate, and tartrate anions to a greater extent than K and Na (see the Series III of our group). If we bring this into relation with analogous action of urea $CO \begin{array}{c} \diagup NH_2 \\ \diagdown NH_2 \end{array}$ we may in general attribute to the NH_2 and NH_4 groups the property of aiding diffusion and we also understand the ease with which protein cleavage products are absorbed, for they occur in the intestines largely split into substances with free NH and NH_2 groups.

Martin H. Fischer explains the diuretic action of *digitalis* preparations and of *caffein* as follows. They increase the strength and frequency of the pulse, increase the utilization of oxygen and thus the blood supply of the kidneys is increased and the "free" water in the blood is increased and may be excreted. This agrees with the results of Sobieranski, Hirokowa and Grunwald who found that the diuretic action of *caffein, theobromin* and *diuretin* depended on their interference with reabsorption.

Grunwald was able to show, for instance, that rabbits on a chlorin-free diet when treated with theobromin finally perished for want of chlorin. The chlorin removed from the body by ultrafiltration was not restored by reabsorption.

Purgatives.

If we wish to explain the action of purgatives we must first review the processes in the intestines. The intestine is the place where *secretion* and *absorption* occur. The volume of the *secretion* of the salivary glands, the stomach, bile, pancreas and intestine is, according to H. MEYER and R. GOTTLIEB,* about 3 to 4.5 liters daily. The amount reabsorbed is a still larger quantity. An increased absorption of fluid is followed by an increased secretion of fluid into the intestine. The final result depends on whether more fluid is absorbed or secreted (into the intestine) or *vice versa*. If the secretion exceeds reabsorption the intestinal contents are *fluid* and *voluminous*, and we have one of the conditions for easy defecation On this account substances having a capacity for swelling counteract constipation. Persons suffering from constipation are recommended to eat considerable quantities of *vegetables* and *graham bread*, because the indigestible cellulose they contain retains water. This accounts for the laxative action of agar. In addition, all substances which act on the intestinal nerves by increasing peristalsis will favor defecation.

The effect of alkali salts have been most exhaustively investigated, but before we consider them we must recall the observations of LOEPER.* He found that salt solutions which were introduced orally either in hypertonic or in hypotonic solution, when they reached the intestine were in practically isotonic solution. We can accordingly disregard all hypotheses which seek to explain the action of purgatives by differences of the osmotic pressure of the intestinal contents. If hypertonic or hypotonic salt solutions have an effect notwithstanding, we must explain this by indirect action, for hypertonic salt solutions inhibit gastric movements and thus interfere with the progress of the chyme from stomach to intestine.

We saw that the chlorids and nitrates are diuretics; the sulphates, phosphates, citrates and tartrates are chiefly purgatives, so that the last-mentioned anions must possess properties which either increase secretion, diminish absorption, or strengthen peristalsis.

Some diuretics may purge by reason of increased secretion. Table salt acts in this way and, in mild constipation, it is given in dry form in Spa cures, or as sodium bicarbonate.[1]

In the case of the real purgatives of Group I, it is a question whether their action is directly on the intestinal mucous membrane or whether they increase peristalsis through nerve stimulation. Possibly they may impede the absorption of themselves and other substances by dehydrating and precipitating albumin. This does occur in high concentration (1 gram equivalent Na_2SO_4). G. QUAGLIARI-ELLO * has shown in the case of sodium sulphate that for such salt concentrations as enter the intestine after passing through the stomach, the imbibition of water is no different than for sodium chlorid, and accordingly that *there is no direct action* by such purgative salts on the *intestinal mucous membrane.*

[1] Changes into sodium chlorid with the gastric hydrochloric acid.

We must therefore strive to discover what facts speak for a strengthening of peristalsis by such salts.

Interesting observations by MacCallum* in agreement with observations by J. Loeb *² show, as a matter of fact, that the salts of Group I exert on muscle and nerve a stimulating effect which induces an *increased peristalsis* of the intestines. This occurs not only when citrates, tartrates and sulphates are placed in the lumen of the intestine but also when they are injected subcutaneously or intravenously, and even dropping a $\frac{m}{8}$ solution of such salts on the peritoneal surface of the intestines induces especially strong peristaltic intestinal movement, so that according to Wo. Pauli *³ the intestinal activity may even approach that of a gastro-enteritis. With this increase of peristalsis there is associated an *active secretion* into the intestine, so that according to MacCallum the *empty coils of small intestine* of a rabbit became filled with secretion (20 c.c.) when a drop of sodium citrate solution was placed on the peritoneal coat   I wish to recall that these anions raise the blood pressure, and possibly the increased secretory activity stands in relation to this.

Magnesium sulphate is one of the best known cathartics, although on account of its place in Group III of our table we would hardly expect that it should have any special action. This need not surprise us, since there are in the intestine Na ions which largely inhibit the antagonistic action of Mg ions, and as a result the SO₄ action is brought out. According to MacCallum, if we introduce MgCl₂ (instead of MgSO₄) or CaCl₂ solution into the intestine, or inject them into the circulation, the peristaltic waves which citrates or fluorids, for instance, strongly induce, are inhibited. This agrees completely with our premises, according to which there exists high antagonistic action of divalent cations (see p. 82) as here exemplified CaCl₂ diminishes diuresis as well as defecation

Frankl* and Auer* found certain contradictions to the results of MacCallum. They claim to have observed no diarrhea upon injecting subcutaneously or intravenously dilute purgative salts, and to have observed even constipation upon employing more concentrated solutions. J. Bancroft,* on the contrary, confirms the results of MacCallum From all of which it may be concluded that, as was to be expected, the result chiefly depends upon the conditions of concentration and upon the location where these conditions are active. In this connection the old experiments of von Hay* are very instructive. If he gave large quantities of sodium sulphate by mouth, it abstracted fluid until its concentration had fallen to 3 per cent after which diarrhea occurred. If he deprived the animal of water for 1 or 2 days and gave only a dry diet, even concentrated solutions of Glauber's salt (20 gm. salt) had no cathartic action. The same quantity of salt diluted to a 5 per cent solution resulted in strong catharsis after one or two hours. We see, therefore, that the condition of the tissues and blood colloids in respect to swelling play a most important part in these processes. On this account it is possible to employ the salts of Group I and MgSO4 either to purge or to *dehydrate* the body as may be necessary. It is important to consider how purgative action is to be measured; whether according to the amount of dried substance passed or according to the total quantity including the fluid. A fluid stool permits us to conclude that there is an increase of secretion or a diminution of absorption, an increased amount of solid feces suggests an increase of peristalsis

Astringents.

Constipating substances, *i.e.*, those which diminish the intestinal or even the gastric secretion and peristalsis, are substances which diminish stimuli. As such are employed, as has been mentioned on page 365, hydrophile colloids (mucilages, etc), as well as strongly adsorbent suspensions (talc, bismuth subnitrate, bismuth subgallate). More powerful actions are obtained with such substances which *tan* the intestinal membrane superficially and in this way interfere with the secretion of the intestinal glands, or at least arrest absorption at the point affected. Most important of these is *tannin* and such tannin compounds as are dissolved in the intestinal juice (tannalbin, tannigen).

BALNEOLOGY.

It would certainly be a fortunate circumstance for balneology if we knew but a small fraction as much about the physiological action of medicinal springs as we at present know of their physical and chemical properties. Every mineral spring, no matter how insignificant, has its chemical composition determined to the fifth decimal; its osmotic pressure, conductivity, radioactivity, etc , are investigated and the *possibilities* of its therapeutic activity are lauded and its clinical successes (not the failures) are carefully registered.

The scientifically determinable and explicable effects are considered by very few. From these remarks it must not be concluded that valuable clinical results are not to be obtained by means of balneology, but that its scientific basis is largely undetermined.

Water and Solutions.

In Chapter XIV I stated that the body colloids have a normal state of swelling and that they stand in definite *swelling relations* to each other. Thus, when the condition of swelling in one organ, *i e.*, the muscles, changes, it must in turn influence the condition of swelling of other body colloids; as in the case of every other substance there is for *water*, a definite *distribution* in the organism This *distribution of water* is dependent on the *capacity* of the organ colloids *to swell* and this again largely depends on the amount of electrolytes contained.

It is very probable that during life the crystalloid content of organ colloids suffer certain changes which may even become pathological Under such circumstances, it is conceivable that a thorough flushing of the body with water such as our ancestors were accustomed to undertake every spring to "purify the blood" might be of great value inasmuch as it restores the normal swelling

It would be very desirable for the elucidation of this question to undertake a thorough experimental investigation of the swelling capacity and swelling range of the organs at various ages under normal and pathological conditions.

Just as a drinking "cure" so a thirst "cure" (SCHROTH's "cure") may influence the condition of swelling. [KARELL's Treatment as well as TUFFNEL's owe much of their efficacy to "drink restriction." (See p. 234.) Tr]

In various parts of this book, there have been thoroughly described the great significance of electrolytes for the swelling of cell colloids, the viscosity of the blood, the influence of heavy metals on solubility (urates, lime salts) and the acceleration of fermentative cleavages and syntheses, *i.e.*, the acceleration of metabolism. The introduction into the body of electrolytes in the form of *mineral waters* is the original and essential function of balneology. It is. quite conceivable, that the increase in the body of definite anions or cations might satisfy important therapeutic demands. [Radioactivity should be considered a possible therapeutic adjuvant, see ZWAARDEMAKER, H., Aequi-radioactivity, Am. Jour. Physiol., 1918, XLV, p. 147. Tr.]

We have at present nothing to support even the idea, that concentration of a definite electrolyte is possible.

There are a few indications which favor this view. It may be recalled, that hypertonic salt solutions result in a destruction of tissue; hypotonic solutions, in a diminished metabolism of protein (see E Rosr *) We must also remember that cells are not impermeable for ions, but that accompanying the abstraction of water by hypertonic solutions a penetration or interchange of ions may occur.

For the diuretic and purgative action of neutral salts see page 409 et seq.

SALVES, LINIMENTS.

Salves and similar preparations are frequently employed not only to cover wounds but also with the object of introducing medicines into the body through the skin. The skin absorbs only such substances as are soluble in fat; this has been established by the investigations of W. Filehne.* and A. Schwenkenbecher.*

The colloidal properties of fats deserve our attention. The cooling sensation induced by *cold cream* depends on its capacity for holding water; it takes up about 28 per cent water which is obviously the dispersed phase. Wool fat is "hydrophile" to a still greater extent. It enters commerce as *lanolin* and is the basis for salves. We saw that by means of hydrophile lecithin water-soluble, though ordinarily fat-insoluble, substances, such as sugar, become soluble in fat. Possibly we may attribute to this property, when it is present, the penetration into the body through the skin by means of salves, of medicaments for which the skin is otherwise impermeable. [Wes-eron, Jour. Industr. and Eng. Chem., Vol. IX., p. 1125 gives the method for preparing cetyl alcohol as a substitute for lanolin and eucerin. Tr.]

P. G. Unna* showed that the hydrophile constituent of wool fat is the oxycholesterin group. Five parts of this latter mixed with 95 parts of paraffin ointment are able to unite with 100 per cent of water. (It enters commerce as eucerin.)

CHAPTER XXIII.

MICROSCOPICAL TECHNIC.

THE microscopic study of organisms and parts of organs is one of the most important tasks of biologists and physicians. The principal object of the microscopist is to deduce from the form of an object its nature and whether its appearance is normal or diseased.

Remarkable progress has been made in this field though the chemical interpretation of the methods employed is still in its infancy.

To prepare an object for microscopical examination it must be spread out very thin upon a slide and, if necessary, made transparent. In the case of unicellular organisms (bacteria, protozoa, etc.) no further preparation is necessary. If the presence of bacteria is to be determined it suffices to spread the object in question on a slide with a platinum loop and to dry it at moderate temperature by drawing the slide through a Bunsen flame several times, so as to coagulate the albumin. On account of the intensity with which bacteria and cocci stain with basic dyes (methylene blue, carbol fuschin, etc.) it is usually an easy matter to recognize them in the otherwise structureless coagulum.

Organs of higher plants and animals must be either teased or prepared in thin sections.

The least deceptive object is naturally the living organism, as we see it, for instance, in hanging drops, in the moist chamber or the microscope stage aquarium of J. Cohn, etc.; even in higher animals some investigations may be made while they are still alive by spreading out portions of organs still connected with the animal so that they are transparent. In this way we may see, for instance, the circulation of the blood in the lungs and in the web of a frog's foot. Much more frequently an opportunity to examine surviving tissue presents itself. It is by no means necessary that at the moment that the animal itself dies, a given organ or cell should die. Let me recall that the heart may be isolated immediately after an animal (cat, frog, etc.) has been killed and may continue to beat for a long time if suitable means are employed. Leucocytes of warm blooded animals show protoplasmic movements, if observed at 37°, even as long as a half day after the animal's death. It goes without saying that this must occur in a medium which causes neither swelling nor

417

shrinking   Pure water is never suited for this; a salt solution which approaches in its composition that which bathes the organ is best   In many cases "physiological salt solution" is ample, in mammals this contains 0.85 per cent common salt, in other kinds of animals this may advantageously be reduced to 0.5 per cent   Even though the living or surviving organism presents a microscopical picture devoid of artifacts, on the one hand it is rarely possible to examine it and, on the other, many details are concealed, since the refraction of the different cell elements is almost equal.   On this account we are compelled to section and stain the organs.

Since even the death of the cell causes changes in structure, these changes with the chemical manipulations about to be described may reach a grade which leads to the gravest errors   Only absolute ignorance of colloid processes explains how artificially produced flocculations, coagulations and striations (after treatment with silver nitrate and potassium bichromate), etc , could be considered definite constituents of cells, and it is a pity that numerous painstaking investigations must, as a result of this, be considered mere waste paper.   By indicating these errors A. FISCHER and WALTHER BERG, as well as TH. v. WASIELEWSKI, performed a great service. Accordingly, A. FISCHER distinguishes reagents which form granules (nuclei) and those which form congula, and W. BERG, also calls attention to those which produce granulated pellicles and cavities.

If then, as may be seen from the foregoing, we may obtain different structures by means of different reagents acting on the same bodies and, conversely, with the same chemical substance produce the same microscopic picture on different bodies, we may by accurate comparative experiments make valuable deductions.   It is hardly possible to employ such methods in determining form, but for the understanding of the colloidal nature of the object examined they offer a broad, uncultivated and promising field for colloid research.

The preparation of dead material for microscopic examination may be divided into maceration and isolation, fixation and hardening, decalcification, bleaching, embedding, sectioning and mounting, and finally staining.[1]

Maceration and Isolation.

Maceration and isolation are for the purpose of dissolving apart the constituents of an organ (cells) and thus to recognize their connection and to make it possible to examine the isolated cells.   The

[1] I have for the most part followed here the directions given in the "Lehrbuch der Mikroskopischen Technik" of Prof. Dr B GRAWITZ (Leipzig, 1907), whose numerous detailed directions should be of valuable assistance to every biochemist

objects are placed (depending on the variety) in 15 to 35 per cent alcohol or in physiological salt solution which contains 2 cc of 40 per cent formaldehyd per liter, or into 0.1 per cent to 0.005 per cent chromic acid, or 1 per cent osmic acid, dilute picric acid, 20 per cent nitric acid, pure HCl, javelle water or many other solutions recommended for particular purposes. Obviously, with the first mentioned substances we may dissolve the connections *by a differential shrinking of the cell constituents,* because as we shall see the identical substances are employed in different concentrations for fixation and for hardening. Substances such as 20 per cent nitric acid, pure HCl, etc., obviously change the cement substances chemically. We understand the action of digestive fluids (pepsin-HCl, pancreatin) to be similar, yet they have not proven very satisfactory. After successful "maceration" it is sometimes sufficient to shake violently the object which has been treated to cause it to fall apart or it may be teased on the slide with needles or a coarse brush.

Fixing and Hardening.

Whereas the methods previously described permit the recognition of individual elements of a tissue, they do not permit a study of the relations of the tissue elements, their connections and, in short, the entire tissue structure. For this purpose a thin section of tissue must be prepared and stained Before doing this it is frequently necessary to fix and harden the object to be studied

Fixation is undertaken for the purpose of making the partly fluid and partly semifluid constituents firm, so that they stop changing, neither swelling, shrinking, coagulating nor the like and so that their appearance shall remain as nearly lifelike, or at least as fresh as possible, in order that this condition shall be maintained through all the later manipulations. By fixation, the relations between the different tissue elements are made permanent. The object is frequently too soft to section, so that it must be subjected to a special procedure, hardening. Viewed colloid-chemically, tissues may be considered to consist of (1) *irreversible slightly elastic gels,* (2) *reversible elastic gels,* (3) *sols.* All sorts of transition states exist

Accordingly, fixation renders each constituent completely insoluble, unshrinkable and incapable of swelling, the sols are changed to gels, and no shrinking or swelling should occur during the fixation. Finally, it must be possible to stain the objects well, and consequently their chemical properties must not be too radically changed. It is a problem almost impossible to solve. For the sake of comparison, every one knows how great and almost insuperable difficulties are often presented by the fusing together of a metal wire and a glass tube because of the different degree of contraction (shrinking) upon cooling. Cracks frequently occur. Now imagine how very complicated the problem becomes whenever three, four or perhaps a dozen fused ingredients are subjected to a manipulation to which they react differently. This simple consideration teaches us that we can never expect a piece of tissue that is fixed and hardened to show the same appearance as when it is alive. Only by comparing pieces of tissue, treated in different ways, can we recognize what is normal and what is due to fixation, but even in these distorted pieces we can see the places of least resistance where inequalities of staining exist, and by careful consideration we can learn much even from such pieces as are regarded as spoiled by histologists

Of course, a fixative must not block its own path. If massive organs, *e.g*, the brain or liver, are to be fixed, the fixative solutions have a great distance to travel before they reach the center, if shrinkages or precipitates are formed at the periphery, the diffusion paths are closed at the outset and the fixative could never reach the center even if such objects should lie in the fluid for weeks   It is quite reasonable to expect that in such large organs the central portion will show a different kind of fixation than the periphery

We can well understand how temperature plays an important rôle, conditioning not only the rate of diffusion but also governing the processes of coagulation.

Wherever feasible the objects are cut into small pieces and placed in very large quantities of fixative fluids (50–100 times the volume of the object) so that too great a dilution shall not occur and the action shall be quite uniform, if the fixation is prolonged the fluid must be renewed from time to time.

Among the fixatives an important rôle is played by certain electrolytes (chromic acid, bichromate, mercuric chlorid, picric acid, etc); they cause swelling in solutions that are too dilute, shrinking in too concentrated solutions.   On this account C. DEKHUYSEN and W STOELTZNER prepared "isotonic" solutions which cause neither swelling nor shrinking.   These authors, as may be seen from their method of expression (hypertonic, hypotonic), evidently proceeded from premises which depend upon osmotic pressure, a factor involved only to a very limited extent.   By treating the whole practice of fixation from a colloid standpoint, doubtless a whole series of valuable new methods of fixation would be evolved for histologists   Such a study would furnish us with more definite rules for knowing why, on the one hand, one solution is more suitable for marine animals, and on the other, why other solutions are more suitable for mammalian organs.

It is quite clear that the action of the same fixative differs, depending upon the variation of the electrolyte content of various animals and plants.

From what has been said, it may be concluded that alkaline solutions are not to be considered fixatives, since they produce only swelling. The salts of the light metals are not included among fixatives; they usually form reversible gels; but, on the contrary, certain heavy metals as well as acids, especially the acid mixtures, are of great importance. Many have an oxidizing action, as a result of which the organic substances lose their ability to swell.[1]

Acids are obviously employed with the object of changing sols into gels, and since a chemical change must simultaneously occur, it follows that all acids are not available for this purpose and that they must always be employed in high concentration Hydrochloric acid and sulphuric acid (the latter, at least, never unmixed) are not employed as fixatives, but we do frequently employ nitric acid in 2 to 10 per cent concentration. Its use is not general since it frequently alters the stains For organs with epidermal coverings, nitric acid is unsuitable since it raises the epithelium in blisters from the tissues supporting it.

Chromic acid (introduced by HANNOVER in 1840) is the oldest and most used fixative and hardening agent for cell protoplasm and nucleus. It is used in concentrations of from 0 33 per cent up to 1 per cent. It is employed preferably in the dark, since daylight causes a sort of tanning of the periphery so that the chromic acid penetrates very slowly and amorphous deposits form very easily in the preparation.

Objects fixed in chromic acid or its salts become green in time (reduction to chromic oxid) and are poorly stained. Many methods for regenerating the staining capacity of such specimens have been proposed (L. EDINGER and MAYER, B. GRAWITZ).

Osmic acid (0.5 to 2 per cent) is especially recommended for the fixation of protoplasm and nucleus. It is soluble in fat and consequently can penetrate the living cell. It does not penetrate far, however, and on this account is available only for small or thin objects. With the fixation there is a blackening, especially of the fats and some other substances (reduction to colloidal osmium). Opinions on the use of osmic acid are very divergent. Though praised by some, A. FISCHER, as the result of his studies of non-biological material, considers it a weak, unsatisfactory precipitating agent, since it precipitates only acid reacting structures.

---

[1] To fix tissue practically, the exact directions as they are found in the books must be followed, they are employed just as a cooking recipe would be. Only a few generalizations can be given here.

Acetic acid alone (in concentration up to 1 per cent) causes swelling, but is suitable for combination with reagents which cause shrinking, especially for the fixation of nuclear structures

Trichloracetic acid (5 per cent to 10 per cent) penetrates rapidly, destroys the most delicate structural relations of protoplasm and nucleus but fixes well centrosomes, chromosomes and spindles   Since fibrillar connective tissue swells strongly in trichloracetic acid, the preparation must be placed at once in absolute alcohol.

Picric acid does not change all sols and reversible gels into irreversible gels. This follows from the results of A. FISCHER who showed that precipitations with picric acid are dissolved again by water, and this is confirmed by the experience of histologists with actual specimens   Only when combined with other acids (acetic acid, chromic acid, sulphuric acid, nitric acid and osmic acid) does picric acid attain its importance as a fixative, and under these circumstances it is highly praised.

Since picric acid is lipoid soluble and forms insoluble dye salts with dye bases it is suitable for fixing specimens after "vital staining."

Salts. Among these, the chlorids next to the chromates enjoy especial popularity. I attribute this to their ease of diffusion and to the fact that in respect to swelling and shrinking, the chlorin ion occupies approximately a middle position.

Copper chlorid and *copper acetate* are suitable for delicate lower plants but are very seldom employed.

Mercuric chlorid in concentrated aqueous solution is very suitable for the fixation of animal preparations. I have had very good results in fixing leucocytes. It may not be employed for any molluscs or for fresh water crustaceans; it also seems not quite suitable for plant cells   As a result of a certain amount of lipoid solubility it is able to penetrate the living cells and on this account in vital staining it serves to fix the dye. Obviously, part of the mercuric chlorid is in this case bound by the protoplasmic albumin; the resulting combination is somewhat insoluble in water.

Ferric chlorid in alcoholic solution is recommended for pelagic marine animals.

Platinum chlorid (0.1 to 1 per cent), *palladious chlorid* (0.1 per cent) and *iridium chlorid* are recommended for special purposes (usually in mixtures).

Potassium bichromate is rarely used as a pure solution, since it markedly changes the structure, but used in combination with other substances it is a very popular fixative (with acetic acid for cell substance and nuclear structure; with sodium sulphate for the central nervous system; with copper sulphate for bulky objects; with sublimate, etc.).

Nonelectrolytes.

Alcohol. Although diluted alcohol causes shrinking, by employing absolute alcohol (not under 99.5 per cent) we obtain in the case of compact structures (spleen, kidneys, digestive glands, etc.) a fixation without shrinking. The explanation of this is found in the double action of alcohol, both precipitating and chemical. The latter which effects the transformation of sols and reversible gels into irreversible gels requires a certain time and indeed more time the more dilute the alcohol is, so that we must endeavor to hurry the chemical action as much as possible by employing concentrated alcohol. The double action of alcohol may be easily demonstrated: If a solution of albumin is poured into alcohol a moderate amount of precipitate is formed which dissolves again upon diluting with water; the longer the time that elapses before diluting, the less is dissolved and the further has the chemical coagulation process advanced. Besides ethyl alcohol, methyl alcohol may be employed.

Formaldehyd (Formol or Formalin). The 40 per cent formol solution in the shops is usually diluted 10 times with water; if we speak of 10 per cent formol solution we mean that it contains 4 per cent of formaldehyd. Such a solution is preferable for uniform fixation and preservation of compact organs (liver, brains); it is less desirable for cell and nuclear structures. A 4 per cent formaldehyd solution is the best preservative for scientists on collecting expeditions, even though it is not well adapted for fixation. After formol fixation the staining is often not all that could be desired. The preeminent properties of formol depend on the fact that it is chemically very active, easily diffusible and hardly at all adsorbed by organic substances. The *chemical* process of tanning which is very similar to fixing, is much less complicated with formol than with *tannin* and *pyrogallic acid*, with which an adsorption precedes the chemical change. These two substances are hardly ever employed alone; at times they follow fixation with osmium.

We have now reviewed the most important substances used as fixatives. In practical histology almost all of them are used in mixtures. We employ chromic acid + acetic acid, potassium bichromate + sublimate + glacial acetic acid, nitric acid + potassium bichromate, osmic acid + potassium bichromate, chromic acid + picric acid + nitric acid, alcohol + glacial acetic acid, etc. Directions for fixing tissues are legion, but they are "cooking recipes" without any thought whatsoever of the chemistry involved. For a truly scientific "theory of fixation" it would be necessary first to consider the condition of the solutions involved, so that even the fundamental facts would have to be experimentally determined, and then only would we be in a position to determine their action on colloids. At present we lack almost the very essentials for the development of a rational method from this wilderness of directions.

Hardening.

Hardening follows fixation. For this purpose alcohol is almost exclusively used; it is gradually concentrated, beginning with 50 per cent alcohol and then increasing the strength 10 per cent until 96 per cent alcohol is reached A preliminary washing out of the fixative is required, only if it forms precipitates with alcohol.

In order to make thin sections with the microtome or razor it is usually necessary to embed the preparation; in structures containing lime, siliceous or chitinous deposits, these must be removed first by employing suitable acids. Finally, the sections must be mounted. We shall not discuss these manipulations at greater length, since they are purely technical.

From our viewpoint, however, a very important procedure is

Staining.

Unstained specimens are usually so uniformly transparent that it is difficult or almost impossible to distinguihs their intimate structure. In order easily to recognize the individual structures, histologists make use of stains. As has been said, they are chiefly concerned with a *morphological* classification, to see cells, it usually suffices to stain the nuclei, cell division, spermatogenesis and secretion require specific stains. It is remarkable that but few, especially P. EHRLICH, P. G. UNNA among others, have considered what conclusions concerning the *chemical nature* of the stained substance may be derived from staining. We are unacquainted with any conclusions concerning the *physical* nature (density) of tissues. The elaboration of these investigations would be of great importance, since staining pictures for us the action of drugs, toxins and disinfectants.

The Theory of Staining.

Though supporters of the chemical and of the physical theories of dyeing were until recently actively disputing, there are mutual concessions at present. We have recognized that dyeing does not occur in response to a fundamental law but that various complicating factors enter, great variations being possible by reason of the variety of dyes and fabrics.

OTTO N. WITT proposed the theory that the dye occurred in the fiber in *solid solution*. This assumption can only apply to the initial stages as G. V. GEORGIEVICS showed, in experiments on the absorption of acids by wool. The further absorption of dyes, in general, corresponds to an adsorption. This is the result of quantitative studies of the distribution of dyes between fiber and liquor (the technical name for the dye solution).

We owe this knowledge to the researches of J. R. APPLEYARD and J. WALKER, W. BILTZ, H FREUNDLICH and G. LOSEV, G. V. GEORGIEVICS and L. PELET-JOLIVET; these experiments show, moreover, that there is no essential difference between the adsorption of formic acid by blood charcoal and of indigo-carmine by silk. What applies to textile fibers we may apply as well to animal and plant tissues.

In technical dyeing which has formed the chief basis of theoretical studies, the addition of electrolytes (NaCl, Na₂SO₄, etc.) are important factors which modify the state of swelling of the fabric and markedly influence the tendency of the more or less colloidal dye to precipitate; in biological staining electrolytes are not used to such an extent, but they always enter as factors.

The course of the adsorption curve requires that proportionately much more dye shall be removed from a very dilute solution than from one that is more concentrated, an observation which impresses every one who investigates dyes

It must be assumed if adsorption phenomena are involved, that the entire dye may be removed by sufficiently prolonged washing, *i.e.*, that the process is reversible; this, as is well known, is contrary to the facts. The adherents of the adsorption theory maintain that traces of the strongly adsorbed dyes which can no longer be recognized in the dye bath or wash water are in adsorption balance with the dye taken up by the fiber.

In most cases of true dyeing, fixation may be brought about by secondary intercurrent chemical processes between fiber and dye This firm union between fiber and dye is what the adherents of the chemical theory of dyeing (M. HEIDENHAIN, E. KNECHT, W. SUIDA and his pupils) chiefly advance in support of their theory. They say, in general, that the textile fiber is a complex organic substance which undergoes a double decomposition with a dye salt, just the same as any other salt, the result of this double decomposition is on the one hand an insoluble compound (textile fiber-dye) and on the other a soluble compound which passes into the bath, e.g.,

wool + rosanilin hydrochlorid = wool rosanilin base + ammonium chlorid.

The adherents of the adsorption theory insist that the dye salts are frequently strongly hydrolyzed in solution, so that there is, accordingly, only an adsorption of the color base or color acid, but on this account no chemical double decomposition is required in the staining, inasmuch as fibers, as well as dye, are often colloids of opposite charge which mutually precipitate each other. In favor of this view is the fact that a dye solution stains the better, the more colloidal it is. The numerous minute additions employed in microscopical stains (methylene blue with a trace of alkali, gentian violet with anilin water, etc.) are usually added for the purpose of making from a true solution one less dispersed. P. G. UNNA, who first recognized this, applied the characteristic term "incipient precipitation" to the condition of a staining fluid most suitable for staining. Finally, we shall indicate another point made by adherents of the adsorption theory; that in those cases in which hydrolytic cleavage is not demonstrable, we frequently observe, — not only in the case of textile fibers but also in adsorption by charcoal and silicates, — that with the taking up of the dye, a cleavage of the dye salt occurs (demonstrated for crystal violet, fuchsin, etc.), whereby the cation (dye base) goes to the adsorbent and the anion goes into the solution. (This is chiefly true of basic dyes.)

Such phenomena were first demonstrated by J. M. VAN BEMMELEN in the adsorption of potassium sulphate by hydrated manganese dioxid; free sulphuric acid is found in the solution while KOH is adsorbed. MASIUS* has shown in the case of the very strongly hydrolyzed anilin salts, that more anilin than acid is adsorbed by charcoal.

To explain these cleavage processes, especially in dyeing, it must be assumed that the easily adsorbable dye ion displaces a cation K, Na or the like, which is already present and adsorbed, though possessing little capacity for adsorption.

The weak point in the argument for the *chemical* theory resides in the fact that we do not know the real constitution of the adsorbent, that is, the fiber (silk, wool, cotton, etc.), so that we do not know what chemical groups are involved in a dye combination. H. BECHHOLD accordingly strove to solve this question by using as adsorbent a group of substances whose composition is accurately known, namely, naphthalin $C_{10}H_7OH$, naphthylamin $C_{10}H_7(NH_2)$ and amidonaphthol $C_{10}H_6OHNH_2$. The result of this experiment is reproduced on page 30 and shows that acid groups in the adsorbent fix color bases especially, that basic groups fix acid colors, and that the amphoteric amidonaphthol stains very well with both acid and with basic dyes.

In the matter of cell staining not only is the chemical nature of the cell constituents and of the dye involved, but the *physical prerequisites for the penetration of the dye* must be supplied

In the dyes we have a group of substances, most of them chemically well defined, which exhibit all transitions from true crystalloid (e g , methylene blue) to the highly colloidal hydrosols (*e.g.*, benzoazurin) There is, already, an extensive literature in reference to the colloidal properties of dyes which has been collected in the work of L. PELET-JOLIVET *

The experiments of R HOBER and S CHASSIN * showed that, in general, the more colloidal a dye is, the more difficult is its absorption by the kidney epithelium of frogs. Some exceptions are probably associated with specific chemical properties

The idea that the staining of a living plant tissue depends on the dispersion of the dye was developed into a comprehensive theory by RUHLAND in his "ultrafilter theory" which points to a satisfactory explanation of the staining processes in organized tissues [1]

An important element in staining capacity seems to me to have been disregarded hitherto, it is the question of the *density of the substance to be stained* in its relation to the diffusibility of the dye It is quite clear that an easily diffusible dye will penetrate everywhere, and that a dye possessing no diffusibility will always remain on the external surface of the tissue If we are dealing with substances of medium density, it will depend upon the density of the tissues whether it will penetrate at all, and to what extent. If we know our dyes from this point of view we will be in a position to draw conclusions from their penetration as to the structure of the tissue examined. Some experiments performed with this end in view will explain what is meant.[2] In solving the previous question I employed paper strips which were soaked in glacial acetic acid collodion [3] of different concentrations (8 per cent, 4.5 per cent, 1 5 per cent

---

[1] I am glad to learn that J TRAUBE and F KÖHLER, obviously without knowing my views (see 1st edition of this book, 1912, p. 49), in a recent publication, 1915, likewise point out the significance of "the variability of the dispersing gel by added substances," inasmuch as dyes producing swelling increase permeability and dyes causing shrinking diminish it. I do not consider satisfactorily established the proof of swelling and the shrinking properties on *irreversible gels* and the conclusion drawn from them since the experiments of the author depend only on reversible gelatin gel.

[2] These investigations have not been published before.

[3] A solution of collodion in glacial acetic acid.

and 0), gelatinized and then placed in running water until every trace of acid was removed. These strips were then placed in 0.5 per cent dye solutions for 10 minutes and then washed in running water until the wash water was almost entirely colorless. The results are shown in the table on page 429.

It follows from these experiments that the staining is more intense, the denser the stained substance, in the case of easily diffusible dyes, as aurantia, methylene blue and crystal violet. Conversely, in those difficultly diffusible, as chrome violet and benzopurpurin, the intensity of the staining diminishes with the density. Obviously, the particles of the dye are largely colloidally distributed and too large to penetrate the pores of the filter. In between there are substances of medium particle size in which the staining of the different samples does not vary much one way or the other, as, e.g., in the case of alizarin, janus red, bismarck brown, etc. An important factor in these experiments is the time element, as may be seen in the first column (8 per cent). The slower a dye diffuses the longer the time that must elapse for it to penetrate a dense tissue and the slower the color constituents that are not firmly bound by the fibers will diffuse away.

In this connection experiments of E. KNOEVENAGEL * and of O. EBERSTADT * are of interest; they tested samples of acetyl cellulose swollen to various degrees, for their capacity to take up methylene-blue solution of 0.05 per cent. They found that the speed of adsorption was approximately proportionate to the swelling, so that dyes which penetrated greatly swollen acetyl cellulose in a few minutes required months in the case of acetyl cellulose that was not swollen

Elsewhere we have discussed whether there are not other factors involved besides the speed of diffusion and the size of the particles.

The methods of analysis proposed by me, which have not as yet been applied to organized tissues, promise fewer results in microscopic preparations and microtome sections since the surfaces to be penetrated are so thin that sufficient differences are not noticeable. However, we might expect new information in the case of coarse pieces of tissue which are to be examined after they are sectioned.

In what precedes, the discussion of the dyeing process has been studied only from the standpoint of the chemist and the physico-chemist. Somewhat independently of it and with other means the same discussion will be carried into biology.

The dye chemist deals with the coloring of a few fibers of almost constantly the same constitution, with silk and wool, which dye easily with most dyes, and with cotton and related fibers which are

INTENSITY WITH WHICH STRIP OF GLACIAL ACETIC ACID COLLODION IS STAINED.

	8 per cent collodion	4 5 per cent collodion	3 per cent collodion	1 5 per cent collodion	Untreated filter paper
Aurantia	Deep orange (stained throughout)	Orange	Faint orange	Faint yellowish orange	Very faint orange
Methylene blue	Deep blue (stained throughout)	Rather dark blue	Blue	Medium blue	Bright blue
Crystal violet	Deep dark violet (stained about half through)	Dark violet	Deep violet	Violet	Violet
Gallein	Violet	Faint violet	Faint violet	Faint violet	Faint violet
Eosin	Pink (stained throughout)	Faint pink	Faint pink	Faint pink	Faint pink
Alizarin (dissolved in NaOH)	Deep violet (stained only on the surface)	Rather deep violet	Violet	Violet	Violet
Carbol fuchsin	Deep red (stained throughout)	Deep red	Deep red	Deep red	Red
Manson's blue	Deep blue (only the superficial layers are stained)	Deep blue	Deep blue	Blue	Light blue
Picric acid	Yellow, stained throughout (may be washed out completely in 24 hours)	Very faintly stained	Unstained	Unstained	Unstained
Chrome violet	Almost unstained	Very light violet	Faint violet	Faint violet	Faint violet
Bismarck brown	Brown (only the superficial layers stained)	Brown	Brown	Brown	Brown
Janus red	Red (only the most superficial layer stained)	Red	Red	Red	Red
Benzopurpurin	Almost unstained (only the most superficial layer)	Faint red	Deep red	Deep red	Red

dyed directly only by certain groups of dyes. On this account he is able to obtain almost uniform dyeing. The biologist, on the contrary, has to stain much more tenacious parts of tissue and it is quite wonderful what different shading and even what different colors the individual tissue element of a tissue often shows after treatment with a single stain. If we consider, moreover, that each individual tissue element frequently selects its own particular constituent from a mixture of stains thus forming the brightest pictures we shall understand why the chemical theory of dyeing is the most consuming to biologists.

The following is a resumé of the results to date of the investigations upon dyeing with basic and with acid dyes. *By adsorption the dye is concentrated upon the tissues with chemical action, may occur as the result of chemical process.*

Hitherto we have only considered the so-called substantive dyeing, by which the fabric stains directly in the dye solution without any previous preparation, wool, silk. Vegetable fibers such as cotton, flax, paper, etc., take up very little color from most dye solutions and do not hold it very firmly, they require a mordant to chain the color to them, namely a mordant. This type of dyeing is known as *adjective dyeing*, a term introduced into industrial dyeing technology by J. Bancroft. In biological staining the chief mordants are alum and ferric oxid salts. The combinations of mordants with dyes (hemotoxylin, hematin and alizarin colors) are called lakes. W. Biltz has definitely proved that in addition to physical adsorption, chemical combination occurs in adjective dyeing.

Histologically, staining with dye mixtures is much employed. P. Ehrlich found that if aqueous solution of an acid dye e.g. acid fuchsin or orange G, were mixed with a basic one e.g. methylene blue or methylene green so that one remained in excess, then no precipitate was formed. From colloidal solutions of dye mixtures certain tissue elements remove the base and others the acid dye. It is thus possible to obtain with one solution double stains or even triple stains (triacid). (See above.)

According to the investigations of O. Fischer and B. H. Hexner acid and basic dyes precipitate most completely if they are mixed in equimolecular proportions. An excess of one dye interferes with precipitation, i.e. it acts as a protective colloid and in fact the interference zones are wider the more colloidal the dye. Especially important for the histologist is the fact that highly colloidal dye mixtures are bound more firmly together than those that are slightly colloidal.

We must consider very critically histochemical reactions and stains which arise from the interaction of *two* chemical substances with the formation of an insoluble precipitate. R. Liesegang[*6] has called attention to the phenomena involved in his investigations of *Golgi's stain*. If a piece of brain is placed in potassium bichromate, and after it is completely soaked through, it is then immersed in silver nitrate, some of the ganglion cells in which silver chromate has been precipitated are stained reddish brown.

The interior of the brain substance is never thoroughly stained, notwithstanding the fact that potassium bichromate is present after the first process and silver nitrate after the silver bath. The reason is as follows: when the chromatized portion of brain is placed in the silver nitrate solution, silver chromate forms in the outer layers; the potassium bichromate present in the interior diffuses outward where it is arrested by the silver so that the interior is more and more depleted of chromate. The irregularities in the Golgi staining depend upon similar interferences with diffusion and nucleus actions of silver chromate, on account of which only a portion of the ganglion cells are stained. After staining peripheral nerves with Golgi's stain we obtain stratifications in the axis cylinders (Fromann's lines). These have been shown to be artifacts.

The Technic of Staining.

We distinguish *staining en masse, section staining* and *vital staining*.

In *staining en masse* the entire object is immersed in the stain solution subsequent to hardening. If this is soluble in alcohol, it requires no special precautions, it is otherwise with solutions containing alum, in which case alcohol in the object must first be replaced by water.

After staining, the dye is washed away with water or alcohol until the fluid remains colorless. After staining in aqueous solution the piece must be rehardened in alcohol. The subsequent treatment is then the same as in unstained pieces.

Section staining is much more frequently employed, since not only details are brought out better, but the staining can be watched more closely and later counter-stains may be added intermittently. According to the dilution of the stain solution and the length of time the section is stained, we may obtain on the one hand contrasting, or on the other finely shaded pictures with much more detail.

Vital staining, the staining of *living* tissues, was introduced by P. Ehrlich and was applied by this investigator in his classical work on "The Oxygen Requirements of the Organism" to the processes of living cells. At present it has the center of interest, and from it we may expect most valuable discoveries on the physiology and pathology of living tissue as well as concerning the mechanism of the action of drugs. E. GOLDMANN, R. HÖBER and W. SCHULEMAN have in recent years contributed much concerning the utilization and theory of vital staining They studied healthy and sick animals, whereas KÜSTER and RUHLAND applied vital staining to plants. As yet vital staining of bacteria and other microörganisms has not been definitely attained (EISENBERG). The stain must not be poisonous or the cell will die before it has the desired color.[1] We have numerous dyes at present which fulfill this condition. A few of the most useful are mentioned, methylene blue, neutral red, toluidin blue, trypan blue, trypan red and isamin blue. The studies of RUHLAND on plants, as well as those of EVANS, SCHULEMAN and WILBORN on animals, indicate strongly that the extent of dispersion of the dye chiefly determines its suitability for vital staining, so that the cell behaves like an utrafilter (see p. 428). A dye that is too diffusible distributes itself too readily in all the organs and is accordingly quickly excreted by them; one that is highly colloidal remains at the site of injection. The studies of RUHLAND include both basic and acid dyes while the experiments of EVANS, SHULEMANN and WILBORN were only with acid dyes.

It was formerly believed that only lipoid soluble dyes penetrated living tissues, but this view has not been sustained (see also GARMUS) Many vital stains are known which are insoluble in fats. The colloidal metals are included among these; they have proven useful agents in studying "distribution" in J VOIGT'S method of investigation. This does not by any means imply that lipoid insoluble vital stains may not be especially suitable for some of the organs which are rich in lipoids Thus, for instance, axis cylinder and ganglion cells of the nerve substance are most intensely stained by methylene blue. It is remarkable that the cell nucleus which stains most intensely with basic dyes when the object is dead, with vital staining is constantly colorless; nuclear staining occurs only when the cell dies.

If vital stains are to be fixed, *i.e.*, made insoluble, ammonium molybdate, sublimate, picric acid, etc., are employed.

If this fixation is omitted, the dye diffuses away after death, *i.e.*, according to the changed condition of the tissue, physical and chemical, and a different distribution results.

---

[1] The lack of toxicity of vital stains is only *relative*, in concentrated solution they are all poisons and may be used only in extreme dilutions. Safranin and methyl violet, especially, are quite poisonous, and on this account they cannot be employed for injections into the higher animals

THE TISSUE ELEMENTS IN THEIR RELATION TO FIXATIVES AND DYES.

With iodin-potassium iodid solution, *starch grains* give a blue adsorption compound (see p. 135).

Glycogen forms with it a red adsorption compound The stain with strongly alkaline potassium carmine recently recommended by BEST is so complicated that it cannot yet be interpreted.

The Lipoids.

The fixation and staining of lipoids can hardly be regarded as other than a colloid-chemical question. Fixation is generally accomplished with osmic acid by means of which the fat is simultaneously blackened and the acid is reduced to colloidal metallic osmium; similarly, gold, silver and palladium salts are reduced to the colloidal metal. Of the true dyes, we must especially consider those which are very soluble in fat, though quite indifferent chemically, and which are very slightly adsorbed by the other constituents of the cell. Among these are Scarlet R (fettponceau) and Sudan III. Both are amphoteric dyes in which the basic as well as the acid character is so indefinite that they seem quite indifferent and do not form salts with aqueous caustic soda. Employed in alcoholic solution, staining results.

Protoplasm.

We may attribute to protoplasm chemical properties similar to those of the albumins Protoplasm may be amphoteric, on which account neither acid nor basic properties become more prominent. Consequently, protoplasm stains only faintly with either basic or acid dyes, even though its water content is relatively high.

Nucleus.

The chief constituents of the cell nucleus are the *nucleoproteins*. These are strongly acid in character; to them may be attributed the intense staining of the nucleus with basic dyes, and to them the intensely staining constituent of the nucleus is indebted for the name *chromatin* or *chromatic substance* among histologists The union with the color base becomes firmer with the lapse of time, since in the beginning it is possible to effect almost complete decolorization with alcohol, whereas when the dye acts for a longer period the nuclei retain their intense staining and only clouds of color leave. For nuclear staining any basic dye may be employed; safranin, fuchsin, methyl violet, methyl green and bismarck brown are recommended most highly.

Another favorite nuclear staining method is with the *mordant dyes*, e g., hematoxylin or carmine. In this instance, also, the acid character of the nuclear proteins explains the action of the dyes. The nuclear proteins adsorb the mordants, usually colloidal aluminium hydroxid (from alum), and these form an insoluble compound with the acid hematoxylin or one of its oxidation compounds, or with acid carmine.

Finally, we may mention the *double staining of* ROMANOWSKY, which has been modified by G GIEMSA. Its underlying principle is that a basic blue dye (methylene azur or methylene blue) is mixed with an acid dye eosin (see p. 426). At first the preparation stains blue in the mixture; gradually there occurs a differentiation into blue and red elements or combination violet shades whereby the nuclei become red   For the present, all interpretations of this phenomenon are quite hypothetical, it presents a very interesting colloid-chemical problem   If methylene azur and eosin are mixed, a colloidal solution of eosin-acid-methylene azur forms, provided that one of the two dyes is present in excess   Nuclear staining may occur in such a way that the basic methylene azur serves as mordant for the eosin, it is also possible that the nuclei stain better with colloidal eosin-acid-methylene azur than with crystalloidal methylene azur, and that in a reaction which requires time (possibly hydrolytic cleavage) the red color base of methylene azur becomes free.   In this double staining there enter as factors phenomena involving the colloidal condition of both dye and specimen with respect to the diffusibility of the dye and perhaps also other circumstances which have not been considered here.   This may be assumed both from the accurate directions which are given for the preparation and age of the solution, the thickness of the preparation, the duration of staining, etc , and from the fact that every departure from the directions gives a different result.

Connective Tissue, Capillary Walls, Membranes, Etc.

From the numerous reports I gather that only easily diffusible stains, especially the sulphoacids (acid fuchsin, soluble blue combined with picric acid), are suitable for this purpose.   This probably depends upon the fact that connective tissue, etc., are among the tissues poorest in water and least swollen, so that dyes of more colloidal character are unable to penetrate them.

For the staining of *elastic fibers*, which is best performed by the orcein method of P G. UNNA and TAENZER or by WEIGERT's method, we have no explanation whatever.   The recent investigations of the *keratins* by L GOLODETZ and P. G. UNNA show that we are dealing with a number of chemically very different substances (ovokeratin, neurokeratin, elastin) [VAN GIESON's stain contains picric acid and stains elastin specifically. Tr.]

The Staining of Bacteria.

Most cocci and bacteria have a definite acid character evidenced by the fact that they migrate to the anode in the electrical current (see p. 205).

Though they usually stain intensely with basic dyes (fuchsin, methylene blue, thionin, etc.), nevertheless bacteria exhibit considerable differences in staining capacity. Though all cocci with which I am acquainted stain very intensely, some bacteria, *e.g.*, paratyphoid and bacilli of hog erysipelas, are stained more faintly. *Spores* stain with especial difficulty, the more poorly the older they are; it is obvious that the solid capsule offers great resistance to the penetration of the stain. The *tubercle bacillus* is most difficult to stain, which may be attributed chiefly to its high keratin content, inasmuch as other keratin-containing substances (bristles, hair, epidermis, etc.) stain just as poorly. The difficulty in staining the tubercle bacillus was formerly attributed to the wax contained. HELBIG, however, showed that complete removal of the wax did not increase the staining capacity.

GRAM's stain is quite unique; it is extensively employed for the classification of bacteria (we distinguish Gram-positive and Gram-negative) It is performed as follows: we first stain with methyl violet or some related basic dye and then subject the specimen to the action of iodin (dissolved in KI). After this treatment, some bacteria readily give up the dye to alcohol and are decolorized, whereas others firmly retain it. In the latter case, a firm combination has been formed. A thorough study from modern points of view would be of great value, since it would explain the difference in the nature of the two groups of bacteria It is important to mention that, by GRAM's method, a differentiation of the structure of individual bacteria may be revealed. The so-called BABE's corpuscles are not decolorized by a brief action of alcohol. Upon this fact depends M. NEISSER's method for identifying diphtheria bacilli.

We have as yet little insight into the actual basis of differentiation by GRAM's stain It has actually only been established that GRAM positive bacteria show a greater permeability for dies, stain more quickly and intensely and retain the dye more strongly upon decolorization with alcohol. Probably the only purpose of the treatment with iodin is to increase the size of the dye molecule or increase its fixation by the bacillus (EISENBERG).

AUTHORS' INDEX

ᶠⁿ refers to footnote in text
* refers to reference given

SUBJECT INDEX

157

D. VAN NOSTRAND COMPANY

25 PARK PLACE

NEW YORK

SHORT-TITLE CATALOG

OF

Publications and Importations

OF

SCIENTIFIC AND ENGINEERING BOOKS

This list includes
the technical publications of the following English publishers:

SCOTT, GREENWOOD & CO.   JAMES MUNRO & CO., Ltd.
CONSTABLE&COMPANY,Ltd   TECHNICAL PUBLISHING CO.
BENN BROTHERS, Ltd.

for whom D Van Nostrand Company are American agents.

SHORT=TITLE CATALOG

OF THE

Publications and Importations

OF

D. VAN NOSTRAND COMPANY
25 PARK PLACE, N. Y.

All Prices in this list are NET.
All bindings are in cloth unless otherwise noted.

Abbott, A. V. The Electrical Transmission of Energy. .. . .8vo, *$5; oo
—— A Treatise on Fuel. (Science Series No. 9.).............16mo, o 75
—— Testing Machines. (Science Series No. 74.)............16mo, o 75
Abraham, Herbert. Asphalts and Allied Substances. .. ..8vo, 5 oo
Adam, P. Practical Bookbinding. Trans. by T. E. Maw......12mo, *2 50
Adams, H. Theory and Practice in Designing.,..... .. . 8vo, *2 50
Adams, H. C. Sewage of Sea Coast Towns.. .... 8vo, *2 50
Adams, J. W. Sewers and Drains for Populous Districts..... . 8vo, 2 50
Addyman, F. T. Practical X-Ray Work.................. ..8vo, 5 oo
Adler, A. A. Theory of Engineering Drawing....... ...... 8vo, *2 oo
—— Principles of Parallel Projecting-line Drawing. ....8vo, *1 oo
Aikman, C. M. Manures and the Principles of Manuring,....... .. 8vo, 2 50
Aitken, W. Manual of the Telephone.................. ...... 8vo, *8 oo
d'Albe, E. E. F.; Contemporary Chemistry.................. . 12mo, *1 25
Alexander, J. Colloid Chemistry.... .... 12mo, 1 oo
Alexander, J. H. Elementary Electrical Engineering 12mo, 2 50
Allan, W. Strength of Beams Under Transverse Loads. (Science Series
 No. 19.) .... 16mo, o 75
—— Theory of Arches. (Science Series No. 11.)........ . 16mo,
Allen, H. Modern Power Gas Producer Practice and Applications 12mo, *2 50
Anderson, J. W. Prospector's Handbook. 12mo, 1 50
Andés, L. Vegetable Fats and Oils............. .... 8vo, *6 oo
—— Animal Fats and Oils. Trans. by C. Salter. 8vo, *5 oo
—— Drying Oils, Boiled Oil, and Solid and Liquid Driers....... 8vo, *6 oo
—— Iron Corrosion, Anti-fouling and Anti-corrosive Paints. Trans. by
 C. Salter. .... 8vo, *6 oo
—— Oil Colors, and Printers' Ink. Trans. by A. Morris and H.
 Robson.. .... 8vo, *4 oo
—— Treatment of Paper for Special Purposes. Trans. by C. Salter.
 12mo, *3 oo
Andrews, E. S. Reinforced Concrete Construction... .... 12mo, *2 oo
—— Theory and Design of Structures 8vo, *3 50
—— Further Problems in the Theory and Design of Structures 8vo, *2 50

Cornwall, H. B. Manual of Blow-pipe Analysis 8vo,   *2 50
Cowee, G. A. Practical Safety Methods and Devices   .   8vo,   *3 00
Cowell, W. B. Pure Air, Ozone, and Water.. .   12mo,   *2 50
Craig, J W., and Woodward, W. P. Questions and Answers About
    Electrical Apparatus   .   .   .   12mo, leather,   1 50
Craig, T. Motion of a Solid in a Fuel. (Science Series No 49.) 16mo,   0 75
—— Wave and Vortex Motion. (Science Series No 43.) 16mo,   0 75
Cramp, W. Continuous Current Machine Design 8vo,   *2 50
Creedy, F. Single Phase Commutator Motors   ...   8vo,   *2 00
Crehore, A. C. Mystery of Matter and Energy 8vo,   1 00
Crocker, F. B. Electric Lighting. Two Volumes. 8vo.
    Vol. I. The Generating Plant 3 00
    Vol II. Distributing Systems and Lamps   .   . ..
Crocker, F. B., and Arendt, M. Electric Motors   . .   . 8vo,   *2 50
Crocker, F. B., and Wheeler, S. S. The Management of Electrical Ma-
    chinery   .   .   .   12mo,   *1 00
Crosby, E. U, Fiske, H. A, and Forster, H. W Handbook of Fire
    Protection .   .   .   12mo,   4 00
Cross, C. F., Bevan, E. J., and Sindall, R. W. Wood Pulp and Its Applica-
    tions. (Westminster Series.)   ...   8vo,   *2 00
Crosskey, L. R Elementary Perspective   .   . 8vo,   1 25
Crosskey, L R., and Thaw, J. Advanced Perspective   .   . 8vo,   1 50
Culley, J L. Theory of Arches. (Science Series No. 87)   ... 16mo,   0 75
Cushing, H. C , Jr., and Harrison, N. Central Station Management. .   *2 00

Dadourian, H. M. Analytical Mechanics 12mo,   *3 00
Danby, A. Natural Rock Asphalts and Bitumens   .   `.... ..8vo,   *2 50
Davenport, C. The Book. (Westminster Series.) 8vo,   *2 00
Davey, N. The Gas Turbine 8vo,   *4 00
Davies, F. H. Electric Power and Traction 8vo,   *2 00
—— Foundations and Machinery Fixing. (Installation Manual Series.)
            16mo,   *1 00
Deerr, N. Sugar Cane 8vo,   9 00
Deite, C. Manual of Soapmaking. Trans. by S. T. King .   . 4to,
De la Coux, H. The Industrial Uses of Water. Trans. by A. Morris 8vo,   *5 00
Del Mar, W. A. Electric Power Conductors   .   . 8vo,   *2 00
Denny, G. A. Deep-level Mines of the Rand...   .   .. 4to,   *10 00
—— Diamond Drilling for Gold *5 00
De Roos, J. D. C. Linkages. (Science Series No. 47.) .. . 16mo,   0 75
Derr, W. L. Block Signal Operation   . ..   . Oblong 12mo,   *1 50
—— Maintenance-of-Way Engineering   .. (In Preparation)
Desaint, A. Three Hundred Shades and How to Mix Them .. 8vo,   *9 00
De Varona, A. Sewer Gases. (Science Series No. 55.) . 16mo,   0 75
Devey, R. G. Mill and Factory Wiring. (Installation Manuals Series.)
            12mo,   *1 00
Dibdin, W. J. Purification of Sewage and Water .   .   8vo,   6 50
Dichmann, Carl. Basic Open-Hearth Steel Process .   12mo,   *3 50
Dieterich, K. Analysis of Resins, Balsams, and Gum Resins ..8vo,   *3 50
Dilworth, E C Steel Railway Bridges   . 4to   *4 00
Dinger, Lieut. H. C Care and Operation of Naval Machinery 12mo,   *3 00
Dixon, D. B. Machinist's and Steam Engineer's Practical Calculator.
            16mo, morocco,   1 25

Dommett, W. E   Motoi Car Mechanism 12mo,   *2 00
Dorr, B F.   The Surveyor's Guide and Pocket Table-book.
                                                  16mo, morocco,   2 00
Draper, C. H.   Elementary Text-book of Light, Heat and Sound   12mo,   1 00
--- Heat and the Principles of Thermo-dynamics   .   .   .   12mo,   *2 00
Draper, E. G.   Navigating the Ship 12mo,   1 50
Dron, R. W.   Mining Formulas 12mo,   1 00
Dubbel, H.   High Power Gas Engines   .   .   . 8vo,   *5 00
Dumesny, P., and Noyer, J.   Wood Products, Distillates, and Extracts.
                                                          8vo,   *5 00
Duncan, W. G , and Penman, D   The Electrical Equipment of Collieries.
                                                          8vo,   *5 00
Dunkley, W. G   Design of Machine Elements   Two volumes 8vo,each,   2 00
Dunstan, A. E., and Thole, F. B. T.   Textbook of Practical Chemistry.
                                                          12mo,   *1 40
Durham, H. W.   Saws. 8vo   2 50
Duthie, A L.   Decorative Glass Processes.   (Westminster Series.) 8vo,   *2 00
Dwight, H B   Transmission Line Formulas 8vo,   *2 00
Dyke, A. L.   Dyke's Automobile and Gasoline Engine Encyclopedia.8vo,   4 00
Dyson, S. S.   Practical Testing of Raw Materials 8vo,   *5 00
Dyson, S. S., and Clarkson, S S.   Chemical Works   . .   8vo,   *9 00

Eccles, W H.   Wireless Telegraphy and Telephony   .   .   .   12mo,   *3 80
Eck, J.   Light, Radiation and Illumination.   Trans by Paul Hogner.
                                                          8vo,   *2 50
Eddy, H T   Maximum Stresses under Concentrated Loads   8vo,   1 50
Eddy, L C.   Laboratory Manual of Alternating Currents   . .   12mo,   0 50
Edelman, P. Inventions and Patents   .   .   12mo,   *1 90
Edgcumbe, K   Industrial Electrical Measuring Instruments   8vo,   5 00
Edler, R   Switches and Switchgear.   Trans. by Ph. Laubach .   8vo   *4 00
Eissler, M.   The Metallurgy of Gold. 8vo.   9 00
—— The Metallurgy of Silver 8vo.   4 00
- ---The Metallurgy of Argentiferous Lead 8vo,   6 25
—— A Handbook on Modern Explosives 8vo,   5 00
Ekin, T. C   Water Pipe and Sewage Discharge Diagrams . . . .   .folio,   *3 00
Electric Light Carbons, Manufacture of... .   .   .   . .8vo,   1 00
Eliot, C. W., and Storer, F. H.   Compendious Manual of Qualitative
         Chemical Analysis. 12mo,   *1 25
Ellis, C. Hydrogenation of Oils. 8vo,   7 50
—— Ultraviolet Light, Its Applications in Chemical Arts . .   12mo,
                                                          (In Press)
Ellis, G.   Modern Technical Drawing.   .   .   8vo,   *2 00
Ennis, Wm. D.   Linseed Oil and Other Seed Oils 8vo,   *4 00
- -— Applied Thermodynamics 8vo,   *4 50
- - Flying Machines To-day 12mo,   *1 50
- - Vapors for Heat Engines 12mo,   *1 00
Ermen, W. F. A.   Materials Used in Sizing 8vo,   *2 00
Erwin, M.   The Universe and the Atom 12mo,   *2 00
Evans, C. A.   Macadamized Roads.   .   . . . (In Press.)
Ewing, A. J.   Magnetic Induction in Iron. 8vo.   *4 00

Fairchild, J F.   Graphical Compass Conversion Chart and Tables . .   0 50
Fairie, J   Notes on Lead Ores. 12mo,   *0 50
—— Notes on Pottery Clays   .   .   .

Gratacap, L. P.   A Popular Guide to Minerals................ 8vo,   *2 00
Gray, J.   Electrical Influence Machines 12mo,   1 00
—— Marine Boiler Design..   ....12mo,   *1 45
Greenhill, G.   Dynamics of Mechanical Flight... .. .. 8vo,   *2 50
Gregorius, R.   Mineral Waxes.   Trans by C. Salter..........12mo,   *1 00
Grierson, R.   Some Modern Methods of Ventilation. 8vo,   *3 00
Griffiths, A. B.   A Treatise on Manures. 12mo,   3 00
—— Dental Metallurgy 8vo,   3 50
Gross, E.   Hops... ...   .8vo,   *5 00
Grossman, J.   Ammonia and Its Compounds 12mo,   *1 45
Groth, L. A.   Welding and Cutting Metals by Gases or Electricity.
        (Westminster Series) 8vo,   *2 00
Grover, F.   Modern Gas and Oil Engines.. ....   8vo,   *3 00
Gruner, A.   Power-loom Weaving.. ....   8vo,   *3 50
Grunsky, C. E.   Topographic Stadia Surveying.   .   ..   16mo,   2 00
Güldner, Hugo.   Internal Combustion Engines.   Trans. by H. Diederichs.
                                                               4to,   *15 00
Gunther, C. O   Integration 8vo,   *1 25
Gurdea, R. L.   Traverse Tables   .   .   ...   folio, half morocco,   *7 50
Guy, A. E.   Experiments on the Flexure of Beams. 8vo,   *1 25

Haenig, A.   Emery and Emery Industry 8vo,   *2 50
Hainbach, R.   Pottery Decoration.   Trans. by C. Salter.........   12mo,   *1 50
Hale, W. J.   Calculations of General Chemistry.... ....   12mo,   *1 25
Hall, C. H.   Chemistry of Paints and Paint Vehicles 12mo,   *2 00
Hall, G. L.   Elementary Theory of Alternate Current Working .   8vo,
Hall, R. H.   Governors and Governing Mechanism..   ... .   12mo,   *2 50
Hall, W. S.   Elements of the Differential and Integral Calculus   8vo,   *2 25
—— Descriptive Geometry   ...   .   8vo volume and a 4to atlas,   *3 50
Haller, G. F., and Cunningham, E. T.   The Tesla Coil.... .   12mo,   *1 25
Halsey, F. A.   Slide Valve Gears.....   ...   12mo,   1 50
—— The Use of the Slide Rules.   (Science Series No. 114.) 16mo,   0 75
—— Worm and Spiral Gearing.   (Science Series No. 116.).....   16mo,   0 75
Hancock, H.   Textbook of Mechanics and Hydrostatics   8vo,   1 50
Hancock, W. C.   Refractory Materials. (Metallurgy Series.) (In Press)
Hardy, E.   Elementary Principles of Graphic Statics....... .   12mo,   *1 50
Haring, H.   Engineering Law.
     Vol. I.   Law of Contract 8vo,   *4 00
Harper, J H.   Hydraulic Tables on the Flow of Water..... .   16mo,   *2 00
Harris, S. M   Practical Topographical Surveying.... ... ...(In Press.)
Harrison, W. B.   The Mechanics' Tool-book 12mo,   1 50
Hart, J. W.   External Plumbing Work 8vo,   *3 50
—— Hints to Plumbers on Joint Wiping.. . ...   8vo,   *3 50
—— Principles of Hot Water Supply........................   8vo,   *3 50
—— Sanitary Plumbing and Drainage.. .   . ..   8vo,   *3 50
Haskins, C. H.   The Galvanometer and Its Uses....   ..   16mo,   1 50
Hatt, J. A. H.   The Colorist.. . ... .square 12mo,   *1 50
Hausbrand, E.   Drying by Means of Air and Steam.   Trans. by A. C.
        Wright 12mo,   *2 50
—— Evaporating, Condensing and Cooling Apparatus.   Trans. by A. C.
        Wright

ausmann, E. Telegraph Engineering. 8vo, *3 00
ausner, A. Manufacture of Preserved Foods and Sweetmeats. Trans.
    by A. Morris and H Robson 8vo, *3 50
awkesworth, J Graphical Handbook for Reinforced Concrete Design.
                          4to, *2 50
ay, A. Continuous Current Engineering 8vo, *2 50
ayes, H. V Public Utilities, Their Cost New and Depreciation 8vo, *2 00
—— Public Utilities, Their Fair Present Value and Return 8vo, *2 00
eath, F. H. Chemistry of Photography .. 8vo (In Press)
eather, H. J. S. Electrical Engineering . 8vo, *3 50
eaviside, O. Electromagnetic Theory. Vols. I and II . 8vo, each, *6 00
                    Vol. III. 8vo, *10 00
eck, R. C. H. The Steam Engine and Turbine .. 8vo, *3 50
—— Steam-Engine and Other Steam Motors. Two Volumes.
    Vol. I. Thermodynamics and the Mechanics 8vo, *3 50
    Vol. II. Form, Construction, and Working .. . 8vo, *5 00
—— Notes on Elementary Kinematics . 8vo, boards, *1 00
—·— Graphics of Machine Forces 8vo, boards, *1 00
eermann, P. Dyers' Materials. Trans. by .A C. Wright ..12mo, *2 50
ellot, Macquer and D'Apligny. Art of Dyeing Wool, Silk and Cotton. 8vo, *2 00
enrici, O. Skeleton Structures. . 8vo, 1 50
ering, C., and Getman, F. H Standard Tables of Electro-Chemical
    Equivalents 12mo, *2 00
ering, D. W. Essentials of Physics for College Students . 8vo, *1 75
ering-Shaw, A. Domestic Sanitation and Plumbing. Two Vols 8vo, *5 00
ering-Shaw, A. Elementary Science .. 8vo, *2 00
erington, C F. Powdered Coal as Fuel 8vo, 3 00
errmann, G. The Graphical Statics of Mechanism. Trans. by A. P.
    Smith.. . . . . . 12mo, 2 00
erzfeld, J. Testing of Yarns and Textile Fabrics . . 8vo.
                  (New Edition in Preparation.)
ildebrandt, A. Airships, Past and Present 8vo,
ildenbrand, B. W. Cable-Making. (Science Series No. 32) 16mo, 0 75
ilditch, T. P. A Concise History of Chemistry . 12mo, *1 50
ill, J W. The Purification of Public Water Supplies. New Edition.
                    (In Press)
——Interpretation of Water Analysis . . . . (In Press)
ill, M. J. M. The Theory of Proportion . .. 8vo, *2 50
illhouse, P. A. Ship Stability and Trim 8vo, 4 50
iroi, I Plate Girder Construction. (Science Series No 95.) 16mo, 0 75
—— Statically-Indeterminate Stresses. . 12mo, *2 00
irshfeld, C F. Engineering Thermodynamics (Science Series No. 45.)
                      16mo, 0 75
oar, A The Submarine Torpedo Boat 12mo, *2 00
obart, H M Heavy Electrical Engineering.. . . .. 8vo, *4 50
——Design of Static Transformers 12mo, *2 00
—— Electricity 8vo, *2 00
—— Electric Trains . . 8vo, *2 50
——Electric Propulsion of Ships 8vo, *2 50

Inness, C H. Problems in Machine Design. 12mo, *3 00
—— Air Compressors and Blowing Engines. 12mo,
—— Centrifugal Pumps 12mo, *3 00
—— The Fan 12mo, *4 00

Jacob, A., and Gould, E. S. On the Designing and Construction of
    Storage Reservoirs. (Science Series No. 6.) 16mo, 0 75
Jannettaz, E. Guide to the Determination of Rocks. Trans. by G. W.
    Plympton.....   . ...   12mo,   1 50
Jehl, F. Manufacture of Carbons... ...   .   8vo, *4 00
Jennings, A. S. Commercial Paints and Painting. (Westminster Series.)
                                                        8vo, '4 00
Jennison, F. H. The Manufacture of Lake Pigments 8vo (In Press)
Jepson, G. Cams and the Principles of their Construction.   .. 8vo, *1 50
—— Mechanical Drawing ..   ..   .. 8vo (In Preparation.)
Jervis-Smith, F. J. Dynamometers 8vo, *3 50
Jockin, W. Arithmetic of the Gold and Silversmith   .   12mo, *1 00
Johnson, J H. Arc Lamps and Accessory Apparatus. (Installation
    Manuals Series.) 12mo, *0 75
Johnson, T. M. Ship Wiring and Fitting. (Installation Manuals Series.)
                                                       12mo, *0 75
Johnson, W. McA. The Metallurgy of Nickel.. . . (In Preparation.)
Johnston, J. F. W., and Cameron, C. Elements of Agricultural Chemistry
    and Geology 12mo,   2 60
Joly, J. Radioactivity and Geology. 12mo, *3 00
Jones, H. C. Electrical Nature of Matter and Radioactivity ... .12mo, *2 00
—— Nature of Solution 8vo, *3 50
—— New Era in Chemistry. 12mo, *2 00
Jones, J. H. Tinplate Industry.. .... .8vo, *3 00
Jones, M. W. Testing Raw Materials Used in Paint. 12mo, *2 50
Jordan, L. C. Practical Railway Spiral .. .. 12mo, leather, *1 50
Joynson, F. H. Designing and Construction of Machine Gearing . .8vo, 2 00
Jüptner, H. F. V Siderology: The Science of Iron.... ... ... 8vo, *5 00

Kapp, G. Alternate Current Machinery. (Science Series No. 96.)
                                                       16mo, 0 75
Kapper, F. Overhead Transmission Lines............... ....4to, *4 00
Keim, A. W. Prevention of Dampness in Buildings.... .... .8vo, *2 50
Keller, S. S. Mathematics for Engineering Students. 12mo, half leather.
——and Knox, W. E Analytical Geometry and Calculus *2 00
Kelsey, W. R. Continuous-current Dynamos and Motors. 8vo, *2 50

Kemble, W. T., and Underhill, C. R. The Periodic Law and the Hydrogen
    Spectrum...   . . . . 8vo, paper, *0 50
Kemp, J. F. Handbook of Rocks 8vo, *1 50
Kennedy, A. B. W., and Thurston, R. H. Kinematics of Machinery.
    (Science Series No. 54.) 16mo, 0 75
Kennedy, A. B. W., Unwin, W. C., and Idell, F. E. Compressed Air.
    (Science Series No 106) 16mo, 0 75

Kennedy, R. Electrical Installations. Five Volumes. 4to,   15 00
 Single Volumes   .   . . . each,   3 50
 —— Flying Machines, Practice and Design. 12mo,   *2 50
 —— Principles of Aeroplane Construction 8vo,   *2 00
Kennelly, A. E. Electro-dynamic Machinery 8vo,   1 50
Kent, W   Strenth of Materials   (Science Series No. 41.) .   16mo,   0 75
Kershaw, J. B. C. Fuel, Water and Gas Analysis   .   8vo,   *2 50
 —— Electrometallurgy. (Westminster Series.)   .   8vo,   *2 00
 —— The Electric Furnace in Iron and Steel Production   12mo,
 —— Electro-Thermal Methods of Iron and Steel Production   8vo,   *3 00
Kinzbrunner, C. Alternate Current Windings   . .   8vo,   *1 50
 —— Continuous Current Armatures   .   . .   8vo,   *1 50
 —— Testing of Alternating Current Machines   .   8vo,   *2 00
Kinzer, H., and Walter, K. Theory and Practice of Damask Weaving,
                8vo,   4 00
Kirkaldy, A.. W., and Evans, A. D   History and Economics of
 Transport 8vo,   *3 00
Kirkaldy, W. G   David Kirkaldy's System of Mechanical Testing   4to,   10 00
Kirkbride, J. Engraving for Illustration   .   8vo,   *1 00
Kirkwood, J. P. Filtration of River Waters 4to,   7 50
Kirschke, A. Gas and Oil Engines 12mo,   *1 50
Klein, J. F   Design of a High-speed Steam-engine 8vo,   *5 00
 —— Physical Significance of Entropy   .   . 8vo,   *1 50
Klingenberg, G. Large Electric Power Stations.   . . .   4to,   *5 00
Knight, R.-Adm. A. M. Modern Seamanship   . .   . 8vo,   *6 50
 —— Pocket Edition   . . . .   .12mo, fabrikoid,   3 00
Knott, C. G., and Mackay, J. S. Practical Mathematics   .   . . 8vo,   2 50
Knox, G. D. Spirit of the Soil 12mo,   *1 25
Knox, J. Physico-Chemical Calculations 12mo,   *1 25
 —— Fixation of Atmospheric Nitrogen. (Chemical Monographs.)   12mo,   *1 00
Koester, F. Steam-Electric Power Plants 4to,   *5 00
 —— Hydroelectric Developments and Engineering   . .   4to,   *5 00
Koller, T. The Utilization of Waste Products   . . . 8vo,   *5 00
 —— Cosmetics 8vo,   *2 50
Koppe, S. W. Glycerine 12mo,   *3 50
Kozmin, P A. Flour Milling. Trans by M. Falkner   . . .8vo,   7 50
Kremann, R. Application of the Physico-Chemical Theory to Tech-
 nical Processes and Manufacturing Methods. Trans. by H
 E. Potts 8vo,   *3 00
Kretchmar, K. Yarn and Warp Sizing 8vo,   *5 00

Laffargue, A. Attack in Trench Warfare 16mo,   0 50
Lalher, E. V. Elementary Manual of the Steam Engine   . . .12mo,   *2 00
Lambert, T   Lead and Its Compounds   .   . .   8vo,   *3 50
 —— Bone Products and Manures   .   . 8vo,   *3 50
Lamborn, L. L. Cottonseed Products 8vo,   *3 00
 —— Modern Soaps, Candles, and Glycerin   8vo,   *7 50
Lamprecht, R. Recovery Wo k After Pit Fires. Trans by C. Salter,
                8vo,   *5 00
Lancaster, M. Electric Cooking, Heating and Cleaning 8vo,   *1 00
Lanchester, F W. Aerial Flight. Two Volumes 8vo.
 Vol. I. Aerodynamics. *6 00
 Vol. II   Aerodonetics *6 00

Marsh, C. F.   Concise Treatise on Reinforced Concrete 8vo,   *2 50
— — Reinforced Concrete Compression Member Diagram.   Mounted on
   Cloth Boards *1 50
Marsh, C. F., and Dunn, W.   Manual of Reinforced Concrete and Con-
   crete Block Construction...   16mo, fabiikoid (In Press)
Marshall, W J, and Sankey, H. R.   Gas Engines.   (Westminster Series.)
                                              8vo,   *2 00
Martin, G.   Triumphs and Wonders of Modern Chemistry .   .   . 8vo,   *3 00
— — Modern Chemistry and Its Wonders. 8vo,   *3 00
Martin, N.   Properties and Design of Reinforced Concrete .   . 12mo,   *2 50
Martin, W D.   Hints to Engineers 12mo,   *1 50
Massie, W. W., and Underhill, C. R.   Wireless Telegraphy and Telephony
                                   12mo,   *1 00
Mathot, R E.   Internal Combustion Engines 8vo,   *4 00
Maurice, W.   Electric Blasting Apparatus and Explosives   .   .   . 8vo,   *3 50
— — Shot Firer's Guide 8vo,   *1 50
Maxwell, F   Sulphitation in White Sugar ' anufacture   .   . 12mo,   3 75
Maxwell, J. C.   Matter and · Motion.   (Science Series No. 36.).
                                 16mo,   0 75
Maxwell, W. H, and Brown, J. T.   Encyclopedia of Municipal and Sani-
   tary Engineering 4to,   *10 00
Mayer, A. M.   Lecture Notes on Physics 8vo,   2 00
Mayer, C., and Slippy, J C   Telephone Line Construction   8vo,   *3 00
McCullough, E.   Practical Surveying 12mo,   *2 00
— — — Engineering Work in Cities and Towns 8vo,   *3 00
— · · · Reinforced Concrete 12mo,   *1 50
McCullough, R. S.   Mechanical Theory of Heat 8vo,   3 50
McGibbon, W. C.   Indicator Diagrams for Marine Engineers   .   . 8vo,   *2 50
— — — Marine Engineers' Drawing Book .   .   .   .   .   .oblong 4to,   *2 50
McGibbon, W. C.   Marine Engineers Pocketbook   .   .   . 12mo,   *4 50
McIntosh, J G   Technology of Sugar 8vo,   *6 00
— — · Industrial Alcohol 8vo,   *3 50
— — — Manufacture of Varnishes and Kindred Industries.   Three Volumes.
   8vo.
   Vol. I.   Oil Crushing, Refining and Boiling.   .   .   .   .
   Vol. II   Varnish Materials and Oil Varnish Making.. .   .   .   .   . *5 00
   Vol.. III.   Spirit Varnishes and Materials *6 00
M:Kay, C. W.   Fundamental Principles of the Telephone Business.
                              8vo. (In Press.)
McKillop, M., and McKillop, A. D.   Efficiency Methods   .   . 12mo,   1 50
M·Knight, J. D., and Brown, A. W.   Marine Multitubular Boilers .   *2 50
McMaster, J. B.   Bridge and Tunnel Centres.   (Science Series No. 20.)
                                16mo,   0 75
McMechen, F. L.   Tests for Ores, Minerals and Metals   .   .   . 12mo,   *1 00
McPherson, J. A.   Water-works Distribution 8vo,   2 50
— — de, A.   Modern Gas Works Practice. 8vo,   *8 50
Mellick, C. W.   Dairy Laboratory Guide 12mo,   *1 25
'Mentor.'   Self-Instruction for Students in Gas Supply.   12mo.
   Elementary 2 50
   Advanced 2 50
Merck, E.   Chemical Reagents, Their Purity and Tests   Trans by
   H. E. Schenck 8vo,   1 00
Merivale, J. H.   Notes and Formulae for Mining Students   .12mo,   1 50
Merritt. Wm H   Field Testing for G· · · · · ·

Mertens. Tactics and Technique of River Crossings. Translated by
  W. Kruger 8vo,   2 50
Mierzinski, S.   Waterproofing of Fabrics.   Trans. by A. Morris and H.
  Robson 8vo,   *2 50
Miessner, B F.   Radio Dynamics 12mo,   *2 00
Miller, G. A.   Determinants.   (Science Series No 105.)   .   16mo,
Miller, W. J.   Introduction to Historical Geology 12mo,   *2 00
Milroy, M E. W   Home Lace-making   .. . 12mo,   *1 00
Mills, C. N.   Elementary Mechanics for Engineers   .   8vo,   *1 00
Mitchell, C. A.   Mineral and Aerated Waters.   8vo,   *3 00
Mitchell, C. A., and Prideaux, R. M   Fibres Used in Textile and Allied
  Industries 8vo,   3 50
Mitchell, C. F., and G A.   Building Construction and Drawing.   12mo.
  Elementary Course *1 50
  Advanced Course   .   *2 50
Monckton, C C. F   Radiotelegraphy.   (Westminster Series.)   8vo,   *2 00
Monteverde, R. D.   Vest Pocket Glossary of English-Spanish, Spanish-
  English Technical Terms   ...   64mo, leather,   *1 00
Montgomery, J. H.   Electric Wiring Specifications .   16mo,   *1 00
Moore, E. C. S   New Tables for the Complete Solution of Ganguillet and
  Kutter's Formula 8vo,   *6 00
Moore, Harold.   Liquid Fuel for Internal Combustion Engines   8vo,   5 00
Morecroft, J. H., and Hehre, F. W.   Short Course in Electrical Testing
  8vo,   *1 50
Morgan, A. P.   Wireless Telegraph Apparatus for Amateurs   12mo,   *1 50
Moses, A. J   The Characters of Crystals   .   ,   8vo,   *2 00
——and Parsons, C L.   Elements of Mineralogy   ..   8vo,   *3 50
Moss, S. A.   Elements of Gas Engine Design.   (Science Series No
  121.) 16mo,   0 75
———The Lay-out of Corliss Valve Gears   (Science Series No 119)
  16mo,   0 75
Mulford, A. C.   Boundaries and Landmarks   .. . 12mo,   *1 00
Mullin, J. P.   Modern Moulding and Pattern-making   .   . 12mo,   2 50
Munby, A. E.   Chemistry and Physics of Building Materials.   (West-
  minster Series.) 8vo,   *2 00
Murphy, J. G.   Practical Mining   .   .   . 16mo,   1 00
Murray, J. A.   Soils and Manures.   (Westminster Series.). . .   8vo,   *2 00

Nasmith, J.   The Student's Cotton Spinning. 8vo,   4 50
—— Recent Cotton Mill Construction   .. 12mo,   2 50
Neave, G. B., and Heilbron, I. M.   Identification of Organic Compounds.
  12mo,   *1 25
Neilson, R. M.   Aeroplane Patents 8vo,   *2 00
Nerz, F.   Searchlights.   Trans. by C. Rodgers.   .   .   8vo,   *3 00
Neuberger, H., and Noalhat, H   Technology of Petroleum.   Trans. by
  J. G. McIntosh 8vo,   *10 00
Newall, J. W.   Drawing, Sizing and Cutting Bevel-gears   8vo,   1 50
Newbigin, M. I., and Flett, J. S.   James Geikie, the Man and the
  Geologist 8vo,   3 50
Newbeging, T.   Handbook for Gas Engineers and Managers   8vo,   *6 50
Newell, F. H., and Drayer, C E.   Engineering as a Career   12mo, cloth,   *1 00
  paper,   0 75
Nicol, G.   Ship Construction and Calculations 8vo,   *10 00
Nipher, F. E.   Theory of Magnetic Measurements   ...   .12mo   ...

Perkin, F. M. Practical Methods of Inorganic Chemistry..	12mo,	*1 00
Perrin, J. Atoms...	8vo,	*2 50
—— and Jaggers, E. M. Elementary Chemistry .	12mo,	*1 00
Perrine, F. A. C. Conductors for Electrical Distribution .	8vo,	*3 50
Petit, G. White Lead and Zinc White Paints .. '. .. .	8vo,	*2 00
Petit, R. How to Build an Aeroplane Trans. by T. O'B. Hubbard, and		
J. H. Ledeboer	8vo,	*1 50
Pettit, Lieut. J. S Graphic Processes. (Science Series No. 76)	16mo,	0 75
Philbrick, P. H. Beams and Girders. (Science Series No. 88.)	16mo,	
Phillips, J. Gold Assaying	8vo,	*3 75
—— Dangerous Goods......	8vo,	3 50
Phin, J. Seven Follies of Science	12mo,	*1 50
Pickworth, C. N. The Indicator Handbook. Two Volumes 12mo, each,		1 50
—— Logarithms for Beginners .... 12mo. boards,		0 50
—— The Slide Rule	12mo,	1 50
Pilcher, R B., and Butler-Jones, F. What Industry Owes to Chemical		
Science	12mo,	1 50
Plattner's Manual of Blow-pipe Analysis. Eighth Edition, revised. Trans.		
by H. B. Cornwall	8vo,	*4 00
Plympton, G. W. The Aneroid Barometer. (Science Series No. 35)		
	16mo,	0 75
—— How to Become an Engineer. (Science Series No 100.)	16mo,	0 75
—— Van Nostrand's Table Book. (Science Series No 104)	16mo,	0 75
Pochet, M. L. Steam Injectors. Translated from the French. (Science		
Series No. 29.). 16mo,		0 75
Pocket Logarithms to Four Places. (Science Series No. 65)	16mo,	0 75
	leather,	1 00
Polleyn, F. Dressings and Finishings for Textile Fabrics	8vo,	*3 50
Pope, F. G. Organic Chemistry . . .	12mo,	2 50
Pope, F. L. Modern Practice of the Electric Telegraph ..	8vo,	1 50
Popplewell, W. C. Prevention of Smoke	8vo,	*3 50
—— Strength of Materials	8vo,	*2 50
Porritt, B. D. The Chemistry of Rubber. (Chemical Monographs,		
No. 3.) . . .. .12mo,		*1 00
Porter, J. R. Helicopter Flying Machine	12mo,	1 50
Potts, H. E. Chemistry of the Rubber Industry. (Outlines of Indus-		
trial Chemistry)	8vo,	*2 50
Practical Compounding of Oils, Tallows and Grease . ..	8vo,	*3 50
Pratt, K. Boiler Draught 12mo,		*1 25
—— High Speed Steam Engines	8vo,	*2 00
Pray, T., Jr. Twenty Years with the Indicator........	8vo,	2 50
—— Steam Tables and Engine Constant 8vo,		2 00
Prelini, C. Earth and Rock Excavation	8vo,	*3 00
—— Graphical Determination of Earth Slopes	8vo,	*2 00
—— Tunneling. New Edition	8vo,	*3 00
—— Dredging. A Practical Treatise.................... ..8vo,		*3 00
Prescott, A. B. Organic Analysis . .	8vo,	5 00
Prescott, A. B., and Johnson, O. C. Qualitative Chemical Analysis	8vo,	*3 50
Prescott, A. B., and Sullivan, E. C. First Book in Qualitative Chemistry.		
	12mo,	*1 50
Prideaux, E B. R. Problems in Physical Chemistry..........	8vo,	*2 00
—— The Theory and Use of Indicators	8vo,	5 00
Primrose, G. S. C. Zinc. (Metallurgy Series). . (In Press)		

e, G. T. Flow of Water 12mo, *2 00
, E. Manual of Chemical Analysis. 8vo, 6 00
E   Modern Steam Boilers 8vo, 5 00
1, W. W. F. Application of Graphic Methods to the Design of
    Structures 12mo, *2 50
Injectors. Theory, Construction and Working 12mo, *2 00
ndicator Diagrams 8vo, *2 50
Engine Testing 8vo, *5 50
:h, A. Gas and Coal-dust Firing. 8vo, *2 50
bon, T. R. Introduction to Chemical Physics. . .8vo, 3 00

:r, G. W. Mechanics of Ventilation. (Science Series No 33.) 16mo, 0 75
Potable Water. (Science Series No. 103) 16mo, 0 75
Treatment of Septic Sewage (Science Series No. 118.) 16mo, 0 75
r, G. W., and Baker, M. N. Sewage Disposal in the United States.
                                    4to, *6 00
:s, H. P. Sewage Disposal Works 8vo, *4 00
au, P. Enamels and Enamelling 8vo, *5 00
ine, W. J. M. Applied Mechanics.. . ... 8vo, 5 00
Civil Engineering 8vo, 6 50
Machinery and Millwork. 8vo, 5 00
The Steam-engine and Other Prime Movers..... .... 8vo, 5 00
ine, W J. M., and Bamber, E. F. A Mechanical Text-book....8vo, 3 50
ome, W. R. Freshman Mathematics 12mo, *1 35
.ael, F. C. Localization of Faults in Electric Light and Power Mains.
                                    8vo, 3 50
b, E. Electric Arc Phenomena. Trans. by K. Tornberg.. 8vo, *2 00
bone, R. L. B. Simple Jewellery 8vo, *2 00
au, A. Flow of Steam through Nozzles and Orifices. Trans. by H.
    B. Brydon.. . .. . 8vo *1 50
enberger, F. The Theory of the Recoil Guns.. ...... 8vo, *5 00
enstrauch, W. Notes on the Elements of Machine Design.8vo, boards, *1 50
enstrauch, W., and Williams, J. T. Machine Drafting and Empirical
    Design.
Part I. Machine Drafting.......... . ... 8vo, *1 25
Part II. Empirical Design .. .. (In Preparation)
nond, E. B. Alternating Current Engineering 12mo, *2 50
ier, H. Silk Throwing and Waste Silk Spinning. ... 8vo,
:es for the Color, Paint, Varnish, Oil, Soap and Drysaltery Trades,
                                    8vo, *5 00
:es for Flint Glass Making...... ....12mo, *5 00
ern, J. B., and Savin, J. Bells, Telephones (Installation Manuals
    Series.).... ....16mo, *0 50
rove, H. S. Experimental Mensuration... .. .. 12mo, *1 25

rood, B. Petroleum (Science Series No. 92) 16mo, 0 75
, S. Turbines Applied to Marine Propulsion *5 00
's Engineers' Handbook 8vo, *9 00
Key to the Nineteenth Edition of Reed's Engineers' Handbook. .8vo, 4 00
Useful Hints to Sea-going Engineers . . 12mo, 3 00
, E. E. Introduction to Research in Organic Chemistry. (In Press)
1ardt, C. W. Lettering for Draftsmen, Engineers, and Students.

Reinhardt, C W. The Techmc of Mechanical Drafting,
oblong, 4to, boards,   *1 00
Reiser, F. Hardening and Tempering of Steel. Trans. by A. Morris and
H. Robson 12mo,   ¹2 50
Reiser, N. Faults in the Manufacture of Woolen Goods. Trans. by A.
Morris and H Robson 8vo,   *2 50
——Spinning and Weaving Calculations 8vo,   *5 00
Renwick, W. G. Marble and Marble Working . . 8vo,   5 00
Reuleaux, F The Constructor Trans by H. H Suplee .. . 4to,   *4 00
Rey, Jean. The Range of Electric Searchlight Projectors. . 8vo,   *4 50
Reynolds, O., and Idell, F. E. Triple Expansion Engines. (Science
Series No 99.) 16mo,   0 75
Rhead, G. F. Simple Structural Woodwork.. .... 12mo,   *1 25
Rhead, G. W British Pottery Marks 8vo,   3 50
Rhodes, H. J. Art of Lithography 8vo,   5 00
Rice, J. M., and Johnson, W. W. A New Method of Obtaining the Differ-
ential of Functions . . 12mo,   0 50
Richards, W. A. Forging of Iron and Steel 12mo,   1 50
Richards, W. A., and North, H. B. Manual of Cement Testing, 12mo,   *1 50
Richardson, J. The Modern Steam Engine .. 8vo,   *3 50
Richardson, S. S. Magnetism and Electricity 12mo,   *2 00
Rideal, S. Glue and Glue Testing 8vo,   ˣ5 00
Riesenberg, F The Men on Deck .. . 12mo,   3 00
——Standard Seamanship for the Merchant Marine 12mo (In Press)
Rimmer, E. J. Boiler Explosions, Collapses and Mishaps . 8vo,   *1 75
Rings, F. Reinforced Concrete in Theory and Practice.. 12mo,   *4 50
——Reinforced Concrete Bridges . . 4to,   *5 00
Ripper, W Course of Instruction in Machine Drawing . folio,   *6 00
Roberts, F C. Figure of the Earth. (Science Series No. 79) 16mo,   0 75
Roberts, J., Jr. Laboratory Work in Electrical Engineering 8vo,   *2 00
Robertson, L. S. Water-tube Boilers 8vo,   2 00
Robinson, J B. Architectural Composition . .. 8vo,   *2 50
Robinson, S. W. Practical Treatise on the Teeth of Wheels. (Science
Series No. 24) .. .. .16mo,   0 ₃5
——Railroad Economics. (Science Series No. 59.) . 16mo,   0 75
——Wrought Iron Bridge Members (Science Series No. 60.) 16mo,   0 75
Robson, J. H Machine Drawing and Sketching .. .8vo,   *2 00
Roebling, J A. Long and Short Span Railway Bridges . folio,   25 00
Rogers, A. A Laboratory Guide of Industrial Chemistry 8vo,   2 00
——Elements of Industrial Chemistry 12mo,   *3 00
——Manual of Industrial Chemistry 8vo,   *5 00
Rogers, F. Magnetism of Iron Vessels. (Science Series No 30.)
16mo,   0 75
Rohland, P. Colloidal and Crystalloidal State of Matter. Trans. by
W. J. Britland and H E Potts 12mo,   *1 25
Rollinson, C. Alphabets . . Oblong, 12mo,   *1 00
Rose, J. The Pattern-makers' Assistant.. 8vo,   2 50
——Key to Engines and Engine-running . 12mo,   2 50
Rose, T. K. The Precious Metals. (Westminster Series.) . 8vo,   *2 00
Rosenhain, W. Glass Manufacture. (Westminster Series.) 8vo,   *2 00
——Physical Metallurgy, An Introduction to. (Metallurgy Series.)
8vo,   *3 50
Roth, W. A. Physical Chemistry 8vo,   *2 00

n, M. Electric Lamps. (Westminster Series.) 8vo,   *2 00
scales, A. N. Mechanics for Marine Engineers 12mo,   *2 00
echanical and Marine Engineering Science   . . .   8vo,   *5 00
n, J. W. The Marine Steam Turbine .   . .   8vo, *12 50
erbal Notes and Sketches for Marine Engineers . .   . 8vo, *12 50
n, J. W., and Sothern, R. M. Elementary Mathematics for
   Marine Engineers. 12mo,   *1 50
mple Problems in Marine Engineering Design .   12mo,
r, E. G. W. Design of Factory and Industrial Buildings 8vo,   4 00
ombe, J. E. Chemistry of the Oil Industries (Outlines of Industrial Chemistry.). 8vo,   *3 00
t, D. H. Dyeing and Staining Marble. Trans. by A. Morris and
   H. Robson 8vo,   *2 50
nburg, L. Fatigue of Metals. Translated by S. H Shreve.
   (Science Series No. 23).. .   . . . .16mo,   0 75
, G. J., Hardy, A. S., McMaster, J. B., and Walling. Topographical
   Surveying. (Science Series No. 72.). 16mo,   0 75
r, A. S. Design of Steel Framed Sheds .   8vo,   *3 50
's, C. L. Text book of Physical Chemistry   . .   . 8vo,   *1 50
l, L Chemical Constitution and Physiological Action (Trans.
   by C Luedeking and A. C. Boylston.). 12mo,   1 25
ir, E. H Hydraulics 12mo,   2 00
lements of Graphic Statics. 8vo,   1 00
tability of Masonry 12mo,   2 00
lementary Mathematics for Engineers. 12mo,   2 00
tability of Arches . .   . .   * .8vo,   2 00
trength of Structural Elements 12mo,   2 00
loving Loads by Influence Lines and Other Methods . .   12mo,   2 00
A. W. Transmission of Power. (Science Series No. 28.) 16mo,
A. W., and Woods, A. T. Elementary Mechanism   ..   12mo,   *2 00
, C., and Pierson, G. S. The Separate System of Sewerage. .8vo,   *3 00
age, H. C. Leatherworkers' Manual 8vo,   *3 50
ealing Waxes, Wafers, and Other Adhesives 8vo,   *2 50
vglutinants of all Kinds for all Purposes. 12mo,   *4 50
y, H. Practical Applied Physics . . . .(In Press)
ie, J. H. Iron and Steel. (Westminster Series.). 8vo,   *2 00
nan, F. M. Unit Photography. 12mo,   *2 00
r, G. E. Cork. Its Origin and Industrial Uses 12mo,   1 00
icil, A., and Voit, E. Applied Optics. 8vo,   5 00
an, D. B. Suspension Bridges and Cantilevers. (Science Series
   No. 127.) 0 75
lelan's Steel Arches and Suspension Bridges .   .   8vo,   *1 00
is, E. J. Field Telephones and Telegraphs .   .   1 20
is, H. P. Paper Mill Chemist . . . .   16mo (In Press)
is, J. S. Theory of Measurements 12mo,   *1 25
ison, J. L. Blast-Furnace Calculations .   . .   12mo, leather,   *2 00
rt, G. Modern Steam Traps 12mo,   *1 75
A. Tables for Field Engineers 12mo,   1 00
a, A. Steam Turbines. Trans. by L. C. Loewenstein   8vo,   *5 00
H. The Timbers of Commerce 8vo,   3 50
i, M. Ancient Plants 8vo,   *2 00
he Study of Plant Life 8vo,   *2 00
rough, J. J., and James, T. C. Practical Organic Chemistry. 12mo,   *2 00
ng, F. R. Treatise on the Art of Glass Painting. 8vo,   *3 50

Sullivan, T. V., and Underwood, N   Testing and Valuation of Building and Engineering Materials   ...   .   (*In Press*)
Sur, F. J. S.   Oil Prospecting and Extracting.   .   .   . 8vo,   *1 00
Svenson, C. L.   Handbook on Piping 8vo,   4 00
—— Essentials of Drafting 8vo,   1 50
Swan, K.   Patents, Designs and Trade Marks.   (Westminster Series.).
8vo,   *2 00
Swinburne, J., Wordingham, C. H., and Martin, T. C   Electric Currents.
(Science Series No   109) 16mo,   0 75
Swoope, C. W.   Lessons in Practical Electricity... .. .. .. 12mo,   *2 00

Tailfer, L.   Bleaching Linen and Cotton Yarn and Fabrics.... . 8vo,   7 00
Tate, J. S.   Surcharged and Different Forms of Retaining-walls.   (Science
Series No. 7.) 16mo,   0 75
Taylor, F. N.   Small Water Supplies   .   .   .   12mo,   *2 50
—— Masonry in Civil Engineering. 8vo,   *2 50
Templeton, W.   Practical Mechanic's Workshop Companion.
12mo, morocco,   2 00
Tenney, E. H.   Test Methods for Steam Power Plants   (Van
Nostrand's Textbooks) 12mo,   *2 50
Terry, H. L.   India Rubber and its Manufacture.   (Westminster Series.)
8vo,   *2 00
Thayer, H. R.   Structural Design. 8vo.
Vol   I.   Elements of Structural Design *2 0C
Vol. II.   Design of Simple Structures. *4 00
Vol. III.   Design of Advanced Structures ....   (*In Preparation*)
—— Foundations and Masonry   .   (*In Preparation*)
Thiess, J. B., and Joy, G. A.   Toll Telephone Practice   .8vo,   *3 50
Thom, C., and Jones, W. H.   Telegraphic Connections.   oblong, 12mo,   1 50
Thomas, C. W.   Paper-makers' Handbook   .   (*In Press*)
Thomas, J. B.   Strength of Ships..   ... .   8vo,   2 50
Thomas, Robt. G.   Applied Calculus   .... 12mo (*In Press*)
Thompson, A. B.   Oil Fields of Russia 4to,   *7 50
—— Oil Field Development 7 50
Thompson, S. P.   Dynamo Electric Machines.   (Science Series No. 75.)
16mo,   0 75
Thompson, W. P.   Handbook of Patent Law of All Countries   .16mo,   1 50
Thomson, G   Modern Sanitary Engineering   ... .12mo,   *3 00
Thomson, G. S.   Milk and Cream Testing   . ... .12mo,   *2 25
—— Modern Sanitary Engineering, House Drainage, etc   ... 8vo,   *3 00
Thornley, T.   Cotton Combing Machines 8vo,   *3 50
—— Cotton Waste 8vo,   *3 50
—— Cotton Spinning. 8vo.
First Year *1 50
Second Year *3 50
Third Year *2 50
Thurso, J. W.   Modern Turbine Practice   .   .   . 8vo,   *4 00
Tidy, C. Meymott.   Treatment of Sewage.   (Science Series No. 94)
16mo,   0 75
Tillmans, J.   Water Purification and Sewage Disposal. Trans by
Hugh S. Taylor. 8vo,   *2 00
Tinney, W. H.   Gold-mining Machinery. 8vo,   *3 00
Titherley, A. W.   Laboratory Course of Organic Chemistry. .   8vo,   *2 00

CPSIA information can be obtained
at www.ICGtesting.com
Printed in the USA
LVOW13*1437120318
569547LV00015B/956/P